ADAMS

BUSINESSES YOU CAN START

ALMANAC

The Adams Almanac Series:

Adams Cover Letter Almanac
Adams Resume Almanac
Adams Job Interview Almanac
Adams Jobs Almanac
Adams Businesses You Can Start Almanac

ADAMS

BUSINESSES YOU CAN START
ALMANAC

KATINA JONES

ADAMS MEDIA CORPORATION
Holbrook, Massachusetts

Published by Adams Media Corporation
260 Center Street, Holbrook, MA 02343

ISBN: 1-55850-602-0

Printed in Canada.

J I H G F E D C

Library of Congress Cataloging-in-Publication Data
Jones, Katina Z.
The Adams businesses you can start almanac / Katina Jones.
p.   cm.
Includes index.
ISBN 1-55850-602-0 (pbk.)
1. New business enterprises—Handbooks, manuals, etc. I. Title.
HD62.5.J657   1996
658.1'1—dc20   96–12166
CIP

This publication is designed to provide accurate and authoritative information with regard to the subject matter covered. It is sold with the understanding that the publisher is not engaged in rendering legal, accounting, or other professional advice. If legal advice or other expert assistance is required, the services of a competent professional person should be sought.
— From a *Declaration of Principles* jointly adopted by a Committee of the American Bar Association and a Committee of Publishers and Associations

This book is available at quantity discounts for bulk purchases.
For information, call 1-800-872-5627 (in Massachusetts 617-767-8100).

Visit our home page at http://www.adamsmedia.com

This book is for Lilly Eleni Romestant, who is already
a budding entrepreneur in her own right.

CONTENTS

Start-up between $1,000 and $5,000 / 105

Start-up between $5,000 and $15,000 / 273

Part III: Appendices

Acknowledgments

There are so many people who made this book come together, and for their help I am eternally grateful: first and foremost, the editorial wizardry of Ruth Dean at The Writing Toolbox and Kathy Baker at The Write Choice; Teri Peters, Paula Powles, Jolene Colant, Anna Hall, and Jesse Adkins, who all contributed small yet important parts of the book; and Jennifer Annandono, Dianna Knox, and Norma Rist for their inspiration and guidance.

Thanks, too, to Pam Liflander, the kindest editor anyone could work with, and to Frank Weimann and Jessica Wainright at The Literary Group in New York City for being such terrific agents.

Special thanks to John Yaceczko, the most patient, tolerant, loving, kind man on the planet. Your love and support carried me through.

INTRODUCTION

There has never been a more exciting time to start your own business! New businesses are springing up every day all across the country. Whether these new ventures are inspired by women re-entering the job market, young people starting their careers at home-based businesses, previously employed middle managers, or just regular folks looking to earn some extra cash on the side, everyone is finding themselves caught up in the entrepreneurial spirit.

What has led to this entrepreneurial boom? First, there has been a sharp increase in downsizing at both large corporations and medium-sized businesses. As you may be aware, many of the larger corporations in the United States, like IBM and General Motors, have been laying off workers in record numbers, and the end is not yet in sight. Nearly one-third of companies surveyed by major outplacement firms say they are considering cutting their work force in 1996 by as much as 30 percent.

As companies are learning to be leaner and meaner, career-minded professionals cannot expect job security the way they could in the past. In today's economy, chances are good that you will probably not stay at one company throughout your professional career. And a growing number of people feel that the best way to prevent an almost inevitable layoff is to take the skills they have and open up shop for themselves.

Changes in government programs and tax benefits for minority-owned businesses provide still more clues why entrepreneurship is on the rise. And despite affirmative action programs, it is still a statistically proven fact that there is a lack of opportunity for women and minorities within medium- to large-sized companies. Thus, thousands of women and minorities are recognizing that their earning potential is much higher "on their own" than it would be in the corporate world, and that there is no "glass ceiling" to deal with when you are your own boss. In addition, it is now easier for minorities and women to get financing to start new ventures, either through local banks or government programs.

The success rate is good for new minority and women-owned startups. In a report released in December 1995, the U.S. Census Bureau stated that women owned 34.1 percent of all non-farm businesses in 1992, and that woman-owned firms earned an average of $246,000 annually. More than 50 percent of minority-owned firms hit the million-dollar mark in sales in 1993—and nearly half of these businesses were launched at a cost of $25,000 or less.

Other population groups are jumping on the entrepreneurial bandwagon as well. Burgeoning technological advances have opened up new opportunities for the physically challenged. In the past, these people were limited in their professional choices by their physical handicaps. Affordable computers, the Internet, and greater public acceptance of home offices have opened up a wide range of opportunities for those with physical limitations, and many have launched successful ventures as a result. An exceptionally high percentage of the businesses profiled in this book are terrific opportunities for the physically or developmentally challenged to earn an income equal to that of any other working professional.

The concept of the home office continues to rise in popularity. Many entrepreneurs have even been able to start new ventures while still employed at another firm, thus increasing their capital and minimizing their day-to-day financial risk. With an answering machine, a second phone line, a computer, some letterhead, and business cards, many home-based businesses can literally run themselves while you keep your day job, leaving you to fill orders or talk to clients on your off time. A few years ago, this type of business practice would not have been considered acceptable. But now, many new businesses are getting off the ground just this way. And if you do choose to quit your day job and work at home full-time, a fax machine, modem, and Internet access can help keep you connected to the outside world during business hours, too.

All of these cultural changes working together have created an atmosphere of opportunity in the entrepreneurial environment. It's now up to you. Making the decision to be an entrepreneur was the hard part. All you have to do is choose the type of business that meets your financial, emotional, and intellectual requirements, and get going!

WHY THIS BOOK?

The Adams Businesses You Can Start Almanac is unique among the plethora of business ideas books. The majority of businesses highlighted here are based on the assumption that you already have some area of interest, or skill, that you would like to apply to your own business. Most of the businesses are considered to be "white collar," but there are also plenty of ideas for the person looking to work with their hands. All of the businesses are significant and realistic ventures, the majority of which can be started right in your own home.

This book emphasizes the potential for many businesses to become offshoots of others. Not every business can exist on its own as a full-time enterprise, although many can be used as opportunities for supplemental income. You can look for companion-type businesses in the index to merge two part-time opportunities into one profitable venture.

Most importantly, this book also provides a view from the trenches. In researching this book, I spoke with business owners across the country about how they did it, why they did it, and what they would have done differently. Aside from discovering hundreds of up-and-coming business ideas, I was amazed by the frank and honest answers I received. Many business owners were quick to tell me about their mistakes, and even more willing to talk about what they would have done differently if they knew then what they know now. Many of their interviews, and all of their advice, are included in full detail.

Lastly, my emphasis is your bottom line. Aside from the explanations on what the crux of each business is, there is a thorough analysis of what it will take to get each new venture up and running, and what kinds of profits you can expect. I've tried to uncover all of the hidden costs for each business, so that you can make an educated decision as to which business is truly the best for you.

HOW TO USE THIS BOOK

There are three ways you can use this book to find a business that is compatible with your background and interest level. First, you could determine what kind of business to enter by understanding what financial resources are available to you. The five hundred businesses profiled are sorted into five start-up cost categories:

Under $1,000—These businesses can be started with very low out-of-pocket expenses. They require no more capital than what you could raise using credit cards, if you had to. Generally, these are businesses that can turn a profit right away, to keep funding the costs you'll be incurring.

$1,000-$5,000—These businesses require some preplanning. The necessary start-up capital should come from your prior savings or through creative personal financing (for example, a home equity loan). The financing for these businesses would probably not require—or qualify for—a small business loan. They are excellent part-time opportunities that can be turned into full-time careers once your business is established.

$5,000-$15,000—You might be able to call on relatives and friends to help raise the necessary capital for these businesses. Otherwise, you will definitely need a significant savings cushion before you embark on any of these opportunities as full-time endeavors.

$15,000-$40,000—You would probably qualify for a small business loan or second mortgage with any of these opportunities. At the very least, you will need a few firm commitments from clients lined up before quitting your day job. Putting together a thorough business plan is essential, so that your financiers can gauge your potential success level.

Above $40,000—At this start-up level, you'll usually need to obtain a bank loan or look for investors just to get the business off the ground. The businesses in this category usually require the purchase of large machinery, specialized equipment, sizable inventories, or warehouse space. As with the previous category of businesses, you'll definitely need a thorough business plan.

Another way to use this book is to use the category index to search for your area of interest. You might get some ideas for jobs in a related field to yours, or find a niche for something that you've always wanted to try.

Lastly, you can simply scan through the book at your own pace to learn more about all of the different types of businesses out there. You might just stumble onto something that addresses a lucrative skill you didn't even know you had.

As you read each business description, you'll notice some specific statistical information at the beginning of every entry. It is organized as follows:

Start-up costs: These costs are calculated by adding together all equipment, advertising, and operating capital costs. I tried to consider every possible cost, and then asked the question: "What's the least amount of money you would need to start this business?"

Potential earnings: This range is calculated by multiplying typical fees by the 2,080 billable hours in each year (40 hours a week for 52 weeks). This is a gross figure and does not account for costs and overhead.

Typical fees: I researched each field to determine the average hourly rate or per-job rate. For many entries, you will see a range instead of one flat fee. This is because your geographic location may dictate the demand for your goods or services, and demand is what drives prices up.

Advertising: Here, I rounded up all of the possible ways you could promote each type of business, from methods that cost nothing, such as networking, to long-term media contracts that cost several thousand dollars. The advertising costs are built into the start-up costs.

Qualifications: This category contains everything you need to know about professional certifications, personality requirements, and other information pertinent to what it takes to run your business.

Equipment needed: I researched and surveyed the equipment purchases you'll likely need to make to run your business effectively. You may need anything from a basic home office set-up to specific industry-related machinery.

Home business potential: Many of the businesses can be launched and run out of your own home. I've also identified those that really need more space (such as a manufacturing facility), and those that you can run from your home even if you are not actually doing the work there.

Staff required: A high percentage of the businesses profiled can be one-person operations, but those needing additional staff are identified, often with a suggested number of employees.

Handicapped opportunity: I've identified the businesses that can be run by those with physical or developmental handicaps. The good news is that a significant number of the businesses listed fit into this category.

Hidden costs: This is probably the most important element of each entry. The costs that you don't think about are often the ones that drive your business into the ground. I've tried to uncover costs you might not have thought of when developing your business plan or strategy. They include insurance coverage, workers' compensation, and even fluctuating materials costs. Many of these are costs you simply cannot predict—or might not have realized are incurred by state and federal government requirements.

The balance of each entry, divided into three sections, provides a comprehensive guide to each individual business. With each, you'll get a total picture of what's involved in successfully running the kind of business that best matches your background and expertise.

Lowdown: This section supplies the details of exactly what each type of business demands of its owner, what your day-to-day activities will be, and who your customers are. This section also includes information on specific marketing opportunities.

Start-up: Here, you'll find an in-depth breakdown of your startup costs, including everything from office furniture, computer equipment, and advertising costs. You'll also find valuable information on how to arrive at specific earnings goals for each business.

Bottom Line: This section points out the positive and negative aspects of each business, so you'll know exactly what you're in for. Remember, there are positives and negatives for every opportunity.

But what is running your own business really like?

As a small business owner myself, I thought I knew everything about starting a business. Through my research and interviews for this book, I found I still had much to learn.

In 1992, I started my own small business, a resume service, with about $500, a laptop computer, and some specialty paper that I bought from catalogs. If I'd known then what I know now about the financial struggles, the managerial challenges, and the near-impossibility of overnight success, I would have never done it. Fortunately, I tried to make it work in spite of my ignorance. Today, I wouldn't have had it any other way.

One business owner recently told me that the best thing about owning your own business is that it's your own business, and the worst thing about owning your business is, well . . . that it's your own business. While owning your own business is the opportunity of a lifetime, you might come to find out that the opportunity to work—or worry—24 hours a day is not one worth having. But you'll never know until you try. And what might be one person's burden is another person's ticket to financial independence and personal fulfillment.

The trick is to manage your entrepreneurial journey well enough to expect the good with the bad—and not pressure yourself to perform perfectly every time After all, this is new ground for most of us. While this book certainly does not provide all the answers, it lets you address several issues you'll need to think about to determine if this lifestyle is really right for you.

As a potential new business owner, the most important place you can start is with a solid idea of what you want to do, and what will it take to achieve those goals. I wish you good luck as you embark on what will become the most interesting journey of your professional life!

WORDS OF ADVICE
FROM THE EXPERTS

LAWRENCE H. CARLTON, CPA

On Getting Started

In order to excel at accounting, there is a need not only to understand accounting, but to understand today's technology, and to have good communication skills. It's a shame to see people coming out of school who are technically proficient, but can't really communicate the information they have. So the accounting profession as a whole has decided there is a need for more education, and by the end of the century, accounting graduates will be required to have at least one additional year of education after a bachelor's degree in order to meet certification requirements. The additional classes will not be accounting-oriented, but will allow students more time to develop the technology and communication skills they will need in order to operate successfully in the business world.

If you're think of working independently, you will be starting out at the small firm end of the profession. The small firm today really has to find a niche. It is no longer sufficient to be a generalist, as was true in the past, or to only provide accounting or tax services. You might also have to provide financial planning work or consulting for your tax clients, or other information technology work for other clients. In short, you will have to be broader-based than the traditional bean-counter of the past to succeed in today's more competitive environment.

ELIZABETH C. HATCH,
TRAVEL AGENT

On Improving Your Skills

I would definitely say: get experience. Don't open up an agency just because you are a person who likes to travel. When I started out, I was able to do everybody's job. I could be an account manager, I could take reservations, I could deliver tickets. I did everything.

If you're just a vacation agent, you're going to have to learn how to service corporate clients. If you're just a corporate agent, you're going to have to know how to do vacation sales. So get as much experience as you can in all of those different areas because you're going to need them when the opportunity arises.

On Personnel

When starting your own agency, or starting your own business in general, you need to be able to fill in for absent personnel in case of an emergency. When I first started and only had one other agent, if I was unable to work, I effectively lost 50 percent of my staff. You can't afford to be down to 50 percent of your staff when service is your product.

Being able to do everyone else's job also gains you greater respect from your employees. When they have a challenge or a question, I'm usually a good source for answers because I do understand what they are going through.

KAREN TUCKER, MEETING PLANNER

On Getting Started

You need to be well-connected within your industry. In my industry it is crucial to be a member of Meeting Planners International, and you should also consider joining SITE (Society of Incentive Travel Executives). You should also have some really solid contacts within one of the hospitality industries. When you start out, I would suggest letting all of those people within your industry know about your business, and then pick a focus. What market are you going to be focusing on for sales?

There are several universities—I think Columbia University in New York City is one of them—that have courses in event planning, perhaps leading up to a hospitality degree. In addition, you can also be certified as a meeting planner, which requires experience and some sort of exam.

On Burnout

My week is often comprised of days when I get up at between 5 and 6 in the morning and don't get home until midnight. I carry a walkie-talkie and a cellular phone, and at any given time may have three people standing in front of me saying, "What do I do?" It's a pretty stressful job, so you have to love it in order to stick with it.

When I was first starting out, I asked advice from more experienced planners. One of the things I heard again and again is the importance of keeping balance in your life. After you've done this for a couple of years, you might think, "I'm going to burn out. I can't do this." I used to lose my voice after big meetings or sometimes just fall apart for a week. I know people who even get physically ill from the stress of it all.

So back to the big question: How do I achieve balance? Balance, to me, means planning your day saying, "I can only do so much. Do I need to farm out some of the work to a subcontractor? And if I have to subcontract out to other people to help me during projects, how do I adjust the price of my services?"

KEN LIZOTT, CAREER COUNSELOR

On Money Issues

Many solo practitioners, such as career counselors or therapists, love working with people but are uncomfortable with the financial aspect of their profession. Of course they want to earn a living, but they usually feel that they are not in their chosen profession for the money. They may hate sending out invoices, and might leave them undone for months. They might be afraid to ask for a fee or to ask for a more substantial fee. In short, there are a lot of issues surrounding money, marketing, and selling that a small business person must work out in order to be successful.

On Advertising

Word of mouth is by far the best means of promoting your business. In a relationship-based business, advertising does not work. Even if you have the best-placed, most expensive ads, you may not get any response from them. However, having a more relationship-oriented approach to getting the word out about your business, such as a job fair, is usually a good bet.

In our first year, we attended a job fair that included four hundred employers with booths. My coworkers and I were the only career counselors there. For two days, ten thousand people came through the job fair, and perhaps half of them came to our booth. Some of those became clients, and others who didn't still spread the word about our operation.

ADAM SCHLINGENBAUM,
DATABASE CONSULTANT

On Getting Started

There are two main areas to this particular job: the computer side and the people side. A lot of people are good at either one area or the other, but there are very few that are really good at both. So you need to ask yourself if you can really be a people person as well as a technology person. This is probably necessary in any technology-driven field.

A good way to get started in this business is to find a way to work on some projects, even if you're not going to make any money. That's how I got started. If you look at your own business needs, or at the needs of your friends or family, somebody probably needs help with a database.

One key thing in this business is to do at least one thing very well. For example, I think it's really too much to expect yourself to really understand more than one, or at most two, platforms or programming languages or database systems, and still work proficiently with each one of them. I've chosen to focus on just one language, one database system, and because of that, I feel like I have as good or better an understanding of it than almost anyone. However, there is a risk with this business model. The technology could change, and your platform or program could go out of business. Hopefully, what you've learned is transferable to another mode of programming.

Networking with your peers is important in this business. Regardless of what platform or technology you're focusing on, there's a place on the Internet where folks like you are talking about it. You should use this resource to learn from other people who are doing what you do, or who are doing what you want to do. I have relationships with people around the country whom I've met through these electronic forums.

NANCY HAHN,
INFORMATION CONSULTANT

On Advertising

To advertise my business, I first had to look at the clientele I already had, and what areas of business they were in. From there, I was able to determine what category of business to target. After that, I compiled names, addresses, and phone numbers of people in my chosen category. As soon as I generated that list, I started contacting people by direct mail. Direct mail works.

I made a few mistakes when I first started out. I tried advertising in local papers, with negligible results. I also advertised in a lot of trade magazines, but it was the same story. Finally, I went to all the trade shows. It's called "working the other side of the table." I would go in, act like a potential customer, and hand out my stuff. I also got lots of names from business cards I collected, and later contacted these people by direct mail.

I always use first-class postage for my mailings; people don't want to read the things they receive by bulk mail. And the envelopes are always handwritten. I've learned that people are far more prone to open envelopes if their name and address are handwritten.

On Working Alone

I really don't want people to know that this business is really just one person, so I always talk in terms of "we." When someone is asking me something that I can't answer right away on the phone, I simply use the line, "I'll have to discuss that with my colleagues and get back to you."

ALISON E. HUTCHINSON, COMMERCIAL ACTOR

On Networking

In order to build a stable career as an actor, you need to work constantly. While you will not always be able to get the role of your choice, do anything you can in your down time, whether it is working as a stage manager or acting as an extra in a local film production.

If you want to stay employed, you will have to build a network of peer contacts. Try to meet as many new people as possible, and find out what they've tried, where they are going, where the auditions are. You can also learn from their mistakes. Your professional peers can also provide a forum so that you can bounce your ideas off of others.

Taking acting classes is one way to help you get to know other people in the business with the same interests. Classes really worked for me because I was able to put together a group of supportive people who were always there to cheer me on and boost my confidence when I didn't get the part I wanted. Community theater is another good way to build up your experience and make contacts. Although this work is generally unpaid, it can help you build your resume, sharpen your skills, and feel that you are part of the scene.

Most actors I know have part-time jobs, but many have full-time office jobs, and use their vacation time to audition or work in community theater. You don't have to feel like a failure if you are not a full-time actor right away.

Be leery of agencies that want you to pay them money before they have found you a job. Most reputable agencies will not require any money from you up front. Your chief out-of-pocket expense should be paying a professional photographer for a good head shot, which you will need for auditions.

NATHAN EVANS,
AUTOMOTIVE DETAIL SPECIALIST

On Following Trends

Trends are set by the customers. Watch for repeat requests. If a new customer says he wants leather seat covers, I will recall that I've been asked a couple of times to supply leather seat covers, and will consider branching out into that area. Then I'll do the research and find the materials to help me produce them in a cost-effective manner. I may not make a profit on the first couple of jobs, because I will probably spend too many hours learning how to do the job, but after a while, it should prove to be a moneymaker.

Keep in mind that trends change, and you've got to go with the flow. Your original skills may not gel with the current trends, so you should always try to keep your skills updated.

On Organization

When you're self-employed, it's very easy to squander the entire day. You've got to allocate your time very carefully and figure out how to use it efficiently. It might be only a fifteen-minute trip to a potential client to do another estimate, which could lead to a $250 job. In short, you should always try to maximize the moneymaking potential of your days. Even if you think that you don't have a full schedule, you can't goof off for the morning. Instead, get the stuff that you do have to do completed in the morning because the phone is going to ring and there's bound to be some kind of emergency. You're probably going to have to go out and tend to a customer. Who knows, you may make half the money you earn that week in that one afternoon, which you wouldn't have made if you closed up shop and went fishing.

ELISH McPARTLAND,
MASSAGE THERAPIST

On Advertising

I think the most important thing is to have the right attitude of respect and care for your clients, and convey that to them. If you can do that effectively, word of mouth will take care of your advertising needs. It is amazing how a small group of satisfied clients—perhaps as few as five or six—can lead to well over a hundred clients.

The best thing to do is when you're starting out in my business is to give massages to a lot of people who have never had a professional massage. They will generally give you wonderful feedback, which boosts your confidence, and they are likely to become repeat customers.

ROBERT FRANGIOSO,
COMMERCIAL PHOTOGRAPHER

On Continuing Education

Probably the toughest part of photography, or perhaps of any business, is to pull in the customers. You may not be the best photographer in the world, but you can still make a good living as long as you can run a business. When I started as a photographer, I didn't have any business background and had to learn everything the hard way. So, take some business courses along with your photography classes. It'll pay off in the end.

As well as beefing up your knowledge of how to run a business, you need to keep abreast of changes in your industry. Photography is one art that has changed dramatically with the technological revolution. Most of the professional photographers' associations have seminars and schools to help you stay current. Professional Photographers of America also offers a Master's Program. In short, unless you go back and add the skills you need, you're going to be left behind and out of business.

For example, you can fix a photograph on a computer screen in a few minutes, which would have taken you hours to do by hand in the past. The latest technology can save you hours of time, and time is money.

AMY KITTS, ARTS ADMINISTRATOR

On Getting Started

At first, I didn't really know what artistic administration was. I didn't know all the different job titles that go into making a play happen onstage. So I just started talking to people in the business. I went to theater companies and offered to help them out, just so I could pick their brains and find out what my career options were. And I then got a job through a publication called "Art Search," which is a very valuable resource for anyone who is looking to get into arts administration.

In this business, you need to be very, very organized and detail-oriented. You also have to be outgoing and really understand the artistic temperament, yet be able to maintain a businesslike demeanor. And that's straddling two very different worlds.

This job also involves a lot of networking. You need to be prepared to sell yourself to other people, and you need to have good connections. For instance, in regional theater, I run into the same actors and administrative people again and again. I am sure that it works the same way in film and television. Once the members of a creative team begin to work well together, they're going to stick together. Trying to break into an established group is really difficult.

Finally, you need to know that you've made the right career choice. In this field, you could make twice as much money with your skills somewhere else, so it's important that you do love it.

LARRY ROSENBERG, PH.D., COUNSELOR/PSYCHOLOGIST

On Continuing Education

Psychologists spend much of their day hearing about very serious problems that other people are facing. I work in a field where people are recovering from trauma and abuse, so some of the stories I've heard about people's suffering is pretty intense. So you need to be able to learn how to both be available and engaged with your clients, and, at the same time, not carry the emotional burden of their stories with you. In short, you have to be able to separate your work life from your personal life.

Most psychologists are not well trained in the business aspects of being a psychologist. Once they begin their own practice, most have to learn how to set fees, collect fees from delinquent clients, and other administrative and management aspects of a practice. These are quite a different set of skills from the clinical and listening skills gained through schooling.
It is also helpful to have some basic understanding of the law. In the 1990s, with malpractice and liability concerns being very salient, it is beneficial to understand the many legal aspects of being a psychologist.

LAURA SAPELLY,
COMPUTER TRAINER

On Improving Your Skills

One way to improve your teaching style is to sit in on classes taught by other computer trainers. When I was starting out, I sat in on a variety of classes: beginner, advanced, and ones featuring different platforms. I tended to sit in on classes that covered subject I was already familiar with, and concentrated on trying to broaden my range of teaching styles, and skills. I also learned what approaches students respond to best. I saw a lot of good teachers, and a lot of bad ones. The more I observed teachers interacting with students, the better I was able to assess what the students were and were not getting out of their classes. For me, that was the best way to learn how to train others effectively. I also was a teaching assistant in some of the classes, and that was very, very helpful.

I could spend a million dollars upgrading my software with all the latest releases, but I just can't afford that. So I joined a user group of a computer society. They have the software upgrades and the books, and you can train yourself. I find that I can use my time most effectively by reading a third-party book on the software before I try it out.

JUDITH FORTIN,
DANCE INSTRUCTOR

On Knowing Yourself

Not everyone who is a good dancer is going to be a good teacher. It doesn't work that way. A lot of people think that if they can perform at a very high level, they can walk into a studio and be able to teach. Teaching is a gift, and the principles that you use to teach dance are the same that you use to teach algebra.

When I first started teaching, I was renting a shared space. A lot of dance schools start out in church halls or school buildings. They may have use of the space for three hours, and then somebody else will be in there for the next three hours. I didn't really like that. So when I found my present studio, I chose a place I love and that is close to my home. But if I had placed it in a more commercial location, I think I could have done even better.

JOY BENJAMIN,
DATING SERVICE OWNER

On Friends

When you start a dating service, your first priority is signing up members. Some people give memberships away just to get a group together. I remember when I started out, I had a hard time getting that first group of members together, and I mistakenly counted on my friends to help me out. I thought that they would all join because they wanted dates and because they liked me and wanted to help out. But even your friends don't necessarily want you to know about their broken romances, or that their daughter is looking for a husband. So learn from my mistake and realize that you won't necessarily be picking up a lot of business from people you know. I think that this is probably true for any business that you go into. You can't rely on your friends in any business as a source of revenue.

ED LIZOTTE, FINANCIAL PLANNER

On Certification

A person cannot just wake up one morning and decide to be a financial planner, as is true of many other popular start-up businesses. Aside from the necessary educational background, there is a licensing process that is critical. You need state licenses in health insurance, securities, and life insurance. In addition, the Securities Exchange Commission delegates the National Association of Security Dealers to test prospective financial planners. They offer different exams that, if you pass them, allow you to discuss and distribute securities. These are called the Series 6 and the Series 7 exams. The Series 7 is the one you want to get.

It's really a tough test. So before you begin studying for it, you're forced to ask yourself, "Do I have what it takes?" It's a very, very long and arduous exam. However, once you pass it, you can really begin to get started in the field.

One good place to get your training is the College of Financial Planning in Denver, Colorado. This institution offers extension courses in six key areas of financial planning: financial position, protection planning, investment planning, tax planning, retirement planning, and estate planning. Typically, a degree program to become a certified financial planner takes three to four years. The Association of Financial Planners bestows that designation on you, and it's a registered trademark. You can't put "certified financial planner" on your business card unless you've passed all the exams in the six key areas, plus a comprehensive two-day exam, and of course, the previous education requirement and an experience or "years in the business" requirement.

JOHN HENRY, MAGICIAN

On Getting Started

To get a magic business going, try performing for your friends free of charge. Do some free work in hospitals, or for community groups. Also, you should let prospective clients know that you're just starting out and practicing to be a better magician. That way, no one's disappointed.

You can also home your skills and pick up tricks of the trade through attending conventions and meetings sponsored by professional organizations. National organizations like the Society of American Magicians and the International Brotherhood of Magicians are always a good bet.

When you're not actually performing, you need to keep up with the same kind of boring operations stuff any business person does. You need to get information from your clients, such as what kind of a show they want and on what date. You've got to keep excellent records and contracts. People are always amazed when I say, "I'm just overwhelmed with paperwork." Maybe they think a magician can just wave a magic wand, but my business is just that—still a business.

MYRA MAYMAN,
ARTS FESTIVAL PROMOTER

On Planning an Event

In my field, every event requires the tedious, nuts-and-bolts work of setting things up—the planning process. Early on, you have to schedule the meetings, send out memos to get people to the meetings, and have your databases updated, so that when the time comes to put on an event, you can contact people from a list without additional research. For every one-weekend event, there's a lot of preparation work going on throughout the year.

A good way to get into this business is to have some experience doing smaller-scale productions—anything from special events at institutions, to producing a play, to putting on a concert. You might also gain relevant experience by being a community activist—a person who gets people together and making something happen. In general, you need to be a person who can cope with adrenaline rushes and crisis management—all that is part of putting on a show.

MARK TALANIAN,
INSURANCE AGENT

On Customer Service

The bottom line in this business is how you treat your customers. In fact, your customer service is probably the most valuable advertising you can do, because satisfied people will tell others about you and generate new business.

The first couple of years in this business can be really dry years. I mean, you're just starting from scratch. As you develop your clientele, you get commissions on the policies you write year after year after year, so the more policies you accumulate, the more money you receive. You have to have some staying power in order to get through those early years, and you need to limit your expenses, or have some other means of support.

MARY LOU ANDRE,
PERSONAL SHOPPER

On Using the Telephone Effectively

When I first started my business, I had no idea how to use the telephone. It was so scary. When someone called, I would get very excited about what I do because I love it, and start to blabber out my ideas.I learned the hard way that once it is out of my mouth and I'm not yet billing for my time, I'm giving my product away! So I got a sales trainer to help me with a script for receiving phone calls. Now, if I get a call from an interested client, I book an appointment right away. I never walk into anybody's home or office not on the clock.

To determine my fees, I started with the Yellow Pages. I called everybody that was in my field, and asked them what they charged. I determined an initial rate at the low end of the spectrum at first. As I found out the extent of my talents, efficiency, and uniqueness, I gradually raised my prices.

I started my newsletter three years ago. My first mailing went to everybody who had come to my wedding! After that, I added in everybody that I worked with, and then new people that I met at networking events. That's how my business started to grow.

ERICA KLEINKOPF, RETAILER

On Communication Skills

I think that having good communication skills and being able to speak with different people in different situations is crucial when you have your own store. One of the things you must be able to do is go out there in the marketplace and talk to people. It's difficult to talk to your competition, so I recommend going to another state. Even if you're on vacation, if you see people in a business that you're interested in, just strike up a conversation, or ask them if they could speak with you at a later time, or if you could take them out for coffee. You can also use your local Small Business Development Center (SBDC) or Small Business Association (SBA) to find other business owners who are willing to have a chat.

I've found that when you are the principal in a business, you are responsible for many different things, but you can't be expected to be an expert at every single part of the business. So I feel it's very important to hire the appropriate people to help you out. Every small business owner should have their own attorney and their own accountant. Many businesses don't thrive because the person in charge thinks, "I have to be great at everything I do."

DONALD MARTINI,
SECURITY SYSTEMS CONSULTANT

On Defining Your Market

I think if I were first starting in this business, I would look closely at the existing market for my services. What potential clients exist in my geographical area? What are some potential opportunities?

Second, I'd look at what competition is already out there. Are there other companies that are already doing an excellent job? Maybe there's really no room for me to start from the bottom up. I'd be really careful to determine that up front.

The third thing I would do is dedicate an hour a week, or whatever I could afford, to public relations. Public relations doesn't necessarily need to be sponsoring a baseball team. It can be as simple as writing a piece relating to your line of work for your local newspaper. Getting your name in print will make some people perceive you as an expert in your field, and two or three years down the road, you'll be in demand.

A good time to market to potential customers in my business is when people are doing work on their property. One easy way to locate potential customers is to check local building permits, which are almost universally required for people who are building a new structure or adding on. Building permits are public records. So you can go to three, four, or five surrounding towns, and all of a sudden, you have 200 or 300 potential customers to call. The next thing you know, you've got more appointments than you can handle.

JEFF CHIN AND TIME REGAN, WORLD WIDE WEB HOME PAGE CREATORS

On Having a Business Plan

When we first started our business together, we said, "We don't need a business plan. We know what we're doing. We know where we're going with this, and the business plan might actually inhibit our opportunities." We were so wrong! No matter what your business is, develop a plan, and structure that plan with some realistic objectives and benchmarks, and stick with it. And once you get to a point where you've allowed yourself the room to shift a little bit, then do it. But a business plan is absolutely critical. We missed perhaps six or eight months of business opportunities because we didn't have a plan.

To sustain your business for any length of time, you're going to need to invest money as well as time. When you're first starting out, you should have some money from your last job in reserve for basic expenses. Even if you're starting your business on the side, you're going to have to spend money on marketing and hardware. The more you have tucked away, the more comfortable you will be.

If we could start our business over again, we would put more money into marketing up front. We spent a lot of money on equipment, software, and education. The learning process was long and expensive. In retrospect, we should have approached smaller potential clients and offer to handle assignments while we were still going through the learning process. It probably would have been easier too, if we had two or three more people on board.

MARY MCCARTHY, BOOK BINDER

On Working with Clients

Besides knowing the basic skills of your trade, you have to have true business skills if you're going to make money. You have to be able to work with people, and you have to be able to ask lots of questions because sometimes people really don't know what they want. In the past two years, I've worked with lots of corporations, marketing strategy people, advertisers, designers, and design groups. And my clients will often ask for materials that don't work together. So you also have to know your materials, besides knowing how to create the objects that your clients want.

Setting fees was probably the most difficult thing that I've had to do. I looked at some handmade work and then went to binderies and asked how much things cost, and then I tried to price projects on an hourly basis. After a while, I found out that I was really selling myself short, and I could charge more money. So I just raised my hourly fee. When I take on a new job, I tell people that I charge by the hour, so if they waste my time, it's their money.

Whenever I work with advertisers or marketing people, I always make them a sample. It might not be exactly what they want when they're finished, but if they tell me they want something and I say I can't make that, or those materials are not going to go together, I'll prove it to them. Sometimes I make a dummy that's just a small model of what they want. If the clients have something to look at, they have a real sense of what they're going to get when the project is finished.

CAROL HAMBLET ADAMS, MOTIVATIONAL SPEAKER

On Getting Started

If you want to be a motivational speaker, you have to be able to choose an effective topic. I think it pays to be different. It's very helpful to ask yourself, "What makes me different? What can I bring to an audience that someone else might not?" Zero in on your uniqueness. Don't try to be like everybody else.

Make sure you have a good promotional piece on yourself for any client who wants one. You can start off with a one-page black-and-white piece that you can mail or fax to potential clients. Mine has endorsements on it from some of my clients, and briefly describes who I am and what I do. You can also develop a brochure, which should include letters of reference from people in your audience, and any kind of available press releases or clippings about your work.

Speak...wherever you can. And start off local. For example, Rotary clubs and Kiwanis clubs need speakers every week. Church groups are also a good bet. You should never lose sight of the fact that whatever group you speak before, you have potential clients listening to you.

When I speak, people always say, "Gee, can I buy a tape of yours? Do you have any books?" As a speaker, you should have a product. If you have a speech, you have potential for an audiotape or videotape. And if you go home and type out your speech, you have potential for a book. Begin developing your product as early in your career as possible.

Hooking up with a professional organization is also important when you're just starting out. Get involved in the National Speakers Association. Every state has a chapter. You can learn how to market yourself, how to develop better presentation skills, how to dress, and what kind of written materials are needed.

DONNA O'LEARY ABKOWITZ,
TECHNICAL WRITER

On Improving Your Skills

A very marketable skill today is writing on-line help for software programs, which can also be a lot of fun. You need to know the productivity tools like Doc-to-Help or Robohelp to be able to do that. And if you're writing printed documentation, you need to know Microsoft Word for Windows or probably Framemaker for desktop publishing. Once you're up and running, you certainly can demand a very good hourly rate.

A challenge for a lot of technical communicators right now is how to deal with information. In the past, a great deal of technical information was published in books and manuals. Now, most of my work ends up on the World Wide Web. Writing skills, research skills, and interpersonal skills are still very much in demand, but you have to keep up with technological trends.

On Employment Agencies

Some technical writing consultants work through agencies, but I don't feel that you are self-employed if you're going that route. I consider myself self-employed because I get paid as a freelancer, using a 1099 tax form for payment, which means that I can deduct certain business expenses. It's not a bad idea if you're new to the work to go through an agency because then you might be able to get real work assignments on your resume. After you've established yourself, you can work with clients directly.

PART I

PUTTING YOUR BUSINESS TOGETHER

LEGAL ISSUES FOR SMALL BUSINESSES

Many start-up businesses do not have a lawyer, and some companies operate for years without ever needing legal advice. The owners have done their homework and understand the legal situations likely to arise in their area of business. They know the government rules and regulations affecting them and have set up systems to assure that they dot the i's and cross the t's consistently, keeping accurate records to prove it.

DO YOU NEED A LAWYER?

Generally speaking, though, entrepreneurs find that working with an attorney who specializes in small business issues saves them time, worry, and (possibly) large sums of money over the long run. This should be one of the "business advisor" relationships that strengthens your organization rather than draining its resources. You will definitely need to work with an attorney:

- If you decide to incorporate or form a partnership.
- When you need to sign a contract or agreement—understanding the legal language so you know exactly what you are committing your business to do.
- Whenever you prepare a contract or agreement for others to sign.
- If someone sues you.

FINDING AN ATTORNEY

To find a good attorney, ask friends and business associates for recommendations. It is important to check each lawyer's business experience and learn about his or her general approach. You want direct, no-frills service that provides substance at the least possible cost. You need a real relationship—someone who responds to your calls within a reasonable time period, answers your questions in plain English, and takes an active interest in your business success. Most attorneys provide an initial consultation at no charge. Ask about fees. Once you have chosen your lawyer, develop a fee or retainer plan that fits your budget.

Finding a compatible attorney can be a somewhat lengthy process, and it is much better to do this before the crisis hits. In fact, good legal advice can be the stitch in time that saves you from tedious, expensive trouble later on. What is your exposure to lawsuits? If the danger is high, you might also consider insuring your business against legal costs.

AVOIDING LEGAL TROUBLE

Most businesses never incur these costs, and clearly you want to do everything you can to be in that category. Set your business up and conduct it with the aim of keeping legal troubles from arising. Get business agreements in writing, and maintain clear, organized records of each transaction. Add to the files your notes on what is said in any additional telephone calls or meetings that discuss expectations, promises, modifications, and other issues.

Follow laws and regulations, those that apply generally to businesses, and those that apply to your specific business type. Make sure your employees and customers know what your policies are, and follow them yourself. This is an area where your leadership will have a more powerful effect than all the memos and employee handbooks in the world. When you do what you promise and follow through immediately to resolve complaints, you set up an atmosphere of trust. That's the best legal protection your business can have.

AGREEMENTS

New business owners may not recognize situations that actually involve an agreement or contract, even though no official piece of paper has been written to label them as such. Do you get paid in advance for a service or product to be delivered later? Do you send payment to a supplier and receive delivery of the materials later? These are really agreements: money is exchanged on the expectation that the desired result will occur.

Many slightly more experienced business owners discover a painful truth: agreements aren't always honored by the other party. You may provide a service, an expensive service that involves buying the paper to produce a catalog, hiring an associate, or accumulating travel costs. You intend to send a bill when the job is complete, but the client wants one small change after another. You finally send the bill—but it never gets paid. Unless you have excellent records of what was asked for and what you promised, as well as what you delivered, you may have no way of recovering this loss. One situation like this can destroy a fledgling business. For safety's sake, check with your attorney to set up a formal agreement procedure before your fingers get burned.

CONTRACTS

If contracts are part of your business, you will also need to work with your attorney, to protect yourself. Getting the requests, plans, and promises down on paper is actually a good selling technique: your customer knows exactly what to expect, and you have a checklist to make sure that you perform the work to expectations. Then there will be no gray areas that could lead to discomfort, disagreements, and disappointment later. You are protecting your business, and you are guaranteeing customer satisfaction as well. It's a win/win activity.

Contracts tend to be more formal than agreements. If you write your own, have your attorney create the first one and check any major variations that occur in later versions. If you are asked to sign a contract prepared by another organization, READ ALL OF IT. Have your attorney read it, too, and explain the murky parts to you. Again, you can't provide complete customer satisfaction if you don't know what you're supposed to do. Renegotiate whatever provisions you do not wish to meet. The other party has the option of doing this as well. Carrying out this process in a positive manner can be a key to selling successfully. You're simply working toward a situation of mutual benefit: providing your products or services to meet their needs in a mutually agreeable way.

COPYRIGHTS

Copyrights and trademarks are methods of protecting your rights to "intellectual property," that is, ideas, words, names, and so on. The two types of protection are very different in ease of use, and they have different effects. Additionally, neither is a guarantee of anything. They simply give you the right to try to enforce your ownership. Major legal cases involving copyright infringement occasionally receive national attention in the news media, but the day-to-day application of copyright and trademark protection is extremely complex.

The copyright symbol is familiar to almost everyone. You can simply apply it yourself to the beginning of a literary, musical, dramatic, choreographic, or visual work you have created. Typically, a copyright claim takes this form: Copyright © 1996 by Mary Smith. You can't copyright an idea or a title, but you can use a claim to protect an article, photograph, painting, record, or tape. The copyright gives the creator the sole right to copy or reproduce a work. Registering a copyright with the federal government costs $20. This is an additional step, not a requirement.

Anyone who works with business material knows, however, that copyrights are infringed regularly. Intentionally or otherwise, people steal or "borrow" others' work. It's a frustrating situation, and there is no squad of government enforcers riding out from Washington, D.C., in defense of the injured parties. Definitely claim any copyright you deserve, but realize that you'll have to enforce it yourself. It can be hard to identify what is original, what is a slight alteration of your work, and what is simply material that is "common knowledge" and should not be considered original at all.

TRADEMARKS

Trademarks apply specifically to business situations. You trademark your business name, product name, symbol, or combination of symbol and name so that no other organization can use it. The reputation for quality and service attached to your business name is protected in this way from use by sleazeballs who want to ride on your coattails.

Registering a trademark is essential, and the process is complex enough to require the assistance of an attorney who specializes in this area. An extensive search is necessary first to be sure that no one else has used "General Motors" as the name for their car company. Given the size and dynamics of the U.S. economy, it can be quite difficult to create a business name that is not already in use. Another purpose of the national trademark search, therefore, is to avoid unintentionally infringing the trademark of an established business.

Again, there is no guarantee that a trademark will protect you, but it will help prevent accidental use by another organization of your name. And it will at least discourage copycatting. To some extent, your name conveys the value and quality of your business. Your customers find you by your name, and they use your name to spread the good word to others about the value of what you provide. Your business or product name is far more, then, than just a phrase to print on your business card. Trademarking helps protect this symbol of your enterprise.

PUTTING TOGETHER A SOLID BUSINESS PLAN

A business plan is a detailed document that describes the vital elements of your enterprise, outlines the basic assumptions you are making as you develop the organization, and details your financial projections. The plan establishes your goals: what are you trying to achieve?; what specific steps will you take to achieve these goals?; what resources will be required? A well-thought-out, well-written plan is essential for gaining funding from banks and other investors. More importantly, though, producing the plan forces you to think through your business concept in a systematic way.

The plan is also a living document. Every six months, you should take the opportunity to reassess the effectiveness of the strategy you have laid out in the plan. How accurate were your assumptions? What do you now know that you can use to help the business?

Business plans can vary depending on the type of business, what is customary in a geographic area, and the specific audience. If you are submitting your plan to a bank, obtain a model plan from the loan officer for guidance. Read as many other plans as you can, and work with your business advisors as you write. Keep your readers in mind, and be sure to address their concerns. Do not assume that your readers will be familiar with the jargon and technical terminology of your business. Above all, state the assumptions behind your financial projections. Offer evidence to support each claim you make. Why is your market attractive? What information supports your projected sales figures for each of the next five years? How have you calculated your materials costs?

All business plans include these basic elements: an executive summary, a company profile, a product or service analysis, a market analysis, a marketing plan, a financial analysis, and a description of your management team.

EXECUTIVE SUMMARY

The executive summary is critical because most investors will read it first to gain a sense of your business as a whole. (Write it last, after all the details have been worked out.) Within a few pages, you should:

- Define your company and describe the management team—their expertise, management ability, and experience with start-up businesses.
- Outline your products or services and highlight the benefits they provide to your target market.
- Show evidence that your product or service is accepted by your market.
- Describe your target market.
- Analyze your competition.
- Summarize your financial prospects.
- State the amount of money you need.
- Show how the money will be used.
- Explain why your business will be successful.

COMPANY PROFILE

This section describes your planned company in detail. It outlines the products, markets, and history of the business. The goal of this section is to convince your readers that you are able to produce the results that you are projecting. Here is where you establish your competitive edge—the factors that make you stand out above the competition and appeal to your target market. This section also contains your general, long-term business goals.

PRODUCT OR SERVICE ANALYSIS

This section establishes exactly why and how your product or service is different from what is already available from other businesses. What are you offering that your target market can obtain in no other way? The features of your product are important, but what you must clarify here are the benefits.

- Outline the resources you will need to deliver the product or service: raw materials, skilled technicians, packaging, office space, etc. Discuss availability and cost.
- Describe your facility and delivery methods, equipment needed, utility costs, and other factors in the day-to-day operations of the business. Transportation, suppliers, and manufacturing issues must be outlined here.
- Explain why your product or service is unique. What value will it add to your customers' lives? Is your technology legally protected? How will you keep what you offer up to date?

MARKET ANALYSIS

A market analysis supports all successful businesses and requires a great deal of research. Use the library, local trade associations, and business groups such as the Chamber of Commerce for data. The point is to illustrate the potential demand for your specific product or service. What needs are currently not being met, and why? What trends affect your market area? What changes are occurring in the business climate?

Describe your competition, what they offer, what segment they appeal to, and the reasons why their customers buy from them. Describe your likely customers: number, demographics, trends, location. Clarify the pluses and minuses of your products versus those of your competition: price, quality, appeal to the market.

MARKETING PLAN

The marketing plan shows how you will reach your target market. How will those who need your product or service come to understand that it is available from your business? This plan covers pricing, and the relationship of these prices to similar products and to the competition. It covers distribution, delivery, returns, and replacements.

You will outline your plans for the sales process and the methods of payment you will accept. You will describe your promotions and advertising approaches. Most importantly, you will project your sales month by month for the first year and, in general, for the four years after that.

FINANCIAL ANALYSIS

Investors with a serious interest in your business will read this section in detail. It's the heart of your business plan. The financial analysis describes where the money will come from and how it will be spent, with projections of cash flow, income, and debt. This section includes:

- A balance sheet, a snapshot of your company's assets, liabilities, and net worth;
- An income statement, comparing your revenues and expenses over a specific period of time to show your net profit or loss;
- Projected income statement, which estimates income and expenses at a future period;
- Projected cash flow, which shows how you will manage the most difficult problem for many businesses: spending and collecting cash;
- A break-even point, the date at which your company will begin to make a profit!

MANAGEMENT AND ADVISORY TEAM

You need to explain how your company is organized and who fills each role. Outline the responsibilities planned for each position. Some plans place the background information on each member of the management team in this section, while others put detailed resumes in an appendix.

Include enough details on key people to allow a background check. Describe their experience and highlight the strengths they bring to your specific business. Describe what each person has invested in the business and their compensation plans. Include here the names of outside owners and such business advisors as your attorney, your accountant, and other people important to the enterprise.

WHY SOME START-UPS FAIL
(AND WHAT YOU CAN DO TO SURVIVE)

It has been said that some 60 percent of new businesses fail within their first five years. How can you protect yourself when you think you're hitting hard times?

Primary reasons businesses fail:

- **Undercapitalization.** You don't have enough to pay the bills and keep the creditors off your back. The phone is ringing, but you hate to answer it because it's more likely a creditor than a customer. The problem is, you're spending more than you're actually earning.
- **Poor Leadership/Direction.** Your staff is running around in circles, and nothing seems to get accomplished. You spin your own wheels trying to assess blame rather than solve the problem. Maybe you just weren't trained to be a good manager; get training now.
- **Shaky Business Plan.** Remember that all-important document you were supposed to work on—the one that answered all the questions about where your money would come from and how you would keep it rolling in? Maybe it's time for a look back; such time-travel can often provide important clues to what's happening and what's not in your business. But, then, you should have been looking back and updating your business plan every few months or so anyway, right?
- **Miscalculated Market Potential.** Your marketing strategy should have pointed out all of your areas of opportunity, but what if you were flat wrong? What if your idea was a good one for New York City but not for Boise, Idaho? Let's face it: when we're first working on our marketing plan, we're always overly optimistic. That's why it's a good idea to have another (more cynical and objective) person look over your marketing data; they'll play devil's advocate, and you'll thank them for it later.

- **Ineffective Marketing.** You've spent tons of money on advertising and wonder why it isn't paying off. Could it be that you were advertising in the wrong place—or, worse yet, to the wrong people? Once you've committed advertising budget to one or more media, you'll have a hard time pulling the dollars out when you get no response. Test your markets, and don't commit to long-term contracts until you've gotten at least a 15 percent return on three consecutive ads.

Primary Strategies for Survival:

- **Take a hard look at your debt.** Too many of us shy away from what we fear most. Have the courage to get it all out into the open—and, if you don't have any courage left, call a professional bookkeeper who can help put everything in the right column again.
- **Work out alternative payment plans where you can.** Often, all you'll need to do is tell your creditors you're thinking of filing bankruptcy. The word alone makes them jump at accepting payments that are significantly less than they would have gotten (to them, some money will be better than no money).
- **Sell whatever you can, if you can.** If you've got equipment that's worth something, put it on the market as soon as you can. If it's critical to your business, you obviously can't sell it; if it's a piece that you could just as easily lease, it could bring in the money you need.
- **Don't think of expansion as the answer.** Too many entrepreneurs think that if one aspect of their business isn't working, they should add another (rather than subtract the one that's not working). Don't make the mistake of growing bigger to avoid problems; you're only distracting yourself from the real issue at hand.
- **Cut expenses across the board.** Some entrepreneurs get narrow-minded about controlling expenses; you'll lose your business for sure if you're not flexible in where you can save money.
- **Consider the worst thing that could happen.** In your survival plan, you'll need to picture the most terrible thing that can happen in order to be able to work back to the most positive. Know it, face it, then work your plan.
- **Keep a positive attitude.** It's hard to remain positive when you feel as though you're losing control of your business, but you need to remember that all businesses go through trying times. Moreover, you'll need to be positive for your employees and your customers, so that they don't lose faith in you during what might wind up being only a temporary problem.

Part II

500 Businesses You Can Start

START-UP FOR UNDER $1,000

AIRBRUSH ARTIST

Start-up cost:	$500-$1,000
Potential earnings:	$25,000-$50,000
Typical fees:	Varies; could be as low as $125 and as high as several thousand per project
Advertising:	Local art galleries, art studios, art supply houses
Qualifications:	Graphic design, art background or degree
Equipment needed:	Airbrush, paints, hose, canvas, cloth, masks
Home business potential:	Yes
Staff required:	No
Handicapped opportunity:	Yes
Hidden costs:	Ventilation system, rising materials costs

LOWDOWN:

Airbrush art is found in many different places, such as on billboards or T-shirts. An art background is a must for this job. It's essential that you can separate colors as well as mix them. The ability to think in fine detail and visualize is also essential. Build your reputation as an artist wherever you can find work (try magazines, ad agencies, and public relations firms). There are several ways to do this; the most simple is to enter a contest or show or try to get your work exhibited locally. The icing on the cake would be to get your work commissioned for private or public display. Either way, this shows that someone (hopefully with big money) has noticed your work and is willing to pay for it. You're well on your way.

START-UP:

Most of your initial investment will be in trying to enter your work in contests and art galleries. Some charge a fee for this. You should already have the tools you need because of your background training (start-up could be as little as $500). Be prepared to start out slowly until you build your reputation. If you hit some craft shows and are lucky enough to get into an exhibit, your monthly income could be approximately $1,000-$3,000 per month. But don't quit your day job just yet, since your income is bound to be unpredictable. It's the nature of the creative beast to live paycheck to paycheck.

BOTTOM LINE ADVICE:

If you live for creativity, the sky is the limit. You can airbrush on all types of materials: wood, shirts, brick, film—you name it. Sure, it will take a while before you'll make really big money, but in the meantime you can console yourself with the fact that this is a growing industry and you will have repeat business once you've done at least a few good projects for your clients.

ANIMAL REGISTRATION/ID SERVICES

Start-up cost:	$500-$1,000
Potential earnings:	$15,000-$30,000
Typical fees:	$6-$10 per license, $20-$40 for electronic ID service
Advertising:	Yellow Pages, veterinarians' offices, local trade fairs, word of mouth
Qualifications:	You may need to apply for a license to sell dog licenses
Equipment needed:	Electronic ID patches, computer, dog tags/licenses
Home business potential:	Yes
Staff required:	No
Handicapped opportunity:	Yes
Hidden costs:	Insurance

LOWDOWN:

Pet registries contain photos and identifying information about household pets, primarily in case an animal gets lost or stolen. This information can be matched with descriptions from the Humane Society, police departments, local animal shelters, and even classified ads. Your job will be to maintain these records and conduct a little bit of a search through these channels if Fido's missing in action. You can start this business by selling dog licenses and work up to peddling the ID products as an add-on service. You will be providing a service that is as valuable to animal lovers as their pets—and that kind of loyalty can go a long way in your bank account. To really maximize your potential, you could try networking with veterinarians (who might help you via referral or by simply letting you post flyers in their offices).

START-UP:

You can launch this one without much hassle—and with as little as $500 (mostly to cover a small product inventory). Charging $6-$10 per license and $20-$40 for electronic ID products (which must be inserted by a veterinarian), you could make anywhere from $15,000-$30,000. That's not too shabby, especially if you offer this service as an add-on to an existing business (such as a hardware store, for example).

BOTTOM LINE ADVICE:

People are just plain crazy about their pets, and they can be easily convinced that your products are of value to them. However, you'll need to make sure that you have a genuine interest in their animals, or it'll show.

APARTMENT PREPARATION SERVICE

Start-up cost:	$500
Potential earnings:	$20,000–$30,000
Typical fees:	$50 and up per apartment
Advertising:	Yellow pages, direct contact with apartment owners
Qualifications:	Knowledge of cleaning procedures and painting skills
Equipment needed:	Cleaning supplies, sweeper, mops, buckets, painting equipment
Home business potential:	Yes
Staff required:	No
Handicapped opportunity:	No
Hidden costs:	Insurance, equipment maintenance

LOWDOWN:
You add the finishing touches to apartment buildings before the next tenant moves in. To increase your marketability, offer several services, including carpet cleaning, wall washing, painting and wallpaper repair, and overall cleaning services. Set fee schedules appropriately depending on individual services (or offer an all-inclusive package price). Advertise your services to many apartment complexes. To cut down on driving, try to get a contract with a multi-unit apartment complex offering short-term lease options.

START-UP:
Invest in good quality cleaning equipment, including a sweeper and carpet cleaner. Start-up costs can be as low or as high as you want, depending on what services you are going to offer and the quality of equipment you purchase. This business can be started for a relatively low cost with high return on investment.

BOTTOM LINE ADVICE:
This business is not for someone who is afraid of good hard elbow grease. Be prepared to encounter some messy situations. An apartment preparer might spend quite a bit of time on their hands and knees cleaning baseboards and floors—consider the health of your back and always wear a back corset. In addition, invest in a good pair of knee pads and rubber gloves.

ARTS FESTIVAL PROMOTER

Start-up cost:	$500-$1,000
Potential earnings:	$20,000-$45,000+
Typical fees:	40 percent of registration fees from artists; often, you'll also make a commission from each ticket sold
Advertising:	Word of mouth, ads in artists' newsletters and publications, direct mail to artists, newspaper/billboard ads for the event itself
Qualifications:	Strong organizational skills
Equipment needed:	Computer with desktop publishing software and laser printer
Home business potential:	Yes
Staff required:	No (you can solicit volunteers to work at each festival)
Handicapped opportunity:	Possibly
Hidden costs:	Insurance and low attendance due to poor advertising or inclement weather

LOWDOWN:

Annual arts festivals abound in nearly every community, and you could cash in on the public's interest in the arts by sponsoring or promoting your own group of arts festivals. Give your events a flashy name so that you can win instant recognition with your buying public and among artists (who get barraged with requests to appear in shows all over the country). You'll need to promote your festivals two ways: first, to artists who might like to participate; second, to folks who might like to attend. So, your advertising budget must be split to cater to both "customers." Set your festivals apart somehow by inviting only particular types of artists/crafts-men or by attaching your festivals to some sort of theme (such as an Oktoberfest arts festival). That way, you've set an annual time for the show to be expected to recur; build your mailing list for the following year by requiring everyone to sign in (or, better yet, by offering a drawing for an exquisite work of art).

START-UP:

You'll need $500-$1,000 to launch this interesting and artistic enterprise; this seed money will primarily cover your computer costs (printer, desktop publishing software) and a little advertising until you've got one or two shows under your belt. Once you've established a name for your arts festivals, you could have annual repeat business in certain areas and begin to make more than $45,000 per year doing something you truly enjoy.

BOTTOM LINE ADVICE:

You love the arts, and know that others like artsy events. So what's the downside? The only real negative is that sometimes the weather rains on your parade of artists. You could avoid such mishaps if you hold all of your events indoors; even though it may raise your space rental cost, the payoff might be worth it.

ATHLETIC RECRUITER/SCOUT

Start-up cost:	$1,000
Potential earnings:	$15,000 or more
Typical fees:	$25 per hour or more
Advertising:	Networking, referrals, participation in athletic boosters clubs, attendance at games
Qualifications:	Knowledge and love of sports, enthusiasm for young people, ability to spot talent, commitment to the team or school for which you want to recruit
Equipment needed:	Car
Home business potential:	Yes
Staff required:	No
Handicapped opportunity:	No
Hidden costs:	Transportation costs, telephone bills

LOWDOWN:

You do this anyway, right? Every game you go to, you notice the players who stand out, who make the great catches, who come through in the final minutes with the setup that leads to the winning score. You see the "unsung heroes" who support the stars, and you have a sense for the kids with commitment. You can turn your interests into a business by contracting with a college or professional athletic team or teams as a scout. As a recruiter, you will establish the initial contact with the player and his or her family. You will show them the opportunities that may be available for scholarships and for participation in a sports program with spirit and great coaching.

START-UP:

All you really need to do is get yourself to the games (not much more than $1,000 needed initially). If you have to write reports, a secretarial service can type them for you. Depending on how much time you put in, or if you work for colleges, $15,000 can be achievable for part-time work.

BOTTOM LINE ADVICE:

You'll need to be the kind of person in whom athletic directors, coaches, players, and parents feel confident. You'll need the patience to sit through the games that lack excitement and the games that are played in bad weather. Converting yourself from a fan to a worker means losing some of the spontaneity of just watching and enjoying the contest. Instead, you'll be analyzing all the time: how is this player progressing? Who was able to spark the team to greater effort in the second half? Will this player look so good at the next level of competition? This is not a way to get rich, but it has the satisfaction of bringing out excellence and helping young people find opportunities.

AUCTION HOUSE

Start-up cost:	$500-$1,500
Potential earnings:	$15,000-$25,000
Typical fees:	10 to 15 percent of total auction take
Advertising:	Yellow Pages, community newspapers, flyers, word of mouth
Qualifications:	Some states offer certification as an auctioneer
Equipment needed:	None (although a gavel seems to go with the territory)
Home business potential:	Yes (but you'll be working at each auction site)
Staff required:	No
Handicapped opportunity:	Yes
Hidden costs:	Insurance

LOWDOWN:

Auctioneers speak a language all their own . . . at such a rapid rate, it's a wonder that those bidding can hear themselves think. As an auctioneer, you'll auction off everything from fine china to farm animals; mostly, however, your work will entail auctioning off the remains of estates. You'll need to work with the executors of wills, attorneys, and others when participating in an estate auction; often, they'll pay you a small fee ($25-$50) in addition to your commission of what's sold. The advantage is obvious: you'll get better pay when handling estates than when working with smaller auctions such as those involving animals. However, don't rule out auctions of big-ticket items (such as farm equipment); here, your commissions may be higher than you would at first imagine (perhaps bringing in $5,000 or more per auction). Sometimes, particularly when dealing with antiques or fine art, you may have to appraise each item for its value; if you aren't trained as an appraiser, you'll need to hook up with a good one (and maybe trade referrals with each other).

START-UP:

Your start-up will be relatively low ($500-$1,500) and will mostly cover your certification or training costs, plus some business cards. Since you don't need an office or a basic office setup, your overhead will be extremely low. All you need to do is get out there and sell, sell, sell—and you could make $15,000-$25,000.

BOTTOM LINE ADVICE:

This is a fun, fast-paced occupation, but to make a good, strong living at it, you'll need to position yourself in the more affluent neighborhoods. In other words, you'll need to be where the rich folks are, since their "toys" are the ones that will bring you the most in commissions. If you don't know how to smell money a mile away, you probably won't do very well as an auctioneer.

AUTO PAINT TOUCH-UP PROFESSIONAL

Start-up cost:	$500-$1,000
Potential earnings:	$15,00-$25,000
Typical fees:	$30-$50 per job
Advertising:	Memberships and active participation at car enthusiast events, direct mail, flyers, referrals from dealers and auto repair stores, radio spots, classified ad in auto sales section of newspaper
Qualifications:	Some experience with auto paint work, sales skills
Equipment needed:	Inventory of popular paint colors, sander, brush
Home business potential:	Yes
Staff required:	No
Handicapped opportunity:	No
Hidden costs:	Inventory and disposal of used chemicals

LOWDOWN:

It's not the big things that drive us crazy, sometimes, it's the dings in our car doors and the chips off the hood. For an entirely new paint job, or the replacement of a crumpled fender, plenty of sources are available in most communities. But how can people keep those little scratches and chips from slowly ruining the appearance and resale value of their cars? That's where your service comes in. You can fix the small stuff, which is important nowadays just to keep a car's body panel warranty in effect. Your business meets the need for a smaller, less expensive way to maintain the smooth surface that your customers' vehicles had when new.

START-UP:

Costs are low (about $500 for materials); your skill in doing neat-looking paint touch-ups is your main product. On a part-time basis alone you could earn in excess of $15,000.

BOTTOM LINE ADVICE:

Can you find a way to combine customers? Would it work to fix the scratches in every car in the parking garage or lot of a huge company? Can you be an add-in to the work of a local detailer, car wash, or used car lot? You decide—and market yourself accordingly, perhaps offering group discounts.

AUTOMOTIVE LOAN BROKER

Start-up cost:	$500-$1,000
Potential earnings:	$50,000-$70,000
Typical fees:	Percentage of loan amount, from lender or borrower
Advertising:	Classified ads in local and national newspapers and magazines
Qualifications:	Finance background would be helpful
Equipment needed:	Office furniture, computer, suite software, printer, fax, modem, business card, letterhead, envelopes
Home business potential:	Yes
Staff required:	No
Handicapped opportunity:	Yes
Hidden costs:	Utility bills

LOWDOWN:

A loan broker brings together the people who need money with the institutions that are in the business of lending it. As an automotive loan broker you will be specializing in a type of loan applicable to almost every household in the country. There are roughly 1.8 vehicles per household in the U.S., and most of the new vehicles sold are purchased through loans. That's a huge potential market. How can you become a part of this picture? You have a list of lenders, a long list. You have obtained their trust with a well-organized business plan. You advertise for borrowers. It is possible that local auto dealerships might be good referral sources for you. But you don't have to restrict yourself to your own geographical area; much of this business can be done by phone. It is important to have a written agreement before you begin the loan search process, as most of your clients will use your service over a bank for credit reasons (i.e., they've had trouble securing credit in a more traditional way).

START-UP:

The borrowers will visit the lenders, not your office. Your only start-up costs are your advertising and the equipment to support your paperwork and communications; all of these should be under $1,000. Considering that, if you have marketing savvy, you could earn as much as $70,000. In short, the potential for success in this business is high. All you need is the ability to produce.

BOTTOM LINE ADVICE:

Clarity on goals and expectations is vital to the professional, ethical conduct of a loan brokering business. You make it clear to the potential borrower what expenses are to be reimbursed, and you take a fee only as a commission on a completed loan. Skill at bringing the two sides of the automotive transaction together can enable you to earn a very high income once you are established. Persistence pays off here, as it so often does in the world of small business.

BAND MANAGER

Start-up cost:	$500-$1,000
Potential earnings:	$15,000-$25,000
Typical fees:	10 percent to 25 percent of a gig
Advertising:	Industry trades, local paper, direct mail, nightclubs, bulletin boards, musicians' associations
Qualifications:	An ear for what will sell, management skills
Equipment needed:	Computer, laser printer, phone, letterhead, business cards
Home business potential:	Yes
Staff required:	No
Handicapped opportunity:	Yes
Hidden costs:	Band could fire you without notice; it might be a good idea to represent several

LOWDOWN:

You're into the club scene; you know instinctively what's hot and what's not. You see a few up-and-coming bands who need representation (because, truthfully, most musicians lack business skills). If you've got the ability to convince musicians that you can really sell them and make their jobs easier by handling all of the business details they'd probably rather not think of anyway, you could make a decent living. You'll need to be well-connected on the club scene, and if you are clued in on where to plug your band(s), you could successfully book them for regular gigs and earn a steady flow of income for yourself in the meantime. Of course, you need to really believe in your band, because if you don't, you won't be able to develop and promote them properly and it will show in your presentation. Good negotiation skills are a must.

START-UP:

You'll need some initial capital ($500-$1,000) to help get the band off the ground and lay the ground for some publicity. The ability to negotiate good contracts is important not only to the band, but to you because you get roughly 10 to 25 percent of what they make. With percentages like that, you could make $15,000-$25,000 (depending on how many bands you represent).

BOTTOM LINE ADVICE:

Expect to spend long hours on the phone trying to get bookings. At the start, you'll probably still have a day job, so expect your evenings and weekends to be tied up. Start out at small clubs and work your way to bigger ones as your band(s) get more confident.

BANKRUPTCY SERVICES

Start-up cost:	$500-$1,000
Potential earnings:	$25,000-$40,000
Typical fees:	$350 per client; sometimes an additional percentage (5 to 10 percent) from the creditors
Advertising:	Classified ads, local newspapers, seminars, and public service speaking engagements
Qualifications:	Financial planning expertise, good people skills
Equipment needed:	Office furniture suitable for client conferences, business card, letterhead, envelopes, marketing materials
Home business potential:	Yes
Staff required:	No
Handicapped opportunity:	Yes
Hidden costs:	Errors and omissions insurance

LOWDOWN:

Overextended is one thing; completely out of financial control is another. Your clients are the people who realize that they can't manage the debt they've accumulated, and they can't manage the bankruptcy process either. You assist them in developing a clear picture of their financial problem, filing for bankruptcy, and planning for the consequences. In today's world of easy credit, many people find themselves in bankruptcy without quite realizing what hit them. They're distressed, humiliated, and probably very confused as well. Your assistance with the painful process of sorting out the facts from the feelings is a very significant benefit.

START-UP:

Costs can be low ($500-$1,000), depending on the furniture and space you already have. If you're good at what you do, you could earn between $25,000-$40,000.

BOTTOM LINE ADVICE:

You are meeting your clients at a real low point in their lives, but you are the first step on their way back up. So the emotional temperature of your workday is going to be fluctuating wildly. Keeping a good psychological balance will be as important as getting the paperwork filled out correctly. Some of your clients will just have been irresponsible, but other have been dealt an impossible hand by fate. Historically the bankruptcy process has been designed to help these people by wiping the slate more or less clean. Nevertheless, people facing bankruptcy are not generally easy to work with. Your skill in dealing with the human side of your business will be essential.

BARTENDING SERVICES

Start-up cost:	Under $1,000
Potential earnings:	$10,000-$20,000
Typical fees:	$15-$30 per hour, or a flat per-event rate
Advertising:	Classified ads, bulletin boards, community newspapers
Qualifications:	Must be legal age (and should know how to make drinks without looking them up)
Equipment needed:	None
Home business potential:	Yes (but you'll be traveling to the party sites)
Staff required:	Might be a good idea to have one or two other bartenders
Handicapped opportunity:	Possibly
Hidden costs:	None apparent, so just watch your mileage

LOWDOWN:

Being a traveling bartender service for private parties is an exciting way to meet people and make money at the same time. You'll mix libations for everyone from wealthy executives to people at a family celebration, and the time will always pass quickly. You'll need to make sure that if you are expected to bring the beverages, you secure funds for that ahead of time to avoid excessive outlay of your own cash. Be sure to add in the cost of delivering the goods as well. The best way to get started is to produce professional-looking business cards and leave them prominently displayed at a few of your first jobs. In fact, you may want to do your first five jobs for free (if you feel you'll get a lot of attention)—that may be a great way to start the highballs rolling!

START-UP:

With virtually nothing to lose but your time, you could do far worse than start a bartending service. Invest in a few good mixology handbooks and you're off to a great start! You also may want to visit the more progressive bars in your area to see if the bartenders know of any interesting new drinks—the more you can offer your clients, the happier they will be.

BOTTOM LINE ADVICE:

You'll really absorb the energy and variety of bartending work, but it can be tiring to stand on your feet in one place for too long. Remember to bring a bar stool for yourself—and invest in a good pair of shoes with soothing inserts!

BARTER SYSTEMS

Start-up cost:	$500-$1,000
Potential earnings:	$15,000 and up
Typical fees:	$15 or more per transaction
Advertising:	Penny savers, community newspaper classifieds, bulletin boards, flyers, networking, participation in community activities related to recycling, cooperative grocery stores
Qualifications:	Friendliness, detail orientation
Equipment needed:	A computer would help you keep track of the information, but you could use a paper system as well
Home business potential:	Yes
Staff required:	No
Handicapped opportunity:	Yes
Hidden costs:	Phone bill may be higher than expected

LOWDOWN:

You know everyone. You never waste a penny. You love to solve problems, and to help other people solve theirs. That's why you will derive great satisfaction from your barter system business. It's really just putting two and two together: what someone has, with what someone needs, and vice versa. Making it all work as a profitable business will be a bit more challenging than just this (which you have probably been doing on an amateur basis most of your life). Many barter systems are warehouse operations, with individuals buying bulk odd lots and then trying to trade them. You will need to become known, to gather the data, the offerings, and the needs, and to work continually at the matches. Creating some kind of valuation system for disparate objects and services may pose difficulties also: how does a carwash match up with a soccer ball? Trading small ski boots for larger ones is easier.

START-UP:

Costs will be minimal (only about $500 to start). You'll need some way for your clientele to reach you, and some way to track what is bartered. Your thoughtfulness is your real product in this business. A part-time business should net you around $15,000.

BOTTOM LINE ADVICE:

Barter systems appeal to people who try to live inexpensively and not wastefully—the cooperative market types, people in academic communities, and creative thinkers who are trying to step off the whirl of consumerism that keeps the rest of us in debt. You'll develop repeat customers if you can help people achieve their wants, and get rid of their don't-wants, without the exchange of large sums of money—just a small fee to you for the privilege. This business is a classic example of making something out of nothing. Virtually no investment, no training required, nothing but hard work on your part.

BLADE-SHARPENING SERVICE

Start-up cost:	$500-$1,000
Potential earnings:	$8,000-$15,000
Typical fees:	$5-$15 per blade
Advertising:	Yellow Pages, community newspapers, word of mouth, cold calls
Qualifications:	None
Equipment needed:	Blade sharpener
Home business potential:	Yes
Staff required:	No
Handicapped opportunity:	Yes
Hidden costs:	Insurance, equipment maintenance

LOWDOWN:

Knives get dull, and most households and small businesses don't have the sharpeners or time to deal with such an inconvenience. You can market your service through the Yellow Pages and through cold calls to restaurants and other places where many knives are used on a regular basis. You could offer package deals (i.e., 12 knives for $25) or special promotions. You could network with kitchen and restaurant equipment suppliers to provide counterreferrals. Still, the work is quite simple and the hours few—you get the knives, put them through the sharpener, and return them in tip-top condition. It's an excellent retirement possibility or opportunity for supplemental income.

START-UP:

You'll spend $500 or less on your blade sharpener and the rest on your Yellow Pages and other forms of minor advertising (such as business cards to leave at kitchen supply stores). Of course, this is a sporadic and highly specialized type of business, so your income potential is limited to $8,000-$15,000 per year (unless you somehow manage to work out regular contracts with large restaurants and restaurant supply houses).

BOTTOM LINE ADVICE:

It's simple, it's straightforward—what's not to like? Well, the low-income potential could be troubling . . . but then, you probably chose this type of specialized service knowing it would only provide a supplemental income.

BOARDINGHOUSE OPERATOR

Start-up cost:	$500
Potential earnings:	$20,000-$60,000
Typical fees:	$100 per week per room
Advertising:	Classified ads, community bulletin boards, penny savers
Qualifications:	Capacity for hard work
Equipment needed:	Furnished rooms
Home business potential:	Yes
Staff required:	No
Handicapped opportunity:	No
Hidden costs:	Increased utilities, insurance, wear-and-tear replacements

LOWDOWN:

Through the centuries people have supported themselves by taking in boarders. Many people need an inexpensive place to live, and if you have a house with extra rooms, you can meet this need. The classic boardinghouse operator is a woman whose family is grown and who does not want to give up the house that is now too big. She can rent some of the rooms, avoid living alone, and bring in some income at the same time. Other boardinghouse operators make a business out of supplying rooms near universities and other organizations that attract a large group of transient people who need to save their pennies and have a decent place to live. You don't need a college degree or any special training to start this type of business. You do need a willingness to work hard, a sense for who will be a suitable renter, and a firmness about collecting rent when it's due.

START-UP:

If you are using rooms and furniture you already have, start-up could be as little as $500. If you buy or rent a house specifically to start this business, that's another matter. You should make at least $20,000 the first year.

BOTTOM LINE ADVICE:

Overall, most people are wonderful human beings who are a privilege to know. But there are others. This is the challenge in the boardinghouse business. Possibly you will always rent to friends who cause no trouble and always pay their rent on time. But you will need ways to deal with the difficult boarders.

BOOK INDEXER

Start-up cost:	$500-$1,000
Potential earnings:	$15,000-$30,000
Typical fees:	$2.50-$4.00 per printed book page
Advertising:	Direct mail to book publishers, Yellow Pages, industry newsletters
Qualifications:	A strong eye for detail and subject matter; impeccable organizational skills
Equipment needed:	Computer with alphabetical sorting capability, printer
Home business potential:	Yes
Staff required:	No
Handicapped opportunity:	Definitely
Hidden costs:	Your time—indexes are complex and time-consuming, and must be accurate

LOWDOWN:

When you're reading a book and you want to find information on a specific topic, you look in the index first. But it probably didn't occur to you that putting together an index is a job dependent upon painstaking accuracy and attention to detail. It's an area of specialization that sets professional indexers apart from other editorial types. These folks are typically not writers (although they can be), and they are not really editors, either. Their expertise is sought after the book is written and edited, but prior to publication; they provide readers with a service that enables them to conduct research or just locate topics of interest to them, saving them time in combing through the entire book. Obviously, indexers work with nonfiction books, but the subject matter can be extremely varied and could include everything from automotive manuals to business or self-help guides. A good place to start if you feel that your organizational skills are up to this kind of work is the American Society of Indexers in New York City. Joining organizations such as this prestigious association could instantly raise your credibility level.

START-UP:

Start-up costs are almost negligible for indexing. Begin with memberships in key organizations, then submit a letter of interest or resume to book publishers in and out of your area. Set aside at least $500-$1,000 for working capital; you may need it to furnish your office with a comfortable chair (a must). Charge anywhere from $2.50-$4.00 per printed book page; for example, a 200-page book will net you $500 minimum for your indexing work.

BOTTOM LINE ADVICE:

Low initial investment makes this a win-win if you don't mind detail-oriented work. The hours may be long, the turnaround time may be quicker than you had hoped, but the ability to generate income is there for those with talent.

BOUNTY HUNTER

Start-up cost:	$500-$1,500
Potential earnings:	$1 million+
Typical fees:	Extremely varied; could be as high as $500,000 per job (plus expenses)
Advertising:	Word of mouth, referral from federal/municipal law enforcement agencies
Qualifications:	Extensive training in fugitive tracking and self-defense
Equipment needed:	Computer with printer and on-line services, cellular phone/pager
Home business potential:	Yes
Staff required:	No
Handicapped opportunity:	No
Hidden costs:	Insurance, threats to your life

LOWDOWN:

While it may seem far-fetched at first to consider quitting your MBA-track job to become a bounty hunter, it isn't as unusual as you might think. In fact, many FBI retirees or ex-CIA investigators opt for a career as a bounty hunter, since they've already learned tracking techniques and know how to find criminals in a nanosecond. Granted, it won't all be as dramatic as the search for the Oklahoma City bombers, but it will be every bit as challenging to locate a deadbeat dad who's on the run from paying child support. Bounty hunters are a necessary component to our criminal justice system, primarily because they have the tenacity and resources to track relentlessly—while police stations and federal investigators simply don't have the time or funds to conduct as thorough a search.

START-UP:

You'll need minimal amounts of cash ($500-$1,500) to start this business, because your first clients will pay you enough to keep you financially sound for a long time. You may want to purchase a computer for on-line detective work, but your office expenses should stay as limited as possible since you'll be traveling constantly. If you're good at what you do, and produce tangible results in a short period of time, you could earn $1 million or more; your clients will pay you anywhere from $100,000-$500,000 per job (plus expenses).

BOTTOM LINE ADVICE:

Well, not everyone can afford to pay you for their services, and there will be some work you do pro bono (free). Ask these folks to offer testimonials that you can use to get other clients. Network regularly with the law enforcement community to let them know of your availability; sometimes, they may offer you contract work to handle cases they simply don't have the resources to handle in-house, particularly if it's a high-profile or high-publicity case. P.S. Remember: As in the Old West, you'll have to bring 'em in alive to collect the highest bounty.

CAKE DECORATOR

Start-up cost:	$100-$200
Potential earnings:	$5,000-$25,000
Typical fees:	$10-$1,000 per cake
Advertising:	Word of mouth, newspaper ads, neighborhood bulletins
Qualifications:	Cake baking and decorating knowledge
Equipment needed:	Baking pans and utensils, decorating supplies, ingredients, oven
Home business potential:	Yes
Staff required:	None
Handicapped opportunity:	Yes
Hidden costs:	Make sure you have enough kitchen space for finished cakes; may need a second oven or other facilities as business grows; need vehicle if you deliver

LOWDOWN:

People love home-baked goodies. All it takes to satisfy that need is an oven, some recipes, and a way (brochure, advertisement) to tell customers you're in business. Birthday cakes for children are especially popular; a home baker can customize and personalize them in countless ways to please the customer. Wedding cakes can be very lucrative but require more time and equipment than cakes for other occasions. Nowadays people want to choose from more than chocolate, vanilla, or yellow cakes—the sky's the limit!

START-UP:

Start-up costs for a cake-baking business are minimal. Some great recipes, baking pans, decorating supplies, utensils, and an oven (your kitchen range will do just fine) are all that you need. If you can't easily learn to decorate cakes from a book or by trial-and-error, you may want to invest in an inexpensive cake decorating course. If you plan to deliver the cakes, you will need an appropriate vehicle.

BOTTOM LINE ADVICE:

The potential market out there is huge, especially since most working women and men don't have time to bake, but still want homemade cakes. There are so many special occasions to celebrate, and most of them feature great cakes: graduations, birthdays, anniversaries, retirement parties, baby and wedding showers, weddings . . . the list is endless! A cake that can be made for as little as 60 cents can sell for as much as $9—a nice profit for your efforts! On the downside, it may take some practice to make beautiful cakes. You also need patience and good marketing skills to build your business.

CALLIGRAPHER

Start-up cost:	$150-$500 .
Potential earnings:	$10,000-$15,000
Typical fees:	$50-$75 per invitation, other items on a per-job basis
Advertising:	Classified ads, bridal magazines, bulletin boards
Qualifications:	A steady hand and a love for lettering
Equipment needed:	Calligraphy pens and ink, parchment or specialty paper
Home business potential:	Yes
Staff required:	No
Handicapped opportunity:	Possibly
Hidden costs:	Don't spend too much on advertising until you're sure of your market

LOWDOWN:

The fine art of calligraphy began in medieval times, when monks joyously and laboriously produced biblical text using intricate, artistic lettering. This regal writing appears today in items such as wedding invitations, birth notices, and certificates of merit. You could also produce suitable-for-framing family trees (the customer would, of course, need to supply the data). Without a huge initial investment, you can offer your services to schools (for diplomas), brides-to-be (for addressing invitations), athletic teams, and even corporations that are involved in recognition programs where certificates are in order. The market is large, diverse, and challenging—because there are many paper companies that offer programs for producing certificates having the same look as a hand-produced one. Consider branching out and offering both hand-produced and computer-generated calligraphy, and you'll stand a good chance of continuing this fine and delicate tradition.

START-UP:

Calligraphy pens and paper are all you need to start this business, although you will have to work hard to get the word out. Perhaps you could mail invitations to those who might need your service, inviting them in for a free consultation. Networking with bridal salons may also help build business. Charge at least $50 for your services, since they are specialized and time-consuming.

BOTTOM LINE ADVICE:

The freedom and creative nature of this age-old art form is in demand by those who still place value on the handmade; but, with the ability to quickly generate calligraphic style on a computer, you may find the market challenging, at best. Also, being a professional calligrapher isn't necessarily going to make you rich—but it's not a bad way to earn some extra pocket money, either.

CANDLE MAKER

Start-up cost:	$150-$500
Potential earnings:	$3,000-$5,000
Typical fees:	$2-$20 or more (depending on size and intricacy) per candle
Advertising:	Local craft shows, specialty retailers, festivals
Qualifications:	The ability to learn a skilled trade
Equipment needed:	Wax wicks, scented oils, molds, flowers, baking soda
Home business potential:	Yes
Staff required:	No
Handicapped opportunity:	Yes
Hidden costs:	Fire prevention and storage coolers

LOWDOWN:

The great thing about candle making is anyone can do it and it's really inexpensive. You won't get rich, but you could earn a tidy little side income if you work the arts and craft shows throughout the year. Your investment is low because nearly all of the equipment you need can be picked up at your local craft store or at grocery stores. There are different types of candles: hand-dipped, beeswax, honeycomb, confectionery, molded, and decorative. Decide early on what you'd like to specialize in, and try to set yourself apart by coming up with your own unique style. If you want to make some serious money at this, try to market to a crafts distributor (if you can really set yourself apart enough from the others they represent). If you're wanting to add variety, you might want to network with other candle makers and form a cooperative (that way, you can all save money on booth rentals).

START-UP:

Investment is so low that the first dozen or so candles you sell will more than double your profit (you could invest $150 at first). Depending on the kind of volume you want to produce, you could gross $3,000 for part-time work.

BOTTOM LINE ADVICE:

Minimal skill is involved, so you can produce large quantities very quickly. If you want to specialize, for example, in confectionery (making wax look like a dessert, such as ice cream) or decorative (adding dried flowers), the process will take just a little longer, but you will be able to sell the items for more. The only drawback about candle making is that wax is highly flammable. If you're going to do this inside, use caution and keep your insurance policy up to date.

CANING SPECIALIST

Start-up cost:	$50-$150
Potential earnings:	$1,000-$2,000 per month
Typical fees:	$25-$75+ per chair
Advertising:	Country magazines, furniture manufacturers, local paper, craft publications
Qualifications:	Should be an apprentice first
Equipment needed:	Cane, splints, rush, razor blades, scissors, tack hammer/puller
Home business potential:	Yes
Staff required:	No
Handicapped opportunity:	Yes
Hidden costs:	Mileage for deliveries

LOWDOWN:

Before venturing into this profession on your own, you should be an apprentice, since caning is a time-honored tradition. It takes patience and an eye for detail to reweave wicker that has worn with time, or to add wicker to a piece of furniture that didn't have it to begin with. It helps if you are dedicated to the task at hand, because if you're good at what you do, you'll get lots of referrals, since there are so few caning specialists around these days. Still, caning is a slow process. Once you get an order, allow for soaking (about one day), drying (about two days), and making the chairs (approximately four hours per chair). You might want to partner with a chair maker to make your business more profitable; the two of you can copromote each other and provide a constant flow of referrals both ways.

START-UP:

Cane is sold in hanks (1,000 feet)—enough to make four chairs. Plan to pay close to $10-$15 per hank, depending on where you buy it. Total cost for materials is so low that, if you market yourself well, you could make a decent living of around $15,000-$24,000 per year.

BOTTOM LINE ADVICE:

This could be a high-risk venture if you haven't done your homework or let potential clients know about your services; expect to spend a great deal of time promoting yourself in the beginning. The best part is you are considered a craftsman and artist for the beautiful work you weave. For this, you'll need to like working by yourself and have enormous amounts of patience.

CARTOONIST

Start-up cost:	$150-$500
Potential earnings:	$15,000-$40,000 (if regular at a daily newspaper)
Typical fees:	$15-$20 per hour, or $20-$500 per piece
Advertising:	Send work to art editors at newspapers and magazines
Qualifications:	Natural talent, ability to express ideas
Equipment needed:	Drawing media, postage, access to a copier
Home business potential:	Yes
Staff required:	No
Handicapped opportunity:	Yes
Hidden costs:	Postage

LOWDOWN:

Do you have a burning need to present a particular viewpoint in pictures? Have you always turned to the comics page first in the newspaper, before reading the top story of the day? If so, you may be a cartoonist in the making. Of course, you'll need to have some artistic ability, as well as a unique way of expressing your viewpoints. Competition in this field is fierce, and only the truly innovative (or downright wacky) seem to survive. Assertiveness is the most important trait needed to start this business. Mailing out pieces of work is the only way to get noticed, so do it often and everywhere. Leave no stone unturned. Advertising businesses pay the best ($20/hr.+) if they decide to use a piece; try to secure a regular column at a newspaper or for corporate newsletters. Local and specialty publications use cartoonists more, but their pay is usually less ($20+ per piece). Best advice: try to sell your cartoons to a computer software company; more and more programs featuring creative clip art are being produced and sold to companies that would prefer to keep their art production in-house (and inexpensive).

START-UP:

This is an inexpensive business to begin, because the real product being sold is your innate ability to create (which can't be bought for any price, right?). Artistic materials can be bought at local stores as needed for various prices ($5-$150), and copies to send out can be made at any corner store for a dime or less each. Postage costs can really add up as large-scale mailing begins; stay on top of changes in postage, too.

BOTTOM LINE ADVICE:

As with any creative undertaking, frustration is inevitable. It can take many tries before your work is published. Although there is a lot of opportunity in this field, competition is tough. Art editors use only a small percentage of the thousands of submissions they receive each year. Believing in yourself and the uniqueness of your work is vital to surviving the numerous rejections before the final success. If you really believe in what you're doing, don't give up—but don't quit your day job, either!

CHILD CARE REFERRAL SERVICE

Start-up cost:	$500
Potential earnings:	$10,000-$35,000
Typical fees:	$25 per client
Advertising:	Classified ads, bulletin boards
Qualifications:	Should be good at handling multiple tasks and somewhat detail-oriented
Equipment needed:	Answering machine, pager, or cellular phone
Home business potential:	Yes
Staff required:	No
Handicapped opportunity:	Yes
Hidden costs:	None

LOWDOWN

This is a perfect match for those who like to work alone and as a valued resource person. As a child care referral agent, you would provide names and phone numbers of reputable child care professionals in your area—at a cost of about $25 per caller. You would most likely get your start by placing a classified ad in your local newspaper, then scheduling a meeting time with the prospective client to discuss their needs and particulars with regard to the type of professional they're seeking. For instance, some career couples are in need of a caregiver to watch their kids all week long, while others just need part-time care for their children. Some will want individual care, others will want you to check out the local service.

START-UP

With a $500 minimal start-up covering mostly your advertising and telephone costs, you could begin to pull in a profit almost immediately. You will need to build a vast network of child care professionals, which you can easily accomplish by posting flyers in public places (such as Laundromats and grocery stores) and combing the ads in your local newspaper to find baby-sitters who are offering their services. If you have a little bit of extra money to play with at the beginning, you should also invest in professional-looking stationery and business cards to convey the best-possible image to your baby-sitters as well as your clients.

BOTTOM LINE ADVICE

What's not to like about setting your own hours and having essentially complete control over a low-overhead business? The only obstacle would be limitations with respect to the availability of child care providers or those in need of them. If you live in a small, rural area, this business could max out in a month—but if you are in suburbia, you could really make some decent cash.

CHILDBIRTH INSTRUCTOR

Start-up cost:	$500-$1,000
Potential earnings:	$15,000-$35,000
Typical fees:	$175 per couple
Advertising:	Bulletin boards, parents' newsletters, OB/GYN offices
Qualifications:	A nursing degree would be helpful—and respected by those needing your service
Equipment needed:	No
Home business potential:	Yes
Staff required:	No
Handicapped opportunity:	Yes
Hidden costs:	None very serious (but you may want to invest in some educational materials such as models, books, and videos)

LOWDOWN:

Giving birth is a very natural experience that doesn't come naturally—that's why we need childbirth instructors to show us the way. First-time parents are especially uneasy (even frightened) about the pending event, and their fears are best calmed with detailed and expert information from a reliable source. If you've been in a delivery room, and have a nursing degree or related training, you would be a terrific candidate for this type of work. A childbirth instructor is essentially a teacher, so you must develop (and stick to) a teaching plan much the same as any other teacher. Most childbirth classes meet once a week for four to six weeks, so space your materials out accordingly. Begin with the basics and end with a strong visual, such as a childbirth film. Be sure to answer all questions, even the most common ones, courteously and compassionately—after all, many of your customers haven't a clue what they're in for, and it's your job to make their fears subside for a calm, secure birthing experience.

START-UP:

You will be competing against hospitals (unless you contract with them), so you will need to spend some advertising dollars to get your name out there. In addition to advertising in parents' newsletters, you might also want to consider advertising at a children's consignment store—they often have bulletin boards for related services and you could provide some referrals for them in return. Speaking of referrals, you should also get to know a few obstetricians and midwives; they will comprise your strongest source of word-of-mouth business.

BOTTOM LINE ADVICE:

The birth experience is a joyous occasion, and you will likely enjoy telling and retelling the story of this miracle of life. On the downside, the repetition can get on your nerves . . . after all, how many different ways can you tell people how babies are born?

COLLEGE APPLICATION CONSULTANT

Start-up cost:	$500-$1,000
Potential earnings:	$15,000-$30,000
Typical fees:	Extremely varied; some consultants charge as high as $1,000 for this service
Advertising:	School and local papers, direct mail, Yellow Pages
Qualifications:	Familiarity with various colleges and programs
Equipment needed:	Computer, variety of available databases, reference materials
Home business potential:	Yes
Staff required:	No
Handicapped opportunity:	Yes
Hidden costs:	Long distance phone calls and on-line time

LOWDOWN:

Nowadays the hardest part of getting into a college is choosing the right one; it's a vital decision for a young person's future, with far-reaching implications. Now more than ever, a bachelor's degree is almost a requirement to secure a decent, well-paying job. And although some high schools do have respectable advising departments, many do not invest the time and money into this important aspect of continuing education that they could and should. That's where you come in. As an independent college application consultant your services are in high demand in a low-competition field. What more could a business person ask for? If you are amenable to long hours of research and documentation, this business could provide you with just the academic challenge you need. Your biggest hurdle is problem-solving for high school seniors and their families, dealing with emotional/sentimental issues (primarily of the parents), and helping anyone else interested in entering college who doesn't have access to the information they need. You would conduct a skills/needs assessment, match them to an appropriate choice of universities, assist the customer in obtaining and filling in financial aid and application forms properly (and mailing them on time). You will also relay necessary facts about: ACT/SATs, placement tests (such as math, English, and foreign languages), degrees, and extracurricular activities offered by the school that might be of interest to the student, program requirements, etc.

START-UP:

A computer is the largest expense at about $1,500, if you choose to buy one. It isn't a necessity but it will tremendously speed the search process. College catalogs show listings of offered courses and a description of each, as well as some information about application procedures, fees, deadlines, and requirements and other general facts about the school. Buying many of these, as well as a few specialized publications that rate universities or give little-known information about them, will cost several hundred dollars, but it's the basis for your business. Placing only small ads will help keep advertising costs down to $100 or so, but the price of calls to colleges may add up quickly, so remember to monitor your phone time.

Charges for these tasks could be determined a number of ways: per task, per package of tasks, hourly, or however else seems reasonable for the area and best covers the particular request.

BOTTOM LINE ADVICE:
Good listening skills and problem-solving ability are your biggest assets in this business. Customers are trusting you with a very important part of their lives: their futures. High self-motivation and research skills will also help keep you enthused and knowledgeable about colleges and what's new on campus. If you enjoy being the middleman, then college consulting is for you.

Marketing on a Shoestring

Whatever business you enter, you must do marketing. The people who need your product or service must be able to reach you. Take every route you can to communicate your message to prospective customers. That does not mean pouring money into untested ad campaigns or producing expensive giveaways. Creativity is much more important than money in marketing a new venture. Your ideas and commitment to the value of your product or service are the central factors in marketing success.

The first step to successful marketing is self-analysis. What are you really selling? What are the values of your business? What makes you different from similar companies? What do you offer that your customers can't do without, and can't get anywhere else? It can be difficult to come right out and tell people the answers to these questions—but you and everyone else in your organization must learn to say in one sentence what your business offers.

Advertising is only a small piece of the marketing puzzle, and some businesses thrive without ever doing it. Others use one or another type of advertising exclusively, but they go through a process of discovery first. What works well? Any cost is too much if it does not result in sales. Experiment, tracking results carefully. Repeat only those methods that work. Otherwise you will go broke fast.

An effective marketing plan is essential. Work with it for a year, and reassess. Do not neglect some of the proven techniques for marketing that cost very little and serve to make your name known in your community.

- **Cooperate with other businesses**—consider a joint promotion (for fitness classes and nutrition counseling, as an example).

- **Be an expert**—give speeches before community groups, write articles on topics related to your service offerings, etc.

- **Participate in trade shows**—with careful planning, you can gain follow-up opportunities, do many product demonstrations, and make contacts with prospects.

- **Gain free media exposure**—get publicity at no cost, receive third-party presentation for your story.

- **Consider direct mail**—guided by an expert, you can create an effective mailing list to reach your target market.

- **Become involved in your community**—genuine public service on boards and committees enhances your reputation, makes friends for your business, and gets your name out.

- **Publish a newsletter quarterly**—include information of interest to your target market, appealing graphics, and a focus on one of your products or services.

COMEDY WRITER

Start-up cost:	$100-$1,500
Potential earnings:	$10,000-$30,000+
Typical fees:	$25-$1,000 per stand-up piece
Advertising:	Industry trade publications, word of mouth, comedy clubs
Qualifications:	Sense of humor, ability to write clearly and for audiences
Equipment needed:	Computer, laser printer, video camera/tape recorder, business card
Home business potential:	Yes
Staff required:	No
Handicapped opportunity:	Yes
Hidden costs:	Travel, union dues

LOWDOWN:

Do you have a talent for making people laugh—at themselves, each other, and the world? If so, and if you have the writing ability to boot, you could make a living as a professional comedy writer. However, it is an extremely competitive field, and you'll need to be decidedly different (albeit unusual) to set yourself apart from the rest of the funny people. Your best bet for starting out is to write your own material and perform it at a local comedy club's open mike or amateur night. Or, you can write material and try peddling it to your local radio personalities—they often buy material for their morning shows. To be a successful comedy writer, you should be organized, concise, and dedicated. You also have to be confident that your material is funny and be persistent in shopping it around.

START-UP:

The sky's the limit on what you can make, but be prepared to shell out some savings for hotels, travel, postage for your scripts, and union dues to protect your material. Expect to spend between $100-$1,500; expect to earn $10,000-$30,000 or more (if you write for Jay Leno, you'll obviously be paid accordingly).

BOTTOM LINE ADVICE:

Not everyone has the same funny bone. The trick will be to find someone—anyone—who likes your material well enough to pay for it. There are lots of long hours involved shopping the studios, agencies, and other writers during the day and the comedy clubs and stand-up comedians at night. Keep in mind that many stand-ups write their own material.

COMMERCIAL PLANT
WATERING SERVICE

Start-up cost:	$800-$1,000
Potential earnings:	$30,000-$60,000
Typical fees:	$25-$50 per day; some work on monthly retainers of $500 and up
Advertising:	Referrals, Yellow Pages, affiliations with nursery businesses
Qualifications:	Knowledge of plants' requirements
Equipment needed:	Vehicle for traveling to client businesses
Home business potential:	Yes
Staff required:	No
Handicapped opportunity:	No
Hidden costs:	None

LOWDOWN:

Interior plantings are more significant in some parts of the country than in others, but almost all large businesses maintain some kind of greenery to soften their offices. Once you show these organizations that you can care for their plants and make them stay healthy and attractive, you will have the opportunity to develop an ongoing business that brings you a steady income stream.

START-UP:

Costs are minimal. You will need a car or truck to drive from client to client, and perhaps should consider business cards that you could leave near the plants to generate more business. Most larger plant maintenance services charge a flat monthly rate of $500 or more; if you're smaller, however, this will likely be a part-time job, earning you between $25-$50 per day.

BOTTOM LINE ADVICE:

This is definitely a business for plant lovers. If you enjoy making things grow, you'll find plant watering to be a rewarding enterprise. However, there isn't much change from day to day, although you are in and out of different environments as you go from customer to customer. This is not a business for people who thrive on excitement—and not exactly a get-rich-quick enterprise, either.

COUPON DISTRIBUTOR

Start-up cost:	$500-$1,500
Potential earnings:	$10,000-$35,000
Typical fees:	$3-$5 per drop site or a bulk rate for mailings (usually $300 per thousand)
Advertising:	Word of mouth, cover letter with resume
Qualifications:	Postage meters and knowledge of postal regulations; a clean driving record
Equipment needed:	Solid, dependable vehicle
Home business potential:	Yes
Staff required:	No
Handicapped opportunity:	Yes
Hidden costs:	Insurance, mileage

LOWDOWN:

Coupon books are a quick, positive means of getting a company's message across to consumers; what better incentive to buy than a discounted price for doing so? Producers of coupon books often don't have the time or resources to distribute the books themselves, so they hire out services such as yours to make sure that potential buyers receive their "golden" opportunities. You'll either drive around your community distributing such books by hand, or you'll use direct mail to ensure delivery by a specific date. Because coupons are of a time-sensitive nature, you'll always need to stay on track—invest in a good time-management system (a personal organizer or even a simple planner) to make sure that you never miss a deadline. Familiarize yourself early on with postal regulations; post offices regularly hold classes that teach you all the ins and outs of mass mailing. Networking with printers, advertising agencies, and coupon book producers will bring you the most business (rather than advertising your services in a publication).

START-UP:

If you already have a dependable vehicle, you'll spend between $500-$1,500 getting this business off the ground. Mostly, you'll spend it on postage equipment and your own self-promotion. You'll charge about $300 per thousand, or $3-$5 per drop site if you're doing it via your own vehicle. You can expect your annual earnings to be between $10,000-$35,000 (depending on which method you choose to deliver the books).

BOTTOM LINE ADVICE:

This is a good part-time profession, but it isn't exactly dependable, as many coupon book producers are disreputable or go out of business in a short period of time. Align yourself with the tried and true, and all will go smoothly. Otherwise, you might consider becoming a coupon book producer yourself.

DOLL REPAIR SERVICE

Start-up cost:	$500-$1,000
Potential earnings:	$20,000-$40,000
Typical fees:	Depends on what needs to be replaced and whether the doll is an antique (could be $50-$300 or more)
Advertising:	Yellow Pages, antique shows, specialty shops, hobby magazines
Qualifications:	Enjoying the art of doll-making and repair; special knowledge of antique dolls
Equipment needed:	Spare parts, precision tools
Home business potential:	Yes
Staff required:	No
Handicapped opportunity:	Yes
Hidden costs:	Liability insurance, shipping

LOWDOWN:

This is a thriving business. As dolls get older, they become more popular to collect—and if they're going to be worth anything later on, they need to be in the best possible shape to command the highest dollars. One early Barbie doll can be worth as much as $500, but only if she's in mint condition. That's where you come in: you repair and restore dolls to their original state—and sometimes that means purchasing used dolls for spare parts. Keep all types of doll parts on hand and network with other repair services to locate spare parts. Pay attention to detail and have the hands of a surgeon. Dolls aren't just plastic—there are many different types, such as bisque, china, wax, and mechanical. Know what is special about each doll and what precautions to take when repairing them. Market your service especially hard at antique fairs and specialty shops. Have them keep your business cards by their cash register. You may want to offer related services such as collectibles connections (matching buyers and sellers) and a retail doll shop as well.

START-UP:

Advertising will be key to generating most of your business (about $1,000); the rest of your cost will go to spare parts (about $500 to start). Some may be expensive, so you may want to hold off ordering until there is a need. You will be repairing high-end and antique dolls, so gauge your earnings between $20,000-$40,000.

BOTTOM LINE ADVICE:

Some doll repair services have given the business a bad name. You'll have to overcome this by knowing the ins and outs of doll-making. It is much easier to repair something if you know how it is put together. Take your time and know what you are doing; if you ruin a doll you may have to buy it. Be sure your packaging is secure when you deliver or ship to avoid any damage.

ETIQUETTE ADVISER

Start-up cost:	Under $1,000
Potential earnings:	$20,000-$50,000
Typical fees:	$15-$35 per class
Advertising:	Newspapers, business publications, networking with community organizations
Qualifications:	Extremely good taste and a sense of moral superiority
Equipment needed:	Good resource materials
Home business potential:	Yes
Staff required:	No
Handicapped opportunity:	Yes
Hidden costs:	Networking in high places could set you out some considerable cash in your entertainment budget—be careful not to live too well until you're making enough money to cover it

LOWDOWN:

You've always known the answer to seemingly eternal questions: which fork do I start with, and what is that spoon across the top of my plate really for? People rely on your expertise for such sticky situations as who to invite to a wedding, where to place divorced parents in a room together, when not to send a thank-you card, and how long is too long to respond to an RSVP. That's why your talents are needed, but how do you charge for them and still maintain your dignity? Easy—you offer your services in six simple courses. It's too difficult for an etiquette advisor to make serious money handling each question piecemeal, so develop a curriculum and offer your classes to the public or (better yet) the Corporate Confused seeking to become the Corporate Elite. You could offer tips on everything from proper conversation to handling potentially embarrassing situations; for instance, what should you do if your crouton shoots out from your plate to your bosses' during lunch?

START-UP:

Your start-up costs are so minimal, you needn't worry about whether it is proper to launch this business. Just make sure you have good reference materials for the questions that stump you—and leave a little extra for entertaining (which could be your main course to bringing in business).

BOTTOM LINE ADVICE:

You'll love the authority and power of being a moral authority—but try not to let it get to your head. The last thing any one of your clients wants is a know-it-all. Be matter-of-fact, and try to inject some humor into your profession. Believe it or not, humor is the best teacher in a delicate, personal subject such as etiquette.

FIRST AID/CPR INSTRUCTOR

Start-up cost:	$300-$500
Potential earnings:	$15,000-$20,000
Typical fees:	$10-$20 per participant
Advertising:	YMCA, hospitals, churches, associations, schools, swim clubs
Qualifications:	American Red Cross or American Heart Association certification required
Equipment needed:	"Annie-are-you-okay" dummy for practice
Home business potential:	Yes (but you will be traveling to various sites to teach)
Staff required:	No
Handicapped opportunity:	Possibly
Hidden costs:	Some educational materials could cost you more than expected; you'll find out what you really need and what you don't from your training instructor

LOWDOWN:

The blond woman is stretched out on the floor, with a small crowd of people around her. "Annie, Annie—are you okay?" someone asks. She is not breathing, and one person gives mouth-to-mouth resuscitation while another provides heart massage to bring her back to life. Does this scene ring a bell? Many of us have been given CPR training at schools, churches, or swim clubs, and if you've always been interested in teaching people to save lives, this could be your calling. It is not particularly profitable (as volunteers from many associations offer similar courses), but you could set yourself apart by adding on a related service, such as a speakers bureau that offers tips on CPR in the Age of AIDS or some other topic of current concern.

START-UP:

It really doesn't cost much to instruct others on the benefits of life-saving techniques; your biggest up-front cost will be for the practice dummy and related resource materials such as models and diagrams. One innovative place you could offer your services is to restaurants; their staffs always have diagrams of what to do in an emergency, but do they really read them and have they actually practiced on anyone? Not likely. Offer them a group discount!

BOTTOM LINE ADVICE:

The challenge of setting yourself apart from competing services offered free of charge can seem overwhelming at first—but get creative and you can make a small, yet profitable, business for yourself. Be positive and look for the big guys who can help provide a steady flow of business (i.e., health clubs, restaurant associations, and human resource managers at large corporations).

GARAGE SALE COORDINATOR

Start-up cost:	$500-$700
Potential earnings:	$15,000-$25,000
Typical fees:	Often a flat fee of $25-$50 per garage sale; sometimes an additional percentage (5 to 10 percent)
Advertising:	Classified ads, bulletin boards, community newspapers, condo associations
Qualifications:	Organizational skills, strong marketing ability
Equipment needed:	Phone, computer with letter-quality printer, fax, hammer and nails for posting signs
Home business potential:	Yes
Staff required:	No
Handicapped opportunity:	Yes
Hidden costs:	Gas and mileage may get out of hand; try to cover these costs in your fee

LOWDOWN:

Are you a garage sale goddess? Do you spend your entire weekend cavorting around town in search of great bargains? This could be a business made in heaven expressly for you. As a garage sale coordinator/marketer, you would first advertise your services stressing your skill at saving folks time and energy so that they can relax and make money from their old stuff. Then you would organize all of the details involved in putting together a successful garage sale, including marketing (posting signs and placing publicity in newspapers, etc.), and running the sale itself (tagging, bartering, and keeping a record of what's been sold). Don't wait for the individual, single-home customers to build your business; try to work with condo associations, churches, and apartment complexes to organize large-group garage sales—these will bring in your best dollars and provide you with the greatest marketing opportunity, since many bargain hunters like the idea of one-stop shopping.

START-UP:

This business could be a real bargain for you, because it involves minimal start-up cost and the ability to be paid for something you truly enjoy. Advertising in the newspaper classifieds will be your biggest cost, averaging $500-$700. You can earn a pretty good penny for yourself in all of this, especially when you work with large groups. Charge between $25-$50 per individual garage sale, and add on a percentage of the profits if you'd like (5 to 10 percent is typical).

BOTTOM LINE ADVICE:

Many large newspapers offer free garage sale kits, complete with signs, records, and tips for making a garage sale a success. Call or write to request one of these kits—they could become a standard for your business and make your job even easier.

GENEALOGICAL SERVICE
(FAMILY HISTORY WRITER)

Start-up cost:	$500-$1,500 (depending on whether you have a computer)
Potential earnings:	$15,000-$25,000
Typical fees:	$25-$125 per search; $200-$500 per written family history
Advertising:	Magazines with a historic slant, newspapers, Yellow Pages
Qualifications:	None
Equipment needed:	Computer with family tree software program
Home business potential:	Yes
Staff required:	No
Handicapped opportunity:	Yes
Hidden costs:	If you're billing on a per-job basis, don't spend too much time on each project

LOWDOWN:

Everyone would like to know their roots, and what better way to find out than through a genealogical service? By hiring such a service, you could learn about everyone from the first generation of your family to the black sheep that every family seems to have. As a family history writer, you would meet with family members to obtain every known detail about a family—and then compile the information into a family tree diagram or a written report. Mind you, not all is known about every member of every family, but the Mormon church has an extensive genealogical service that you could use to find seemingly obscure bits and pieces. And this service is provided for everyone, not just for Mormons. There are also census reports at major metropolitan libraries to assist you with your search. If you aren't afraid of a lot of research and detail-oriented writing work, this could be a great business for you. Every family has a different, yet fascinating, story to tell.

START-UP:

You'll need to have a good computer system and genealogical software to produce the kinds of detail-oriented reports necessary in the family history writing business. Expect to spend anywhere from $500-$1,500 on those items alone, then factor in your advertising costs at around another $350-$500 and up (depending on the size of the publication you advertise in).

BOTTOM LINE ADVICE:

Your work is much in demand in these nostalgic times, and while there is not a high upfront investment, your time is worth money—and you could spend more of that than you are paid for. Make sure you budget your time accordingly or you could easily (and quickly) come up short.

GERONTOLOGY CONSULTANT

Start-up cost:	$500
Potential earnings:	$25,000-$40,000
Typical fees:	$20-$40 per hour
Advertising:	Direct mail, networking with psychologists and medical professionals, speaking engagements
Qualifications:	Background in psychology or sociology
Equipment needed:	No
Home business potential:	Yes
Staff required:	No
Handicapped opportunity:	Yes
Hidden costs:	None (but watch your mileage)

LOWDOWN

Into the next century, the population over the age of 60 is expected to rise to as high as 65 percent of the total population. That's because many of us have chosen healthier lifestyles—but also because life expectancy itself is on the rise. With more and more folks still in control of their lives after age 80, the need for skilled professionals to help others understand the process and effects of aging will become more apparent. As a gerontology expert, you will work in conjunction with hospitals and psychologists to help patients and their families adjust to the many changes and challenges of their loved ones growing older. You will counsel them on issues ranging from health care to assisted living programs, and may be called on frequently as a resource person for hospitals and the community at large.

START-UP

Assuming that you have the necessary credentials (i.e., a college education in psychology or a related field), your start-up costs should be minimal. The first thing you'll need is professional-looking stationery and business cards, so allow about $500 for that and some preliminary advertising. A gerontology consultant works primarily on-site; that is, at the place where your services have been contracted. Because of this, you can easily use your home as an office, but do make sure you have dependable transportation.

BOTTOM LINE ADVICE

You will probably enjoy the favorable attention you'll receive from people in need of your services, but you should also keep in mind that many of your clients are under unbelievable stress because they are balancing their careers with the need to care for aging relatives. They simply can't be in two places at once, and they may be difficult to deal with at times as a result.

GRAPHOLOGIST

Start-up cost:	$500-$1,000
Potential earnings:	$10,000-$50,000
Typical fees:	$30-$50 per hour; if working with banks, often a monthly retainer of $1,000
Advertising:	Classified ads, business publications, banking publications/newsletters, networking
Qualifications:	Training in character details/nuances of handwriting; certification would lend greater credibility
Equipment needed:	A good eye, magnifier; some use computer and scanner to analyze handwriting on the computer
Home business potential:	Yes
Staff required:	No
Handicapped opportunity:	Yes
Hidden costs:	Travel expenses

LOWDOWN:

With inventions like computerized scanning and computer programs that can mimic a person's handwriting, it doesn't take a genius to see that the job of the forgery expert has been made easier than ever. Important items such as checks, credit cards, and insurance policies can be processed by tellers and other professionals who are skilled in their work but not in detection of fake signatures. That's where the graphologist's, or handwriting expert's, special ability comes in. As a handwriting expert, you will work on a contractual basis with banking institutions and insurance companies, combing through suspect documents to look for the nuances that make each individual's written words different and distinct. You will identify and mark each curve of every letter in your search for similarity, and assist in prosecuting the guilty forgers once they are apprehended. You may even have to appear as an expert witness, and can sell your services to the criminal market in this manner as well. In other words, to maximize your earning potential as a graphologist, you would do well to work on a contract basis with banks and other institutions, but to offer yourself as an expert witness for hire as well. Expert witnesses can earn up to $500 per day for their time and opinions in criminal matters.

START-UP:

You may need certification in some states to work in federal institutions; if you do, set aside another $500 or so for courses and/or testing. However, keep in mind that, even with certification costs, your start-up will be minimal for this business. You'll need some business cards, stationery, and related office materials (about $500-$700); spend a little more than that ($300) on direct mail or advertising in a business publication. You'll charge at least $30-$50 per hour for your work, and you'll earn about $1,000 per month if on a retainer for a bank or other large business.

BOTTOM LINE ADVICE:

If you aren't afraid of detailed work that can affect people's lives in a very negative way (especially if they're wrongly accused of forgery), graphology has a lot to offer you in terms of job security and financial reward. Still, you'll need to be aggressive in marketing your services to be able to attract enough business to stay afloat.

Marketing Trends of the Future

How your business will look in the future depends upon your changing consumer base. Here are just a few trends:

- **The Age Factor.** The number of Americans over 65 exceeds the total population of Canada. Aging bodies have distinct needs in everything from health care to cosmetics. Aging minds may be in search of nostalgia as well as retirement planning.

- **Alternative Lifestyles.** Notice this in health issues (aromatherapy, organic foods, wellness programs) and in the move to the home office, to a slower pace of life, to spiritual fulfillment.

- **Cocooning.** People are claiming control of their immediate environments. This shows itself in increasing gun-ownership (particularly among women), in the rise in home-schooling, in people's reluctance to go to a business. You may have to go to your customers.

- **Adventure.** People want excitement, but they want it safely. The trend is toward exotic foods, sports, and travel.

- **The Informed Consumer.** Access to information allows a consumer to research your product before speaking to you. Be ready to listen, to get to know your customer, to establish trust.

These are some of the broad trends. Get to know the narrower trends, too, in your neighborhood and business area.

HANDBILL DISTRIBUTION

Start-up cost:	$200-$500
Potential Earnings:	$15,000-$20,000
Typical fees:	$5-$10 per drop-off
Advertising:	Flyers or classified ads
Qualifications:	Marketing sense, time-management skills
Equipment needed:	None
Home business potential:	Yes
Staff required:	Yes
Handicapped opportunity:	Yes
Hidden costs:	Spot-checking the distribution crew

LOWDOWN:

Businesses are moving beyond the traditional marketing avenues (magazine and newspaper advertising, radio spots, etc.) to develop less expensive, more effective alternatives. In many areas there is a return to a very old advertising method, handbill distribution. If you live in an area with a high concentration of people on foot, near a mall or in a large city, you can develop a handbill distribution service that forms a significant part of your clients' marketing strategies. You will need a crew of people to do the actual distribution, and you should carry out spot checks to see that they are actually handing each bill out and not dumping them. If all goes well, handbill distribution can be a very effective and direct marketing approach.

START-UP:

The flyers with which you advertise your own business are about the only cost for a handbill distribution business, aside from what you pay to your crews. You may need to carry insurance for work-related mishaps; check with your agent. Expect to bill between $5-$10 per drop-off or location; add extra for those jobs involving more time and effort.

BOTTOM LINE ADVICE:

The simplicity of this business has great appeal. It's person-to-person, face-to-face. Creating a business that is an almost pure service can be very satisfying to those who love to make something out of nothing. A lot of your energy will be consumed in marketing your operation, however, and more will be needed to hire and manage your crew.

HANDYMAN NETWORK

Start-up cost:	$500-$1,000
Potential earnings:	$20,000-$45,000
Typical fees:	10 to 20 percent of the repair cost
Advertising:	Yellow Pages, community newspapers, coupon books
Qualifications:	Good communications skills
Equipment needed:	Phone, well-stocked van(s) with tools
Home business potential:	Yes
Staff required:	Yes (stable of handymen willing to work on-call)
Handicapped opportunity:	Possibly
Hidden costs:	Workers' compensation, tool maintenance costs

LOWDOWN:

A handyman network is the perfect way to find employment for the retired tinkerer; here, you'll run a business similar to a referral service, where you get the call and then match a fixer-upper to a customer in distress. You will dispatch one of your dozen or so handymen to a caller, then sit back and let the work happen. When it's done, the handyman will bring you a completed work order and a check for the service rendered. At regular intervals (typically twice per month), you'll cut a check to each handyman for his percentage of each completed job. You'll be handling everything from dripping faucets to deck-building or possibly even roofing—the possibilities are limited only by your staff's capabilities. Make sure to hire a wide variety of specialists, so that you have enough workers to cover any anticipated project.

START-UP:

If you've already got a van for carrying your tools and equipment to house calls you make, you'll need only $500-$1,000 to get started in this business. With some hard work and heavy promotion, you can turn a profit of $20,000-$45,000. One tip: make sure you advertise on your van; it's surprising how many handyman networks get referrals that way.

BOTTOM LINE ADVICE:

It's a win-win . . . you're helping out retired and possibly displaced workers who need to do something to make ends meet, but you're also helping a customer solve a problem in his or her home. The income is not fantastic, but it's respectable.

Home Schooling Consultant

Start-up cost:	$300-$1,000
Potential earnings:	$15,000-$45,000
Typical fees:	$25-$45 per hour
Advertising:	School boards, Yellow Pages, local newspapers
Qualifications:	Degree in education plus a teaching certificate
Equipment needed:	Books, teachers' guides, monthly planners
Home business potential:	Yes
Staff required:	No
Handicapped opportunity:	Yes
Hidden costs:	Mileage

Lowdown:

Communication, organization, and the ability to juggle several things at once are needed in this field. Your job will be to set up the school curriculum and schedule classes for parents who seek to teach their children at home instead of in public (or even private) schools. You could possibly consult for a parent who doesn't want the child in the school system for religious or intellectual reasons, or whose child has to be out of school for a long period of time due to illness or injury. If you are establishing a new curriculum, you will need the ability to evaluate the child's skill level. If you are helping the student who is out for a long period, you will have to communicate with their original school on a regular basis.

Start-up:

Start-up is low (after you have obtained your degree). Be prepared to buy books up front and be reimbursed for them later. Charging $45 per hour on a regular basis could earn you up to $45,000 per year

Bottom Line Advice:

You may need to join a national, state, or local education association program in order to get a job. This business allows for excellent, high-standard teaching without all the hassles of dealing with a classroom. You don't have to answer to a boss and if you find you don't care for the environment, you can quit. Networking is a definite necessity, but with enough contacts, you could find yourself with year-round work.

HORSE TRAINER

Start-up cost:	$800-$1,000
Potential earnings:	$10,000-$20,000
Typical fees:	$25+ per hour
Advertising:	Referrals from vets, equestrian clubs, interest groups
Qualifications:	Love for horses and skill in handling them
Equipment needed:	Riding gear, stable, horse trails
Home business potential:	Yes
Staff required:	No
Handicapped opportunity:	No
Hidden costs:	None

LOWDOWN:

Riding is popular in many areas of the country, and all horses must be carefully trained to be suitable for this activity. A skilled, sympathetic trainer can make a decent living breaking horses to the saddle and teaching them to respond to their riders' commands. If you have the skills and experience necessary to consider training horses as a business, you probably have observed other trainers at work and can choose one as a mentor. Once you become known, you can depend on referrals for new business. Your days will be spent working with the animals you love and also teaching their owners to respect these powerful creatures to avoid injury. Therefore, you should also be trained in first aid when working with animals and people.

START-UP:

Costs are very low for this business unless you decide to offer boarding services, in which case you will need a barn or stables and paddocks. This equipment will run anywhere from $10,000-$50,000, depending on how elaborate you want to get. Charge an hourly rate of at least $25 to make a decent profit; your time is worth it, and the clients are out there.

BOTTOM LINE ADVICE:

For people who love horses, this business can almost be its own reward. All horses need training and skillful work can greatly increase its value. For outdoor, active people who love animals, horse training can be a wonderful business. You may find that to make ends meet you will need to add boarding or breeding services. Horse owners can sometimes be difficult to please, and of course your work depends on something outside your own control, the horses themselves. This is hard work, requiring strength, agility, and a tolerance for bad weather.

HOSPITALITY SERVICE

Start-up costs:	$500-$1,000
Potential earnings:	$15,000-$25,000
Typical fees:	$10 to $15 per person
Advertising:	Personal contacts with bus companies, Chambers of Commerce, hotels/motels, local restaurants
Qualifications:	Knowledge of the culture or area in which you are operating
Equipment needed:	Dependable transportation and a stack of local newspapers, city guides, and coupon books
Home business potential:	Yes (but you'll be on the road constantly)
Staff required:	No
Handicapped opportunity:	No
Hidden costs:	Insurance, mileage

LOWDOWN:

Weary travelers entering a new city have literally no idea where the best of anything is (restaurants, shows, shopping, etc.). As a professional host or hostess, you could offer your services through hotels or local travel bureaus and would spend your days assisting those travelers with finding suitable entertainment or special places of interest in your own hometown. You won't necessarily get rich doing this job, but if you enjoy meeting people and like to show strangers around town or to travel, this is worth looking into. You can devise your own walking tours of the town you live in, especially if it is a large urban center, or contract with bus companies that need tour guides. Familiarize yourself with everything that's happening in your town; read every entertainment paper your city publishes.

START-UP:

You'll spend at least $500 on business cards to spread all over town (to restaurants, hotels, and travel agencies), but that's really your major expense. Charge your customers about $10-$15 per person, or work out package deals with hotels to help their own customer service efforts look even better.

BOTTOM LINE ADVISE:

Cultivate contacts with personnel at the concierge desks of hotels and convention managers, as well as your local Chamber of Commerce. Even if you don't live in an urban center, if your area attracts out-of-towners or is known for something special, you can still make this business work for you.

ICE SCULPTING

Start-up cost:	$500-$1,000
Potential earnings:	$15,000-$25,000
Typical fees:	$125 per sculpture is not uncommon
Advertising:	Yellow Pages, flyers, direct mail pieces to fund-raising groups and caterers, networking
Qualifications:	Artistic ability
Equipment needed:	Chisel, hammer, and related sculpting equipment
Home business potential:	Usually this work is done on-site to avoid melting
Staff required:	No
Handicapped opportunity:	Possibly
Hidden costs:	Travel expenses; also, you might decide to buy a portable freezer

LOWDOWN:

The Iceman Cometh! Despite the short-lived nature of this art form, ice sculpting is becoming increasingly popular—particularly for hotels, caterers, and special events planners. Why? There's something about watching an artist carve a figure out of a challenging medium, one that could begin melting at virtually any moment. But the effects of ice sculpture can be lasting if done in an air-conditioned environment, and the aesthetic appeal can add sparkle to any buffet table. As an ice sculptor, you'll be contracted to perform specific, yet detailed work in environments where others will likely be watching you. If you don't mind such artistic voyeurism, this will be an enjoyable, even educational, experience. If you prefer to work alone, you'll probably need to buy a portable freezer to move your work from your studio to the requested party.

START-UP:

Materials and equipment should cost you no more than $1,000 total. Charges for your services will vary according to the size and complexity of the project, but it's not atypical for a sculpture to run $125 or more.

BOTTOM LINE ADVICE:

Be sure to cover more than your costs in this business; you'll need to be compensated not only for materials but also for your expertise and talent. Otherwise, you might experience your own meltdown.

IN-HOME MAIL SERVICE

Start-up cost:	Under $500
Potential earnings:	$10,000-$15,000
Typical fees:	25 to 50 cents per envelope
Advertising:	Flyers and mailings to companies without in-house mailing services
Qualifications:	Knowledge of postal regulations
Equipment needed:	None (except for an envelope folder/sealer)
Home business potential:	Yes
Staff required:	No
Handicapped opportunity:	Yes
Hidden costs:	Watch out for clients who seek to pay one flat fee and then dump extra work on you

LOWDOWN:

Companies who use direct mail in their advertising or promotional campaigns need help stuffing the envelopes and getting them properly prepared for the post office. If you're skillful at the manual end of this business (folding/stuffing/sealing envelopes), you'll be amazed at how much you can earn with only a few hours' worth of work. You'll need to market your services well—and if you find that you have too much business, it's a perfect opportunity to hire handicapped and retired folks who might be on the lookout for such straightforward, low-pressure work. Make sure you schedule your jobs realistically to allow for quick turnaround, because that is what will likely be expected of you from most of your clients.

START-UP:

You may spend a few hundred dollars or so on items such as letter folders and envelope sealers, but this business still shouldn't cost more than $500 to launch. Get the word out by networking with small- to medium-size companies; they usually have the need for others to help them on projects of this kind. Charge between 25 and 50 cents per envelope, and try not to quote a flat rate if you can help it; you may be taken advantage of after the ink is dry on your agreement.

BOTTOM LINE ADVICE:

Let's face it—stuffing envelopes is pretty boring work. If you don't mind the tedium—if you can manage to do your work and still catch *Oprah* when you want to—this could be a perfect way to either supplement an existing income or build a modest single income. However, remember that your success depends largely on your own marketing ability.

INCORPORATION SERVICE FOR BUSINESSES

Start-up cost:	$500-$1,000
Potential earnings:	$25,000-$45,000
Typical fees:	$175-$300 (depending on area)
Advertising:	Yellow Pages, business publications, direct mail to entrepreneur groups, classified postings on on-line services or Internet
Qualifications:	A good working knowledge of incorporation law
Equipment needed:	Computer, fax, legal forms, business cards
Home business potential:	Yes
Staff required:	No
Handicapped opportunity:	Yes
Hidden costs:	None

LOWDOWN:

With more business start-ups than ever before, the need for quick, inexpensive help in forming a corporation is greater than ever. Many people who consider starting a business simply have no idea which form of business is more advantageous for them. A nice benefit to incorporating is that you are personally protected from any lawsuits filed against the company (in other words, you probably won't lose your house or car). As an incorporator, you'll be networking with entrepreneurial groups to find clients in need of your services (or fielding calls from your advertisements), then meeting with the client(s) to fill out the necessary, and often straightforward, forms required by the government. You may also have to set up the client's Employer Identification Number, and you'll present them with their corporate package, which will include easy-to-fill-out forms such as the Articles of Incorporation, any minutes from board of director meetings, stock certificates, etc. Essentially, you'll be getting a company started on the road to greater growth or expansion potential.

START-UP:

Advertising will be your largest out-of-pocket expense (between $500-$1,000). It would also help you to have business cards for networking (add another $100-$200). But you could charge as little as $175 and as much as $300 for your services, depending on your area or the size and complexity of the client company.

BOTTOM LINE ADVICE:

If you like working day in and day out filling out the same forms, this job could be just what you're looking for. If, on the other hand, you thrive on excitement and variety, perhaps you should look into starting a business that specializes in putting together business plans.

JEWELRY DESIGNER

Start-up cost:	$500-$1,000
Potential earnings:	$25,000-$75,000
Typical fees:	Some pieces sell for $50-$75; others for thousands
Advertising:	Jewelry trade shows, newspapers, jewelry retailers, craft shows
Qualifications:	Geological Institute of America (GIA) certificate may be helpful but not required; some formal art training and knowledge of jewelry
Equipment needed:	Vices, pliers, jeweler's loop, magnifying glass, molds, melting equipment
Home business potential:	Yes
Staff required:	No
Handicapped opportunity:	Yes
Hidden costs:	Travel expenses

LOWDOWN:

For those who like to create intricate detail with their hands and have an artistic flair, this business could be ideal for you. Some people just jump into this with their natural ability; others who really make it big have some form of formal art training and have also been picked up by a major distributor. In the meantime, hit the jewelry trade shows, craft shows, and antique shows with a vengeance and take a lot of business cards with you. A GIA certificate will be helpful with the respect that you'll have studied different types of precious and semiprecious stones and you'll be able to better price your pieces. This certificate also allows an additional income potential as a licensed jewelry appraiser; you could also buy back old jewelry and reset the stones in your own designs.

START-UP:

Jewelry has one of the highest markups going (100 percent minimum). So with little investment (around $500), a lot of imagination, and some smart marketing, you could be well on your way to a first-year income of $25,000. Try to get noticed by the press, and you'll nab more business than you can handle because people really appreciate having one-of-a-kind jewelry.

BOTTOM LINE ADVICE:

Ever hear of the expression the "small but mighty"? Jewelry has been known to bring in thousands of dollars for a single piece. Here's your opportunity to cash in on your one-of-a-kind creation. Since not everyone's tastes are the same, you can create until you're out of ideas (which, hopefully, will never happen). The only problem with the GIA certificate is that it's a six-month program and offered only in New York and California.

KNITTING/CROCHETING LESSONS

Start-up cost:	$100-$300
Potential earnings:	$3,000-$15,000
Typical fees:	$5-$10 per class
Advertising:	Craft shows, local library, flyers
Qualifications:	Knowledge of knitting and crocheting
Equipment needed:	Needles, thread, yarn, material, scissors
Home business potential:	Yes
Staff required:	No
Handicapped opportunity:	Yes
Hidden costs:	Fluctuating materials costs

LOWDOWN:

Beautiful baby blankets, sweaters, and booties have an heirloom quality in addition to their warmth factor. After all, you don't buy or make a special, handmade blanket merely for its practicality. You choose such items for their sentimental value—and what better way to make a living if that's what you already enjoy doing? You could teach others your craft if you have patience and an eye for detail. You already know how much time is involved with each project and you can read intricate patterns, but can you teach others without winding up doing it all yourself? Marketing yourself at craft shops and networking with related fields will be some of your best advertising. Sell some of your work at art and craft shows to showcase your abilities. Always have plenty of business cards on hand.

START-UP:

If you are giving lessons, you most likely have all the equipment you need. Keep some extra supplies on hand. Have your students purchase their supplies before they come to class, which relieves you from making an up-front purchase. Plan on grossing around $5,000 per year; this would be a great sideline business.

BOTTOM LINE ADVICE:

This can be a very relaxing venture to do in your home. You get to be creative and pass down these centuries-old techniques to others. Be prepared to hold class at hours convenient for your students, including weekends and evenings. On the downside, there is always the possibility that a student may drop out without notice. Try to fill your classes with more students than you think you need.

LACTATION CONSULTANT

Start-up cost:	Under $1,000
Potential earnings:	$25,000-$40,000
Typical fees:	$40+ per hour
Advertising:	Doctor's offices, Yellow Pages, visiting nurse centers
Qualifications:	Nursing or related degree; some states merely require certification
Equipment needed:	None
Home business potential:	Yes (but you'll be working with clients on-site)
Staff required:	No
Handicapped opportunity:	Possibly
Hidden costs:	Mileage

LOWDOWN:

The womanly art of breast-feeding is not always an easy one to master for new mothers. For one thing, many of them are frightened by the prospect of having to be completely responsible for another human being; for another, many hospital professionals are simply not well-trained in teaching new moms how to breast-feed properly. As a result, there are many young women out there who are breast-feeding incorrectly—and quite painfully so. Your prospects look good for this consulting business if you are patient and caring enough to show them the way, and with hospitals increasingly being forced to release mothers and their newborns in a short period of time after the birth, there will be plenty of room (and need) for outside professionals. Your word-of-mouth advertising could bring in quite a few referrals, since many new moms like to share their positive experiences.

START-UP:

Your start-up costs are minimal; mostly, you'll need to make sure you have an adequate amount of resource materials and dependable transportation. For marketing materials, invest in professionally designed business cards—something that gives off a warm, caring feeling. Your fees should start at $40 per hour, collected at time of service.

BOTTOM LINE ADVICE:

It can be stressful dealing with frightened new mothers and helpless fathers; you'll need a cool head to deliver this service. On the bright side, once you've accomplished teaching the mother how to feed her baby properly, the stress level will sharply subside and you'll have at least three happy customers.

ADVICE FROM THE EXPERTS

What sets your business apart from others like it?

Service is what sets apart International Board Certified Lactation Consultant Barbara Taylor's Breast-feeding Specialties in Lake Jackson, Texas. "I offer the added bonus of breast pump rental services as well as one-on-one work with new moms. Also, I have an extremely high referral rate."

Things you couldn't do without:

"My own business line with an answering machine; also, my own office space in my home for professionalism and confidentiality."

Marketing tips/advice:

"Network with other professionals . . . being in a small town, I often feel cut off. Most of my networking involves a long-distance call! Also, you need to find out what mistakes others have made and share ideas about how to promote your businesses as an industry."

If you had to do it all over again . . .

"It would be much easier to succeed in this business if I had been a Registered Nurse."

LAUNDRY/IRONING SERVICE

Start-up cost:	$100-$1,000
Potential earnings:	$20,000-$30,000
Typical fees:	$10 per pound of clothes (this includes "The Works": wash/dry/iron)
Advertising:	Local papers, bulletin boards, flyers, Yellow Pages
Qualifications:	Knowledge of fabric do's and don'ts
Equipment needed:	Extra-large capacity industrial washer/dryer; iron/board or a professional press
Home business potential:	Yes
Staff required:	No
Handicapped opportunity:	Yes
Hidden costs:	Insurance or "mistake money"

LOWDOWN:

Have some business cards handy for this profession and lots of happy customers to refer additional business to you. You should especially seek out professional women who simply don't have the time for laundry detail. There is no other business where word of mouth can make or break you as much as this one. You'll need to be a perfectionist and pay attention to every detail: people tend to think that the clothes make the person and if you make a mistake on their clothing, they take it personally. You should have a room especially devoted to this venture. Have clotheslines available for drip-dry, special laundry soap on hand, softeners, and starches. If you don't invest in a professional steam press, have more than one iron available, just in case. Be sure to keep all of your warranties up to date on your machines, since they are the lifeline to your business.

START-UP:

Overhead has the possibility to be low (under $1,000) if you already have the machines. Any washer or dryer in good working condition will do, but the extra-large capacity will cut your time in half allowing you to do more laundry in a shorter period of time. The large capacity also allows you to do big-ticket items such as comforters. Since your start-up cost may be low, you could easily make $20,000 in 40-hour work weeks.

BOTTOM LINE ADVICE:

You either love or hate to do laundry. Since this is a home-based business, you still have time to catch a soap opera or talk show and feed your baby. Be prepared to correct any mistakes, even if they are not your fault (i.e., replace missing buttons, fix a shoulder pad, or totally replace the garment). For this reason, keep some extra "mistake money" on hand. If you make small repairs at no charge, it tends to be good for business, and the word will spread.

LAW LIBRARY MANAGEMENT

Start-up cost:	$500-$1,000
Potential earnings:	$35,000-$80,000
Typical fees:	$50-$75 per hour or a retainer fee
Advertising:	Networking, personal contacts, direct mail, brochure
Qualifications:	Background in legal reference work, knowledge of on-line services
Equipment needed:	Computer and printer, office furniture, business card, letterhead, envelopes
Home business potential:	Yes
Staff required:	No
Handicapped opportunity:	No
Hidden costs:	None

LOWDOWN:

Your market is medium-size law firms and corporate law departments. These clients are large enough to have a law library but too small to have a librarian. Law librarians have to keep the constant stream of updates filed correctly. The physical books and reference materials must be kept in order and available for frequent use by the lawyers. On-line research projects provide another opportunity for service. Lexis, Nexis, and Westlaw are used as frequently as the printed materials, and you can offer assistance with on-line searches. You will need experience with the specialized world of the law library, and you'll need on-line skills as well.

START-UP:

Costs are minimal because your work is done at the client location; therefore, your earnings could be enough to support yourself in a short period of time.

BOTTOM LINE ADVICE:

This business provides steady work once you have developed your client base because updates are produced regularly. Many law firms experience difficulty keeping track of their reference materials, so your services will be highly valued. You should be able to get referrals easily after the initial marketing effort to gather the first few clients. You will need considerable patience to keep repeating the same exacting filing process from client to client, and from month to month. Hours can be long.

LAWN CARE SERVICE

Start-up cost:	$500-$1,500
Potential earnings:	$15,000-$25,000
Typical fees:	$12-15 per hour or a flat rate of $50-$75 per job
Advertising:	Flyers left in front doors, ads in local or community newspapers
Qualifications:	Love for working outdoors and some knowledge about lawn care
Equipment needed:	Power mower, rakes, power trimmer and spreader, pickup truck or station wagon
Home business potential:	Yes
Staff required:	No
Handicapped opportunity:	No
Hidden costs:	Insurance, transportation, some equipment rental

LOWDOWN:

Most people can squeeze in time to mow their own lawns, but it's the weeding and trimming, fertilizing, aerating, and leaf removal that takes up the extra time. By providing these services, you can rake in profits for yourself. Don't try to compete with neighborhood youth who mow lawns or with professional lawn services that include landscaping and related services. Plant your seeds, develop your niche, and cultivate the business.

START-UP:

You'll shell out at least $300 for basic equipment; more for a power lawn mower. Double or triple those costs if you decide to have a team of workers mowing a lawn simultaneously (as is often done). You'll make roughly $50-$75 per job in a residential lawn care business; more if handling corporate accounts in addition. However, your income isn't limited to flat fees, because many happy customers also include a tip for your trouble.

BOTTOM LINE ADVICE:

By scheduling some or all of these services with the same customers in the same neighborhoods, you will save on transportation and rental costs. One day you might be mowing lawns and another you'll be aerating. You might have to rent an aeration roller for $25 a day. But if you schedule aerations in one neighborhood for the same day, you'll easily recoup the investment.

"Must-Have" Checklist for New Businesses

Here are some of the more critical items you'll need for your new business:

- Computer system with a printer, fax/modem, and special software packages pertaining to your business and its needs (accounting, desktop publishing, etc.)

- Phone system with voice mail capability or answering machine

- File cabinets with a filing system

- Comfortable, ergonomically designed chair (often a last thought, but incredibly important to your productivity)

- Desk with plenty of arm space (for working on projects without bumping into your computer)

- Guest chairs and a conference table for meeting with employees, clients, and suppliers

- Bookshelf to hold your numerous resources

- Office supplies: stapler/staples, paper clips, pens/pencils, tape, corrective fluid, date stamp

- Storage shelves or cabinet (usually to house supplies)

- Garbage bins (don't forget one for recyclable paper)

- Background music (if that's important to you or your customers)

- Aesthetically appealing, yet professional-looking decor. Whether traditional or contemporary or eclectic, you need to send a solid visual message about your company through your decorative ability. If you are decoratively impaired, hire a professional to help (work out a trade for services).

- Most important: good lighting. One tiny desk lamp just won't do, and your staff will work as productively as you do if you invest in proper, clear lighting.

LITERARY AGENT

Start-up cost:	$500-$1,500
Potential earnings:	$20,000-$60,000+
Typical fees:	15 percent commission on domestic sales, 25 percent on foreign rights, 20 percent on film rights
Advertising:	Listing in the *Guide to Literary Agents* and *Art/Photo Reps*; ads in *Writer's Digest* and *The Writer* magazines, networking at writer's conferences
Qualifications:	Should know a good book a mile away
Equipment needed:	Computer, printer, fax/modem, copier, phone system
Home business potential:	Yes
Staff required:	No
Handicapped opportunity:	Yes
Hidden costs:	Insurance, copying, postage, phone expenses

LOWDOWN:

The literary life is indeed a glamorous one, especially if you're a literary agent. Imagine entire days filled with power meetings at large publishing houses, where you're negotiating for the best deal for one of the many writers you represent. You'll be offering everything from the right to publish to film and foreign rights (for publication overseas). Your business may also extend to book promotion, as you could negotiate book tours and publicity for your client in addition to the sale of the book project itself. Of course, you would hope to represent that one unknown client who could really score big in the publishing industry, such as Robert James Waller did with his *Bridges of Madison County*; look everywhere for talent—even in remote cities or small rural towns. No matter how hard you try, realize that not all literary agents can represent a Stephen King—and you should go in with an open mind whenever you look through the piles of manuscripts and queries on your desk. The successes could really surprise you.

START-UP:

Your start-up is relatively low ($500-$1,500) and mostly covers your initial advertising costs and basic office equipment setup. With your commission, you stand a good chance of earning a respectable income of at least $20,000—but look forward to making as much as $60,000 or more (depending on whether you get that "big break").

BOTTOM LINE ADVICE:

On the one hand, you'll be making a good piece of change hanging around the best media minds in the business. On the other hand, you'll have to know when to give up on a particular project, even if it seems totally worthwhile. Often in the publishing world, trends take over and dominate what's likely to be published (remember, for instance, the Mafia book craze a few years back?). You'll need to constantly stay on top of what's hot.

ADVICE FROM THE EXPERTS

What sets your business apart from others like it?

Marie Dutton Brown, President of Marie Brown Associates literary agency in New York City, says her business is unique because her agency primarily represents African-American authors. "We connect clients to the publishing industry and provide counsel for writers . . . we focus on black life and culture as well as books of general interest."

Things you couldn't do without:

Phone, fax, copier, computer, and typewriter.

Marketing tips/advice:

"Start small, think big, and follow your niche," says Brown. She enjoys the process of bringing an interesting creative project to fruition, and thrives on positive publicity. She has been profiled by the Associated Press, and that has certainly been a profitable marketing tool.

If you had to do it all over again . . .

"I would have started with more capital. As it was, I started at home with only $1,000. It takes more than that to get things rolling."

MAGICIAN

Start-up cost:	$500-$1,000
Potential earnings:	$6,500-$20,000 or more
Typical fees:	Not necessarily carved in stone, but generally $50 per two-hour children's party, $300 per two-hour adult event
Advertising:	Yellow Pages, entertainment section of newspapers, bulletin boards, networking with civic organizations
Qualifications:	Ability to perform magic tricks convincingly, outgoing personality
Equipment needed:	Magic trick equipment, business cards
Home business potential:	Yes
Staff required:	No
Handicapped opportunity:	Possibly
Hidden costs:	Advertising

LOWDOWN:

To be a good magician, you must have the ability to learn magic tricks and perform them quite convincingly (despite the audience's willing suspension of disbelief). You can buy kits from party centers/entertainment retailers or possibly take a continuing education course from your local university/college. Working as an assistant for an established magician is also a good way to learn the business. Having a good personality and the ability to work well with people is a strong selling point.

START-UP:

Start-up should be minimal depending on what you invest in. Visit the local library to find books on magic for an inexpensive way to learn the art. Investing in magic kits from retailers will cost you a little more. The most expensive start-up cost would be to take a class.

BOTTOM LINE ADVICE:

Perform for free at your friends' parties or children's school functions to get exposure. Once your name gets on the streets, start charging for your services. Attempt to work with your city's parks/recreation department for leads or a convention center to get jobs at conferences. Working with an events planner or advertising agency is another good way to get your own name pulled out of the hat.

MAKEUP ARTIST

Start-up cost:	$500-$1,500
Potential earnings:	$20,000-$40,000
Typical fees:	$20-$30 per session
Advertising:	Newspapers, beauty salons, bridal consultants, funeral homes, department stores
Qualifications:	Eye for color and contour
Equipment needed:	Makeup samples/kits, brushes, cotton swabs, a director's chair
Home business potential:	Yes
Staff required:	No
Handicapped opportunity:	Possibly
Hidden costs:	Insurance

LOWDOWN:

If you enjoy making eyes for people, or just plain giving them lip, you will revel in the opportunity to be a professional makeup artist. Your services are needed in extremely diverse areas, from the life and action of the stage to the stately composure of the funeral home. You could offer makeovers for brides-to-be, new moms, college graduates, and those simply in the mood for a new look. Or, you could specialize in helping those who are disfigured due to accident or illness. Whomever you choose as your clientele, you will need to be familiar with all skin types and problems, matching your products carefully with each client's basic needs. With an astounding array of cosmetic products currently available (even at wholesale prices), you could produce professional and fabulous-looking results for just about any client in no time. Study facial structure to know where to shade and what to hide, and you're on your way to a beautiful new beginning!

START-UP:

Your costs are relatively nominal. Start out with some makeup kits and samples, supplies, and a sturdy chair for your clients to sit on—then add your brochures, business cards, or flyers. All of this should cost you no more than $1,000—but add a little more if you decide to sell the products you're using, because you'll need to secure a vendor's license.

BOTTOM LINE ADVICE:

While you may enjoy the freedom and creativity of being a professional makeup artist, you may also find the lack of predictable income unnerving. Try to offer your services to groups to maximize your marketing moments, because the one-customer-at-a-time philosophy doesn't cut it with this business.

MALL PROMOTION

Start-up cost:	$500-$1,500
Potential earnings:	$30,000-$45,000
Typical fees:	$500-$1,000+ per project or a monthly retainer of $1,000-$3,000
Advertising:	Networking with corporations owning shopping malls
Qualifications:	Background in events planning, promotion, and/or advertising
Equipment needed:	None
Home business potential:	Yes (but you'll mostly be working on-site)
Staff required:	No
Handicapped opportunity:	Yes
Hidden costs:	Travel (reimbursement may take 30-45 days)

LOWDOWN:

In the competitive retail sector, professionals like you are needed to constantly reel in potential customers with exciting events (such as bridal and fashion shows or antique fairs) and special promotions (discount programs for multiple purchases made within the mall). Although some mall promoters work as permanent staff at a single mall, you can make a business of working as a consultant to malls if you have the right connections in the corporate world. Meet with executives at companies that own several malls to maximize your earning potential in this ever-challenging market. When you do land the first client, you'll spend your days with a calendar, planning the best times of year to bring creative events and promotions to each mall on your client list. Then you'll work with the mall staff to ensure that everything comes off without a hitch; more than likely, there will be postevent meetings to evaluate each program's success or failure. Naturally, you will need to be able to work in two worlds at all times—both corporate and consumer. Having a keen understanding of what makes people want to buy will be your most useful asset.

START-UP:

This is a great business to start with little cash, largely because you'll be working out of your clients' offices and several malls across the country. You'll really need to spend your money ($500-$1,500) on self-promotion; business cards and networking are your primary ways of getting the word out about your services. If you have the right connections, you should be able to pull in $30,000-$45,000 in no time.

BOTTOM LINE ADVICE:

Being on the road all the time might get to you after a while, even if you are a self-confessed "mall rat." Just remember that, on the plus side, you are getting paid to put together fun events that will be profitable for the mall—and in the long run, for you.

MERCHANDISE DEMONSTRATOR

Start-up cost:	$500-$1,000
Potential earnings:	$20,000-$35,000
Typical fees:	$150-$1,000 per event
Advertising:	Yellow Pages, direct mail to manufacturer's representatives or marketing departments, networking
Qualifications:	Good people skills and selling ability
Equipment needed:	None
Home business potential:	Yes (but you'll be on the road)
Staff required:	No
Handicapped opportunity:	Possibly
Hidden costs:	Insurance, slow reimbursement for travel expenses

LOWDOWN:

This is definitely a "who-you-know" sort of business; if you know a key marketing official at a large automobile manufacturer, you've got it made if you want to be a merchandise demonstrator at a big trade show for automobiles. Many "product specialists" (as some prefer to be called) can travel year-round to trade shows demonstrating products for one specific company, while others circulate their talents to many different types of product manufacturers. For instance, you can start as small as handing out samples at your local grocery store (of course, the pay for that is usually $25-$50 per day) or you can work toward establishing relationships with larger corporations in order to represent them at trade shows. The days of the gimmicky product demonstrator are virtually over, however, so keep in mind that today's consumers want intelligence and answers to all of their questions. You'll need to learn everything about the products you demonstrate by talking with everyone from the engineering team to the marketing department.

START-UP:

You can get started in this business for less than $1,000, because all you really need are some terrific self-promotion pieces (such as business cards and perhaps a postcard for direct mail purposes). Be sure to allow a few extra dollars for advertising, but really limit what you spend since your success will ultimately depend on how well you network. If you're a Les Brown-caliber speaker and promotional genius, you can make a fairly respectable $20,000-$30,000 per year— and get to travel all over the country on the house.

BOTTOM LINE ADVICE:

Travel gets tedious, even for the adventurous. You'll be expending huge amounts of energy up there on stage, and you'll have to work at sounding extremely knowledgeable about everything you show off. Get some rest, drink plenty of fluids, and be sure to collect an advance when possible.

MOBILE BOOK/MAGAZINE DISTRIBUTOR

Start-up cost:	$100-$500
Potential earnings:	$15,000-$25,000 (sometimes slightly more, if the market is large)
Typical fees:	$3-$5 per stop
Advertising:	Word of mouth, ads in trade journals, business cards
Qualifications:	Excellent driving record and valid license
Equipment needed:	Delivery vehicle (car or truck)
Home business potential:	Yes
Staff required:	No
Handicapped opportunity:	Not typically
Hidden costs:	Mileage (be sure it's covered in your contract), insurance

LOWDOWN:

Many local publications need to hire delivery subcontractors to make sure their distribution base is covered. If you find this kind of work appealing, you should have no problem securing customers, because turnover is often so high. Why is that? Often, it's because these publications tend to hire a staffer's grandparent or retired parent to make deliveries, and that person gets tired of the job because it can be a little stressful (particularly if the press run is late). You can set yourself apart from the rest by developing professional-looking business cards and making the rounds to different publishers, positioning yourself as a delivery professional and not just another flunky. The nice aspect about your work is that you'll get to meet so many members of the local business establishment, as many bars, restaurants, and bookstores carry the publications you'll be delivering to them on a weekly basis. You'll know everyone in town after a short period of time—and that can be helpful in ways beyond your delivery service.

START-UP:

Your initial costs will be low, especially if you've already got a delivery vehicle of some kind (a station wagon or small pickup can work perfectly). Expect to earn $15,000-$25,000 (depending on the size of your market and the number of publications you're delivering for).

BOTTOM LINE ADVICE:

It's a cool job, with lots of independence and autonomy; basically, you're in and out of a great many places in one day. On the downside, you may have to endure the complaints of customers whose papers are late, but that isn't as bad as getting chewed out over a million-dollar deal gone wrong. Seriously, there isn't much here you can complain about.

MORTGAGE LOAN BROKER

Start-up cost:	$600-$700
Potential earnings:	$15,000-$50,000
Typical fees:	Commission equal to 4 percent or less of the value of the mortgages placed, paid by borrower
Advertising:	Classified ads, real estate magazines, newspapers, referrals
Qualifications:	Extensive knowledge of real estate finance, license (in some states)
Equipment needed:	Business cards, letterhead, envelopes
Home business potential:	Yes
Staff required:	No
Handicapped opportunity:	Yes
Hidden costs:	Advertising is necessary on an ongoing basis

LOWDOWN:

Borrowers (people and firms) who want second mortgages come to you to find a lender. Third, fourth, and even higher levels of mortgages are possible in certain cases. You may operate entirely independently or work as a subcontractor with a real estate agent or attorney. You will need to keep putting your message before the public because for the most part each transaction will be with a new client. Occasionally mortgage brokers find borrowers for lenders, rather than the reverse.

START-UP:

Costs to start are very low (around $600 to start) if you already have a computer. All you'll need is a good mortgage program. You could earn your first $15,000 easily enough, charging only 4 percent of the total mortgage.

BOTTOM LINE ADVICE:

Once you develop a reputation for effectiveness, you may find that repeat business from one or more lenders will bring in an excellent income. But most mortgage brokers focus on finding would-be borrowers and then linking them with the dollars. You'll need an ability to inspire confidence and to speak the language of people on both sides of the transaction. Patience and active listening are also very applicable in this type of enterprise.

MOTOR VEHICLE TRANSPORTATION

Start-up cost:	$1,000
Potential earnings:	$5,000-$10,000
Typical fees:	$7-$10 per hour plus tolls, gas, lodging, and food expenses
Advertising:	Yellow Pages, flyers to colleges, vacation communities, mailings to auto dealerships
Qualifications:	Good driving record, valid driver's license
Equipment needed:	None
Home business potential:	Yes
Staff required:	No
Handicapped opportunity:	Not typically
Hidden costs:	Insurance

LOWDOWN:

Mrs. Smith in Portland, Oregon, needs to have a very specific vehicle: it's a peach-colored Cadillac with white tires and a white leather interior. The problem is, the only one like it is in Sarasota, Florida. If the dealer really wants to make the sale, he'll have to send someone down to the sunshine state to get the one-and-only Caddy with a personality. That's where a motor vehicle transportation service comes in; typically, the car dealership calls on such a service to make "runs" for customer-specific vehicles, and pays an hourly fee in addition to incidentals (such as tolls, parking, and food/gas/lodging). Or, an individual might hire you to drive their car to their destination, while they fly. In this business, you'll be driving across the country, from one car dealership to another—and you'll be expected to deliver the new vehicle within a fairly short period of time (so don't try to work in much sightseeing). It's a great way to earn a supplemental income, particularly if you're retired and have spare time.

START-UP:

You won't need to spend anything to get yourself started in this business, except for marketing. If you're working with several different dealerships, you could make the high end of $10,000—but, more than likely, you'll be in the $5,000 range, because this work is so sporadic and specialized.

BOTTOM LINE ADVICE:

The good news is, you can get paid to do a little traveling . . . the bad news is, you won't ever be able to make a full-time living at this business. Perhaps you could parlay it into something else—or add it onto another service, such as automotive detailing (also a customized automotive business).

MOVIE SITE SCOUT

Start-up cost:	$500-$1,000
Potential earnings:	$10,000-$25,000
Typical fees:	Usually a retainer fee of $3,000-$5,000 per month
Advertising:	Industry trade publications, word of mouth
Qualifications:	Ability to visualize; knowledge of general history and geography
Equipment needed:	Computer, cellular phone, business cards
Home business potential:	Yes (but, of course, you'll be on the road a lot)
Staff required:	No
Handicapped opportunity:	Possibly
Hidden costs:	Passport; union dues

LOWDOWN:

For every beautiful landscape in a film, there was a site scout who searched for the perfect spot. As a movie site scout, you'll need to be well-connected and able to sell yourself to some pretty high-powered folks, but once you get one job, the others become easier to get. What will you do all day? You'll likely start by reading the script, doing a little research (especially if it's an historical or period film), then scanning the globe. Sometimes, it's just a one-shot deal, where you find one place for the entire film to be shot. Often, however, you'll be working on two coasts, or maybe even in different countries, to meet all of the script's required shots. The ability to visualize is incredibly important in this profession, because you are responsible for selecting the absolute perfect setting for a movie that costs millions of dollars to produce. Take into consideration the architecture of the area, geography, weather conditions, and people when selecting your site. A background in the movie industry would be helpful. This is definitely a "schmoozing" position, as you'll be forming relationships with people all over the world.

START-UP:

Most of your money will go toward socializing, since your business depends on who you know. Get your face out there and start passing out those business cards. Getting the job will be the hard part, so plan on spending at least $500 to secure your first assignment.

BOTTOM LINE ADVICE:

You will likely have started in a lower position and worked your way up to this one. Hopefully, you have made a lot of friends along the way to help you break into scouting.

MULTILEVEL MARKETING

Start-up cost:	$500-$1,000
Potential earnings:	$20,000-$50,000
Typical fees:	Percentage, plus bonus for new distributors
Advertising:	Networking, memberships in business and community groups, direct mail
Qualifications:	Salesmanship
Equipment needed:	Basic computer setup, phone
Home business potential:	Yes
Staff required:	No
Handicapped opportunity:	Yes
Hidden costs:	Marketing materials like catalogs or leaflets may become necessary, membership dues

LOWDOWN:

Some products don't seem appealing unless they are demonstrated. The classic example is Tupperware, which just sat on store shelves until the company realized that buyers needed to be shown how the top is burped to create a vacuum seal. Many other products, with vitamins being an outstanding example, are sold as Tupperware is, person to person. Often, a business starts when someone develops enthusiasm for, and commitment to, a product or company. The sales process for that product then seems to happen almost naturally. If you have recognized something like a line of cosmetics that is especially effective for you, or a nutritional supplement that has made a difference in your sense of well-being, you should consider participating in multilevel marketing. You will be selling not only the product, but the opportunity for others to sell it as well. That's what sets multilevel marketing apart from direct sales—here, you're aiming to maximize your own income potential by deriving percentages from other salespeople you recruit.

START-UP:

This is another business where you begin with nothing but your own energy and commitment (as little as $500 to start). Potential earnings of $20,000 and more.

BOTTOM LINE ADVICE:

Do you know that you can sell? More importantly, do you love the sales process? Do you enjoy helping your customers discover products that will improve their lives? With this approach, you can make an excellent, if not wonderful, living in the multilevel marketing world. However, far more people have tried it than have made the easy millions that are sometimes promised. You really do have to work very, very hard. You can't give up when your first 74 efforts end in no sale. You will have to manage your time well, and you will have to find a company whose products are worth this much of your commitment.

MYSTERY SHOPPER

Start-up cost:	Less than $500
Potential earnings:	$10,000-$20,000
Typical fee:	$25 to $50 per shopping experience
Advertising:	Personal contact with stores, hotels, corporations
Qualifications:	Knowledge of area to be evaluated, being a good actor or actress so as not to be noticed, being highly observant
Equipment needed:	None
Home business potential:	Yes
Handicapped opportunity:	Yes
Hidden costs:	Mileage

LOWDOWN:

Mystery shoppers are used in a variety of settings: retail stores, typically where the owner is absent, hotel chains, restaurants, charitable organizations, government organizations, collection agencies, and banks. Their purpose is to observe the business from a customer's point of view and to report to management its short-comings and strengths for the sake of improving service. A mystery shopper acts like a customer, observing the quality of the service, employee theft, plus shopping the competition for valuable information. Companies use mystery shoppers because they are less expensive than electronic surveillance.

START-UP:

You won't spend very much at all launching this one, but you probably won't become a Rockefeller, either—earning $10,000-$20,000 per year would probably be as good as it gets.

BOTTOM LINE ADVICE:

You might want to stick to a particular industry where you already have experience or knowledge. Chains would provide multiple sites to shop without being known as a shopper, besides providing continuing business. Provide a written and oral report of your findings. In some states mystery shoppers are considered private investigators and therefore must be licensed: look into your state's laws regarding licensing.

Notary Public

Start-up cost:	$100-$200
Potential Earnings:	$6,000-$10,000
Typical fees:	$10 per requested service (average)
Advertising:	Yellow Pages, location
Qualifications:	License as Notary Public, usually upon recommendation of two lawyers
Equipment needed:	Seal
Home business potential:	Yes
Staff required:	No
Handicapped opportunity:	Yes
Hidden costs:	None

Lowdown:

Notary publics usually add this service on to a related business. Witnessing signatures and administering oaths will bring you a small fee each time, but you will not become a magnate by this route alone. A surprising number of transactions must be notarized, though, so if you can draw in foot traffic or position yourself next to a business related to your services (such as a photocopy shop, license bureau, or post office), it can be well worth the trouble of obtaining the license. Check the requirements in your state, since each are different.

Start-up:

Start-up costs are minimal, aside from the license fee and whatever your seal will cost you (not more than $500). A sign directing people to your location will bring walk-ins to have you witness their signatures. Fees are low, but so is the cost of providing the service.

Bottom Line Advice:

Why not? What have you got to lose? If people are going to pay notary public fees, why not have them be paid to you? Creativity in developing an associated service will enable you to make a business enterprise out of the enthusiasm for having things notarized that runs throughout American bureaucracies. Document typing is one possibility. Dreams of glory may pass you by, but the challenges are negligible, too.

NUTRITION CONSULTANT

Start-up cost:	$500-$1,000
Potential earnings:	$10,000 and up
Typical fees:	$15-$30 per hour
Advertising:	Brochures, ads in health-related publications
Qualifications:	Knowledge of nutrition and healthy diet; different states may require degree in dietetics or related discipline
Equipment needed:	Computer (probably), reference books
Home business potential:	Yes
Staff required:	None
Handicapped opportunity:	Yes
Hidden costs:	Make sure legal and health ramifications are understood

LOWDOWN:

Nutrition is increasingly important to Americans these days—and most people are still not eating a healthy diet. Since people are seeking better, healthier foods and guidance in selecting them, you can learn about nutrition and share this information with others via classes, seminars, individual counseling, articles, and cookbooks. Nutrition consultants are also employed by hospitals, health clubs, and large corporations. If you enjoy helping and motivating others, this might be a great business for you.

START-UP:

Start-up costs are minimal. You can easily run this business from your home with nothing more than a basic computer and a minimum of office equipment. You will need to investigate applicable zoning and health regulations. Expect to spend some time and money on marketing materials to promote your business.

BOTTOM LINE ADVICE:

Depending on which area of nutrition you pursue, you may need certain credentials (such as a degree in dietetics). You cannot instantly become an expert on nutrition; you may need additional knowledge of physiology, food, management, marketing, and psychology. One route to consider is the preparation of computer-generated, healthy meal plans for institutions. If motivating and assisting people in being healthier would be satisfying to you, this field may be the perfect choice.

Packing/Unpacking Service

Start-up cost:	$500
Potential earnings:	$15,000-$20,000
Typical fees:	$20-$30 per hour or a flat rate (usually $75-$100)
Advertising:	Bulletin boards at apartment complexes and grocery stores, classified ads
Qualifications:	None
Equipment needed:	None
Home business potential:	Yes (but you'll be traveling to the client's site)
Staff required:	None
Handicapped opportunity:	Possibly
Hidden costs:	A good insurance policy can be worth a lot to you

Lowdown:

Today's society is an extremely mobile one; people move nearly three times as much as they did in the last few decades. With such a transient population, there are often no relatives or friends living close enough to the person moving to volunteer a helping hand. That's one reason packing services are becoming more popular; the other is that society as a whole is becoming increasingly dependent on "convenience" services (i.e., services that save them time or aggravation so that they can spend their free time doing things they truly enjoy). You will carefully pack (and sometimes unpack) items for the pending move, labeling everything so that each item can be easily located at any time during the move. Decide early whether you want to provide the boxes and packing materials to your clients; if you choose to, you'll need to make sure you cover the cost of such items in your fee.

Start-up:

For practically nothing, you can start a packing and unpacking service for the upwardly mobile. All you need are some flyers to spread the word—and you can place them at Laundromats, apartment complexes, and possibly even at moving van rental agencies. Charge either by the hour ($20-$30) or by the job ($75-$100).

Bottom Line Advice:

If you're well-organized and know how to pack delicate items for often-turbulent travel, you would likely enjoy this line of work. Developing a system will help you manage each project efficiently and keep your hours down. On the downside, some clients could be difficult to work with—particularly if their move is due to a bad situation such as a divorce. Try to keep a cool head.

PARAPSYCHOLOGIST

Start-up cost:	$500-$1,500
Potential earnings:	$10,000-$20,000
Typical fees:	$150 per visit
Advertising:	Yellow Pages, metaphysical publications, museums
Qualifications:	Certification as a parapsychologist (available in California and New York)
Equipment needed:	Resource materials
Home business potential:	Yes
Staff required:	No
Handicapped opportunity:	Yes
Hidden costs:	Travel expenses

LOWDOWN:

Some things just can't be explained . . . but your job as a parapsychologist is to find ordinary explanations for the paranormal event. For instance, when there is a claimed UFO sighting or ghostly visitor in an old theater, you'll be called in to see if there is a logical reason for the perceived apparition. This is a skilled profession, but the skills are primarily of a higher nature; you'll be trained as a metaphysician (studying not only paranormal occurrences, but also the folklore and belief systems involved in mythology and fortune-telling). You'll need to know the history behind every supposed sighting and try to experience a re-creation of each event in the place where it has occurred; obviously, you're trying to rule out human intervention in such events. Many people are just plain weird, and enjoy making up ghost stories for the sake of gaining public attention. You have to weed through these folks, find the holes in their stories, and educate the public as to your findings.

START-UP:

Your start-up will be wrapped up in your certification and related educational resources (i.e., books on ancient history/mythology, etc.); you'll spend between $500-$1,500 (depending on where you go for certification; universities are more expensive). Expect to earn $10,000-$20,000, as your services are not always going to be in high demand. (In other words, don't quit your day job.)

BOTTOM LINE ADVICE:

Okay, so your profession is perceived as a little bit flaky . . . but who are the folks we call on for explanations when there is no one else out there with a background in the paranormal? A "Ghostbusters"-type service would be a little far-fetched, but essentially you're going to be working around some pretty strange stuff. Still, recognize that there are literally hundreds of parapsychologists around the country today—so there must be something for you to do.

PARTY PLANNER

Start-up cost:	$500-$1,000
Potential earnings:	$20,000-$40,000
Typical fees:	Charge a base fee of $300-$500 per party or a percentage of total cost of party (typically 15 to 20 percent)
Advertising:	Yellow Pages, direct mail, flyers, referrals/networking
Qualifications:	Resourcefulness, creative ability, exceptional organizational skills
Equipment needed:	Planning system (hand-held electronic planner or a good planning book), phone, fax, camera or camcorder (to record parties so that other potential clients can see the results of your work)
Home business potential:	Yes
Staff required:	No
Handicapped opportunity:	Yes
Hidden costs:	Travel expenses, spending too much time on each project for the amount being paid

LOWDOWN:

A party planner tends to all the details for any given social function—from hiring the caterer, florist, and musician(s) or entertainer(s) to addressing and sending invitations. Planners should have a creative flair and be able to suggest a variety of party themes to fit the occasion. For instance, you could come up with a Caribbean theme where all the party-goers must dress in tropical attire, all the music is calypso-inspired, and giant papier-mâché palm trees sprout from various corners of the room. Or, plan a party that is a surprise for your client's family members—with a little Sherlock Holmes-style caper for guests to solve upon their arrival. Whatever your plan, you'll need to be extremely well organized to maintain a good reputation, and since your business will grow primarily based on referrals, you'll need to keep this uppermost in your mind. More than likely, you'll put in way more hours than you should for each job, but the return will be worth it if your ideas are exciting or innovative and your execution of those ideas is first-class. In other words, do your job, and do it well—the payoff will be directly related to what you put into it.

START-UP:

It's a good idea to purchase some party planning guides from a bookstore (or borrow books from the library). Advertising costs will be your biggest start-up expense; be sure to get a Yellow Pages ad ($30-$100 per month, depending on ad size) since this is where many people who don't know you personally will be apt to look. You can charge either on a percentage basis (15 to 20 percent of total party cost) or a flat fee of $300-$500 per party.

BOTTOM LINE ADVICE:

While getting started, you might want to plan some friends' parties for free. This will give you valuable experience and build a portfolio, so to speak, of your successes and innovations. Keep at least a photo album of your parties so that you have something to show potential clients. Nothing sells better than demonstrated success. On the downside, expect there to be difficulties in dealing with the personalities involved in planning a party. Remember, too, that your tastes (even though they may be better) will not always be the prevailing ones.

5 Steps to Better Time Management

1. **Know your company's goals** and set your own priorities accordingly. Give your tasks priority according to what must be done today, and what can be done tomorrow.

2. **Delegate wherever possible.** Invest the time at the outset to explain the task, the result you expect, and the deadline. You'll soon notice the benefit.

3. **Clear your desk each day,** at a time when you can prevent interruptions, or before they begin. You can manage interruptions by using voice mail to prioritize your calls and focusing on completing tasks by the end of each day.

4. **Make "wasted" time productive.** This may call for investment in a cellular phone or a laptop, but much of the time you spend waiting for planes or sitting in lobbies can, with preparation, become productive.

5. **Give yourself creative time.** Spend it alone with your ideas, or over coffee with an employee, but be sure it's in your schedule.

PERSONAL INSTRUCTOR/
FITNESS TRAINER

Start-up cost:	$100-$1,000
Potential earnings:	$20,000-$65,000
Typical fees:	$50-$75 per hour
Advertising:	Business cards, brochures, flyers, bulletin boards in health clubs
Qualifications:	Experience, physical fitness, knowledge of equipment and CPR
Equipment needed:	Membership to a gym; your own equipment if you want to do it directly out of your home
Home business potential:	Yes
Staff required:	No
Handicapped opportunity:	No
Hidden costs:	Travel time needed to meet clients where they work out

LOWDOWN:

Do you keep yourself physically fit, have a great personality, and enjoy teaching others? If you answered "yes" to all three, pull out those business cards and start a personal trainer business. You'll have to market yourself like a pro—give seminars about being fit and cover the benefits of working out to get your name and face out there in this highly competitive occupation. Experience will be on your side. Remember, you are marketing yourself and motivating others to become physically fit at the same time, so you must also be in excellent physical shape and condition. Be prepared to work out right alongside your clients if they request it, teaching them all the latest ways to get and stay in shape. Keep a couple of before and after photos of yourself and others whom you've helped tone and shape. Do a video and sell it through local health clubs.

START-UP:

Start-up costs can consist solely of a gym membership; or, if you want the client to come to your home, you'll need a full set of equipment including free weights, Nautilus and weight training equipment. That could send you into the $100,000 range for start-up costs. You have the potential to stay in shape and make a decent living in the range of $20,000-$65,000 or more, depending on how affluent your clients are.

BOTTOM LINE ADVICE:

How many people can say that going to work relieves stress? Not only can you have fun and stay in shape, you get to have a social life on the job. Working out has become very social and everyone can do it, but the downside is, a client may quit without warning. Some people consider working out to be seasonal, so you'll really have to go out there and establish a good client base.

PERSONAL MENU SERVICE

Start-up cost:	Under $1,000
Potential earnings:	$10,000-$30,000
Typical fees:	$20-$50 per project
Advertising:	Brochures, advertisements in newspapers, food/health magazines
Qualifications:	Knowledge of basic nutrition and dietary requirements
Equipment needed:	Computer (helpful), nutrition resource materials
Home business potential:	Yes
Staff required:	None
Handicapped opportunity:	Yes
Hidden costs:	None

LOWDOWN:

Most people lack a good understanding of proper nutrition, but they know it is important. They are also too busy with work and family responsibilities to learn about the components of a good diet. If you have a solid background in this field and access to a computer, you can fill that need. You simply create weekly or monthly meal plans, based on the specific requirements of your clients. Not only individuals need such services; so do hospitals, retirement centers, schools, overworked restaurant owners, and many others.

START-UP:

Other than the cost of a computer and advertising, this business can be started on a shoestring.

BOTTOM LINE ADVICE:

It may be tedious at times to create brand-new menu ideas on a constant basis. You may also have difficulty selling your services to some institutions if you don't have credentials in dietetics. It is important to check out legal and health ramifications of any business that relates to food consumption.

PERSONAL SHOPPER

Start-up cost:	$500-$1,000
Potential earnings:	$10,000-$25,000
Typical fees:	$20-$40 per shopping excursion
Advertising:	Brochures, classified ads, personalized notes to busy executives
Qualifications:	An eye for a great deal and the ability to match gifts to personalities
Equipment needed:	Dependable transportation
Home business potential:	Yes
Staff required:	No
Handicapped opportunity:	Yes
Hidden costs:	Watch your mileage and be sure that you bill on an hourly rate rather than a per-job basis; otherwise, people may try to take advantage of you

LOWDOWN:

Do you consider yourself to be the "shopping goddess of the universe?" Are you able to consistently choose tasteful and well-received gifts? If so, this business could be your dream come true. Many of today's executives are simply too busy to spend an hour or two shopping for the perfect gift, so you can do it for them by offering your services at an hourly rate. You'll need to make sure that the client provides you with some method to purchase the gifts—or arrange for the items to be held for pickup by the client. Build a strong network of places to shop; familiarize yourself with every gift/specialty store, retail store, and florist in your area. You'll need this vast resource (and plenty of catalogs) to come up with refreshingly new approaches to gift-giving. Another part of your business might be purchasing items for busy executives themselves; they could provide you with a personalized size (and preference) card, then send you off on a buying odyssey.

START-UP:

Brochures and personal notes sent to managers of large corporations are a good way to introduce yourself and your services. Be sure to stress the advantages of using a shopping service (chiefly, the time-saving and money-saving factor) and be clear about the way you bill up front. Then, you'll need to start collecting catalogs, visiting malls and unusual shops, and combing the newspapers for sales. Your clients will expect you to know everything possible about shopping—so take the time to prepare!

BOTTOM LINE ADVICE:

If you only want to do this job part-time for individual clients, you won't make as much as you would working full-time for large companies. Difficult situations may occur when the client isn't happy with the purchase, but you should be able to return anything you buy. All in all, the joy of spending other people's money is hard to resist—it gives you all the pleasure with none of the guilt.

PET PSYCHOLOGIST

Start-up cost:	$500-$1,500
Potential earnings:	$50,000-$75,000
Typical fees:	$25-$75 per office visit or house call
Advertising:	Veterinary offices, pet stores, Yellow Pages, newspapers
Qualifications:	Degree in veterinary science or psychology (or even both)
Equipment needed:	None
Home business potential:	Yes (but you'll probably be making lots of house calls)
Staff required:	None
Handicapped opportunity:	Yes
Hidden costs:	Mileage can get out of control; keep good records and make sure to include those costs in your fee structure

LOWDOWN:

What do you do when Fido's got the blues? Or when Chance the Cat's carpet-wetting problem is not physically motivated? You call a pet psychologist, of course. This professional will meet with furry clients to determine the source of the emotional problem. Is it a new baby in the house, or what about that new job that takes you away on business trips frequently? A pet psychologist specializes in finding solutions to problems such as these and suggesting appropriate behavioral changes. As a "pet shrink," your biggest challenge will be to get the word out—as well as to assure others of your credibility. After all, this job is a little out of the ordinary—so you'll need to network with veterinarians, pet store owners, and even the Humane Society and adoption shelters to educate them about the need for services such as yours in order to get them to act as referral agents. But when you consider that people spend an average of $1,000 annually on each of their animals, it's not far-fetched to assume that you could build a nice nest egg helping animals sort out the messier details of their lives.

START-UP:

After you earn your degree or professional certification, you'll only need to get the word out about your services. This should cost you in the neighborhood of $500-$1,000 (for brochures, business cards, and a Yellow Pages ad). But keep your advertising costs low initially by networking with people who will provide you with referrals. Charge an hourly rate of $25-$75 per hour, and collect when services are rendered.

BOTTOM LINE ADVICE:

This business could go to the dogs if you aren't careful about maintaining a high level of professionalism. People who are serious pet owners expect others to take their pets seriously—and if you approach each job in a caring, sensitive, and authoritative manner, you'll have no problem getting to the heart of the problem. Otherwise, you're providing a helpful service, as well as indirectly saving the lives of pets who might otherwise be given over to the pound.

PRIVATE TUTOR

Start-up cost:	$500
Potential earnings:	$15,000-$20,000
Typical fees:	$10-$20 per hour
Advertising:	Classified ads, Yellow Pages, word of mouth (school principals would be a good group to network with)
Qualifications:	Teaching experience or degree in area of expertise
Equipment needed:	None
Home business potential:	Yes
Staff required:	None
Handicapped opportunity:	Yes
Hidden costs:	Watch your mileage

LOWDOWN:

Since classrooms are getting larger and larger, many students' needs are getting overlooked. Your services may be needed to bring a struggling student up to speed—and the best part about this type of business is that it is recession-proof! As long as there are students, there will be a strong need for capable individuals to guide them to scholastic success. Determine where your area of expertise lies (is it in history? English? mathematics?) and meet with teachers in this subject to ask for referrals. Once you get a few clients, your word of mouth will grow quickly, and you may find that you need to network with other tutors to build referral systems of your own. At any rate, as a tutor you will find out the student's needs (probably in a written report from their teacher) and develop lesson plans tailored to that specific need. The opportunity to be creative is up to you, so try to make the lessons interesting and empower the student so that each success feels like their own.

START-UP:

Purchase a few used textbooks (preferably with teacher's guides) and buy yourself some good books on learning challenges and motivation to succeed. To be a good inspiration to your student, you'll need to demonstrate your own willingness to learn. Your only other start-up cost will be advertising, and that will generally stay under $500.

BOTTOM LINE ADVICE:

Encouraging a young student's success while fostering a thirst for knowledge can be richly rewarding if you are genuinely interested in education. Helping a student overcome what seemed like an obstacle offers you—and the rest of the world—optimism about our own possibilities. Aside from an occasional obnoxious child, what's there to hate about that?

PROFESSIONAL ORGANIZER

Start-up cost:	$500-$1,000
Potential earnings:	$25,000-$45,000
Typical fees:	$25-$40 per hour
Advertising:	Write articles for your local newspapers on time management and organizing space, Welcome Wagon, direct mail coupons; conduct seminars through local community continuing education; network
Qualifications:	You must be a highly organized person by nature, with drive for efficiency; knowledge of systems, furniture, products, supplies and accessories are a must
Equipment:	Pager or cellular phone, computers
Home business potential:	Yes
Staff:	No
Handicapped opportunity:	No
Hidden costs:	Mileage and cellular phone bills

LOWDOWN:

Most organizers specialize in one of five areas: space planning (organizing office arrangement of furniture, traffic, lighting, noise, and leisure space); time management (setting goals, developing action plans, scheduling, and delegating tasks); paper management (organizing the steady flow of information materials by setting up filing and retrieval systems, sometimes with the aid of a computer); clutter control (finding the proper and efficient placement for things to keep clutter to a minimum); closet/storage design (organizing closet and storage space). Choose one or two and market your services accordingly. This business would thrive in highly urban areas with busy professionals who want their home life to run as smoothly as the office—and it's much more fun to organize other people's lives than to run our own.

START-UP:

You'll spend at least $500 or so on business cards for networking—but that's almost negligible considering that you'll be charging $25-$45 per hour for your expertise.

BOTTOM LINE ADVICE:

Look into the National Association of Professional Organizers for more information. Hook up with an organization that conducts seminars, and offer your services as an instructor. This can supplement the income of your consulting service rather nicely.

REAL ESTATE AGENT/
HOME RESEARCHER

Start-up cost:	$500-$1,000
Potential earnings:	$25,000-$100,000
Typical fees:	Commissions of 30 to 40 percent are common
Advertising:	Yellow Pages, memberships in local business and charitable organizations, local newspapers, penny savers, referrals from agencies
Qualifications:	Real estate license
Equipment needed:	Phone, computer, printer, fax/modem and copier, business cards, letterhead, envelopes
Home business potential:	Yes
Staff required:	No
Handicapped opportunity:	No
Hidden costs:	Travel, marketing

LOWDOWN:

You will be focusing here on one part of the residential real estate agent's job. You will be doing the basic research rather than carrying out the entire process through to closing. You will develop a range of choices based on the buyer interview. This gives the agent and the buyer an opportunity to plan, clarify wants and needs, and consider the financial implications. It is reassuring for a family making a transcontinental move to know what choices are available to them within their price range, general preferences for neighborhood type, and so on. Your job, essentially, is to match your clients to their "perfect" home; you're different from a relocation specialist in that your territory is limited to your own immediate community. You provide information on the homes in your geographic area as opposed to helping clients relocate elsewhere around the country.

START-UP:

Start-up costs are low (could get by for $500), but marketing efforts will be ongoing unless referrals or subcontracting can bring you adequate business. You could earn $25,000 annually.

BOTTOM LINE ADVICE:

You will need to prove, consistently, that your services add value, don't threaten agents, and make sense to transferees. Keeping good records of your effectiveness will support your marketing efforts. Projecting an enthusiasm for your local area, its different communities, and its varied attractions, will enhance your work. This is a good choice for someone who loves houses and enjoys thinking about what type of family would choose each one, but who finds the "sale" process unappealing. Not everyone wants to spend all weekend showing picky buyers house after house, only to see the sale evaporate. As a home researcher you can create a service that suits you as well as it does your clients.

REMINDER SERVICE

Start-up cost:	Under $1,000 ($500 to cover flyers and advertising); add $1,500 if you buy a computer
Potential earnings:	$10,000-$15,000
Typical fees:	$20-$35 per month
Advertising:	Bulletin boards, direct mail, networking at business meetings
Qualifications:	Strong organizational and time-management skills
Equipment needed:	Computer and software program with built-in reminders, a detailed planner
Home business potential:	Yes
Staff required:	No (although you may want someone to cover the late shift)
Handicapped opportunity:	Yes
Hidden costs:	Telephone costs may be high if you're not careful; also, be sure to keep accurate records for billing purposes

LOWDOWN:

If you consider yourself exceptionally well-organized and have the ability to stay on top of a million details at once, then setting up a reminder service should come naturally to you. Your days will consist of talking with clients to determine the scope of their needs, entering their data onto a computerized tracking system, and keeping on top of what you need to remind them of and when. Set regular hours to maintain continuity; this cannot be a job that you work at only when you feel like it. Also, since many of your customers are too busy to remember important details of their lives (such as when to pay bills, birth dates of family and friends, and other such data), they may forget to pay you. That's why it is suggested that you collect at least half of your fee up front, offering standard hourly rates and/or specific packages geared toward themes. For instance, you could offer a "Birthday Blitz" package, where the only service the customer buys from you is that of being reminded of important birthdays as they occur throughout the year.

START-UP:

There are quite a few good time-management and reminder-type software packages out there, so do yourself a favor and buy the best one you can afford. You'll also need a powerful computer (about $1,500). After you get your computer system plugged in, all you really need are your marketing materials (flyers and business cards).

BOTTOM LINE ADVICE:

Helping others to keep track of the important details of their lives, both personally and professionally, can be interesting and different work nearly every day. The downside is pretty clear-cut, however: mess up once, and your business could get a bad reputation. That's why you should protect yourself with a good software program to help manage your business.

ROOMMATE REFERRAL SERVICE

Start-up cost:	$500-$1,000
Potential earnings:	$10,000-$25,000
Typical fees:	20 to 50 percent of a month's rent
Advertising:	Yellow Pages, flyers at apartment complexes, coin-operated laundries, and supermarkets, newspaper classified ads
Qualifications:	Excellent organization skills
Equipment needed:	Database management software, computer modem, printer, phone, credit card processing equipment
Home business potential:	Yes
Staff required:	No
Handicapped opportunity:	Yes
Hidden costs:	Insurance

LOWDOWN:

With the rising cost of living in many major cities, and the rise in displaced folks who need to share rent with the ideal roommate, you could make a fine living playing matchmaker for live-ins. Ideally, you would have a method for screening each of the candidates (police checks at the very least) and a method for securing your payment ahead of time (credit card processing equipment would be helpful). Advertise in places where people generally look for a place to live, and you'll have found your special niche. Develop a good questionnaire that really asks the kinds of questions a potential roommate would want answered. To double your income potential, you could add on other services such as mediation between rumblin' roomies or budget development assistance. The best advice is to focus on one area first, then branch out your services as you move successfully along.

START-UP:

Your costs are incredibly low when compared to most other businesses, mainly because you can create your own flyers to post in noticeable, highly trafficked areas. That's why your income potential, while seemingly low, is actually somewhat appealing—you have such low overhead, most of your income ($10,000-$20,000) will be sheer profit.

BOTTOM LINE ADVICE:

The only advice is to be sure you carefully screen your applicants—bad matches are sure to strike you if you don't.

SCANNING SERVICE

Start-up cost:	$600-$1,000
Potential earnings:	$15,000-$25,000
Typical fees:	About $3 per page or image
Advertising:	Yellow Pages, local business newspapers
Qualifications:	Ability to manipulate the software and scanner
Equipment needed:	Scanner, computer, optical character recognition and image scanning software
Home business potential:	Yes
Staff required:	No
Handicapped opportunity:	Yes
Hidden costs:	Software upgrades

LOWDOWN:

Anyone who deals with document production beyond simple word processing will probably be needing a scanner anyway. So why not make some additional money with it by scanning for others? Paper records are scanned for businesses so that data can be stored, indexed, and accessed electronically. But many organizations that need this process do not own scanners and will bring their paperwork to you. Your other main market will be scanning images. Pasteup is going the way of the carrier pigeons. Everything must be part of the electronic file nowadays. You can scan images and store them as .TIF files for manipulation later by graphic designers, artists, and document production specialists.

START-UP:

Adding the scanner to your current office setup will not be excessively costly ($600-$1,000), especially in view of the fee you can charge for its use ($3 per image average). Be sure to buy a high-resolution scanner; and save yourself a lot of aggravation by not purchasing a hand-held model (even though they are less expensive). For a scanning business, you'll need to produce your results quickly and accurately—and a hand-held model doesn't produce quality results.

BOTTOM LINE ADVICE:

You're not going to build a business empire out of scanning alone, but it will likely round out other services you already offer. Marketing will bring some people to your door for scanning services alone, but you are most likely to be selling scanning to people you already work with.

SILK FLOWER ARRANGER

Start-up cost:	$500-$1,000
Potential earnings:	$20,000-$40,000
Typical fees:	$25-$300
Advertising:	Yellow Pages, newspapers, bridal salons, restaurants
Qualifications:	Some training with flower arranging, creativity
Equipment needed:	Phone, floral accessories (vases, baskets, floral tape, access to a wide variety of silk flowers)
Home business potential:	Yes
Staff required:	No
Handicapped opportunity:	Yes
Hidden costs:	Watch materials costs

LOWDOWN:

There's nothing in the world like fresh flowers, but they only last a short while. That's why silk flowers are the mainstays of interior decorating; all you've got to do is dust them every once in a while and they retain their beauty forever. You'll always have plenty of customers if you choose to work in this field, from brides who don't want to worry about wilting flowers, to mourners who want to give the bereaved family a lasting token of their remembrance. You'll work many hours in your office, putting together the arrangements that have been ordered by your customers. The only problem is, you'll have to work hard to get some business, since there are plenty of others like you. Think about what makes you different, and let your customers know exactly what your unique marketing point is. Finally, network with funeral homes, churches, and wedding shops for cross-marketing opportunities.

START-UP:

Obtain a vendor's license (approximately $25) and buy your supplies at a wholesale store. Check with local craft stores to see if they offer additional discounts if you have a vendor's license. When starting the business, invest a few hundred dollars in floral supplies and silk flowers so you can make arrangements to sell at craft shows. Also, set aside money for booth space rental ($25-$100). Your products will sell anywhere from $25-$300.

BOTTOM LINE ADVICE:

Gain experience by working with florists or taking classes at craft stores. Once you have some knowledge of floral arranging, sign up to sell your goods at holiday craft fairs. Always have plenty of business cards/brochures to accompany each sale, and keep an album with pictures of your work to show clients.

STORYTELLER

Start-up cost:	$100-$500
Potential earnings:	$5,000-$15,000
Typical fees:	$15-$25 per storytelling event
Advertising:	Boards of Education, day care centers, libraries
Qualifications:	Ability to tell and retell stories with enthusiasm
Equipment needed:	None (except a great archives of stories)
Home business potential:	Yes
Staff required:	No
Handicapped opportunity:	Yes
Hidden costs:	Books

LOWDOWN:

Do you have a flair for telling (and retelling) stories? Can you paint pictures in listeners' minds as they hear every exciting detail? You may be skilled in the ancient art of storytelling; it's a tradition that first reached popularity during the time of Homer's *The Odyssey*. Now, storytellers for children are especially popular; many schools regularly bring in such professionals and parents are increasingly seeking storytellers for parties and special events. But storytelling isn't just reading well from a book; it's memorizing the stories, adding your own personal touches where necessary, and enlivening stories in a way only you would choose to do. You'll need a good repertoire to choose from, and you'll have to practice regularly to ensure that your vocal abilities and versatility stay up to the job. More than likely, this will be a part-time business opportunity.

START-UP:

You'll have virtually no start-up cost except business cards or flyers and the books from which you'll glean your tantalizing tales. Spend about $100-$500 on these items and subscribe to magazines that contain storytelling tips or new stories. You won't get rich doing this (especially charging $15-$25 per event), but if you really love storytelling, the joy of sharing with children will be reward enough.

BOTTOM LINE ADVICE:

Get involved with libraries in the area that feature children's activities. Place your business card in toy stores and bakeries, anywhere parents would go to plan for a child's birthday party.

STRESS MANAGEMENT COUNSELOR

Start-up cost:	$500-$1,500
Potential earnings:	$50,000-$65,000
Typical fees:	$20-$40 per session
Advertising:	Newspapers, magazines, bulletin boards, associations, physician referral, direct mail
Qualifications:	Some states require certification or license
Equipment needed:	Materials such as books, videos, audio tapes
Home business potential:	Yes
Staff required:	No
Handicapped opportunity:	Yes
Hidden costs:	Certification can cost you anywhere from $200-$500, depending on your area. Also, corporate clients may have a 45-day payment delay policy, tying up your cash flow (so insist on at least 50 percent down)

LOWDOWN:

In the high-tech, fast-food '90s, we are all getting stressed out to the max—and that's why stress management counselors have been cropping up everywhere, from church groups to Corporate America. Large companies hire such professionals to keep their employees sound, sane, and productive—recognizing that a well-balanced worker is also as much as 45 percent more effective on the job. As a stress management counselor, you would work with individuals or groups, assessing their problem areas and assisting them through innovative, inspiring materials and exercises. You will encourage them to perform at their happiest and healthiest best.

START-UP:

To begin with, you'll need to promote your services to literally hundreds of people; however, you should pinpoint the top 50 or so prospects and exhaust your efforts there before embarking on the rest of the world. Buy or develop a list of human resource professionals to mail information to—and don't forget to secure a vendor's license if you plan to offer resource materials for sale.

BOTTOM LINE ADVICE:

You'll feed off of the creative energy generated by helping others solve stress problems; after all, it is much easier for an outsider to identify what's working and what's not. After a few years, though, you may burn out yourself . . . make sure you've got a support person who will remind you of that which you preach.

TASTE TESTER FOR FOOD COMPANIES

Start-up cost:	$500
Potential earnings:	$10,000-$15,000 (most work part-time hours)
Typical fees:	$10-$15 per hour
Advertising:	Direct mail to food product manufacturers
Qualifications:	A good culinary sense and strong tastebuds
Equipment needed:	None
Home business potential:	Yes
Staff required:	No
Handicapped opportunity:	Yes
Hidden costs:	Mileage can become a problem; see that you are reimbursed or that you've covered these costs in your pricing structure

LOWDOWN:

The ultimate dream job for those who love food! Companies that are producing food products often use outside individuals for taste testers; although it is not a particularly lucrative field, it can be an interesting and satisfying one filled with variety. As a taste tester, you will taste new or improved food products and record your impressions, usually on a checklist predesigned by the company. You may have to wear a blindfold for some tests, while others may simply require a thumbs-up or thumbs-down. It is important that you can communicate to others the palatability of food; its taste, texture, and desirability are all of critical importance to the developers and marketing professionals working on the new product.

START-UP:

Buy a good list of companies that produce food items and you're off to a great start! With as little as an introductory letter detailing your interest in becoming a taste tester, you could let companies know of your availability—but do be sure to include some of your qualifications (such as having worked in a restaurant, or as a gourmet cook). You should have dependable transportation to and from company sites, because very rarely will you taste food in your own home.

BOTTOM LINE ADVICE:

While working in a "food festival of the senses" can be easy to digest, it can also cause heartburn if you are seeking to build a large nest egg. Nowhere will you find a wealthy taste tester basking in just desserts. Still, if financial reward isn't as necessary or important to you, you could really eat your heart out with this small business opportunity. And the hours aren't all that bad, either.

TOY CLEANING SERVICE

Start-up cost:	$500-$1,000
Potential earnings:	$20,000-$30,000
Typical fees:	$15-$20 per toy
Advertising:	Yellow Pages, direct mail, cold calls, referrals
Qualifications:	None (just elbow grease)
Equipment needed:	Standard germicidal spray/janitorial cleaning supplies, towels, gloves
Home business potential:	Yes
Staff required:	No
Handicapped opportunity:	Yes
Hidden costs:	Excessive mileage (be sure to stay within a 40-mile radius unless you charge extra for work outside your territory)

LOWDOWN:

One innovative new business to hit the scene is a toy cleaning service for doctors' offices, playgrounds, restaurants, and child care centers that could use a helping hand keeping their toy collection clean and germ-free. All of these facilities leave hundreds of small toys in their waiting and play areas for children to use freely—often forgetting that each toy must be cleaned on a regular basis to avoid contamination among the children. You offer peace of mind to the folks who have the play center, while at the same time offering peace of mind to parents who worry about their children catching a cold or virus from dirty toys. And all you're doing is showing up, cleaning the toys properly, and returning everything neatly to its place. It's simple, it's straightforward—and the best part is, it's profitable because it's just one less chore for the customer to worry about.

START-UP:

All you really need is some germicidal spray and other cleaning solvents, gloves, and towels—everything under $500. Spend another $500 or so on advertising via direct mail or Yellow Pages (but keep in mind that until people know what you do, you're better off spending your advertising budget on direct mail and networking functions). If you build enough contacts, you could earn between $20,000-$30,000 per year—more if you grow and hire additional help.

BOTTOM LINE ADVICE:

It's an innovative, yet totally sensible idea. All you need to do is get out there, convince others that you can save them time and money in the long run, and roll up your sleeves. It's a terrific little niche market for those who enjoy the cleaning business.

VACATION RENTALS BROKER

Start-up cost:	$500-$1,000
Potential earnings:	$45,000-$60,000
Typical fees:	Usually a percentage (10 to 15 percent)
Advertising:	Advertising in real estate magazines and real estate section of newspaper, Yellow Pages, referrals
Qualifications:	Experience in real estate rentals, good organizational skills
Equipment needed:	A basic office setup for record keeping
Home business potential:	Yes
Staff required:	No
Handicapped opportunity:	No
Hidden costs:	Insurance, vehicle maintenance

LOWDOWN:

A vacation rentals broker keeps track of all the details related to renting property for distant owners. Many people with second homes rent them for the better part of the year, reserving a week or two for themselves and their families. Renting helps with the costs of this additional residence, but it also creates a number of headaches and problems that are very difficult for someone who lives far away to deal with. Your service finds renters, writes the rental contract, and makes sure that the agreements are carried out. You collect the rent, check for any damage, answer the million and one questions renters always have, and generally keep an eye on things.

START-UP:

Costs are minimal; you just need an effective way to keep track of information and money. Since your business depends directly on how much time you put into it, expect to earn as much as you work for (and that could be anywhere from $45,000-$60,000 or more).

BOTTOM LINE ADVICE:

Consider becoming a vacation rentals broker if you live in an area that has a high appeal for renters and a large stock of available summer (or winter) homes to rent. Once you develop a reputation for dependability, referrals will bring other homeowners to you. The amount of advertising you will need to do will vary depending on your area and the presence or absence of competing services.

WELLNESS INSTRUCTOR

Start-up cost:	$500-$1,500
Potential earnings:	$25,000-$40,000
Typical fees:	$20-$40 per hour
Advertising:	Human resource association newsletters, Yellow Pages
Qualifications:	Some states require certification
Equipment needed:	Fax, phone, pager or cellular phone
Home business potential:	Yes
Staff required:	No
Handicapped opportunity:	Yes
Hidden costs:	Photocopying materials for classes can add up—be sure to include them in your price or cost analysis

LOWDOWN:

Rising medical costs have driven many companies to wellness programs as a preventive measure for cost containment. You can provide seminars for these companies on topics such as stress-cutting foods, the importance of drinking water throughout the day, and even breathing exercises. You'll rely on resource materials such as audiocassettes, books, and videos that give added credibility to what you teach. The fact is, most of us are leading potentially destructive lifestyles (drinking too much caffeine and smoking, for example) and need to be given some empowerment in our lives to conquer these bad habits. As a wellness instructor, your job will be to help clear out the cobwebs in mind, body, and spirit—and to do it in such a way that the students feel empowerment over their own bugaboos.

START-UP:

You can start a healthy business with a minimal investment if you have the right credentials (a degree in nursing, social work, or psychology). Advertising will initially cost you in the neighborhood of $500-$1,000, because you need to be where human resource and other professionals can readily find you (more specifically, in their trade association newsletter). One easy way to get your foot in the door is to attend professional functions and spread your brochure or business card; most associations will allow nonmembers to attend meetings at a slightly higher cost than members. Take advantage—and promote the positive benefits of your work!

BOTTOM LINE ADVICE:

Inspiring others to take charge of their lives and active roles in their health and longevity can be a richly rewarding field. But you'll need to make sure you follow your own rules; be a good role model and never, ever let them see you sweat!

START-UP BETWEEN
$1,000 AND $5,000

ABSTRACTING SERVICE

Start-up cost:	$2,500-$8,000
Potential earnings:	$20,000-$40,000 per year
Typical fees:	At least $5-$15 per article (full abstract with index)
Advertising:	Solicit database publishers, corporations, respond to newspaper ads for abstract work
Qualifications:	Knowledge in the areas you are abstracting, ability to research a wide range of topics, ability to organize and consolidate data, good writing and communication skills, knowledge of database services and CD-ROM publishers
Equipment needed:	Computer and modem, fax, printer, software, office furniture, business cards, letterhead, reference books, dictionaries
Home business potential:	Yes
Staff required:	No
Handicapped opportunity:	Yes
Hidden costs:	Keep an eye on on-line time if using these services

LOWDOWN:

Abstracters read articles from various publications, summarize them, and store the data on a computer. Some abstracters also index the articles by key words or terms that help the computer locate them quickly. Often abstracters specialize in areas such as engineering, science, and other technical fields; some work in medical and legal fields. A keen interest in reading is very important to your success, as is the ability to retain what you read. Good writing skills and knowledge of the topics you are abstracting is essential, especially for condensing the material. This business could also fit well with an existing editorial services or technical writing business. If you don't have actual paid experience as an abstracter, you can select articles of interest to certain potential clients, make up a portfolio of samples, and pitch your services to them. You might also talk with database publishers to discuss how you might help them, and vice versa.

START-UP:

In addition to basic computer equipment and a word-processing package, you don't need much beyond office furniture and reference books. Your business can be launched for as little as $2,500. Charge $5-$15 per article.

BOTTOM LINE ADVICE:

Many larger corporations, in particular, rely on abstracting services to keep them updated about competitors and innovations in products and services relating to their businesses. This work allows considerable flexibility in your schedule and requires only a modest investment. Abstracting demands great concentration and careful organization, but also exposes you to a wealth of knowledge and contacts. You also will have the satisfaction of knowing that your work provides a valuable service to your clients.

ACCOUNTANT

Start-up cost:	$3,000-$6,000
Potential earnings:	$20,000-$80,000
Typical fees:	$35 and up per hour
Advertising:	Membership and active participation in community groups, newspapers, ads in publications for local fund-raisers, referrals
Qualifications:	CPA, some experience in services on which you choose to focus
Equipment needed:	Office, furniture, computer, suite software, printer, business cards, letterhead, envelopes
Home business potential:	Yes
Staff required:	No
Handicapped opportunity:	Yes
Hidden costs:	Errors and omissions insurance, subscriptions and membership dues, continuing education

LOWDOWN:

This is a service that virtually everyone needs. The challenge is to show potential clients how you can improve their lives by helping them manage their financial affairs better. The two major approaches chosen by solo accountants are to work with individuals on tax issues and personal financial planning, or to serve the burgeoning small business market with bookkeeping setup, payroll, tax planning, and all the other financial activities that enterprises require. You will need to be creative in distinguishing yourself from this rather crowded field. How are your accounting services better than those of the six other accountants who have called a business that week, looking for work? How can you show an individual that you can serve him better than the big storefront operations that prepare taxes for low fees during the winter and early spring?

START-UP:

Will you meet clients in your office, or will you travel to their homes or businesses? These decisions will control your start-up costs (could be as little as $3,000). Potential earnings of $20,000 and more.

BOTTOM LINE ADVICE:

Being an excellent accountant and being able to create a profitable business are two different things. The people skills required have probably been completely neglected in your education, and possibly in your experience if you have worked for a large firm. Gaining the confidence of potential clients is far more than simply having excellent accounting skills up your sleeve. You'll need to find a way to present your services in a way that appeals to people who want your help but don't really understand numbers and like to tell condescending accountant jokes at parties. On the downside, there is a seasonality to your services; you'll be busiest in December and March/April.

Advice from the Experts

What sets your business apart from others like it?

Personalized service and affordable rates are what set apart
Kelly M. Zimmerman, CPA's business in Cuyahoga Falls, Ohio.
"I take a genuine interest in my clients' businesses. I really care
about whether or not they succeed."

Things you couldn't do without:

Zimmerman says she couldn't do without a computer,
telephone, and calculator.

Marketing tips/advice:

"Get involved in an organization that you believe in personally
and where you can also promote your business. Marketing for
accountants is basically word of mouth, so be sure to do
everything you can to keep your current clients happy. They'll
send you more clients if they know you've gone out of your way
for them."

If you had to do it all over again . . .

"I would try to be more organized and focused on the types of
clients I really want to serve."

ADOPTION SEARCH SERVICE

Start-up cost:	$2,000-$3,000
Potential earnings:	$25,000-$40,000
Typical fees:	$150-$250 per job or an hourly fee of $15-$25 per hour
Advertising:	Yellow Pages, referrals from social service agencies and associations
Qualifications:	Experience with the field, sensitivity, understanding of state laws, rules, and records regarding adoption, persistence
Equipment needed:	Computer, modem, printer office furniture, business cards, letterhead, envelopes
Home business potential:	Yes
Staff required:	No
Handicapped opportunity:	Yes
Hidden costs:	On-line time, phone bills

LOWDOWN:

Adoption search services provide opportunities for birth children or birth parents to retrace the steps that separated them from their blood relatives. This is a challenging business, and it is still encircled with complex regulations that vary from state to state. Another source of challenge is the infinite variation of human nature. Some reunions are filled with joy, but not all discoveries are happy ones and some people would rather not be found. A vocal minority of the population strongly opposes the adoption search process. Overall, however, bridging the chasm caused by adoption decisions can be a viable service for a small business to offer.

START-UP:

Some of the searching process may be done on-line (spend $2,000-$3,000 for a computer), but the telephone and shoe leather will be your major tools. You may opt to charge a flat rate ($150-$250) or an hourly fee of $15-$25 per hour. If the client has some information for you to go on, opt for the flat rate. If it looks like a wild-goose chase, you might seriously consider the hourly rate plus related expenses.

BOTTOM LINE ADVICE:

Marketing will be a challenge. How will adoptees and birth parents come to know about your service? And since you will only work once for each client, marketing must be an ongoing part of your strategy. Linking people can heal old and painful wounds, so you will get more than monetary rewards from your successful searches. On the other hand, it could throw salt into a wound that was somewhat healed. How will turning someone's life around, for good or ill, affect you?

ADVERTISING SALES REPRESENTATIVE

Start-up cost:	$1,000-$1,500
Potential earnings:	$40,000-$150,000
Typical fees:	Commission-only is standard and ranges from 5 to 25 percent
Advertising:	Direct mail, trade journals, referrals
Qualifications:	Experience with an advertising agency or periodical sales rep
Equipment needed:	Basic office equipment, business cards, letterhead, envelopes
Home business potential:	Yes
Staff required:	No
Handicapped opportunity:	Yes
Hidden costs:	Expect high phone bills and mileage costs

LOWDOWN:

This business must be built on extensive experience in the field. Your expertise lies in matching the need to the availability. If you know how, you can sell advertising space in all magazines to the advertisers who need it. Your job is to find a buyer at a good price that might never have discovered this advertising venue unaided. You'll need contacts and experience to make a success of this enterprise, but room exists for the independent rep and many earn $100,000 or more. Much depends on the media you're selling ad space for; for instance, if you're selling ads in a trade journal or well-known national publication, your income will be quite high. However, if you're selling ads for a community newspaper, your income may reach its peak at $35,000.

START-UP:

The telephone is your major tool, and you may discover a great need for a car phone (which brings with it monthly charges and high incoming-call fees). You'll need access to reference books listing periodicals, rates, and dates. Expect a $1,500 initial start-up cost for this business.

BOTTOM LINE ADVICE:

If you love selling, this is selling in its purest form. No limitations bind you to one focus, one time, or one perspective. Businesses need to advertise, and finding space for their commercial messages can be a real challenge. Your services are the perfect answer to their needs. The same old way of doing things will be your biggest hindrance. Established agencies are your competitors, and you will need to market your services vigorously.

ARBITRATION SERVICE

Start-up cost:	$3,000-$6,000
Potential earnings:	$40,000-$70,000
Typical fees:	$35-$65 per hour
Advertising:	Referrals from courts and law firms, Yellow Pages, memberships in legal organizations, business groups, community organizations
Qualifications:	Law degree, extensive experience in arbitration, ability to market and sell your services
Equipment needed:	Office furniture, computer, modem, fax, cellular phone, printer, business cards, letterhead, envelopes
Home business potential:	Yes
Staff required:	No
Handicapped opportunity:	Yes
Hidden costs:	Errors and omissions insurance, memberships dues

LOWDOWN:

Arbitration is becoming an essential facet of the American legal process. Increasingly, it is a required step in the effort to find a resolution to legal conflicts. Lawyers are officers of the court, and as an arbitrator you will be embodying that concept. You'll work as a go-between for parties who can no longer communicate directly but who still seek an equitable solution to their problem. Once you become known for your ability to achieve a consensus between opposing parties, you ought to have a steady stream of referrals. Commercial conflicts, especially, often cannot wait the years that are now required for a case to pass through the clogged court system. Sometimes you will be able to sell your services before the lawsuit stage has been reached. Creating a solution that works effectively for both sides in a dispute is a valuable—and rare—ability.

START-UP:

You're selling yourself, not your premises. The equipment needed is just what will allow you to prepare your own paperwork and do your bookkeeping (about $3,000 to start). Realistic earnings of $40,000 are possible.

BOTTOM LINE ADVICE:

Becoming established will take time and persistence. Keep careful records of your successes to use in future marketing efforts. A supportive network will be vital; you can't build an arbitration service on cold-calling. Wisdom about people, knowledge of the law, and a good ability to clarify issues are all essential to success. In effect, you are doing what a lawsuit ought to do but really can't today, because of the high costs and long time frame involved. Excellent arbitrators are in very high demand, but it might take many years to achieve success.

ART BROKER/
CORPORATE ART CONSULTANT

Start-up cost:	$1,000 plus
Potential earnings:	$35,000-$100,000
Typical fees:	$50 per hour
Advertising:	Trade publications, business periodicals, service on boards or in community charitable organizations, networking, referrals
Qualifications:	Degree in art or related field, extensive gallery or museum experience, interior design credentials
Equipment needed:	Business cards, letterhead, envelopes, phone
Home business potential:	Yes
Staff required:	No
Handicapped opportunity:	No
Hidden costs:	Membership dues, subscriptions to art periodicals, travel

LOWDOWN:

The corporate art consulting business is where connoisseurship and corporate image issues come together. It's a rarified combination, and you'll need a strong eye for art and a reputation for awareness of business requirements to create a successful enterprise. The art world often has trouble communicating with business people. Your ability to move in both worlds is a major factor in your success. To a large degree you will be selling yourself, and you will do this by listening well, grasping the needs of the corporate culture of your client, and presenting each organization with choices that will enhance their workplaces and their image. You will transform your own appreciation for art into a service that adds value to your clients' enterprises.

The ability to locate the perfect piece of art for the corporate environment is rare. You'll need to visit every art show or trade convention you can, and collect catalogs from dealers worldwide. Then, you'll negotiate fair prices—as an expert, you can help the newly discovered artist price to sell.

START-UP:

You'll be working at your clients' premises, in galleries, etc., not at your own office, which only needs to support your business needs, not to impress (as little as $1,000 to start). Depending on your clients, you could easily earn up to $100,000.

BOTTOM LINE ADVICE:

Establishing yourself as an art broker or corporate art consultant will take time, determination, and persistence. Your location will control your avenues of approach; probably operating independently will be possible only in one of the major U.S. cities. Elsewhere, you'll need to be associated with a commercial interior design firm or an art gallery.

ASSOCIATION MANAGEMENT SERVICES

Start-up cost:	$2,000-$9,000
Potential earnings:	$20,000-$50,000
Typical fees:	Monthly retainers of $1,000-$5,000 are not uncommon (directly dependent upon the association's size)
Advertising:	Network with professional and trade associations, advertise in related publications
Qualifications:	Good organizational, writing, marketing, communication, and motivation skills, an eye for detail, office management or administrative experience is helpful
Equipment needed:	Office and computer equipment, phone, fax, copier, business cards, letterhead, supplies
Home business potential:	Yes
Staff required:	None
Handicapped opportunity:	Yes
Hidden costs:	Membership in associations; subscriptions to related publications

LOWDOWN:

From the Association for Association Management (yes, there really is an association for everyone) to the Association for Children for Enforcement of Support, most organizations need help in managing their operations. Especially well-suited to a management service are groups too big to rely solely on volunteers but not big enough to justify hiring someone to do it on a full-time basis. Your services for each client may vary, but may include maintaining membership lists, publishing a newsletter, mailing out information about the organization, keeping records, collecting dues, and handling meetings, events, and fund-raising activities. Not only can you work for an existing organization, you could also start an association of your own. Best bet: base it on your own profession or something else with which you have personal experience.

START-UP:

Office and computer equipment are your biggest expenses (about $2,000). You may be able to get the organization(s) you represent to pay for some supplies, but that is not something to rely on at the business plan stage. Charge a monthly retainer of $1,000-$5,000 for your services to make sure you cover all of your expenses; since many of these associations work with volunteers, they may try to take advantage of your expertise, too. Don't let them.

BOTTOM LINE ADVICE:

Association management provides a great variety of duties and an opportunity to interact with interesting people. You will also get opportunities to learn about an array of topics at meetings and conventions. This is a great opportunity for those with philanthropic tendencies.

Juggling Family and Work

Let's face it, raising a family and growing a business are each full-time jobs. So, how can you give 100 percent to each and still maintain your sanity?

First of all, set aside a special time each day or week that is designated "family time." During this time, you will accept no phone calls, set no appointments, and not even think about your business. You will probably not even want to stay near your office. Think about going out to dinner and sharing the three best things that happened to each family member during that week.

Or, if you feel you can incorporate your family into parts of your business, it might help them to better understand your needs and constraints. It's one thing for your spouse or children to see you completely stressed out; it's quite another for them to be in your office when that high-volume order comes in on short notice. Especially for children, it is a good idea to demonstrate your commitment to your work.

Smaller children, particularly females, need positive workplace role models—and who better to pave the way than Mom or Dad? Historically, children who are raised by entrepreneurs do tend to become entrepreneurs themselves.

What should you do in the event that a client or customer wants to meet during one of your special family times? You can handle it one of two ways: first, you could rearrange your family time. But the better solution might be to simply say, "I am already meeting with a client at that time . . . is there another time that works for you?" Others will respect your attention to commitments, and you never have to offer an explanation for whom you're meeting with, and why.

However you decide to work your children into your business, or your business into your family life, one thing is for sure: there will never be a time without challenges and disruptions.

You will need to develop the skill to work around any obstacle or challenge, and the best way to accomplish a good balance between work and home life is to learn to follow a time-management program. Scheduling your time is the best way to make sure everything gets done. The rest is just recognizing that it is possible to have two loves: your business and your family.

AUDIO RECORDING FOR TRADE SHOWS AND SEMINARS

Start-up cost:	$2,000-$5,000
Potential earnings:	$25,000-$45,000+
Typical fees:	$100 per hour to tape a show/seminar, $2 per dub; or, you can tape for free and sell the tapes directly to attendees for $10-$35 a pop
Advertising:	Industry trades, flyers, direct mail
Qualifications:	Knowledge of audio equipment
Equipment needed:	Duplicators, small soundproof recording booth, mixing board, business cards
Home business potential:	Yes
Staff required:	No
Handicapped opportunity:	Yes
Hidden costs:	You may eventually need to move to a studio (see if you can rent space before buying it)

LOWDOWN:

There are hundreds of people giving seminars every day, so the field is ripe for your audio taping services because seminar attendees often like to take tapes for their colleagues to listen to later. You may be taping on a contractual basis (for an hourly fee) with a particular association, or you may be taping each seminar at a trade show and dubbing as quickly as possible to produce copies of the sessions for sale at your own booth. This unique business requires that you have knowledge and skill in the audio trade; read up on your industry and only buy used equipment if you're sure of what you're doing. A degree or certification in the radio industry may be helpful. Your challenge will be to market your service to the biggest marketers of all. They know every trick in the book, so your best bet is to take an honest approach and sell them on the benefits of your services.

START-UP:

Equipment will be your biggest expense ($2,000-$5,000); you'll have to build a soundproof room if you don't have one (tack on an additional $10,000). Don't limit yourself to hotel meeting rooms; think hospitals, schools, churches, and businesses, too. If you tap into every market, you could earn $45,000 or more.

BOTTOM LINE ADVICE:

Be prepared to give up your weekends and evenings. Some seminars are conducted when the majority of people will be able to attend; if you get a free night, plan on dubbing. On the plus side, this job will give you somewhat of a flexible schedule, since you won't be working 8:00 A.M. to 5:00 P.M. weekdays.

ADVICE FROM THE EXPERTS

What sets your business apart from others like it?

For Kathy Vanaman, co-owner (with husband Jonathan) of Listen Again Recording in Tallmadge, Ohio, it's immediacy that makes her business unique. "We do on-site recording and duplicating, so that conference attendees can purchase tapes of seminars the day of the seminar. They can take them home and listen to them right away."

Things you couldn't do without:

Vanaman's business depends on a duplicator, tape recorders, microphones, a computer and printer, and a labeling program.

Marketing tips/advice:

"Networking has been the most effective method of marketing by far," says Vanaman. She is a member of at least one organization that has used her services for large conferences.

If you had to do it all over again . . .

"We'd do it all the same way over again . . . there's actually not much you can change about this type of business."

AUTO MAINTENANCE

Start-up cost:	$2,000-$5,000
Potential earnings:	$25,000-$50,000
Typical fees:	$25 and up per job (usually an hourly rate of $45 plus parts costs)
Advertising:	Newspaper, radio, billboards, neighborhood flyers, direct mail, location
Qualifications:	Certified Automobile Mechanic
Equipment needed:	Automotive repair tools, inventory of wipers, motor oil, garage space (rented or owned)
Home business potential:	No
Staff required:	No
Handicapped opportunity:	No
Hidden costs:	Inventory, insurance, ongoing advertising

LOWDOWN:

On average, each American spends half of one year's wages on his or her car. To put it another way, we value our autos very highly, and we want excellent care for them. An auto maintenance service can be a wonderful way to reach this large group of customers, most of whom are keeping their cars years longer than they did in the past. You can focus your business just on maintenance and leave the complicated computer diagnosis and repairs, and the big parts inventory, to the dealers and garages. You'll have a limited, repeated set of procedures to follow, and you can build a loyal clientele if you keep people's cars running well, and do it in a way that is convenient for their drivers.

START-UP:

Costs will be fairly high to equip your business, unless you can buy a set of tools from another business for a reasonable sum. It will take some expensive marketing to launch your enterprise, and you will need to keep a certain level of advertising going throughout each year. If you are good, word of mouth could get you at least $25,000 the first year.

BOTTOM LINE ADVICE:

So, what makes you think you can compete with Minit-Lube? The answer, of course, is personal service. You're not just a well-trained teenager in a clean uniform, you're an experienced, well-organized, customer-oriented maintenance person. You're the answer to the dreams of the little old lady on the corner who relies on her car for safe travel, of the incredibly busy executive who demands rapid, accurate service, and of the car nuts who drop in and want to "talk cars" with someone else who cares about them as much as they do.

Advice from the Experts

What sets your business apart from others like it?

Paul Taylor, owner of a Midas Muffler franchise in Lawrence, New York, says his business is set apart because it's run by him. "I believe in the highest standards of equipment and service, and my customers know that about me."

Things you couldn't do without:

"It really depends on the types of services you're providing. If it's just a muffler shop, you'll only need an air compressor, cutting torches, a MIG welder, and lifts; you'll need more equipment if you start adding brake services and other automotive repair services." Taylor says he couldn't do without multiline phones, an answering machine, fax, and printer in his office.

Marketing tips/advice:

"As an independent, you'll need to do more guerrilla-type marketing, going after wholesale work within a trade as a subcontractor for body shops or transmission services. If you're in a franchise operation, you should be getting all the marketing and technical support they can offer; after all, that's really the only reason for buying into a franchise."

If you had to do it all over again . . .

"I think I've done all the right things, but the climate is awfully discouraging for newcomers due to heavy environmental and government regulations. If I had to do it all over again, I'd probably think twice."

BACKGROUND MUSIC LEASING

Start-up cost:	$1,500-$5,000
Potential earnings:	$30,000-$65,000
Typical fees:	$125-$350 per month or more, depending on how much music clients buy and how often they want to change it
Advertising:	Industry trades, local and business papers, direct mail
Qualifications:	BMI, ASCAP licensing (rights to resell music)
Equipment needed:	Editing and duplicating equipment, tapes, soundproof room
Home business potential:	Yes
Staff required:	No
Handicapped opportunity:	Yes
Hidden costs:	Equipment maintenance and upgrades

LOWDOWN:

It ain't just elevator music anymore; many offices and facilities are leasing music that moves, inspires, and calms workers or folks on hold. New Age music is a top seller these days, primarily because of its soothing and mind-expanding qualities. Many shopping centers, malls, and bookstores use music aimed at making the shopper feel comfortable and in a buying mood. Regardless of the type of music you're selling, getting companies to use prerecorded music takes some tremendous marketing ability. First, you'll have to go to BMI or ASCAP (the folks who regulate prerecorded music) and tell them that you are interested in purchasing some music from them. You will pay a blanket fee to the label the music is recorded on or directly to the composer. From there, you'll try to get places such as hospitals, offices, or hotels to rent or sublease from you. Having a background in the music or radio field would be helpful and lend you much in the way of credibility.

START-UP:

After your start-up cost, you'll have to figure in the blanket fee charged and the licensing fee. Add in your marketing and travel time and you can still make a pretty decent living at $30,000-$65,000. You'll want to suggest that your client change music a minimum of once a month, if not more.

BOTTOM LINE ADVICE:

If you can understand all the licensing jargon and you like reading and drawing up contracts, look into this profession. It could be a low-stress job because lots of companies use this service—and they're not just using Muzak anymore.

BOAT MAINTENANCE/CLEANING SERVICE

Start-up cost:	$2,000-$10,000
Potential earnings:	$30,000-$60,000
Typical fees:	$55 per hour
Advertising:	Marinas, boat retailers, Yellow Pages, brochure
Qualifications:	Know the mechanics of a boat and the types of boats
Equipment needed:	Tools, cleaning supplies, dock, storage space
Home business potential:	No
Staff required:	No
Handicapped opportunity:	No
Hidden costs:	Repairs, insurance

LOWDOWN:

Boat owners are nuts about their boats and while they enjoy being out on the open seas, they often hate keeping up with the maintenance end. After all, boating is about getting away from it all, right? Usually, your clients have a lot of disposable income, since they've invested a great deal of cash in the boat itself; that's how you can be sure of your own earning potential. On a more practical note, this business is for you if you don't mind a little grease under your nails and working out in the hot sun occasionally. Know your boat types (fiberglass, wood, steel, aluminum) and what type of chemicals you can use on each without causing any damage. Certification as a boat mechanic will be helpful but not required. Advertise where people buy dock space and at boat retailers. Try to get the businesses (such as restaurants) along the shore to carry your brochure.

START-UP:

If you are a good mechanic to begin with and have your own tools, your start-up costs could be minimal (about $500). You'll need storage space, possibly a dock, and all types of cleaners, paint, and detergents. Your basic fee to do a tune-up would likely be $50 per hour; add another $25 per hour to clean. Your salary will be in the $30,000-$60,000 range.

BOTTOM LINE ADVICE:

This is a big undertaking, as boat owners usually pamper their boats. You have to be truly committed. If you like working with your hands and tinkering with engines, this would be a great opportunity for you. The pay-off in the end could be great, too, as there are hundreds of thousands of registered boaters today. If you space your jobs out well, this could be a full-time job, and you could add staff before you know it.

Book Binder

Start-up cost:	$1,500 and up
Potential earnings:	$25,000-$40,000
Typical fees:	$3-$5 per page or a per project fee (varied)
Advertising:	Yellow Pages, newspaper classified, book dealer newsletters and industry publications, direct mail or business cards to libraries
Qualifications:	Apprentice experience or training
Equipment needed:	Press, page cutter, stamping machines
Home business potential:	Possibly
Staff required:	No
Handicapped opportunity:	Yes
Hidden costs:	Materials costs, insurance

Lowdown:

While many book binders assemble the pages and cover of books, the majority specialize in repairing them. Damage can be caused by a wide variety of things: misuse, vandalism, fires, water damage, and simple wear-and-tear. To save books that are rare or out of print, libraries and book dealers often need the services of a book binder who can restore the natural beauty of the original binding. That often means sewing together pages by hand or machine and producing a new cover that looks remarkably like the old one. Why go to so much trouble for old books? Because many are worth money, and money is of particular importance to the rare book dealers in need of your services. The best way to get started in this field is to accept an apprenticeship with another, more experienced book binder. Then, after you feel confident enough to break out on your own, start networking with owners of bookshops and library administrators. These people are always looking for reliable help in maintaining the quality of their products.

Start-up:

This one can be expensive if you purchase new equipment ($10,000 or more); look for used equipment in auctions and newspaper classifieds to keep start-up costs to a minimum. In terms of fees, most book binders charge $3-$5 per page for smaller projects and a per-project fee (varied according to level of damage) for the more complex or intricate jobs.

Bottom Line Advice:

Like carpenters and artisans, your work is highly specialized and depends on quality and finesse. You could burn out if you get too bogged down in detail. On the other hand, if you like working in solitude, this profession could be tailor-made for you.

Types of Business Insurance

- **Property Damage:** Covers fire, storm damage, vandalism, etc., for the replacement costs of the contents of your business.

- **General Liability:** Provides protection from personal injury and property damage.

- **Product Liability:** Protects from claims for damages or injuries related to defects in the products you make or sell. Regardless of outcome, litigation in these cases is time-consuming and expensive. Judgments often run to multimillion-dollar sums.

- **Disability:** Provides income replacement should you miss work through injury or illness. This is important if you are the major income source for your family.

- **Workers' Compensation:** Covers employees for loss of income and for medical costs arising from a job-related injury or illness. This coverage is required by law in all fifty states. You are legally required to: 1. provide a safe workplace, 2. hire competent employees, 3. provide safe tools, and 4. warn employees of existing dangers. Check the coverage of any contractor you hire.

- **Business Interruption:** Covers extra expenses and loss of income caused by an interruption of normal business due to an unforeseen event, such as fire. Lost income is defined as the difference between normal income and the income earned during the interruption of normal business.

- **Key Person:** Protects your business in case of the death or disability of an owner, partner, or key employee.

- **Health or Medical:** Protects against the costs of major medical expenses.

- **Special Insurances:** Many special types of insurance are available, such as automobile, crime, computer, life, malpractice, and glass insurance. Take a close look at your business to see what may be advisable.

- **Financial Insurances:** Depending on the structure of your business, you may need Sole Proprietor Insurance, Partnership Insurance, or Shareholder Insurance. Fidelity Bonds protect against loss from embezzlement.

BOOK PACKAGER

Start-up cost:	$1,000-$5,000
Potential earnings:	$45,000-$80,000
Typical fees:	Sometimes a percentage of total production costs; often, a flat consultant's rate
Advertising:	Writers' publications, industry trade magazines, direct mail, word of mouth
Qualifications:	Editorial background and top-notch organizational skills; broad understanding of publishing process
Equipment needed:	Computer with printer, fax/modem, desktop publishing software, phone
Home business potential:	Yes
Staff required:	No
Handicapped opportunity:	Yes
Hidden costs:	Insurance, cost of sales (it often takes a lot of socializing to get work)

LOWDOWN:

Book packagers are often hired by publishers whose staffs are too limited to work on a multitude of projects simultaneously; in other words, they are maxed out on projects and need outside help in handling additional ones. Some book packagers handle as much as 75 percent of a publishing house's projects, allowing the in-house staff to concentrate on future projects and expansion. You would do well as a book packager if you have an editorial background, a knack for organizing and pulling together all the details of a book project, and the foresight to set realistic goals about accomplishing publication. You will likely handle everything from hiring writers and photographers to production and sales/marketing management. You would do well to pick an area of expertise, such as high-quality illustrated books, since many publishers don't have that kind of in-house expertise and will gladly pay you for yours.

START-UP:

Expect to spend between $1,000-$5,000 on your start-up, which will cover your initial advertising in addition to your complete computer setup (with printer, fax/modem, and desktop publishing software). You'll need to work hard to make $45,000-$75,000 or more in this field, but it isn't uncommon (especially for those in close proximity to the publishing capitals of New York and San Francisco).

BOTTOM LINE ADVICE:

Things could easily get out of hand when you are pulling together many different creative forces for a special project; try to work out your worst-case scenarios early enough to form a game plan around them—and set deadlines that are in reality far ahead of when you actually need a project to be turned in. You'll see why after only one project.

ADVICE FROM THE EXPERTS

What sets your business apart from others like it?

Andy Mayer, President and co-owner (with Jim Becker) of becker & mayer ltd. in Seattle, Washington, says the ability to produce very complicated, production-intensive books is what sets his business apart from others like it. "My partner and I both have backgrounds in toy invention and design, and we can produce really interesting books as a result."

Things you couldn't do without:

"Our staff! We couldn't do anything without them . . . so many good ideas come from them. From an equipment standpoint, we couldn't do without a phone, a computer, and a color printer to produce mock-ups for publishers."

Marketing tips/advice:

"Bring a lot of who you are to your company. Find out what your passions are and try to put that into the things you produce. Also, don't listen to people who try to tell you there's only one way to do something. Freely break the rules and see what happens."

If you had to do it all over again . . .

"I would have focused the business on book packaging much earlier . . . we tried to do both book packaging and toy invention, and that didn't work as well."

Bookkeeping Service

Start-up cost:	$2,000-$9,000
Potential earnings:	Typically $20,000-$50,000 per year
Typical fees:	$25-$35 per hour; more for financial statements and other tasks. Certain clients may pay a flat monthly fee rather than hourly charges
Advertising:	Ads (phone book, trade publications), networking, referrals (from CPAs, for example)
Qualifications:	Knowledge of basic bookkeeping principles, some legal and tax knowledge, ability to use a computer, accounting/spreadsheet software, good eye for detail, honesty, good communications skills
Equipment needed:	Basic computer and office equipment, a financial calculator and accounting software
Home business potential:	Yes
Staff required:	No
Handicapped opportunity:	Yes
Hidden costs:	Organizational dues, if applicable

LOWDOWN:

Small business owners, in particular, use bookkeeping services to keep up with the ever-changing tax laws and the constant flow of bookkeeping details they don't have time for. Clients need help with such tasks as making deposits, reconciliation of bank statements and preparing financial reports, payroll, billing, and accounts payable and receivable, to name a few. What's the difference between bookkeeping and accounting? Bookkeepers are the record keepers; an accountant's job is to analyze and audit the records. If you have a clear, logical mind and common sense, this may be a great business for you. It is recession-proof, essential work that can be challenging and fun.

START-UP:

The required computer and office equipment can be acquired for as little as $2,000. Add another $500 or so for your first six months of advertising, and you'll be all set. You might consider joining business owners' associations or your local Chamber of Commerce to generate business. Charges for your services will vary according to the extent of the project, but the average fees are $25-$35 per hour.

BOTTOM LINE ADVICE:

This work gives you a great opportunity to learn more about the business world—and about specific fields of business. The work requires close attention to each detail and necessitates your staying current about tax-law changes relating to payroll and record keeping. Mistakes may cause problems for your client with the government; clients may also blame you for mistakes that they made. If you like numbers and enjoy working independently to solve problems, bookkeeping may be a great career for you.

BRIDAL CONSULTANT

Start-up cost:	$1,000-$3,500
Potential earnings:	$25,000-$60,000 (depending on volume and location)
Advertising:	Bridal magazines (many areas have their own, local versions), bridal salons, newspapers, word of mouth
Qualifications:	An eye for detail and a cool head
Equipment needed:	Cellular phone, computer plus software for contacts and clients
Home business potential:	Yes
Staff required:	Sometimes
Handicapped opportunity:	Yes
Hidden costs:	Keep accurate records of the time you spend with each client, or you could short-change yourself.

LOWDOWN:

Wedding planning can easily turn any reasonable family into a temporary war zone—and that's where bridal consultants have entered the picture. With most families spending anywhere from $10,000-$15,000 and up on the wedding extravaganza itself, what's a few extra dollars to take the headache out of the blessed event's planning? Your rates would range from $50 per hour to a flat fee of $1,000 or more for the entire wedding, so it is easy to see how you could earn a profitable amount of money in a short period of time. But don't think you won't work hard for it. As a bridal consultant, you will handle every minute detail, from the number of guests to invite to what kind of champagne to buy. You are essentially in the hotbed of the action, with total responsibility for every aspect of the wedding.

START-UP:

You will need to develop strong word of mouth (try forging reciprocal referral arrangements with florists and bridal and hair salons) to build a good reputation. Also, since this is a people- and image-oriented business, you will need to make sure you look like you're worth it; dress professionally and carry yourself with poise and an air of diplomacy. But the bulk of your start-up will be in producing business cards and brochures in addition to placing newspaper and bridal magazine ads (count on forking over at least $1,000 for those items).

BOTTOM LINE ADVICE:

The flash and excitement of impending nuptials can be intoxicating, as can the power involved in directing others to perform their best. Be careful not to offend anyone or step on their toes. Listen to what your customers tell you they want—and have the good sense to make them think all of the good ideas were theirs. While such ego-suppression is hard to accomplish in a high-profile job like this one, remember that the customer is always king.

BROADCAST SALES/
ADVERTISING BROKER

Start-up cost:	$2,000-$3,000
Potential earnings:	$20,000-$40,000
Typical fees:	Often a 10 to 25 percent commission
Advertising:	Business publications, Yellow Pages, referrals, networking
Qualifications:	Wide experience buying advertising, good connections with the media, marketing savvy
Equipment needed:	Computer, fax/modem, printer, office furniture, business cards, letterhead, envelopes
Home business potential:	Yes
Staff required:	No
Handicapped opportunity:	Yes
Hidden costs:	Dues to trade/business groups, phone bills, mileage

LOWDOWN:

Very few business people have enough knowledge of advertising to shop for the best deals for the advertisements they plan to place. Small businesses must especially make the most of each dollar spent. Your knowledge of the broadcast opportunities available (e.g., rates, frequency, discounts) will enable you to act as an agent for your small business clients, getting them the best deal in the right medium for their product. You can help each business deliver its message to their target market, and educate them against costly long-term contracts that seemed like good deals at the time. Many exceptional deals are available for knowledgeable bargainers who understand where advertising slots may be available for a fraction of the usual cost. Some advertising brokers will carry their service one step further and negotiate the media contract for a business as well.

START-UP:

Equipping your office will be the main expense ($2,000-$3,000). Your energy and your phone time are the principal ingredients in this service, so expect to spend at least $200-$300 per month on the phone and mileage bills. Billings typically include a 10 to 25 percent commission.

BOTTOM LINE ADVICE:

Media reps will try to sell an advertiser the moon—at a far higher cost than necessary. But this fact makes them poor advisers to their customers. Businesses can achieve much more with less cost by going through you. You will need to have considerable media-buying experience under your belt. Being a quick learner is also necessary, as you must be fast at scoping out where the target market really is for a range of different businesses. The organizations who need your service the most are probably the least aware of it, so marketing your own business must be continual.

BULLETIN BOARD SERVICES

Start-up cost:	$1,000-$3,000
Potential earnings:	$5,000-$15,000
Typical fees:	Monthly subscription fees start at $10; annual are $20-$50
Advertising:	On-line services
Qualifications:	On-line marketing skills
Equipment needed:	High-power computer with fax/modem, printer, phone
Home business potential:	Yes
Staff required:	No
Handicapped opportunity:	Yes
Hidden costs:	On-line time can get expensive

LOWDOWN:

In the computer age, more and more folks are seeking special places to communicate with others who have similar interests. If there is no official on-line bulletin board on a subject such as baseball card collectors or movie buffs, your business can provide one. You would advertise the availability of such a bulletin board, then post as many pieces of related information as possible to generate the number of users tapping into your service. The more information you have on-line, the more you'll be able to charge individuals for getting to this data. A related service that is even more important is to check the messages frequently and remove outdated ones. You can see that messages are arranged neatly and any inappropriate material is removed on a regular basis. Check with major carriers to familiarize yourself with their bulletin board regulations—and any possible charges you may incur from them for use of their on-line services.

START-UP:

All you will really need to start is a computer with a modem (about $2,000). Bulletin boards are widely available; check carefully to avoid duplicating another service or you may have some problems. What you earn is directly dependent upon how many people use your service, so make sure your topic is of wide-range interest.

BOTTOM LINE ADVICE:

Selling skills and patience are the two vital ingredients here. To gain repeat business, you have to keep up with the bulletin boards under your care. A large clientele is needed to make an adequate profit overall—and remember that some competing BBS are offered for free.

BUSINESS BROKER

Start-up cost:	$2,500-$7,000
Potential earnings:	$100,000 (based on one sale a month for ten months of the year)
Typical fees:	Standard 10 to 12 percent of the selling price of the business
Advertising:	Direct mail, telemarketing, networking, referrals, ads in Yellow Pages and business publications
Qualifications:	Ability to understand financial reports, solid business background, considerable legal knowledge, good sales and "people" skills
Equipment needed:	Computer and office equipment, telephone, answering machine or voice mail
Home business potential:	Yes
Staff required:	No
Handicapped opportunity:	Yes
Hidden costs:	Some states require a real estate broker's license

LOWDOWN:

Business brokers match clients interested in selling a business with others who want to buy—and many are home-based. This field is growing; many people think it's less risky to buy an existing business than to start a new one. Nearly all brokers represent the client who is selling a business, but a few choose to represent the buyer. Specializing in a particular size or type of business, or in a particular geographic area, brings success to many home-based brokers. Excellent communication skills are vital, particularly empathy and an ability to listen carefully. Strong sales skills, coupled with the essential legal knowledge and business background, will help you establish what may be a most lucrative business.

START-UP:

Computer, printer, and software (some specialized) will cost an average of $3,500. Add to this at least $700 for office furniture, phone, letterhead, and supplies. Your earnings will hinge on whether you're able to strike a deal; if so, take a 10 to 12 percent cut on the selling price.

BOTTOM LINE ADVICE:

Network, network, network! Talk to people who own businesses, figure out what associations they belong to, and join them. Take some adult education courses, if necessary, to help you learn more about the unfamiliar aspects of your new business. Get referrals from lawyers, accountants, and bankers. Getting businesses to sell is hard work (although specialization helps) and you don't get paid until you sell something, but it's fun to act as matchmaker and satisfying to help your clients succeed. Your expenses and start-up costs are low, and the opportunity to make a great living is excellent. Nothing succeeds like success, so once you make a great match, you'll have a basis on which to build future business.

BUYER'S INFORMATION SERVICE

Start-up cost:	$3,000-$6,000
Potential earnings:	$30,000-$50,000
Typical fees:	$25 and up
Advertising:	Trade journals, local and national business periodicals, Yellow Pages, memberships in business associations and community groups, networking, referrals
Qualifications:	An understanding of and experience in the purchasing world
Equipment needed:	Office furniture, computer, high-speed modem, fax, printer, cellular phone, on-line accounts, business cards, letterhead, envelopes
Home business potential:	Yes
Staff required:	Yes
Handicapped opportunity:	Yes
Hidden costs:	On-line account fees, utility costs

LOWDOWN:

A buyer's information service does the legwork for overburdened purchasing departments. Researching the features and availability of new or unusual products, parts, or materials takes a great deal of time, experience, and persistence. Outsourcing this specialized work makes sense for many organizations, and your business supplies the need. You will probably specialize in a business type (electronics manufacturing, sports retail) or in a materials area (chemicals, lumber). Having an excellent network will enable you to gather the information your clients want quickly and thoroughly.

START-UP:

Communications are vital; you'll be on the phone a lot, and the Internet will supply much of the information you need ($3,000 to start). Once you build your network, $30,000 and up should be easily attained.

BOTTOM LINE ADVICE:

This business is a facet of the "information age." Yes, there's lots of information available, but finding what is needed, when it's needed, is possibly even more difficult than it was in the past. Sorting through the blizzard of product data, materials sources, prices, and requirements for the relevant facts is a real challenge. You'll need to be very persistent, detail-oriented, and focused on your clients' needs to make a success of this business. Once you become known as "the answer," you'll have a steady stream of repeat business and referrals.

CALENDAR SERVICE

Start-up cost:	$3,000-$5,000
Potential earnings:	$10,000-$25,000
Typical fees:	$150/year for each subscription
Advertising:	Business and trade periodicals, organization membership, networking, direct marketing
Qualifications:	Energy, a very high level of organization, an outgoing personality, good writing skills
Equipment needed:	Computer, office suite software with powerful database program, high-quality fax/modem, copier, printer, office furniture, business cards, letterhead, envelopes
Home business potential:	Yes
Staff required:	No
Handicapped opportunity:	Yes
Hidden costs:	On-line time, attendance at functions, organization dues

LOWDOWN:

This business is among the newest emerging businesses. You'll create a master calendar of public events for your community, or an annual publication that is sent to your client list of hotels, motels, restaurants, and other high-traffic businesses. The excitement comes from the fax; each week you fax a reminder-and-update sheet to everyone on your list. As you become established, gathering the information will become easier, as planners, public relations people, and event sponsors will be sure to inform you about their dates and events. Why does this work? Many individuals and businesses need to know this information, and they appreciate the opportunity to have information to offer free of charge to their customers. Everyone from politicos to florists needs to have event dates at their fingertips, and your service will be faxing it to them weekly. In short, it is your business to make other businesses look "in the know."

START-UP:

You will need the equipment to gather and print the information, and above all, the fax capability to broadcast it weekly. This should cost you between $5,000-$10,000; but, by billing $150 per year for a company's subscription to your service, you could easily earn back your investment in two to three years.

BOTTOM LINE ADVICE:

Keeping track of dates is hard—that's why all those meeting planners and impresarios are going to pay you to do it. You'll need to be the kind of person whom bigwigs like to talk to, both for info-gathering and sales of your service. Writing it all up in an accurate, amusing manner is important, because you're competing against a myriad of free arts and entertainment newspapers and similar publications. Creating a service like this means a super marketing effort until you get established.

CARPET/UPHOLSTERY CLEANING

Start-up cost:	$1,000-$3,000 if leasing equipment initially; $4,000-$10,000 if buying equipment
Potential earnings:	$35,000-$50,000
Typical fees:	20 cents per square foot first room; $40 each additional room
Advertising:	Direct mail, Yellow Pages, newspaper ads, coupon books
Qualifications:	Physically able to do manual labor, some prior experience
Equipment needed:	Cleaning machine, large quantity of chemical cleaners, some mode of transporting materials
Home business potential:	Yes
Staff required:	No
Handicapped opportunity:	No
Hidden costs:	Fuel for vehicle

LOWDOWN:

If "Out, damned spot!" is your battle cry, getting others to enlist your services in the carpet/upholstery cleaning business shouldn't be too hard. After all, we've all spilled seemingly unremovable food or drink on at least one piece of furniture in our homes—and we've all thought of paying a professional every once in a while to freshen up the house with a clean-smelling carpet, right? That's why this is such a recession-proof business; the need for clean places to live never goes out of favor with consumers. You could offer your cleaning services to everyone from individuals to apartment complexes or even corporations, and the best way to get your name out there is through excellent, timely service and its resultant good word of mouth. You'll sweep the surface dirt from furniture and floors, perform an overall general cleaning, and use industrial-strength spot removers on tough stain areas. Since each room takes approximately an hour to service (if there are few stains requiring more attention), there is the potential for making lots of money once you learn to work quickly and efficiently while maintaining high-quality standards. One final note: Buying cleaning fluids will be slightly more expensive if environmentally safe products are chosen, but many people prefer "green" cleaning products, especially for health reasons. Customers will feel safer and more satisfied when they know there are no toxic residues in their house.

START-UP:

Deciding whether to buy or lease equipment at first will depend upon how much capital is available to invest. A carpet cleaning machine itself will cost from $600-$3,500, while leasing will run about $300-$400 per month. Rotary shampooers and steam extractors are the two current types available, and each has its advantages and disadvantages, but rotary shampooers are the preferred method because they clean more deeply. A good, strong vacuum cleaner is the next most vital tool, and buying a sturdy canister model with a variety of attachments will cost $400-$600. The leasing option will be anywhere from $100-$200 per month. Access to a reliable vehicle large enough to tote around all equipment and supplies (and gasoline to run it) is another expense involved in this business, but really won't amount to much if you already have a station wagon/truck/van. Include advertising in your budget, which could run anywhere from $600-$3,000 for half a year. Coupon books seem to be fruitful ground for carpet cleaning businesses as a starting point for bringing in new customers. For carpets, fees are often 20 cents per square foot plus an additional $40 or more per each extra room depending on size. Upholstery cleaning is usually done per piece, with fees ranging from $50-$150.

BOTTOM LINE ADVICE:

Working for another local company first may give you a good idea of what's needed to get started and how to proceed from there. As in most trades, experience is essential to success: knowing which contracts to take and which are just impossible, what are appropriate fees for your area, how billing works, and other general questions will make your start-up smoother. Sales skills are a plus since most people don't realize that they might need your service, or know how often they need it. Calling former customers to find out if the work was performed satisfactorily and offering to repeat it will keep you busy.

CHIMNEY SWEEP

Start-up costs:	$1,500-$5,000
Potential earnings:	$35,000-$60,000
Typical fees:	$60-$80 per job is common
Advertising:	Yellow Pages, local newspapers, direct mail
Qualifications:	Knowledge about cleaning chimneys and willingness to get dirty
Equipment needed:	Brushes, tarpaulins to protect customer's floors, high-pressure dust collectors
Home business potential:	Yes
Staff required:	No
Handicapped opportunity:	No
Hidden costs:	Insurance

LOWDOWN:

Many homes have wood-burning fireplaces or stoves with chimneys that should be cleaned at least once a year—for health reasons in particular. As a chimney sweep, you will work with different people on a short-term basis—and if this variety and flexibility appeals to you and you don't mind working on your own, this business could be ideal for you. Using specially designed brushes, a skilled sweep can clean a chimney in a maximum of an hour and a half; an efficient, experienced sweep can accomplish the job in even less time. By doing up to eight cleaning jobs per day at about $60-$80 each, you can really clean up the profits.

START-UP:

Mostly, you'll need to spend money on brushes and related cleaning equipment ($1,000 or so) and advertising your services in the Yellow Pages or by distributing flyers. Try to get repeat business by leaving behind a promotional item with your company's name or logo on it—people need to have a physical reminder of your service, since they can't necessarily see the results of your work!

BOTTOM LINE ADVICE:

Many people aren't aware of the need to clean chimneys annually. But this is a vital service, since chimney fires are among the most common cause of house fires. This gives you the opportunity to educate your clients and ensure repeat business. Consider dressing the part. In Dickens's time, sweeps wore tails and top hats. Although it's a little gimmicky, wearing top hats can add to your appeal and help promote your business. Whatever brings in the money . . . .

CITY PLANNER

Start-up cost:	$3,000-$6,000
Potential earnings:	$40,000-$200,000
Typical fees:	Varies according to length and extent of project
Advertising:	Referrals, membership in civic, charitable, and trade organizations
Qualifications:	Degree in related field, proven track record of success, ability to deal with overlapping governmental structures, excellent oral and written communication skills
Equipment needed:	Computer, modem, fax, suite and presentation software, laser printer, cellular phone, business cards, letterhead, envelopes
Home business potential:	Yes
Staff required:	No
Handicapped opportunity:	Yes
Hidden costs:	Errors and omissions insurance, membership dues, conferences for networking and continuing education

LOWDOWN:

City planning affects the use of land, the development of neighborhoods, the implementation of incentive programs for new factories, and many other factors in the welfare of a community. As an independent city planning consultant, you will work on large or small projects with a number of different communities rather than serving on the staff of one municipality as an employee. Each new project will involve a lot of learning as you familiarize yourself with the needs of the specific community, the challenges it faces, its infrastructure, and its unique politics and culture. Cookie-cutter approaches do not work any better in this type of consulting than they do in other types. These demands mean constant learning for you, as well as a heavy draw on your creativity and problem-solving skills.

START-UP:

You will need to keep in communication with your clients, especially when projects overlap. Professional-looking reports are also essential. Spend at least $3,000 on a good computer system with graphics capability; you'll probably need a 3-D software program, too. But, when you consider that your services are offered in a specialty area and that cities are always growing (just look at the trend toward Edge Cities—those little towns burgeoning into mini-cities), an income between $40,000-$200,000 doesn't seem all that unreasonable.

BOTTOM LINE ADVICE:

Marketing yourself and your services will be very demanding. Excellent work will lead to referrals, but probably you should not rely on repeat business to carry you. Small municipalities will do one big project and then wait a considerable time before embarking on another one, so you will need a small but steady stream of new clients. Dealing with fickle, politics-driven city governments can be a challenge. Decisive action can come hard in a democracy, and that delayed decision may be the one about whether to go ahead with your project or not.

CLIP ART SERVICE

Start-up cost:	$3,000-$5,000
Potential earnings:	$15,000-$35,000
Typical fees:	$10-$15 per image or, preferably, a monthly clip service where you provide new images each month for a fee of $30-$40 per month
Advertising:	Business publications, direct mail to advertising/public relations firms
Qualifications:	A graphics or art background will help build credibility
Equipment needed:	Computer with high-resolution laser printer and scanner
Home business potential:	Yes
Staff required:	No
Handicapped opportunity:	Yes
Hidden costs:	Your resource materials will run high at first if you use other people's clip art; if designing your own, watch for best prices on art materials

LOWDOWN:

Downsizing has severely affected the art departments of many corporations, with many now outsourcing to freelancers or buying predesigned work to paste into their presentations. Smaller agencies are also turning to nontraditional solutions for quick, inexpensive art. What is quicker and easier than copyright-free pictures that can be copied and pasted (or even scanned) into any of your business publications in a matter of minutes? The fact is, there are thousands of decent illustrations out there, whether in clip art books (available in most book stores for a nominal fee) or in software programs dedicated to specific themes (such as business art, sports art, cartoons, and religious art). The obvious problem with running a clip art business is that you're competing against literally hundreds of software programs that can do the same thing. Your major strategic selling point, then, becomes the fact that you have it all to choose from in one place, and that your availability is even better than overnight delivery. If you can sell your customers on those two concepts, you stand a fighting chance of making it. However, it would be wise to come up with an add-on service, such as cartooning or small-scale art production, to help you keep a steady income rolling in. Also, think of producing your own clip art and selling clients on the fact that it was specially designed by you.

START-UP:

Your start-up fees could be quite high, especially compared to your first-year potential earnings. You'll need to invest in just about every clip art book and software program you can get your hands on in order to build a sufficient enough library for clients to choose from, and that could cost anywhere from $1,000-$1,500 total. Next, you'll need to advertise in business publications or through direct mail to advertising and public relations companies, and that could run as high as $3,000. When you consider that your charges may be as little as $10 per image, it doesn't take a wizard to see that the return on investment will take a while. Your best bet is to try to design your own clip art and market it on a subscription basis to local companies; for a monthly fee of $20-$40, you could earn more money on a more regular basis.

BOTTOM LINE ADVICE:

You'll really need to network with advertising and promotion specialists to get this business off the ground. Understand that people buy people, not just art, and that your biggest asset is personalized service. You can save companies time by searching through a myriad of resources for that perfect image—stress that point in everything you do.

Writing Grant Proposals and Loan Applications

Applying for a grant or loan requires much the same thinking process you went through in preparing your business plan. The reason is the same: you are presenting the facts and assumptions about your new venture to an outsider for the purpose of gaining financial resources.

A business development grant may be available to you if you are a member of a special group, depending on the state you live in. Subsidized loans may also be a possibility. Women and minority business owners should make special efforts to discover what financial support programs are available to them. Most of these are administered at the state level.

The persistence that has allowed you to develop a business concept and get it off the drawing board needs to be applied to the process of seeking a grant or loan as well. You will probably have to ask many, many people before you find the right door to open, the right office to call in your state government, and the helpful person who can finally assist you with your search. A professor at a local business college may know where to guide you. A women's business group could offer assistance. Try calling the office of your state representative. Consult your library for resource guides.

A loan could be all you need to start you on the road to success, and a grant, which need not be paid back, would be an even bigger boost!

TIPS ON FILLING OUT THE PROPOSAL OR APPLICATION:

1. Make sure your business plan does an outstanding job of presenting your concept, marketing approach, and financial projections.

2. Follow the loan or grant guidelines to the letter. If possible, obtain a model application and study it carefully.

3. Have your business advisors check your completed application.

4. Include all required elements:

- Credit request (the amount of money needed, its intended use, and the plans for paying it back if a loan).

- A copy of your business plan.

- Federal Income Tax returns, for the last three years, for all significant members of the management team and the business owners.

- Your projected income statement, monthly for a year and quarterly for the following three years.

- Cash flow projected similarly.

- Specifics on all business debt.

- Resumes for significant participants in the enterprise.

- Source of equity, describing the contribution of each significant business backer.

- Other requirements as needed depending on the business type (construction contract for a building business) or loan type (SBA Compensation Agreement, etc.).

CLIPPING SERVICE

Start-up cost:	$1,500-$3,000
Potential earnings:	$15,000-$25,000
Typical fees:	$2-$4 per clip (or a monthly fee for a predetermined number of clips)
Advertising:	Local papers, business publications
Qualifications:	Be observant and read voraciously!
Equipment needed:	Access to a copier and various publications, word processor/typewriter, envelopes
Home business potential:	Yes
Staff required:	No
Handicapped opportunity:	Yes
Hidden costs:	Subscriptions could run high as a whole; try to negotiate the best possible rates or use on-line services; postage

LOWDOWN:

Have you always clipped articles and pinned them to your bulletin board for future use? Or are you an avid reader who's always clipping and mailing articles to people you know? You just might be able to make a living with this rather obsessive behavior. A clipping service finds and copies articles of interest to various businesses, including pieces on the company itself and/or its products, employees, the industry of the business, competitors, and related subjects of interest. Being familiar with the local library system is vital, but even more critical is the ability to search using the proper keywords (in the Information Age, you can accomplish such searches fairly easily on the computer). Good research skills and use of a periodical index will save a lot of time and hassle. Patience and curiosity are richly rewarded for folks in this field.

START-UP:

A moderately powerful computer, a pair of scissors, access to a copy machine, and a little extra time and money are all you need to get started in this business. None except the computer costs very much (about $2,000), so you shouldn't have much getting in the way of an easy start-up. The service that is really being paid for is the time spent searching through literally hundreds of publications. Being paid by the hour rather than by the piece is best; there's no reliable way to know just how much press each company is generating without putting in a considerable amount of time. Get started by calling the public relations offices of local corporations to find out if they need this service; network in their professional organizations to drum up initial business.

BOTTOM LINE ADVICE:

The most positive aspect of this business is its versatility. If you don't have a computer, finding a local library with convenient hours is likely the most difficult task involved. Using your own subscriptions is not recommended, since it limits the number of copies available and is more expensive. Watch that on-line time (write down all possible keywords before connecting).

COLLEGE INTERNSHIP PLACEMENT

Start-up cost:	$1,500-$3,000
Potential earnings:	$20,000-$50,000
Typical fees:	$75-$175 (paid by student/parents)
Advertising:	College newspapers, campus bulletin boards, direct mail to parents
Qualifications:	Background in placement services would be helpful
Equipment needed:	Computer with printer, fax/modem, e-mail address
Home business potential:	Yes
Staff required:	No
Handicapped opportunity:	Yes
Hidden costs:	Insurance, on-line time

LOWDOWN:

It used to be that companies offering internships contacted colleges to find students for summer or short-term work. But, in the ever-competitive '90s, such companies are relying increasingly upon services such as yours to bring them talent in exchange for small pay and experience. It's challenging work to find a suitable internship for a student (and vice versa), and you'll have enough resources to choose from at your local library. There are plenty of books that detail such opportunities, and there should be plenty of postings for internships through on-line services or the Internet. You'd have to work pretty hard to exhaust all of the possibilities. You'd be wise to market to the parents of students, as they are typically the ones with the foresight to see the importance of an internship; they also are typically the ones with all the money, too!

START-UP:

You'll need to have at least $1,500 for your computer system and another $1,000 or so for advertising in your first six months. Charging customers $75-$175 (depending on the size of the university or college market you're serving) will likely lead you to an annual salary of $20,000-$50,000 per year.

BOTTOM LINE ADVICE:

Your work will be different every day, and the challenges will present themselves on a regular basis, too. Often, you'll work with folks you simply can't seem to please, or who don't come across as highly motivated. Remember that part of your job is to sell the student on the importance of internships—what they can mean later on to a job-seeking student is immeasurable.

COLOR CONSULTANT

Start-up cost:	$2,000-$4,000
Potential earnings:	$30,000-$50,000
Typical fees:	$35-$75 per hour analysis
Advertising:	Local newspapers, business publications, direct mail
Qualifications:	Possibly training through cosmetic firm, paint company, or similar business
Equipment needed:	Color swatches, color charts
Home business potential:	Yes
Staff required:	No
Handicapped opportunity:	Yes
Hidden costs:	Travel expenses

LOWDOWN:

Have you ever wondered exactly how the major automobile manufacturers and appliance makers decide which colors to use on their products? Or where the world of fashion comes up with the latest hues? They use color consultants—experts who know the entire spectrum of the rainbow, including minute variations and redefining nuances that are invisible to the untrained eye. It is essential that a color consultant have a strong understanding of color dynamics (how color affects people) in addition to the natural ability to distinguish slight color variations. The former is a learned skill, while the latter is an inherent talent that must be present to ensure acceptance into training and success in the field. Once established in this business, your days will consist of working with anyone from cosmetic companies to corporate consultations to group workshops to appliance/furniture manufacturers to individual analyses. People will look to you for the trends of the future.

START-UP:

Training with a company that is heavily dependent upon color and color dynamics is the biggest initial expense involved in becoming a consultant. Most often, the program is a week of intensive instruction on color theory and analysis, marketing techniques, and applications; expect to spend at least $1,200 on classes/certification (if available in your area). Other costs are directly related to visual materials to use in consultations and demonstrations (anywhere from $25-$1,000). Consultations often last an hour, with the average fee being $50-$75, depending upon the industry and geographic area of the country.

BOTTOM LINE ADVICE:

Working with people is always a challenge, but more so when it involves personal issues such as what's aesthetically pleasing and what's not (which can be quite subjective). Staying on top of what's new in the ever-changing fashion world can be an exciting challenge, so if you like the idea of making other people look good and making money while doing it, this could be the career for you.

COMMERCIAL ACTOR

Start-up cost:	Put away at least six months' worth of living expenses ($1,000-$5,000)
Potential earnings:	$5,000-$100,000 or more (depending on your "star" quality)
Typical fees:	Extremely varied; actors are usually paid union rates for commercials, guest appearances, and feature film work; per diems are varied according to "screen time" (amount of time you're on camera)
Advertising:	Resumes, photos, and videos profiling your work or talents
Qualifications:	Dramatic ability; perhaps singing or dancing talent as well
Equipment needed:	None
Home business potential:	Work is done on location
Staff required:	No
Handicapped opportunity:	Possibly
Hidden costs:	None

LOWDOWN:

There are hundreds, perhaps even thousands, of actors in this country—and not all of them are working on a regular basis. Of course, anyone who's interested in acting as a profession has already heard about the competitive, cutthroat nature of show business (if not from books, then most definitely from other family members). But year after year, many new "wannabes" enter the scene, and some are actually lucky enough to make it. The best way to break into this business is to work with local advertising agencies, production companies, and public television stations. From these places, you can gain the experience that will build your portfolio. You'll need to have a professional presentation, including photographs of yourself, a strong résumé, and a sample of your work (preferably on video). It's a hard way to make a living, but not impossible if you set your goals in manageable portions.

START-UP:

Your start-up will mainly be your living expenses; you'll need to figure out exactly how much you'll need to survive on until that first big break comes. Multiply that figure by six, and you'll have six months to land your first job. Union dues (and you should join if you want to earn "scale") are typically $200-$500. The union will provide you with a list of typical fees for each kind of acting job you may encounter.

BOTTOM LINE ADVICE:

If you've been bitten by the acting bug, nothing except a lack of funds will keep you from doing it. No amount of discouragement . . . no disheartening unemployment figures. Nothing will hold you back until you're out of money and have to take another job. But even then, you can keep trying your hand at it—and that, oddly enough, is a great benefit.

COMMERCIAL PHOTOGRAPHER

Start-up cost:	$3,000-$5,000
Potential earnings:	$35,000 and up
Typical fees:	$35-$50 per hour
Advertising:	Classifieds, trade publications, business groups, referrals, direct mail
Qualifications:	Photographic skills, excellent time management skills, ability to market and sell your services
Equipment needed:	Excellent camera equipment, office furniture, preferably a computer and printer, fax, business cards, letterhead, envelopes
Home business potential:	Yes
Staff required:	No
Handicapped opportunity:	No
Hidden costs:	Equipment upgrades and repair, travel costs

LOWDOWN:

Commercial photography is an ideal business for the individual who can produce. If you can "see" the images needed by a business segment in your community, and produce them on time for a competitive cost, you can probably develop relationships with your customers that will bring you an ongoing stream of business. Photos always seem to be needed, but at the last minute. You will need to produce what is wanted under pressure, and have a reputation for getting it right the first time. Commercial photography requires an interesting combination of technical, artistic, sales, and business skills. If you have this mix, or can develop it, you can go far.

START-UP:

The photographic equipment you use is, of course, the vital component of this business (should get started on $3,000). Having an effective home office is also necessary for supporting the "business" side of your business: receiving assignments, preparing invoices, and so on. You could earn upward of $35,000.

BOTTOM LINE ADVICE:

Most successful commercial photographer specialize. And some have gone beyond providing the photographic image alone to offering related services—preparation of brochures, scanning and retouching images, or working in close association with graphic artists and copywriters to provide a completed piece. If you become known for excellence in photography of construction projects, retail store installations, or company board retreats, you will have a leg up on the competition. This is another crowded field with plenty of room at the top.

ADVICE FROM THE EXPERTS

What sets your business apart from others like it?

Tom Uhlman, owner of Tom Uhlman Photography in Cincinnati, Ohio, says that he stands apart from other commercial photographers by offering sound editorial judgment in addition to providing quality photographic work. "I'm dependable at finding interesting situations, giving publications the kinds of unusual photos they want and need without having to wait for assignment." Uhlman's photos have been picked up by the Associated Press and have appeared in *Newsweek*, the *New York Daily News*, and *USA Today*.

Things you couldn't do without:

Uhlman says he couldn't do without top-quality cameras with motor drives, flash equipment, better-than-average lenses, and dependable transportation. "I would also buy a police scanner, so you can shoot 'hard' news as it happens. It's the best way to break into newspapers, because they often don't have the staff or time to get these shots."

Marketing tips/advice:

"Look at the work of others and learn from it. But you'll probably learn the most from being out there and getting your own experience. Find photos that tell good news stories, and you should never have a problem selling."

If you had to do it all over again . . .

"I pretty much did everything in the right way and time, mainly because I didn't know any better. I learned early on that doing is what gets you there."

CONFERENCE CALL FACILITATOR

Start-up cost:	$2,000-$5,000
Potential earnings:	$15,000-$40,000
Typical fees:	$25-$50 per hour
Advertising:	Trade journals, business periodicals, direct mail, referrals
Qualifications:	Telecommunications skills, marketing ability
Equipment needed:	Computer, teleconferencing equipment, printer, fax, modem, office furniture, business cards, letterhead, envelopes
Home business potential:	Yes
Staff required:	No
Handicapped opportunity:	Yes
Hidden costs:	High telephone bills, equipment maintenance

LOWDOWN:

Here's a true niche market. You are bringing far-flung people together for the direct discussions that cannot be replaced by messaging, letters, or e-mail. Setting up conference calls involves the people skills of planning the time and date, along with the technical skills of linking phone systems. You will be completing a time-consuming task once performed by an administrative assistant. You will need to educate your market about the usefulness and availability of your service. Once a group of businesses have become your clients, you should be able to develop an ongoing relationship with them; if possible, offer a list of your clients to potential ones to build your credibility.

START-UP:

The cost is in your teleconferencing equipment ($2,000-$3,000) and in the basic office computer, printer, and furniture that almost all businesses need.

BOTTOM LINE ADVICE:

This field is for skilled marketers who can jump on a trend or even create it themselves in their service areas. You will be plowing new ground in the business-to-business service arena, and you will know that your offering has value to your clients. Newness has its disadvantages, though. The need for this service is there, but awareness has a long way to go. Also, people can be annoying. Some individuals just don't keep to planned times and dates.

CONSTRUCTION MANAGEMENT SERVICES

Start-up cost:	$3,000-$6,000
Potential earnings:	$40,000-$60,000
Typical fees:	$50-$75 per hour or a flat monthly retainer ($1,000-$2,500)
Advertising:	Business publications, membership in business and civic groups, referrals
Qualifications:	Extensive background in commercial construction, excellent management ability, detail orientation, selling skills
Equipment needed:	Office furniture, computer, modem, fax, suite software, printer, cellular phone, business cards, letterhead, envelopes, marketing materials
Home business potential:	Yes
Staff required:	No
Handicapped opportunity:	No
Hidden costs:	Errors and omissions insurance, vehicle maintenance

LOWDOWN:

As a specialist in construction management, you guide the building process through to completion for an expanding business. The word "construction" covers many different processes, steps, plans, purchases, subcontractors, and schedules. Integrating all these in time, space, and design sometimes seems like an impossible task; an effective manager can make an enormous difference in the cost and quality of the final product, the factory or store being built. The best market for your consulting services will be businesses that are growing rapidly from a small-to-medium beginning. These enterprises have a great need for support in the construction process because they do not have sufficient staff and administrators to keep track of everything in-house. You will need a reputation for effectiveness and cooperativeness with all sides in what can be a contentious process if things start to go wrong.

START-UP:

You probably won't have much time to spend in your office, as much of your work will be on-site. But the planning and tracking functions that you are being paid for need to be supported by computer and communications equipment, so you'll need to shell out at least $3,000-$6,000 for a good computer and a cellular phone or pager system. However, if you're good at what you do, your referrals could bring you lots of business—and you could earn at least $40,000-$60,000 managing projects.

BOTTOM LINE ADVICE:

Toughness, decisiveness, and superior organizational skills are absolute musts for success in construction management. You have to be able to see the big picture—what is going well, when a subcontractor needs a decision to be made, what will be a reasonable compromise when things can't be done as planned. Being outstanding will get you referrals.

CONSUMER RESEARCHER

Start-up cost:	$2,500-$5,000
Potential earnings:	$25,000-$59,000
Typical fees:	$25 per hour
Advertising:	Business periodicals, trade journals, Yellow Pages, networking, referrals, business organizations
Qualifications:	Business background, experience in consumer research, proven track record, excellent written and oral communication skills
Equipment needed:	Office furniture, computer, suite software, laser printer, modem, fax, cellular phone
Home business potential:	Yes
Staff required:	Probably
Handicapped opportunity:	No
Hidden costs:	Preparation of materials, utility bills

LOWDOWN:

Your experience in communicating with consumers will allow you to provide essential information to your corporate clients. How is their product viewed in the marketplace? How do people feel about it? What would they like to buy to go with it? How were they treated as they bought it? Would the average consumer be interested in trying a certain type of new sports equipment or baby chair? What is the most appealing approach right now in window treatments? Thousands of questions like these are the grist for your mill, and you'll arrive at answers via phone, mail, or in-person surveys. You will need to market your own services to show that you can find the answers to the questions that affect your clients' businesses. Each successful project should lead to further work. Estimating costs, and price, accurately will be challenging. Managing the workflow will also require considerable skill. You'll be moving from the big picture to the details and back again constantly.

START-UP:

Keeping in communication, tracking data, and reporting information clearly are all essential. Your office needs to support these functions (for a start-up cost of about $2,500). You could earn around $25,000 after the first year.

BOTTOM LINE ADVICE:

Writing an effective questionnaire, or interview script, is no easy task. Clarity, simplicity, and effectiveness are all vital. Gathering and interpreting the data is much more challenging than just talking to people about a topic. You'll be helping your clients decide what knowledge about their customers is important. Then you'll present the results of your research in a clear, concise form. Business will build slowly as organizations become more confident in your skills.

COOKING CLASS INSTRUCTOR

Start-up cost:	$1,000-$5,000
Potential earnings:	$10,000-$20,000
Typical fees:	$20-$45 per class
Advertising:	Newspaper ads, brochures, flyers
Qualifications:	Cooking experience, teaching ability, some marketing skills
Equipment needed:	Cooking equipment and supplies, a place to teach (if not teaching at home)
Home business potential:	Yes
Staff required:	None
Handicapped opportunity:	Yes
Hidden costs:	Possible need to rent a facility to teach the classes; must have adequate stove(s), generous counter space

LOWDOWN:

Gourmet cooking and dining are both very popular right now. There are many television shows featuring chefs and cooks whose creativity pleases the palate, and gourmet restaurants and cooking supply stores abound. If you have (or can learn) the basics of cooking and have an interest in teaching others to do the same, this might be the business for you. You might check out the possibility of teaching in a home economics room at your local high school. This business can also be conducted easily from your home.

START-UP:

Start-up costs can be minimal if you already have the cookware and utensils needed. In addition, factor in the purchase of a professional stove, if you don't have one, and the cost to rent a facility for the classes, if you don't want to teach at home. Teaching at home is only recommended if you have a large kitchen. The costs of your raw materials will need to be factored into your class fees.

BOTTOM LINE ADVICE:

A cooking class business can be very rewarding. Everyone loves to eat, and learning to produce delightful meals will please your students. Marketing is probably the big hurdle for this type of business. You will need to advertise; you might be able to find related businesses to sponsor you or to spread the word about your classes. For instance, you could build a relationship with the owner of an upscale kitchen products company or offer your classes as "continuing education" through a high school's home economics department.

COUNSELOR/PSYCHOLOGIST

Start-up cost:	$3,000-$5,000 (after college expenses)
Potential earnings:	$35,000-$65,000
Typical fees:	$40-$75 per hour
Advertising:	Newspapers, referrals from physicians, Yellow Pages
Qualifications:	Degree and certification
Equipment needed:	Phone, fax, and answering service to field calls when you are not available
Home business potential:	Yes
Staff required:	No (possibly an assistant for scheduling insurance claims)
Handicapped opportunity:	Yes
Hidden costs:	Keep scrupulous records of every meeting you have with a client—emergency meetings are frequent and could slip through the cracks if you aren't watching

LOWDOWN:

Do you have a knack for getting to the heart of a problem? Are you on top of all the self-help ideologies out there—their potential for both helping and worsening the problems of others? If so, you are well-suited to the profession of counselor/psychologist. You will not only listen to your clients' problems, but you'll also guide them to finding their own healthy solutions. You'll offer them resources to expand their own abilities in problem-solving—and provide creative exercises to get the clients to relax and open up their lives to you. But your job doesn't stop there. You must also keep accurate records of your meetings and what transpired, spending time reviewing these records before and after each meeting. Therefore, you must love detail and be able to budget your time appropriately in order to stay on top of your workload while helping your clients go on with their lives.

START-UP:

Your initial costs are moderate and primarily cover advertising and promotion. You'll need business cards and stationery to invoice your clients with if you don't ask for cash up front (which most experts highly recommend). Add to that the cost of continuing your education via seminars and conferences (generally around $1,000 annually). Finally, you'll need someone who can process medical claims if you are not able to—and the insurance companies can be tricky to deal with if you're a novice.

BOTTOM LINE ADVICE:

You may relish the opportunity to make sense out of someone else's life, but being a successful counselor or psychologist often means giving with a capital "G"—and not all of us are such martyrs. Your clients will be dependent upon you very heavily at first, then may possibly disappear altogether when they feel they are better. These up-and-down cycles can contribute to feelings of depression—and not even "couch" professionals are immune to that.

CREDIT CARDHOLDERS' SERVICE

Start-up cost:	$1,000-$5,000
Potential earnings:	$45,000-$75,000
Typical fees:	$50-$75 per membership fee
Advertising:	Heavy telemarketing
Qualifications:	Finance/sales background
Equipment needed:	Computer, suite software, presentation software, laser printer, modem, fax, business cards, letterhead, envelopes, marketing materials
Home business potential:	Yes
Staff required:	Yes (telemarketers)
Handicapped opportunity:	Yes
Hidden costs:	Insurance, excessive phone expenses (shop for best current rates)

LOWDOWN:

A credit cardholders' service is a very specialized form of business-to-business financial product. You'll sell a program of bonus offers and discounts (also called enhancement products, because they enhance the use of credit cards at each participating establishment) on products and services that credit card customers will likely use and benefit from. You'll need to develop strong relationships with key vendors, negotiating package discount deals (such as 20 percent off all restaurants on a particular list). You will then turn these discount packages into bonus programs for credit card users, selling credit card companies on the fabulous deals you're offering so that they may, in turn, sell their customers on using their cards at each of the participating businesses offering discounts. Everyone benefits; the consumer pays a little more up front, but gleans the savings ultimately from your discount programs. The credit card company benefits from the positive publicity.

START-UP:

Your office needs to support your paperwork and communications. In addition, you will need to prepare professional-looking presentations for each establishment you are hoping to serve by developing their credit card program. Expect to spend at least $1,000-$5,000 setting up your equipment and office alone. Your income will depend on how many sales you can generate; each membership fee will bring in $50-$75. Your annual earnings could be $45,000-$75,000.

BOTTOM LINE ADVICE:

What you are really doing in this business is making connections and package deals that seem like winning propositions for everyone; however, remember that establishing relationships takes time and effort. You'll need to spend extraordinary amounts of time on the phone until you develop a reputation for success in your endeavor—and that could be costly.

CREDIT CARD MERCHANT BROKER

Start-up cost:	$1,000-$2,000
Potential earnings:	$30,000-$40,000
Typical fees:	Commission on accounts accepted by bank; often an application fee of $125 or more per client
Advertising:	Classified ads, magazines targeting business people, membership in local business groups
Qualifications:	None (except sales ability)
Equipment needed:	Basic office setup
Home business potential:	Yes
Staff required:	No
Handicapped opportunity:	No
Hidden costs:	Telephone bills for long-distance sales; mileage and car phone expenses

LOWDOWN:

Credit cards aren't always as welcome as they seem. That is, not all merchants accept them, or accept all kinds. Merchants want to deal with credit cards linked with banks, or set up their own credit cards through a solid bank. You will advertise your representation of one or more banks for credit accounts. You will help the merchants fill out their account applications. When an account application is accepted, you will receive your commission. You'll need to keep developing new customers, but businesses are being created every day in almost all communities. Most of these new businesses are potential customers.

START-UP:

This is not an expensive type of business to enter, but you will have to pay for your initial ads before commission revenue can cover the next batch. Expect to spend $1,000-$2,000 to develop professional-looking materials and good working relationships with several banks.

BOTTOM LINE ADVICE:

Keep careful track of which advertising venues are productive for you. In this way you will gradually learn what publications should receive your advertising dollars. The grapevine is valuable to anyone like you who needs to know about new businesses being established nearby, although advertising and direct mail marketing can be targeted at new enterprises nationwide. You'll need to travel to the customer's location for the application fill-out process; after that, you'll do occasional follow-up to make sure their in-store credit cards are actually bringing in more business.

CREDIT CONSULTANT

Start-up cost:	$2,000-$3,000
Potential earnings:	$25,000-$40,000
Typical fees:	Percentage of debt from client and from creditor (usually 10 to 15 percent from each)
Advertising:	Yellow Pages, seminars, speeches to community groups, classified ads, newspapers, radio spots
Qualifications:	A background in finance would be ideal
Equipment needed:	Business cards, letterhead, envelopes, computer, printer, fax, spreadsheet software
Home business potential:	Yes
Staff required:	No
Handicapped opportunity:	Yes
Hidden costs:	Insurance, secretarial support if needed

LOWDOWN:

As a credit counselor you work with people who have overextended themselves financially. Your clients will come to you for help in dealing with an unmanageable credit burden. How big is this market? We've all heard the stories about the credit cards that pour into people's mailboxes, even cards with "Fido" printed on them in gold letters. Fido's credit rating has "already been preapproved." Credit card debt is at an historic high right now, and not everyone has budgeted for the payments. You will negotiate with the creditors to develop a manageable payment plan. Your client pays you a small percentage of what is owed, and the creditors also compensate you, as the plan you work out prevents the debt from most likely being a complete loss.

START-UP:

Your office can be quite minimal at first; you should be able to get away with spending $3,000-$5,000 maximum. Since your business depends on how many clients you can secure (i.e., how many stay with the program, so to speak), you should be able to make a decent living ($25,000-$40,000).

BOTTOM LINE ADVICE:

You're providing a valuable service to desperate, guilty, and frustrated people. This situation can be rewarding or draining, depending on the individuals involved. For most debtors, dealing with the pain feels much better than watching it spiral out of control. You will probably have the opportunity to add some education and psychological support into your services. This will allow you to gain the satisfaction of knowing that you have improved a person's or family's financial standing.

DANCE INSTRUCTOR

Start-up cost:	$1,500-$3,000
Potential earnings:	$25,500-$35,000
Typical fees:	$15 per lesson
Advertising:	Yellow Pages, entertainment sections of local papers, brochures, dance-wear retailers
Qualifications:	Experience, a degree to teach at the college/conservatory level
Equipment needed:	Studio, dance equipment
Home business potential:	Yes
Staff required:	No
Handicapped opportunity:	No
Hidden costs:	Insurance, advertising

LOWDOWN:

Fred and Ginger made it look so good that everyone wanted to try it—and that's pretty much how the Fred Astaire School of Dance got its start so long ago. If you are an excellent dancer/choreographer yourself, and don't mind being patient with younger folks who aren't as focused as you are yet on the art of dance, you could dance your way into a respectable living. Physical strength, endurance, coordination, and creativity will help your business take off—but not more than referrals. Many dance instructors have years of training themselves or are retired from the profession. Some instructors will specialize in one area of dance such as tap or ballet in order to keep a cohesive following; others offer special packages where students can learn several different dances over a period of six to eight weeks.

START-UP:

The cost includes the rental of studio space if you do not have a large room to hold classes in (start-up costs could be as little as $500). The other part of your expense will be advertising your services ($1,500-$3,000). Earnings, however, are pretty decent if you have a good reputation and get regular referrals. At the college level, a dance instructor could make $40,000+ and a private instructor $27,000.

BOTTOM LINE ADVICE:

The long hours, especially evenings and weekends, may hinder some from pursuing this career. However, the grace, beauty, and strength of dancers are admired by many. Patience and the ability to critique without being hypercritical should come naturally if you want to be successful.

DATA RETRIEVAL SERVICE

Start-up cost:	$3,000-$5,000
Potential earnings:	$18,000-$50,000
Typical fees:	$45-$75 per hour
Advertising:	Networking, contacts in fields where you have experience, referrals
Qualifications:	Familiarity with business software in your specialized field
Equipment needed:	Computer, printer, office furniture, business cards, letterhead, envelopes
Home business potential:	Yes
Staff required:	No
Handicapped opportunity:	Yes
Hidden costs:	Business insurance, magazine subscriptions, and training to keep abreast of the field

LOWDOWN:

Lost data is a disaster. Businesses rely on data for countless types of operations from banking transactions to premium fulfillment. Yet even the best-maintained information system will have breakdowns and glitches from time to time. Mechanical failures, electrical problems, and human error will cause problems that are opportunities for you, if you have the expertise to retrieve lost data. When your clients need you, they really NEED you. This is another specialized computer consulting field where you must combine a high level of computer hardware/software knowledge with excellent communication skills in order to create a successful business of your own. If you can do these things while managing to control the company's stress level, the sky's the limit.

START-UP:

A computer will be your basic tool in this business; expect to invest at least $5,000 for equipment costs alone. Since your work is of a short-term, emergency nature, you should always charge an hourly rate ($45-$75 per hour).

BOTTOM LINE ADVICE:

You'll be the hero of the hour when you recall the first-quarter sales data from oblivion. Data retrieval expertise is highly valued, and you can find enough challenges to keep even the most active intellect fully occupied. The risks are fairly high here, but so are the rewards, if you can establish a relationship of trust with a few clients and then build on their referrals. You'll need to be the personality type that thrives under pressure, even in apparent chaos, and you'll be working with organizations that may not understand exactly what they have hired you to do. This is not a business for the laid-back; you're a technician who specializes in resurrecting the dead.

DAY CARE SERVICE

Start-up cost:	$3,000
Potential earnings:	$25,000-$40,000
Typical fees:	$40 per child per week or $50 per adult per week
Advertising:	Referral service, bulletin boards, classified ads
Qualifications:	Some states require a license and insurance
Equipment needed:	For children: cribs, toys, movies, and games; for adults: arts/crafts supplies and some form of entertainment
Home business potential:	Yes
Staff required:	No (but many states impose a limit on the adult-to-child ratio; for example, in Ohio you may have no more than six children to one adult)
Handicapped opportunity:	No
Hidden costs:	Insurance

LOWDOWN:

The day care business has been growing in direct relation to the rising number of women choosing careers in addition to families—and never has it been more flexible. There is a need to care for both seniors and children—and a few innovative entrepreneurs have integrated both at their care centers, so that the two groups can enjoy and learn to appreciate one another. You can easily start a day care center in your home if you meet the necessary zoning requirements of your community. It works best if you have a large yard and extra room (perhaps a finished basement) so that there is plenty of room to play. You'll need to be clear in your rates/policies (especially about regular hours, vacations, and payment due dates), and be careful not to let the parents treat you like a baby-sitter who is at their beck and call. Be assertive about protecting your personal time with your own family.

START-UP:

Your main start-up cost will be getting the word out about your service. Classified advertising, bulletin boards, and mothers' groups are a good way to build word of mouth. Your larger expenses will likely come from updating your home to meet zoning regulations; your home may have to pass inspection before licensing. If you decide not to license or not to carry insurance, be sure to let the parents/families know, because you will be held liable in the event of a disaster if you don't. Along those lines, be sure to familiarize yourself with safety procedures in case of an emergency.

BOTTOM LINE ADVICE:

If you love to be around little people or seniors, you'll enjoy the opportunity to do so daily. Also, if you have children of your own, you can be paid for watching them play with others—not a bad position to be in. On the downside, although you are responsible for the children you watch, you are not their parent—a fact the parents themselves may constantly remind you of. Be sure to meet with the parents of children or the families of seniors on a regular basis to keep communications straight.

DESKTOP PUBLISHER:
COMMUNITY-BASED COUPON BOOKS

Start-up cost:	$1,000-$5,000
Potential earnings:	$15,000-$30,000
Typical fees:	Ad rates vary (but generally start at $300-$500 per ad); plus, you can sell the books to the public for an average cover price of $29.95
Advertising:	Yellow Pages, community newspapers, local radio
Qualifications:	Ability to relate to both businesses and the public, one-on-one
Equipment needed:	Computer, software, printer
Home business potential:	Yes
Staff required:	Yes
Handicapped opportunity:	Yes
Hidden costs:	Phone and mileage for ad sales reps

LOWDOWN:

You'll be providing a useful service for both the businesses and the public. Businesses offer discounts to attract customers; you are aiding them in their marketing strategies by publicizing these discounts. You will sell advertising space in your coupon books, produce them with a printer, and then sell them to consumers through the mail. If you enjoy people and are good at presenting your "product," you will find that many customers in your community are receptive to receiving discounts from businesses they know and respect. The best part is, your revenue is collected from both sides (the advertiser and the buyer)—so you have a double stream of income.

START-UP:

It requires a lot of legwork to get a business like this started, but the end-product—an inexpensively printed booklet—is your major cost. Perhaps you can strike a deal with a local printer, offering a percentage of the take. Or, shell out the $1,000-$5,000 in your first six months of start-up—if you sell enough ads and begin to generate simultaneous interest from the public, you'll make enough to cover printing (and still have quite a bit left over).

BOTTOM LINE ADVICE:

You're creating a business enterprise out of almost nothing as you develop and sell your coupon book. This is truly a business that depends on hard work. Many individuals find a deep sense of satisfaction in knowing that they have provided a useful community service while making a profit at the same time. However, gathering enough coupon commitments from businesses is difficult: selling has its discouraging days. This is an enterprise for people with a lot of determination and a great deal of free time to successfully promote the book to the public.

DIRECT MARKETING/SALES

Start-up cost:	$1,000-$3,000
Potential earnings:	$20,000-$50,000
Typical fees:	Percentage basis
Advertising:	Word of mouth, direct mail, cold calling
Qualifications:	Energy, persistence, ability to manage time well
Equipment needed:	None
Home business potential:	Yes
Staff required:	None at first
Handicapped opportunity:	No
Hidden costs:	Some organizations charge for catalogs and other sales materials, attendance at meetings, inventory replacement

LOWDOWN:

Many, many people try their hand at direct sales, yet only a few of them make it big. What is the difference? Consider your goals. Do you want to make a few bucks and sell a line of products you like to family, friends, and acquaintances? Is your main goal to make your own purchases at a discount? Or are you planning to put the effort and commitment into direct sales that you would into establishing any other type of small business? Many products are best sold person-to-person because they benefit from demonstration. Finding an excellent product line to work with is vital, and you should feel confident in the company as well. The rest is up to your selling skills and personal drive. Many direct sales-oriented companies encourage their salespeople to create networks, additional salespeople whose sales bring a percentage to the person who recruited them. This practice acts as an incentive to everyone in the sales force. It is the way to large earnings, if you can achieve it.

START-UP:

Costs to start are very low (around $1,000), but watch out for hidden charges and fees from the manufacturers. These should warn you off the companies that might exploit you. An income of $20,000 in the beginning is realistic.

BOTTOM LINE ADVICE:

How many opportunities are left in this country in which your own hard work will define your success? Direct sales is one of them. Are you comfortable with cold-calling? Are you committed enough to keep yourself going with no one to answer to but yourself? Do you genuinely like people and enjoy helping them find products that will add something to their lives? Or, on the other hand, would you be satisfied with direct sales as an add-on to some other/activity? Be sure you're clear on what you want, and what you will need to do to achieve it. If you have big ambitions, you'll need a very big commitment to achieve them in direct marketing and sales.

DISABILITY CONSULTANT

Start-up cost:	$2,000-$4,000
Potential earnings:	$50,000-$75,000
Typical fees:	$60-$80 per hour
Advertising:	Direct mail, referrals, membership in business organizations
Qualifications:	Extensive experience in field, college degree in related area, ability to communicate well with employers and employees, good writing skills
Equipment needed:	Computer, printer, office furniture, business cards, letterhead, envelopes
Home business potential:	Yes
Staff required:	No
Handicapped opportunity:	Yes
Hidden costs:	Insurance, dues for organizations, conferences and seminars

LOWDOWN:

As a disability consultant you will advise corporations on disability claims and assist them in meeting the requirements of all government and regulatory bodies. Nothing is cut and dried about the disability field, and rapid changes have left even the best-intentioned employers confused about what they must do to be in compliance. Disability claims made by employees are a major cost in some industries, and your recommendations for alterations in the setup of the workplace or refinements in work processes could be seen as extremely valuable.

Managing medical claims is another important function. The conflicts arising from the most common worker problem—back pain—need expert management, both for medical treatment and for the maintenance of good relations with the employee. The third aspect of this field is the requirement to make reasonable accommodations for disabled workers. Creative consultants can often find ways to make small alterations, for example, in the height of a counter, that can enable a wheelchair-bound person to fill a position at the company.

START-UP:

Most of your work will be carried out at the companies you are assessing and handling claims for, but you will need your own office for production of reports and possibly for client meetings. Expect to spend $2,000-$4,000 for your computer system and first few months of rent. Charge $60-$80 per hour for this service that can save a company thousands of dollars per year.

BOTTOM LINE ADVICE:

If you have experience in this complex field and can communicate with both sides, the disabled and the employer, you can build a business as a disability consultant. In fact, many disabled people do just this, using their own perspectives to enrich the services they can offer to other organizations. Enabling challenged people to hold a job is an important service, and it keeps employers on the right side of the law as well.

DOG TRAINER

Start-up cost:	$1,000-2,000
Potential earnings:	$35,000-$45,000
Typical fees:	$300 for a three-week session is fairly common
Advertising:	Flyers, direct mail, Yellow Pages, classifieds, referrals from vets, free clinics
Qualifications:	Experience with different breeds, track record of success, patience, and credibility
Equipment needed:	Space for pets to roam, be fed, etc., kennel area for sleeping
Home business potential:	Yes
Staff required:	No
Handicapped opportunity:	No
Hidden costs:	Advertising, travel

LOWDOWN:

Working dogs need considerable training, depending on the jobs they have to perform. Drug-sniffing dogs, guard dogs, guide dogs, movie dogs, and herding dogs all have their specialized training systems. Often these dogs receive much of their training from their breeders or owners, although some trainers of working dogs have national reputations for their skill and effectiveness.

A much bigger market is training services for pets. Most pet owners wake up a bit late to the need for training (usually after half of the carpet has been eaten), but you can present your service as the solution to those nagging problems that make pet dogs so frustrating at times. Some trainers give classes for owner and dog together while others go to a pet's home and provide individual sessions. Network with veterinarians; they are usually the first to hear about animal problems.

START-UP:

Your main start-up cost is for whatever marketing and advertising approaches seem best for your community. Somewhere between $500-$1,000 would be an average amount to spend on launching this business. Remember, though, that you'll be charging as much as $300 per dog for a three-week session—that can add up to a tidy profit early in the game.

BOTTOM LINE ADVICE:

This job is immensely enjoyable if you love dogs and can tolerate their owners (remember, you'll be training them, too). Gaining the trust of an animal is an essential part of any training process, but some trainers find that getting the human side of the equation to cooperate is even harder. Once the pets in your class begin to give up eating the curtains and jumping all over Grandma, however, you will seem like a genius. Then the class can proceed to the really hard stuff such as coming when called (the pet) and being patient (the owner). For most trainers this is not a route to wealth, but a decent living can be made if you keep up your marketing.

ECONOMIC DEVELOPMENT CONSULTANT

Start-up cost:	$1,000-$5,000
Potential earnings:	$35,000-$50,000
Typical fees:	$50-$75 per hour
Advertising:	Yellow Pages, affiliations with civic and government agencies (particularly Chambers of Commerce)
Qualifications:	Degree
Equipment needed:	Computer, printer, fax, phone, letterhead, business cards
Home business potential:	Yes
Staff required:	No
Handicapped opportunity:	Yes
Hidden costs:	Travel expenses

LOWDOWN:

For a city experiencing a major financial tailspin, economic development consultants provide the compass by which businesses can gain new ground. As an advisor to such businesses, and often through a Chamber of Commerce, you will provide guidance and direction to higher profitability, and perhaps even offer the city developers new ideas or opportunities to cash in on their location. For instance, it is the economic development consultant who typically suggests such moneymakers as convention centers, sports arenas, and other key profit-boosters. Recognize, though, that although the city is primed for change, you could be entering into a potentially volatile environment (politically speaking). Keep a cool head, stick to the facts, and show the decision-makers where the money's really at.

START-UP:

Your start-up is low because your service is mainly in your mind and your accumulation of experience. Set aside $1,000-$3,000 for your basic office equipment, and be sure to invest in a cellular phone or pager—you'll need it. Earnings will range from $35,000-$50,000, depending on your reputation and proximity to cities in need.

BOTTOM LINE ADVICE:

Build a name for yourself by doing some volunteer work in your community; that will help you get networked with key people and those people generally know people like themselves in other communities. Once you get your name out there, you should have little trouble making the phone ring.

EMERGENCY RESPONSE SERVICE

Start-up cost:	$1,000-$5,000
Potential earnings:	$15,000-$25,000
Typical fees:	$5-$10 per client per month
Advertising:	Yellow Pages, referrals from physicians/hospitals, direct mail, community newspapers, coupon books
Qualifications:	Superior organizational skills and the ability to respond quickly and professionally
Equipment needed:	Computer system with specialized software that recognizes alarms or signals, phone
Home business potential:	Yes
Staff required:	Yes
Handicapped opportunity:	Yes
Hidden costs:	Insurance, system downtime (can be costly)

LOWDOWN:

Lots of elderly and handicapped folks have a limited number of caregivers, and many rely on the false hope that nothing bad will happen to them when they are alone. Your service provides peace of mind to both the homebound and their support people, because you are tied into their homes with a signal transmitter or push-button system that immediately contacts your computer. A signal goes off in your home, and you are in charge of sending immediate help to the client's location (which you've already got stored in your computer). It's fast, it's safe, and it's necessary for those who really don't have much family around to call on them regularly. You will be in a noble profession, and there are some franchises you can buy into to get the benefit of technical support and even the specialized software program you'll need.

START-UP:

Your start-up costs will reflect a franchise fee (which, at $2,000-$5,000 is significantly lower than most buy-ins of a franchise operation). You will need to spend a little on advertising, but your computer system is what will cost you the most in the beginning (about $1,500). Some franchises include your computer as part of your buy-in. With or without a franchiser, you'll be charging between $10-$15 per client per month for your service; expect to earn $15,000-$25,000.

BOTTOM LINE ADVICE:

Your clients will depend heavily on you for life-and-death situations; one time is all you'll get to make a serious mistake. You need to decide if you're in this to make money or to help people; ideally, it will be a mix of both.

EMPLOYEE HARMONY CONSULTANT

Start-up cost:	$3,000-$6,000
Potential earnings:	$40,000-$60,000
Typical fees:	$2,000-$3,000 per engagement
Advertising:	Trade publications, business newspapers, association memberships, community activity, seminars and public speaking, referrals, word of mouth
Qualifications:	Background in related field, proven track record in consulting, human relations, total quality management, or related specialty, ability to market you own services, excellent presentation and facilitation skills
Equipment needed:	Office furniture, computer, suite and presentation software, fax, modem, printer, business cards, letterhead, envelopes, marketing materials
Home business potential:	Yes
Staff required:	No
Handicapped opportunity:	No
Hidden costs:	Time and support for marketing efforts, cost of materials, travel

LOWDOWN:

You're not going to be able to call the vice president for human resources at Mega Corp. Inc., and immediately get an assignment as an employee harmony consultant. Instead, your marketing will probably have to focus on educating your potential clients on the nature and value of your work. More and more demands are being placed on most employees in large organizations today, and tensions and conflict have risen as well. Life for many employees is more tense than harmonious, and the quality of the customer service they provide is suffering as a result. This problem ought to be your opportunity. Your workshops, exercises, and self-discovery projects do meet a direct need in many organizations, and your persistence in selling these values will eventually allow you to build a business.

START-UP:

All you really need to do is equip your office and produce whatever materials you plan to use. You should be able to do this for about $3,000 in start-up costs, to potentially earn about $40,000 annually.

BOTTOM LINE ADVICE:

As with any new type of business, the challenge is to make people understand what it is. The idea is quite viable if it can be sold effectively. Your skills in interpersonal relations and team building are very applicable; the difficulty will be to persuade organizations to let you make your contribution.

ENVIRONMENTAL
CONSULTANT/CONTRACTOR

Start-up cost:	$3,500-$5,000
Potential earnings:	$50,000-$100,000
Typical fees:	$150 per hour and up (depending on area or field of expertise)
Advertising:	Association memberships, referrals, networking
Qualifications:	Master's or preferably Ph.D. in related field, at least five years' experience, excellent research/writing skills, ability to work well with people of many different views
Equipment needed:	Sophisticated computer, suite software, printer; additional heavy equipment, depending on specialty, such as materials for oil-spill clean-up, collection methods for lab samples, and a lab for analysis
Home business potential:	Yes
Staff required:	No
Handicapped opportunity:	Not typically
Hidden costs:	Insurance, on-line time, publication subscriptions

LOWDOWN:

This is a growing field in most parts of the country. Environmental regulations are becoming more stringent and concern for the welfare of the natural world around us motivates public and private organizations alike to call experts in for specialized advice. Even a seemingly simple decision such as the siting of a factory can have environmental consequences, depending on the effect of the building process on the flow of ground water, the need for safe disposal of any effluents, and possibly the need for highway upgrades to handle increased traffic. Farmers and fishermen must have a clean environment to operate successfully, yet their practices can have a harmful effect on the same resources that support them. Creative environmental consulting can help balance between competing interests and clarify the issues upon which political decisions must be made. Your ability to draft and complete an effective report will be an important selling point for your skills.

START-UP:

Even at the basic level this field is relatively expensive to enter, particularly when you factor in the cost of your education. Environmental contracting could move you out of the one-person home office category, considering the capital expenditures for the equipment your specialty may require. Bill your services at $150 per hour or more; after all, you're a highly credentialed professional.

BOTTOM LINE ADVICE:

People with the background to consider becoming an environmental consultant usually have a deep personal commitment to this type of work. The result is that each project has special meaning and offers rewards of the psyche in addition to the fees earned. If you can help create a governmental policy that improves man's relationship to the environment, you are achieving something of which to be proud. If you can help a business act responsibly, work effectively, and stay competitive, you will probably receive enthusiastic referrals and repeat business as well. But getting established is very hard in this field. You will need to build trust and earn the respect of politicians or business people, some of whom wish that the whole environmental movement would just quietly fade away.

ADVICE FROM THE EXPERTS

What sets your business apart from others like it?

Anne Hayden, environmental consultant for Resource Services in Brunswick, Maine, says her company stands out because of the value of its particular focus: there are not a lot of other people doing marine-related work. Her clients are typically government agencies and nonprofits.

Things you couldn't do without:

A computer, a modem, and access to a well-stocked library, as Hayden's work is largely research-intensive.

Marketing tips/advice:

"I try to promote myself as an objective expert in my field. Many of the issues I'm dealing with are controversial. Also, I offer my first hour pro bono (free) to tell what I know about a particular environmental issue. It's been an effective marketing tool."

If you had to do it all over again . . .

"I would buy time-management software. Ideally, it would track time for planning purposes to give a more accurate estimate of my time spent on any particular project."

FACTORY LOCATING CONSULTANT

Start-up cost:	$3,000-$6,000
Potential earnings:	$50,000 and more
Typical fees:	$35-$50 per hour or a flat retainer of $500-$1,000
Advertising:	National business periodicals, memberships in trade associations and manufacturers organizations, networking referrals
Qualifications:	Extensive business real estate experience, understanding of manufacturing, knowledge of urban geography, wide network of contacts, excellent oral and written communication skills
Equipment needed:	Office furniture, computer, high-speed modem, on-line accounts, fax, printer, cellular phone or pager, business cards, letterhead, envelopes
Home business potential:	Yes
Staff required:	No
Handicapped opportunity:	No
Hidden costs:	Travel, on-line account fees, telephone bills

LOWDOWN:

The search for a new factory location can often be an extensive one. First, the requirements must be outlined. These include workforce availability, transportation needs, land requirements, availability of power, and environmental concerns. Given the differences among the laws of the fifty states, researching the legal issues alone can be a major challenge. Finally, what state and local business development programs are available, and how do their offerings compare? Your ability to outline the desired factors, gather data, and present several alternatives for consideration will allow you to establish a business as a factory locating consultant. There are thousands of pieces to this jigsaw puzzle, and you won't find a crowded field of competitors for the business. On the other hand, the potential market for your services must be national, not local, so your marketing efforts must be extensive.

START-UP:

You'll need to be able to plow the ground first by computer. And most of all, you'll need to be able to keep in touch with your clients. Depending on how knowledgeable you are, you could soon be earning $50,000.

BOTTOM LINE ADVICE:

You'll need to know when a company is beginning the search process so you can market to them. This means having a network of people in the know who can clue you in. Also consider working on a subcontractor basis for the business development department of a large state. You could help them offer sites that are well-suited to businesses that are considering relocating. A very few factory locating consultants operate internationally. Getting established will be challenging, but once you have proven your abilities, referrals may bring all the business you need.

FAN CLUB MANAGEMENT

Start-up cost:	Minimal, if artist pays for expenses; $3,000-$5,000 if you're totally self-sufficient
Potential earnings:	$10,000-$30,000
Typical fees:	$10-$25 each for memberships; you can also derive a percentage from merchandising products
Advertising:	Direct mail and word of mouth
Qualifications:	Membership in the National Association of Fan Clubs
Equipment needed:	Computer, printer, fax/modem, copier, database/label and desktop publishing software, phone system with voice mail capabilities
Home business potential:	Yes
Staff required:	Not initially
Handicapped opportunity:	Possibly
Hidden costs:	Postage and printing costs

LOWDOWN:

When a celebrity becomes a celebrity, the last thing they want to do is sit around answering fan mail. Still, many celebrities do realize that their fans are who put them where they are, and they don't necessarily want to ignore them. That's why it makes sense for popular artists to hire fan club managers to keep in touch with their many admirers: they recognize the importance of staying where they are by staying in touch with those whose opinions ultimately matter the most. If you have the right credentials (such as having been a professional writer or prior experience in radio or television), then you might be able to convince a celebrity to let you take charge of his or her mail. In addition to opening and answering huge bags of mail, you'll offer services such as quarterly or semiannual newsletter and merchandising (offering promotional products like T-shirts, posters, and autographed photos for sale and taking a small percentage for yourself). Like the celebrity, if you're in the right place at the right time, this could be the right opportunity for you.

START-UP:

You won't need very much at all to get started if you can convince a celebrity to foot the bill for his or her fan club; some celebrities actually do see the worth of paying someone else to handle the mail and requests for signed photos. However, most fan clubs operate on their own (with or without celebrity endorsement, but obviously it's easier with), leaving you with a start-up cost of $3,000-$5,000 if you operate on a shoestring. You could sell memberships for $10-$25 each, and offer incentives for joining (such as a free T-shirt or baseball cap). At any rate, you'll be producing newsletters (at $500-$1,000 each) a few times per year, so you'll need to be sure you've sold enough memberships to cover printing and postage rates. If all goes well, you could make $10,000-$30,000 per year doing something enjoyable and high-profile; not enough to make you rich, but certainly enough to make you smile.

Bottom Line Advice:

This seems on the surface to be a glamorous job, and it is—until you get barraged with unreasonable requests, tight deadlines on newsletters, and ego-maniacal celebrities who think treating "underlings" accordingly is the path to greater success. It might help if you continually remind the celebrity just how much more money the fan club is ultimately making them in boosting record or ticket sales.

ADVICE FROM THE EXPERTS

What sets your business apart from others like it?

"We are an authorized fan club management company and I have a highly specialized background in radio," says Joyce Logan, President of Fan Emporium, Inc., a Branford, Connecticut-based firm representing entertainers such as Michael Bolton, Carly Simon, John Mellencamp, and Mariah Carey. "I put myself in the fan's shoes and give every fan the personal touch . . . we produce newsletters, answer fan mail, sell authorized merchandise, and even have a 900-number service for fans to get concert updates and messages from their favorite superstars."

Things you couldn't do without:

Computer with a good database management program, printer and labeling program, fax, and modem.

Marketing tips/advice:

"Start with just one celebrity, and know that you can't just run a fan club for a little while. This is a serious commitment to the celebrity and the fans. You're dealing with people's emotional links to their favorite celebrity . . . you are a 'merchant of emotions.'"

If you had to do it all over again . . .

"I would have made contracts with the artists a little bit differently, so that they would assume all the costs of printing and mailing. We are a public relations firm just like any other, and we need to be recognized as such to stay profitable."

FARM-SITTING

Start-up cost:	$1,000-$5,000
Potential earnings:	$19,000-$25,000
Typical fees:	$1,500-$2,000 per month
Advertising:	County fairs, farm equipment shops, personal contacts
Qualifications:	Optional certificate as an accredited farm manager; knowledge of agriculture, equipment, state/federal regulations
Equipment needed:	None
Home business potential:	Yes
Staff required:	Possibly
Handicapped opportunity:	Not typically
Hidden costs:	Bonding, insurance, licensing fee

LOWDOWN:

If you don't mind the strenuous physical work involved in farming, farm-sitting could be a great business for you. Here, you have all the benefits of running a farm minus the regular daily headache (since you're only doing it on a short-term basis, perhaps while an owner is on vacation). Word of mouth means a lot in rural communities and could become the lifeline to this job. It will help if you have grown up on a farm and already have some knowledge of what needs to be done each day. Being in good physical condition will come in handy when it's time to slop the pigs and clean the stalls. Be prepared for any emergency (have the veterinarian's phone number handy at all times) and know how to handle livestock. Organization and dependability are also key ingredients; if you can work from the crack of dawn to dusk, this would make a fine profession. The best part is, you only have to do it when you choose to—in other words, you don't have the tremendous burden of running your own farm full-time.

START-UP:

Since you'll be going to well-stocked farms, all you'll really need to take along are a good pair of boots, socks, and overalls. Expect to earn roughly $20,000 and up if you have a certificate.

BOTTOM LINE ADVICE:

This temporary assignment will demand that you give up a lot of your time until the job is done. A farmer's work is never really done. Don't lull yourself into thinking that this is a glamorous job; you'll really appreciate the fact that it is only temporary unless you are considering owning your own farm. If you're doing it as a learning experience before embarking on your own as a farmer, you'll get to see firsthand the inner workings of a farm without making a huge personal investment.

FARMER OF FRUITS OR VEGETABLES

Start-up cost:	$1,000-$5,000
Potential earnings:	$15,000-$40,000 (or more)
Typical fees:	Prices are based on what the market will bear for each particular item
Advertising:	Newspaper ads, word of mouth, grocery stores, catalogs
Qualifications:	Knowledge of growing fruits/vegetables, marketing skills
Equipment needed:	Planting and harvesting equipment, soil, implements, packing materials, land
Home business potential:	Yes
Staff required:	None at first
Handicapped opportunity:	No
Hidden costs:	A cash reserve or other income is needed to get through weather-related setbacks; competition may be stiff in some areas, crops are usually seasonal

LOWDOWN:

If you enjoy working the land and watching fruits and vegetables grow, this may be a satisfying business for you. How much land you need depends on the crop you're growing and the amount of profit you want to realize. Americans are hungry for home-grown (especially organically grown) produce; farmers' markets are gaining popularity everywhere. You will find a market for your crops in groceries, gourmet shops, health-food stores, and even (in some cases) mail-order catalogs. This business spells hard work, but the opportunity for success is excellent.

START-UP:

Start-up costs depend on the crop you wish to grow. Most likely, you will require a plot of land (up to several acres to start), located near a well-populated area. You will also need plants, seeds, or trees (depending on what you're growing), planting and harvesting equipment, farm tools and implements, fertilizers, etc. In addition, plan on using or purchasing a truck or other vehicle for deliveries, and be sure to check out any applicable zoning or health regulations of your products. You may also need to lease farm equipment, such as a tractor or rototiller.

BOTTOM LINE ADVICE:

Growing fruits and vegetables is hard, dirty, physical work. It is often frustrating, as well, due to weather and seasonal conditions. You must safeguard your plants with tender care, which means you have little time off (unless you have help with your business). You may eventually have to lease or buy additional land in order to expand. On the upside, if you love the outdoors and enjoy watching plants grow, this endeavor will be a very satisfying one. You will get a chance to live a country lifestyle, while selling your produce in cities. You can take satisfaction in supplying people with one of the basic necessities of life—food.

FEED CONSULTANT/BROKER

Start-up cost:	$2,000-$3,000
Potential earnings:	$20,000-$35,000
Typical fees:	10 to 15 percent from dealers and $300 per day from individual clients or small farms
Advertising:	Farm journals, local newspapers, direct mail, Yellow Pages, referrals
Qualifications:	Degree in animal nutrition or extensive experience with livestock or poultry, awareness of agricultural economics, wide network of contacts in your region's farms
Equipment needed:	Basic office setup, cellular phone, business cards, letterhead, envelopes
Home business potential:	Yes
Staff required:	No
Handicapped opportunity:	Not typically
Hidden costs:	Travel between farms, cellular phone bills

LOWDOWN:

You can use your understanding of animal nutrition and ability to work with the farming community to establish a solid and profitable business as a feed consultant/broker. The science of animal nutrition is growing ever more complicated, and even the most modern farmer can benefit from the advice of a specialist in making feed decisions. Different mixtures of feed must be designed depending on the intended result—fattening beef cattle is quite different from feeding milk cows—and the cost of each feed mix must be considered as well. Add in seasonal variations and you have a potentially challenging situation. Profit margins on many farms are so low that even a few percentage points change in cost or productivity can have a big effect. As a consultant, you will advise your clients which feed mix to choose. As a broker, you will help them buy it at the best possible price from the most reliable source.

START-UP:

You will be relying on your knowledge and your contacts, not so much on your equipment. Therefore, you shouldn't have to spend more than $3,000 on start-up costs. Your money will be earned from two sources: first, your daily fee of $300 or more for consulting; second, your percentage (usually 10 to 15 percent) of the sale from dealers. With low initial investment and high profits, you can make a killing in this field—all you need is the know-how to back it all up.

BOTTOM LINE ADVICE:

As with so many consulting fields, you are not going to be jumping into this one cold. You will be known for your expertise, and you will be respected by the larger community in which you live. Agriculture is a tough business dependent on many factors (weather included), and you must have enough capital or cash flow to ride out the low times.

FINANCIAL AID CONSULTANT

Start-up cost:	$2,000-$4,000
Potential earnings:	$15,000-$40,000
Typical fees:	Flat rates of $150-$500
Advertising:	Yellow Pages, classified ads, direct mail, membership and participation in community organizations related to education, seminars and speeches for community groups, networking, referrals from high schools
Qualifications:	Experience as a school guidance counselor or college admissions officer, extensive knowledge of the field, ability to relate well to college applicants and their parents
Equipment needed:	Office with conference table for meeting clients, computer, suite software, modem, fax, printer, business cards, letterhead, envelopes
Home business potential:	Yes
Staff required:	No
Handicapped opportunity:	Yes
Hidden costs:	Subscriptions, on-line time, dues

LOWDOWN:

The cost of higher education continues to escalate. And while it is always said that many types of financial aid are available, finding them is quite another matter. Families need guidance and assistance in preparing the paperwork and in finding the sources to which they can apply. Your services as a financial aid consultant will be in great demand once your name gets known to the community at large. Word of mouth from students you have helped, and their parents, will bring you new business regularly. You will need a lot of familiarity with financial aid options to make a success of this type of consulting, and you will need excellent people skills as well. Some financial aid consultants research options on the Internet, while other specialize in aid for secondary, or even elementary school tuition. The bulk of the market, though, is for students entering college.

START-UP:

Keeping your own knowledge up to date and providing a suitable place for interviewing clients are your two main expenses ($2,000 to start). Part-time could earn you $15,000; rates could range anywhere from $150-$500 per job.

BOTTOM LINE ADVICE:

Many parents experience major sticker shock when they first realize how much having one or more children enrolled in the ivied halls is going to set them back. And even the "simple" financial aid forms for determining basic financial need are far from easy to cope with. Beyond that, you can give vital help in finding the multitude of special scholarships for students with a certain heritage, a special academic interest, or some other unusual characteristic.

FLEA MARKET ORGANIZER

Start-up cost:	$1,000-$5,000
Potential earnings:	$25,000-$50,000
Typical fees:	$5-$100 from vendors per day, depending on size and reputation of market; from attendees, some flea markets charge an admission or parking fee of $3-$5 per carload
Advertising:	Flyers, classified ads, rent-a-sign
Qualifications:	Basic knowledge of the area and merchandise
Equipment needed:	Large piece of land (rented is better than owned), insurance, some form of shelter in case of rain
Home business potential:	No
Staff required:	Not at first
Handicapped potential:	Possibly
Hidden costs:	Liability insurance, crowd control, promotion

LOWDOWN:

Are you the type who simply cannot pass up a bargain? Do you consider yourself an authority on decent used or collectible items? If so, you might make a terrific "head flea." As a flea market promoter/organizer, you would round up as many vendors as you can safely fit into a designated area, and advertise everywhere your clientele would be likely to look for flea markets. The main jobs of the organizer are to promote the event to sales people and customers alike and schedule the flea market so that there are no large competitors running theirs nearby at the same time. Another opportunity for the promoter is in selling goods to the public, and even to other dealers who've run short; you could make basically as much money as you have the energy to generate.

START-UP:

Two large expenses are the land rental and insurance coverage, each approximately $300-$500 depending upon the area. Advertising is key, but not very expensive (average quarterly budgets are $500-$1,000). Creating and making copies of a flyer is a good way to get the word out, as well as posting signs on local bulletin boards and en route to the site itself. Buying a supply of goods to sell is not necessary, but could increase profit by as much as 40 percent. Finally, two or more police officers acting as crowd control/problem prevention should be hired for at least $15 per hour. Charge anywhere from $5-$100 per table for vendors who wish to rent space; some flea markets also tack on an admission or parking fee for attendees ($3-$5 per carload is typical).

BOTTOM LINE ADVICE:

The number-one priority in considering this business is organizational skills. A well-run flea market can make a great deal of money. Conversely, a poorly run event can be a disaster financially and logistically. (P.S. Make sure all of your vendors have valid vendors' licenses, or you could be fined considerably.)

FOOD DELIVERY SERVICE

Start-up cost:	$1,000 or more
Potential earnings:	$25,000 and up
Typical fees:	$5-$10 per "run"
Advertising:	Brochures in office buildings, newspaper ads
Qualifications:	Ability to create attractive, healthy, portable meals
Equipment needed:	Kitchen, cooking supplies and equipment, food packaging
Home business potential:	Yes
Staff required:	Part-time delivery person, if needed
Handicapped opportunity:	Yes
Hidden costs:	May need delivery vehicle; check out legal and health requirements

LOWDOWN:

Food delivery to the home or office is an idea whose time has come. Delivering lunches to office workers is especially lucrative. Harried people will love seeing your delicious dinner brought to their door as they arrive home after a long day at work. The menus need not be extensive, which simplifies the operation. You can "pick up" from a variety of local restaurants, or prepare your own meals. Challenges include safe food handling practices "on the road," keeping foods hot or cold, as appropriate, and maintaining on-time deliveries.

START-UP:

This business isn't costly to start up, especially if you opt to offer a lunch-only service. If you offer sandwiches and soups, salads and rolls, beverages and dessert, for instance, you need very little equipment to prepare the meals. You will need to invest in packaging for the foods (disposable plastic bowls, cellophane or foil wrapping, for instance); the cost will vary depending on the foods you're selling. Create a flier that can be posted in heavily populated office complexes to get started; always deliver the next day's menu with each meal as you drop them off. Make sure your insurance policy will cover your vehicle while it is being used for deliveries and, if you are hiring a delivery helper, make sure your insurance covers that employee in your car.

BOTTOM LINE ADVICE:

Most people in the food delivery business get up early in the morning to bake and/or cook; night owls may not survive! Expect a long day of work, especially if you deliver at dinnertime in the evening. You'll need an ability to deal successfully with vendors and suppliers to keep your costs down and the food quality consistent. On the upside, the future is bright for food delivery businesses. More and more people have less and less time to cook; everyone is tired of the typical "fast food." Start-up costs in most cases are modest, and you can net $70-$100 a day right from the start (the sky is the limit after that, as you add more routes).

FOOD ITEM MANUFACTURER

Start-up cost:	$500-$5,000 (depending on the food product)
Potential earnings:	$30,000-$75,000
Typical fees:	As high as $50 for some items, but most range $2-$25 each
Advertising:	Mail-order catalogs, brochures, direct mail, groceries, farmers' markets
Qualifications:	Knowledge of how to manufacture and market the item
Equipment needed:	Depends on the item
Home business potential:	Yes; at least until the business outgrows your home
Staff required:	None
Handicapped opportunity:	Yes
Hidden costs:	Legal advice

LOWDOWN:

The sky is the limit in food production—anything from eggs and bottled water to candy and organically grown tomatoes can be manufactured by a home-based entrepreneur. What's involved in such a business varies greatly, depending upon which product you choose, but either offering a unique food item or marketing a tried-and-true favorite in a new way spells success. A package of pasta, for example, can be produced for as little as 46 cents and sold for $3.50 or more. How about pizza? Everyone loves pizza, it's easy to make and, with your own marketing or recipe twists, you can make a tremendous amount of money. Want more ideas? How about food by mail order, a food-preserving business, specialty breads, sassafras tea, holiday cookies, or maple syrup? If you are willing to learn the ins and outs of producing and marketing a particular food product, you can establish a profitable business.

START-UP:

Start-up costs depend on the food product you choose. If you need ovens or an assembly line to manufacture your products, it may be relatively expensive to begin. On the other hand, a product such as soup can be started on a shoestring. Packaging and marketing costs for any product must be carefully considered; explore your market area, examine packaging of similar products, and research the costs.

BOTTOM LINE ADVICE:

Your livelihood is greatly affected by weather and the seasons, if it requires growing a crop. You may need considerable knowledge about fertilizers, plant diseases, etc. You must have a consistent supply of ingredients and a consistent manufacturing method to ensure that your products always taste the same. Any food product is subject to safety and health regulations. The good news is that many food manufacturing operations are quite simple, requiring few ingredients and no great technical skills. Everyone loves to eat, so food products are always in vogue.

Food Manufacturing Consultant

Start-up cost:	$1,500-$5,000
Potential earnings:	$45,000-$80,000
Typical fees:	$125 per hour is common; some opt for flat, per-job rate
Advertising:	Industry/trade publications, direct mail, word of mouth, Internet
Qualifications:	Extensive manufacturing or food industry background
Equipment needed:	Computer with printer and on-line services, fax/modem, phone (also cellular phone, since you'll be on the road a lot)
Home business potential:	Yes
Staff required:	No
Handicapped opportunity:	Not likely
Hidden costs:	Insurance, travel costs

Lowdown:

We all know what food manufacturers essentially do, but what about food manufacturing consultants? Well, if you decide to become a player in this competitive field, you'd better have a background in the food industry; you'll need it just to walk into a trade show and take in everything you see. As a food manufacturing consultant, you'll study how the best food producers get their product to market; you'll relish sumptuous facts such as how a particular company chose an innovative label to sell its product effectively, and you'll know all of the major food success stories out there (waiting, of course, to be told to your client, the budding entrepreneurial food maker). You will assist a company in everything from production to marketing, and you will likely charge an hourly consulting fee of about $125 for such knowledge and expertise.

Start-up:

You'll likely spend $1,500-$5,000 launching this very specialized business; these dollars will be split between equipment and advertising costs. Count on purchasing a computer/printer with fax/modem capabilities ($2,000). Also, spend some money on a dynamic direct mail piece that will somehow set you apart from competitors. You could make $45,000-$80,000 or more in this high-energy, highly competitive field.

Bottom Line Advice:

If you're already so into this industry that you want to be a food manufacturing consultant, then it's probably too late to tell you the downside. Here it is, anyway: You will work long, long hours and never be able to walk down the grocery store aisles in peace again.

FORENSIC CONSULTANT

Start-up cost:	$2,000-$3,000
Potential earnings:	$40,000-$60,000
Typical fees:	$50 and up per hour
Advertising:	Referrals, professional memberships, networking
Qualifications:	Medical degree with specialty in pathology or related field, extensive experience, law degree desirable as well
Equipment needed:	Office furniture, computer, printer, suite software, cellular phone, pager, business cards, letterhead, envelopes
Home business potential:	Yes
Staff required:	No
Handicapped opportunity:	No
Hidden costs:	Errors and omissions insurance, ongoing training, organization memberships

LOWDOWN:

Forensic consultants sit on an interesting conflict line in American culture, between the exponential growth in technological tools on the one hand, and the inability of governments and police forces to keep up with the demands of criminal investigations on the other. The O.J. Simpson trial highlighted this contrast, with evidence at the level of DNA analysis combined with demonstrations of the serious management problems within the Los Angeles police lab. As a forensic consultant, your services will be needed by overburdened prosecutors and police departments, as well as by defense teams (in the case of the few defendants wealthy enough to pay for extensive trial preparation). You are the expert who looks at the physical remains of a crime scene—analyzing wounds, suggesting time of death, establishing identity, and providing factual supporting details for a criminal investigation. The need is great; the challenge will be obtaining the funding in these days of budget cutbacks to pay your fees.

START-UP:

An adequate office will support the "business" side of this business. Lab work and other services will be performed by subcontractors. Your main product is your expertise. Communication equipment will be vital, though. You could earn upward of $40,000.

BOTTOM LINE ADVICE:

Streetwise is definitely what you will need to be, to make a success of this type of business. You'll be selling yourself, your expertise, and your ability to work through the technical data to produce results that support the defendant—or the prosecution. The forensic expert has been a character in thousands of TV dramas, but the real-life specialty is much less glamorous, and much more technical. If you prove effective, you'll have all the business you can handle, once your name gets known. This is no place for amateurs.

Advertising Effectively— and Economically

You've started a business and you need to get the word out. The problem is, you simply don't have the kind of budget that General Motors does to advertise your products or services. What can you do? You could try one or more of these economical methods:

- **Press releases.** Free press is the best, when you are lucky enough to get it. Try to offer tips to a particular group of people, and you'll have a better chance of catching the interest of an editor.

- **Flyers.** Post them everywhere your potential customers go. If you've got a moving or packing service, a flyer strategically located at a laundromat or apartment complex bulletin board might yield some quick results for you. Be where they are, and you'll go far.

- **Get an Internet address, or design a Web Page.** The advertising wave of the future is on the 'Net. Why? Because it is so inexpensive compared to print media. Will it help you get all the business you need? That remains to be seen, but all indications are good. One pie baker sold a thousand pies the first few months after she posted her Web Site. If she can do that, imagine what you could do.

- **Offer coupon deals regularly.** Coupons are ads that come with souvenirs for your customers; you get the sale, they walk away with a prize for doing business with you: a lower price or a better deal. Who can beat that?

- **Trades for advertising space.** Often, you might have a service that a local newspaper or TV/radio station needs. You can sometimes trade your services for free space or airtime.

- **Direct mail.** You can spend a small amount of money and reach a large number of potentials through direct mail pieces. Be sure to design something that's interesting and captivating. Your clients are deluged with such pieces (sometimes referred to as "junk mail") so yours needs to be fairly innovative and attention-getting. Work with a professional (you can trade services here, too) to write and design your direct mail pieces.

FREELANCE
WRITER/EDITOR/ILLUSTRATOR

Start-up cost:	$2,000-$5,000
Potential earnings:	$22,500-$50,000
Typical fees:	$50-$150 per hour, depending on area and experience level
Advertising:	Personal contacts, trade publications
Qualifications:	Writing and communication skills; attention to detail and organizational ability, sense for graphics and design
Equipment needed:	High-end computer with light pen or graphics tablet and a high resolution graphics video card, scanner, laser printer, word processing, design, and contact management software, fax, office furniture, reference books, business cards
Home business potential:	Yes
Staff required:	No
Handicapped opportunity:	Yes
Hidden costs:	Maintaining personal contacts (business lunches, etc.), memberships in trade organizations, software upgrades

LOWDOWN:

Many people have made careers out of freelance writing, editing, and illustrating—and many more are trying. Success will come for you when you can distinguish your services from those of others who will work for peanuts. Excellent communication skills are required to discover exactly what your clients want and need. You then turn those skills around to produce the corrected materials, written texts, or illustrations that will support your clients' marketing plans. This is a personal business that requires building up trust slowly and carefully before you can obtain the big projects that bring in enough income to make you successful. Creativity and goal-directedness are both essential. No detail can slip by your eye. But successful projects will bring you referrals, and each small step can lead to a bigger one.

As a writer, you will work on special editorial projects for clients ranging from small business owners to universities to newspapers—and you may even be lucky enough to snag a corporate client or two in the meantime. Your projects might be as specialized as an article for a trade journal or a corporate history; then again, you could be a generalist who writes articles on a wide variety of topics for various magazines and newspapers. Your best bet, at least in the beginning, is to produce brochures for small businesses.

As an editor, you will focus your energies on making sure everything that you see goes back out to a publisher totally free of mistakes—including grammatical errors, spelling and punctuation mistakes, and even poor sentence flow. Your job is to ensure that all the words on the page make sense and have a certain rhythm to them, so that the reader is carried along through the book logically and concisely, You may end up editing thousands of projects, from annual reports to menus to book-length manuscripts.

As a freelance illustrator, you will market your work to various publishing houses, ultimately in search of a regular contract with at least one. If you do secure a contract, you may design and produce book covers as well as any artwork to go into the book itself. This area of expertise is particularly lucrative for those who can produce lively, entertaining illustrations for children's books. If you should decide to stay unaffiliated with a large publishing house, your projects will always be varied and you'll have the challenge of getting to know what each of your client companies wants—over and over again. Many illustrators adore that challenge.

Start-Up:

You'll be spending a lot of time in your office, so whether you plan to meet clients there or not, you'll need to make it an effective work space. The high-end computer equipment needed to produce professional results is costly, averaging $2,000-$5,000. Your hourly rates should cover all of your overhead, so price yourself competitively in the $75-$150 per hour range.

Bottom Line Advice:

You can indulge your love of words and graphics to the max in this field. You will be learning something new with each project, and you will have the satisfaction of seeing everything you produce be published (unlike poets and novelists). Working to support your client businesses can result in a satisfying partnership. However, pricing your services can be very difficult. Nonwriters often do not appreciate the time and effort that goes into producing an effective piece of writing, and there are many writers out there in the marketplace who are likely to undercut you. You'll have to spend long hours staring at your blank computer monitor and then actually completing the projects you have fought so hard to get. Deadlines are always too short, and sometimes it can be difficult to obtain the background information needed from a client. Freelance writers have earned the circles under their eyes the hard way.

ADVICE FROM THE EXPERTS

What sets your business apart from others like it?

Ruth Dean, owner of The Writing Toolbox in Akron, Ohio, says her business is unique because she listens well and helps clients clarify their ideas and plans. She specializes in technical marketing communications and gets her best results by writing to appeal to the client's intended audience, not just to the client.

Things you couldn't do without:

"The fax is essential. Clients want instant communication." A computer and laser printer would also be necessities.

Marketing tips/advice:

Dean markets by networking. "I just ask clients about their business and listen. That's all it takes. It's important to have writing samples available in simple 'packages' so that clients who are not accustomed to working with writers can figure out how to hire you."

If you had to do it all over again . . .

"I wouldn't have waited so long to go out on my own."

FUND-RAISING FIRM

Start-up cost:	$2,000-$5,000
Potential earnings:	$25,000-$35,000
Typical fees:	Some fund-raisers charge a flat fee (varied) while others are paid about 20 percent of the total funds they raise
Advertising:	Direct solicitation, networking, referrals
Qualifications:	People skills, selling ability, excellent writing ability
Equipment needed:	Computer, printer, office suite software, fax/modem, office furniture, business cards, letterhead, envelopes
Home business potential:	Yes
Staff required:	No
Handicapped opportunity:	Yes
Hidden costs:	On-line time, telephone charges

LOWDOWN:

You need to able to make the general public see the worthiness of the causes for which you are raising funds. This process has similarities to marketing any intangible product. Fund-raisers know a lot about the organizations they support and they believe in the importance of their missions. The other side of the equation is friendliness. You need to be someone that people like, respect, and feel comfortable with. They are effectively taking your word about the charity you are working for, so your word needs to be very convincing. A range of public and private organizations survive on fund-raising, so once you can demonstrate success, you will have a large market for your services.

START-UP:

Equipping your office is the main expense here, and you can add elements over time, once your telephone is installed. If you don't already have a computer, expect to spend at least $2,000 on one. Your earnings will largely depend on what kinds of funds you're able to bring in—not an easy way to earn a living, but profitable for the most tenacious.

BOTTOM LINE ADVICE:

Fund-raising is done by charities and service organizations of all types, and even government-funded groups need to supplement their annual budget with funds gathered from donations. If you can help bring in donations, you can take this business wherever you want it to go. Unfortunately, a lot of other people have had the same idea, and some of them have been so dishonest as to cast the whole profession in a very bad light. Separating yourself from the sleaze will be an ongoing task for you. Expect a lot of hang-ups from cold calls, too.

GOVERNMENT CONTRACT CONSULTING

Start-up cost:	$3,000-$6,000
Potential earnings:	$40,000-$65,000
Typical fees:	$50-$150 per hour or a flat rate of $175+
Advertising:	Trade journals, association memberships, direct mail, networking, referrals
Qualifications:	Experience in obtaining government contracts, contacts in Washington, writing skills
Equipment needed:	Computer, suite software, fax/modem, copier, printer, mobile phone, office furniture, business cards, letterhead, envelopes
Home business potential:	Yes
Staff required:	No
Handicapped opportunity:	Yes
Hidden costs:	On-line time, telephone bills

LOWDOWN:

As companies downsize, they no longer employ people who can thread their way through the complex world of government contracts. Yet these contracts can be a source of business growth to many companies. Your clients should not be ignored on the basis that the requirements seem too difficult. Instead, you will guide these organizations into the land of business opportunity that government contracts represent. Your experience with the special language that government agencies use (and the number of pieces of red tape involved in each transaction) plus your contacts in different departments and agencies will help you help your clients in doing business with the government. This is a specialized field, but it can be a very rewarding one. Often success in gaining one contract will smooth the path for future work. If you can produce the contracts, you have a very large potential market of companies that would love to have your services.

START-UP:

Equipping your office is the main expense; expect to spend at least $3,000-$6,000. But, considering that some government contract consultants charge as much as $150 per hour for their valued service, your expenses will be minimal in relation to your earnings.

BOTTOM LINE ADVICE:

This is an insider business, so you'll need to sell yourself as an insider if you aren't one already. Don't worry—as you begin to achieve success, you will become more of a real insider. The other factor here is a good business sense. What approach to obtaining a government contract would be most appropriate for each of your clients? How can you guide a specific business organization through the process? You are doing a lot of good for your clients each time you are successful, and that should make up for the frequent need to work under time pressure.

GRANTS/PROPOSAL WRITER

Start-up cost:	$1,000-$2,000
Potential Earnings:	$45,000-$100,000
Typical fees:	$500+ per project or an hourly rate of $25 or more
Advertising:	Networking, direct mail, word of mouth
Qualifications:	Knowledge of the regulations governing formal proposals, knowledge of technology and industry, ability to write clearly and logically
Equipment needed:	Computer, office suite software, laser printer, fax, modem, office furniture, business cards, letterhead, envelopes
Home business potential:	Yes
Staff required:	No
Handicapped opportunity:	Yes
Hidden costs:	Printing and publishing documents

LOWDOWN:

Organizations that want to do business with the federal or state government, cities, counties, and special districts often must respond in writing to a request for proposal (RFP). Writing an effective proposal is a highly skilled activity, and often businesses must contract out the work. A related activity is grant writing, which helps a charitable organization establish its relationship to a foundation. In either case, the piece of writing must conform to the specifications in the RFP, outlining the methods to be used, the needs to be met, and the financial background and expected outcomes of the project.

Some proposal writers are generalists, while others focus on one field, such as education or health care administration. The emphasis, though, is on good writing skills applicable to any field—clear organization, logical exposition, and excellent grammar. Aptitude with numerical data in graphs and spreadsheets is required; business communication savvy is necessary to work with the client's group of employees who are planning the bid or funding request.

START-UP:

You will need to be able to produce professional-looking documents that may include graphs, charts, and tabular data. Buy a computer system with high-resolution and graphics capabilities (around $2,000-$3,000). Your physical office needs to function well as this is a desk-intensive job (buy a comfortable chair, around $200). You can bill hourly ($25-$50 per hour) or on a per-job basis ($500 and up).

BOTTOM LINE ADVICE:

A skilled grant and proposal writer provides the essential link between the client and the funding, whether it is a grant for a nonprofit organization or a contract for a business. It's challenging work that involves constant learning and creative solutions. It can take a long time to gain enough experience and contacts to be effective. Pricing is always a challenge unless you can negotiate an unlimited hourly rate.

HERB/FLOWERS FARMING

Start-up cost:	$1,000-$5,000
Potential earnings:	$10,000-$80,000 per year
Typical fees:	Usually between $5-$125 (from single item to large arrangement)
Advertising:	Ads in catalogs; signage in groceries and other stores
Qualifications:	Knowledge of plant growing, fertilizers, etc.; marketing/bookkeeping skills
Equipment needed:	Land, fertilizers, seeds, pots, supplies; optional: greenhouse, vehicle, computer, and office equipment
Home business potential:	Yes (but may outgrow your available land)
Staff required:	None at first
Handicapped opportunity:	Possibly
Hidden costs:	None

LOWDOWN:

Backyards, basements, or a few small acres is all you need to begin growing herbs. Americans have a good appetite for exotic, unusual, and healthy foods. Restaurants, groceries, and health-food stores are anxious to stock such products. Farmers' markets have grown increasingly popular recently, too, and herb growers can charge premium prices for their produce. Potpourri, dried flowers, and produce grown without the use of pesticides are also "hot" items to consider. Such a business is great if you want to get "back to nature" or stay in a rural area. You can also produce herbs and tropical plants in a greenhouse.

START-UP:

You will probably need a plot of land to grow your products; the amount you need depends on what you are growing, whether you wish to earn a full-time paycheck from your plants, and whether crop rotation is an issue. You will definitely need seeds, fertilizers, plant boxes and pots, hoses, and general gardening supplies, which can cost from $500-$2,000 to start. A greenhouse can cost from $500-$20,000, depending on its size and the materials used. You will need a vehicle to service your accounts, and can probably purchase a used truck for as little as $4,000 (new vans or trucks cost at least $14,000). Business cards and stationery cost about $100-$400; you may also wish to purchase a computer and office furniture (approximately $1,500).

BOTTOM LINE ADVICE:

Herb farming offers you many choices of products in which to specialize. You have the freedom of working close to the earth while still remaining close to cities. In addition, you can meet many others who have similar interests through the marketing of your goods. However, your livelihood is vulnerable to the weather and the seasons. You may also face stiff competition because of the current popularity of certain "trendy" herbs and flowers. Land near cities can be expensive, which can shrink your profit margin. Keep in mind, too, that growing any kind of crop is hard, dirty, physically demanding work.

IMAGE CONSULTANT

Start-up cost:	$1,500-$5,000 (depending on equipment choices)
Potential earnings:	$20,000-$50,000
Typical fees:	$50-$200 per session
Advertising:	Classified advertising or ads in women's or business newspapers, bulletin boards, coupon books, direct mail
Qualifications:	None except to be a good example yourself
Equipment needed:	You may wish to use a computerized video system to demonstrate what your suggestions will look like on your client
Home business potential:	Yes
Staff required:	No
Handicapped opportunity:	Yes
Hidden costs:	Mileage costs

LOWDOWN:

How many times have you seen a misguided soul wearing colors that should only be on a flag—or makeup that dates back to Cleopatra? Did you have the guts to pull that person aside and offer suggestions on self-improvement? Probably not. Yet that is exactly what image consultants are paid to do. Particularly in the business world, people are concerned about the way they come across—and your most frequent clients are likely to be those embarking on career changes or job searches, recent college graduates, and brides. Your mission: to help them make a more positive impact on others through look and attitude. In some respects, you will be like the mother who tells it like it is: "You should wear cool blues instead of muddy browns, which make your face appear yellowish." If you are fashion-minded and have an impeccable sense of balance and color, you are likely to find clients nearly anywhere.

START-UP:

If you're just starting out, you really needn't invest in much more than mirrors, color swatches, and makeup samples. Once you become a little more established, however, you might add on innovative pieces of equipment such as a computerized video system that "morphs" changes on a picture of your client. A good place to set up shop in a heavy-traffic area would be a mall kiosk (carts can be rented for $300-$500 per week, but the attention might be worth it). Also, wouldn't it be interesting to form a cooperative marketing venture with a related (but noncompeting) business, such as a hairstylist or resume service? You could each offer discounts for the other's service as an incentive for clients to buy your own.

BOTTOM LINE ADVICE:

It is fun to play "dress-up" with people who are in the mood for a change, but keep in mind that these people are probably going through some emotional changes that prompted them into action. Be careful, then, of hurting their feelings . . . criticism is easier to take if it sounds encouraging rather than critical.

ADVICE FROM THE EXPERTS

What sets your business apart from others like it?

Janet Neyrinck, Image Consultant and Certified Color Analyst in Akron, Ohio, says her business is set apart by the fact that it offers many services. "We're not just trying to sell makeup; our goal is to create a total harmonious image, including everything from dress and makeup to hair color. We believe in 'personality' dressing."

Things you couldn't do without:

"I need to have my makeup kit and, most important, my fabrics (for color draping). These are the basis of everything I do."

Marketing tips/advice:

"Be out there, be everywhere you can and introduce yourself. Also, be prepared to do a lot of research before buying your equipment."

If you had to do it all over again . . .

"I think that before I'd commit to one method or company's approach to image consulting, I would investigate all of the options out there. I would check the Directory of Image Consultants and ask others what's worked for them."

INTERIOR DESIGNER

Start-up cost:	$3,000-$5,000
Potential earnings:	$30,000-$50,000
Typical fees:	$50 per hour or a flat, per-job rate
Advertising:	Yellow Pages, newspapers, networking with builders/contractors
Qualifications:	Some states require certification; you should be a member of at least one professional association related to this field
Equipment needed:	Swatches, sample books, catalogs, computer, cellular phone or pager
Home business potential:	Yes
Staff required:	No
Handicapped opportunity:	Possibly
Hidden costs:	Getting set up with distributors and manufacturer's reps can run your phone bills up at first; budget accordingly

LOWDOWN:

As more people buy older homes with fix-up potential, there is more work for interior designers who are skilled at filling spaces with dynamic statements about the presence of a room. Do you read *Metropolitan Home* regularly? Are you addicted to the latest home fashions and accessories? If so, you may make a fine interior designer. But the work is more than plaster-deep; you'll need the ability to work with builders and contractors if a room is being redesigned with a specific aesthetic effect in mind. If you apprentice with an interior designer first, you'll gain much more detailed knowledge about the intricacies and nuances of this incredibly subjective business. Personalities are the most difficult aspect of the job—getting others to cooperate and work as a team with a unified vision is probably your biggest challenge. Keeping up with fast-changing trends is another. Still, if you like meeting with people and helping to create the (interior) home of their dreams, you'll enjoy the challenges and learn to overlook the difficulties.

START-UP:

Your start-up costs with an interior design service will be in the $3,000-$5,000 range, primarily to cover your first six months of advertising. You'll need classy business cards and brochures about your service, so set aside $500-$1,000 for these items alone. Set your fees at $50 per hour (or a per-job basis for larger work), and re-evaluate your prices after your first year of business. The more clients with prestige, the higher your prices.

BOTTOM LINE ADVICE:

If you truly like working with people in their most intimate surrounding, this is the job for you. However, expect there to be difficulties such as timing (what if you get too many clients at once?), and clients who request too many changes and wind up costing you money. Learn to set some policies in writing ahead of time to avoid these annoyances; add a surcharge for any work that goes above and beyond your initial agreement.

ADVICE FROM THE EXPERTS

What sets your business apart from others like it?

"I seem to be the remedy person," says Linda Chiera, President of Studio Space Design in Akron, Ohio. "People usually come to me after they've experienced a problem elsewhere . . . I'm working on getting them to think of me first!" Chiera feels that her business is unique in that it provides expert service and assistance with complex projects. "We learn a person's work style and incorporate that into whatever we do for them, whether it be redecorating a home or redesigning their office space."

Things you couldn't do without:

Chiera couldn't do without a computer and CAD system, fax, phone, sample books/resources, tape measure, scale, and business cards.

Marketing tips/advice:

"Get sales training and get out there . . . join networking organizations such as the Chamber of Commerce, and if there's a mentoring program available in your area, enlist in it. Offer yourself as a speaker, advertise wisely (knowing your exact market), and hire seasoned professionals to do the things you can't." Finally, says Chiera, don't be afraid to make mistakes.

If you had to do it all over again . . .

"I would have been wiser about target marketing and advertising. I should have been more careful about selecting the right niche and also should have tried to become more comfortable earlier on about the selling aspect of my job. I'm trained as a designer, and sales and self-promotion have been a bit of a challenge for me until recently."

INTERNET MARKETING SPECIALIST

Start-up cost:	$2,000-$4,000
Potential earnings:	$20,000-$40,000
Typical fees:	Hourly rate of $45+
Advertising:	Bulletin Board Services, direct mail, trade journals, business publications
Qualifications:	Knowledge of marketing, business savvy, awareness of the unwritten rules and limitless possibilities out there on the Internet
Equipment needed:	Computer, modem, printer, fax, office furniture
Home business potential:	Yes
Staff required:	No
Handicapped opportunity:	Yes
Hidden costs:	On-line time, time spent educating client

LOWDOWN:

Marketing is always creative; Internet marketing is even more so. You'll be creating the actual marketing approaches for a variety of different businesses to get the word out on the Internet. So if newness is your bag, then this is your game. Even more than with conventional marketing, you will need to deliver more than you promise, to tell more than you sell, and attract the attention of potential customers rather than push products at them. The Internet is the perfect way to inform people about some products and services, but it is still useless for others. You'll spend enough time developing your own markets, but once you do, expect to earn more of a cutting-edge salary for your toils.

START-UP:

The ability to create effective Internet messages will require increasing levels of computing power (equipment costs $2,000-$4,000). Expect to spend a pretty penny initially for on-line services, because you'll likely end up subscribing to all of them in addition to the Internet. Subscriptions to newsletters and magazines on the computer industry are also essential as resource guides—estimate spending at least $2000 per year to keep up-to-date. You can charge $45 per hour until you feel you're experienced enough to command (and get) $75 per hour; you may decide to accept MC/Visa over the 'Net, so be sure to include in your price the surcharge for such capabilities.

BOTTOM LINE ADVICE:

Experience, good sense, and highly refined marketing skills will make you successful at this new game. You'll need to be persistent in creating your own market before you can begin creating customers for your clients. You'll need a high tolerance for monitor-staring, and you'll need to watch out for the uncharted pitfalls that accompany any cutting-edge activity (such as time spent educating and rewriting).

ADVICE FROM THE EXPERTS

What sets your business apart from others like it?

Tim DiScipio, President of Easton Media Group in Greenwich, Connecticut, says he has a unique niche in the electronic marketplace. "I've got valuable years of experience in this field; something others can't claim in an emerging industry. It's attractive to companies that want someone who's been in the industry for a while and knows their way around."

Things you couldn't do without:

Obviously, DiScipio couldn't do without a 586 computer (he has two), but he also needs a high-speed modem, a two-line telephone, and a fax machine.

Marketing tips/advice:

"If you're going to thrive in this business, you really need to network and expand your contacts regularly. Everyone in this industry has a different, unique niche . . . align yourself with the real players who can help you expand to where you need to be. Stay within your own niche; don't try to be everything to everyone."

If you had to do it all over again . . .

"I would have relinquished the time-consuming business operations duties and focused on my areas of specialty. It would have simplified my problems and allowed me to remain focused."

INTERVIEWER

Start-up cost:	$2,000-$3,000
Potential earnings:	$30,000 and more
Typical fees:	$35 and up
Advertising:	Referrals, trade association memberships, networking
Qualifications:	Master's degree in organizational psychology or related field, experience in human relations with a focus on interviewing, a proven record of effectiveness
Equipment needed:	Business cards, letterhead, envelopes, marketing materials
Home business potential:	Yes
Staff required:	No
Handicapped opportunity:	Yes
Hidden costs:	Ongoing marketing to maintain workflow, membership dues, professional associations

LOWDOWN:

Business organizations are placing more and more importance on selecting the right employees and placing them in the most suitable positions. As organizational structures become flatter and managers must take on a wider range of duties, they have less time to perform the vital interviewing functions that allow them to find and hire appropriate people. As a professional interviewer, you can meet these corporate needs. Your training in interviewing techniques, combined with your background in organizational psychology, enable you to do a far better job of selecting employees than can be achieved by a busy executive with no training. You can design a series of questions related to the company's mission and the job functions of the position that will allow a meaningful comparison to be made among the candidates interviewed. You will need to be able to show that you can save the company money by reducing turnover and increasing employee effectiveness.

START-UP:

You will be meeting clients and performing the interviews at their client locations, so your own setup need not be too expensive (about $2,000). In the beginning, about $30,000 can be achieved.

BOTTOM LINE ADVICE:

Selling this service will be a challenge—not that almost every business couldn't benefit from working with a professional interviewer, but the service is a new idea. Many business people also seem to assume (in spite of all evidence to the contrary) that they can "take someone's measure" quickly and make the right judgment just by instinct. Getting your message out about the value of a more scientific and systematic approach will take determined marketing. Ideally, you will eventually build a client base that offers ongoing opportunities and a steady income flow.

INVENTION CONSULTANT/BROKER

Start-up cost:	$1,500-$3,000
Potential earnings:	$30,000-$50,000+
Typical fees:	Upfront fee of $500-$1,500 plus percentage of invention's final sale price (usually 15 to 20 percent)
Advertising:	Yellow Pages, business/trade publications, direct mail to inventors' associations or on-line services
Qualifications:	Degree or extensive background in product development
Equipment needed:	Computer, phone, fax, modem
Home business potential:	Yes
Staff required:	No
Handicapped opportunity:	Yes
Hidden costs:	On-line service connect time can get costly; if you wind up with a Web site, it will cost extra to maintain it regularly

LOWDOWN:

Where would we be without inventors? Without Edison, there would be no street-lights; without Thomas Jefferson, there would be no dumbwaiter. You can take an up-front fee plus a percentage of each invention if you are the consultant or broker who helps bring it to the marketplace. The area most ripe for invention is in personal services (a massaging chair is but one great idea an inventor came up with); think of the things people buy and why they buy them. Usually, consumers want something unique—a product that does something no other product on the market does. Your challenge is to be able to spot such potential moneymakers a mile away—and the only way to do that is to stay in constant touch with inventors' associations and museums (such as the National Inventors Hall of Fame in Akron, Ohio). You'll need to, at some point, get on the Internet and advertise your services there; so many inventors live overseas and want to sell products or ideas to the United States. The hardest part of your job will be finding a suitable outlet for each invention—but your sales ability should be able to handle that quite nicely, right?

START-UP:

Your start-up will consist of a basic office setup (computer, printer, fax/modem, phone, and sales-tracking software package); you'll spend $1,500-$3,000 total for these items. Considering the double-faceted nature of your earning potential (up-front fee plus percentage), you should be making $30,000-$50,000 once you get established in your field.

BOTTOM LINE ADVICE:

You're on the cutting edge of product development—that's the best part of your chosen profession. The downside is, many inventions never quite make it to market (and that's why it's so essential that you charge an up-front fee to cover your own marketing expenses).

INVESTMENT BROKER/CLUB

Start-up cost:	$1,000-$5,000
Potential earnings:	$25,000-$75,000
Typical fees:	Percentages (usually 5 to 15 percent) or a flat fee for your services ($150-$300) as a broker
Advertising:	Classified ads, business publications, bulletin boards, and (most importantly) networking
Qualifications:	Certification often required; check with local authorities
Equipment needed:	Computer with high-speed modem and on-line services, software programs that can produce financial projections, cellular phone and/or pager, TV with cable (to watch special financial programs), and subscriptions to the best financial newspapers
Home business potential:	Yes
Staff required:	No
Handicapped opportunity:	Yes
Hidden costs:	Your own income may fluctuate like the markets you're selling others on; be sure to plan for ups and downs

LOWDOWN:

Investment clubs are the wave of the financial future, as many baby boomers throw their hats into the world of investments, stocks, and portfolios—words that aren't typically part of their vocabulary. They need to grow into investing, and what better way than with an investment broker or through an investment club. The two are so closely related that, in many cases, the clubs are run by investment brokers as a way of introducing the masses to the idea of building a nest egg for the future based on healthy, expanding markets. As a broker running your own service, you'll be assisting others in the art of speculation—that is, putting up money in the hopes of (but not promise of) making more money. You'll identify some thriving markets for them to get their feet wet in, and tell clients when to stay in and when to get out. You'll be doing lots of hand-holding, because the thought of potentially losing money does tend to frighten folks away from investing until they learn more about it. That's why the investment clubs are such a good idea—they break people in on many of the key concepts and methods of investing without high risk.

START-UP:

You'll need some computer strength to crunch numbers and identify "happening" markets. Expect to spend at least $2,500 on a computer system with modem and on-line capabilities (for the latest up-to-date financial information). Spend another $1,000 or so on advertising. Your earnings could be as little during your first year as $5,000 or as high as $30,000—as with most things, you'll get out of it what you put in. The more clubs you run, the better; if you're qualified to do both clubs and brokering, you can reap the rewards of your own investment—your company—in a short period of time and with little up front cash of your own. If you work hard that first year, you could see a return as high as $30,000. After you're more established and have several clubs running simultaneously, you could earn as much as $75,000.

BOTTOM LINE ADVICE:

If highs and lows don't frighten you, go for it! You're a financial wizard, you're in touch with both the markets and your clients on a moment-to-moment basis . . . now all you have to do is make money for your clients. Once you do that, referrals should be no problem.

Lease vs. Buy Decisions

If your start-up venture requires a lot of equipment purchases, you would do well to look into a "lease-option to buy" program that allows you to pay as you go. Why is this scenario more desirable than an outright purchase? Two reasons.

First, a lease allows you the flexibility of using equipment without long-term commitment to it. If, for some reason, your business goes under, you can usually negotiate your way out of a lease—and you're not faced with the prospect of having to find a buyer for your used equipment.

Second, your cash flow isn't tied up in equipment expenses—freeing you up to invest your capital in other, more immediate return areas (such as advertising).

Most leases run thirty-six to sixty months, but you can often negotiate your terms in addition to your rates. Since leasing is a very competitive field, your chances of finding a deal that is suitable to your needs is quite high.

JEWELRY/CLOCK/WATCH REPAIR

Start-up cost:	$1,000-$5,000 (more if you need a storefront)
Potential earnings:	$1,800 per month for jewelry; $1,500-$3,000 per month for watches/clocks
Typical fees:	Depends on the jewelry/clock/watch and what is being repaired (can be as low as $5 and as high as several hundred)
Advertising:	Jewelry trade shows, craft and antique fairs, newspapers, jewelry retailers, Yellow Pages
Qualifications:	Gemological Institute of America (GIA) certificate is helpful but not required, knowledge of jewelry and clocks
Equipment needed:	Vices, pliers, jeweler's loop, magnifying glass, jeweler's tools
Home business potential:	Yes
Staff required:	No
Handicapped opportunity:	Yes
Hidden costs:	Replacement stones, parts

LOWDOWN:

Nothing takes a licking and keeps on ticking forever—even the best watches, clocks, and pieces of jewelry need to be repaired every once in a while. You should have steady hands and good eyesight to do this trade well. You'll need to be exceptionally skilled at detailed work, and enjoy the solitude of working alone with a strong light and a magnifier. Your customers will find you through the Yellow Pages primarily, but you can seek out additional customers at jewelry trade shows, craft shows, and antique fairs. It would be helpful, but not absolutely necessary, to have a GIA certificate. Not only will you have studied stones, but you'll be a licensed appraiser as well—and that can bring you extra dollars.

START-UP:

Your basement would make the perfect work area for your repair shop (about $500 to start). Most of your expenses will be in advertising. Depending on whether you want to specialize in jewelry or watch repair, you could make $20,000-$35,000.

BOTTOM LINE ADVICE:

Here's a chance to work with fine jewelry, semiprecious/precious stones, and valuable watches or clocks worth hundreds of dollars. Some jewelry repair shops have given the business a bad name by using deceptive practices, but register yourself with the Better Business Bureau and be honest and you should overcome the general public's distrust.

LABOR RELATIONS CONSULTANT

Start-up cost:	$2,000-$4,000
Potential earnings:	$50,000 and up
Typical fees:	$35-$50 per hour
Advertising:	Referrals, memberships in professional associations and trade groups, advertisements in business publications, direct mail
Qualifications:	Degree in related field, extensive experience in labor relations for a well-respected corporation, ability to gain the confidence of potential clients
Equipment needed:	Office furniture, computer, modem, fax, printer, business cards, letterhead, envelopes
Home business potential:	Yes
Staff required:	No
Handicapped opportunity:	No
Hidden costs:	Errors and omissions insurance, utility bills, travel expenses

LOWDOWN:

This is a field for a few outstanding individuals who can show that their expertise in labor relations is applicable to an organization's specific labor challenges. Many companies still operate in a mode of opposition and suspicion between management and employees. Dangers of this approach include unionization, reduced productivity, and an inability to focus as a team on achieving the organization's goals. You will need to reach the top executives of organizations with these or other labor problems and convince them of your ability to bring the two sides together and forge better working relationships. Successful projects will launch your enterprise forward.

START-UP:

Keeping yourself available to your clients is central. Having an impressive office is not, as you will be working at your clients' premises (around $2,000 to start). Earnings of $50,000 could be achieved after the first year.

BOTTOM LINE ADVICE:

Setting up a business as a labor relations consultant is not for the faint of heart. You will need boundless self-confidence, an ability to work with angry people to achieve compromise, and excellent teaching skills. Essentially, you will be teaching groups of people how to pull together, and in the same direction, for the mutual good. In this age of teams and employee empowerment there is still a great deal of need for the services you can provide.

LICENSING AGENT

Start-up cost:	$3,000-$6,000
Potential earnings:	$50,000-$100,000
Typical fees:	Percentage of the deal (typically around 15 percent)
Advertising:	Referrals, association memberships, networking
Qualifications:	Salesmanship, outgoing personality, confidence, ability to communicate with the technical people, the business types, and the manufacturing specialists
Equipment needed:	Computer, fax/modem, copier, laser printer, office furniture, business cards, letterhead, envelopes
Home business potential:	Yes
Staff required:	No
Handicapped opportunity:	Yes
Hidden costs:	Insurance, attorney's fees to draw up contracts

LOWDOWN:

The licensing agent acts as a go-between, helping a technology-driven company find a manufacturer for its invention. In addition, you help manufacturers or service companies find organizations that offer the technology they need. The service provided by a licensing agent is often transnational. Possibly you will be finding technology for Chinese companies that cannot develop it locally. Licensing agents usually specialize in one industry—shoe products, electronic products—in which they have developed extensive experience and contacts. This way they already know many people on both sides of the street before they start. Some technical competence in the field is required, but this can be gained through experience. The other important quality for a licensing agent is patience. You may work for a long time on several deals, only one of which pays off.

START-UP:

Equipping your office to produce professional-looking reports and keep in touch with the world is the main start-up cost; expect to spend at least $3,000 on that alone. However, considering that your 15 percent is spread across a wide range of potential projects, your earnings could be as high as $100,000.

BOTTOM LINE ADVICE:

Becoming a licensing agent is an excellent way for a newly laid-off person to use his/her contacts. It can be a welcome alternative to simply struggling to get the same job with a competitor. If you've got the sales skills, the contacts, and the ability to communicate with the "techie" dreamers as easily as the hard-nosed business types, you can build a successful enterprise. Keep in mind that you will be paid a percentage of the final deal. This can take a long time to bear fruit, and it is essential to have the agreement in writing from the start. There tend to be a lot of disputes if that percentage turns into big money.

LIQUIDATOR

Start-up cost:	$2,000-$6,000
Potential earnings:	$20,000-$60,000
Typical fees:	Percentage of sales
Advertising:	Trade publications, memberships in business organizations, direct mail, classifieds, networking, referrals
Qualifications:	Extensive experience in the field
Equipment needed:	Office furniture, computer, modem, fax, suite software, printer, cellular phone or pager, business cards, letterhead, envelopes, marketing materials
Home business potential:	Yes
Staff required:	No
Handicapped opportunity:	No
Hidden costs:	Storage fees, high utility bills, loss insurance

LOWDOWN:

Liquidators are business people who are fast on their feet, who can see gold where others see only problems, who don't take "no" for an answer. You will be dealing with the merchandise no one else can work with, the odd lots that didn't match, the leftover inventory from bankrupt businesses, and the reclaimed goods ready to be sold after a contract dispute. What sets you apart from a barter service is the plain and simple fact that you are an unloader—getting rid of stuff as quickly as possible without bothering to match your needs to anyone else's. Often, you'll be selling directly to wholesalers or the general public. You need the confidence to assess the possibilities quickly, develop a pricing and sales strategy in difficult circumstances, and persist until the goods have been liquidated. You need excellent connections and the ability to engender trust in difficult situations.

START-UP:

Your office needs to support the intensive marketing by phone that a liquidator practices to find a buyer/seller match. You don't need a walnut desk, but the chair had better be comfortable. And you need to have excellent communications equipment, all of which could get you $20,000 annually.

BOTTOM LINE ADVICE:

You're working hard to provide a necessary service, but you're not usually stepping into a bed of roses with each new customer. You're not going to offer as much as the seller hoped to get for the material, and you're going to sell for as high a price as you can manage—as any other salesperson would also be doing, of course. But none of your transactions will have the mellow, customer-service kind of feeling that can develop in a regular supplier-customer relationship. The excitement of the chase and the need to be on one's toes at all times are pluses for most liquidators, who thrive on the adrenaline. It can be a great way to build a business if that's the environment in which you feel most alive.

LOBBYIST

Start-up cost:	$3,000-$6,000
Potential earnings:	The sky truly is the limit; some lobbyists earn as much as $100,000 or more
Typical fees:	Whatever clients will pay you to further their cause
Advertising:	Networking, word of mouth, and friends in Washington
Qualifications:	People skills, knowledge of your specialty area
Equipment needed:	Computer, fax/modem, printer, mobile phone, pager, business cards, letterhead, envelopes
Home business potential:	Yes
Staff required:	No
Handicapped opportunity:	Not typically
Hidden costs:	Travel expenses, phone bills

LOWDOWN:

It is fashionable to assume that lobbyists somehow cause all the problems we experience with our democratic form of government. The reality is that lobbyists help different groups within the country put forward their views. Without the assistance of lobbyists, many state legislatures would have a difficult time producing effective bills. Even the U. S. Congress draws on the expertise of lobbyists for a range of services related to the preparation of legislation. Lobbyists specialize in a field, or even represent one company alone, and they must have a good ability to develop relationships with the people they hope to communicate with. You'll need to be a good listener and know how to master large amounts of information quickly. Being able to explain issues clearly, with regard to the interests of your listener, will make you an effective representative of your clients. Patience, strong familiarity with the legislative process, persistence, and good humor are the other necessary ingredients in this recipe for lobbyist success.

START-UP:

You'll need to dress the part of someone who deserves to be listened to, so count clothes as a business expense. And you'll need as many means of keeping in touch as you can manage, including cellular phone, pager, and answering service. Spend a maximum of $6,000 on your start-up costs so that you can enjoy the fruits of your labor early in the life of your business—you'll be making the kind of money that will enable you to take a nice vacation once or twice a year.

BOTTOM LINE ADVICE:

If you're effective as a lobbyist, you can write your own ticket. It will take incredible effort to achieve that level of success, though. Getting started is hard, and finding ways to have your clients' messages be heard above the roar is even harder. It's a very stimulating business. You'll be learning all the time, and your studies of human nature will not go unrewarded. Time management is difficult, if not impossible; no nine-to-fivers need apply.

MANUFACTURER'S REPRESENTATIVE

Start-up cost:	$2,500-$9,000
Potential earnings:	Up to $150,000 (gross) in first three years
Typical fees:	Commission basis, usually 5 to 15 percent of product sale (depends on product, level of difficulty in selling it, size of territory, and other factors)
Advertising:	Cold-calling, networking, presentations, reference publications
Qualifications:	Sales experience or expertise in a particular field, good people skills, an ability to negotiate
Equipment needed:	Computer, fax, phone, cellular phone, office furniture, business cards, letterhead
Home business potential:	Yes
Staff required:	No
Handicapped opportunity:	Yes
Hidden costs:	Mileage

LOWDOWN:

Companies are operating with slimmer sales forces these days, creating a need for other alternatives in marketing and selling their products. Independent reps can take on an interesting variety of products to sell—everything from gifts and sporting goods to chemicals, adhesives, and heavy machinery. Many experts recommend that manufacturing agents handle eight to ten lines of goods in order to make a nice profit. In addition to a thorough understanding of your product's features and benefits, you also need a solid customer base for each line and enough money to carry you while you get established, which can take up to a year. Having a background in the product(s) you rep is the easiest way to succeed. Look for opportunities with emerging companies, such as those profiled in entrepreneurial publications and business newspapers. Be sure to include a client list or background sheet on yourself when approaching new companies—they appreciate and often require that level of professionalism.

START-UP:

As mentioned, costs start at approximately $2,500 for computer and office equipment. You may also need a laptop, cellular phone, and modem to use while "on the road;" if so, tack on another $5,000-$6,000. At 5 to 25 percent commission, it could take a while to develop cash flow—but one good sale is all you need to turn into more business.

BOTTOM LINE ADVICE:

Sales can be one of the most lucrative home businesses of all. Meeting and working with people can be very rewarding, as can the freedom of choosing the companies you will represent and setting your own hours. On the downside, repping for a living can mean long periods of travel and, sometimes, a long wait to be paid for your services. Also, sales in some fields will require you to be aggressive and highly competitive to succeed. Can you swim with the sharks—or will you be eaten alive?

MASSAGE THERAPIST

Start-up cost:	$1,000-$5,000
Potential earnings:	$15,000-$35,000
Typical fees:	$45-$60 per hour session
Advertising:	Newspapers, Yellow Pages, bulletin boards, direct mail to corporations
Qualifications:	Must be state-certified (in most states)
Equipment needed:	Massage table, products such as oils and relaxing music
Home business potential:	Yes (but corporate massage therapists work on-site)
Staff required:	None
Handicapped opportunity:	Not likely
Hidden costs:	You may have to carry liability insurance

LOWDOWN:

If you can't keep your hands off of anyone, being a massage therapist could bring you immediate (financial) satisfaction. Seriously, massage therapists are finally entering their own as certified professionals rather than as euphemisms for other, less desirable types of professionals. They must study human anatomy as clinically and carefully as a paramedical professional would, and must have the ability to make people relax enough to enjoy the service itself. With many of us leading increasingly stressful lives, such professionals should be welcome almost anywhere—from health clubs to wellness centers and even metaphysical bookstores. Many massage therapists offer their services to harried executives, and visit them on-site to work out the kinks in their backs and necks. Still others work out of their homes or in small, quiet offices.

START-UP:

If you decide to lease a small office, you can expect to spend at least $350 and up per month on rent alone. Add to that your massage table (about $500) and some relaxing music, soothing oils, and clean towels (allow another $250 or so for these). Finally, you must get the word out via advertising and/or direct mail to individuals or corporate clients, so expect to spend about $500-$1,000 on marketing, too.

BOTTOM LINE ADVICE:

Working in a relaxing atmosphere while helping others relieve stress can be positively exhilarating for you—but it can also be tiring. Are you sure you can stand up to the physical demands of this business—which usually leaves you on your feet most of the day. If the answer is yes to that question, the rest will, like tense muscles, fall back into place.

MEDICAL MANAGEMENT CONSULTANT

Start-up cost:	$3,000-$6,000
Potential earnings:	$30,000-$75,000
Typical fees:	$5,000-$10,000 per contract
Advertising:	Referrals, trade publications, memberships and participation in professional groups, networking, seminars and public speaking
Qualifications:	Academic degree in related field, extensive experience in medical practice development and management
Equipment needed:	Office furniture, computer, suite software, printer, fax, cellular phone, business card, letterhead, envelopes, marketing materials
Home business potential:	Yes
Staff required:	No
Handicapped opportunity:	Yes
Hidden costs:	Research, membership dues, subscriptions, errors and omissions insurance, additional secretarial services

LOWDOWN:

As the health care marketplace becomes more challenging, the demand for professional assistance in setting up or maintaining a medical practice is increasing. Few medical graduates have received adequate training in the business side of providing health care services. In addition, meeting government regulations and managing the complexities of insurance billing require sophisticated office planning and staff training. Medical management consultants offer the services that most physicians require to make a financial success of their practices. You will need a demonstrable record of success, and excellent referrals, to market yourself effectively. In fact, marketing will be an ongoing part of your business life. Knowing how to make a physician's office run well, and being able to persuade a busy doc to engage your services are two completely different skills. Some medical management consultants put together a package to offer to new doctors who are establishing their practices. Other specialize in working with group or multilocation practices.

START-UP:

Most of your client interaction will take place in their offices, so your own workplace can focus on function rather than fanciness at first (around $3,000 to start). Earnings could be $30,000 the first year.

BOTTOM LINE ADVICE:

Physicians are not the easiest people to communicate with; they are always pressed for time, and they receive a blizzard of marketing messages every day. The word has gotten out, however, that each practice needs an excellent business structure, staff, and strategic plan to succeed. You will be helping your clients focus on what they are trained to do—provide patient care—so they can stop wasting their time and money on ineffective management.

MEETING PLANNER

Start-up cost:	$2,500-$6,500
Potential earnings:	$25,000 to start per year; possibly as high as $100,000 per year after you get established
Typical fees:	$40-$60 per hour or $400-$500 per day; planners handling large events such as conventions may get 15 to 20 percent of the overall projected budget for the entire event
Advertising:	Networking with convention and visitors' bureaus, caterers, and travel agents to hear about conferences and conventions, plan a civic or charitable event on a volunteer basis to gain experience, advertise in meeting magazines
Qualifications:	Excellent organizational and negotiation skills; detail-oriented; good business background; good communication and troubleshooting skills
Equipment needed:	Office and computer equipment, fax, telephone, reference books, business cards, stationery, envelopes
Home business potential:	Yes
Staff required:	No
Handicapped opportunity:	Possibly
Hidden costs:	Phone costs could easily run higher than you budget

LOWDOWN:

If you like handling the myriad of details involved in planning formal events and if you have the organization, negotiation, and communication skills necessary to pull it off, you can have a great career as a meeting planner. There are many sources of business, from corporations and associations to conventions and trade shows. As companies become "leaner," employees can no longer be spared to handle meeting planning projects; also, meetings and events are increasingly viewed as great sales and marketing opportunities. Therefore, creative, talented meeting planners are in demand. You will need to be knowledgeable about many areas—everything from hotels to catering to travel. You may need to negotiate a block of hotel rooms, find exotic locales for company meetings, book speakers and entertainers, set up promotions, and handle all the many small and large details that make for a successful event. In return, you may get to travel and stay at exclusive resorts and hotels, you will meet interesting people from many walks of life—and you will have the satisfaction of seeing people enjoying your event.

START-UP:

A computer and modem will cost from $1,000-$3,000. Software, printer, telephone, and fax will add from $900-$3,000 or more. Office equipment, reference books, insurance, letterhead, etc. will bring the total costs to $2,700-$8,500. Fees are typically $40-$50 per hour or $400-$600 per day. To get more assignments from the get-go, you should do a few "free" events to give potential clients a good idea of how spectacular your meetings really are.

BOTTOM LINE ADVICE:

Meeting planning can be very rewarding, but it often requires long days and hard work. If you are good at handling details, you're halfway to success already, because all those little pieces of the puzzle are crucially important. In addition to making sure you have adequate money for your start-up, bear in mind that a meeting planner's livelihood is often tied to economic conditions, since companies may tighten their meeting budgets to cut costs. However, meetings and conventions will always be popular and productive, and the trend toward outsourcing them to professional meeting planners will continue—good news for you!

When to Hire a Consultant or Subcontractor

Your desk is piling up with unpaid bills, tax forms, and work orders. Your time is eaten up in the all-encompassing aspects of running your business entirely by yourself—and the work just keeps rolling in anyway. What can you do?

You could hire a consultant or a subcontractor to pick up the slack, help arrange your office so that it runs neatly and efficiently, or simply to offer you advice in an area where you are weakest. You can bring in such additional help on a short-term, per-project basis, by using the professional one time only or once per month.

But how do you find such a professional, and how do you know if their services are worth their price? If you're looking for an accounting subcontractor, for example, you might start in the Yellow Pages, or contact a local association for accounting professionals (they meet regularly and often have a directory of members).

You could also ask for referrals or recommendations from your own association members, as they have likely had the same needs as you and have probably used the services of a subcontractor at least once before. These folks will tell you everything you need to know about the pros and cons of hiring outside help, but be prepared to hear a lot of horror stories.

One way you can protect yourself against the false claims of a so-called consultant (one who is unethical or who really lacks the skills necessary to help you effectively) is to check them out with the Better Business Bureau as soon as possible. You might also do well to interview more than one possible candidate for the job: often, entrepreneurs get duped into thinking that there is only one real expert on a given topic and end up following bad advice rather than switching "experts."

One final way to protect yourself against harm is to request a list of references or testimonials from the consultant's clients. Ask if you may call any of these folks to provide you with details of how well the consultant worked for another company.

Hiring a consultant or subcontractor can lessen your load as a busy entrepreneur, but it can make your life more complicated if:

- the consultant isn't up front about each fee you'll be charged for the duration of the project

- the workload and estimated hours of the project are off in calculation by several hours or even days

- a "no compete" clause is missing from the contract, leaving your business wide open for exploitation by an unscrupulous subcontractor

- you simply cannot communicate well enough or agree with the consultant on key issues of importance to the project

Take the time to thoroughly check out anyone you plan to work with on short-term (or long-term) projects. You have the right to be sure that the professional has a solid track record and is worth the hourly rate you'll be paying. There's nothing worse than paying lots of money for a job miserably done. Remember, you have the power to keep from being taken advantage of if you spend a few minutes conducting a thorough check.

METEOROLOGICAL CONSULTANT

Start-up cost:	$2,000-$3,000
Potential earnings:	$20,000-$50,000
Typical fees:	$50-$75 per hour
Advertising:	Trade journals, networking, direct mail
Qualifications:	A strong background in meteorology, business awareness
Equipment needed:	Computer, modem, fax, printer, office suite software, office furniture, business cards, letterhead, envelopes
Home business potential:	Yes
Staff required:	No
Handicapped opportunity:	Yes
Hidden costs:	On-line time for research

LOWDOWN:

The weather is extremely important to a vast range of enterprises across the country, from agriculture to resorts to construction. You can develop a business in which you refine the information gathered by weather satellites and prepare a detailed forecast related to the interests of your clients. A high level of meteorological expertise is required, as well as the marketing savvy to match the information you can develop with the needs of a client base. Recent hurricanes and floods have highlighted the effects that extreme weather systems can have on a broad geographic area, but small changes in precipitation and ambient temperature are significant to many businesses as well. Once you develop your client base, you ought to be able to provide regular forecasting on a long-term contract basis.

START-UP:

You will need the computer equipment to receive, interpret, and report the weather data needed by your clients. You can bill an hourly rate of $50-$75, or opt for a flat daily rate ($500+).

BOTTOM LINE ADVICE:

If you have the advanced skills necessary for this business, you won't find a competitor on every corner. A proven track record will bring you referral business. Considerable marketing may be required to achieve the number of clients necessary for an adequate income. Your biggest competitor is the U.S. government, but keep up-to-date on congressional cuts that will allow you an entrée into this field.

MOBILE HAIR SALON

Start-up costs:	$1,000-$5,000
Potential earnings:	$30,000-$50,000
Typical fees:	Depends on the service (haircuts cost a lot less than perms, or hair color, but services can run anywhere from $20-$75)
Advertising:	Local newspapers, direct mail, coupons, contacts with nursing homes and hospitals
Qualifications:	Must be a licensed cosmetologist
Equipment needed:	Scissors, electric trimmers, rollers, combs, brushes, portable hair dryer, blow dryer, curling wands, towels, capes, and supplies (shampoo, etc.)
Home business potential:	Yes (but you'll be mobile, of course)
Staff required:	Yes
Handicapped opportunity:	No
Hidden costs:	Insurance, continuing education, cellular phone

LOWDOWN:

A cosmetologist who makes house calls? Without the overhead of a salon, this could be a lucrative business. However, you will have to come up with your own transportation such as a station wagon or van. Just think of all those who could take advantage of this convenient service—busy executives, stay-at-home moms, shut-ins, nursing home residents, and hospital patients. You'll have to figure in travel time. But if you plan to service a specific area on a set day of each week, you'll reduce time and travel expense. You can work with clients in their natural habitat; that can be very helpful to these clients and they will probably tip you well for your trouble.

START-UP:

Spend between $1,000-$5,000 on getting this show on the road, so to speak. Mainly, you'll be covering your equipment and supply costs (and, as a licensed cosmetologist, you can buy everything wholesale, of course). Charges will vary from $25-$75, but be sure to tack on your mileage in the fee structure.

BOTTOM LINE ADVICE:

You might want to hire a receptionist or answering service to take incoming calls and book appointments.

MONEY BROKER

Start-up cost:	$1,000-$5,000
Potential earnings:	$40,000-$60,000
Typical fees:	Commission/percentage (usually 5 to 15 percent)
Advertising:	Direct mail, classified ads
Qualifications:	Familiarity with financial news reporting, detail orientation, persistence
Equipment needed:	Computer, fax, on-line account, word processing software, printer, business cards, letterhead, envelopes
Home business potential:	Yes
Staff required:	No
Handicapped opportunity:	Yes
Hidden costs:	Printing materials for reports, utility bills, on-line account fees

LOWDOWN:

Tracking down money can be surprisingly challenging and time consuming. Yet many businesses depend on loans, either directly or as part of the buying process. Real estate agencies and automobile dealerships, for example, need up-to-date information on the availability of loans because almost all of their transactions will depend on this source of money. Your service saves countless phone calls and prevents missed opportunities because you gather this information and report it to your client companies. They can then transmit it to their buyers. Loan rates, money rates, exchange rates, and a realm of other financial listings are printed in magazines and newspapers. You will be spending time at the library and on the Internet assessing the data your clients need. You report it to them monthly.

START-UP:

Your clients won't have to see your office, but you'll spend a lot of time there reading, compiling, and writing reports. The computer is changing this type of business, but the wealth of information now available makes your service of gathering and assessing it even more important. Expect to spend $1,000-$5,000 setting up this business. With commissions of 5 to 15 percent, you could make $40,000-$60,000 if you are savvy enough.

BOTTOM LINE ADVICE:

Consider becoming a money broker if the world of finance is not dry, meaningless numbers to you but a fascinating area of shifting relationships and monetary opportunities. You'll need a love of the details to sustain the tedious fact-gathering required here. Financial acumen is reasonably rare, so if you've got it, market it.

MOTIVATIONAL SPEAKER

Start-up cost:	$1,000-$5,000
Potential earnings:	$40,000-$100,000 (depending on the scope and appeal of your message)
Typical fees:	These vary widely according to experience level and your own personal magnetism; individuals will pay $100 and up to hear speeches they feel will change their lives
Advertising:	Newspapers, Yellow Pages, business publications, networking with associations (that always need speakers)
Qualifications:	Excellent presentation skills and communicative ability that truly inspires
Equipment needed:	None really; you'll be renting items from the facilities you speak at
Home business potential:	Yes
Staff required:	No (unless you're selling tapes, books, or other materials)
Handicapped opportunity:	Yes
Hidden costs:	Travel expenses; make sure you cover these in your fee structure

LOWDOWN:

Dale Carnegie did it . . . so did Les Brown, Lee Iacocca, and Anthony Robbins. They spoke to millions of people from all walks of life and business, and inspired them to feel empowerment, to accomplish things they never thought possible, and to win friends and influence people. All got their start speaking to smaller groups, collecting testimonials, and growing their speaking businesses to a national level through related book, tape, and workshop products. Do you feel like awakening the giant within you as a motivational speaker? Do you have a unique spin on how to improve oneself, or ones relationships? If so, your presentation should be top-notch. Study the many programs out there, watch how the other guys do it, then work every day at making your presentation better. Be sure you add value by telling your customers how much you can change their lives for the better—don't just try to sell them on a trendy, yet meaningless topic. Your ability to lift them to greater heights is what will ultimately lift your sales to new heights. Be prepared to travel—and consider marketing your presentation to any one of the larger seminar promotion companies. You might have to give up a piece of your profits, but it could be worth your while if they do all the legwork in rounding up audiences.

START-UP:

Start-up costs are very low for this business, mostly involving $1,000-$5,000 for advertising/promotion. After that, you needn't have anything else except a pager or cellular phone to stay connected to those who need you. As a motivational speaker, you can charge anywhere from $25-$150 per person for a seminar, depending on your experience level and the uniqueness of your message.

BOTTOM LINE ADVICE:

Your business hinges on your ability to stay busy—plan to offer at least one speaking engagement per month to start. Organize your speech well, and videotape it for your own viewing before you throw yourself in front of a crowd. Get opinions from others, iron out the details, and practice, practice, practice!

ADVICE FROM THE EXPERTS

What sets your business apart from others like it?

"Mine is a high-energy presentation that leaves audiences with messages that they can use in everyday living," says Barbara Greavu, owner of Something Else & More in Canton, Ohio. "I present them with things they can remember in a humorous format that's easily understood."

Things you couldn't do without:

"I'm finally buying a fax machine. I have believed for the longest time that, if you have a passion for what you do, you don't really need much technology."

Marketing tips/advice:

"Read, read, read—anything and everything that's pertinent to your speaking business. You don't have a tangible product with this kind of work, so speak to other speakers to get the ins and outs of the business."

If you had to do it all over again . . .

Greavu wishes she had spent more time networking with other speaking professionals. "I would have researched better in the beginning, and I would have made a greater effort to talk with others in the business. They would have warned me or given me a better sense of direction, I'm sure."

MOVER

Start-up cost:	$1,500-$3,000
Potential earnings:	$20,000 and up
Typical fees:	$35 or more
Advertising:	Classified ads, radio spots, direct mail, flyers, community bulletin boards, referrals
Qualifications:	Physical strength, experience
Equipment needed:	Truck, pads, straps, packing materials
Home business potential:	Yes
Staff required:	Yes
Handicapped opportunity:	No
Hidden costs:	Insurance, truck maintenance

LOWDOWN:

To set up a successful small business as a mover, you will need to carve out a niche for yourself. What can you specialize in? What type of moving service is not readily available in your community? The companies that provide enormous vans to move households across the continent are too expensive for a move within the same community, and they are too hard to schedule. Small household moves are an underserved market, and meeting these needs in a flexible, cost-effective way could allow you to fulfill your entrepreneurial ambitions and use your knowledge of how to get heavy stuff from here to there, down and up the stairs. Other local movers specialize in commercial moving: relocating businesses, office expansions, etc.

START-UP:

The truck is the major expense, and locating a reliable staff will also cost you (you could start out for as little as $1,500 if you rent a truck). Your physical endurance will determine your earnings, but you should make at least $20,000.

BOTTOM LINE ADVICE:

Your market may well be people who originally plan to do their moves themselves, and realize at the last moment that the task is too big. You will need to position your business so that these frustrated, desperate people can find you easily and realize that the cost of your service is far outweighed by the value they will receive: less breakage, no backaches, a faster completion of the move process, and so on. You will need to inspire confidence in your customers so that they trust you with their valuables. That way, they will recommend you to others, and word of mouth will eventually carry your business.

MURDER MYSTERY PRODUCER

Start-up cost:	$1,000-$5,000
Potential earnings:	$20,000-$40,000
Typical fees:	$25-$50 per person (more if providing overnight accommodations)
Advertising:	Entertainment publications, newspapers, bulletin boards, city magazines, Yellow Pages
Qualifications:	None, but theater experience is helpful
Equipment needed:	Costumes, props
Home business potential:	Not typically
Staff required:	Yes (actors who can convincingly stage a "murder")
Handicapped opportunity:	Possibly
Hidden costs:	Advertising could get expensive

LOWDOWN:

Imagine, if you will, a quaint restaurant in the middle of Ohio. You and your guests are seated at a lavish table, complete with Victorian niceties and delicious food. You don't know all of the people at the table, and this isn't a problem until a dark figure walks into the room and begins arguing with one of your dinner mates. Suddenly, your dining companion is "shot" and "killed"—and you and your remaining companions must now embark upon your own sleuthing in order to solve the "mystery." Sound like fun? It should, because producing such murder mysteries is getting to be quite a popular business —particularly for those with backgrounds in theater. The challenge is staging a convincing enough murder to make solving it compelling for the guests. It's all in fun, and they usually know what's going to happen in advance. However, you'll need to provide them with clues (and don't forget the infamous "red herrings" that will occasionally throw them off the trail). You'll need to constantly come up with innovative twists and thicker plots. Feel up to it?

START-UP:

What good are theatrical events such as murder mysteries without sufficient advertising? Plan to spend about $1,000-$5,000 on this expense alone; then set aside another $1,500-$3,000 for costumes, props, and a good script. Charging $25-$50 a head for these charming little adventures could become profitable in a reasonably short period of time—but remember, you'll have to pay your actors something, too (unless you use university students in need of stage experience).

BOTTOM LINE ADVICE:

There is a huge market out there for murder mystery productions, and it can be done even more cost-effectively if you work out arrangements with large local businesses such as theaters, restaurants, and hotels. Offer them a percentage of the take and you might be off to a more profitable start!

NEWSPAPER DELIVERY SERVICE

Start-up cost:	$1,000-$5,000
Potential earnings:	$10,000 or more
Typical fees:	Usually a flat rate
Advertising:	Cold-calling
Qualifications:	Stick-to-itiveness
Equipment needed:	Van, canvas bags
Home business potential:	Yes
Staff required:	Yes
Handicapped opportunity:	No
Hidden costs:	Maintenance, fuel

LOWDOWN:

You will be providing newspaper delivery on a subcontracting basis within a specific geographic area. With the move toward morning newspapers in many localities, it has become more difficult for newspaper publishers to find reliable delivery people. It is very difficult for the preteenagers who used to fulfill this role to get up way before dawn, deliver papers, and still get through a full day of school. You take over, delivering one or more routes yourself and hiring a crew to complete the rest.

START-UP:

You may need a van to pick up bundles of newspapers or to drop them off at your assistants' routes (could get by with just about $1,000 start-up cost). For a part-time job, $10,000 a year to start is easy money.

BOTTOM LINE ADVICE:

This is another American classic: a job that depends on hard work (and an excellent alarm clock) rather than on education, social position, or good luck. You'll probably need to have others working with you to earn an adequate return on your efforts, and managing others always requires thought and effort. There's no glamour to the job of delivering newspapers, but it's good, honest work, and you'll get plenty of exercise.

OIL AND GAS FIELD SERVICES

Start-up cost:	$2,000-$4,000
Potential earnings:	$30,000-$40,000
Typical fees:	Hourly rate of $150 or daily rate of $500+
Advertising:	Relationships with energy companies, referrals, advertising in trade journals
Qualifications:	Extensive experience, scientific training in geology or related field, good negotiating and people skills
Equipment needed:	Camera, mobile phone
Home business potential:	Yes (not that you will be home much!)
Staff required:	No
Handicapped opportunity:	No
Hidden costs:	Travel, telephone bills

LOWDOWN:

America runs on energy. You can make an excellent living if you have the skills and experience to find new sites where wells should be drilled to capture more of these vital resources. You'll need to be a trained geologist, and you'll need that "sense" which tells you where the black gold lies. Developing the contracts that give drilling rights is the "people" part of this interesting business. You will probably be working in many different areas, each with its own landscape and its own human culture.

START-UP:

You'll need to write up your reports in a professional manner, so basic word-processing equipment might be all you need, along with a mobile phone or pager ($2,000-$3,000). Bill hourly ($150 per) or daily ($500 and up).

BOTTOM LINE ADVICE:

In the past, this field has had its shady practitioners, and the reputation for hoodwinking naive farmers out of their cow pastures tends to linger today. In fact, exploring for oil and gas is essential to everyone's comfortable way of life. You are in charge of your own reputation, and you will slowly build up your name for accuracy and honesty as you work. You may set up a cozy home office, but you won't be spending much time there. So you had better develop an enjoyment for your own company and a knack for making friends with strangers.

ON-LINE JOB SEARCH

Start-up cost:	$3,000-$6,000
Potential earnings:	$25,000-$50,000
Typical fees:	$25 or more per hour
Advertising:	Home page, referrals, electronic and personal networking, Yellow Pages
Qualifications:	Human relations or other job search experience, extensive familiarity with on-line searches, ability to draw people out and help them assess their career goals
Equipment needed:	Computer with sufficient memory for high-speed operation, high-speed modem, on-line accounts, printer, office furniture, suite software, business cards, letterhead, envelopes
Home business potential:	Yes
Staff required:	No
Handicapped opportunity:	Yes
Hidden costs:	On-line account fees, utility fees (especially telephone)

LOWDOWN:

Most people don't realize what practical applications the Internet can have for their lives, even if they have discovered e-mail and the Web Crawler. You can provide a valuable service to job seekers by guiding their path through the many on-line career services available. Preparing a resume that will be effective electronically can be a significant part of your service. The scannable resume, which focuses on the keywords that allow computerized sorting, is quite different from the graphically attractive resume on fancy paper that has until recently been the standard. When you start an on-line job search business, you are serving as the link between your client and a very large but invisible world of potential employers.

START-UP:

Computer speed will cut down on search times and on-line account costs (about $3,000 to start). You'll need comfortable furniture and a monitor that is easy on the eyes to minimize your fatigue. Hopefully you'll make at least $25,000 the first year.

BOTTOM LINE ADVICE:

This is a new field, which can be fun and exciting if you like being on the cutting edge of the business world. It does mean, however, that your marketing efforts will be intensive and will have to contain a large element of education. The people who can use your help the most are exactly the ones who won't immediately understand what an on-line job search can do for them. Keep careful track of your successes to support your later marketing and sales claims.

ON-LINE SERVICES CONSULTANT

Start-up cost:	$4,000-$6,000
Potential earnings:	$10,000-$30,000
Typical fees:	Hourly $50-$75, or per job $150 plus
Advertising:	Bulletin Board Services, flyers, publications, word of mouth
Qualifications:	Technical knowledge of hardware and software, good written communications skills, self-marketing ability
Equipment needed:	PC with high-speed modems; at least five phone lines
Home business potential:	Yes
Staff required:	No
Handicapped opportunity:	Yes
Hidden costs:	On-line time

LOWDOWN:

As an on-line consultant, you will assist those in need of specific pieces of information or directions to a BBS or other on-line service. You will trouble-shoot for them, providing help in areas where the user is not as knowledgeable. Charges may be for the service received (employer/job searcher) or the knowledge gained (ability to use a certain piece of software). Some on-line consultants charge a flat monthly fee (average: $8-$10 per month); others have a low fee and add-on charges for time above a certain amount per month. You may need to send invoices or to obtain credit card capability to receive payments. The easiest way to be certain you're paid for your services is to obtain credit card information early in the process.

START-UP:

Your initial investment is relatively high, since this is a very technology-dependent business. A computer, high-speed modem, and five phone lines—so that you can have many different on-line services running simultaneously—are the minimum equipment necessary to begin. Of course, if you are very familiar with on-line and bulletin board services, you will likely have a good start on your equipment already.

BOTTOM LINE ADVICE:

Electronic links between individuals have added a new dimension to life in the '90s. You can take your enjoyment of this new way of communicating and make it into a business. Once you have found a niche, a group of potential subscribers with a strong interest in a topic and an enthusiasm for learning more, you can use your electronic communications skills to guide them on their way. BBS subscribers often expect immediate, or at least rapid, responses from their sysop (system operator), so you will need to be available several hours each day. And developing a method of charging that is competitive while bringing in enough income can be difficult.

PARALEGAL

Start-up cost:	$3,000-$6,000
Potential earnings:	$45,000-$65,000
Typical fees:	$40-$65 per hour
Advertising:	Yellow Pages, local business periodicals, direct mail, association memberships
Qualifications:	Degree in field, experience, proven track record, excellent organizational skills, service orientation
Equipment needed:	Fully equipped office with computer, suite software, laser printer, fax/modem, copier, office furniture, business cards, letterhead, envelopes
Home business potential:	Yes
Staff required:	No
Handicapped opportunity:	Yes
Hidden costs:	Office supplies, software upgrades

LOWDOWN:

More and more lawyers are setting up small firms or even starting single-shingle practices. Meanwhile, the cost of their support services is skyrocketing. Independent paralegal businesses can find a niche in this market by offering to complete many of the routine legal tasks that must be done but drain lawyers' time and energy. In other words, your paralegal service will be providing the services that large firms and corporate law departments have staff to perform. Having an effective paralegal company as a resource means that a small law firm can provide service to its clients for much less cost than it would have to charge if all the tasks were performed by a lawyer. This can be a vital marketing approach now that legal bills are being scrutinized closely and clients are striving to reduce fees.

START-UP:

It will be quite expensive to set up the required computer equipment ($3,000-$5,000). You may discover that much of your work is completed on your clients' premises, or you may prepare a considerable amount of the paperwork at your own office. Charge $40-$65 per hour for your services (keeping in mind that many attorneys in small firms work for $100 per hour).

BOTTOM LINE ADVICE:

There seem to be more lawyers now than there are legal positions open, but the opportunities for paralegal work are increasing. You will need to offer excellent service, complete tasks correctly, ask good questions about the areas that are unclear, and deal with the time crunches that always seem to go hand-in-hand with the practice of law. Once the lawyers in your community come to see you as the solution to some of their problems, you will have a successful enterprise.

PARENTING SPECIALIST

Start-up cost:	$1,000-$5,000
Potential earnings:	$5,000-$50,000+
Typical fees:	$30-$50 per hour
Advertising:	Nursery schools, play groups, day care centers, YMCA, hospitals, bulletin boards
Qualifications:	Being a parent yourself helps
Equipment needed:	Good resource materials, i.e., books, magazines, tapes, etc.
Home business potential:	Yes
Staff required:	No
Handicapped opportunity:	Yes
Hidden costs:	Travel expenses

LOWDOWN:

There was a time in our society when everything was passed down from generation to generation, particularly parenting advice. But in today's high-tech, dual-income families (who are often also 3,000 miles away from relatives), there doesn't seem to be as much time for history, or even for moms and dads to teach their daughters and sons how to be parents. Some new parents actually need to be taught how to be parents. Your job as a parenting specialist will be to ease their "parent-anoia." With the patience of a saint you will go into their home and teach the bewildered parents everything from changing a diaper to handling a tantrum in public and planning a birthday party for a two-year-old. Marketing yourself will be easy in big metropolitan cities, but don't overlook the possibility that your services may be needed in the suburbs and rural areas, too.

START-UP:

Your biggest expense will be in marketing yourself and keeping a library of up-to-date reference material on hand to help in unique situations. Since your start-up cost will be relatively low (under $5,000), in large cities you could earn an easy $45,000 in one year.

BOTTOM LINE ADVICE:

You really need to love children of all ages to be in this business, and you have to be an excellent example for the parents to follow. When you watch a frazzled parent turn into a calm, loving, caring parent, this job can really be rewarding. On the downside, even though you're not Dr. Spock, you'll be looked upon as such and you should expect to be on call 24 hours a day, seven days a week. We all know that time is relative to babies and children—they often pick undesirable hours to have problems.

Payroll Administrative Services

Start-up cost:	$3,000-$6,000
Potential earnings:	$40,000-$60,000
Typical fees:	$25-$40 per hour
Advertising:	Trade publications, direct mail, networking, memberships in community and business groups
Qualifications:	Bookkeeping skills, expertise in payroll technicalities, taxes
Equipment needed:	Office furniture, computer, suite software, fax, modem, printer, business cards, letterhead, envelopes
Home business potential:	Yes
Staff required:	No
Handicapped opportunity:	Yes
Hidden costs:	Errors and omissions insurance, software upgrades

Lowdown:

Supposedly the new accounting software packages make payroll easier for small business owners to manage. In reality, the drain on time and energy in setting the system in place is far more than the cost of having you take over this hated chore. You'll need to gain the confidence of business owners, which can be quite challenging, but once you do, you will have ongoing, regular business. As long as federal, state, and local governments keep making the rules and regulations more complicated, you will have plenty of opportunity to make a positive difference in your customers' lives. You'll need to be completely accurate and totally reliable. This is a business for the detail-oriented, careful person who just loves to see all the columns add up neatly.

Start-up:

Your office/computer setup needs to support the accounting/bookkeeping nature of this work (usually $3,000 to start). An annual income of $40,000 can be reached.

Bottom Line Advice:

Feelings seem to run high over payroll issues. Secrecy, accuracy, and just getting all the information you need to do your part all pose challenges. But the complexity of the task works to your advantage. Doing an excellent job may bring you referrals as well.

PERSONALITY ANALYSIS/
TESTING SERVICE

Start-up cost:	$1,000-$5,000
Potential earnings:	$35,000-$50,000
Typical fees:	$125-$300 per test
Advertising:	Direct mail, human resource publications, networking with executives
Qualifications:	Background in psychology would be helpful (but may not be necessary)
Equipment needed:	Computer, standardized tests, a system for recording results
Home business potential:	Yes
Staff required:	No (unless you grow quickly or have several corporate clients)
Handicapped opportunity:	Yes
Hidden costs:	Telephone bills will be high due to long-distance interviewing for corporate clients; keep accurate records and hold your terms at 30 days

LOWDOWN:

With the alarming rate of disgruntled employees suddenly opening fire on their former bosses and colleagues, it's no wonder that there are a growing number of businesses aimed at security and preventive methods. One of the best ways a company can protect itself is to hire a personality analyst to interview all current and prospective employees, determining their personality types (using a standard psychological test such as the Briggs-Meyers) and identifying their potential hot spots. You'll spend at least three hours with each individual, either on the phone or in person, and you may decide to hire on additional staff to cover several interviews at once.

START-UP:

Most of your initial investment will cover the cost of resource materials (and there may be a licensing fee involved for some of the tests you'll use). Aside from that, you may need to rent office space (from $350 a month) and place ads in professional publications (average cost: $500) to reach key management and human resource professionals in need of your services.

BOTTOM LINE ADVICE:

You will enjoy the diversity of the people you interview, particularly if you have a background or interest in psychology or sociology. But the work itself is very repetitive, and could prove tedious. Also, making sure you always have more details than seemingly necessary to protect yourself from potential lawsuits later—after all, not everyone likes to be hired (or fired) on the basis of one professional opinion!

PERSONALIZED CHECK SERVICE

Start-up cost:	$3,000-$5,000
Potential earnings:	$15,000 or more
Typical fees:	Generally $15-$30 per set of 250 checks
Advertising:	Yellow Pages, local interest periodicals, programs for community fund-raisers, word of mouth, referrals, home parties
Qualifications:	Printing knowledge and experience
Equipment needed:	Check printing equipment (unless subcontracting)
Home business potential:	No
Staff required:	No
Handicapped opportunity:	No
Hidden costs:	Materials, maintenance, equipment replacement

LOWDOWN:

People aren't satisfied with the plain old yellow checks from the bank. And they don't want to pay the higher prices that banks charge for the limited selection of more interesting check designs they offer. Your business helps your customers express themselves, make a statement, or even create a marketing image for their own businesses through the medium of their checks. The personalized checks that you create for them offer one more way to establish spark in the day-to-day routine of exchanging money (in the form of checks) for goods and services. Part of the business could be creating checks as fund-raising tools for nonprofits, colleges, etc.

START-UP:

Equipping your new business will not be inexpensive. And you will need good relations with your supplier of designer check materials to keep your variety up and your costs down (could get by on about $3,000 to start, for advertising your services heavily in a few choice markets). Part-time work alone could net you $15,000 annually.

BOTTOM LINE ADVICE:

Many of your potential customers will be unaware that they have a choice in suppliers of checks. Once the message gets out about the range of choices you offer, and your competitive prices, you will have an excellent opportunity to develop a successful business. Keep up your good relationship with your materials distributor, and maintain excellent quality during the printing process.

PERSONNEL SAFETY CONSULTANT

Start-up cost:	$3,000-$6,000
Potential earnings:	$30,000 and up
Typical fees:	$35 per hour
Advertising:	Business publications, membership in business and trade groups, referrals, networking
Qualifications:	Degree in organizational psychology or related field, experience in corporate security or industrial hygiene, proven track record, ability to market and sell your own services
Equipment needed:	Office furniture, computer, modem, fax, laser printer, suite software, business cards, letterhead, envelopes, marketing materials
Home business potential:	Yes
Staff required:	No
Handicapped opportunity:	No
Hidden costs:	Travel, errors and omissions insurance, attendance at seminars or conferences for ongoing education, membership dues

LOWDOWN:

This is a growing field as the American workplace changes. Tensions can arise that blow up into major crises; we read about the worst of these in the news media. But simmering hostility and negative attitudes occur in many organizations. Your business is founded on your ability to recognize these and other potentially serious problems, such as dangerous doorways. You help companies recognize the triggers, be they physical structural problems or management issues, and then mediate crises. This is a high-profile, high-stress form of consulting. It requires outstanding presentation skills, the ability to communicate effectively with all types of people, and the self-confidence to be an effective change agent. You are different from employee harmony consultants (who specialize in making sure everyone gets along) and labor relations professionals (who primarily translate corporate policies).

START-UP:

You'll need to keep in communication with your clients as you travel, and you'll need the basic office to support your work (about $3,000). Most projects are carried out at the client's site, and to earn $30,000 annually should not be difficult.

BOTTOM LINE ADVICE:

You'll need to feel comfortable dealing with crises as a regular part of your work. Of course organizations ought to bring you in to prevent hostility from arising, but realistically, that's not what happens. On the other hand, there will be no doubt about the importance and value of the services you provide. The other big requirement is the ability to market yourself. Getting established is likely to be very difficult.

PHARMACEUTICAL RETURNS
CONSULTING

Start-up cost:	$1,000-$3,000
Potential earnings:	$20,000-$40,000
Typical fees:	Percentage of value of returns
Advertising:	Trade journals, participation in professional organizations, association with health care management consulting firms, direct mail
Qualifications:	Pharmacy degree
Equipment needed:	Home office, manuals, pharmaceutical listings
Home business potential:	Yes
Staff required:	No
Handicapped opportunity:	Yes
Hidden costs:	Errors and omissions insurance, ongoing marketing, ongoing training for yourself and anyone else on the payroll

LOWDOWN:

Hospital pharmacies could save enormous amounts of money, and meet tightened quality standards, by reviewing the inventory in their pharmacies and returning expired drugs that can still be returned to the manufacturer. Busy hospital pharmacies, with thousands of different drugs to track, almost always have an extensive quantity of such expired material that cannot be administered to patients and should be returned. Your expertise in the field of drug returns can be marketed directly to hospitals, or you can subcontract your services to health care management consulting firms with projects related to pharmacy operations. Cutbacks in funding mean that no health care organization can ignore any means of recovering dollars, and your business can provide them with an excellent way to achieve this goal.

START-UP:

The primary value of the business is your expertise. The ability to produce a decent-looking report is important, but a secretarial service can prepare this for you. Potential earnings of $20,000 or more are possible.

BOTTOM LINE ADVICE:

Success builds success. Your challenge will be to get started, to get your foot into the door of the clannish world of health care administration. Most hospital pharmacists would be only too glad to have your assistance in clearing up the inventory in their departments, but a vice president who is relatively unfamiliar with the issues involved will probably be making the decision about whether to engage you. Here, as with so many other businesses relying on expertise, you will have to do what you can to become known and to gather a small nucleus of clients.

POLITICAL CAMPAIGN MANAGEMENT

Start-up cost:	$3,000-$6,000
Potential earnings:	$40,000-$100,000
Typical fees:	Extremely varied according to level of government, but can range from $40,000-$75,000
Advertising:	It's who you know
Qualifications:	A track record of success
Equipment needed:	Office with phone, fax/modem, copier, mobile phone, pager
Home business potential:	Yes
Staff required:	No
Handicapped opportunity:	Possibly
Hidden costs:	Phone bills

LOWDOWN:

This is often a combination business and crusade. Usually political campaign managers are identified with one of the political parties. And unless you are able to join the very few who work at the national level, your success is strongly related to your familiarity with the attitudes, issues, and expectations of your state or region. This is a profession for dynamic, incredibly energetic, intuitive, and very well-organized people who want to act out their commitment and beliefs by supporting candidates they believe in. The cynical manipulator who can package some faceless candidate to hoodwink the electorate is a myth. Not that the process of getting someone elected is entirely pretty and nice. Money, influence, the varying demands of the people, and attacks by the opponent can all make a campaign manager's life miserable. But winning the election is an incredible high—and your ticket to the next challenge in two or four years.

START-UP:

You probably won't be working much out of your own office, but you need to be available when you are there. Include a cellular phone into your office costs. Since the time you put into a campaign may equal a year's worth of work or more, it's easier to count your earnings by annual salary ($40,000-$100,000, depending on who you're representing). You may need a secretary if managing a large campaign.

BOTTOM LINE ADVICE:

Some people love the exciting give and take of the political process, the opportunity to meet public figures, and even the chance to affect policies. Other people hate all the hysteria. One good way to see if this is for you is by volunteering in several campaigns. You'll answer the phone, lick the stamps, and tie up the balloons for the victory celebration. You'll need to be a risk-taker and definitely a self-promoter to make this a career. If you go into it professionally, it will take over your life.

POLLSTER

Start-up cost:	$1,000-1,500
Potential earnings:	$15,000-$40,000
Typical fees:	$10-$20 per hour or a flat rate of $150 and up
Advertising:	Connections, referrals, networking, newspaper ads
Qualifications:	Energy, patience, people skills
Equipment needed:	Computer, office suite software, printer, office furniture, business cards, phone
Home business potential:	Yes
Staff required:	Yes (1-2 people)
Handicapped opportunity:	No
Hidden costs:	Time is money, so plan well

LOWDOWN:

To become a pollster you will need an ability to get people to talk to you. You can take your energy, your determination to keep going in the face of rejection, and your genuine interest in what people have to say and turn this into a business. Constructing the questions to ask is one of the jobs of a pollster. Another may be finding the right people to carry out polls devised by someone else. Typically pollsters focus on one geographic or demographic area.

START-UP:

You can probably make do with very little equipment to start but will be able to produce more professional-looking reports with a computer and printer. Tabulating results will be much easier with a good spreadsheet program (around $100-$300). Charge by the hour ($10-$20 per) when you can, because this is a time-consuming business. If your client wants to pay a flat fee, a good starting point is $150.

BOTTOM LINE ADVICE:

This can be a fascinating field. You will be gathering and analyzing information that can be gleaned no other way. But marketing your services will be extremely challenging. Polling requires connections in government as well as industry, so your marketing skills need to be top-drawer. Your network will lead you to further referrals. Be careful; this business ebbs and flows depending on the electoral season, the weather, and other factors out of your control.

PRINTING BROKER

Start-up cost:	$1,000-$3,000
Potential earnings:	$35,000-$50,000
Typical fees:	10 to 15 percent commission on sales
Advertising:	Yellow Pages, trade publications, direct mail, cold calls
Qualifications:	Printing sales background
Equipment needed:	Cellular phone, computer, printer, fax, copier, phone
Home business potential:	Yes
Staff required:	No
Handicapped opportunity:	Yes
Hidden costs:	Insurance, mileage

LOWDOWN:

For those who are inexperienced in the world of printing and publishing, a printing broker can be a godsend. Relying on an extensive background in printing sales, a printing broker can actually save the client hundreds of dollars in printing costs by shopping for the best (and most current) rates. The broker does not work for one specific printer, but represents all of them, in a sense, because he or she will offer a client the best going rate without sacrificing quality. Clients could be anyone from advertising agencies to community newspapers and book publishers. To be successful, you'll need to have a natural sales ability and the technical know-how to get printing jobs accomplished. You're servicing two sides here: the customer who needs a brochure or book printed, and the printing house itself (because you are working with them as an outside representative, and you'll need to work at preserving that relationship). If ink is in your blood, this could be a terrific opportunity for you—since most unknowledgeable folk are on the lookout for the lowest prices when they need items printed.

START-UP:

Your start-up costs are low ($1,000-$3,000), because you'll only need to have a basic office setup (with computer, printer, fax, copier, and phone) and some advertising to get things off the ground (assuming, of course, that you already have a printing background, complete with contacts). With some heavy shoe action, you could make $35,000-$50,000 per year—especially if you can build a solid reputation with documented savings for your clients.

BOTTOM LINE ADVICE:

Your contacts will make or break you in this business; always be honest and reputable, and you'll reap the benefits threefold. Why threefold? Because your satisfied clients will tell at least two other contacts about your services and how much money you saved them. On the sour side, you could wind up spending a lot of your own time trying to negotiate deals that don't materialize—and that means you'll have to eat the related costs.

PRODUCT DEVELOPER

Start-up cost:	$3,000-$5,000
Potential earnings:	$25,000 and up
Typical fees:	$500+ per project (could be as high as several thousand dollars)
Advertising:	Referrals, networking, memberships in business and trade organizations
Qualifications:	Record of success, business background, creativity, ability to be a self-starter
Equipment needed:	Office furniture, computer, suite and presentation software, laser printer, business cards, letterhead, envelopes, marketing material
Home business potential:	Yes
Staff required:	No
Handicapped opportunity:	Yes
Hidden costs:	Research, subscriptions to newspapers and trade journals

LOWDOWN:

Tens of thousands of new products are introduced every year into the American economy. Every consumer item we use each day was once someone's bright idea for a new product. And then there are the fads . . . . We all laugh about the pet rock, but it was a lot of fun, it was incredibly popular, and quite a few people got rich in the process of developing and selling it. As a product developer, you'll be drawing together your awareness of the needs of your corporate clients (who provide you with their input and ideas), the temper of the marketplace, and your own creativity. Lots of people have great ideas, but yours are the ones with legs. They work for you, for the organization that will produce and market them, and for the final consumer. This is not a game for sissies. You'll need a major dose of self-confidence and a generous helping of right-brain creativity to succeed as a freelance product developer.

START-UP:

Are you just thinking, or are you tinkering? The difference will affect your costs ($3,000 to start). You'll definitely need to be able to produce professionally written materials as part of your marketing process. You could make $25,000 your first year.

BOTTOM LINE ADVICE:

There is a big gulf in this business area between the many voices crying for attention and the few who can produce valuable ideas. Some product developers are truly freelance, while others focus on serving one or two corporations, with which they have long-term relationships. Your personal reputation for creativity, reliability, and awareness of the perspective of the consumer is central to success.

PROFIT SHARING PLAN CONSULTANT

Start-up cost:	$2,500-$4,000
Potential earnings:	$25,000-$50,000
Typical fees:	$50-$75 per hour
Advertising:	Participation in business-oriented community groups, trade publications, direct mail
Qualifications:	Certification as a financial planner, industry experience as a benefits advisor
Equipment needed:	Office furniture and equipment (including computer, printer, copier, fax, and phone), business cards, letterhead, envelopes
Home business potential:	Yes
Staff required:	No
Handicapped opportunity:	Yes
Hidden costs:	Continuing education, subscriptions and membership dues

LOWDOWN:

Profit sharing is becoming an increasingly important benefit, but designing an effective plan requires expertise and experience. Goal setting is vital: what is the company trying to achieve with the profit sharing plan, what level of employee with be targeted, and how will the specific elements of the plan be designed? Establishing the cost-benefit analysis alone is often a major challenge. Evaluation of the effectiveness of the chosen plan over the short and long term is also essential. As a consultant in this field, you will need to find growing companies that are not yet large enough to have a human resources staff capable of handling these questions. A history of successful plan design will be your major marketing tool.

START-UP:

You need the marketing materials and personal image to appeal to your corporate market. A functional office for your own work is all that is required (about $2,500 to start). You should make $25,000 your first year, considering that you'll be charging $50-$75 per hour for your services.

BOTTOM LINE ADVICE:

This business appeals to a narrow but potentially very profitable market niche: growing companies with a vision for the future. Unfortunately, many others are clamoring for the attention of this market. Your record of success, and your ability to present your ideas in terms that will appeal to these clients, will define your success.

PROPERTY MANAGEMENT SERVICE

Start-up cost:	$3,000-$6,000
Potential earnings:	$25,000-$50,000
Typical fees:	$25 per hour or a monthly retainer of $500-$2,500
Advertising:	Classified ads, referrals, memberships in community and business real estate groups
Qualifications:	Experience in the field, related degree helpful, outstanding management skills, good ability to communicate and work with people, knowledge of basic bookkeeping, understanding of building maintenance issues
Equipment needed:	Office furniture, computer, suite software, possibly specialized property management software, printer, fax, modem, business cards, letterhead, envelopes
Home business potential:	Yes
Staff required:	No
Handicapped opportunity:	No
Hidden costs:	Insurance

LOWDOWN:

This is the business for someone who likes juggling a thousand balls at one time, pulling many different pieces together, and keeping track of the people and data that go with the projects. If you're good, you'll become indispensable to the owners of the properties you manage, and you'll have a well-established enterprise that will keep you busy and well-rewarded indefinitely. Why are good property managers so valuable? You maintain all the financial records for each property, which include income and expenses, bills, and taxes. Skill at auditing bills is extremely valuable just on its own. The ability to keep repair and maintenance schedules up to date is essential, so you will need to be able to pay great attention to detail and also have the people skills required for relating to the individuals who carry out the work on your buildings. Collecting rents is the other central piece of this puzzle.

START-UP:

Your own office needs to support you well, especially in communicating to building owners, repair personnel, and tenants. The computer is the tool used most for tracking all the financial information related to the properties (around $3,000 to start). Depending on your location, you should make at least $25,000 annually.

BOTTOM LINE ADVICE:

The owners of properties—your prospective clients—will need to place great responsibility on your shoulders. Things can degenerate very quickly in a poorly managed building, and once the financial records become tangled, it can be very difficult to bring them into order, or even to learn if the expenses are exceeding the income. You are asking your clients to have a large amount of confidence in you, and marketing these services successfully may depend on how well you can engender that sense of trust. It may be, however, that you will only need a few clients. This is one small business where constant marketing may not be necessary.

RECREATION ACTIVITIES CONSULTANT

Start-up cost:	$1,000-$3,000
Potential earnings:	$30,000-$50,000
Typical fees:	$500-$1,000 per job (plus travel expenses)
Advertising:	Recreation associations (for networking and advertising in their publications)
Qualifications:	A degree in recreations management would be extremely helpful
Equipment needed:	Good resource materials and perhaps some road atlas software (with points of interest mapped out and profiled)
Home business potential:	No (you'll be on the road a lot or may work through a particular resort)
Staff required:	Usually a low-paid staff of college interns majoring in hotel or sports management, on an as-needed basis
Handicapped opportunity:	Yes
Hidden costs:	Association dues

LOWDOWN:

What does a recreation activities consultant do besides get paid to show others a great time? Not too much, actually. You may be hired as a regular consultant to a particular resort, handling the details and finer points of hospitality and fun. Often, you'll be hired by corporations sending groups of people on trips to interesting places—and you'll be in charge of making sure that everything goes smoothly for the travelers, from dining to activities and sightseeing. Whatever you choose, you'll enjoy the challenge of choosing interesting, offbeat things to do—with the added bonus of getting to travel all over the world yourself. What could be more desirable than that? On the downside, you'll be putting in long hours, and often will need to be up and at 'em long before any of your clients. You will be paid to worry and fuss over these people, constantly making sure that their every need is met. In that sense, you're in the same league as a concierge—except you get to play outside, too.

START-UP:

Your start-up is considerably low ($1,000-$3,000), but your income potential will be driven by your ability to network. If you get out there and make yourself available (even during holidays), you could reap $30,000-$50,000. The icing on the cake is that you'll get your own travel costs paid for by the hiring company, in addition to commanding $500-$1,000 for your time.

BOTTOM LINE ADVICE:

Who could blame you for wanting to get paid for having fun? Expect to be harassed by your family and friends, because yours is truly an enviable job. The only problem you may have is keeping everyone happy—remember to be patient and kind at all times.

RECYCLING

Start-up cost:	$1,000-$2,000
Potential earnings:	$10,000-$20,000
Typical fees:	Not applicable
Advertising:	Flyers, referrals, networking
Qualifications:	Driver's license, knowledge of state and federal guidelines, often state certification
Equipment needed:	Pickup truck
Home business potential:	Yes
Staff required:	No
Handicapped opportunity:	No
Hidden costs:	Mileage, insurance, vehicle maintenance

LOWDOWN:

A ton of newsprint seems like a lot, but that ton can be worth $50 to $75, and it's yours for the gathering. The increasing popularity of recycling means that more and more recycling centers are accepting newspapers, cardboard, office paper, and aluminum. You can make a good living picking up these materials and selling them to the center. You will need contracts with regular customers and a vehicle that can carry relatively heavy loads. As you pick up unwanted materials, you are also making the world a better and cleaner place.

START-UP:

You may distribute flyers to let home owners and businesses in your service area know of your business. The only other cost is a car or truck for carrying the materials to the recycling center. You make most of your money on whatever the recycling center will pay you for what you bring in. There aren't very many recycling services making millions.

BOTTOM LINE ADVICE:

It's outdoor work—no sitting behind a desk day after day. For active, friendly people, recycling can be an ideal occupation. While some are in it just for the profits, others feel strongly about the wise use of resources and the importance of reusing what we can. Many people who are unable to recycle their own waste materials will be grateful for your assistance so that they also can participate in this worthwhile activity. On the other hand, it's just trash, trash, trash. The routine of picking up and sorting, whatever the weather, can be numbing. Carrying heavy loads is back-breaking and can be tedious as well.

REFERRAL SERVICE

Start-up cost:	$3,000-$5,000
Potential earnings:	$5,000-$40,000, depending on experience level
Typical fees:	Varied according to type of service
Advertising:	Yellow Pages, newspapers, bulletin boards
Qualifications:	None
Equipment needed:	Phone, computer with extensive database of businesses
Home business potential:	Yes
Staff required:	No
Handicapped opportunity:	Yes
Hidden costs:	Updating your database annually will cost you some money

LOWDOWN:

How many times have you been stuck in the middle of nowhere with absolutely no idea who to call for what you need? A referral service eliminates the time you'd spend thumbing through every category in the Yellow Pages, not knowing who is reputable and who is not. With one phone call, a referral service can locate all of the reputable businesses in any given category and within a specific geographic area. As a referral service operator, you would gather every piece of information about these companies, perhaps aligning yourself closely to Chambers of Commerce or the Better Business Bureau to ensure the credibility of each company you refer. You may work out a commission with the companies you represent, or you may set up an on-line service or 900-number for folks in need of referrals so that you can earn income from them. Some referral services do a combination of the two methods. At any rate, you'll need to establish yourself as an authority on a wide variety of businesses, so research is vital to success.

START-UP:

Expect to spend anywhere from $3,000-$5,000 on computer and related databases to keep your research time down to a minimum. On-line services, the phone book, and bulletin boards provide you with various avenues of income; your fees will depend on which method(s) you choose.

BOTTOM LINE ADVICE:

If you don't mind dealing with people and vast amounts of data, and if you're skilled in matching the two, you'll likely succeed in this business. However, unless people know about you, they won't call . . . be sure to advertise in the most high-profile places you can afford.

RELOCATION CONSULTANT

Start-up cost:	$3,000-$6,000
Potential earnings:	$15,000 and more
Typical fees:	$25-$35 per hour
Advertising:	Trade publications, networking, memberships in real estate and general business organizations, referrals
Qualifications:	Real estate experience, close knowledge of your area's neighborhoods, attractions, amenities, schools
Equipment needed:	Office furniture, computer, printer, fax, modem, business cards, letterhead, envelopes
Home business potential:	Yes
Staff required:	No
Handicapped opportunity:	No
Hidden costs:	Telephone bills, membership dues, entertainment

LOWDOWN:

Your ideal market will probably be companies that do some relocations but are too small to provide much assistance in-house to the executives they are transferring to your community. Moving is a challenging experience for almost all families, and enlightened employers will see the value of your assistance in making the transition go as smoothly as possible. You will provide advising as the transferees begin to make decisions: What neighborhood will we like best? Where can we find eldercare or child care? What sports are played at local high schools? Can we find a house with enough land for trail riding? Your relocation consulting service will assist transferees with questions like these. You work with the employees before they are ready to choose a real estate agent.

START-UP:

Equipping your office will be the main expense (about $3,000). You will do some work by computer and fax, but most of your time will probably be spent driving to the different areas of your city, or having a restaurant meal with a transferee. Annual wages of $15,000 is realistic for part-time work.

BOTTOM LINE ADVICE:

You're doing two kinds of marketing here, first, for your own service, and second, for your community. Many organizations use relocation consultants to help persuade a prospective employee to take the job with that company. How the prospect and his family feel about moving to your area can be a major factor. Your services can offer an unprejudiced look at what the locality has to offer. Hospitals recruiting a certain physician and companies recruiting someone for an upper-management position will both value your service highly.

RESPIRATORY EQUIPMENT REPAIR

Start-up cost:	$2,000-$3,000
Potential earnings:	$30,000 or more
Typical fees:	$20-$50 per service call, plus parts and labor
Advertising:	Direct mail to hospitals and other inpatient health care facilities, trade journals, business publications, referrals, participation in professional organizations
Qualifications:	Technical training with the related equipment, familiarity will all brands used in your service area, a can-do attitude, an aptitude for mechanical tinkering
Equipment needed:	Van for pickup, delivery, and on-site service, tools, parts, and repair equipment, answering service, cellular phone
Home business potential:	Yes
Staff required:	No
Handicapped opportunity:	No
Hidden costs:	Training in new equipment brands

LOWDOWN:

Service, service—that's what every organization wants. In health care, service is everything, and the escalation of costs means that equipment is being stretched further and further. Your business, which keeps vital respiratory therapy equipment in top working order, has a ready and eager market with few competitors. You will need to find the people (and machines) that need you, and to get to them when things break down. If you can resolve equipment problems, fix things right the first time, and keep your transportation expenses down, you'll have an excellent enterprise and probably find a need to expand relatively soon. As our population ages, more and more patients are going to be needing respiratory therapy, and fewer dollars will be available for buying new equipment. Keeping everything in running order is not a "nice-to-have" service for health care providers, it's a "must-have." A "must-have" business is the ideal business to be in.

START-UP:

It will take you a while to find your customers, but repeat business will eventually keep you going. You'll need to be able to do a complete service job from the beginning, and supplying yourself to do that will be a significant expense (about $2,000 in good tools to start). You could make $30,000 in the beginning.

BOTTOM LINE ADVICE:

Making a profit will take business as well as mechanical sense. Many people who are wonderful at the delicate work necessary to repair a sophisticated piece of equipment lack the people skills that are essential for marketing their skills. These skills can be learned, and you will be glad for every bit of training you allow yourself in this area. The third essential factor in your success is managing your costs, including the cost of time. With these three ingredients in place, there's nowhere to go but up.

RESUME SERVICE

Start-up cost:	$1,000-$5,000
Potential earnings:	$20,000-$50,000
Typical fees:	$150-$500 per resume (depending on your demographics)
Advertising:	Yellow Pages, newspaper classifieds, referrals
Qualifications:	Writing ability, attention to important detail, strong organizational ability
Equipment needed:	Computer, printer, fax/modem, paper, extra computer disks
Home business potential:	Yes
Staff required:	No
Handicapped opportunity:	Yes
Hidden costs:	Insurance, spending too much time with one client

LOWDOWN:

Thousands of people are looking for new work these days, and they all have one need in common: they simply must have a dynamic resume. Those who really want to put their best foot forward with a trend-setting (yet somewhat traditional-looking) resume and cover letter will come to you for a package that looks visually appealing yet businesslike enough to get even a stuffed-shirt hiring professional to glance twice. Your resume service needs to reflect the trends of the future in order to survive, because the small typing service-variety resume service simply can't keep up with technological demands and self-promotional waves of the future. Some folks are even posting their resumes on the Internet, and you could offer additional services such as this if you choose. Regardless, your days will be spent meeting with a wide variety of clients from all walks of life (from foundry supervisors to attorneys), writing down specific job histories, and adding pertinent skill information that will make a potential employer jump with glee. It's a time-consuming job, but it gets easier the more you work at it.

START-UP:

Your start-up is relatively low ($1,000-$5,000) because all you really need is a good computer setup and a small advertising budget to get the word out. You can expect to earn $20,000 or so in most medium-size markets; in New York City and other large metropolitan areas, you'll be charging much more for your services (up to $500) and could easily make $50,000 per year.

BOTTOM LINE ADVICE:

If you're a writer, this is a pretty easy way to make a living (or an additional income to support your quest for the Great American Novel). However, you do need to enjoy working with people: they will hound you day and night until their project is finished, and possibly even afterward. If you don't like to be hounded, stick to novel writing.

ADVICE FROM THE EXPERTS

What sets your business apart from others like it?

Katina Z. Jones has a nontraditional resume service called Going Places Self-Promotions, Inc., in Akron, Ohio. She says that her business is unique because it breaks many of the traditional rules of resume writing. "We do resumes that are not only eye-catching, but also go beyond providing a mere rundown of a client's job history. We like to add a sense of not only what a person has accomplished in their career, but also who they are and how they might fit into an organization. We have a 98 percent success rate in helping clients secure interviews because of that personalized approach."

Things you couldn't do without:

"I couldn't do without my computer, laser printer, phone, pager, and fax. My clients want fairly quick turnaround, and these items help me to accomplish that. Also, I need to have plenty of paper catalogs on hand, as I use a ton of specialty preprinted stationery to produce resumes on."

Marketing tips/advice:

"Set yourself apart from the people who are glorified typists . . . recognize that the resume industry is changing rapidly, and the resumes of the past (with cookie-cutter objectives and meaningless buzzwords) are just not getting people results anymore. After you've got your niche, network like crazy. Anywhere you go, introduce yourself; you're bound to meet someone who either needs a resume or knows someone who does."

If you had to do it all over again . . .

"I would have started networking much sooner and would also have put together a more meaningful marketing plan; I don't think I strategized nearly enough in the beginning."

RETAIL BAKERY/SPECIALTY FOOD STORE

Start-up cost:	$1,000-$5,000
Potential earnings:	$2,000-$5,000 per month
Advertising:	Newspapers, flyers, brochures, direct mail, press kits
Qualifications:	Knowledge of baking and/or cooking; ability to prepare a specialty food item
Equipment needed:	Oven, kitchen equipment, knowledge of sanitation and food safety
Home business potential:	Yes
Staff required:	Not initially; may be needed to grow
Handicapped opportunity:	Yes
Hidden costs:	None

LOWDOWN:

People are hungry for homemade baked goods and specialties (such as gourmet desserts, for example). No one has time to bake anymore; the "personal touch" is greatly desired by consumers who are tired of mass-produced, commercial foods. Packaging and marketing are important in this type of business, so you will need to be an astute marketer, as well as a good baker or cook. To grow your business, you will need to include the cost of additional staff in your budget. Maintaining top quality by using the finest ingredients is important. Some stores make their name with an entirely new food product or baked item (or several); others succeed with a tried-and-true item, such as macaroon cookies or muffins. A hot item that can brew up big profits is gourmet coffees.

START-UP:

The gourmet coffee business can be quite expensive (up to $20,000) to start up but profit margins are high and repeat business is almost guaranteed. Establishing a niche as a baker of pies, donuts, and other baked goods can be done on a shoestring budget. For instance, cakes can cost as little as 60 cents to produce and can be sold for an average of $9 each.

BOTTOM LINE ADVICE:

Providing a food product or beverage that tastes twice as good as commercial varieties will give you loyal customers who will come out of their way to buy your wares. There is a huge market out there for foods with the personal touch. On the downside, marketing will require a chunk of your budget, as will staffing (if you require employees). Food safety considerations and zoning regulations can be a headache.

RETIREMENT PLANNER

Start-up cost:	$1,000-$2,000
Potential earnings:	$20,000-$40,000
Typical fees:	Set fee of $150-$1,000 (depending on scope of project)
Advertising:	Newspapers, publications of local interest groups, membership in community organizations, word of mouth, direct mail
Qualifications:	Expertise in financial planning (certification helpful), experience in a related field
Equipment needed:	Computer, printer, fax, phone, copier, marketing materials, business cards, letterhead, envelopes
Home business potential:	Yes
Staff required:	No
Handicapped opportunity:	Yes
Hidden costs:	Conferences for continuing self-education

LOWDOWN:

We're an aging population in this country, and the baby-boom generation is notorious for its poor planning for retirement. It used to be something that people just didn't want to think about, but the tide is changing. Now, with widespread fears about the future of Social Security, retirement planners are finding a rising demand for their services. You will be distinguishing yourself from the hundreds of "financial planners" searching for customers in every community by your focus on this one vital piece of the financial puzzle. As with lawyers, accountants, and other professionals who operate as small businesses, your challenge will be to gain the confidence of your clients so that they prefer your excellent personal service over the security of dealing with a large institutional business that claims to offer the same type of advice. You'll sell them on how meticulous you are at developing financial strategies tailored to their own unique financial situations (instead of a grid in a book). You'll take a good look at their plans for retirement and work out a sensible budget based on that information. You may also suggest financial products or options, such as mutual funds.

START-UP:

Minimal (about $1,000)—you just need adequate materials to present the image of reliability that will make people feel confident in your knowledge and expertise. If you travel to your clients' homes, you do not need an elaborate office setup.

BOTTOM LINE ADVICE:

The difficulty in selling retirement services is that, while almost everyone needs them, they're afraid to contemplate the reality that they should be saving more, spending less, and keeping to a budget. Your "hook" for this market may be to find a way to send a reassuring message, to plan for retirement without taking all the fun out of today.

Reunion Organizer

Start-up cost:	$2,000-$3,000
Potential earnings:	$15,000-$50,000
Typical fees:	$5-$10 for each classmate who attends
Advertising:	Word of mouth and warm calling
Qualifications:	A big network of friends and acquaintances in your community, patience, determination, organizational ability
Equipment needed:	Computer, database and suite software, fax, copier, office furniture, business cards, letterhead, envelopes
Home business potential:	Yes
Staff required:	No
Handicapped opportunity:	Yes
Hidden costs:	Telephone bills

LOWDOWN:

Changing life patterns are making reunions seem more appealing to many kinds of groups; more women in the workforce leaves fewer people with the time to pull such events together. High school reunions are a major focus of this business and finding the "lost" members is an important part of the process. Your persistence and sheer determination need to be applied to the search process, which usually starts one year before the event. Former employees of some organizations also occasionally hold reunions, and there is a niche market in putting together reunions for today's far-flung families. Once you discover the whereabouts of the people, you may turn your attention to the event itself, arranging the catering, photos, band, decorations, and mementos.

START-UP:

Basic office equipment ($2,000-$3,000) should get you started, but you will need to get the database program ($175-$300) as soon as possible. Set your charges differently for the time involved and the number of people you're expected to locate; many charge between $5-$10 per attendee, but others charge a flat rate commensurate with an hourly fee of $10-$15 per hour.

BOTTOM LINE ADVICE:

Most communities are excellent markets for this service, but they don't know it yet. Reunion organizing is an obvious service to offer, but people won't be expecting it to be available. Consider the organizations and groups in your locale that have reunions, such as schools and colleges. Get a foothold, do one excellent job, and you will find that the referrals will begin to roll in. Your success will depend to some extent on the material and information you have to work with, but once you refine your people-searching skills, you should have a service to offer that can't be matched by amateurs. One tip: Use on-line phone books or the new telephone directories on disk or CD-ROM; these can help you locate nearly anyone in the country.

How to Stay Positive

Let's face it, the best thing about owning your own business is that it is your own business. But, it has also been said that the worst thing about owning your own business is that it is your own business. When things are going great, it's easy to be positive, but what can you do when you have some slow times?

- **Take inventory of all the good things that have happened in the last month.** Write them down, and really appreciate them.

- **Put a "plus" sign over your desk.** At eye level, so you remember to try and remain positive at all times (especially when on the phone with customers).

- **Concentrate on the opportunities you still have.** So often, we expend all of our energy on negative things that happen. Focusing on the future will keep you from ignoring potentially great opportunities that you might have missed while wallowing in your sorrow.

- **Surround yourself with positive people.** If you've got friends in business, try to support one another in times of despair. Offer positive advice and encouragement—but, most of all, learn to accept it when it's given to you.

- **See, then be.** Picture yourself succeeding again, and your chances of success will nearly double. Never underestimate the power of creative visualization.

- **Don't give up.** Even the most successful entrepreneurs have experienced setbacks, so you're not the only one. Have the courage to go on.

SALES OF NOVELTY AND PROMOTIONAL PRODUCTS

Start-up cost:	$1,000-$5,000
Potential earnings:	$30,000-$60,000
Typical fees:	Each product sells anywhere from a few dollars to several hundred
Advertising:	Trade publications, business periodicals, direct mail, catalogs
Qualifications:	Sales ability
Equipment needed:	Computer, suite software, modem, fax, laser printer, business cards, letterhead, envelopes, marketing materials
Home business potential:	Yes
Staff required:	Probably
Handicapped opportunity:	Yes
Hidden costs:	Inventory, reprinting of catalogs and other sales materials

LOWDOWN:

This is the business for you if you know what will amuse people (namely, your clients' customers) and catch their attention. You are providing one facet of the activity that is essential to every business: marketing. Novelties and promotional materials put the name and message of a business out before the public. They can be an enormously effective way of reaching out for customers. In this process, you are far more than just a writer of orders. You present ideas for the new and different. Promotional materials can take many forms, and fitting the object to the message takes a special kind of business insight. You'll need to have an enthusiasm for sales and marketing in your blood. You need to be as creative and off-beat as possible to attract the attention of companies who want to attract attention to themselves.

START-UP:

Your relationship with your distributor will control your need for inventory, which ideally will be kept to a minimum. Demonstration samples and catalogs may be quite expensive, though. Try to secure a good arrangement with your manufacturers and their reps before trying to produce your own. You can earn a living selling these types of products; just look at how well companies such as Successories are doing and you'll know that the market is profitable.

BOTTOM LINE ADVICE:

Your devotion to the needs of your clients will make you stand out from the crowd. There is quite a lot of competition in this field, but many of the other businesses just throw a catalog at prospects and expect them to do the creative work. You, on the other hand, develop a presentation focused on each client's distinctive needs and expectations. You give them several appealing options, and you carry out the detailed ordering and delivery process. It is work, but it's also fun.

ADVICE FROM THE EXPERTS

What sets your business apart from others like it?

"We have not only created a specialty product, but something that has a life and character all its own," says Mark Juarez, President and CEO of Tender Loving Things, Inc., in Oakland, California, which produces tiny wooden creatures with massage capability.

Things you couldn't do without:

"Birch or maple wood, drilling machine, glue, smiley-face brander and office equipment to run shipping, production, art, marketing, customer service, and administrative departments."

Marketing tips/advice:

"We turn profits into social responsibility; we donate 10 percent of our product to non-profit organizations and other groups that might benefit from the caring touch."

If you had to do it all over again . . .

"One of our biggest external challenges has been combating knockoffs and copycats." Juarez suggests protecting yourself as early as possible within federal trademark regulations.

SEAMSTRESS/ALTERATIONS BUSINESS

Start-up cost:	$1,000-$5,000 (depending on whether you have to rent space)
Potential earnings:	$20,000-$40,000
Typical fees:	Varied, but charges normally start at $5 and go all the way to $75, depending on what needs to be done
Advertising:	Newspapers, bulletin boards, fashion shows
Qualifications:	The ability to create fashions and apparel without patterns would be useful
Equipment needed:	Sewing machine and materials
Staff required:	No
Handicapped opportunity:	Possibly
Hidden costs:	Remakes could take up more than an inch of your time; make sure your work meets even the toughest standards

LOWDOWN:

If all you need is a needle and thread to design a business you feel comfortable in, then the alterations/sewing business is a perfect match. In this recession-proof business, you will repair or alter clothing that belongs to your client—but you can also offer custom-sewn clothing to busy executives who appreciate fine threads designed expressly for them. Creativity and the desire to make good clothes even better are the only requirements you'll need, and the higher the quality of your work, the more people will hear about your service. Word of mouth is nearly always the best way to grow the alterations business, although you may want to consider posting your business card on all the bulletin boards you can find in your community. Also, leave some extra cards for owners of dress shops—they often refer their customers to good tailors or seamstresses.

START-UP:

Your biggest up-front cost will be a good sewing machine (up to $1,000 or more); you might look into buying a used commercial sewing machine, because they are more durable and can be purchased for as little as $400. Be sure to invest in professional-looking business cards, because you'll need a lot of them to spread the word about your service. Use a rate card to keep track of what you're charging per job; some alterations are simple and inexpensive ($5-$10), while others are time-intensive and require you to charge $75 or more.

BOTTOM LINE ADVICE:

If you like to work sparingly with people and spend much of the time by yourself, you'll love this type of work. However, the hours can be long and the rewards not as frequent as you might like. Sewing is tedious work except to those who truly enjoy it—so make sure that you enjoy it enough to spend 65 percent of your workday doing it.

SECRETARIAL SERVICE

Start-up cost:	$3,000-$5,000
Potential earnings:	$20,000-$40,000
Typical fees:	$10-$20 per hour (depending on size of the company you're working for)
Advertising:	Classified ads, Yellow Pages, phone contacts
Qualifications:	Good typing and clerical skills
Equipment needed:	Computer or word processor, paper
Home business potential:	Yes
Staff required:	No
Handicapped opportunity:	Yes
Hidden costs:	Invest in a freelance proofreader or proofreading software, as mistakes could cost you repeat business

LOWDOWN:

The executive stretches in his chair, puts his feet up on his desk, and calls for his secretary . . . only, in the age of downsizing, he's likely to be kept waiting—because he's sharing with ten others who are already in line with their requests. The old days where everyone had a personal secretary are gone; many functions have been replaced by small secretarial pools or computers. But the need for personalized service has not gone away, and often a beleaguered company, its small administrative force stretched to the max, needs to farm out work. That's where you come in. You can assist them for a short period of time, typing letters or producing manuals that would be simply too costly to employ a full-timer with benefits to do. Training and/or experience as a secretary will help you understand the types of skills that you need and an idea of who to offer them to (dictation, shorthand, filing, and form typing are just a few). There is a lot of flexibility possible with this type of business: after-regular-hours work for out-of-towners to temporary fill-ins for local companies to contracting overflow and everything in between.

START-UP:

A computer is the recommended choice for running a secretarial service since it has greater versatility and a variety of available programs (compatible, of course, with your client's), but a word processor could work in a beginning pinch. Computers will cost anywhere from $1,000-$3,000, while a simple word processor can be bought for as low as $500. Whichever you choose, buying used models only a year or two old will help keep start-up costs down. Advertising in the Yellow Pages for $50-$100 per month, in the classifieds for $10 per week, and leaving flyers at hotels where businesspeople from out-of-town might need some help are some easy, inexpensive ways to get word out about the services being offered. Remember, the amount of time it will take to finish one assignment will vary and is generally unknown at the start, so charging an hourly fee of $10-$15 will prove more profitable than working for a set price per task.

BOTTOM LINE ADVICE:

Since it's likely that this job will involve working with many different people, tolerance of personality quirks will make jobs—and time—go more quickly and smoothly. The hours will be varied, which could become stressful for you (and your bank account) at times. This business needs a high-energy, go-getter type of person; do you have what it takes (and can you take the orders placed upon you by others)?

ADVICE FROM THE EXPERTS

What sets your business apart from others like it?

"I'm incredibly fast, accurate, and affordable," says Jana McClish, owner of Paragon Word Services in Akron, Ohio. "I can offer a quicker turnaround than most of my competitors."

Things you couldn't do without:

McClish needs a computer, answering machine, and a 10-key adding machine to run her business effectively.

Marketing tips/advice:

"You have to be persistent and market almost constantly. You must be confident and be able to sell that confidence in order to get in the door. You really need to have a special skill that sets you apart, too."

If you had to do it all over again . . .

"I'd research my equipment purchases better. I needed to buy new equipment a year and a half into my business because I did not purchase wisely. Also, I would've started with a much bigger base of prospects . . . I got kind of discouraged in the beginning because I didn't have huge amounts of work."

SOFTWARE CONVERSION SERVICE

Start-up cost:	$2,000-$3,000
Potential earnings:	$20,000-$30,000
Typical fees:	$50-$75 per job or $25-$30 per hour
Advertising:	Referrals, advertising in trade journals, public speaking, networking
Qualifications:	Expertise in a wide range of systems and programs
Equipment needed:	Computer and printer for your own office, office furniture, business cards, letterhead, envelopes
Home business potential:	Yes
Staff required:	No
Handicapped opportunity:	Yes
Hidden costs:	Risk and error insurance

LOWDOWN:

This is a narrow but vital field. When a business upgrades equipment, installs different software, or merges with another company, clashes often occur in information systems. Files may need to be converted from one program to another. Business owners or managers frequently fail to grasp the implications of decisions to change systems, and the apparent loss of files will seem like a major crisis to them. If you have expertise in computer systems, you can serve this niche market by converting files so they can be read by the new system. Technology and programs are changing so rapidly that the need for this service will be great into the foreseeable future.

START-UP:

Start-up costs are relatively low, as your work will be conducted principally on your clients' premises. You will need to subscribe to several computer magazines to keep on top of software developments, so put aside at least $250 annually for this purpose. Charge your clients $50-$75 per job—but if the hours start to get long, switch to an hourly rate of $25-$30.

BOTTOM LINE ADVICE:

Once established as a software converter, a detail-oriented person can develop a satisfied clientele. You understand disk architecture and the means by which electronic information is stored in files—use your skills to keep your client businesses operating. This can be a very satisfying and profitable process. As with many computer-oriented services, though, panicky clients can make your work life tense. You will be serving people who don't understand the problems they are having or exactly what you are doing to resolve them.

Speechwriter

Start-up cost:	$1,000-$1,500
Potential earnings:	$20,000-$60,000
Typical fees:	$50-$75 per hour or a flat rate of $500 or more
Advertising:	Referrals, networking
Qualifications:	Excellent writing and presentation skills
Equipment needed:	Computer, printer, fax, business cards, letterhead, envelopes
Home business potential:	Yes
Staff required:	No
Handicapped opportunity:	Yes
Hidden costs:	None

LOWDOWN:

Excellent speechwriters become like trusted advisors to their clients. If you can develop speeches that work well for different speakers, you can earn an impressive living in this field. Depending on the topic of the speech, you may need to do extensive research in the library or on-line. Success will depend on your sense of what is effective in a spoken format, and what kinds of language and ideas can be delivered effectively by your clients. Businesses executives, politicians, and public figures often give many speeches each year and lack the time and skill to write these themselves. Write a speech that really moves people, and your career will advance quickly.

START-UP:

Start-up costs are low, but you will need a computer and printer ($1,500-$2,000). You can bill anywhere from $25-$50 an hour for your service, or charge a flat rate for 10-, 30-, and 60-minute speeches.

BOTTOM LINE ADVICE:

Writing an effective speech is a highly skilled, creative activity. Many speechwriters develop a sense of partnership with the people who will be delivering their speeches. Once you prove yourself, you become invaluable to your clients. Yet this can be a very hard business to break into. Many writers offer speechwriting as just one of their services, and you must find a way to distinguish yourself from all the rest. This work is often done under tight deadlines and extreme pressure.

STANDARDIZED TEST PREPARATORY SERVICES

Start-up cost:	$1,000-$5,000
Potential earnings:	$30,000-$45,000
Typical fees:	$75-$175 per client
Advertising:	Yellow Pages, direct mail to students/parents
Qualifications:	Familiarity with all standardized tests (including SAT, ACT, GED, LSAT), teaching degree helpful (and required in some states)
Equipment needed:	Practice tests, pencils, timers
Home business potential:	Yes (but you can rent testing space from schools at a low cost)
Staff required:	No
Handicapped opportunity:	Yes
Hidden costs:	Insurance

LOWDOWN:

Thousands of students each year must take standard tests for entry into college, and they usually must spend weeks preparing for these all-encompassing tests. There are sections on math and language usage in most of these tests, and you can help students prepare for each by presenting them with similar questions or problems as practice guides and answering their questions. Perhaps you'll choose to work with a more specialized test such as the LSAT that undergraduates must pass before being accepted to law school. Whatever area you choose to specialize in, you'll need to work with groups of students at one time to make it truly profitable.

START-UP:

Your start-up costs will be low, because you'll only need some workbooks, pencils, and timers to start with—and, since your clients will be paying up front for your services, you needn't worry about maintaining an inventory prior to accepting clients. You may want to spend $35 or so per test prep session on space rental (check with local schools for their after-hour rates). At $75-$175 per student, you can easily see an income potential of $30,000-$45,000.

BOTTOM LINE ADVICE:

If you enjoy repetition, this could be a relaxing and comfortable way to make a living; all you have to do is provide the same services over and over, and collect your checks as you do. On the other hand, it could become too repetitious, and therefore less challenging than most entrepreneurs would like. You decide what your comfort level is.

STENCILING

Start-up cost:	$1,000-$2,000
Potential earnings:	$1,000-$3,000 per month
Typical fees:	$25-$1,000 per project
Advertising:	Business cards, bulletin boards, craft stores, specialty clothing shops, paint and wallpaper stores
Qualifications:	Some artistic flare, ability to handle repetitious work
Equipment needed:	Various paint brushes, sponges, stenciling patterns, paint and varnishes
Home business potential:	Yes
Staff required:	No
Handicapped opportunity:	Yes
Hidden costs:	Insurance

LOWDOWN:

This is a centuries-old technique believed to have started in the Fiji Islands. Even today, folks like having their walls and homes decorated, so you should have no problem getting business. There are as many techniques of stenciling as there are surfaces to stencil. Many people are afraid to stencil their own walls, so they'll hire a professional like you to come in and do the dirty work (which can actually be quite fun once you know what you're doing). You can also stencil floors, furniture, and all types of fabrics. If you want to get into home interior stenciling, hook up with custom builders who provide referrals or contract the work out themselves. Take along some pictures of other stenciling you've done in your own home. If you want to hit the craft shows, the sky's the limit on what you can stencil on—and what you can sell. At shows, the more unique the item, the better it sells.

START-UP:

Stenciling is relatively inexpensive to start ($1,000-$2,000). Your hidden cost may come in the form of a bolt of cloth or a bench to stencil on (about $300 to start). Also, if you do the craft shows, know that you'll have to pay for table or floor space (typically $150-$400 a pop). Most nonprofessional stencilers do this as a hobby; others make $1,000-$3,000 per month, depending on how many jobs they can get.

BOTTOM LINE ADVICE:

Stenciling can be done on everything, from food to kites to cars. If you don't see a stencil out there you like, you can make your own with minimal effort. If you don't want to pay for a stencil pattern, your local library is full of them. Stenciling may require long periods of standing or sitting. You might want to work in a ventilated area because of fumes from the paint and varnishes.

STENOGRAPHY SERVICE

Start-up cost:	$3,000-$6,000
Potential earnings:	$30,000-$40,000
Typical fees:	$15 per page, or $20 per hour
Advertising:	Newspapers, Yellow Pages, publications targeting the business community, referrals
Qualifications:	Secretarial skills, good organizational ability
Equipment needed:	Word-processing equipment, dictation machine, excellent printer, fax
Home business potential:	Yes
Staff required:	No
Handicapped opportunity:	Yes
Hidden costs:	Software upgrades, office supplies

LOWDOWN:

Stenography is a service that can be marketed widely to businesses that are under-staffed or have very lean organizational structures. Your ability to get dictation transcribed accurately onto paper, on time, can be a valuable addition to your clients' work processes. Senior managers have assumed that the advent of the computer has removed the need for stenographic services. They're no longer available in many corporations, but the need is definitely still there, and you can fill it. With the growth of small business establishments in most areas, you could find another market in the very small enterprises that have no support staff at all.

START-UP:

Your furniture must allow you to work comfortably. You'll need equipment compatible with that of your clientele ($3,000 to start). You could earn upward of $30,000.

BOTTOM LINE ADVICE:

Depending on your locality you may find quite a bit of competition for the services you offer. Pricing your work so that you can meet the competition and make an appropriate profit may be a challenge. It may take you a while to learn to give accurate estimates and set appropriate prices. You'll also need to be a self-starter, able to keep going without the stimulation of a busy workplace to keep you on task. Of course, some people find it easier to get work done without the hubbub of the social scene that's usual in a large organization.

SYSTEMS INTEGRATOR

Start-up cost:	$1,000-$5,000
Potential earnings:	$37,500-$100,000
Typical fees:	$150+ per hour
Advertising:	Referrals, direct mail, publications, networking
Qualifications:	Technical knowledge and expertise in systems, time-management skills
Equipment needed:	Computer, software, modem, fax, office furniture, letterhead, envelopes
Home business potential:	Yes
Staff required:	No, but subcontracting may be required depending on project needs
Handicapped opportunity:	Yes
Hidden costs:	Time and expense of staying current in this demanding field

LOWDOWN:

Computers are wonderful business tools; few organizations can begin to operate without them today. Yet no one would disagree with the premise that the design and planning of computers, both hardware and software, has a long way to go. Operations and compatibility problems are enormous, and as businesses grow, they must resolve issues related to the necessary growth in their information systems. If you have the expertise to be a systems integrator, nearly every growing company in the U.S., possibly the world, needs your services. One successful project should enable you to easily move on to another. You will need some people skills to work with the employees involved with information systems at your client's office. Your principal offering will be your detailed understanding of how the current systems work, what the needs are, and how to move the systems into effective integration.

START-UP:

Most of your work will be carried out at your client's premises and on their equipment, so you needn't spend too much on your own office and equipment. However, keep in mind that you'll need to be familiar with many different types of equipment, some of which you'll own and some of which you can lease. You'll need to be billing at a rate of at least $100 per hour.

BOTTOM LINE ADVICE:

Many businesses need your service, so if you live within commuting distance of an urban area, you ought to be able to create an excellent and profitable business of your own as a systems integrator. A longtime commitment to one client, necessary to complete most projects in this field, can limit your contacts—but it also should provide you with an excellent referral base. This is an extremely challenging field; however, one problem is that the people making the decision to hire you often have little understanding of what their information system needs. Education, then, is a major part of each sales effort. Systems integration is often carried out under high pressure. Bidding jobs is challenging as well.

TAXIDERMIST

Start-up cost:	$1,000-$3,500
Potential earnings:	$17,000-$25,000
Typical fees:	$45-$60 per animal
Advertising:	Yellow Pages, referrals from gun shops, fishing tackle and bait suppliers, and outdoor equipment stores, location
Qualifications:	Experience with taxidermy
Equipment needed:	Chemical preservatives, scalpel, inventory of replaceable parts
Home business potential:	Yes
Staff required:	No
Handicapped opportunity:	No
Hidden costs:	Mounts and supplies

LOWDOWN:

Your major market will be hunters and fishermen, although some taxidermists specialize in pets or museum exhibits. Location will be important for you. Taxidermy is often a home-based business, but you will need to make your presence known. It will be helpful if you can set up signs drawing people into your shop. Having a location near a hunting or fishing area will improve your flow of business. The popularity of hunting and fishing continues to increase, so if you are capable of creating an attractive mounted trophy or specimen, you could earn a steady if not spectacular income. Taxidermy is not just a craft. You will need to have a certain artistic sense and an understanding of unique characteristics of wild creatures to produce an effective result.

START-UP:

Your start-up costs consist primarily of the chemical preservatives that keep the animal looking lifelike beyond death. These chemicals and related items of equipment could run between $1,000-$5,000 to start—but, remember that you'll be using these chemicals on more than a few animals. Charge at least $45 per animal to cover your costs.

BOTTOM LINE ADVICE:

Building your market will be slow at first. Many hunters and fishermen are fundamentally conservative people who do not jump on the latest trend. You will need to provide excellent work over several years before referrals keep a reasonable clientele coming to your door. Taxidermy is not simple, and it will require great care to develop a pricing structure that compensates you adequately for the time, materials, and labor involved in your business.

TIME-MANAGEMENT SPECIALIST

Start-up cost:	$1,000-$6,500
Potential earnings:	$20,000-$40,000
Typical fees:	$75-$100 per hour or a set fee ($100+ per person) for classes you offer
Advertising:	Free workshops/seminars and other public speaking, word-of-mouth referrals, networking, news releases, written articles
Qualifications:	High level of organization, analytical ability, punctuality, ability to deliver on your commitments, an open mind
Equipment needed:	Computer with fax/modem, printer, phone, time-management software, handout materials
Home business potential:	Yes
Staff required:	No
Handicapped opportunity:	Yes
Hidden costs:	Preparation time if you are not already using a previously written program, licensing fees if you are

LOWDOWN:

Bringing relief to people under inordinate stress is just one of the many benefits of being a time-management specialist. In addition to making the workplace a little less of a sweatshop, you'll be assisting clients in goal-setting, developing action plans, defining priorities, and scheduling/delegating tasks and activities. You may decide to work as a consultant, identifying problems for harried company execu-tives in search of an answer in the pursuit of higher productivity. But you may also decide to add on additional services, such as seminars for large groups or individ-ual personal productivity training. The opportunities to make money from time are there, you just need to send the message out to the people most in need of your services (and they are nowhere near as limited as you at first might think). Quick profitability is a definite possibility with this low overhead business—but you need to charge appropriately for your time and expertise. One last tip: Don't forget to offer periodic refresher courses for repeat business; you'd be surprised how many customers say they'd benefit from another session.

START-UP:

Word-of-mouth advertising keeps initial costs low in this business, because it is based on credibility and trust of the specialist. To present a professional image, allow a minimum of $250 for business cards, letterhead, and brochures. Computer costs can range from $1,500-$5,000. Remember that organizational dues will be necessary to continually network and prospect for clients; set aside at least $250 per year for this valuable lead-generator. Charge at least $75 per hour for corporate consulting; more ($1,000 per day is typical) if you're conduct-ing seminars for groups of professionals.

BOTTOM LINE ADVICE:

The art of timeliness and organization is relatively new to businesses. Hence, com-petition may not be a significant problem. If you enjoy leading others to dramatic results in a short period of time, this career can be extremely enjoyable. But you should be advised that this work demands a lot of your own time and energy to get started; are you able to practice what you preach? It may take as much as a year or two before you are able to make a full-time income; hopefully, you have been gifted with patience yourself.

ADVICE FROM THE EXPERTS

What sets your business apart from others like it?
Jennifer Annandono, Managing Partner of the Kent, Ohio-based Progressive Leadership Center, says her business is unique because she is. "I greatly enjoy demonstrating to others how to have a more balanced work and personal life. My feeling is that time management is about setting goals, and the implementation of new tools, which will promote achievement."

Things you couldn't do without:
Annandono says she could not do without a second telephone line with answering or voice mail capability. "My computer and laser printer allow me the convenience of professional correspondence."

Marketing tips/advice:
"It is always more effective to market your service as the 'benefit' customers will receive rather than focusing on various features you might offer. Much of my marketing success is based in community interaction and word-of-mouth referral. The best advice is: always be a product of the service you provide!"

If you had to do it all over again . . .
"I would have spent the months preceding the opening of my business selecting centers of influence. If you are not already established in the community, it is never too early to identify and communicate with those individuals who know and trust you and clearly understand what service you provide."

TRADEMARK AGENT

Start-up cost:	$1,000-$1,500
Potential earnings:	$40,000-$65,000
Typical fees:	Usually a flat fee of $175-$250 (more for larger corporations)
Advertising:	Business publications, direct mail, referrals, networking
Qualifications:	Extensive experience in field, familiarity with computer searches, residence near Washington, D.C.
Equipment needed:	Computer with fax/modem, business cards, letterhead, envelopes
Home business potential:	Yes
Staff required:	No
Handicapped opportunity:	No
Hidden costs:	Insurance, on-line time

LOWDOWN:

The business cliché of today is that perception is reality. Whether you agree with that idea or not, the image of a product or service is undeniably a factor in its value. Since medieval times, a trademark has been a way of protecting an essential element of that image, the name. Since medieval times, however, an incredibly large number of names have been trademarked, and your clients need to know if they can call their stunt act Angelic Skydiving Service or if someone in Hawaii has already used that name. You will discover if the name has already been used by conducting a search of the paper records at the Trademark Office in Washington, D.C. Database information such as records from all 50 Secretaries of State is proprietary—owned by your giant competitors—so as a small business person, you must rely on manual searches. Many trademark agents specialize in a field they know well, such as tire names.

START-UP:

Costs are relatively low, especially if you already have a computer (add $2,000 if you don't). The outlay of your own labor, however, will be high for each search; if you are an attorney, you'll likely use a computer database, but if you're not, you'll have to do it all manually—and time is money. Charge $175-$250 per search/registry; more if working for a larger corporation (although many of these companies already have in-house or on-retainer attorneys who would accomplish the same work).

BOTTOM LINE ADVICE:

Skill and sometimes intuition are required to establish the validity of a given trademark. Finding the proper trademark files is an art. You can't simply look up a name, like "sword," in an index. Instead, you must consider all words with similar meanings, like "rapier and "saber," as well as the words with similar sounds, like "sod" and "sore." Then you must consider designs that might include swords. It all becomes quite complicated, so be sure you enjoy minute details before embarking on this one.

TRANSLATION SERVICES

Start-up cost:	$1,000-$2,000
Potential earnings:	$20,000-$30,000
Typical fees:	$25-$35 per hour
Advertising:	Trade journals, Yellow Pages, referrals, personal contacts
Qualifications:	Proficiency in a foreign language, excellent writing and communications skills
Equipment needed:	Computer, modem, fax, printer, software, office furniture, business cards, letterhead, envelopes
Home business potential:	Yes
Staff required:	Yes, for languages you cannot translate yourself
Handicapped opportunity:	Yes
Hidden costs:	Telephone costs, marketing

LOWDOWN:

Thousands of languages are spoken across the globe, and even within the U.S. texts often need translation into French or Spanish. For most business communications in the global marketplace, a translation service can be useful to develop, among other things, a glossary of terms to use in the translation process. Additional services can relate to development of icons and illustrations that are effective across cultures. You can specialize in a business field such as medical instrument sales, or you can focus on one particular language. Producing effective, accurate results under deadline will enable you to build your translation business into a very successful enterprise.

START-UP:

Reference materials and the normal office equipment are the major start-up costs. You'll need a printer that can produce all of the characters and accent marks used in your specialty languages. Grand start-up total should be somewhere from $1,000-$2,000; earnings will come from $25-$35 per hour fees.

BOTTOM LINE ADVICE:

The market for translation services is growing rapidly and will continue to do so in the future. English is by no means a universal language, and few Americans are fluent enough in a foreign language to produce their own translations. You'll be learning as you translate while providing a very significant service to your clients. Problems can result from lack of awareness, though. Translating is not a question of simply plugging words into slots (e.g., one foreign word for one English term). It's a creative and challenging activity to communicate the total meaning of a sentence or paragraph accurately, and your pricing needs to reflect the time needed to do this.

TRAVEL AGENT

Start-up cost:	$2,000-$5,000
Potential earnings:	$25,000-$45,000
Typical fees:	Commission of 10 percent is fairly common on each sale; some airlines have been cutting those commissions considerably, however
Advertising:	Travel, meeting/hotel magazines, Yellow Pages, direct mail, location
Qualifications:	Knowledge of the travel industry and particular destinations; often, certification is required through an accredited travel school; training on the customized computer systems most travel agencies use.
Equipment needed:	At minimum, a computer and phone
Home business potential:	Yes
Staff required:	No
Handicapped opportunity:	Yes
Hidden costs:	Phone expenses

LOWDOWN:

Would you find satisfaction helping others fly the friendly skies to exotic places? Have you always been a travel nut? If you answered yes to both questions, you could potentially succeed as a travel agent. As an outside travel agent, you would associate with a travel agency willing to work with you. You can refer business to them (for perhaps a 10 percent commission) or actually arrange travel bookings for which the agency will cut the tickets (because restrictions on ticketing won't allow you to do it). For the latter work, you can make as much as 60 to 70 percent of the commission. There are also networked travel agencies that rely almost solely on home-based agents, so your options are many if you decide to embark on this exciting and interesting business. The best part is, many travel companies offer incentives and special perks for agents like you—and you could wind up doing some sightseeing yourself.

START-UP:

You need a budget for advertising, the appropriate computer and office equipment, software, and phone, and may have to pay small fees (such as $50) to use your associate's name and ticketing number.

BOTTOM LINE ADVICE:

The travel business is huge—and still growing by leaps and bounds. Many opportunities exist to make money in this field. The cost of running a travel business is modest if you are working as an outside agent; little more than computer and office equipment is required. Opening your own agency is an expensive proposition; it also takes time to get established, and competition from larger agencies capable of booking large corporate accounts can be daunting.

ADVICE FROM THE EXPERTS

What sets your business apart from others like it?

"My agents and I have traveled to almost every destination in the world, so I would say that personal experience set us apart from other travel agents," says Helen Meek, owner of Helen Meek Travel in Fairlawn, Ohio.

Things you couldn't do without:

Computers with specialized reservation programs (leased from airline companies) and telephones are the primary pieces of equipment needed to run this travel agency. "We also couldn't do without our experienced, wonderful staff."

Marketing tips/advice:

"You need to look at location and market demographics; I knew my area would grow, and now I'm an established leader in my geographic location." Meek also advises entrepreneurs to get their names out there any way possible while building credibility.

If you had to do it all over again . . .

"Nothing. It's worked for thirteen years, and if you can get past those first five, you are probably going to make it."

TREE SERVICE

Start-up cost:	$1,000-$5,000
Potential earnings:	$25,000-$35,000
Typical fees:	$120-$350 per day
Advertising:	Classified ads, Yellow Pages
Qualifications:	Experience
Equipment needed:	Pickup truck, chain saw
Home business potential:	Yes
Staff required:	You may need a helper, depending on the size of the job (and the tree)
Handicapped opportunity:	No
Hidden costs:	Permission of local authorities, health and liability insurance

LOWDOWN:

A tree service can be a good business for an energetic and relatively fearless person with experience in climbing up where the squirrels run and using heavy, dangerous tools like chain saws at the same time. You'll need to have expertise in tree health, too. Which limbs are about to fall? How should a tree be pruned so that it will become strong and graceful? When a tree must be cut down, you'll need to know the art and science of making it fall safely and avoid crushing your customer's sunporch. You may be able to sell the logs as firewood for an add-on business. Some tree services specialize in pruning orchard trees. Pruning is essential for productive orchard trees.

START-UP:

Tools, heavy boots, and a truck are all you need. You could make a killing if you live in the country and bill $150-$350 per job. Make sure that you can keep their wood—turning that wood in to lumberyards or firewood services could net you as much as an additional $500 per month.

BOTTOM LINE ADVICE:

Most people who make a success of the tree service business have a deep love of the outdoors and of growing things. It sometimes takes imagination to see which limbs to keep and which to cut. If you'd rather climb a tree than sit in an office and look at one through a skyscraper window, this may be the business for you. The major negative here is the physical danger. You may love the treetops, but insurance companies have a different perspective. And you'll need to plan for seasonal ups and downs.

TROPICAL FISH SERVICING

Start-up cost:	$1,000-$2,000
Potential earnings:	$10,000-$20,000
Typical fees:	$25-$35 per job (depending on tank size)
Advertising:	Flyers, bulletin boards, Yellow Pages
Qualifications:	Knowledge of aquarium maintenance
Equipment needed:	Cleaning equipment, business cards, letterhead, envelopes
Home business potential:	Yes
Staff required:	No
Handicapped opportunity:	No
Hidden costs:	None

LOWDOWN:

This is a business opportunity for a person with patience and enthusiasm for the underwater world and self-marketing ability to go with it. Tropical fish aquariums can require a surprisingly high level of maintenance, and your challenge will be to make your services known to the businesses and individuals who would appreciate being relieved of this tiresome, ongoing chore. The tanks must be cleaned regularly and replenished with fresh water and chemical treatments to ensure that the fish remain healthy. Experience caring for your own fish will help you to recognize what is needed by each aquarium that you service.

START-UP:

Costs are minimal for a maintenance service but will increase if you decide to move into sales of aquarium equipment or the actual fish. You should charge $25-$35 per cleaning job, and remember to include your mileage as overhead.

BOTTOM LINE ADVICE:

This is a nice part-time job for a self-starter. Many people are simply happy with the opportunity to make a hobby into a business. You must plan your service deliveries so you don't spend too much time traveling between clients. Remember, too, that marketing your services can be quite demanding of your time.

UPHOLSTERER

Start-up cost:	$1,000-$5,000
Potential earnings:	$20,000-$40,000
Typical fees:	Varied; could be as low as $50 and as high as $1,000
Advertising:	Yellow Pages, community newspapers, coupon books, referral
Qualifications:	Skilled apprenticeship
Equipment needed:	Upholstery tools, tacks, fabric
Home business potential:	Yes
Staff required:	No
Handicapped opportunity:	Not typically
Hidden costs:	Insurance

LOWDOWN:

There's nothing like a terrific-looking accent chair to make any room stand out . . . and you can help your customers highlight any of their furniture pieces as a quality-driven upholsterer. If you've got the background or skill in the centuries-old art of upholstery, you could go into business as quickly as you can hang up a sign. All you need to do is make sure you're reaching the more affluent types; they'll generally pay better and have furniture re-covered more frequently. Once you've established yourself as a trusted name in the business, you'll be surprised how quickly referrals will start rolling in. Then you can spend your days helping customers choose new and exciting fabrics, style-enhancing accents (such as decorative tacks or tassels), and other details that will change the look and personality of each piece of furniture you work on. You'll provide an estimate, then set about the work itself (after you've ordered the requested fabric and materials). It's a challenging, creative business for those who truly love furniture.

START-UP:

You'll need $1,000-$5,000 to get started in this business, mainly to cover your equipment and supply costs. Of course, there will be at least $1,000 or so in advertising, too. However, if you are conscientious and pay attention to small details, your reputation could bring you $20,000-$40,000 per year.

BOTTOM LINE ADVICE:

The work is exacting, physical—and, to some, quite tedious. If you prefer working alone in a quiet place, and if you are especially very task-oriented, this could be a wonderful opportunity for you. Remember, too, that there is plenty of room for creativity—and some furniture designers look to upholsterers for fresh ideas.

VENDING MACHINE OWNER

Start-up cost:	$1,000-$20,000
Potential earnings:	Depends on the machine location and type; a possible annual potential income of $20,000-$35,000
Typical fees:	Can be as low as $100 per month and as high as $500 per month (per machine)
Advertising:	Direct mail, Yellow Pages
Qualifications:	Excellent sales ability
Equipment needed:	Vending machines and the product to fill them
Home business potential:	Yes
Staff required:	No
Handicapped opportunity:	No
Hidden costs:	An average of 10 percent on what you earn from each machine is given to the property owner

LOWDOWN:

Although they seem to be everywhere, some research will be required to determine what type of vending machine is needed and exactly which spots might be most profitable for you. Without a doubt, you'll need good marketing and sales skills for this occupation. For example, solicit large factories to find out if they have round-the-clock shifts and need 'real food' such as soup and sandwiches—or, if it's a small firm, will only soda and candy machines do? Once you've obtained a client, that customer should be able to tell you what to stock, but ask to tour the facility so you can get a good idea of where to actually place the machine. If you go with soda and candy, make sure your client company will place your machine in a high-traffic area.

START-UP:

Start-up costs depend on what type of vending machine you will want to use. Bubble gum machines cost as little as $100 and cappuccino machines can run as high as $1,000 or more. Whatever machine you decide to go with, it should be a winner if you market correctly, and you could earn $20,000-$35,000.

BOTTOM LINE ADVICE:

Our recommendation is to hit the big factories and large businesses. They usually pay you to come to them and don't require the 10 percent fee. You will also have to follow up on your machines; every day in a large business and a minimum of once a week for smaller-volume vending machines. This can pretty much be a five-day-a-week job, since most businesses close for the weekend.

VENTURE CAPITALIST

Start-up cost:	$1,000-$2,000 (more if you are the primary investor)
Potential earnings:	$15,000-$40,000+ per deal
Typical fees:	Percentage of investment or stock in company
Advertising:	Classifieds in business publications
Qualifications:	MBA or serious investment experience
Equipment needed:	Business cards, letterhead, envelopes, typewriter or computer and printer
Home business potential:	Yes
Staff required:	No
Handicapped opportunity:	Yes
Hidden costs:	Travel time and costs to visit client businesses

LOWDOWN:

There's nothing more exciting than seeing a business grow and develop. As a venture capitalist, you are participating in the process in a unique way. You've got a bird's-eye view of the possibilities, the energy, the creativity, and the drive of new enterprises that will become the Microsofts and Chryslers of tomorrow. Meanwhile, they desperately need capital, the lifeblood of growing businesses. Your contribution is to assess the nature and value of the enterprise and find a source of capital that will be a good match. High-technology areas are the most fertile grounds for your services, but many other types of businesses also are searching for the capital to start or expand.

START-UP:

The cost of your advertisements is the main expense, but you'll need a professional office setup to write reports, model business plans, and so on; spend at least a few thousand setting up. If you have a solid network of financing sources available, and you are good at convincing them to invest in your clients' businesses, you could make $40,000 or more per deal.

BOTTOM LINE ADVICE:

Homework pays off. The value you are adding is really in terms of knowledge. Gather your list of sources of available capital first, and keep it up to date. The shortage in the venture capital world is not with the borrowers but with the "venturers." The fact that you can find and work with them is your contribution. Often the challenge is one of presentation. Sometimes funds are only accessible when a professional business plan has been prepared that reflects the new enterprise in business-oriented terms.

WATER PUMPING SERVICE

Start-up cost:	$4,000-$6,000
Potential earnings:	$30,000-$45,000
Typical fees:	Often a per-job rate of $200-$300
Advertising:	Yellow Pages, direct mail, classified ads
Qualifications:	Knowledge of pumping systems and machinery repair
Equipment needed:	Pickup truck, tools, spare parts inventory
Home business potential:	Yes
Staff required:	No
Handicapped opportunity:	No
Hidden costs:	Insurance, wear and tear on equipment

LOWDOWN:

For homes and businesses that receive water from a well, a breakdown in the pump means an immediate call for help. If you have the knowledge and experience to work with this type of system, you can set up a very healthy business. You will need to live in an area where wells are a common form of water supply, and you must be able to diagnose breakdowns and repair the pumps. Beyond these two requirements your major challenge will be making the availability of your services known to the public.

START-UP:

For a repair service, this type of business is relatively inexpensive to set up ($4,000-$6,000). With a reliable supplier of parts, you can get by with little investment. Bill out at a flat rate of $200-$300 per job, or set an hourly rate of $45 and up.

BOTTOM LINE ADVICE:

It's great to have a business that provides an essential service. Well pumps can be tricky, and when one goes out, the owner will be eager to become your customer. You may find yourself working outdoors in unpleasant weather, and often you'll be responding to a crisis, and agitated customers.

WINDOW TREATMENT SPECIALIST

Start-up cost:	$1,000-$5,000
Potential earnings:	$25,000-$35,000
Typical fee:	$20-$30 per hour or a per-job basis
Advertising:	Personal contacts with interior decorators, fabric and drapery stores, Yellow Pages, local newspapers
Qualifications:	Basic sewing skills, ability to accurately measure
Equipment needed:	Heavy-duty sewing machine
Home business potential:	Yes
Staff required:	No
Handicapped potential:	Yes
Hidden costs:	Materials can get costly; buy wholesale

LOWDOWN:

You can provide a year-round service with a heavy-duty sewing machine, space to create, and an interest in interior decorating. With the continuing influx of housing developments and condominium complexes, you should have no shortage for customers in need of fine window detail such as curtains, valances, or swags. Network with condo associations and apartment complex owners; they may provide you with regular referrals and a steady flow of business. Cultivate contacts with local fabric stores and interior designers. Remember, accuracy is a must because mistakes in measuring can get expensive if you have to replace fabric.

START-UP:

Even with your equipment costs considered, you'll still be in the $1,000-$5,000 start-up range with this business. The biggest cost, really, is your advertising— you'll need to get the word out in community newspapers, the Yellow Pages, and through coupon books, so expect to spend $3,000 or more on advertising alone. Your hourly rate should be somewhere near $20-$35 per hour.

BOTTOM LINE ADVICE:

Make a portfolio with photographs of samples of your work to show prospective clients. Display some of them in fabric stores, and make business cards available to store owners and interior designers.

WINDOW WASHING SERVICE

Start-up cost:	$1,000-$5,000
Potential earnings:	$25,000-$45,000
Typical fee:	$25-$50 per hour (slightly more for corporate work)
Advertising:	Business and consumer Yellow Pages, local newspapers, coupons through direct mail and Welcome Wagon, networking
Qualifications:	Enthusiasm, willingness to work hard—and no fear of heights
Equipment needed:	Ladders, scaffolding, platforms, cleaning solutions, squeegees, buckets, rags
Home business potential:	Yes
Staff required:	Perhaps as business grows, especially for high-rise buildings
Handicapped opportunity:	No
Hidden costs:	Insurance and workers' compensation

LOWDOWN:

How many times do folks use the classic line, "I don't do windows?" If you choose this business as your line of work, you'll have a clever answer ready for those people. As a window washer, you'll be working outside in various locations, and the work is pretty straightforward: you come, you clean, and then you move on. With a little elbow grease, this can be a business with few initial costs, especially where small jobs are concerned. If you plan to go after more lucrative commercial work, greater expenses and more personnel might be required—such as health insurance and workers compensation costs. Still, it's a fairly recession-proof business; after all, no one really likes to clean windows (except you).

START-UP:

Set aside $100 or so for your business cards, then add $3,000 or so for advertising in the Yellow Pages (both business and consumer are recommended). Use the remainder of your start-up funds to get your vehicle packed with solvents and other cleaning chemicals. Ladders, scaffolds, and other equipment can be leased until you're more sure of yourself and your business.

BOTTOM LINE ADVICE:

Everybody's windows get dirty—homeowners and businesses alike. But the big bucks are probably in jobs such as high-rise apartments and commercial office buildings. Decide what kind of niche you want to fill, and plan your business accordingly. You'll use different methods of advertising depending on whether you target your business to commercial buildings or homeowners.

Wood Splitter

Start-up cost:	$1,000-$5,000
Potential earnings:	$25,000-$40,000
Typical fees:	$80-$150 per cord
Advertising:	Flyers, local newspapers, Yellow Pages
Qualifications:	Knowledge of tree and wood types, physical strength
Equipment needed:	Chain saw, wood splitter, large truck
Home business potential:	Yes
Staff required:	No
Handicapped opportunity:	No
Hidden costs:	Gas to run machines and vehicle

Lowdown:

How many times have you seen large trees come down during a heavy storm? Or had trees that needed to be cut into firewood, but you didn't have a chain saw (or the slightest idea how to use one)? That's precisely why wood splitting can be extremely profitable—because few of us know how to cut wood ourselves without cutting off our own limbs. If you're in this type of business, you'll spend your time working with customers who have trees that need to be cut and/or removed. You may also try finding a place to cut for little or no cost, chop down the trees, split them by hand or hydraulic machine, and transport the final product to storage or directly to a customer/sales area. Selling cords of wood in urban areas will net you $150 or more each, while customers in rural areas, where wood is plentiful, will buy a cord for around $80. The best advertising will be your vehicle (with your company information on it) and word of mouth; it would be a good idea to let realtors know of your service, as they often refer clients to specialized services such as this.

Start-up:

A log splitter is not a necessary part of this business, but it sure will make the job a lot easier. You can buy this machine for $600-$4,000, depending on whether it is new or used. Another big expense could be finding an area to harvest. Most often, landowners with forests will charge a fee to let people cut down their trees. Occasionally, however, farmers who want their land cleared will let businesses come chop for free, or even pay them to do it and let them keep the wood. A chain saw ($500-$1,000) is a must, and the two final entries on your start-up list are a truck for transporting and a storage shed.

Bottom Line Advice:

Without physical fitness, you won't go far with wood splitting. Stacking and loading/unloading bundles is strenuous, even if the machine does all the actual splitting. A love for the outdoors in all weather is also very important—withstanding heat in particular—since most splitting is done during the summer when the wood is dry and easier to chop.

Checklist for Success: Can You Be a Successful Entrepreneur?

Here are some questions you might ask yourself before embarking on a new business:

❑ Are you unhappy with your current situation—and ready for a change?

❑ Are you completely self-directed; that is, able to come up with and complete your own job requirements?

❑ Are you able to meet with and sell to many different types of people?

❑ Are you an expert planner—someone who can see not only the big picture, but every tiny line that created the big picture?

❑ Can you set and keep deadlines?

❑ Are you a clock-watcher, or someone who quickly loses track of time?

❑ Can you commit to projects and follow them through to completion every time?

❑ Are you adaptable and open to learning new ways of doing things?

❑ Do you have the mental and physical stamina you need to run your business?

❑ Are you afraid of risk?

❑ Do you have adequate savings to cover your first year's salary?

❑ Are you a positive person?

WORLD WIDE WEB HOME PAGE CREATOR

Start-up cost:	$2,000-$3,000
Potential earnings:	$15,000+ (it's an emerging market, so the true ceiling isn't known yet)
Typical fees:	$500+ per creation
Advertising:	Word of mouth, bulletin board services, trade journals, on-line account
Qualifications:	Marketing skills, computer graphic skills, experience in cyberspace
Equipment needed:	Computer, modem, office furniture
Home business potential:	Yes
Staff required:	No
Handicapped opportunity:	Yes
Hidden costs:	Be sure to watch your connect time with on-line services

LOWDOWN:

This is about as cutting edge as you can get in the world of marketing. Industries of almost all types are exploring the Internet; many have found that a home page connects them with their customers in new ways. An effective full-color home page works much better than a dull list of products available with their specs. Producing an effective home page is an entirely different experience from developing an old-fashioned paper brochure; if you can make the Web come alive for a client by designing a home page that is visited often, you can be one of the first in this emerging field. Businesses need to understand that surfers will spend time at a location on the Internet that offers something they want: an interesting, informative home page that engages their imaginations and offers them products related to their needs.

START-UP:

Power up your modem and go. On-line time will probably be a significant cost and you will want to advertise on-line as well; these rates will vary according to carrier but run $8-$10 a month for basic services and an average of $4 per hour on extended services. Set your fees according to what the market will bear—check out what competitors are charging by visiting their Internet site.

BOTTOM LINE ADVICE:

This business depends on several kinds of creativity at once. The process of making home pages isn't something you can follow step-by-step out of your old college textbooks. You're covering new ground here. It will take creativity to market yourself as well, because the whole idea of computerized marketing is so new. Learning about your client companies so you can represent them creatively and effectively will keep you on your mental toes. You'll find it takes quite a bit of time to find clients creative and futuristic enough to understand the advantages of your service.

ADVICE FROM THE EXPERTS

What sets your business apart from others like it?

"We're based in the fundamentals of advertising and design," says Larry Rosenthal, President of Cube Productions, Inc., in New York City. "We are also on the cutting edge; if it's new technology, it's been in here for an experimental run. Our clients appreciate the fact that we try everything out first."

Things you couldn't do without:

Rosenthal says he couldn't do without a computer and modem, Internet lines, software tools, and external, peripheral equipment such as scanners.

Marketing tips/advice:

"Get yourself a home page, and make it a well-constructed, easy-to-use one with a clear point of view. Also, use e-mail to market directly to those who might be interested in your services."

If you had to do it all over again . . .

"I would have started working on the Web even earlier. I would've also e-mailed Mark Andreeson from Netscape and ask to work with him!"

START-UP BETWEEN
$5,000 AND $15,000

ACCIDENT RECONSTRUCTION SERVICE

Start-up cost:	$10,000-$15,000
Potential earnings:	$50,000-$100,000
Typical fees:	Flat fees of $500-$1,000 per job
Advertising:	Law journals, referrals, direct mail
Qualifications:	Extensive experience, technical training, writing skills, ability to give effective testimony in court
Equipment needed:	Computer, modem, fax, suite software, laser printer, business card, letterhead, envelopes, camera
Home business potential:	Yes
Staff required:	No
Handicapped opportunity:	No
Hidden costs:	Travel, insurance

LOWDOWN:

Automobile accidents are all too common, and often the serious crashes result in a court case. It can be surprisingly difficult to establish the facts of what happened. Witnesses offer different stories based on different perspectives. Memories can be clouded by shock and by the suddenness of the accident. Passengers in the vehicles often remember little beyond the first terrifying crashing sounds. Your accident reconstruction service will be hired by one side in the case to develop a portrait of what happened that supports the claims they are making. You will use testimony, evidence collected immediately after the accident, and even a fact-gathering trip to the site itself to build your reconstruction. This is a skilled activity; it will take persistence to build your reputation for developing accurate, convincing reconstructions. You will write a report and often give a deposition as to your findings. If the case is not settled and goes to trial, your expert testimony will be called on to support the presentation of your client's case. Some reconstruction services work for police departments rather than preparing evidence to support one claim against another.

START-UP:

You will need a well-equipped office in which to develop and print out your reports, along with some design-oriented software to build computer models of the accident site and those involved. Expect to shell out at least $10,000 for all of these items. Many accident reconstruction services charge $500-$1,000 per job: it takes time to generate a clear image of what occurred. Obviously, if the accident was very straightforward and there were plenty of witnesses, your fee will be considerably less (possibly as low as $250).

BOTTOM LINE ADVICE:

Attention to accuracy, focus on small pieces of evidence to re-create past events, and a creative imagination to build the data into a convincing picture all are necessary for success in this field. Each case is different, and each has challenges. This will never be a dull job, but it won't be an easy one either. It will take persistent marketing to establish the value of your services in the eyes of the legal community.

ACOUSTICAL SERVICES

Start-up cost:	$5,000-$15,000
Potential earnings:	$25,000-$45,000
Typical fees:	$150-$1,000+ per job (depending on size of work area) plus materials costs
Advertising:	Yellow Pages; direct mail to schools, auditoriums, and concert halls, cold calls
Qualifications:	Background in noise control and some working knowledge of architecture
Equipment needed:	Van for transporting materials and tools
Home business potential:	Yes
Staff required:	Not initially
Handicapped opportunity:	Not typically
Hidden costs:	Insurance, fluctuations in materials costs

LOWDOWN:

Because they rely so heavily upon quality sound effects and reverberation during performances, school auditoriums and performing halls often need the services of a good acoustical professional. If they use your service, they're likely to first get an initial consultation (you might need to attend a rehearsal or performance to experience the room's true acoustics and how sound gets absorbed by a full house). After you've made some notes about the sound quality in the performing venue or rehearsal room, you will then proceed to offer suggestions on how to improve the tonal qualities and general acoustics. It could entail simply hanging carpet squares over old speakers no longer being used, or it could be an extensive job of applying sound-dampening foam insulation throughout an auditorium. At any rate, you'll need to become extremely familiar with every type of sound barrier-type material out there—in addition to being adept at customer service. It's your reputation, after all, that will bring you more business.

START-UP:

Your start-up costs ($5,000-$15,000) will consist of preliminary materials and a work van with tools. Your income will vary according to how large or small your clients are (they should pretty much run the gamut); expect to charge anywhere from $150-$1,000 or more for each job. Your earnings will likely be in the $25,000-$45,000 range.

BOTTOM LINE ADVICE:

Once you've helped a customer boost acoustical efficiency and quality, where do you go from there? It's not likely you'll have repeat sales—although the potential exists for you to go back and service your client base and make a few extra dollars per year from them. While the positive side of this business is that you can make a pretty decent cut from each installation, the downside is that you're going to be constantly on the lookout for new business.

ADVERTISING AGENCY

Start-up cost:	$7,000-$16,000
Potential earnings:	$35,000-$75,000
Typical fees:	$75-$150 per hour, a monthly retainer, or a per-job basis
Advertising:	Networking, trade publications, teaching at a community college or adult school
Qualifications:	Knowledge of design, layout, and typography; writing skills; experience
Equipment needed:	Computer with modem and high-resolution printer, presentations, desktop publishing, and photo software, scanner, CD-ROM, fax, copy machine, business card, letterhead, envelopes
Home business potential:	Yes
Staff required:	No
Handicapped opportunity:	Yes
Hidden costs:	Organizational dues and schmoozing may get costly

LOWDOWN:

You're probably not going to be doing the Cadillac ads for General Motors, but if you are motivated and highly skilled you can build up a home-based ad agency serving clients in a specialized area. To get a foothold, you'll need to have experience from a larger agency, or a source of clients who know you and respect your interest in what they do. Activities such as collecting or participating in a special sport could be your lead-in to a small but profitable market. Or you could specialize in one type of store, one product, or a type of service. You will get to know your client organizations well, and you will draw on all of your creativity, both verbal and graphic. New ways of getting a commercial message out to the public are revolutionizing the advertising field, so creativity extends into the nature of the business itself as well. Very few businesses can succeed without advertising in one way or another, so your creativity and awareness of market needs has many possible customers. You'll need to educate your clients about the value of advertising—even when things don't seem to be going very well for the company or when they are overbooked with too much business.

START-UP:

High-end computers with the graphics and print-production software now available enable small agencies to produce ads that once required an entire art department. Setting up this equipment is expensive, though, and could cost from $3,000-$5,000. Bill out between $75-$150 per hour, or determine your rates on a per-job basis that takes into account how much work is actually involved in the project. Many ad agencies also work on monthly retainers of $500 or more; again, look at the workload and the time and expertise involved in each project.

BOTTOM LINE ADVICE:

Advertising is a rewarding occupation because it relies so heavily on ideas and inspiration, connected directly to business results. Successful ad agency personnel (in this case, you) develop close relationships with their clients. You'll be serving an area or group that you know about and enjoy, and you'll be using all of your talents to do so. As a one-man (or -woman) band, you must be able to do all the facets of the advertising process, from sales to writing and pasteup. The pressure never lets up—and the competition for clients is sharklike.

ADVICE FROM THE EXPERTS

What sets your business apart from others like it?
For Carol Wilkerson, owner of Wilkerson Ltd., in Portland, Oregon, it's experience that sets her business apart. "I have over twenty-three years of experience in advertising and public relations, and I have dealt from the bottom up with any kind of promotional effort there is. Also, I'm small and selective about who I work with, because I want to make sure I can really provide the top-notch service the client's looking for, turning things around quickly enough to keep them coming back for more."

Things you couldn't do without:
Wilkerson's business depends on a computer, laser printer, fax, telephone, and overnight delivery services.

Marketing tips/advice:
"Before you start, determine what your strengths are and identify them for your clients. You really run into problems when you start promising things you really can't do . . . you can't fake knowledge and experience. Farm out what you can't do to others who can, and you'll gain a lot more respect."

If you had to do it all over again . . .
"Oddly enough, I didn't promote myself well enough in the beginning . . . I wasn't a big enough cheerleader for my own business. It's so ironic!"

AGRICULTURAL MARKETING

Start-up cost:	$5,000-$10,000
Potential earnings:	$35,000-$60,000
Typical fees:	Percentage of goods sold (usually 5 to 15 percent); sometimes an up-front fee of $500-$1,000 in addition to percentage
Advertising:	Yellow Pages, farm publications, referral
Qualifications:	Commodities background would be extremely helpful
Equipment needed:	Computer, printer, fax/modem, phone, cellular phone
Home business potential:	Yes
Staff required:	No
Handicapped opportunity:	Possibly
Hidden costs:	Insurance, on-line service fees

LOWDOWN:

Farmers are not always the best at selling their product—that's why they often rely on services such as yours. You'll advertise in a respected farming journal or the Yellow Pages, and if you get at least one client for whom you can make a difference, you'll be on the road to referral in no time. Of course, you know that you'll be expected to work long hours trying to get a farmer's goods to market at a profitable (yet competitive) price, since the farmer simply doesn't have the time to be a marketer in addition to all of his other duties. You will develop contacts in your area, and if you're really enterprising, all over the world (through the Internet, naturally). If you can arrange for proper transportation and have a knack for understanding and working through complex customs regulations, you could make a significant amount of money selling farm goods to the rest of the world.

START-UP:

Since some of your work will be done on-line, you'll need a decent computer system as part of your basic office setup (which will also include printer, fax/modem, and phone); between that and your advertising costs, you'll probably spend in the $5,000-$10,000 range to get this business launched properly. On the other hand, you'll likely be earning $35,000-$60,000 annually, so setting a little bit aside for your office shouldn't hurt too much.

BOTTOM LINE ADVICE:

You'll enjoy the independence of working solo and pretty much on your own time schedule; the only potential problem is that you're dealing with a volatile market, so be prepared to spend a lot of time watching the markets for fluctuations.

AMBULATORY SERVICES

Start-up cost:	$6,000-$20,000
Potential earnings:	$20,000-$50,000
Typical fees:	$100-$150 per visit
Advertising:	Direct mail, flyers in health care offices and clinics, referrals from physicians and home nurses
Qualifications:	RN, certification in specific service offered (respiratory therapy, etc.)
Equipment needed:	Small van, medical supplies, and equipment appropriate for your specialty
Home business potential:	Yes
Staff required:	No
Handicapped opportunity:	No
Hidden costs:	Business and professional insurance, licensing fees, vehicle fuel and maintenance

LOWDOWN:

Very few communities in the U.S. have physicians who make house calls. With the reductions in federal support for health care, many smaller hospitals have closed or will be forced to do so. These changes leave an opportunity for an individual with the appropriate medical credentials to create a business providing ambulatory care to patients. Your market will be people who cannot fit the tighter and tighter criteria for admission to a hospital, and who lack the transportation to go to an outpatient clinic for needed medical services. As the population ages, more and more people will be needing these services and will appreciate your ability to deliver them in their homes.

START-UP:

You will need a reliable vehicle that is big enough to carry your equipment and supplies. It needs to present a respectable image of your services as you drive it around town. And you will need the best in equipment. Costs of equipment vary, being much higher if you provide home X rays, for example. All said and done, you'll spend at least $10,000 before you know it, and your income potential annually is somewhere between $20,000-$50,000.

BOTTOM LINE ADVICE:

Getting the confidence of a few physicians with large practices will be the first step in establishing your client base. A home nursing service would also be a wonderful referral base for you. Being reliable, accurate, and totally customer-focused is essential. It may take you a while to discover the right market niche for your service, but referrals will carry you once you do so. This business requires superb time-management skills and a good sense of logistics as well.

ANIMAL BROKER/DEALER

Start-up cost:	$10,000-$15,000
Potential earnings:	$45,000-$70,000
Typical fees:	Often $200 per animal
Advertising:	Trade journals, direct mail, referrals, networking
Qualifications:	Familiarity with CITES, the international treaty on the movement of plants and animals, contacts with zoo personnel, animal parks, and importers
Equipment needed:	Computer, modem, fax, printer, office furniture, business card, letterhead, envelopes
Home business potential:	Yes
Staff required:	No
Handicapped opportunity:	No
Hidden costs:	Travel and conference fees

LOWDOWN:

Zoos increasingly have breeding programs and tend to trade animals amongst themselves. Not all the needed exhibit animals can be obtained by this means, however, and brokers and dealers must fill the rest of the bill. Many animals are bred in private parks and later become available for display in a zoo. There is still some international trade in animals as well, regulated by CITES and various national laws and regulations. To make a go of being an animal broker, you will need many close contacts in the zoo world so you will hear when a particular species is needed. Sources of animals can be even harder to find, and your ability to link the creature with the zoo needing it will set you apart from the competition. Be certain that you like animals and don't mind caring for them in interim situations when they are between places to live. On a smaller scale, you can locate purebred puppies.

START-UP:

The telephone will probably be your most important piece of office equipment, along with some method (probably Internet) of communicating with distant sources.

BOTTOM LINE ADVICE:

This is not the fast-growing fad business of the '90s. Nor is it open to just anyone who has completed a course or two in zoology at the local community college. But if you have a friend in every zoo in the country, and if you care enough about the welfare of animals to plan their new homes successfully, you can establish yourself as an animal broker. Don't expect to grow rich overnight, though. Like the many animals you'll represent, this one will take time to grow.

ARCHAEOLOGICAL SERVICES

Start-up cost:	$5,000-$10,000
Potential earnings:	$15,000-$45,000
Typical fees:	$45-$65 per hour
Advertising:	Yellow Pages, universities
Qualifications:	Degree in archaeology
Equipment needed:	Digging tools, sturdy boots, screens (for sifting dirt), cloth, cellular phone/pager
Home business potential:	Yes (but you'll be working on-site)
Staff required:	Often you can get students to work with you (cheaply) on a large dig
Handicapped opportunity:	Possibly
Hidden costs:	Insurance, workers' compensation

LOWDOWN:

If you're deeply interested in uncovering the secrets of the past, and if you can stand working long hours, archaeological services may be the perfect business for you. Just put on your Indiana Jones hat and start digging! Seriously, though, you'll need to be precise and extremely careful when sifting through layers of sediment in search of works of natural wonder; the slightest scratch or dent could cost the life (and value) of the pieces you'll find. Because you'll likely have a degree in archaeology to begin with, you'll probably have already been on lots of "digs"; however, it is important to realize the delicacy of the work you're doing. First, you'll need to know where to dig (based on historic evidence or detail about a particular culture's habits); then you'll need to clean off each piece you find, number, and tag. Next, you'll wrap the pieces, then transport them to the nearest lab for dating and more meticulous examination. Museum directors and others in the community will always be interested in your findings.

START-UP:

You'll spend around $5,000 on your initial equipment; try to make your own screens to save a little bit of cash. If you work for just a few clients your first year, you'll make about $15,000; however, if you do a lot of work at the corporate level, you can expect to see earnings as high as $45,000. Charge $45-$65 per hour for your work.

BOTTOM LINE ADVICE:

If you like being in the outdoors during different seasons, and you don't mind the long hours of tedium as you uncover layer after layer of sediment, this could be your dream job. The reward is finding something truly unique or of incredible intrinsic value (such as the oldest human remains in your area).

ADVICE FROM THE EXPERTS

What sets your business apart from others like it?

"We have a large in-house staff and the ability to work on multiple projects," says Donald J. Weir, President of Archaeological and Historical Consulting in Jackson, Michigan. "We provide guidance for a complex and confusing process."

Things you couldn't do without:

Weir couldn't do without accounting software, a phone system, and archaeological field and laboratory equipment.

Marketing tips/advice:

Visibility and networking are the best methods of getting more business.

If you had to do it all over again . . .

For Weir, location has been a concern. He would probably move to an area where his services had more of a broad appeal.

ART RESTORATION SERVICES

Start-up cost:	$5,000-$10,000
Potential earnings:	$20,000-$45,000
Typical fees:	$45-$75 per hour
Advertising:	Yellow Pages, art publications, direct mail, cold calls (networking is almost always the best bet)
Qualifications:	Art history degree and artistic background, knowledge of historic technique and materials
Equipment needed:	Paints, brushes, palette, ladders, easel, van for ease of transport
Home business potential:	Yes (but only if you've got a studio)
Staff required:	No
Handicapped opportunity:	Not typically
Hidden costs:	Insurance, travel costs

LOWDOWN:

When the Mona Lisa's smile starts cracking or Van Gogh's sunflowers start to flake off, who does a museum director call for assistance? You can't call on the artist, so you need to call the next best thing—an artist trained in historic technique and "patch" work, a professional who can touch up a masterpiece without destroying it or adding any of his own personal touches to the work. Generally, an art restoration service is made up of one or two artists who are skilled in such matters and who have a reputation for fixing great works of art. That means much of your promotional work will be geared toward getting referrals. Sometimes, you'll take art to your own studio to work on it for a period of a few weeks to several months; other times, the museum's policy will not allow you to leave the premises with its precious objects. You'll painstakingly restore the work, with careful attention to the nuances of each brush stroke. You might spend long hours in unusual positions (as many works of art were created by artists on scaffolds!) and working alone; if it's artistic solitude you're looking for, this could be a rewarding job for you.

START-UP:

If you've already got a studio, or if you're set to work primarily on-site at a museum's studio, you'll need only about $5,000-$10,000 to get started. That will cover your vehicle, paint, and related materials (brushes, drop cloths, ladders, and tools). You'll probably make between $20,000-$45,000, depending on your portfolio or reference list.

BOTTOM LINE ADVICE:

The hours are long, and the insurance you'll need to carry is high (almost in the same category as malpractice insurance, although not as costly). Mistakes could cost you your career, so the pressure can be exceptionally high. On the plus side, you'll be getting paid to help out the masters, and, as an artist, what could be more rewarding than that?

ART/PHOTO REPRESENTATIVE

Start-up cost:	$5,000-$15,000
Potential earnings:	$25,000-$50,000
Typical fees:	20 percent commission on each sale
Advertising:	Trade publications for artists and photographers, listings in *Photographers Market* and *Guide to Literary Agents/Art Photo Reps*, direct mail to related associations
Qualifications:	Ideally, an artistic and/or sales background
Equipment needed:	Computer, printer, fax/modem, copier, phone
Home business potential:	Yes
Staff required:	No
Handicapped opportunity:	Yes
Hidden costs:	Insurance, bad risks (artists whom you care about but who aren't really very marketable)

LOWDOWN:

Behind every successful artist or photographer is an agent who carts around resumes and slides from market to market, seeking the best opportunity to sell works of art to everyone from gallery owners to art catalog publishers and distributors. The key is to juggle several artists and photographers at once, and to spread their work as far out as possible in the hopes that offers will come rolling in. To grow your stable of candidates to represent, advertise in the publications that artistic types generally read. Invite them to respond to your "cattle call" by sending in a detailed resume and plenty of slides; if you should decide to represent someone, provide a contract that clearly spells out what is expected in the give and take of the business relationship; for instance, if you expect to get 20 percent commission on each sale, state it clearly in the contract so that the artist doesn't get snooty with you after you help him become famous.

START-UP:

You'll need to promote your services in each of the respective professional trade publications, and that will likely cost you in the neighborhood of $3,000-$5,000 (some directories, however, allow you a free listing). Next, you'll need to have a set of dynamic, yet professional-looking promotional materials of your own and a basic office setup (computer, printer, fax/modem, copier and phone system) to keep it all running smoothly. With a commission of 20 percent on each deal you make, you should be able to earn an annual paycheck between $25,000-$50,000, depending on where you live and how many successful artists you represent.

BOTTOM LINE ADVICE:

The art world is extremely narcissistic and tight-knit; cliques abound, and if your name isn't known as one of the "chosen" few, you may not succeed as much as you'd like. Work the art show openings and other functions; attend trade shows and the like if you really want to get your name out there fast. Above all else, be knowledgeable about art—if you're not, it will definitely show. The positive side is, there are far more talented artists than there are folks to represent them—so your income potential is quite high.

AUDITING SPECIALIST

Start-up cost:	$5,000-$8,000
Potential earnings:	$50,000-$75,000
Typical fees:	Percentage of the savings you find for clients; often 50 percent for past savings and about 10 percent for two or more years into the future
Advertising:	Business and trade publications, direct mail, membership in business groups, networking, referrals
Qualifications:	Knowledge of area of specialty (utility bills, telephone options), excellent math skills, a detail orientation, good selling skills
Equipment needed:	Office furniture, computer, suite software, printer, calculator, business card, letterhead, envelopes, marketing materials
Home business potential:	Yes
Staff required:	No
Handicapped opportunity:	Yes
Hidden costs:	Ongoing marketing time and materials, continuing education

LOWDOWN:

As bills become more complicated, the opportunity for finding errors and over-charges in them increases. For most businesses, though, the tedious, detail-oriented work necessary to check each bill and interpret all the data is just too time-consuming. An auditing specialist can work through all the paper records, uncover over-charges, collect a percentage of the money saved, and make an excellent living. To be very successful, you will need the ability to consider what lies behind the rows of figures on a utility bill. Something as basic as a misplaced decimal point can have a huge effect, but it's harder to spot incorrect rate assignments, double billing for small segments of the service, or opportunities to use a different rate structure.

START-UP:

You'll need a good place to work. This is a lot of detailed reading, calculating, and thinking, so your equipment needs to fit you comfortably (around $3,000 to start). Earnings could be $50,000 annually.

BOTTOM LINE ADVICE:

If you focus on utility bills, look for organizations that consume large quantities of electricity—businesses that are open all night, for example. Government, churches, and other institutions with big buildings and inadequate staffing are excellent prospects also. Some auditing services focus on insurance costs or telephone charges. In spite of the clear benefits you will offer, however, marketing is a challenge. People aren't used to the idea of auditing specialists, and they probably have no idea how much money they are pouring down the drain each month in their businesses. In other words, they undoubtedly need your service, but they don't realize it. You will succeed when you find a way to help them understand the benefit you offer.

ADVICE FROM THE EXPERTS

What sets your business apart from others like it?

"I don't just punch numbers into a computer . . . I delve deeper to find out more about the customer and how I can help them on a long-term basis," says Dianna Stahl, President & CEO of E.R.S., Inc., in Akron, Ohio.

Things you couldn't do without:

Stahl says she absolutely couldn't do without a computer and a phone.

Marketing tips/advice:

"Find a good mentor in whatever area you're weak in. I was weak in sales, so I found myself a good sales mentor and it helped immeasurably."

If you had to do it all over again . . .

"Know the people you're going to go into business with well before you do it. I was starting my business based on someone else's promises, and they didn't come through. Fortunately, it worked out."

AUTO SWAP MEET PROMOTION

Start-up cost:	$10,000-$15,000
Potential earnings:	$50,000-$100,000
Typical fees:	Participant fees of $25 or more each; admission fees of $5 or more
Advertising:	Automotive newspapers, classified ads, bulletin boards, flyers at auto body and repair shops
Qualifications:	None but an avid interest in cars
Equipment needed:	A parking lot or warehouse to rent for the event
Home business potential:	No (except for handling business details)
Staff required:	Possibly one other person
Handicapped opportunity:	Yes
Hidden costs:	Liability insurance

LOWDOWN:

Auto swap meets, where buyers and sellers gather to buy, sell, and/or trade used vehicles, have been a popular mainstay among car aficionados for several years, and promoting such events can be a profitable business. As a promoter, you would secure the parking lot or large warehouse for those seeking to trade or sell their cars—and participants would pay you as much as $25 each for the opportunity to showcase their vehicles. Attendees would then pay an admission fee of around $5, adding to your income potential. Snack shops fit well with such events, and you could earn even more with this sideline business if you choose popular, easy foods like pizza, hot dogs, and soda.

START-UP:

You'll need to rent temporary space for your swap meets; it's fairly easy to obtain weekend use of a large parking lot. Most rentals will cost you a flat fee of around $50 per day, and some of the more savvy business owners will also ask you for a small percentage of what you'll earn. You'll need to make it clear that you are organizing and running the event, and that you have your own insurance policy to cover any mishaps.

BOTTOM LINE ADVICE:

Once you become established, you should be able to generate cash flow very quickly for auto swap meets you promote. However, if you're not advertising in the right places, your participants won't know about the opportunity. Your success will hinge on your ability to get the word out.

AUTOMOBILE WINDOW STICKERS

Start-up cost:	$5,000-$10,000
Potential earnings:	$15,000-$25,000
Typical fees:	$5-$10 per sticker
Advertising:	Networking and direct mail to car dealerships
Qualifications:	None
Equipment needed:	Mobile printer with preprinted forms
Home business potential:	Yes
Staff required:	No
Handicapped opportunity:	Yes
Hidden costs:	Insurance, equipment maintenance

LOWDOWN:

The used car industry depends on having adequate information about each car on each lot, and the best way to achieve such accuracy regarding a particular auto's history is to have printed labels on each car window, detailing such critical information as mileage, special features, and life cycle of particular items such as tires and timing belts. All of this information needs to be displayed prominently on the inside driver's side window, and in a professional, standard-looking manner. After all, used car dealers base much of their sales on credibility these days, and they depend on items as seemingly unimportant as your product to build customer trust. The buying public is far too smart to be duped by "lemon" automobiles; those who don't know a lot about cars are beginning to hire automotive inspection services to check out a car before they buy it. Your main objective in this straightforward business is to sell to dealers on-site, print out the labels immediately, and collect your cash.

START-UP:

You'll need about $5,000-$10,000 to start this business well, mainly because you'll probably be buying into a franchise (unless, of course, you have access to the specialized forms and printer you'll need to produce labels). Your advertising budget can be rather small, due to the fact that your growth will be based on reputation and networking success. Expect to earn anywhere from $15,000-$25,000 as you run around from dealer to dealer, building lasting relationships based on short-term need.

BOTTOM LINE ADVICE:

This is a simple business to manage and run—but you'll really need to be of immediate and accurate service to your clients to keep the cash rolling in. Any time you're not available to them, they'll use a competitor (and you know what that can do to your bank account).

AUTOMOTIVE DETAILING

Start-up costs:	$5,000-$10,000
Potential earnings:	$30,000-$60,000
Typical fees:	$100-$500 per job
Advertising:	Newspaper, automotive publications, body shops, network with dealers
Qualifications:	A flair for the artistic
Equipment needed:	Cleaning equipment such as polish, rags, brushes, toothbrushes, cotton swabs; equipment such as airbrush, paint, sealer
Home business potential:	Yes
Staff required:	No
Handicapped opportunity:	Possibly
Hidden costs:	Larger building as business grows, hourly wages of additional assistants

LOWDOWN:

Automotive detailing can be done anywhere and at your convenience. A relatively low initial investment will start you on your way. Although the number of auto detailers has grown significantly, you can remain competitive by creating a smart marketing plan, providing superior service, offering lower prices, and exhibiting sound management skills. Continually look for ways to provide services that your competition has overlooked.

START-UP:

Aside from the cost of basic cleaning equipment, an airbrush and related art supplies will start at $2,500. It may be necessary to consider the location of your business. Expect a minimum monthly payment of $250 if you will require a small garage in which to work.

BOTTOM LINE ADVICE:

If you have dreamed of working at your own pace and during the hours you choose, automotive detailing can be a rewarding occupation. Individuals with artistic flair and an appreciation for well-kept automobiles are always in demand as many automobile dealers continue to farm out their detail work. Creativity is the key to keeping the competition at bay. Consider a mobile detail shop as your business van allows on-site work, saving you and your customers valuable time. Your work is different everyday—so what's not to like?

AUTOMOTIVE MARKETING AND TRAINING SERVICES

Start-up cost:	$6,000-$10,000
Potential earnings:	$40,000-$70,000
Typical fees:	$75-$100 per hour or a flat per diem of $500
Advertising:	Dealer publications, business publications, trade association memberships, direct mail
Qualifications:	Proven track record of success in automotive marketing, sales training experience, outstanding oral and written communication skills
Equipment needed:	Office furniture, high-end computer with graphics capability, suite software, presentation software, modem, fax, cellular phone, business card, letterhead, envelopes, marketing materials
Home business potential:	No
Staff required:	Yes
Handicapped opportunity:	No
Hidden costs:	Preparation of presentation materials: workbooks, slides, and overheads, travel time and mileage

LOWDOWN:

In some ways the world of automotive sales is a world apart. Even though automobile ownership is extremely widespread in the U.S., most people are uncomfortable in a dealership. If you have sold cars successfully, if you can communicate with others who work in this field, and if you can demonstrate a record of success to dealership owners and managers, you have a great opportunity to develop a successful enterprise of automotive marketing and training. You'll essentially teach salespeople how to be more effective, and may even work with auto technicians to educate them on their sales potential (after all, they are the ones who work with customers at the repair level—a level ripe for add-on product sales).

START-UP:

You'll need professional, effective materials and support from the outset (about $6,000 for your presentation materials, slides and workbooks, not to mention your own sales/promotional materials, such as business cards and brochures). The office equipment you'll need to produce these is quite an investment. Potential earnings of $40,000 could be yours, if you charge $75-$100 per hour for your services.

BOTTOM LINE ADVICE:

Working with sales professionals to improve their methods can be exhilarating, yet draining because everyone has his/her own style—tread carefully on the egos in each roomful of folks you train. Try to break mind-sets early in the game.

BALLOON DELIVERY SERVICE

Start-up cost:	$5,000-$10,000
Potential earnings:	$25,000-$35,000
Typical fees:	$10-$15 per balloon (some add a delivery fee)
Advertising:	Yellow Pages, classified ads, coupon books
Qualifications:	Valid driver's license
Equipment needed:	Transportation, helium tank supplier, assorted ribbons, and a good range of balloon styles
Home business potential:	Yes
Staff required:	No
Handicapped opportunity:	Possibly
Hidden costs:	Mileage and discount offers (be sure you're still covering costs when you offer specials)

LOWDOWN:

This simple, straightforward service is popular for children's parties, welcome home parties, get well wishes, and birthday surprises. You'll advertise in the Yellow Pages or in local newspapers, take orders more often than not over the phone (be sure you're set up to process credit cards) and then deliver the balloons to the happy recipients. Not too difficult, except when you consider that you'll be competing with florists, who can provide the same services and extras such as flowers and mugs filled with candy. So, how do you set yourself apart? Start with a creative name for your company, one that people will identify with or maybe even chuckle at. The funnier the better, since this is a fun business. Figure out what extras you can provide: is it a singing balloon delivery service, where your delivery people perform a special (and often silly) song when handing over balloons to the intended targets? Or, can you offer them balloons tied to gift items such as a coffee tin filled with gourmet blends? Decide what you can afford to use as a differentiator, then get to work!

START-UP:

You will need reliable transportation, most likely a van or truck to haul helium tanks and supplies. That's why your start-up costs are in the $5,000-$10,000 range. But your helium tank won't be very expensive (around $150 or so) and your orders should bring in about $10-$15 per customer (unless you add on special services or products), so the potential to make money is there if you are clever enough to stand apart from the crowd.

BOTTOM LINE ADVICE:

Network with local party supply retailers and wedding shops; ask them if you can leave pamphlets or business cards for customers. Advertising is critical to the success of this business. This is a competitive business; if you can't find your own niche, you'll have a hard time surviving.

BICYCLE RENTAL

Start-up cost:	$7,500-$12,000
Potential earnings:	$50,000-$80,000
Typical fees:	$12-$15 per half-hour rental
Advertising:	Flyers/brochures (give some to the Chamber of Commerce or travel agencies), Yellow Pages
Qualifications:	None
Equipment needed:	Fleet of bicycles and repair kits
Home business potential:	Yes
Staff required:	No
Handicapped opportunity:	Possibly
Hidden costs:	Liability/theft insurance

LOWDOWN:

Remember the days of the bicycle built for two, when tourists rented bikes to explore island areas where cars either didn't exist or were blessedly limited? Those days are still here—but the majority of bicycle rental businesses are clustered around heavily trafficked tourist spots such as Michigan's Mackinac Island or Florida's sandy beaches. Many bicycle rental shops are now featuring Rollerblade rentals as well, especially in places like California. Regardless of what you decide to offer, you'll be amazed at how much money can be made in this relatively easy business. Each day, you'll take a fee for short-term rentals, offering the possibility of instant repeat business or a large number of daily rentals. And, since most bicycle rentals are cash transactions, you'll have instant money. What could be easier than that?

START-UP:

Your main costs stem from the fact that you must buy a good fleet of bicycles, typically 20-25 of them at a cost of $300 or so each. If you invest in only used bicycles, your maintenance costs will be high. Considering that you'll be earning $12-$15 per half-hour rentals, you could make a sizable amount of money very quickly in this business if you're in a tourist area (especially one that doesn't allow many cars).

BOTTOM LINE ADVICE:

Do your homework and choose the right location for this business. Obviously, it will only be seasonal in northern climates—is that all you want? Or would you rather make money from this relatively simple, straightforward business all year long? You decide. Either way, you're bound to make a decent piece of change.

BOUDOIR PHOTOGRAPHY

Start-up cost:	$10,000-$15,000
Potential earnings:	$15,000-$35,000
Typical fees:	$150-$250 per sitting
Advertising:	Yellow Pages, coupon books, community newspapers, referrals
Qualifications:	Photography background
Equipment needed:	Cameras with soft lenses, soft lighting, touch-up equipment, small studio/darkroom
Home business potential:	Yes (if you have your own studio)
Staff required:	No
Handicapped opportunity:	Yes
Hidden costs:	Insurance, film and processing costs

LOWDOWN:

Many women enjoy the enticing idea of posing for seductive portraits that they turn into gifts for their significant other—and this is definitely a niche market for many photographers as well. Although not every boudoir photographer chooses to specialize in this rather racy field, quite a few are able to market it well and make a decent living to boot. All you need to do is advertise for clients, making your service seem affordable and high-quality enough to interest women who wouldn't normally wear a lace teddy for a formal photograph. One of the best ways for you to find these clients is to advertise in specialty lingerie shops; a business card or brochure is all you really need to leave behind (although you may choose to offer coupon deals from time to time). You will then be challenged with finding the right poses for each of your clients, and making sure that the finished product is tasteful enough to be displayed in your studio for others to dream about what their portrait will eventually look like.

START-UP:

You'll need between $10,000-$15,000 to get your studio and equipment together; at least $3,000 of that will be advertising funds to get your name out there.

BOTTOM LINE ADVICE:

This is an extremely sensitive business, one that depends on your reputation. One lapse in judgment could cost you your entire business, as liability and lawsuit could result from real (or perceived) amorous overtones on your part. Tread carefully.

BRIDAL SHOW PROMOTIONS

Start-up cost:	$5,000-$15,000
Potential earnings:	$20,000-$40,000
Typical fees:	$125 per booth rental space
Advertising:	Flyers, radio ads, newspapers, bridal shops, mailings, billboards
Qualifications:	Exceptional organizational skills
Equipment needed:	Computer with mailing list program
Home business potential:	Yes
Staff required:	Not initially
Handicapped opportunity:	Possibly
Hidden costs:	Radio ads are expensive; try to secure or split costs with sponsors

LOWDOWN:

Bridal shows are popular in every town—there are always young women who seek the best in wedding preparations. You should have no trouble securing an audience if you book in the right places (such as shopping malls, banquet halls, and hotels). Your biggest challenge will be to gain the attention, support, and dollars from participating vendors, who could be made up of businesses like caterers, florists, musicians, and cake decorators. You must be highly organized, however, to pull this one off convincingly. Lose sight of details and you'll instantly lose credibility with your audience as well as your vendors. The best advice is to secure your financial support up front to avoid any of your own out-of-pocket expenses—that way, in the event of a no-show vendor, you'll still have your cash.

START-UP:

The $5,000-$10,000 you'll need to get this business off the ground properly will mainly cover your advertising and promotional costs. Remember that you'll need to have professional-looking materials to sell vendors on in the first place, let alone the flyers and billboards to attract your audience. Do it all correctly and you'll pull in between $20,000-$40,000 yourself, depending on how many shows you run per year.

BOTTOM LINE ADVICE:

If you can't get at least 50 vendors for your first show, maybe you ought to rethink your marketing strategy. Try a novel approach, or try to get a well-known spokesperson or celebrity to appear. Do everything humanly possible to attract attention.

BUSINESS PLAN WRITER/PACKAGER

Start-up cost:	$5,000-$10,000
Potential earnings:	$30,000-$100,000
Typical fees:	$3,000-$6,000 per plan (about two weeks of work)
Advertising:	Teaching courses on business development, networking, business associations, referrals from bankers and entrepreneurship centers, advertising in local business newsletters
Qualifications:	Understanding of financial statements, savvy business sense, excellent oral and written communication skills, ability to get people to work together, experience writing business plans
Equipment needed:	Computer, fax/modem, laser printer, suite software, business-planning software, office furniture, business card, letterhead, envelopes, brochures
Home business potential:	Yes
Staff required:	No
Handicapped opportunity:	Yes
Hidden costs:	Organizational dues, business periodical and newspaper subscriptions, insurance

LOWDOWN:

Businesses are being created all over the country at a phenomenal rate. All of these new enterprises can get two kinds of benefits from having a business plan. First, the plan structures the efforts of everyone involved, outlining what needs to be done and describing the means by which those goals will be achieved. It highlights the feasibility of the products or services the enterprise will be marketing. Most importantly, it estimates expenses and revenues, along with projections. If the revenues won't cover the expenses, it doesn't matter what wonderful things could happen down the road. The cash-starved business won't be able to get there to achieve them.

The second benefit of having a business plan is to obtain financing. A business plan is essential for the process of obtaining bank loans and most other types of outside financing. You can take your good sense of business and finance, your high-level business writing skills, and your ability to communicate with fledgling entrepreneurs and earn a hefty annual income writing business plans.

START-UP:

The equipment and materials to present a reassuringly professional image are fairly costly (in the neighborhood of $3,000-$10,000). You'll need to be able to produce a very polished printout of the final plan, most likely using one of the better-quality business plan software packages available (about $150-$300). But, you can charge $3,000 and up for each package, with hourly fees of $45 and up (depending on your location).

BOTTOM LINE ADVICE:

If you have developed the wide range of skills necessary to do this work, you undoubtedly are the kind of person who loves it and can tolerate the tedious parts. What can be more rewarding than helping a new enterprise take wing and fly? It is very difficult to write an effective business plan, but that is the very reason your market exists. Each situation is different; that means opportunities for constant learning on your part. Once you complete a plan, you will need to find another client, so your marketing must be ongoing. Some business start-ups are shaky, even sleazy, although most failures are due to poor marketing and undercapitalization rather than dishonesty. In any case, try to get at least half your fee up front. You will really be a combination counselor/consultant for the entrepreneurs.

Computer Equipment "Musts"

Here's a checklist for setting up your computer system with everything you will likely need:

- ❏ A 486 or higher computer (preferably with a high-resolution monitor)
- ❏ 640K RAM and hard disk with Windows or MS-DOS Version 3.1 or higher
- ❏ A CD-ROM drive for some of the more innovative (and comprehensive) new programs on the market
- ❏ Near-letter quality or laser-quality printer
- ❏ 3.5" diskettes for file storage and backup
- ❏ 14400 baud or higher modem
- ❏ An accounting program (such as Quicken, QuickBooks, or one-write plus) to keep accurate records and manipulate data to create reports
- ❏ Word-processing software (such as WordPerfect or MS Word for Windows 6.0)
- ❏ Graphics or desktop publishing software (to create your own marketing materials, slides, and graphs)
- ❏ Suite or network program if you have two or more computers sharing information
- ❏ World Wide Web Site construction software (if you feel like creating your own Web page on the Internet)
- ❏ On-line services or Internet launch software
- ❏ Mouse and mousepad

CAREER COUNSELOR

Start-up cost:	$10,000-$15,000
Potential earnings:	$30,000-$65,000
Typical fees:	$350 and up per session
Advertising:	Yellow Pages, classified ads, job fairs, human resource newsletters
Qualifications:	Many states require certification
Equipment needed:	Computer, assessment software programs, TV/VCR (for educational videos), cellular phone, answering service or pager
Home business potential:	Yes
Staff required:	No
Handicapped opportunity:	Yes
Hidden costs:	Any type of counselor must keep an eye on the clock if he or she is billing by the hour. Remember that time is money; clients often need to be told when their time is up

LOWDOWN:

There are literally thousands of careers out there—and many people simply can't follow the road signs. As a career counselor, you can assist them first with personality assessment, then with matching your client's motivations and interests to a potential career. Next, map out a success plan for achieving that new job or business (yes, many people do discover through career counseling that they would really rather work for themselves). You can use formatted questionnaires or conduct personal interviews (or a combination of both) to arrive at some career-forming conclusions. But your counseling efforts don't have to stop there; you can also offer résumé services, viewing of motivational videos, cassette tape rental, and a library of resource books. The best part is, your business is recession-proof and corporations often contract with career counselors during periods of downsizing. The difficult part is reaching those who may need your services but are currently unaware that these services even exist.

START-UP:

Your start-up costs primarily reflect your office furniture and assorted resource/testing materials ($10,000-$15,000 is about right if you don't already have a computer). But the going rate for career counseling services is $350+ (depending on whether you're in a metropolitan area). With at least one good corporate client and a few stragglers, you should be well on your way in your own career path!

BOTTOM LINE ADVICE:

You will be working with many different types of people, but they do have one thing in common: they have no idea what direction to take their careers. This can be frustrating to them, and no doubt that will translate into work for you which is part information-giving, part hand-holding. If you're well-adjusted enough yourself to help others deal with a career catharsis, you'll probably get a lot professionally and personally from this type of service.

CARPET INSTALLATION

Start-up costs:	$10,000-$15,000
Potential earnings:	$40,000-$80,000; many earn $5,000 or more per month
Typical fees:	Usually a per-job rate between $300-$500, but depends on square footage of room to be carpeted
Advertising:	Personal contact with flooring stores, Yellow Pages
Qualifications:	Knowledge and experience with different carpet materials
Equipment needed:	Van to deliver and haul away carpet, tools
Home business potential:	Yes
Staff required:	No
Handicapped opportunity:	No
Hidden costs:	Insurance, transportation

LOWDOWN:

Carpet is a mainstay of our modern lives, despite a trend toward hardwood floors. Virtually every home or business is a potential customer for you; the problem is, it's more than a little competitive out there. So, set yourself apart. You can learn this trade by correspondence or by working with another carpet layer, but once you do, remember that quality workmanship is what ultimately sells your service, along with neatness and an ability to leave a good impression on those you're serving. After making contacts with several flooring stores and providing high-quality workmanship, recommendations should flow from sales personnel and satisfied consumers.

START-UP:

You'll need at least $1,000 to get started, but expect to spend a lot more in your first year of business. You'll need equipment ($1,500-$3,000), advertising ($3,000-$5,000), and possibly a vehicle ($15,000 or more). However, since you'll be charging by the square foot (average jobs run $300-$500 for carpet laying alone), you should have little trouble earning back what you initially lay out.

BOTTOM LINE ADVICE:

Neatness counts. Part of the service should be removal of all carpet remnants (not wanted by the customer) and debris. Offer to haul away the old carpet at a nominal price or include it as part of the package (covering your costs, of course).

CASTING DIRECTOR

Start-up cost:	$5,000-$10,000
Potential earnings:	$5,000 or more per month
Typical fees:	Varies according to size of job; can range from $3,000-$50,000
Advertising:	Industry trade publications, word of mouth
Qualifications:	Experience in the entertainment industry
Equipment needed:	Computer, camera equipment, video setup, cellular phone, business card
Home business potential:	Not likely because you'll probably need ample space for casting calls
Staff required:	No
Handicapped opportunity:	Yes
Hidden costs:	Insurance, phone expenses (especially cellular)

LOWDOWN:

As a casting director, you will work closely with a host of talent agencies and artists to find the right actor or actress for a particular role. What fun it will be to be involved in the movie industry, you might think. However, once you get your foot in the door, you'll begin to see what a difficult and stressful situation you've gotten yourself into. If you're one who thrives on such stress, you'll love the challenges this business will present on a minute-to-minute basis. You'll need the ability to spot potential personality conflicts (those infamous "creative differences") and the creativity to visualize a particular actor in a role that might be a stretch for others to see at first. You'll probably become the proud owner of a huge address book with hundreds of actors' names.

START-UP:

A casting director is employed on a short-term, contractual basis and paid by the hiring studio, network, agency, or producer, so the potential earnings will vary greatly—bringing in as little as $3,000 or as much as $50,000 per job; it just depends on whom you're working with and how big the backing studio is. Your initial investment ($5,000-$10,000) will be to set up an impressive office and get to know the right people.

BOTTOM LINE ADVICE:

Since you are employed by the studio, network, etc., there is no union involvement. Experience will be your best friend here. You will need to work on a lot of different projects simultaneously, so be sure your organizational skills are top-notch.

CLASSIFIED ADVERTISING NEWSPAPER

Start-up cost:	$5,000-$10,000
Potential earnings:	$30,000-$50,000
Typical fees:	Ad space generally sells for anywhere from $4-$500
Advertising:	Cold calling, neighborhood bulletin boards, flyers
Qualifications:	Energy, selling skill, word processing capability
Equipment needed:	Computer, laser printer, copier, fax/modem, light table
Home business potential:	Yes
Staff required:	No
Handicapped opportunity:	Yes
Hidden costs:	Printing can get costly if you don't know what you're doing. Be sure to ask your printer how you can keep production costs down

LOWDOWN:

Did you know that the classified ad section of the newspaper is the most carefully read section? Classified ads, taken together, are big business—and people do pick up and read publications that are classifieds-only when there is something they want to buy or sell. Persistence and a certain eye for detail are the main ingredients you will need to produce your own classified-only newspaper and circulate it. Selling the ads requires a love of that vital business activity. Putting the paper together will demand word processing skills, though not much in the way of design or layout. You will need to develop an effective method for circulating your newspaper; often such publications are distributed for free where there is high foot traffic.

START-UP:

You'll need a location where people can come to purchase ad space (rent can start at $350 per month). You'll need adequate computer equipment for the production side of your enterprise (add another $2,000) and will need to set aside cash for producing the first six months of issues ($10,000). On the upside, if you promote your paper and make sure it gets distributed in the right places, you could make $30,000 or more per year just printing classified ads.

BOTTOM LINE ADVICE:

You're really building an enterprise out of your own energy and sense of business push. No one tells you when to go out selling, how to arrange your material, or where to distribute it. So you'll have a real sense of ownership and pride, supported by happy customers who return to you because your newspaper has helped them complete the sale of what they've advertised. On the other hand, this is a lot of work for one person. Your commitment to complete each issue will be tested and tested again—and if you're turning out a substandard product, your customers will notice.

COFFEE BAR/TEA SALON

Start-up cost:	$10,000-$20,000
Potential earnings:	$25,000-$40,000
Typical fees:	$1.50-$3.00 per cup
Advertising:	Newspaper ads, flyers, magazines/catalogs, location
Qualifications:	Retail experience (especially purchasing and marketing) would be helpful; knowledge and ability to prepare the coffee, tea, and other products
Equipment needed:	Coffee/tea brewing equipment and supplies, cups; furnishings, location
Home business potential:	Probably not (because of zoning restrictions)
Staff required:	None at first; several later on
Handicapped opportunity:	Yes
Hidden costs:	Purchase or rental of location for the shop; meeting zoning, legal, and food service regulations may add to expenses

LOWDOWN:

Gourmet beverage businesses, such as tea shops or salons, are very high-ticket specialty concerns that can brew big profits. People are tired of the same old coffees and teas, and they often want to find lower-caffeine alternatives. Your shop can feature a line of healthy herbal teas to meet that need, as well as attractive add-ons, such as specialty teacups. Profit margins are high; repeat customers are almost guaranteed. Stiff competition exists in some urban locations—especially from the larger chains.

START-UP:

Your biggest expense will be the purchase or rental of a location. You will also need top-quality products, furnishings for the shop, signage, and (probably) a computer. You may also have to pay for legal advice concerning health regulations, and will need to invest in a well-organized marketing campaign.

BOTTOM LINE ADVICE:

Like any small business owner, you may have to work long hours, at least at first. Your business may be affected by the economy, or by the time of year. As you expand, you will experience the usual headaches of staff management. However, this is a business that can generate a very healthy profit, with relatively low overhead and modest equipment requirements. As you become more successful, many other products (such as muffins, teacups, and tea to-go) can be added to keep people coming. You might want to consider serving light sandwiches and pastries from the beginning, but this will add to your cost.

ADVICE FROM THE EXPERTS

What sets your business apart from others like it?

Howard Schultz, Chairman and CEO of Starbucks Coffee Company in Seattle, Washington, says that his company's mission is to establish itself as the premier purveyor of the finest coffees in the world, while maintaining uncompromising principles as the company grows. Today, Starbucks operates more than 565 locations in the United States and Canada.

Things you couldn't do without:

Carrying over thirty varieties of coffee beans that over 2.5 million coffee drinkers consume each week. Retail and restaurant equipment specific to each location.

Marketing tips/advice:

"We are the quintessential product-driven company," says Schultz. "We have the most knowledgeable workforce in our industry, from our head coffee buyer to the skillful baristas in all of our stores. I take great pride in the growth and development of our people." Schultz believes in setting his company apart through its commitment to social responsibility, giving back as much as possible to the community.

If you had to do it all over again . . .

Schultz wouldn't change a thing at his continually growing company.

COLLECTIBLES/MEMORABILIA

Start-up cost:	$5,000-$15,000
Potential earnings:	$500-$20,000
Typical fees:	Varies on what you are selling and the going rate for it
Advertising:	Flea markets, swap meets, antique fairs, flyers, brochures
Qualifications:	Knowing how to spot money from junk
Equipment needed:	20-30 collectibles to start
Home business potential:	Yes
Staff required:	No
Handicapped opportunity:	Yes
Hidden costs:	Table/space rental fees

LOWDOWN:

Everything old is new again! Remember the Morton Salt Girl or the Brady Bunch lunch boxes with radios in them? They are in popular demand right now and bringing in top dollars ($100 or more each). And so is anything retro: salt/pepper sets, board games, clothing, limited edition plates, Presidential items, cereal boxes, you name it—but that doesn't relieve you of the responsibility to heavily market your service. You can specialize in one era like the '50s and carry everything from that time period. Or, you can specialize in one item (like toasters through the century). Try to hit as many antique fairs, swap meets, and dealer conventions as possible; that's where you'll spend a little, but earn a lot.

START-UP:

You will need equipment to show off your stuff, so that will be the biggest expense (about $1,000). The next will be your advertising and marketing. When you go to shows plan on paying $15-$100+ to rent a table or space to showcase your merchandise. Earning potential will be initially slow—$500-$20,000—until you've gotten established.

BOTTOM LINE ADVICE:

People are crazy for the past. In some ways, it represents a simpler time in their lives, and that's something many people are willing to pay for. Collecting has become a $6-billion-dollar a year business, so if you have a collection you're willing to part with, you could make some serious money. Collecting interests tend to run in 20-year cycles, so this has a long-term possibility if you have an eye for what is collectible and what will sell. The danger is getting so caught up in acquiring certain pieces that you aren't willing to part with them yourself. Beware—collecting is intoxicating to those who enjoy it!

Gaining Credibility

Once you've opened your doors for business, how do you get the customers to learn your name and trust it as a reliable source in the community? Ultimately, the way to build credibility is to develop a strong business with a solid reputation for delivering what it promises the customer. But what can you do in the meantime (until you're a household name)? Here are some possibilities:

- **Volunteer at local charitable foundations and corporate events.** Simply being out there where other influential types are likely to be found (either as sponsors or as participants) will put you face-to-face with people who can help spread the word about your business. It's worth the donated hours on your part, and you'll get to widen your circle of acquaintances.

- **Offer yourself as an expert on your topic of interest.** Send regular press releases with tips for consumers to local and regional newspapers and magazines. Editors love such items and you stand a good chance of being interviewed the next time a story on your area of expertise rolls around. Be sure to keep in regular contact with the press, even if it's just a quick phone call to ask if they need any help with upcoming features.

- **Give free speeches at local association dinners.** Or lunches. Or breakfasts. Really, just about anywhere where potential clients gather to learn more about improving their professional (and possibly personal) lives. Association meetings work best because they are always in need for interesting new speakers; so are civic groups and universities.

- **Create and mail a regular newsletter with useful tips.** Giving some information for free can create positive awareness of your company and what it has to offer. People do tend to read newsletters, and even though they may not need your services today, such publications (if well-done) will keep you in their minds tomorrow.

- **Perform to your personal best.** Ultimately, it's going to be a reputation based on fair pricing, high quality, and exceptional service that will gain you the credibility you need to bring in new business. Set high standards and work every day toward achieving them, and you will have your credibility sooner than most.

COLLECTION AGENCY

Start-up costs:	$3,000-$10,500
Potential earnings:	$30,000-$60,000
Typical fees:	25 percent commission
Advertising:	Phone solicitation, networking, writing articles for local publications, public speaking
Qualifications:	Good communication skills, patience, high self-esteem, budgeting skills; clear understanding of the Federal Fair Debt Collection Practices Act, any relevant state laws and health insurance policies and billing practices if working with the medical field
Equipment needed:	Computer with modem, printer, fax, word-processing and spreadsheet software, specialized collection software and phone with optional headset
Home business potential:	Yes
Staff required:	No
Handicapped opportunity:	Yes
Hidden costs:	Organizational dues for networking purposes; state, city, and/or county licenses are typically required; fees for on-line services

LOWDOWN:

Are you an addict of *Unsolved Mysteries?* Collectors are often put to the test as they track down elusive debtors. State laws typically require people who do collections to be bonded and licensed. Generally, it is not difficult to obtain the proper license provided your state does not prohibit home-based agencies. Using special collections software and a PC, a collection service becomes very efficient as it reduces the time and labor for handling mail and accounting. Additionally, on-line services cut the cost of tracking debtors considerably.

START-UP:

It is essential that you take advantage of the many high-tech devices that will make the collection process easier. A computer and modem is essential, as is customized collection software. Costs ranging from $2,000-$7,000 for these basics are average. Don't forget to shop around for the best fee on phone line usage.

BOTTOM LINE ADVICE:

The collection process is often frustrating. Keeping your self-esteem intact in the face of rejection is necessary. Although confrontation of unpaid bills can be emotionally draining, the work never ceases to be challenging and rewarding. In some cases, you are able to solve debtors' financial problems and keep them from bankruptcy. When all parties agree on a suitable payment plan, everyone wins.

ADVICE FROM THE EXPERTS

What sets your business apart from others like it?

"There are a lot of good agencies, and we all basically do the same things," says Deloris C. Lewis, President of Debt Credit Services & Associates in Akron, Ohio. "I cater to the needs of my clients and go out of my way to help them. I try to be fair to both the creditors and the debtors."

Things you couldn't do without:

Items such as an excellent, well-trained staff, speed dialers, computers, integrated skip tracing and bookkeeping software, a phone system, and mailing equipment, Lewis says.

Marketing tips/advice:

"Go after the large-dollar, small-account commercial business that's out there. Stay away from health care; if you're new, it will be too demanding and intense for you. Use networking and advertising to bring in new business, but depend heavily on referrals."

If you had to do it all over again . . .

"I'd have started with more capital . . . that means developing a sound business plan, which I didn't do in the beginning and which has held me back. I winged it—and now I'd be more organized so that I could get better funding."

COMPUTER CONSULTANT

Start-up cost:	$5,000-$13,000
Potential earnings:	$40,000-$100,000
Typical fees:	$75-$150 per hour
Advertising:	Referrals, direct mail, publications, networking
Qualifications:	Technical knowledge, specialty knowledge, people and time-management skills
Equipment needed:	High-end computer, hardware and software, copier, fax, office furniture, business card, letterhead, envelopes
Home business potential:	Yes
Staff required:	No; must be able to subcontract outside of specialty
Handicapped opportunity:	Yes
Hidden costs:	On-line service; time and expense of staying current in fast-changing field

LOWDOWN:

It's getting very hard to operate any business without a computer system, so almost anyone is a potential client if you know how to match up a computer system with their needs. Computer consulting is a big field today and will continue to grow rapidly in the near future. Many computer consultants become as essential to their clients as the systems themselves, earning a steady income in the process. This field is for individuals with wide expertise in hardware and software. Even more important is an ability to see issues from the client's point of view. What are his or her real problems, and what creative solutions to those problems will be best served using computer technology? You will probably need to focus on one area of specialization, such as networking computers, or on one type of business, such as retail outlets or physician offices.

START-UP:

Your own business must have a computer system, including software, that is comparable to those of your clients. This will be your major expense, but if you have the expertise to operate this business, you probably have much of the equipment and software already. You'll also need a high-quality copier and a fax/modem. The essential organizational dues and on-line services can also add surprisingly to your operating expenses. But, if you charge the going rates of $75 and up per hour, you should be able to earn back your initial investment in as little as six months.

BOTTOM LINE ADVICE:

Computer consulting is for big-picture people also skilled in keeping track of details. Each client and situation is different, making for a very stimulating work life. You will be able to function outside of normal time-space restrictions and you won't find competitors undercutting you with cookie-cutter services. But computer consulting is extremely demanding. You will often be working under a deadline or in a crisis situation; you must produce what you promise and be able to train your clients' employees to make the system work under real conditions. Bidding jobs is challenging, especially at first—keeping track of billing is essential.

ADVICE FROM THE EXPERTS

What sets your business apart from others like it?

Lee Hughes, Systems Engineer at Hughes Information Systems in Cloquet, Minnesota, says his business is successful because it streamlines and automates other businesses' operations. "We take an engineering approach to solving problems."

Things you couldn't do without:

"A personal computer, printer, modem, and phone."

Marketing tips/advice:

"It is virtually impossible to accurately estimate project costs. Try to build in a cushion when you provide an estimate."

If you had to do it all over again . . .

"I would educate myself much more in business management, sales/marketing and presentation/negotiation skills."

COMPUTER MAINTENANCE SERVICE

Start-up cost:	$5,000-$10,000
Potential earnings:	$50,000-$70,000
Typical fees:	$50 per hour on cleaning or repairs; $25-$40 per student (if teaching classes)
Advertising:	Word of mouth, Yellow Pages, flyers, business card, opportunities to teach classes
Qualifications:	Knowledge of computer hardware and interfaces, ability to deal with upset clients diplomatically and sympathetically
Equipment needed:	PC with modem, printer, and fax, tools, cleaning supplies, and diagnostic software, spare parts, office furniture, business card, reference books
Home business potential:	Yes
Staff required:	No
Handicapped opportunity:	No
Hidden costs:	Staying abreast of new technology

LOWDOWN:

Computers and dust don't mix. That seems like a simple idea, but many people have little understanding of that concept. They don't understand why computers tend to crash without regular maintenance, and they need much reassurance before they will trust you to remove a cover and begin cleaning the drives. Once you gain trust and develop your clientele, though, you'll be able to negotiate ongoing service contracts that will give you a steady flow of work, and income. Twice a year you can service each client on your list, cleaning the vital components of the machines that keep their businesses running. You may also develop connections to possible add-on services you could offer, such as training, software installation, file backups, and other types of computer-related services.

START-UP:

The computer for your own office is the largest expense because the actual computer cleaning tools are quite simple and not very costly. Fees are usually in the $50 per hour range. Your biggest challenge is to make potential clients aware of the benefit of maintaining their systems—all too often they'll wait until something catastrophic happens before they call you. Consequently, advertising and sending reminder cards will cost you at least $1,000-$2,000 per year.

BOTTOM LINE ADVICE:

If you have the ability to clean computers and peripheral equipment, you can provide a service needed by almost all businesses and many individuals as well. Satisfied customers will probably provide you with plenty of referrals, but you will occasionally be working with distraught clients. You might need to work at your customers' sites, so careful planning is necessary to make best use of travel time.

COMPUTER SOFTWARE SALES

Start-up cost:	$5,000-$15,000
Potential earnings:	$15,000-$40,000
Typical fees:	Software retails anywhere between $5-$500; your commission can be as high as 20 percent (depending on your markup)
Advertising:	Computer magazines, bulletin boards, direct mail
Qualifications:	Knowledge of what is new and hot in consumer software
Equipment needed:	Computer, fax, printer, office furniture
Home business potential:	Yes
Staff required:	No
Handicapped opportunity:	Yes
Hidden costs:	Depends on approach but may include high phone bills and advertising costs

LOWDOWN:

There are a number of avenues open for the creation of a small business that sells already established software. A mail-order business requires considerable advertising and probably an 800 number for customers to call. Your ability to convert phone calls into orders may depend on how you match callers with the packages they need. Use your wide familiarity with different types of software to serve customers better than they can be served by mass-market outlets—and keep your prices competitive as well. Some small software sellers open a retail store, while others find selling opportunities in a range of areas, including flea markets. If you combine knowledge of what is available in software with the selling skills to help your customers buy the right package, you can expect to develop a successful business.

START-UP:

These costs depend on the mode you choose. For mail order, a computer, phone system, 800 number, and office furniture will be the major costs. A retail outlet will require you to stock expensive inventory to meet the needs and expectations of a fickle, fast-changing market in addition to renting or buying a suitable location. Commission depends on what you negotiate with your supplier as your markup, but is typically between 5 and 20 percent.

BOTTOM LINE ADVICE:

It's fun to put products into the hands of customers who need them. Last year, more computers than televisions were sold in the U.S., and all of these machines require your products and their upgrades. So, your market is there. The challenge will be to establish connections with it. To make a profit you'll need to offer better, more knowledgeable service and a competitive price. Keeping up with all the new packages will be an ongoing challenge, and keeping track of your competition will be even more demanding.

COMPUTER TRAINER

Start-up cost:	$5,000-$16,000
Potential earnings:	$40,000-$100,000
Typical fees:	$75+ per hour
Advertising:	Speaking at business meetings, referrals from software companies, networking, direct mail to specific companies, computer and trade publications
Qualifications:	Computer skills and/or certification by software company, writing and presentation skills, ability to handle group dynamics, background in teaching or education design
Equipment needed:	High-end computer, hardware and software, laser printer, comb binding machine for materials, office furniture, brochures and/or presentation folder, business card, letterhead, envelopes
Home business potential:	Yes
Staff required:	No
Handicapped opportunity:	Yes
Hidden costs:	Certification training to teach specific programs

LOWDOWN:

As computers become even more important in the business world, so does computer training. New software is powerful, but added features mean that almost every employee needs training to use it productively. To be a successful computer trainer, you need a range of skills, beginning with expertise in each software package. Beyond the ability to use the software yourself, you need to understand how others use it. Computer trainers may work as tutors with one or two individuals at a time, but more often they teach classes to groups at a business location, so teaching and presentation skills are essential. Computer training can be a successful business for people who have computer skills, find teaching to be a creative enterprise, and like working with adults. You will need to focus on the areas where your expertise is easiest to keep updated: word processing, databases, or accounting programs, for example.

START-UP:

Your computer, software and laser printer will be the largest start-up expenses, totaling as much as $10,000-$15,000. You will also need to produce your own training materials, and these will change as new versions of the software packages are installed by your clients. Most training is conducted on clients' premises, so your own office equipment can be added later. Charge at least $75 per hour to cover your expenses and make a tidy profit.

BOTTOM LINE ADVICE:

If you are good at teaching, you can make a big difference in the work lives of the people you train. They must use computer equipment to complete their tasks, and knowing how the programs operate will greatly increase their efficiency. You will know that the services you provide are important to the employees you train and to the businesses that depend on them. You'll need to be good at defusing their computer anxiety, though. People who don't understand the intricacies of a program start pulling their hair out almost immediately. You will need to coax them gradually through each skill level until they gain confidence. Students who are new to an area often don't ask clear questions; anticipate that and listen carefully to give the right responses. Some adults find it very difficult to become students again. Also, there is a lot of competition in this field today. You will need to find a way to distinguish what you can offer from all the others. Finally, preparing training materials can be time-consuming and labor-intensive if you're not used to step-by-step approaches.

Businesses on the Success Track

What are the top opportunities for making money as an entrepreneur of the '90s? According to *Entrepreneur* magazine, they are actually quite varied, and some of them may be appealing to you:

- Specialty coffee shops/tea salons
- Internet consulting
- Home health care
- Executive temporary services/employee leasing
- Family entertainment centers
- Computer training services/consulting
- Specialized children's stores (educational toys, etc.)
- Exporting
- Environmental services
- Bagels
- Day spas
- Business and management consultants
- Adventure tourism
- Ethnic foods
- Alternative fitness/wellness programs

CONSTRUCTION SERVICES

Start-up cost:	$5,000-$10,000
Potential earnings:	$25,000 or more
Typical fees:	$35 per hour or a flat rate dependent upon the scope of each project ($1,000-$1 million)
Advertising:	Newspapers, real estate magazines, local periodicals, Yellow Pages, radio
Qualifications:	Extensive experience with all phases of the type of construction you specialize in, excellent marketing, pricing, and management skills
Equipment needed:	Well-equipped office plus the equipment necessary for the type of work you perform
Home business potential:	Yes
Staff required:	Probably
Handicapped opportunity:	No
Hidden costs:	Costs for materials can bring you down. Nonpaying customers are another major problem in this area.

LOWDOWN:

Construction services are widely needed. Some individuals build entire homes almost single-handedly, while other construction companies employ many people to do the same projects. Some construction services focus on kitchen remodeling, decks, or skylights. Commercial construction is an option for the small business depending on the size of the project involved. However you configure your service offerings, marketing will be central. How will you reach those wealthy dreamers about a state-of-the-art kitchen? If you focus on the small projects that are just above handy-man level, neighborhood flyers may be an effective way to send out your message. Eventually, referrals may keep you busy. You'll need to be an excellent estimator and judge of people.

START-UP:

Costs will probably be fairly high (at least $5,000) to start, and that's if you start simply (with a few satisfied clients and a stack of business cards). You'll need a cellular phone and computer system, too. With more and more people remodeling these days, you could earn $25,000 fairly soon—possibly on your first job! Be good at what you do, keep your materials costs down, and you could make an exceptionally fine living.

BOTTOM LINE ADVICE:

Many excellent builders cannot make their businesses profitable because time and cost overruns defeat them. Being able to find customers, help them clarify what they want to have done, and doing it at the right price are all essential.

CORPORATE INSURANCE BROKER

Start-up cost:	$5,000-$8,000
Potential earnings:	$50,000-$100,000
Typical fees:	$35-$50 per hour
Advertising:	Direct mail or cold calls, Yellow Pages, ads in business or trade publications
Qualifications:	Extensive insurance experience in specialty
Equipment needed:	Office furniture, computer, printer, suite software, presentation software, database, cellular phone, marketing materials, business card, letterhead, envelopes
Home business potential:	Yes
Staff required:	No
Handicapped opportunity:	No
Hidden costs:	Marketing

LOWDOWN:

The insurance field is crowded, but there is room for you if you can make a difference, a difference available from no other agent out there. Many voices are claiming the attention of your potential customers, but far fewer have a real understanding of the effects of insurance on a business organization. For example, if you specialize in employee benefits, your expertise in assembling the best combination of benefits for your client's specific employee group will set you apart. Assistance with claims processing is another selling point. Most of all, you need knowledge of the insurance field and its costs and benefits; it's this expertise that will allow you to handle everything from group information intakes to claims. Don't forget, too, that you're primarily a salesperson—you're selling peace of mind to your corporate clients, who depend on you for the most thorough, comprehensive, and competitive plans out there.

START-UP:

You'll need the office equipment (around $3,000 to start) to support your marketing and insurance research efforts, but you could see $50,000 annually.

BOTTOM LINE ADVICE:

The key to success here is a good business sense. That is, you need to project more than just your own desire to earn a commission to your potential clients. You need to show them how working with you can meet their strategic goals. As with so many other enterprises, success comes down to a clear focus on what service you're providing and a dedication to marketing as an ongoing part of your business life.

CORPORATE TRAINER

Start-up cost:	$5,000-$11,000
Potential earnings:	$35,000-$100,000
Typical fees:	$500-$2,000 per day
Advertising:	Networking with local personnel managers, speaking before professional organizations and local groups, compiling a detailed portfolio
Qualifications:	Expertise in a specific area like sales or team management, communication skills, facility with group dynamics
Equipment needed:	Office furniture, computer, printer, fax, suite and presentation software, business card, letterhead, and envelopes
Home business potential:	Yes
Staff required:	No
Handicapped opportunity:	Possibly
Hidden costs:	Living expenses for first six months to build client base

LOWDOWN:

Although there has been over the last decade an increase in the percentage of employees who receive formal training, fewer large companies keep a training staff on the payroll. The process of hiring and firing means big losses for companies trying to keep up with changing techniques, technologies, and procedures. Successful training will build a solid reputation, and can be a foothold to other money-making opportunities, such as books, tapes, manuals, and seminars.

START-UP:

The American Society for Training and Development and the American Management Association can be useful resources for developing your own program. You must spend the time and money (about $5,000), to create a specific presentation that will fill an existing niche in the industry, and earn you about $35,000.

BOTTOM LINE ADVICE:

Top trainers make excellent money, but be prepared to take the time to sell yourself and your seminars. Remember that companies are often looking for short-term benefits instead of the long-term value of a good training program. However, once your reputation is established, there is excellent opportunity for repeat business.

ADVICE FROM THE EXPERTS

What sets your business apart from others like it?

For Mike Robinson, Managing Partner of Triad Training & Consulting in Kernersville, North Carolina, it's customized service delivered at great value that sets his business apart from others like it. "With many clients, we'll offer a money-back guarantee."

Things you couldn't do without:

"You'll need a powerful computer system with a good multimedia setup for on-site productions and near-published quality training materials. Also, you'll need audiovisual equipment."

Marketing tips/advice:

"Work on your teaching skills, delivery, and training ability. You'll need to have the ability to read a crowd and fantastic communications skills to get the kind of word of mouth necessary to build business."

If you had to do it all over again . . .

"I didn't have enough clients lined up before I left my previous company. Also, if you're not good in certain areas of business, surround yourself with people who are. Finally, remember that the first few years are going to be difficult—but, if you're persistent, it could snowball soon thereafter."

COST REDUCTION CONSULTANT

Start-up cost:	$5,000-$8,000
Potential earnings:	$50,000-$75,000
Typical fees:	Percentage of the cost savings, for a contracted time
Advertising:	Business and trade publications, direct mail, memberships in business organizations and community groups
Qualifications:	Business experience, some financial background, excellent selling skills
Equipment needed:	Office furniture, computer, suite software, printer, calculator, business card, letterhead, envelopes, marketing materials
Home business potential:	Yes
Staff required:	No
Handicapped opportunity:	Yes
Hidden costs:	Dues to community organizations, publication subscriptions

LOWDOWN:

All businesses want to keep costs down, but with flatter organizational structures and fewer people doing more work, searching for savings often has to take last place behind the needs of the day-to-day operations. As a cost consultant, you can use your creativity and your "nose for money" to keep your clients in the black. Are they really getting the best deal on copier paper? Would it be cheaper to outsource the cleaning? Can they batch orders for a discount? Energy savings can be a significant subspecialty all on its own. You keep a percentage of the savings you find, just as a bill auditor does, and both you and your client profit by your work. This is a great business for people who love a challenge and who are extremely persistent and detail-oriented. You're not only looking at reducing current bills; you're also on the lookout for major savings opportunities.

START-UP:

You will probably do most of your work on your clients' premises, so a basic, functional office will serve you well (about $3,000 to start). If your specialty involves much poring over financial records, you should invest in the furniture to make yourself physically comfortable. Earnings could reach $50,000 quickly.

BOTTOM LINE ADVICE:

Aside from the qualities necessary to look beneath the surface and find savings, you'll need excellent people skills. Allowing someone from the outside to be as involved in the workings of a company as a cost consultant must be is very uncomfortable for many business people. You'll need to gain their confidence with yourself as a person as well as with the service you offer.

DATABASE CONSULTANT

Start-up cost:	$5,000-$13,000
Potential earnings:	$40,000-$100,000
Typical fees:	$100+ per hour
Advertising:	Referrals, publications, trade journal advertising
Qualifications:	A high level of skill in database management and analysis, possible programming skills, awareness of business information needs, excellent communication skills, project management skills
Equipment needed:	High-end computer, database software, modem, printer, fax, office furniture, business card, letterhead, envelopes
Home business potential:	Yes
Staff required:	No
Handicapped opportunity:	Yes
Hidden costs:	Business insurance, need to incorporate to protect your assets against risk, updates on software, training to keep up with developments in field

LOWDOWN:

Companies develop databases to perform a wide range of essential functions; they need information that cross-references their data to make critical decisions and develop corporate strategies. An effective database can reveal all kinds of vital information. For example, an organization can effectively use a database to garner interesting information about its customers, such as what they purchase by mail, what time of year, week, or day they call to place an order, what sizes and quality selections they make, and the types of mailings they find most appealing. If you have the knowledge to create a database system that will present the needed information correctly, efficiently, and accurately, you can sell your services for a very high hourly rate. It may be your responsibility to write the program yourself or you may recommend other programmers—or you may supervise the customization of existing software.

START-UP:

You will need computer equipment to support your work, even though much of your time will be spent at client companies. This could run you in the neighborhood of $10,000 or more, since you'll need a powerful computer that can handle and manipulate huge amounts of data. But, since you'll charge at least $100 per hour for your services, you should be able to see a profit in a short period of time.

BOTTOM LINE ADVICE:

This is an enormously challenging business for people who love working at a high level with abstract ideas. Central to your success will be your ability to understand what information your clients really need. This involves learning in detail how the business operates and having the imagination to realize what a database could do to support that mission, now and in the future. The downside is the size and length of each database project. Some of these people have different agendas and may not share your commitment to making the database work effectively.

DATING SERVICE

Start-up cost:	$5,000-$50,000 (depending on how high-tech you want to be)
Potential earnings:	$50,000-$1.5 million
Typical fees:	$350 per client
Advertising:	Yellow Pages, classified ads, 900 numbers, television ads, singles magazines
Qualifications:	None
Equipment needed:	Extensive phone system for 900 numbers, computer (with many using computer video programs to showcase their clients)
Home business potential:	Not really, if you'd like some respect and privacy
Staff required:	Yes
Handicapped opportunity:	Yes
Hidden costs:	Computerized systems can run as high as $40,000

LOWDOWN:

Matchmaker, matchmaker, make me a living....Today's dating scene is vastly different from the old days, when a village woman made matches based on how her knee was feeling that day. Tired of meeting people in bars and the regular "sweat shops," many young professionals simply want a confidential, efficient way to meet the man or woman of their dreams. Because they don't have the time to screen a hundred or so applicants, you can provide this service for them—and at a competitive rate (just because they don't have time certainly doesn't mean they don't have money). You'll need to first decide what kind of dating service you'd most like to be: a well-respected, high-profile agency or an impersonal (yet profitable) 900 number. Either type requires you to manage profiles of your clients, so you'll need to have them answer questionnaires detailing their hobbies, interests, and desires in a potential mate. The next step is to make this information readily available to your client base—and keep track of your successes!

START-UP:

Your start-up costs can be quite high, based on the fact that most of your competitors (both large and small) are investing in technology that does it all in a few steps: first conducting the interview, then recording the interviewee and, finally, selecting a potential match from the databank. All of this could run anywhere from $40,000-$150,000—so be sure to investigate those costs well enough to document them in your business plan, particularly if you are going to need investors.

BOTTOM LINE ADVICE:

This is the love business, so what's not to love? For one thing, you'll be meeting quite an array of interesting people, and you'll be helping them to find long-lasting happiness. But what if it doesn't work out? Are you prepared to deal with broken hearts, all the while encouraging them to stay in the game? If the answer is yes, you'll be heartily rewarded for your efforts.

DECKS/OUTDOOR FURNITURE

Start-up cost:	$5,000-$10,000
Potential earnings:	$25,000-$65,000
Typical fees:	Can range anywhere from $150-$3,000 for each piece
Advertising:	Yellow Pages, local newspapers, direct mail, home and flower shows, hardware stores or renting your own outdoor space on a busy corner
Qualifications:	Carpentry and sales skills
Equipment needed:	Basic carpentry equipment, saws, blades
Home business potential:	Yes
Staff required:	Yes (for decks)
Handicapped opportunity:	No
Hidden costs:	Insurance and workers' compensation

LOWDOWN:

There's nothing like sitting out on a deck in the summertime, sipping a soda and enjoying a fresh, cool breeze. That's why so many homeowners yearn for additions to their homes in the way of decks and practical (yet tasteful) outdoor furniture. Many retirees have begun businesses like this one; it's the perfect way to cultivate an interest in woodworking and parlay it into a secondary (or even primary, if you're industrious) income. You'll be working with homeowners on everything from concept and design to the actual construction of each custom deck or piece of furniture, so develop strong listening and customer service skills. Remember, too, that even simple home construction projects might need building permits, depending on the community. This is a service that's seasonal, and to meet the demand you might have to hire additional help.

START-UP:

Your start-up fees will include your equipment (saws and other carpentry necessities) more than anything else, so be prepared to spend at least $5,000 on these items. Advertising will be your other main cost (roughly $3,000) and rent may be a consideration if you decide you need a storefront. Fees will vary from $150 for a small piece of wooden furniture (such as an end table) to several thousand dollars for decks.

BOTTOM LINE ADVICE:

Be sure to use the winter months to promote your business. Don't rely solely on homeowners—cultivate contacts with developers of new homes and condos.

DESIGNER/RETAIL ITEMS

Start-up cost:	$10,000-$20,000
Potential earnings:	$50,000-$150,000+
Typical fees:	Varied according to project; can be as low as $500 for a simple design sketch to several thousand for a complete design/technical layout with product specifications
Advertising:	Referral and direct mail
Qualifications:	Degree in product design
Equipment needed:	Computerized product design software (CAD)
Home business potential:	Yes
Staff required:	No
Handicapped opportunity:	Yes
Hidden costs:	Insurance, excessive changes in product specifications (make sure you're clear on what's expected—and get it in writing)

LOWDOWN:

Behind every good product that is made is a strong design team, and you could offer your services to such a team on a contract basis—if you have a reputation for quality product design done on a quick-turnaround basis and within budget. If you can accomplish all of that, you stand a very good chance of building lasting relationships with product manufacturers; they'll depend on your flair and expertise to pull off products that at first seem challenging to make. Your experience in design for manufacturability (i.e., designing products with the manufacturing team's constraints in mind) will be a valuable commodity among your clients; they appreciate working with professionals who understand that good design isn't just artistic; it's practical, too.

START-UP:

You'll need to invest between $10,000-$20,000 in a high-end computer with a large monitor and a computer-aided design (CAD) software package. Your advertising budget will be virtually nonexistent, because your area of expertise depends heavily on word of mouth. If you are successful in building the kinds of contacts you'll need to survive on your own, you'll be making anywhere from $50,000-$150,000 or more; obviously, if you're working for large, well-known manufacturers, your earnings will be on the high end because these companies are more apt to pay big bucks for quality design.

BOTTOM LINE ADVICE:

Your work will not always be your own; since you'll be working on a contract basis most of the time, you will often be brought in to solve design problems or pick up where another designer left off—not the biggest boost to your creativity. Still, the work is solid, it's demanding, and it's profitable for the talented.

DOULA/MIDWIFE

Start-up cost:	$10,000
Potential earnings:	$20,000-$35,000
Advertising:	Parenting newsletters, doctors' offices, word of mouth
Typical fees:	$300-$500 per client
Qualifications:	Certification required
Equipment needed:	Dependable car, pager, cellular phone or answering service
Home business potential:	Yes (although you'll be traveling a lot to birth sites)
Staff required:	No
Handicapped opportunity:	No
Hidden costs:	Liability insurance can be a killer; make sure you have good coverage

LOWDOWN:

If you appreciate the joy of bringing a new life into the world, this could be an ideal match. A *doula* (Greek for "woman's helper") or midwife takes part in the great circle of life on virtually a daily basis. After receiving your certification, you'll need to meet with family physicians to let them know about your services. Not all doctors will react favorably; however, women are demanding such services and look to their doctors for support. The rise in popularity of home births and home-like birthing centers in hospitals is another trend that could easily contribute to your success. One thing is certain: in this field, your best advertising will come from word of mouth.

START-UP:

Your training and certification costs (average: $10,000) will make for a moderate initial investment, but you should be able to recoup within a year after you start. You will, however, need to have liability and/or malpractice insurance, which can often run into thousands of dollars. On the patient side of your business, some insurance companies do not cover midwives—so you may have to work out payment plans (and collection methods) for these clients.

BOTTOM LINE ADVICE:

The demands of being on-call for much of your career can take its toll—as can the occasional life-or-death emergency. Obviously, if you enjoy the challenges and aren't afraid of the risks, you can make a difference in the lives of a new family—and that may be your biggest reward.

DRAFTSMAN/BLUEPRINTING SERVICE

Start-up cost:	$5,000-$10,000
Potential earnings:	$35,000-$65,000
Typical fees:	$150-$500 per blueprint
Advertising:	Yellow Pages, referral, ads in trade publications
Qualifications:	Degree in drafting
Equipment needed:	Blueprint photocopier, drafting table, related small tools
Home business potential:	Yes
Staff required:	No
Handicapped opportunity:	Not typically
Hidden costs:	Insurance, equipment maintenance/upgrade

LOWDOWN:

You're detail-oriented, with a flair for putting the finishing touches on someone else's work. You've also likely studied drafting in college before embarking on this entrepreneurial endeavor; you have the experience that your customers will eventually come to rely on. As a draftsman/blueprinting service, you will ultimately produce the blueprints that architects and builders need to complete their dynamic new projects. You will make any requested number of copies of each blueprint as well. Although individuals may hire you for smaller projects, most of your customers will be architects and building professionals, so you'll need to be well-connected to get any share of the work that's out there. Set yourself apart by adding additional services or special treatment (such as free delivery to work sites).

START-UP:

You'll need between $5,000-$10,000 to get started in drafting and blueprinting, primarily to cover your equipment costs for such items as a blueprint photocopier ($4,000 or so) and drafting table with drafting pencils, etc. You'll likely earn $35,000-$65,000 for your efforts.

BOTTOM LINE ADVICE:

It's very precise work you're doing, and often it's a thankless job (seeing as how the architects and builders take all the glory). Oh, well . . . you should always remember that without you, the project might not have gotten done. Stick close to the builders and architects, since they'll ultimately make up your referral system.

DRIVE-BY BROADCASTING

Start-up cost:	$5,000-$10,000
Potential earnings:	$30,000-$45,000
Typical fees:	$75-$125 per month per system installed
Advertising:	Yellow Pages, direct mail to businesses, restaurants, Board of Realtors, coupon deals for general public or homeowners selling by themselves
Qualifications:	Radio broadcast background would be helpful; possibly FCC licensing
Equipment needed:	Short-range radio transmitting equipment, recording equipment, signs
Home business potential:	Yes
Staff required:	No
Handicapped opportunity:	Not typically
Hidden costs:	Insurance, equipment maintenance and upgrades

LOWDOWN:

How many times have you driven up to a home that's for sale or a business you've never seen before, wondering what each has to offer? With the help of short-range transmitters, you can now drive up to one of these potentials and get the lowdown on it without leaving your car. All you have to do is drive up close to the building, tune in your radio to a specific station, and listen to a prerecorded message detailing the home or business you're interested in knowing more about. You act as the distributor or dealer of such equipment. Your days will mostly be spent combing lists of potential customers, as this is a relatively new service and will consequently require heavy promotion on your part. If you are knowledgeable about the equipment you're leasing, and if you have terrific ideas or unusual messages you can suggest that your clients use in order to boost interest in what they have to offer, you could do quite well for yourself in a drive-by broadcasting dealership.

START-UP:

Your start-up costs ($5,000-$10,000) will likely be wrapped up in securing a dealership with complete technical and sales support; however, expect to spend some money ($5,000 or so) on advertising and promotion. You might have to give away a few transmitters in the beginning, at least on a trial basis, just to gain the testimonials you'll need to convince others. If you are successful, you'll make between $30,000-$45,000 after a few years of hard work.

BOTTOM LINE ADVICE:

This is such a new business, it may seem a little trendy—and trendy is often a hard sell to traditionally conservative industries such as real estate and food service. Have a backup plan in mind in case it takes a while longer than you'd expected to launch this unique business, or you could wind up losing too much money before you make any.

EFFICIENCY EXPERT

Start-up cost:	$5,000-$10,000
Potential earnings:	$35,000-$75,000+ (depending on your market)
Typical fees:	$75-$100 per hour or a monthly retainer of $3,000-$5,000
Advertising:	Trade publications, Yellow Pages, direct mail, business newspapers
Qualifications:	Ability to spot potential problems and time-wasters before and as they occur
Equipment needed:	Computer, fax/modem, printer, resource materials
Home business potential:	Yes
Staff required:	No
Handicapped opportunity:	Yes
Hidden costs:	Insurance, underbilling for amount of time spent (watch your own clock)

LOWDOWN:

Corporations often have CEOs who want the company run like clockwork, particularly if there are production goals to be met regularly. As an efficiency expert, you will come into a company for a period of about two to four weeks and carefully monitor exactly how things are being done. You will ask workers questions such as, "Why are you repeatedly moving across the room to accomplish one simple task?" and "Is there any other way to minimize the steps involved in your particular process?" You are, in a sense, a detective searching for answers to the big question (which is, of course: "How can this company achieve more in a better and more economical way?"). Next, you'll print up a report or make a formal presentation, telling the CEO where he or she can improve operations. You should have a rather broad background in business operations, management experience, and a strong eye for detail. After all, your client companies will be paying you big bucks to figure out what needs to be improved upon at their facilities; you have to convey the idea that you're worth it, so watch your own image and always give it 110 percent.

START-UP:

Start-up will be relatively low (in the $5,000-$10,000 range), but you should do quite well when you consider what you might be able to earn if you're good at what you do ($35,000-$75,000 or more). You'll need a basic office setup and lots of good resource materials to help workers achieve greater effectiveness.

BOTTOM LINE ADVICE:

While some corporate moguls will hire you to tell them what's wrong with their organization, they may not be willing to actually listen. You'll need to be clear from the beginning that you are merely offering your professional opinions and advice—that way, your personal liability will be kept in check.

ELECTRICAL CONTRACTOR/ELECTRICIAN

Start-up cost:	$10,000-$15,000
Potential earnings:	$40,000-$60,000
Typical fees:	$40 per service call; more for parts and labor
Advertising:	Yellow Pages, classifieds, neighborhood flyers, community bulletin boards, word of mouth, radio spots
Qualifications:	Skill and experience as an electrician, ability to manage time and expenses, good people skills. Most states require certification and regular credit hours toward career development
Equipment needed:	Tools, parts, and equipment related to the nature of the work, van, marketing materials.
Home business potential:	Yes
Staff required:	No
Handicapped opportunity:	No
Hidden costs:	Inventory of parts, vehicle maintenance, insurance

LOWDOWN:

Skilled electricians are always in demand, especially ones who can work with undecided homeowners and impatient small business people. As the general population becomes less handy with tools and wires, your electrical knowledge and expertise will become more and more valuable. This is a classic one-person business, and you may find considerable competition. You will need good estimating skills to assess the cost and complexity of the work you are asked to do. Sometimes it seems as if electricians have to be part detective to interpret the hidden wiring in an old house or to trace the cause of a short "somewhere in the wall." Of course, you'll be familiar with code standards in all the communities in your service area.

START-UP:

Costs are relatively high as you must equip yourself to do whatever electrical job is offered. You'll also need to secure certification, and your educational requirements to stay certified may also demand that you take regular refresher courses. Set aside at least $5,000 for all of this—then add your equipment, liability insurance, and related costs.

BOTTOM LINE ADVICE:

Many electricians have made an excellent living by focusing on upgrading the wiring in old houses. If your area has a charming neighborhood of old Victorians, twenties bungalows, or quaint cottages that are being restored, you have a golden opportunity to build a client base. Other electricians work closely with an independent builder to install wiring in new structures. For these jobs, getting the work done according to the overall construction schedule will have a big influence on profits for the builder. Your planning and time-management skills can help build you a steady stream of referrals and repeat projects from builders.

EMPLOYEE BENEFITS CONSULTANT

Start-up cost:	$5,000-$8,000
Potential earnings:	$30,000-$70,000
Typical fees:	$25 and up
Advertising:	Direct mail, networking, memberships in business and community organizations
Qualifications:	Extensive experience in insurance sales, ability to reach business owners, detail orientation, communications skills
Equipment needed:	Office furniture, computer, modem, fax, laser printer, cellular phone, business card, letterhead, envelopes
Home business potential:	Yes
Staff required:	No
Handicapped opportunity:	Yes
Hidden costs:	Preparation of presentation materials, on-line fees, errors and omissions insurance

LOWDOWN:

An effective employee benefits program is an important factor in building a loyal workforce. The challenge is to create a combination of benefits that meets the needs of the organization and also fits its budget. As an employee benefits consultant, you will help growing businesses survey their employees to learn their needs and wants regarding employer-paid insurance. You will work with the business owner to design the best combination of benefits for the dollars available. The likeliest market is businesses with 20 to 200 employees, which are too small to have a large human resources department.

START-UP:

Most of your client contact will take place at their locations, so your office can be functional rather than impressive ($4,000 should get you started). You'll need to be easy for potential and current clients to reach, and you'll need to produce professional-looking presentations to client companies. You should plan to earn about $30,000 in the beginning.

BOTTOM LINE ADVICE:

Many insurance agents have terrible sales approaches. They seem very eager for their commissions and do not give ongoing service throughout the year. As annual review time rolls around, these agents show up again with a plan to change to new providers for a few dollars less. But implementation and employee education are lacking. You will be able to set yourself apart if your focus is on customer service, not your own profit (at least outwardly). Experience in assisting with claims and with any conflicts that may arise is also an important selling point for your enterprise.

EXECUTIVE SEARCH FIRM

Start-up cost:	$5,500-$9,000
Potential earnings:	From $40,000 to as much as $150,000 (gross)
Typical fees:	Varies, but often equals 25 percent of first-year earnings of person placed with client
Advertising:	Cold calls, attending trade shows, newsletter to potential clients, direct mail, ads in publications
Qualifications:	Excellent people skills, patience, self-confidence, knowledge of specialized fields to be able to select appropriate candidates for jobs
Equipment needed:	Computer and office equipment, telephone, business cards, letterhead, brochures
Home business potential:	Yes
Staff required:	None
Handicapped opportunity:	Yes
Hidden costs:	Phone expenses and advertising costs could exceed budget early

LOWDOWN:

Executive recruiters (also known as "headhunters") are paid by companies to fill management, professional, and technical slots within their firms. Most of a recruiter's work is done via phone and E-mail, so you can do this job anywhere, although networking face-to-face is also important. You will collect as many qualified applicants as you can (gleaned mostly from your vast resume collection and a few friends in high places). Many consultants choose niches in which to specialize; others serve all areas. A sales personality is helpful in this business, as is the ability to be self-motivated. Often, finding good people for the positions is easier than finding clients who will hire you to conduct the job search. You will need self-confidence, tenacity, and good networking skills to make it as a recruiter. This career choice gives you a great deal of flexibility and personal freedom, since you can work from any location that has a phone.

START-UP:

A computer and printer are essential, as is database, word processing, and communications software. These items will cost from $2,500 to $5,000. You will need a telephone, a headset, and fax, along with office furniture and business cards, letterhead, and brochures to promote your business. These pieces will cost $1,500-$4,500. You'll earn an average 25 percent of the new hire's salary—so it behooves you to search for the high-end, top-level managers.

BOTTOM LINE ADVICE:

Competition for the best companies and top-notch candidates is stiff, and you get paid only when you successfully match a company with a candidate, but the financial rewards can be considerable, and the satisfaction of helping a good candidate to find a job and your client to fill a key position, make your efforts worthwhile.

EXPERT WITNESS

Start-up cost:	$5,000-$7,000
Potential earnings:	$50,000-$100,000
Typical fees:	Varied (but can be as high as $1,000 per day)
Advertising:	Legal periodicals, referrals, networking, association memberships
Qualifications:	Selling ability, wide range of contacts in technical and business areas
Equipment needed:	Computer, database software, fax, modem, laser printer, office furniture, business card, letterhead, envelopes
Home business potential:	Yes
Staff required:	No
Handicapped opportunity:	Yes
Hidden costs:	Phone bills, on-line time

LOWDOWN:

Expert testimony is frequently required in cases where a consumer product may cause injury. Your business can be a source for lawyers to call when they have clients with unusual claims. You can provide from your database the names of appropriate expert witnesses if you are not an expert yourself—or you can provide referrals in addition to offering your own services. The expert witness often is knowledgeable about a particular type of product and is able to determine if a defect exists in the product in question.

Being an expert witness can be an excellent source of income, especially for someone newly laid off or recently retired. This job is a perfect sideline for doctors and other medical practitioners. Your service can help connect people with technical or business expertise to the lawyers who need the testimony. Expert witnesses must be able to pull complex facts together into simple, understandable sentences. They need to see the big picture and to think quickly on their feet and deal calmly with cross-examination.

START-UP:

You'll need a computer ($2,000-$3,000) for producing credible reports to offer as background information or to be entered as evidence. You may also decide to post your availability on the Internet (since you can reach many more people who might need your services)—especially if you decide to add a referral service to your own. Many expert witnesses charge $1,000 a day or more for their services; it really depends on the nature of your testimony and the extent to which you must prepare for your court appearance.

BOTTOM LINE ADVICE:

This business can thrive on your ability to be an expert witness or to find others with technical or business knowledge who can articulate clearly to the jury—with credibility. Expert witnesses testify in a wide range of cases daily, and they can be very difficult to find for unusual specialties. Once your business is established, referrals should keep an excellent income rolling in.

FABRIC COVERINGS

Start-up costs:	$5,000-$10,000
Potential earnings:	$25,000-$50,000
Typical fees:	Varied according to project and square footage of area; can be as low as $150 or as high as several thousand
Advertising:	Contacts with fabric stores and interior designers, news releases to home improvement editor of local newspaper, Yellow Pages
Qualifications:	Creativity and perhaps training in interior decorating
Equipment needed:	Heavy-duty sewing machine, shears, sample books galore
Home business potential:	Yes
Staff required:	Not initially (maybe for larger installations)
Handicapped potential:	No
Hidden costs:	Insurance and unexpected fluctuations in materials costs

LOWDOWN:

Fabric is a creative alternative to wallpaper for the discerning customer to whom money is no object. The fact is, many Victorian homes used fabric as wall covering to provide a lush, almost ethereal appearance. You'll need special pastes and tools to smooth bumps and trim edges, and you'll need to have plenty of sample materials to show your clients to assist them in selecting the best choices. Network closely with interior designers and fabric store owners to gain some immediate business; consider waiving your fee for the first job or so (or until you get a good portfolio going). Offer a wide variety of styles and designs to choose from, and keep up with trends in the fabric industry by reading every publication you can get your hands on.

START-UP:

You'll spend $5,000-$10,000 in your first year of business, primarily to cover your training and materials. Sample books should be easy enough to come by (and many are offered by manufacturers free of charge). Your own fees will vary widely; they may be as low as $150 for a chair cover to $1,000 or more for wall covering.

BOTTOM LINE ADVICE:

Careful, accurate measuring and treatment of fabric is necessary. Mistakes could be costly—and disastrous-looking, to say the least. Practice on your own walls first.

FAX-ON-DEMAND SERVICE

Start-up cost:	$12,000-$15,000
Potential earnings:	$20,000-$50,000
Typical fees:	$150-$300/month to cover incoming calls, with unlimited responses, or lower monthly fees with charge for each response
Advertising:	Advertising in trade journals, direct mail, direct solicitations, seminars
Qualifications:	Knowledge of technology and software, marketing ability
Equipment needed:	Modified computer with special fax board, customized software, scanner, office furniture
Home business potential:	Yes
Staff required:	No
Handicapped opportunity:	Yes
Hidden costs:	Additional phone lines

LOWDOWN:

You will provide the technology that allows smaller companies and professionals to match the fax-on-demand systems being set up in-house by large organizations. Your clients will make information available to their customers or employees around the clock. These people call to ask for information, and your automated faxing system sends them the newsletter, data sheet, or restaurant menu they have requested instantly. Automatic broadcasting can reach sales reps or members of an interest group. Once businesses understand how their marketing efforts can be supported by fax-on-demand, they will form an ongoing clientele and a source of steady income for you. But your first task will be to help them see the possibilities inherent in this new technology. You're going to be creating the market for this service.

START-UP:

This is an expensive business to get into, with start-up costs averaging $15,000. Getting the funding to set it up may present quite a challenge, since it is a relatively new type of business with little track record to fall back on. Still, if you're creative, you'll find ways to purchase the equipment you need economically; and you'll be billing $150-$300 per client per month, so you will have decent income once you're customer base is well-established.

BOTTOM LINE ADVICE:

You're going to need a silver tongue and a genius for marketing to get a fax-on-demand service off the ground. Finding organizations that need to send out up-to-date printed materials in high volume will be the first step. Creating possibilities that click in with your prospects' needs and assumptions will allow you to get your message through to the people who can see advantages to cutting-edge approaches.

Location, Location

Is it really true that location is everything—to every kind of business there is? Well, yes and no.

While it is important to have an actual location of *some* kind, it doesn't always mean that you need a high-profile storefront or a high-rise corporate office to make your business respected and profitable.

You can get by on a shoestring with a neatly decorated area of your own home, as long as it's separate from the rest of the household activity. An extra bedroom or a den would make a fine office, as would a finished basement or garage. Some home business people simply section off a part of their living room.

The fact is, home offices have become increasingly popular; thousands of people meet with clients every day in their homes and experience no lapse in credibility whatsoever. If you're concerned about your professional image, invest in corporate-looking furniture and high-end equipment; don't meet clients at your kitchen table if you can help it.

If you are opening a retail establishment or other business that depends on high visibility and being located in close proximity to companion-type businesses (such as a clothing store being located next to a tailoring service), you would greatly benefit from renting a small- to medium-size shop. Strip malls and small shopping plazas offer the best choices, and cost considerably less than large shopping mall space.

Above all else, be sure to check the zoning regulations in your area. A florist once failed to do so, and began running her business out of her house only to be subjected to complaints from neighbors. Although she was forced to move out of her house and into a small storefront, her business nearly *quadrupled* in the first two months. The lesson: Higher visibility and drive-by traffic brought the florist the kind of business she'd only dreamed of.

Know where you are likely to be seen and reached by the most customers, but if your customers are buying your product or service because there is no other like it, you may be successful in getting them to come to you, wherever you are.

FINANCIAL PLANNER

Start-up cost:	$5,000-$8,000
Potential earnings:	$40,000-$60,000
Typical fees:	Set fee depending on investments, typically $250-$500 or more
Advertising:	Referrals, networking, memberships in community and business groups, local magazines and newspapers, programs of fund-raisers
Qualifications:	Certification is becoming essential; familiarity with financial issues. Excellent people skills for marketing, and for creating a plan suitable to the client's needs; ability to inspire trust
Equipment needed:	Computer, printer, suite software, fax, modem, on-line account, furniture, business card, letterhead, envelopes
Home business potential:	Yes
Staff required:	No
Handicapped opportunity:	Yes
Hidden costs:	Subscriptions to newspapers and financial periodicals, errors and omissions insurance

LOWDOWN:

The market for financial planning services is becoming very large, especially as the baby boom generation draws close to retirement. Your difficulty in establishing your business will be that so many others are competing with you. You'll probably need to be part of a close network of family, friends, and acquaintances who will work with you and refer you to their friends. This is a very personal business, and your ability to inspire confidence will be vital. Creativity in helping your clients plan their financial future and skill at helping them achieve those goals will set you apart. Is there an underserved group you can target? Can you design plans for self-employed people, the elderly, or investment clubs? Can you work in association with related businesses such as accountant firms to add your service onto their offerings?

START-UP:

Your office needs to give you the up-to-the-moment information you need for proper service to your clients (around $3,000 to start); however, you could earn upward of $40,000.

BOTTOM LINE ADVICE:

Most people manage their money very poorly, if at all. They don't plan well or budget, and they haven't faced up to the question of providing for retirement. All these are difficult topics, and can make dealing with these sensitive issues uncomfortable. You can smooth things over with a reassuring attitude, and by paying attention to the details of your client's finances that they obviously overlook.

ADVICE FROM THE EXPERTS

What sets your business apart from others like it?

Dianne Winnen, a Certified Financial Planner in Akron, Ohio, says she is different because her business caters to middle-income people rather than focusing on seniors with retirement funds. "I'm one of 31,000 CFPs in the country, and I'm proud to be a part of a select group."

Things you couldn't do without:

"I couldn't do without my computer, telephone, and copier."

Marketing tips/advice:

"You really have to want to be in this field to make it successful for you. Read and educate yourself about business matters."

If you had to do it all over again . . .

"I would've gone in with more realistic expectations about what it would take to survive the first couple of years."

FIREWOOD SERVICE

Start-up cost:	$5,000-$15,000
Potential earnings:	$25,000-$35,000
Typical fees:	$65 per cord, delivered and stacked
Advertising:	Local newspapers, bulletin boards, flyers
Qualifications:	Knowledge of wood, good physical condition, ability to manage accounts and records
Equipment needed:	Log splitter, chain saws, various other saws, axes, trailer and/or truck
Home business potential:	Yes
Staff required:	Yes
Handicapped opportunity:	No
Hidden costs:	Equipment maintenance

LOWDOWN:

Some folks just don't relish the idea of getting up on a cold morning and splitting up firewood Abe Lincoln-style; others simply don't have the time and appreciate the convenience of a service like yours. Good physical condition is an absolute must for this position. You can't be afraid to work with your hands for long hours, and hoist loads up to and out of your vehicle. Know the different types of wood that you are cutting down. There is a difference between hardwood and softwood, and your job depends on your knowledge about all kinds of wood (i.e., which burn better than others). Have your marketing materials out well ahead of the fall and winter season, and network with local lumber and hardware shops to see if you can sell smaller bundles through them. Some people like to start buying wood before the cold sets in.

START-UP:

Your initial investment will be relatively low, starting at $5,000 to cover equipment costs (assuming you already have a small truck). In most cases, this job is seasonal, so you really need to get the word out early to gross a high end of $35,000.

BOTTOM LINE ADVICE:

To begin with, this business could be a great second income; you don't necessarily need to start out gangbusters. After you've been working for a few seasons and learn all the ins and outs, you could really make a decent living being a woodsman.

FISHERMAN

Start-up cost:	$10,000-$15,000+
Potential earnings:	$15,000-$25,000
Typical fees:	The going price that day at your co-op or wholesaler
Advertising:	None
Qualifications:	Experience and expertise with water, boats, and fish, appropriate license if required in your area
Equipment needed:	Depends on the type of fish you are aiming for: boat, nets, trawl, rods, crab pots
Home business potential:	Yes
Staff required:	Probably
Handicapped opportunity:	No
Hidden costs:	Fuel and bait, boat maintenance and equipment repair, insurance

LOWDOWN:

You become a fisherman because you love the water and have extensive experience with the ways of the type of fish you intend to catch. You do not become a fisherman to get rich, or to have a soft life. International markets have both negative and positive effects on the profitability of fishing. For example, cheaper cod may be imported from Canada so that your catch cannot be sold. The Japanese market for sea urchins has encouraged many divers to harvest the spiny creatures for export. Prices paid for a fisherman's catch can be volatile, but the costs for fuel and bait always seem to go up. Yet, even in spite of volatile seas, many fisherman would not trade this life for any other occupation. Most commercial fisherman have grown up with the life, although some people do enter this difficult business as refugees from the rat race.

START-UP:

Start-up costs vary enormously, depending on whether you need an ocean-going trawler or a skiff, a simple line with baited hooks, or 150 wire lobster pots. You could wind up spending more than $20,000 if you buy everything new. Look for good, solid, used equipment. Don't expect to get rich; your best income could be as little as $25,000 in a good season. However, if that's all you need to live on, there's plenty of fish in the sea.

BOTTOM LINE ADVICE:

You definitely need insight into both catching your fish and marketing it profitably. Skill, strength, and endurance mark successful fishermen, whatever other variations there may be between them.

FRANCHISE IDEA CENTER

Start-up cost:	$5,000-$15,000
Potential earnings:	$20,000-$40,000
Typical fees:	$5-$15 per idea or a flat fee of $50-$100 to conduct a search
Advertising:	Yellow Pages, ads in national entrepreneurial publications, local newspapers, World Wide Web page, direct mail
Qualifications:	Business background helpful; should be an excellent resource person
Equipment needed:	Computer with printer, high-speed modem and fax, phone, copier, extensive collection or access to resource materials on franchising, credit card processing equipment
Home business potential:	No (unless you work strictly as an on-line service)
Staff required:	No
Handicapped opportunity:	Yes
Hidden costs:	Insurance, constant updating of information (new materials)

LOWDOWN:

Thousands of folks with entrepreneurial dreams set out to find the perfect money-making opportunity, and franchising is appealing because it offers immediate support and a sense of stability. But not everyone knows which opportunities will work best for them, or how to go about researching franchises to determine their feasibility and/or market potential. Your service may be limited to simple printouts of specific franchises available in the United States today, or may include detailed contact and financial information on one or more franchises. If you want to be really progressive, you can set up a World Wide Web home page and sell your services over the Internet (where many entrepreneurs hang out). Either way, you'll need to be an expert on the ins and outs of franchising, and keep up on the constant changes occurring in this dynamic and growing area of opportunity.

START-UP:

You'll spend $5,000-$15,000 launching a business that helps others go into business, but that will cover all of your resource materials (magazine subscriptions, on-line services and directories) in addition to your office setup (including computer, printer, fax/modem). You might consider earmarking $5,000 or so for your first year of advertising, since you'll likely need to advertise in markets larger than your immediate locale in order to make serious money ($20,000-$40,000).

BOTTOM LINE ADVICE:

Your biggest challenge will be to collect your fees up front, particularly on the Internet. You should have credit card processing equipment and make sure that you don't give anything away without securing payment first. On the positive side, you'll enjoy the fact that the information you're selling need only be produced once—and can be sold and resold (profitably) an infinite number of times.

FURNITURE REFINISHER

Start-up costs:	$5,000-$20,000
Potential earnings:	$30,000-$60,000
Typical fees:	$50 or more for a straight chair; $300 for dining set with six chairs; $20 or more per hour
Advertising:	Yellow Pages, local newspapers, contacts with antique shops, interior decorators
Qualifications:	Thorough knowledge and skills of furniture refinishing
Equipment needed:	Dipping tanks, specialized refinishing tools
Home business potential:	Possibly—but be careful about disposal of hazardous chemicals
Staff required:	No
Handicapped opportunity:	Not typically
Hidden costs:	Insurance

LOWDOWN:

Antiques and other priceless pieces of furniture don't always keep their beauty—especially if they're being used on a regular basis rather than simply displayed. Furniture refinishing requires a specialized knowledge and skill. Using the wrong stripping agent, technique, or tool might ruin someone's priceless antique. But if you have the skill and know-how, this business can be lucrative. When it comes to furniture stripping alone, 50 percent of what you can charge covers materials, overhead, and operating costs, so volume is the key to profits. Stripping a simple chair usually takes a veteran about 15 minutes, especially if you use a dipping tank.

START-UP:

Spend $5,000 or so getting started, mainly to cover your advertising fees and initial supplies. Obviously, if you opt for a business space instead of running this out of your home (and, due to EPA regulations, this is highly recommended), expect to shell out another $300-$600 per month for rent. Charge at least $20 per hour for your services; try to develop a price list with specific items on it.

BOTTOM LINE ADVICE:

If you're going to use your home, check out zoning restrictions. Use caution when dealing with corrosive or flammable chemicals; be sure you're very familiar with government regulations regarding disposal of chemicals.

GARDENING CONSULTANT

Start-up cost:	$5,000-$10,000 (more if you need to purchase a vehicle)
Potential earnings:	$40,000-$60,000
Typical fees:	Varied; can be as low as $125 or as high as several thousand per project (depending on whether you're working for an individual or a corporation)
Advertising:	Yellow Pages, community newspapers, city magazines, direct mail, bulletin boards, networking, speaking to community organizations
Qualifications:	Extensive knowledge of plants, growing seasons, and regional climates
Equipment needed:	Gardening tools, hoses, seeds, perhaps a van
Home business potential:	Yes
Staff required:	Yes (1-5 people to work on several projects simultaneously)
Handicapped opportunity:	Not likely
Hidden costs:	Liability insurance and workers' compensation

LOWDOWN:

There's nothing lovelier in the springtime than a perfectly planned garden in bloom. If you've always been the type who can effectively plan such perennial pleasures, you would likely be well-suited to this line of business. Especially if you don't mind working outside in the dirt for long periods of time during the warmest times of the year. As a gardening consultant, you will meet with either homeowners or business owners to work out the details of what will bloom where. Develop a portfolio of your best work, then reel in more business through speaking engagements or presentations to community organizations that are always looking for gardening experts because they appeal to large groups of people. Be sure to always be clear on what your services entail—many well-meaning folks will confuse your services with those of professional landscapers. If you don't cut grass, say so.

START-UP:

If you've already been involved in gardening, you likely have many of the tools you'll need to start. However, keep in mind that you'll probably be adding a staff once the phone starts ringing, so you'll need to double or possibly triple the number of tools you have on hand. Also, if you need a vehicle, such as a van, consider leasing and applying a magnetic sign to the door advertising your services. All said and done, you'll shell out about $5,000-$10,000—more if you add staff. But your fees, which will vary from $125 to several thousand dollars, should help offset any costs.

BOTTOM LINE ADVICE:

Plan your speaking engagements and other forms of promotion during the off-season; chances are, you'll be too busy during the spring and summer months.

GIFT BASKET BUSINESS

Start-up cost:	$5,000-$15,000
Potential earnings:	$25,000-$45,000
Typical fees:	Baskets are individually priced anywhere from $25-$350
Advertising:	Local newspapers, flyers, bulletin boards, direct mail to busy executives, Yellow Pages
Qualifications:	Natural creativity mixed with a strong business sense
Equipment needed:	Baskets and gift materials, glue gun, shrink wrap machine, delivery vehicle
Home business potential:	Yes
Staff required:	No
Handicapped opportunity:	Yes
Hidden costs:	Shipping costs

LOWDOWN:

There's nothing nicer to receive than a basket full of goodies meant especially for you . . . that's why gift basket businesses have been cropping up everywhere. Some are even offered as franchise opportunities. On the surface, this business seems so simple anyone could do it: you just round up a bunch of neat items, place them in a basket, put ribbons and shrink wrap around all and voila! But there is much more to it than that; you must also be a gifted buyer (to get the best bargains on gift items and materials) and a real go-getter of a salesperson to bring in the constant flow of business needed to stay afloat. In other words, you should have all the marketing skills of a seasoned retailer in addition to a dynamic and creative mind. If you can handle all of that, you will likely succeed if your market area isn't already saturated. Be sure to set yourself apart from the others as much as possible: since there are so many in this emerging and trendy business, the competition is fierce and you'll lose out if you don't carve an interesting niche for yourself. Perhaps you could fill your gift baskets with only a particular type of product, such as products manufactured only in your state, or special theme packages.

START-UP:

Your start-up costs hinge on whether you're renting a storefront and whether you're investing in a delivery vehicle or merely using your own car or van. As far as the storefront goes, it could generate some walk-in business, but rent is awful steep for straggler-type businesses. You really should try to keep this one lean and mean for as long as you can, having your clients shop from a catalog rather than in person. You'll need to advertise heavily in places your customers are most likely to think of needing your services, and that will run you in the neighborhood of $500-$3,000. Your money will come from the gift baskets you sell (minus production and commission costs); most gift basket businesses offer a wide range of prices for an array of baskets, anywhere from $25-$300.

Bottom Line Advice:

Since the national recognition of one woman's company, everyone is trying to get into this seemingly easy business. If you feel you can create a gift basket business that truly stands apart in some way, you stand a good chance of earning a living. If you're unsure about this critical piece of advice, think it over or (better yet) rewrite your business plan. It's so competitive that you have to have a niche to survive unless you're in a remote part of the country (but, then, your customer base will also be limited). Still, if you're creative about gift baskets, you'll be creative in coming up with a way to sell them.

Becoming a Networking Giant

Want to move to the networking fast-track? Here are some great tips on becoming a top networking professional:

- **Develop as many contacts as you can.** Add one new person each day, and you'll have met at least twenty new people per month.
- **Tell people the one thing you feel you do best.** Don't give them a rundown of all that you can do. It confuses, and even annoys, some people when the conversation seems one-sided; be concise about what you do so that the other person may reciprocate.
- **Become a host/leader, not a wallflower.** Show initiative; introduce yourself. Don't throw your card at anybody until after you've established a verbal introduction.
- **Cultivate your contacts.** Don't try to use the situation to get immediate business; instead, ask to meet privately later on. Nobody likes to feel pressure in social situations.
- **Extend your own expertise first whenever possible.** Be available to those who call on you for help when they need it.
- **Keep in touch.** Mail or fax articles that might be of interest to your contacts—it shows you were listening when you met them, and that you remembered what they said.

GRAFFITI REMOVAL

Start-up cost:	$5,000-$10,000
Potential earnings:	$10,000-$20,000
Typical fees:	$150-$300 per job
Advertising:	Flyers, door-to-door solicitation, Yellow Pages, classifieds
Qualifications:	Persistence, knowledge of chemical cleaning agents
Equipment needed:	Chemical cleaning agents, business card, brochures or flyers
Home business potential:	Yes
Staff required:	No
Handicapped opportunity:	No
Hidden costs:	None

LOWDOWN:

Graffiti stands out like a sore thumb. All you have to do is find the owner of the defaced property, or the person authorized to contract for work, sell your removal service, and go to it. Graffiti is a serious problem in some areas of the country, especially densely populated places, and, oddly enough, also in relatively deserted places where the spray-can artists feel free to let loose. Letting graffiti remain is an open invitation for more vandalism, so it pays to have the mess cleared up as soon as it occurs. You might be able to develop ongoing contracts for regular checking and cleaning if the graffiti is severe enough. Onlookers may provide referrals on the spot.

START-UP:

Your strong arm is your main tool. You will have to buy cleaning chemicals and some way of transporting them. If you have a rural clientele you'll also need some kind of vehicle, but you can buy a used one with storage capacity. Charge $150-$300 per job, unless there is a lot of time involved (in which case, charge an hourly rate of $50 or more).

BOTTOM LINE ADVICE:

This is a classic American bootstrap-type business. Hard work will be the main ingredient in your recipe for success. This is mostly outdoor work, which is more pleasant in some seasons than in others. After a while the sameness of the task may begin to bore you. The chemicals need to be handled with extreme care as well.

GRAPHIC DESIGNER

Start-up cost:	$6,000-$10,000
Potential earnings:	$30,000-$75,000
Typical fees:	$75-$100 per hour or average retainer fees of $1,000 per month
Advertising:	Business publications, promotional mailings to people in the gift business; referrals
Qualifications:	Background in graphics, type design and color, communication and marketing skills, artistic inclination
Equipment needed:	High-end computer with quality graphics design software, color scanner, large-screen monitor, laser printer; fax/modem, office furniture that includes a light table, business card, letterhead, envelopes
Home business potential:	Yes
Staff required:	No
Handicapped opportunity:	Yes
Hidden costs:	Training in new software programs

LOWDOWN:

In most communities there is a lot of competition in this field, but skilled, creative graphic designers stand out above the rest. Experienced graphic designers who want to work independently can make an excellent living producing work for a range of clients in a home-based setting. Freelance graphic designers work for a variety of different businesses, including book publishers, newspapers, consumer product manufacturers, and even other small start-ups, designing letterhead and logos. Eventually you may decide to set up a studio and employ others to work with you. An ability to communicate well with clients is essential. It is not enough to create designs that appeal to your own aesthetic sense. You need to be part marketer and part psychologist to produce the designs your clients want and need.

START-UP:

The computer equipment required is very expensive. You will need the latest software as well, in addition to an efficient and comfortable work space. Figure your charges to be in the $75-$100 per hour range. Be careful of bidding on a per-job basis; many companies will demand that you do only to take advantage of your time later.

BOTTOM LINE ADVICE:

You can make an excellent living as a graphic designer once you distinguish yourself from the competition and build up a reputation for excellence and on-time work. Good working relationships will lead to a satisfied group of clients that return to you again and again. It can be difficult to bid jobs accurately and sometimes a few clients will be very slow to pay. Working under rush conditions seems to be the norm, and occasionally you will encounter a customer that is impossible to please.

ADVICE FROM THE EXPERTS

What sets your business apart from others like it?

Kelvin Oden, owner of Oh Snap! Design in Brooklyn, New York, says he's had to pay his dues to get where he is. "On the positive side, I'm a young company and can work without limitation or restriction. I can go against the norm."

Things you couldn't do without:

A computer, laser printer with at least 600 dpi, and clients are all Oden says he needs to survive.

Marketing tips/advice:

"The most important thing is to build really good relationships with your clients. If they're comfortable with you as a person, they'll come back to you."

If you had to do it all over again . . .

"I wouldn't change anything . . . I'm extremely happy doing what I'm doing."

GREETING CARD SENDER

Start-up cost:	$5,000-$10,000
Potential earnings:	$20,000-$30,000
Typical fees:	$2-$3 per card
Advertising:	Direct mail, Yellow Pages, networking, business publications
Qualifications:	Highly organized
Equipment needed:	Computer with database and labeling software, laser printer, fax, phone, greeting card sample books or brochures
Home business potential:	Yes
Staff required:	No
Handicapped opportunity:	Yes
Hidden costs:	Postage can be tricky, as can untimely price increases from vendors

LOWDOWN:

Busy executives barely have the time to run personal errands of a critical nature, let alone send out 500 holiday greeting cards to their best customers. That's where you come in. As a professional greeting card sender, you will develop a database of card recipients for as many clients as you can muster—then mail the cards to everyone on the list. It sounds quite simple, really, and it is—except that you need to be exceptionally skilled at organization and time management to be able to stay on top of every holiday, birthday, special occasion, and company announcement that comes along. Buy a software program that features a large calendar that can hold many events. Better yet, buy a software organizer with an alarm system to remind you of your deadlines. The success of your business will depend on the quality of what you send out in addition to your ability to stay on track. Have a large sample book to show the customers you meet with, and offer them nice package deals to avoid piecemeal assignments that don't pay as well.

START-UP:

Your start-up costs will primarily cover the computer system (about $3,000) you'll need to maintain mailing lists and customer information. Expect to spend another $2,000 or so on advertising. Your charges will vary, but will likely be between $2-$3 per card. Add on a database maintenance fee to cover annual updates.

BOTTOM LINE ADVICE:

Since mailing cards is your business, the best way to market is to use direct mail; send creative announcements to businesses on your "hit" list, inviting them to do business with you in the same manner you would extend a wedding invitation. The more creative you are, the more likely you'll be to win their business.

ADVICE FROM THE EXPERTS

What sets your business apart from others like it?

"I feel my company best helps businesses maintain contact with their clients and customers," says Jo Adamczyk, owner of Cards in the Mail in Akron, Ohio. She says that the most interesting and challenging aspects of her business are acquiring customers and explaining her business.

Things you couldn't do without:

Computer, high-quality laser printer, fax machine, and telephone.

Marketing tips/advice:

"It takes time to build business and there is no profit while you are building. Networking will ultimately help you achieve a profitable customer level, as will sending cards of your own to potential customers on a regular basis."

If you had to do it all over again . . .

"I would better identify my target market. Also, I would offer complete packages that companies could purchase in order to bring each client to a more profitable level."

HAULING SERVICE

Start-up cost:	$5,000-$15,000
Potential earnings:	$20,000-$40,000
Typical fees:	$30-$75 per haul (depending on size and content)
Advertising:	Yellow Pages, community newspapers, coupon books, direct mail
Qualifications:	Possibly hazardous waste certification
Equipment needed:	Hauling vehicle (preferably the largest you can afford)
Home business potential:	Yes
Staff required:	Yes (it often takes more than one person to load/unload the truck)
Handicapped opportunity:	No
Hidden costs:	Insurance, workers' compensation, equipment maintenance

LOWDOWN:

You can haul anything from dead trees to old appliances and construction materials if you have a large enough vehicle and the manpower to lift heavy loads. The only restrictions that might apply would be those concerning hazardous materials or waste products—for these items, you'll need to have certification after attending a predetermined number of seminars concerning proper disposal and Environmental Protection Agency (EPA) regulations. Regardless, you'll enjoy the straightforward nature of this work: you get the call, you go to pick up the load, and then deliver it to the designated area. Pretty easy work, right? Except that your knowledge of what can go where (i.e., where to dispose of appliances containing freon) needs to be on the ball, and your ability to work on call needs to be top-notch. You must be dependable in this business if you want to make it work, because customers will call the next guy if you don't show up within a brief period of time. Aside from that problem, there's really not too much to worry about.

START-UP:

Most of your start-up ($5,000-$10,000) will go to your vehicle and its related upkeep. It would be especially wise to lease your vehicle, then upgrade before the terms of your lease are up. If you work hard and promote yourself well via some low-cost advertising, you can make anywhere from $20,000-$30,000 (charging $30-$75 per haul).

BOTTOM LINE ADVICE:

You could make a decent enough living doing this type of work, but keep in mind that it may mean working in hazardous environments or inclement weather. Pack dozens of warm gloves for those cold days.

HERBAL PRODUCTS DISTRIBUTOR

Start-up cost:	$5,000-$10,000
Potential earnings:	$25,000-$35,000
Typical fees:	$25-$75 per herbal product package
Advertising:	Direct mail, networking, trade shows
Qualifications:	Sales ability
Equipment needed:	None
Home business potential:	Yes
Staff required:	No
Handicapped opportunity:	Yes
Hidden costs:	Liability, possible licensing fees

LOWDOWN:

Health-conscious Americans look to herbal products as healthy alternatives to traditional medications, for everything from energy-boosting to sinus troubles. You will purchase a distributorship of established herbal products, then market them to a predetermined list of potential clients (however, you might have to come up with a list of your own). From sports-minded professionals to nursing professionals, your clients will cover a wide range of humanity, all with varying levels of open-mindedness to your products. Perhaps the biggest hurdle for you to overcome would be the negative, fadlike nature of the health food and herbal nutrition industry; you'll need to provide detailed information regarding the features and benefits of using your products as opposed to others with seemingly similar benefits. Don't try to sell your product line (which could include herbs in pill, tablet, or drink mix form) as a "wonder drug." Cynical consumers will see right through that immediately.

START-UP:

You'll need to put down some investment capital or make an outright distributorship purchase of anywhere from $5,000-$10,000. Most of your business will be through cold call and referral, so you needn't worry about a hefty advertising budget. With some aggressive marketing on your part, you could make $25,000-$35,000 per year.

BOTTOM LINE ADVICE:

This is a hard way to make a living, unless you're lucky enough to sell your product to a specialty health food store and reap your percentages from there. If you aren't lucky enough to sell to a built-in market, you'll have to do it customer by customer, and that can take an infinite amount of time.

HOME ENTERTAINMENT SYSTEM SERVICE

Start-up cost:	$10,000-$15,000
Potential earnings:	$35,000-$50,000
Typical fees:	$20-$45 per hour (more for parts)
Advertising:	Classified ads, entertainment magazines and newspaper sections, referrals, neighborhood flyers, direct mail
Qualifications:	Electronics skill, interest in music, knowledge of entertainment systems operation, hookups
Equipment needed:	Tools, cellular phone
Home business potential:	Yes
Staff required:	No
Handicapped opportunity:	Not typically
Hidden costs:	Vehicle maintenance, phone bills

LOWDOWN:

Home entertainment systems can do wonderful things—but only if they are operating properly. Simply getting them installed is beyond the skills of many people, and taking one component out of all the wiring so that it can be delivered to a store for repair seems impossible. All those jokes about not knowing how to operate a VCR really aren't funny. What they do is highlight your market: the owners of home entertainment systems that need help getting them together and keeping them running right. Becoming a home entertainment system service person means that you have a large but very focused market. Each successful job ought to lead to referrals.

START-UP:

You'll need tools and possibly an inventory of parts.

BOTTOM LINE ADVICE:

Referrals from individual customers will take you far, and a relationship with a dealer for service and repairs would also be an excellent marketing tactic. Many homes have the makings of entertainment centers. If the components were purchased at a mass market outlet, or even by mail, the owner may well have no one but you to do the setup and repairs. Your electronics know-how ought to find a ready market.

HOME OFFICE CONSULTANT

Start-up cost:	$5,000-$10,000
Potential earnings:	$30,000-$45,000
Typical fees:	$40-$50 per hour
Advertising:	Direct mail to entrepreneurs, networking with entrepreneurial assistance organizations such as (Service Corps of Retired Executives), Yellow Pages, newspapers
Qualifications:	Business degree or previous entrepreneurial experience
Equipment needed:	Computer, printer, fax/modem, copier, pager or cellular phone
Home business potential:	Yes
Staff required:	No
Handicapped opportunity:	Yes
Hidden costs:	Slow payment for your services as many beginning entrepreneurs have cash-flow problems

LOWDOWN:

Home offices are a large part of the burgeoning entrepreneurial marketplace—and you can cash in on the ground floor if you have the expertise needed to help a home office get off on the right foot. Your biggest problem will likely be in locating those thinking about working from home—although there are a few directions that may prove helpful. One excellent way to find clients is through on-line services and work-at-home forums, where you can offer your expert advice free of charge in an effort to get your name and company information out there. You can also comb the business, professional, and entrepreneurial groups that meet in your community for potential clients. Once you get a client base going, you will work with each client on projects that range from advice on computer systems to office ergonomics to marketing strategy. You really need to be well-rounded in your realm of experience, as you'll be giving the best advice you can on a wide variety of topics. Make sure that you focus heavily on the types of equipment a home office might need, as well as tips on balancing home and family (since both are closely entwined in this venture). The trouble is, your likelihood of having repeat customers is low, since most home offices only launch once; stay on top of things and be constantly on the lookout for new prospects (many will come via referral).

START-UP:

Your launch fees ($5,000-$10,000) will mostly cover your basic office setup and some preliminary list rentals so that you can send some direct mail pieces to folks who work from home. Expect to earn $30,000-$45,000 once you get established; charge $40-$50 per hour for your services.

BOTTOM LINE ADVICE:

While it may be interesting and even exciting to be part of an innovative young company's beginning, it may take a while to secure payment for your services. If you can charge up front, and particularly if you accept credit cards, you'll have a much better chance of collecting what your services are worth.

HUMAN RESOURCE SERVICES

Start-up cost:	$7,000-$10,000
Potential earnings:	$40,000-$70,000
Typical fees:	$35 or more
Advertising:	Referrals, membership in trade associations and business groups, business periodicals
Qualifications:	A proven track record of effectiveness in human resource department management for a medium-size or larger company, degree in related field, excellent selling skills and ability to interact with people
Equipment needed:	Office furniture, computer, printer, suite software, modem, fax, cellular phone, business card, letterhead, envelopes, marketing materials
Home business potential:	Yes
Staff required:	Possibly
Handicapped opportunity:	Yes
Hidden costs:	Errors and omissions insurance, nonreimbursable costs for development of informational materials for clients

LOWDOWN:

Providing human resources services is an excellent business except for the enormous effort that will be required for marketing. Getting your foot in the door will be really tough. Once you're established, you ought to have ongoing relationships with clients for a steady income, year to year. If you can get your sales message through to growing companies with expanding workforces and no human resources departments, you can begin building your business. Some consultants specialize in one area of this complex field, such as developing, writing, and updating employee handbooks. Other human relations consultants function more as recruiters. The training side of human resources work can be marketed effectively if you can show how your presentations are tightly linked to the client company's missions and the specific job responsibilities of their workforce.

START-UP:

You'll be working on-site at your client companies, so your own office can be more functional than impressive (about $7,000 to start up). Excellent communication equipment is vital. Potential earnings of $40,000 or more are possible.

BOTTOM LINE ADVICE:

Many business owners just fumble along with the human resources challenges of their organizations until a crisis forces them to think about how they could do a better job. How can you present your services to these busy people as the solution to their problems and not just a fuzzy, fluffy, feel-good waste of time? This is where you apply your record of success to support your claims. Referrals will probably be your best sources of business.

INCENTIVE PROGRAMS/
PROMOTIONAL MATERIAL

Start-up cost:	$6,000-$10,000
Potential earnings:	$48,000-$75,000
Typical fees:	$35 per hour or a flat fee of $300-$700 or more
Advertising:	Business periodicals, trade journals, memberships in business and community groups, direct mail, referrals
Qualifications:	Extensive experience in advertising, promotions; proven track record
Equipment needed:	Well-equipped office, computer equipment with graphic arts capability, high-end printer, modem, fax, business card, letterhead, envelopes, promotional materials
Home business potential:	Yes
Staff required:	No
Handicapped opportunity:	Yes
Hidden costs:	Development of your own promotional materials, supplies, software upgrades, association dues

LOWDOWN:

Effective incentives and promotions require skill and experience to produce. Everyone wants something new, something that works like magic, something that's cost-effective. Your creativity in designing a program that harmonizes with the mission, goals, and corporate image of your clients will be central to your success in this enterprise. Yes, it's fun. But it's a high-risk, marketing-intensive business as well. People do not really value the jacket or mug so much as they want the feeling of being "in" that the promotional material represents. This is a business for those who have a good sense for what's in, for what's cool, for what works. Your expertise may make you responsible for products all the way through manufacturing or delivery (if you choose).

START-UP:

Client presentations are very important, and they require much time and effort to prepare. Your support systems (about $6,000 to start) need to be adequate from the start to present your services in a professional, appealing manner. Potential earnings can reach toward $48,000.

BOTTOM LINE ADVICE:

You may specialize in internal motivation, programs that recognize and reward employee achievement. Or your work may assist companies in reaching out to their customers with special promotional programs from time to time. You'll need good relationships with distributors and with the business community generally as you build your reputation for effectiveness and creativity.

INFORMATION CONSULTANT

Start-up cost:	$5,000-$11,000
Potential earnings:	$50,000-$75,000
Typical fees:	$30-$100 per hour
Advertising:	Trade groups, public speaking, writing articles for local and trade publications, referrals
Qualifications:	Interest in almost any type of fact or question, skill in database research, ability to market yourself, patience and persistence
Equipment needed:	Computer with large hard drive and plenty of memory, dedicated phone line, on-line database access accounts, high-speed modem, laser printer, software, office furniture, fax, business card, letterhead, envelopes
Home business potential:	Yes
Staff required:	No
Handicapped opportunity:	Yes
Hidden costs:	Memberships, on-line time, utility bills

LOWDOWN:

Managing information is not something most business people plan as an item in their annual budget—but they should. Almost every organization needs to sort through the mountains of data being accumulated each day. Scientific data to support R&D efforts, articles on activities of competitors, and background information for lawsuits are just some of the most needed types of information. You'll probably need to specialize in serving a type of client or in finding a type of data. Demographic information serves marketers, advertisers, city planners, and a host of other potential clients. Recent research on addiction issues could serve health care professionals, counselors, hospital administrators, court officials, and many others. As an information consultant, your creativity in pulling information together must be matched by your initiative in selling these services.

START-UP:

Your work will probably be largely electronic, and the equipment to allow this is your primary investment (at least $4,000 to get you started). Potential earnings can be $50,000 or more.

BOTTOM LINE ADVICE:

To be effective in this business you really need to be one of the few people who enjoy knowledge for its own sake. You'll need to track information through many tangents and subtle clues buried in apparently irrelevant material. Pulling it all together can be tedious and rather exciting at the same time. We talk about information overload in this country, but what we really have is information disorganization. Your presentation of useful, accurate information without the distractions of all the rest is what adds value to your clients' work lives.

ADVICE FROM THE EXPERTS

What sets your business apart from others like it?

Timothy P. Baynham, Esq., President of TPB Information in Winston-Salem, North Carolina, says his business is known as the "public records specialist. We separate ourselves from others by concentrating on providing the highest quality public records report for the least money. My company repackages information and tries to make it easy to comprehend."

Things you couldn't do without:

A computer, laser printer, and fax machine are essential components to Baynham's business.

Marketing tips/advice:

"Despite your basic assumptions, most information is not free. You'll need to be on the Internet or on-line services a great deal. Most people are still not aware of the vast amounts of information that is available through fee-based on-line services. Clients cannot buy something they don't know exists—and that is a marketing problem for you."

If you had to do it all over again . . .

"The biggest lesson I've learned is that less is more. When I started, I wanted to show clients every single thing I could get on-line, hoping they would fall in love with the idea of unlimited information. I now focus on problem-solving; this approach is much more effective, and you don't spend as much on catalogs, copies, etc."

INSURANCE AGENT

Start-up cost:	$10,000-$15,000
Potential earnings:	$45,000-$60,000
Typical fees:	Commissions range from 20 to 35 percent
Advertising:	Cold-calling, membership in community groups, radio, newspapers, community publications, billboards and (of course) your outdoor sign
Qualifications:	License, experience, outstanding selling ability, affiliation with a particular company
Equipment needed:	Office furniture, computer, suite software, printer, business card, letterhead, envelopes
Home business potential:	Yes
Staff required:	No
Handicapped opportunity:	Yes
Hidden costs:	Membership dues, errors and omissions insurance

LOWDOWN:

As a single agent, you will need to develop a focus or specialty to set yourself apart in the crowded field of insurance sales. One possibility is business insurance, with a special focus on insuring home businesses. Dedicated service to your customers is essential in distinguishing your business from the competition. You will be working closely with individuals and small organizations, and you will depend on your financial expertise and your ability to listen to the wants and needs of the buyer. If you can find a way to help people and companies manage their risk appropriately (which is what insurance is all about) without making them feel pushed or confused, you will be performing a useful service. You will be earning your agent's commission many times over.

START-UP:

Knowledge and experience are far more important than equipment, although you will need a computer system that can be networked to your corporate headquarters if you're affiliated or own a franchise. In that case, your start-up costs will be considerably higher (potentially $50,000-$75,000 for training, licensing the company name, and heavy advertising), but you'll get the support you need instead of having to go it alone. However, should you decide to go alone, you can expect to spend between $10,000-$15,000 for your basic office setup, some advertising, and the fees you'll use to take your exam. Either way, your commissions should net between 20 to 35 percent and ultimately lead to an income potential of $45,000-$60,000 or more.

BOTTOM LINE ADVICE:

Being an insurance agent can be tough—but people make fun of lawyers and accountants, too. Once you become established, you will have an excellent business that can support your family and possibly make you rich. Being successful in this type of enterprise requires excellent selling skills, up-to-date information on financial issues, and long hours of hard work. You're using people skills and numerical facility intensively. Most of all, you're unwilling to be discouraged if the first hundred sales calls are no's.

Hiring Smart

Even though there are, generally speaking, more workers available than ever before, you need to be choosy when sifting through the resumes of potential employees. Here are five things you should look for in an outstanding candidate.

- **A willingness to learn new things.** So often, as you embark on your entrepreneurial venture, you'll develop job descriptions that are subject to change. Hiring someone who is flexible and willing to try a new assignment could be the smartest move you could make.

- **Experience in the areas you need to cover most.** If you're looking for an accounting or bookkeeping professional, you'll need to be certain that the candidate's primary area of expertise is in those fields. Even though you may be looking for flexibility, you need to be sure you can adequately cover the necessary areas first and foremost.

- **Demonstrated results.** It's one thing for a candidate to say that their responsibilities included X, Y, and Z; it's quite another to see what kind of impact that employee had on the rest of the organization. Look for key phrases that document some kind of end result, such as "increased profit share by 110 percent" or "boosted credibility and public awareness of product."

- **Creativity.** In a fledgling business, you need to surround yourself with staffers who understand your business and are constantly on the lookout for improvements. These are the people who know that your success will have an impact on their success, and vice versa. You will appreciate creative solutions to problems because they will likely save your company money and increase productivity at the same time.

- **Self-direction.** Let's face it: you're totally consumed by your business; in fact, that's probably why you need help in the first place. Recognize that for everything to work smoothly, you need to give up a piece of your business to someone else who is more focused on that particular area. You'll need to trust that person to take control so that you are freed up to concentrate on growing the business. So make sure new hires can work independently, yet are not afraid to ask questions.

Finally, be sure to check with federal, state, and municipal employment bureaus to make certain you're complying with all regulations. There's more involved in hiring than you might at first imagine; in this litigious society, it will pay for you to familiarize yourself with all components of employment law.

INVENTORY CONTROL

Start-up cost:	$5,000-$8,000
Potential earnings:	$35,000-$50,000
Typical fees:	$15 and up per hour
Advertising:	Business periodicals, direct mail, memberships in trade groups
Qualifications:	Inventory experience, excellent organizational skills
Equipment needed:	Office furniture, computer, suite software, modem, fax, printer, pagers or cellular phones for part-timers, business card, letterhead, envelopes
Home business potential:	Yes
Staff required:	Yes
Handicapped opportunity:	No
Hidden costs:	Record keeping materials

LOWDOWN:

Your inventory control service is another of the businesses that responds to the needs of today's downsized corporation. Taking inventory requires many hours of labor that can no longer be wrung out of an already overburdened corporate staff. The work is outsourced to your group of part-time employees, who track and record the information for your clients. This business is a way of applying people exactly where they are needed, without having them on the client's payroll. Your ability to manage people and data is what enables you to perform these services in a cost-effective manner.

START-UP:

Work is done at the client's site. You'll need your own office functionally equipped for the management of people and projects rather than to impress clients. You'll need to produce data in electronic or printed form for transmission to head offices. Potential earnings could be around $40,000.

BOTTOM LINE ADVICE:

The ability to convince business people to trust you with this vital aspect of their record keeping will be necessary for the launching of a successful inventory control service businesses. Higher-level management skills are also an absolute must. You must track person-hours, data, and client needs accurately and inexpensively to make a go of this type of enterprise. The potential market is wide; your challenge will be to reach it.

INVISIBLE FENCING
SALES/INSTALLATION

Start-up cost:	$10,000-$15,000
Potential earnings:	$30,000-$40,000
Typical fees:	Often $8-$10 per square yard
Advertising:	Newspapers, Yellow Pages, direct mail, flyers, referrals from vets
Qualifications:	Salesmanship, ability to do light digging, some electrical competence
Equipment needed:	Pickup, tools, inventory
Home business potential:	Yes
Staff required:	No
Handicapped opportunity:	No
Hidden costs:	Wear and tear on vehicle

LOWDOWN:

Invisible fencing is growing more popular as more people have dogs but lack time to walk them. Many home owners don't want to solve this problem by making their yards into fortresses. A fence tall enough to keep in a big dog and tough enough to block a digging dog can be a real eyesore. Also, some localities prohibit fences. Here is your market for the invisible fence, which works with a transmitter on Fido's collar to keep him home where he's safe. The electric line is buried a few inches down around the perimeter of the yard, and whenever the dog tries to cross it, he gets a slight shock. It's just enough to remind him that he's supposed to stay—not stray.

START-UP:

You will need some inventory and digging equipment, which could be as much as $15,000. But if you're competitive and charge between $8-$10 per square yard, you should be able to make a sizable profit.

BOTTOM LINE ADVICE:

Your charm and ability to convey a sense of caring for the welfare of your customers' pets will make you successful in this business. Some people start by going door to door, but referrals are a less discouraging approach, once you have broken the ice. Be sure to send a stack of your business cards to veterinarians.

IRRIGATION SERVICES

Start-up cost:	$5,000-$10,000
Potential Earnings:	$15,000-$30,000
Typical fees:	Hourly rate of $100-$200; daily ($500+) or per-job rate
Advertising:	Newspapers, Yellow Pages, direct mail, interest-group meetings, seminars
Qualifications:	Knowledge of irrigation systems
Equipment needed:	Drip irrigation systems, tools for installation
Home business potential:	Yes
Staff required:	No
Handicapped opportunity:	No
Hidden costs:	Permission of local authorities, business insurance

LOWDOWN:

You will have two market segments here: individual gardeners and commercial operations. Many individuals love plants and want their premises to look beautiful and well maintained, but they lack the time to water their gardens on a regular basis. You can set up a drip irrigation system that will replace hours of fussing with muddy hoses and bulky sprinklers. Once the drip system is set up properly, it requires little attention, making it ideal for you and for your customer. Also, many older homes need new irrigation systems to deal with water run-off and avoid watery basements.

Commercial garden and nursery operations have a large investment in plant materials, and the trees, shrubs, and plants must be kept in peak condition to be salable. With the rising cost of labor in most communities, a drip irrigation system will make business sense to these establishments.

START-UP:

You will need an inventory of drip irrigation materials and the tools to set it all up. A pickup or van will allow you to take the bulky materials to your customers' locations. Bill out at an hourly rate of $100-$200, a daily rate of $500 or more, or a per-job rate based on your estimate of the time involved.

BOTTOM LINE ADVICE:

This is a great business for a friendly person with a love for the outdoors, for growing things, and for tinkering with machinery. Drip irrigation systems are not heavy or high-tech, but setting each one up will require some customization to suit the specific location. In many geographic areas your business will be seasonal, so you may want to add a service that blends with irrigation to fill out the year, like snow removal. The steady income from regular customers may compensate, in your mind, for the somewhat limited profit potential of this kind of enterprise.

JOB HOT LINE

Start-up cost:	$5,000-$15,000
Potential earnings:	$15,000-$25,000
Typical fees:	Memberships/subscriptions of $10-$15 per month per client
Advertising:	Yellow Pages, flyers at job fairs/employment agencies, word of mouth
Qualifications:	Good organizational skills
Equipment needed:	Complete computer system with desktop publishing software, multiline phone system
Home business potential:	Yes
Staff required:	No
Handicapped opportunity:	Yes
Hidden costs:	Insurance, printing costs, postage

LOWDOWN:

Thousands of folks are either out of work or looking for new (and perhaps more interesting) work; your product will provide them with just one more way to generate many job leads. As a phone hot line, your service will consist of recorded messages and a phone system that allows clients to scan messages for items they find suitable to their needs. They will be charged a per-minute fee and will generally rack up phone bills of $5-$10. Another way to run a job hot line is to publish a weekly job leads newspaper, with classified listings for jobs posted in your area. You'll charge a subscription rate of $10-$15 per month, and ship these papers out using a bulk rate (if you qualify). For the newspaper hot line, you'll have less timely information than with a phone system, but the capital needed to launch is less with a newspaper than with an expensive phone system. Of course, you could always run your job hot line off the Internet or an on-line service such as CompuServe (see Bulletin Board Service).

START-UP:

You'll spend at least $5,000 on your computer setup, which will include computer/laser printer, fax/modem, and desktop publishing software. Expect to spend an additional $3,000 on advertising. However, if you promote your business well, you can earn at least $15,000 and more likely $25,000 from this low-overhead business.

BOTTOM LINE ADVICE:

It's not exactly easy to make lots of money from folks who are "transitional" and don't have much disposable cash. Your challenge is to make this business appealing not as an "extra" but as an integral part of any job search in your area. Collect up front: once your client gets a job, your product's value is severely diminished (making collection a chore).

LEAD EXCHANGE/
BUSINESS NETWORKING SERVICE

Start-up cost:	$5,000-$10,000
Potential earnings:	$20,000-$80,000
Typical fees:	$200-$300 per year per member
Advertising:	Business publications, newspapers, Yellow Pages, direct mail, networking
Qualifications:	The ability to organize and lead groups
Equipment needed:	You'll need to rent meeting space on a monthly basis (negotiate a special rate based on frequency)
Home business potential:	Yes (but meetings will take place elsewhere)
Staff required:	None initially
Handicapped opportunity:	Yes
Hidden costs:	Phone costs can grow as business owners run on about their business; keep it short and sweet

LOWDOWN:

There are at least 5,000 new businesses launched every day of the week, and all of them need to connect with other businesses to exchange leads and helpful ideas. Your business brings these entrepreneurial minds to the table, encouraging interaction and support. That's what your members essentially get from joining a business networking service. What you get from this service is a steady income and the rewards of facilitating the success of others. You'll round up as many new business owners as you can, invite them to an introductory session, and hook them up with seasoned professionals. Then, secure a financial commitment of anywhere from $200-$300 per year from each member organization, and you've got a business networking service. What sets you apart from other associations (like the Chamber of Commerce, for example) is that you provide expert ability to mix exactly the right combination of professionals, allowing only one company to join in a given category so that there is not direct competition. You can also provide monthly speakers to inspire and motivate the entire group to continued success.

START-UP:

You'll need to advertise your service extensively at first; set aside at least $1,500 for this necessity (until your own networking members bring you additional business). You will also need to rent a monthly meeting place; check hotels, churches, and universities for the best rates. Charges are typically $200-$300 per business member.

BOTTOM LINE ADVICE:

If bringing people and businesses together to work for the group's common good pleases you, you will be pleasing others and making a great deal of money doing it. However, be sure not to invite any unethical businesses into the group; check each out with the Better Business Bureau before accepting their application. It will go miles toward preserving your credibility.

LEGAL COST CONTROL/
LITIGATION MANAGEMENT SERVICES

Start-up cost:	$5,000-$10,000
Potential earnings:	$40,000-$75,000
Typical fees:	Equivalent to the prevailing fee level for lawyers in the community; about $125/hour for small firms outside major U.S. cities.
Advertising:	Local business associations, advertising in trade journals and business publications, referrals
Qualifications:	Law or accounting background, experience in case management and billing assessment, litigation experience
Equipment needed:	Business office, computer, modem, fax, software, printer, business card, letterhead, envelopes
Home business potential:	No
Staff required:	No
Handicapped opportunity:	Yes
Hidden costs:	Insurance

LOWDOWN:

The movement is under way to rein in legal costs. Above all, the astronomical costs of litigation are being managed as closely as possible. For business organizations with a small in-house legal staff or none at all, you can provide this important cost-management service. Assessing ongoing billing can spotlight waste, duplication of services, overbilling, and incorrect entries. This is painstaking work, and often busy in-house lawyers do not have time to comb through the bills their organization receives from outside counsel. The economic benefit of having an outside service perform this function should far outweigh its cost to the organization.

START-UP:

Equipping your office to be functional and present a professional image will be expensive ($4,000-$10,000). This business is not a candidate for running from a corner of your dining-room table. Still, you'll be able to charge around $125 an hour for your services, so you should be able to afford a decent office.

BOTTOM LINE ADVICE:

This service is a creative way to utilize a background that combines legal training with financial and accounting skills. More and more lawyers are competing for the shrinking number of jobs, but few have the combination of expertise and experience that will make you a success in this tightly focused service niche. Marketing your services will be challenging as the concept is new. One success will lead to referrals, though. You will need to allow yourself considerable time to build the business. A thick skin is necessary to face up to possible negative reactions from the lawyers whose accounts you are checking.

GETTING THE WORD OUT: PUBLICITY

---

1. Create the hook. To create your own publicity, you need to develop a "hook" or a compelling reason why someone should listen to your story. Media contacts must feel strongly that your product or service would be of some value to their audience. Take time to build a cohesive "pitch" that really conveys the unique qualities and benefits of your product or service.

2. Make a list. Make a list of media contacts whom you think would be interested in your product or service. Prioritize the list and decide what you want to tell each contact.

3. Create a "mini" press kit. It isn't necessary to send an elaborate press kit. It is often just as effective to send a personalized "pitch" letter and a press release in a standard-size business envelope to your media contacts.

4. Follow up with a phone call. Follow up your mailings with a phone call to each media contact. If you fail to get through the first time or if your media contact is too busy to talk to you, be persistent.

5. Take extensive notes to the interview. Take additional material relating to your product or service to your media contact meeting. Product samples, testimonials, brochures, and a list of current vendors or consumers (with their permission) that use or carry your product or service and will assist you in conveying an interesting and powerful story about your company. Create a list pf possible questions the media representative might ask you. Be ready with answers!

LIE DETECTION SERVICE

Start-up cost:	$5,000-$15,000
Potential earnings:	$45,000-$75,000
Typical fees:	$150 per hour
Advertising:	Word of mouth, Yellow Pages, referral work from police stations and detective agencies
Qualifications:	Training and certification
Equipment needed:	Lie detector and related materials
Home business potential:	Yes
Staff required:	No
Handicapped opportunity:	Possibly
Hidden costs:	Insurance, equipment maintenance and upgrades

LOWDOWN:

When a theft takes place at a jewelry store, often the manager or owner requests that everyone employed therein take a lie detector test to eliminate possible suspects. This is where much of your work will be done: in places where employee theft is suspected and there are no other immediate suspects known. However, you will also do your work at police stations when they request your help in measuring the truthfulness of a suspect's statements. You may accomplish this one of basically two ways: by administering a truth serum (via hypodermic needle) that stimulates the brain to tell the truth, or by administering an electrical lie detector test that measures heart rate, pulse, and sweat produced by an individual under questioning. Since the nature of your tests is precise and heavily dependent upon accuracy of equipment, you can expect to spend money regularly on your equipment maintenance and related costs. Still, if you enjoy helping others get to the bottom of things, you will benefit greatly from this line of work.

START-UP:

You'll need about $5,000-$15,000 for your sensitive lie-detecting equipment, and you should plan to set aside a little extra for networking with law enforcement officials to ensure some kind of referral system. You could make $45,000-$75,000 per year.

BOTTOM LINE ADVICE:

Although it doesn't seem like it on the surface, this could be a potentially dangerous job. Imagine what could happen if you're trying to attach your equipment to a suspect who isn't too happy with being asked about the truth. Fortunately, there will nearly always be another professional with you as you work. Be prepared to be called onto a lot of witness stands; you'll need to really learn how to budget your time effectively.

LOCK BOX SERVICE

Start-up cost:	$5,000-$10,000
Potential earnings:	$30,000-$45,000
Typical fees:	$35 per box (includes one spare key)
Advertising:	Direct mail, brochures, trade journals, networking with real estate companies
Qualifications:	None
Equipment needed:	Lock boxes, adapters, spare keys , tools
Home business potential:	Yes
Staff required:	No
Handicapped opportunity:	Yes
Hidden costs:	Spare keys

LOWDOWN:

This is a highly specialized occupation; not everyone needs a lock box and your job is to be the best at servicing those who do in your area. Who are your clients? Real estate agents, construction companies, and anyone who owns a fleet of vehicles, such as car lots, utility companies, and car rental agencies. Although this is not a very common (or even obvious) service, it is certainly necessary and useful to have lock boxes that keep the wrong people out and let the right people in. Solicit your client industries in person and try to give them the best deal you can; if you can't budge on price, offer them the best service and follow-up care you can muster up. Build relationships with your clients to obtain repeat business.

START-UP:

Lock boxes are generally sold by gross units at $20 each; spare keys go for $6 per spare. Your bare minimum start-up cost will be $5,000, not including any advertising (add another $3,000-$5,000). With the right contacts and a good reputation, you could earn in the neighborhood of $30,000-$45,000.

BOTTOM LINE ADVICE:

There are several obstacles you'll have to overcome to be in this service business; first, it's by no means glamorous, and second, you'll have to make the initial inventory investment yourself. After you have dealt with these two major items, you can enjoy the relationships that you build with your clients and maybe even get a deal on a new car or be the first to hear about the gem of a house for sale on the corner. Small fringe benefits like that abound.

LOCKSMITH

Start-up cost:	$5,000-$10,000
Potential earnings:	$20,000-$35,000
Typical fees:	$1.50 per key or a per-job lock replacement fee (usually $15-$45)
Advertising:	Direct mail, Yellow Pages, bulletin boards near apartment complexes
Qualifications:	Mechanical aptitude
Equipment needed:	Key engraver, product stock/supply
Home business potential:	Yes
Staff required:	No
Handicapped opportunity:	Yes
Hidden costs:	Equipment maintenance costs, insurance

LOWDOWN:

You can do much more than simply make keys in this field. You can offer the following services: change lock tumblers, open locked cars, and pick locks. In addition, you can sell new or even reconditioned locking devices. Your days will be filled with pretty uneventful work—it is straightforward enough that, once you get the hang of it, you may wind up feeling that the work is fairly mundane. However, it is a necessary service that you're providing, as so many of us who have locked ourselves out have experienced. If you do house calls regularly enough, your work will be a bit livelier—and you could actually find yourself in some interesting situations.

START-UP:

Start-up costs will vary depending on the services you choose to provide. If you want to just make keys, you will need to invest in a key duplicating machine. If you plan on selling new locking devices, you will need to invest in some inventory. Also set aside funds for advertising. All said and done, this business should cost between $5,000-$10,000 to launch—and you could sensibly count on an income between $20,000-$35,000.

BOTTOM LINE ADVICE:

This is a trust-based business. If you have a criminal record, you might not be the best person for this business (unless, of course, you're providing insightful tips on how burglars actually do break in). Check with local law offices to determine if there are any requirements or laws that you will need to know about before beginning. You may need signed requests before proceeding with a lock change.

MAID SERVICE

Start-up costs:	$10,000-$20,000
Potential earnings:	$35,000-$150,000
Typical fees:	$25 per hour or a per-room charge of $50
Advertising:	Yellow Pages, local newspapers, Welcome Wagon and direct mail couponing, personal contact with apartment and office building superintendents, and Realtors
Qualifications:	Management skills, ability to motivate personnel and improve their efficiency with superior products
Equipment needed:	Mops, rags, buckets, cleaning solutions; also vehicles
Home business potential:	Yes
Staff required:	Yes
Handicapped opportunity:	Yes
Hidden costs:	Insurance, workers' compensation

LOWDOWN:

This business can really turn a profit if you hire a crew of trustworthy employees. You can run the business from a desk in your home, if you have sales ability and the knack for managing others. Train them to clean efficiently, and you can earn a tidy sum. You might have to arrange for your employees to be bonded and insured since they will be working in other people's homes and workplaces. Always check back with the client to make sure your employees have accomplished the assigned task. Be willing to accept their feedback to improve your business. It's important to offer stellar service, because word of mouth will be the best advertising. Overhead is relatively low if you're not buying into a franchise—once you have an established business, you can buy cleaning supplies in bulk.

START-UP:

You'll spend at least $10,000 launching a cleaning service, but much more if you buy into any one of the fine, established franchises out there (they usually require an initial investment of $50,000 or more). Charge by the hour ($25-$35) or by the room ($50-$75).

BOTTOM LINE ADVICE:

Make contacts with realtors to help new homeowners clean their house before they move in. If you do a good job, there's a good chance they will retain your services. Get clients on a regular cleaning schedule—but make sure you send enough people to do each job. Make sure estimates are in writing.

MAILING LIST SERVICE

Start-up cost:	$5,000-$9,000
Potential earnings:	$40,000-$100,000 per year
Typical fees:	15 to 25 cents per entry (name, address, city, state, zip); about $1 per entry per year to maintain the list. Mailing out 10,000 pieces of mail could cost $800-$1,200
Advertising:	Contacting local stores, associations, churches, clubs, etc. to offer to maintain their lists for them, networking in business organizations, Yellow Pages, direct mail
Qualifications:	Detailed knowledge of postal regulations for bulk mailings, computer expertise, fast, accurate typing skills, ability to meet deadlines
Equipment needed:	Computer, printer, specialized software, database, post office permits, office furniture, business card, letterhead, postage machine
Home business potential:	Yes
Staff required:	None
Handicapped opportunity:	Yes
Hidden costs:	Be sure to invest in backup tapes for your computer system in the event of disaster

LOWDOWN:

Although we all deplore the amount of "junk mail" that is dumped in our mailboxes each day, the amazing growth of direct mail is going to continue—and the opportunity to succeed in running a mailing list service for the companies sending those materials is tremendous. Start-up costs are low, skills needed are easy to acquire, and money is there to be made. Your service can include list maintenance, mailings, creation of lists, list brokering, and even teaching others about mailing lists. Understanding and meeting the changing regulations of the U.S. Postal Service is perhaps the most challenging part of the job. However, software, pamphlets, and seminars abound to bring you up to speed.

START-UP:

You will spend from $5,000 to $9,000 on the equipment and supplies needed for this business. Depending on your specialty, you may be able to begin for even less, especially if you lease a postage meter machine and some of the other equipment. Charges will vary for your services, but you'll need to set two rates from the get-go: a per-entry fee (usually 15 to 25 cents per name) and an annual list maintenance fee of $1 per entry.

BOTTOM LINE ADVICE:

Mailing list businesses are relatively easy to start and to promote. You can have as large a customer base as you wish, rather than relying on just a few key clients. The actual work of creating and maintaining the lists is pretty routine, although it does require attention to detail and great accuracy. A thorough understanding of postal regulations is vitally important—and the regulations are constantly changing. You have to be sure you know what you're doing to gain and keep your customers' business.

MANAGEMENT CONSULTANT

Start-up cost:	$5,000-$15,000
Potential earnings:	$30,000-$60,000 (average); some make as much as $300,000/year
Typical fees:	Varies by market and client needs: average of $500-$1,500 per day (can charge by hour, day, or job)
Advertising:	Networking, referrals, creating audio- or videotapes showing your skills, ads in professional organizations' magazines and newsletters, brochures, direct mail
Qualifications:	Technical knowledge, expertise, and experience, good problem-solving skills, good people skills, excellent communication skills (written and oral)
Equipment needed:	Computer, printer, appropriate software, fax, phone, office furniture, reference books
Home business potential:	Yes
Staff required:	No
Handicapped opportunity:	Yes
Hidden costs:	Special insurance, such as errors and omissions coverage, may be needed. Budget the time and money for continuing education to keep your skills up-to-date (techniques, technology, etc.)

LOWDOWN:

The Institute of Management Consulting has members handling more than 250 specialties. Professional consulting is a fast-growing field that is expected to increase by 25 percent by the end of the '90s, and management consulting is the biggest segment of that field. U.S. companies rely heavily on management consultants, especially in the areas of compliance (with many government agencies) and the introduction of new technologies, and to take the place of permanent staff as companies become leaner. Consultants provide many services, from strategy-planning and implementation to analysis and problem-solving. Many who choose to become consultants are those with top-level skills and experience. They want the freedom and greater variety of working for themselves and recognize the world of opportunity that exists in assisting smaller, entrepreneurial companies get their businesses off the ground.

START-UP:

Start-up costs will vary according to the requirements of the specialty you choose. No matter what you decide, however, you will require the basic office and computer equipment (costing as little as $2,500); depending on the quality and extent of computer equipment needed, this figure could reach $12,000. You will also need to budget $800-$1,800 for continuing education, organizational dues, and reference books.

BOTTOM LINE ADVICE:

To succeed in this business, you must first analyze yourself: decide what sorts of problems you can solve for a client, based on your experience and expertise.

Research the companies (or types of companies) for which you want to offer your services to help you discover needs you can fill. Network with every contact you have in your target areas. Remember, though, that not everyone with good technical skills can be a successful consultant. You need excellent listening and counseling abilities—and patience. Not only does it take time to "grow" your business, but often it takes considerable time to determine if your efforts have paid off for the client. Meeting the challenges of working as a consultant can be financially rewarding. You will have the opportunity to work on a wide variety of projects and enjoy helping clients find creative, successful solutions to their problems.

ADVICE FROM THE EXPERTS

What sets your business apart from others like it?

Norma J. Rist, owner of The Boardroom Group based in Akron, Ohio, says her business assists women business owners to become clear about their goals and to achieve them in a shorter period of time and in an easier way by providing resources and business information in a group setting.

Things you couldn't do without:

A business phone line, fax, copier, and personal computer. Also, a meeting/conference room is useful for generating group discussion and participation.

Marketing tips/advice:

"Segment your niche even more . . . I started 'Spirit Groups' for home-based business owners at the same time so that I could serve a broader population of women owners and generate more income potential simultaneously."

If you had to do it all over again . . .

"I would have segmented much earlier."

MANICURIST

Start-up cost:	$5,000-$10,000
Potential earnings:	$15,000-$35,000
Typical fees:	$50 per set of nails (for length additions) and $15 for a simple manicure or pedicure
Advertising:	Newspapers, coupon books, bulletin boards, Yellow Pages
Qualifications:	Certification in cosmetology or as a nail technician often required
Equipment needed:	Manicuring table with a strong light, credit card processing equipment (if you decide to accept plastic), and nail enhancement or beautification products
Home business potential:	Yes
Staff required:	No
Handicapped opportunity:	Possibly
Hidden costs:	Liability insurance and materials

LOWDOWN:

Luxurious nails are no longer for the rich and famous only—brides want them, society mavens want them, young women want them. You'll only stand to make money from this business if you are a licensed professional, mainly because there are simply not enough skilled nail technicians to go around. Often, the wait to have fiberglass or acrylic nails is two to three weeks (for reputable places) and you could potentially make enough money off of your competitors' overflow. At any rate, you'll be providing a timeless personal service for those who appreciate the finer things in life (translation: don't be afraid to charge a little more than you're worth). You'll create beautiful long nails that would make Cher green with envy, or you'll simply clean and shape nails for folks who are in the limelight often (even if it's only before a board of directors). Yes, men and women alike use the services of a manicurist, so try not to forget that in your marketing pieces.

START-UP:

Essentially, you'll need a good, strong table and a bright enough light to work with, in addition to your nail polishes and assorted nail maintenance equipment. All of this could cost $1,000-$3,000—but add on more if you're planning to rent space somewhere. Charge at least $40-$60 for acrylic, fiberglass, or gel nails; $15 for a simple manicure.

BOTTOM LINE ADVICE:

If you like working with people from several different walks of life, this could be your kind of business—hands down. However, the community gossip might leave you with information you'd rather not know.

MARKET MAPPING SERVICE

Start-up cost:	$5,000-$15,000
Potential earnings:	$30,000-$50,000+
Typical fees:	$1,200-$5,000 per project
Advertising:	Yellow Pages, business/trade journals, newspapers, direct mail
Qualifications:	Background in strategic marketing and/or list rental
Equipment needed:	Computer with on-line services, printer, fax/modem
Home business potential:	Yes
Staff required:	No
Handicapped opportunity:	Yes
Hidden costs:	Insurance

LOWDOWN:

Companies need to know critical information from the get-go, such as where their potential clients are and how close they are physically to competitive markets. You can assist them in their tracking needs by providing a detailed map or listing of names, addresses, phone numbers, and contacts—and, if you want to, you can provide such a listing in the form of a database or mailing labels (which you'll sell on a one-use-only basis). You could, of course, produce a map pinpointing areas of opportunity, but the best way is to provide a listing with contact names and a space for follow-up notes next to each column. Offer your services via direct mail or cold calls after producing a market map of your own to locate your potential clients (usually small- to medium-size businesses). Once you sell a market map, you have the potential to resell to the same client (especially if they expand to include new products or market areas).

START-UP:

Your start-up costs ($5,000-$15,000) will cover your computer system/printer, fax/modem, and copier, along with some preliminary advertising and your cost of building lists (it takes time and plenty of outside resources). You can expect to earn at least $30,000 and possibly more than $50,000—if you target market your own services as well as you can your customers'.

BOTTOM LINE ADVICE:

You'll need to make sure that you can secure payment up front or as early as possible, since the value of your services will diminish significantly upon receipt of the market map. In other words, get the money before the product actually gets used—otherwise, you're giving your services away.

MARKETING CONSULTANT

Start-up cost:	$5,000-$10,000
Potential earnings:	$60,000-$150,000
Typical fees:	Hourly fees range from $50 to $200, while the fee for leading a workshop might be $2,000-$4,000.
Advertising:	Referrals, word of mouth
Qualifications:	Broad expertise in marketing or specialization in one area, business savvy, high energy level, excellent written/oral communications skills, creativity, persistence
Equipment needed:	Computer, laptop, laser printer, fax/modem, copier, office furniture, business card, letterhead, envelopes
Home business potential:	Yes
Staff required:	No
Handicapped opportunity:	No
Hidden costs:	Membership dues, phone bills, on-line time

LOWDOWN:

Customers are the lifeblood of all businesses—and marketing is how companies attract them. Sales are the end result of the entire marketing process, which can take almost as many forms as there are enterprises. Developing ads, writing printed materials and letters, creating promotions, gaining publicity, and designing sales strategies are all facets of marketing. Just developing a focused marketing plan is a demanding activity, and most executives need the services of a marketing professional to produce effective results. Marketing consultants are filling in the gaps left by downsizing at big organizations, as well as supplying these services to small companies. Even though this is the second largest category of consulting after management consulting, opportunities abound if you can produce results.

START-UP:

Marketing materials require a sophisticated and flexible computer setup ($4,000-$6,000). You'll need to be able to produce drafts even if the client's art department or an ad agency creates the final versions. You'll spend an equal amount on marketing efforts of your own (including joining associations in which you can build a strong network). If you're persistent and have the kind of marketing personality that draws customers in, you can earn as much as $150,000 a year.

BOTTOM LINE ADVICE:

Above all, effective marketing takes imagination. What do potential customers want, and what kind of message will enable them to see that your client's product is that very thing? Knowing how to create these interactions will make you a success as a marketing consultant, if you combine that expertise with an ability to scope out your client company. To prove your worth, try to highlight strengths that they may not have realized they had. You may need to structure the goals for the marketing plan and get buy-in from the executives before the ads, promos, or sales letters are developed. Be sure to get a contract with payment milestones in writing as these projects can take many months to come to fruition.

MEDIATOR

Start-up cost:	$5,000-$10,000
Potential earnings:	$40,000-$65,000
Typical fees:	$75-$300 (usually split between the disputing parties)
Advertising:	Yellow Pages, newspapers, bulletin boards, networking with legal groups
Qualifications:	Some states require license
Equipment needed:	Office with comfortable furniture, phones, computer
Home business potential:	Possibly
Staff required:	No
Handicapped opportunity:	Yes
Hidden costs:	Some cases are more complicated than others; try to see the writing on the wall when it comes to the bigger jobs

LOWDOWN:

The wave of the legal future is the mediator, especially with the rising cost of attorneys. While attorneys are paid to reach an eventual settlement, a mediator looks for ways to settle any disputes with compromise and without going to court. Because many marriages end in bitter divorce, mediators have their ripest ground in the domestic sector, where they can save the parties literally thousands of dollars in litigation and get to the heart of the matter through mutual conciliation. Identifying what each party truly wants out of the deal is the most critical part of successful mediation. Keeping the parties from killing each other is the next. Are you skilled at bringing people back to the issues at hand instead of hurling pointless accusations at each other? Can you help them to see the big picture in this situation? If so, you would make a fine mediator. You're essentially being paid to help fighting folks stay out of court. It's an admirable profession—and getting to be more and more profitable for those involved.

START-UP:

You'll need a nice, comfortable office for these transitional customers of yours, so expect to lay out at least $3,000 for your "digs." Next, spend some money advertising in places potential clients typically look for help (namely, the Yellow Pages). You'll charge $75-$300 per job; more if the work gets complicated.

BOTTOM LINE ADVICE:

While this is an admirable profession and is much more respected than others in the legal profession, it's still a personally challenging one. Can you listen all day to folks fighting over trivial and petty things (like who gets the washing machine)? If you're able to keep them focused on the goal of an amicable settlement, you'll do well. But do take time for yourself—you'll need it.

ADVICE FROM THE EXPERTS

What sets your business apart from others like it?

Albert H. Couch, a Family, Divorce and Community Mediator for Akron Family Mediation in Akron, Ohio, says three things set his business apart from others like it. "We have a full-time commitment to mediation, and a lot of mediators don't have that. Second, we cap our fees so that our customers know there's a limit to what they'll spend with us. Finally, we have experience in our field and are aggressive in promoting mediation in general. When I'm not mediating, I'm talking about mediating somewhere."

Things you couldn't do without:

Couch says he couldn't do without a computer, phone and, most important, the training he's had in his field.

Marketing tips/advice:

"Learn mediation inside and out, that's first and foremost." But the second most important thing you can do, according to Couch, is to talk mediation with just about anyone who'll listen. "This is primarily a word-of-mouth business."

If you had to do it all over again . . .

"I'd spend less money up front on advertising, since so much of my business comes from referrals. I advise others to get involved in their community and give as many speeches as you can to promote your business."

MEDICAL CLAIMS PROCESSING

Start-up cost:	$5,000-$12,500
Potential earnings:	$12,000-$48,000
Typical fees:	Monthly rates of $800-$1,500 per client
Advertising:	Direct mail, networking, telemarketing
Qualifications:	Knowledge of insurance billing including CPT coding, Medicare and Medicaid regulations, capitation, changes in legislation and subsequent forms
Equipment needed:	Desk, computer with hard drive and modem, printer, medical billing software, fax, typewriter, CPT coding manual
Home business potential:	Yes
Staff required:	Not initially; may be needed to grow
Handicapped opportunity:	Yes
Hidden costs:	If you are new to the insurance claims arena, it is strongly suggested that you attend various seminars and training sessions

LOWDOWN:

As regulation of the medical field continues, the number of businesses that simplify the claims process will also grow. Due to an aging population and the 1990 federal law requiring physicians to submit claims for all their Medicare patients, many medical offices are inundated with paperwork. This has created the need to hire outside billing services to process the claim and provide various other services such as invoicing, collecting any copayments required from the patient, tracking past due and uncollectible accounts, and answering all patient questions regarding their claim. A minimum of four to six doctors or practices is required to remain reasonably profitable. If you are looking for a challenging opportunity that utilizes computer technology and sharp interpersonal skills this is a very promising field.

START-UP:

Access to a computer, modem, and updated medical billing software is a must to really compete in this market (costs range from $3,000-$5,000). In addition, allow for hourly wages of additional staff as your business begins to grow. Be sure to shop around for the best rate on phone line service since the modem will be used extensively.

BOTTOM LINE ADVICE:

Medical claims processing requires patience and attention to detail. The work is often challenging and interesting due to the ever-changing nature of health insurance and Medicare. Although selling your services may be difficult at first, good communication skills and persistence will result in lasting relationships with those doctors or offices that you service. Once your business is established, processing claims electronically takes little time and can be done at your convenience. Most importantly, a successful medical billing service can be quite profitable.

MEDICAL PRODUCTS MANUFACTURER

Start-up cost:	$10,000 and up
Potential earnings:	$50,000 and more
Typical fees:	Your products should sell for anywhere from $150-$150,000 (more for laser technology)
Advertising:	Trade publications, direct mail, sales calls to physicians or hospital administrators/operations managers
Qualifications:	Scientific, technological and manufacturing skills, medical training for product identification, testing and planning, marketing and finance skills
Equipment needed:	Production equipment related to specific product, fully equipped offices
Home business potential:	No
Staff required:	Yes
Handicapped opportunity:	Yes
Hidden costs:	Planning and development stages can be very long; cost of financing, testing

LOWDOWN:

Medical products continue to be developed, manufactured, and added to the day-to-day arsenal of tools that physicians can use in their practices. As technological advances are made, they are being applied to medical products. If you have one foot in each camp—an extensive technology background, and a knowledge of the medical needs to which a new product might be applied—you can develop your own product (a new type of shunt, a better suture, a more flexible brace), manufacture it, and make a significant contribution to health care, and to your own wealth. Obviously this type of enterprise requires a number of highly developed skills and abilities, but small companies have sprung up in the "research valleys" of the U.S., near universities, and in association with technological enterprises of other kinds.

START-UP:

Costs will be high, and the return can be years down the road. The stakes are big, but so is the opportunity. Your manufacturing costs could run into the million-dollar arena, particularly if you're involved in laser or magnetic resonance imaging systems. You'll spend $10,000-$20,000 alone on marketing; $100,000-$300,000 (potentially) on product development and research.

BOTTOM LINE ADVICE:

Your links to your market—a medical subspecialty like pediatric orthopedics, perhaps, or a group of geriatric care centers—will be vital to the success of your business. You must have a viable idea for a product that is a real addition to what is currently available. And you must be able to test and develop it in service to the patient population it is meant to serve. Marketing, sales, and financial professionals will probably be needed by your new enterprise as it moves out of the tinkering-at-the-workbench stage.

MEDICAL TRANSCRIPTIONIST

Start-up cost:	$5,000-$9,000
Potential earnings:	$30,000-$60,000 (billing 2,000 hours a year)
Typical fees:	$30-$40 per hour
Advertising:	Advertise in publications of local medical societies, direct mail, telemarketing, networking
Qualifications:	Excellent listening skills and good eye, hand, and auditory coordination, knowledge of word processing, dictation and transcription equipment, understanding of medical diagnostic procedures and terminology, good typing skills, impeccable spelling
Equipment needed:	Computer, printer if not using modem, transcriber, word-processing software, reference books
Home business potential:	Yes
Staff required:	Not initially; may be needed to grow
Handicapped opportunity:	Yes
Hidden costs:	As many as one to two years of education may be required if you have little or no experience. Business cards, letterhead, envelopes are necessary to promote a professional image

LOWDOWN:

According to the American Association of Medical Transcription (AAMT), there is a shortage of qualified transcriptionists. This job is in demand for two reasons: many insurance companies are requiring transcribed reports before they will pay doctors or hospitals and transcribed copy provides health care professionals with the necessary documentation for review of patients' history, legal evidence of patient care, data for research, or to render continuing patient care. Since turnaround time of transcription is a primary concern for health care providers, increase your competitiveness by offering pickup and delivery, seven-day-a-week service, same-day service, and phone-in dictation service.

START-UP

Computer hardware and software will run you anywhere from $1,900-$5,000 with a transcriber unit ranging from $200-$800. Do not forget that this job requires hours sitting in front of a computer; a good chair and desk at the proper height is a smart investment.

BOTTOM LINE ADVICE:

Medical transcribing can become somewhat monotonous. You must possess high levels of self-discipline and focus as you work. In addition, the demand for faster turnaround times occasionally necessitates working nights and weekends. On the other hand, medical transcription work is steady and resistant to recession! This field is rapidly expanding with more work than there are trained transcriptionists.

MIDDLEMAN

Start-up cost:	$5,000-$10,000
Potential earnings:	$20,000-$80,000 (net)
Typical fees:	A percentage, varying widely by type of product and manufacturer
Advertising:	Direct mail to obtain line to sell; cold calling, and networking to complete the sales process
Qualifications:	Extensive experience with the type of product with which you plan to deal; a wide network of friends, associates, acquaintances, and people who might be buyers
Equipment needed:	Office furniture, computer and/or laptop with modem, fax, printer, suite software, cellular phone, business card, letterhead, envelopes, business directories and maps
Home business potential:	Yes
Staff required:	No
Handicapped opportunity:	No
Hidden costs:	Development of sales materials

LOWDOWN:

What does a middleman do? In today's economy, this role is expanding. Sales must be central to the operation of all manufacturing businesses, yet in-house sales forces are shrinking. Someone needs to bring the market and the product together—and there you are, right in the middle. Deciding to start a middleman business means that you love this process, you are committed to it, and you are excellent at it. You can explain anything, so that someone who needs it will immediately grasp an idea and take up the opportunity to buy it. First, you persuade the manufacturer to work through you. Then you find his market for him. This may be a step within the process of producing a final consumer product, selling raw materials or parts to a manufacturer. Or you may be "in the middle" between a wholesaler and a retailer.

START-UP:

You'll need an office that supports your efforts, and, of course, a reliable vehicle. You'll be traveling extensively. You could net $20,000 in the beginning.

BOTTOM LINE ADVICE:

Your success will depend on your sales skills, your organization, and your knowledge of the specialty chemical market, or whatever the line is that you have chosen to sell. "Choice" is the significant word here; people who are employed by large organizations tend to have little choice. They have rigid quotas, memos from on high, and a set pattern they are expected to follow, not to mention endless tedious reports to write during time that might better be spent calling on customers. You, on the other hand, have your own time and expenses to manage. You have your own sense of who needs what you've got, and how you can present that information most effectively. This is not an enterprise for people who hate, or even dislike, cold calling. This is an enterprise for people with outstanding personal charm and a huge appetite for work.

MINI-BLIND CLEANING SERVICE

Start-up cost:	$10,000-$15,000
Potential earnings:	$25,000-$35,000
Typical fees:	$10-$20 per blind for standard-size windows, more for larger ones
Advertising:	Yellow Pages, local newspapers, direct mail, coupon books
Qualifications:	Commitment to providing quality service
Equipment needed:	Ultrasonic cleaning system, phone
Staff required:	No
Handicapped opportunity:	Not typically
Home business potential:	Yes
Hidden costs:	Transportation, phone, insurance

LOWDOWN:

Mini-blinds are a versatile window treatment for offices and homes and must be cleaned regularly to be kept in pristine condition. The problem is when you try to dust the blinds off or even use soap and water, the static electricity only pushes the dirt from one side to the other. Professional cleaning from a professional service is the answer. Ultrasonic cleaning systems use sound waves to remove dust, grease, and grime. Because the system is portable, you can take the cleaning process right to the customer in a van or station wagon. The key is doing volume business to recoup the cost of the equipment.

START-UP:

Your ultrasonic cleaning equipment will run between $10,000-$15,000; you'll spend the rest of your start-up funds on a vehicle and advertising. But, if you do enough volume at $10-$20 per blind, you could recoup your investment within the first two years.

BOTTOM LINE ADVICE:

If you decide to do the cleaning yourself, make sure you use a reliable answering service or pager system, or hire someone to answer the phone. You won't want to miss a potential customer. Consider aggressive advertising. This is a relatively new service, and most people aren't aware it exists, so promote your service to consumers and businesses alike.

MOBILE DISC JOCKEY SERVICE

Start-up cost:	$5,000-$10,000
Potential earnings:	$15,000-$25,000
Typical fees:	$75-$150 per job
Advertising:	Classified ads, bulletin boards
Qualifications:	Knowledge of popular music, strong personality
Equipment needed:	Compact disc and cassette players, turntable, sound/mixing systems, microphone, theatrical lighting (if desired), and a larger and varied CD and cassette collection
Home business potential:	Yes (but your work will always be on-site)
Staff required:	No
Handicapped opportunity:	Possibly
Hidden costs:	Buying too much music at full price (try to get on record company or DJ-only promotional mailing lists)

LOWDOWN:

Because live bands cost quite a bit more than mobile disc jockey services, many party-givers book DJs to handle the entertainment needs of their party or celebration; sometimes they even ask the DJ to play "host" for a theme party. Disc jockeys have been around as long as there have been records to play, and they will continue even as equipment gets more sophisticated. For one thing, systems producing excellent sound quality are getting smaller and more portable—making it easier for DJs who travel to several locations in a given weekend. As a DJ, you'll need to develop your own style for building rapport with the audience; study the techniques of professionals you respect and try to emulate them if you can't come up with your own material. You should have a wide variety of music available—and regularly read industry publications such as Billboard and Rolling Stone to learn what's new and what's hot.

START-UP:

Your start-up costs are wrapped up in equipment and your music collection itself, because advertising will cost you no more than a few hundred dollars at the outset (for classified ads). Look for used equipment and CDs before plunking down thousands of dollars extra; you could save $1,000 or more. Scour garage sales and flea markets for the unusual or obscure, and attend record fairs when you can. Since you'll be working an average of 3-5 hours per job, it's not unrealistic to set your fee at $75-$150 per event.

BOTTOM LINE ADVICE:

Your work cycles will be extremely varied, with heavier loads typically in the spring and summer. Most of your work will be done on weekends, cutting into your social life considerably. If you're looking for work that's there when you want it, being a DJ is not for you. On the other hand, if you don't mind the erratic hours and enjoy being with people in a celebrative mood, you'll look forward to each new "gig."

MODELING SCHOOL/AGENCY

Start-up cost:	$5,000-$10,000
Potential earnings:	$40,000-$150,000 (of course, larger and better-known agencies command millions)
Typical fees:	Models earn $25-$1,000 per hour; you get 15 to 20 percent of their income
Advertising:	Direct mail, Yellow Pages, area universities, nightclubs
Qualifications:	Ability to recognize beauty, good marketing skills
Equipment needed:	Cameras, backdrops, stationery, makeup kits, lots of lights
Home business potential:	Yes
Staff required:	Not initially
Handicapped opportunity:	Yes
Hidden costs:	Insurance

LOWDOWN:

Rounding up a bevy of beauties is the easy part, but truly marketing your models is the real challenge. If you start out with just a few terrific (and fresh) faces, and aggressively market them in the right places, you'll build credibility much quicker than you would by filling up your agency with a lot of men and women all dressed up with no place to go. In other words, don't overextend yourself in the beginning—start slow and steadily increase your stable of models over a period of months. Arrange fashion shows through local malls/retail stores, and send photos to area advertising producers to get your models in weekly newspaper advertisements. Contact department stores about your business—and don't forget that many companies seek models to act as demonstrators or to be spokespersons at special events, such as trade shows.

START-UP:

Start-up costs should be relatively low (in the $5,000 range, mostly to cover office expenses). If you have the space and good lighting you can run the operation out of your home, although that may work against your credibility. We've all heard of the infamous casting couch, and for that reason perhaps the home office isn't the best idea. Good camera/video equipment is another wise investment; expect to shell out $2,000 for these items alone. If you succeed at building a solid, reputable agency, you could make between $40,000-$150,000 or more. Think of what the big guys get for models like Cindy Crawford.

BOTTOM LINE ADVICE:

Determination and persistence will get your business off the ground. When first starting your agency, you will most likely need to charge the models enrolling in your modeling school. Try to keep your sign-up fees low, though, to attract a broad range of hopefuls. Try offering two-for-one specials, or give dollar incentives to anyone who brings in new models.

MONEY ORDER SERVICE

Start-up cost:	$5,000-$10,000
Potential earnings:	$15,000-$20,000
Typical fees:	$3-$5 per money order
Advertising:	Yellow Pages, newspaper classifieds, flyers at grocery stores or Laundromats
Qualifications:	Must be bonded in most states
Equipment needed:	Cash register, safe, calculator, money orders
Home business potential:	Possibly (but not desirable)
Staff required:	No
Handicapped opportunity:	Yes
Hidden costs:	Insurance and bonding

LOWDOWN:

There are many good reasons for using money order services: when you're buying a car or big-ticket item from an individual, when you're putting down a security deposit, and of course, when your checks just plain aren't good. On the downside, if you choose this business, you may be competing with electronic banking in the near future, and who knows what could happen to the money order business in general after that. Still, if you like the straightforwardness of a business where money talks and your customers walk after a few minutes' time, this could be the ideal business for you. You might want to consider adding on additional services (such as passport production, notary, or even bill-paying services) so that you can boost your income potential. A final note: you will likely need to be bonded to handle money orders, so check into your state's requirements.

START-UP:

Most of your start-up capital ($5,000-$10,000) will be tied up in your equipment and advertising. Your earnings will be relatively low to start (unless you add on related services); look for them to be in the $15,000-$20,000 range.

BOTTOM LINE ADVICE:

The best thing you can do (although not necessarily the safest) is to position yourself in a low-rent market; it's these folks who typically get into the most trouble using regular bank checks, and they'll be more likely to need your services.

MONOGRAMMING SERVICE

Start-up cost:	$5,000-$15,000
Potential earnings:	$20,000-$50,000
Typical fees:	Varies according to items chosen and number of units/volume discounts, but generally $3.50-$100 each piece
Advertising:	Yellow Pages, local school districts, direct mail to companies
Qualifications:	Some sewing skills or ability to operate monogramming equipment
Equipment needed:	Monogramming equipment, business card
Home business potential:	Yes
Staff required:	No
Handicapped opportunity:	Yes
Hidden costs:	Insurance

LOWDOWN:

You've seen them everywhere . . . baseball caps, sweatshirts, and jackets with company logos on them. You have a knack for knits, and for transferring a company's identity to the appropriate material. Or maybe you simply want to monogram initials onto towels, blankets, and other home accessories for the marriage-minded. Whatever your specialty area, you'll need some equipment and marketing savvy to get your business off the ground. Silk screening is a good place to start; check your local art supply shops for information and creative options. For the more advanced monogrammer, research thermal transfer devices or computer-aided sewing machines in business and trade publications before making a huge purchase.

START-UP:

This business can be started on a modest budget. However, depending on the equipment you invest in, you could spend as much as $15,000 or more to get started. You will most likely need to insure any equipment purchased, plus any supplies. Expect to earn back your initial cash outlay in about two to three years, based on an income potential of $20,000-$50,000 per year.

BOTTOM LINE ADVICE:

Advertising and marketing will play an important role in making this business a successful venture. Monogramming is much more than just initialing towels—and you'll need to convey that in every piece of literature you send out (particularly in your business cards).

MOTION PICTURE RESEARCH CONSULTANT

Start-up cost:	$10,000-$15,000
Potential earnings:	$35,000-$60,000
Typical fees:	$150-$300 per hour
Advertising:	Industry trade publications, word of mouth
Qualifications:	Degree in history, the ability to conduct research, and an inquisitive mind
Equipment needed:	Computer with on-line service, library card, resource materials of your own, business card
Home business potential:	Yes
Staff required:	No
Handicapped opportunity:	Yes
Hidden costs:	Travel expenses

LOWDOWN:

You are the Fact Man (or Woman): your mission is to research a person, place, event (or all three) and put that information together so that actors and movie-goers alike can understand it. If you are inquisitive about history, nosy about people or places, and a history buff in general, then this seek-and-find mission is for you. The motion picture research consultant flushes out all possible angles, much like a reporter, only you remain behind the scenes. Could you imagine *Gone With the Wind* without historical accuracy? A good researcher is invaluable to producers and the movie itself because if there is an error, a critic is bound to find it—even if the movie is good. That's why your services are invaluable; your only challenge is to get the word out there about your availability.

START-UP:

You'll have to rub elbows with directors, producers, and movie people in general, so plan on going to all of the trade shows, cocktail parties, and as many events as possible. It's at these functions that you'll network and get people to know you. Plan on dropping a minimum of $5,000 just to get noticed. As to what your return will yield, that will depend on what you charge per hour per project. Generally speaking, you could charge between $150-$300 per hour (more if it's a major studio) and pull in between $35,000-$60,000.

BOTTOM LINE ADVICE:

Plan on traveling and talking to all types of people to help you in your research. This is a low-profile job that sometimes requires months to complete—and yet it is of critical importance to directors and producers. Plan on using your on-line services regularly (and set aside extra cash to cover related charges).

NETWORKING SERVICES

Start-up cost:	$10,000-$15,000
Potential earnings:	$20,000-$50,000
Typical fees:	$50-$200 per event attendee
Advertising:	Yellow Pages, direct mail (most effective), newspaper ads, billboards (for larger events)
Qualifications:	Strong organizational skills and follow-through
Equipment needed:	Computer, printer, fax/modem, copier, phone, contact management software for keeping up with contacts
Home business potential:	Yes
Staff required:	No
Handicapped opportunity:	Yes
Hidden costs:	List rental fees, insurance

LOWDOWN:

How do most business professionals of the '90s meet other influential types they may need in the future? They go to networking events, such as business trade shows and after-hours mixers. In many cities, it is the larger networking events held at luxurious hotels that bring in the most business; some of these functions chalk up more than 10,000 attendees. Your business, of course, might start out a bit smaller; you could organize a series of small networking dinners or cocktail hours at a local hotel, and advertise them on a regular basis. It works best if you can hold one event per month. After you get a strong enough following to generate more business through referral, you might want to organize larger events or trade shows where folks can get a discount with their business card (that way, you also build your own mailing list, which will save you money over rental fees with mailing list houses). Better yet, find a large corporate sponsor and split the profits with them (it might be worth the boost in credibility).

START-UP:

The $10,000 or so it will take to get you started in the networking services business will mainly cover your basic office setup (computer, printer, fax/modem, copier, and phone system) along with the initial outlay for mailing list rentals and labels. You'll also need to set aside money for additional advertising for each event; newspaper editorial departments will ask that you purchase ad space rather than run you a free event listing. With lots of hard work, you could make $20,000-$50,000 bringing professionals together for the economic benefit of all concerned.

BOTTOM LINE ADVICE:

Your toughest problem will be getting enough people to attend your functions on a regular basis—and keeping the "new blood" flowing in. Since your income potential depends so heavily on people and interesting enough events to attract them, you are at the mercy of the general public—and that's a precarious position for a business owner to be in. On the bright side, once you've got a following, you'll have a strong referral base.

NEW PRODUCT RESEARCHER

Start-up cost:	$5,000-$10,000
Potential earnings:	$40,000-$80,000
Typical fees:	Per-project rates of $1,000-$5,000 or a percentage (15 to 20 percent) of gross sales
Advertising:	Business publications, direct mail, networking with venture capitalists and other investors who can provide referrals
Qualifications:	Should have extensive experience in all aspects of product launch (particularly strategic marketing)
Equipment needed:	Computer with high-speed modem for on-line searches of related or similar products, fax, phone, business card
Home business potential:	Yes
Staff required:	No
Handicapped opportunity:	Yes
Hidden costs:	Always add 20 percent to your pricing to cover the unexpected

LOWDOWN:

Ever wonder where innovative new products such as the Wonder Bra came from? While it could have been an in-house, corporate "think tank" that developed this and other fine products, it's highly unlikely for companies that are too small to afford such a group. For these small, yet progressive companies, hiring a new product researcher to determine the marketability and profitability of a proposed new product can be a cost-effective solution to a timeless problem. Even the oldest companies are looking for new products to add to their established lines, because we live in a society where innovation is rewarded. Your job as a new product researcher will entail extensive research to uncover possible competitors, identify customer need, and break down the cost of producing such a product into palatable portions for management to swallow. In other words, you'll be determining whether it's worth it or not to produce a particular product line.

START-UP:

Your start-up costs will mostly cover advertising your services, either through direct mail pieces to manufacturers or through ads in business publications. You'll spend at least $5,000 on these items alone, and then you'll need to add more to cover equipment purchases such as computer, fax, modem, etc. (around $5,000). But when you consider that your earnings per project could be as high as $5,000 for one month's work, it doesn't take a mathematician to see that your own product is worth it.

BOTTOM LINE ADVICE:

On the positive side, you'll be among the first to know about emerging products. You'll be sitting at conference tables with some of the greatest engineering minds around, hashing through ideas and weighing the pros and cons of every project. However, make sure you're paid up front for your services to avoid misunderstandings should a project lose its backing midway through your work, or at least have a good contract lawyer working with you to protect your interests.

Newspaper Features Syndicate

Start-up cost:	$10,000-$15,000
Potential earnings:	$20,000-$45,000
Typical fees:	$10-$25 per month, per article, per publication
Advertising:	Direct mail to small and large newspapers, industry publications
Qualifications:	Some newspaper experience would be helpful
Equipment needed:	Computer, fax/modem, laser printer, postage scale/machine
Home business potential:	Yes
Staff required:	Yes (freelance writers or cartoonists)
Handicapped opportunity:	Yes
Hidden costs:	Production, postage

LOWDOWN:

Newspapers are always on the lookout for new, exciting, and offbeat articles and cartoons to use as filler material, or even to boost their credibility if they have a small staff. That's why features syndicates work so well: they provide a wide array of usable, printable journalism at a fraction of what it might cost to develop such work in-house. Why pay a staffer a hefty salary (with benefits) to produce movie reviews when you can purchase syndicated reviews for $20 per month? As a syndicate, you'll need to get the word out after building your stable of fine writers and artists; you can't sell papers on using your services without providing some samples of the work you represent. Network with artists'/writers' groups and through universities to scour the journalistic jungle for the best in your area. Or, open your doors to artists across the country by advertising in their publications (*Writer's Digest*, *The Artist Magazine*, etc.); you can tell them you're building a syndicate and they have an opportunity to get in on the ground floor. Since syndication most likely means regular work for them, the artists and writers will be willing to work with you on their percentages (often you can pay them a flat fee per piece).

START-UP:

You'll spend between $10,000-$15,000 getting this operation off the ground, largely due to the fact that you'll need to advertise heavily in the beginning (first to build your stable of artists, then to get the word out to papers). Still, you could make between $20,000-$45,000 if you have a solid group of people producing quality work on a regular basis.

BOTTOM LINE ADVICE:

Keep your freelancers happy, because they'll quit on you—leaving you high and dry and minus some credibility with your newspaper customers. The best thing you can do is negotiate a fair deal for them from the beginning, even if it costs you a little more. It's worth it in the long run to keep a stable image.

NOISE CONTROL CONSULTANT

Start-up cost:	$5,000-$10,000
Potential earnings:	$30,000-$50,000
Typical fees:	$50-$75 per hour is common
Advertising:	Trade publications, business associations, referrals
Qualifications:	Certification as an industrial hygienist, extensive experience with a large employer or a consulting firm, quantification orientation, ability to deal with people in a workplace environment, writing skills
Equipment needed:	Dosimeter, computer, suite software, printer, office furniture, business card, letterhead, envelopes
Home business potential:	Yes
Staff required:	No
Handicapped opportunity:	Not typically
Hidden costs:	Travel, insurance, periodical subscriptions

LOWDOWN:

Noise control is a branch of industrial hygiene. Employers need to track noise levels in their plants because long-term exposure to noise can produce hearing loss, even with noise that does not seem painful. Requiring employees to wear earplugs has not been found to be an adequate response to the problem. Instead, a noise control consultant will measure workplace noise with a dosimeter, write a report, and work with the employer to determine ways to reduce the noise level. The consultant may recommend putting baffles on machines, relocating machines, running them at different speeds, or replacing them with different equipment. Considerable business judgment is required to assess the problem, plan improvements, and present recommendations that meet the expectations of both the employer and the workers.

START-UP:

You'll need some highly sensitive and specialized equipment to start your business, in addition to the standard office outfit. Expect to spend close to $10,000 on these items. Charge $50-$75 per hour for your services; more ($500 per day) if working for a large corporation or factory.

BOTTOM LINE ADVICE:

You will need certification in industrial hygiene to gain credibility as a noise control consultant. More importantly, you will need the acoustical ability to locate different workplace sounds. This numerical analysis has to be performed in relationship to the real people who work in the environment and operate the machines, regardless of the safety regulations. You'll need good people skills and the ability to present abstract measurements clearly on paper. Creative solutions to any problems discovered will set you apart from mere technicians. In other words, you also need a sense of how your recommendations relate to the overall operation of the plant. This is not an easy business to break into. Some working conditions can be difficult and hazardous to your own hearing.

OFFICE EQUIPMENT LEASING

Start-up cost:	$7,000-$10,000
Potential earnings:	$35,000 and up
Typical fees:	Rates range from $75-$1,000 per month for each rental unit
Advertising:	Local newspapers, radio spots, Yellow Pages, flyers, direct mail, memberships in business organizations
Qualifications:	Excellent marketing ability, knowledge of office equipment
Equipment needed:	Inventory of equipment to lease, computer, modem, fax, cellular phone, printer, office furniture, business card, letterhead, envelopes, marketing materials
Home business potential:	No
Staff required:	Possibly
Handicapped opportunity:	No
Hidden costs:	Legal assistance in setting up lease agreements, equipment maintenance, and repair

LOWDOWN:

Today's changed business climate means great opportunity for you. We are see-ing the growth of new businesses that cannot afford the capital expenditures required to purchase outright the equipment they need. Your leasing service is the perfect solution to this problem, allowing enterprises in your service area to rent the equipment they need at a cost they can afford. Leasing in general is growing in popularity—from computers to tractors—so your marketing efforts need not educate but only distinguish you from your competition.

START-UP:

This is a high-cost business to establish. You'll need excellent relationships with your suppliers as well as your customers. Depending on your suppliers, you could earn upward of $35,000. You can get by the first year or so leasing the equip-ment and then subleasing to your clients, but for liability reasons you'll eventually want to buy.

BOTTOM LINE ADVICE:

Outstanding organizational skills are what will enable you to pull the pieces of this business together. Your customers will want what they want, when they want it. And all equipment must be in excellent condition. As needs change, you must keep abreast of the desires of different businesses, as well. Are color copiers going to be wanted in most offices next year? Will shredders rise or fall in popularity?

ON-LINE INTERNET RESEARCHER

Start-up cost:	$4,000-$12,000
Potential earnings:	$18,000-$75,000
Typical fees:	$45-$75 per hour
Advertising:	Networking, contacts in fields where you have experience, seminars, newsletters, advertising in trade journals, bulletin boards
Qualifications:	Familiarity with the requirements of the databases in your specialized field, ability to scan information rapidly and pick out what is relevant
Equipment needed:	Computer, modem, fax, printer, on-line accounts, office furniture, business card, letterhead, envelopes
Home business potential:	Yes
Staff required:	No
Handicapped opportunity:	Yes
Hidden costs:	On-line time, marketing required to sell such a new service

LOWDOWN:

Companies require many kinds of information, but they often do not have the time or skills necessary to find it. Not everyone has the patience and creativity to be an effective, efficient researcher. The information explosion means that a wealth of data is available, but sorting out what is useful to a particular project can be challenging. Increasingly this work is done through computerized databases rather than in the library. Successful on-line research often requires that you specialize in one type of information so that you can draw on your familiarity with Internet locations to produce the information your clients need quickly.

START-UP:

A computer and high-speed modem will be your basic tools in this business. On-line database access and accounts can be expensive, but this cost is spread out over time. Expect to spend at least $2,000 to start; expect to bill at $45 per hour until you develop a strong reputation.

BOTTOM LINE ADVICE:

The task of finding specific data for a client can have the same appeal as solving a puzzle or tracking down the answer to a mystery. Creative thinking is often required to discover new approaches to a search or hidden sources of information. You can use your intellectual curiosity and your desire to leave no stone unturned to develop a successful on-line research business. You will be gaining satisfaction by providing information essential to the growth and development of your client businesses. Costs can be difficult to manage, however, because it is hard to predict how long a search will take. And you may not always be able to find that last piece of data. You will have to keep learning how to use new databases, and you will have to keep educating potential clients about what your service is and be able to justify what might turn out to be an expensive additional cost to their bill.

Outdoor Adventures

Start-up cost:	$5,000-$10,000
Potential earnings:	$50,000-$100,000
Typical fees:	Varied, depending on length of excursion, group size, and corporate versus individual rates (could range anywhere from $300-$1,000 per person)
Advertising:	Magazines with an outdoor or fitness focus, newspapers, public speaking on outdoor and environmental issues, direct mail
Qualifications:	Outdoor leadership skills and experience, knowledge of the natural world, first aid certificate, excellent planning ability
Equipment needed:	Outdoor equipment for yourself and group, van, basic office setup
Home business potential:	Yes
Staff required:	Yes
Handicapped opportunity:	No
Hidden costs:	Insurance, equipment repairs and replacement

LOWDOWN:

There are almost as many ways to conduct an "outdoor adventure" as there are individual personalities. Broadly defined, your business will take groups of people into the outdoors, camping, hiking, and experiencing the vanishing wilderness as participants rather than just seeing it on TV. The popularity of the long-established organizations offering outdoor programs has not nearly met the demand, and many small organizations have been very successful in offering related services. Some focus on learning to exist with little material support in a wilderness environment. Others offer opportunities for self-development, self-reflection, or fitness. Another popular approach is to create group activities that build relationships of trust for business organizations, college freshman orientations, and similar groups.

START-UP:

Your decisions about equipment will affect the cost of your start-up, and of your continuing operations. Advertising will be an ongoing requirement; expect to spend at least $5,000 on that alone. However, if you market yourself well, especially to corporations, you can really carve out a mighty fine living for yourself (to the tune of $100,000).

BOTTOM LINE ADVICE:

An outdoors adventure business will rely on your love of the wilderness and your creativity in designing effective, appealing programs that allow your customers to encounter it. But not everyone who can build a camp out of hemlock twigs and catch mountain trout for dinner is also people-oriented enough to share their expertise with others. Wet, cold campers with blistered feet are not as easy to charm as day trippers on a short hike. So emphasize that experiencing and surviving the full range of challenges builds self-esteem, group solidarity, and an enduring respect for the power and beauty of nature.

Home Alone:
How to Feel "Connected" When You're Home-Based

You work anywhere from thirty to sixty hours per week in your cozy little home office, where you curl up with a cup of coffee and enjoy the solitude of working alone. No office politics, no petty disagreements, no feeling of corporate pressure.

But too much solitude can be a bad thing. When the sound of silence gets to you, where can you go for some human interaction? Here are a few places you can start:

- A home-based business forum available through on-line services such as America Online and CompuServe

- A professional organization made up of business professionals like yourself (check with your Chamber of Commerce for listings of such groups)

- Toastmasters International—this organization offers you the chance to improve your speaking/presentation skills as well as meet with several others in your community (and from all walks of life)

- Volunteer at your local hospital, community organization, or even professional associations

- Work one day per week at your local library

- Take yourself out to lunch; you can bring along an assignment and make it a "working lunch"

- Spend at least one-half day per week networking at a function or event

- Form a "business buddy" system with another home-based worker, sharing trials and tribulations

- Form a success team with a dozen or so other home-based business professionals, where you meet once a week to discuss your business problems and offer one another some solutions

- Stop feeling alone—there are literally thousands of self-employed, home-based workers in the U.S. today

PACKAGING CONSULTANT

Start-up cost:	$8,000-$10,000
Potential earnings:	$40,000-$80,000
Typical fees:	$50-$75 per hour or a per-project fee
Advertising:	Membership in trade organizations, referrals, networking, direct mail
Qualifications:	Extensive experience in commercial design, advertising and sales promotion; outstanding skill at package design
Equipment needed:	Office furniture, high-end computer with graphic design software, laser printer, color printer, modem, fax, business card, letterhead, envelopes
Home business potential:	Yes
Staff required:	No
Handicapped opportunity:	Yes
Hidden costs:	Cost of creating sample packages

LOWDOWN:

Packaging is a separate and very highly developed facet of the product development process. As a consultant, you will work with an advertising agency, a manufacturer, or a product developer to create the ideal package. Do you need to focus on form (perfume bottle) or function (milk carton)? Will the package need to jump off the shelf at a discount store or reach out to an impulse purchaser in a gourmet food shop? Your ability to respond to the market, the materials, the message, and the channel of distribution will make you a valuable addition to the process of bringing many products to market. Consider specializing in the area where you have a record of success to back up your own marketing efforts.

START-UP:

Equipping your office to support your design work will not be inexpensive, but you must have the ability to produce professional-looking results, so spend at least $8,000. At billings of $50-$75 per hour, you'll earn between $40,000-$80,000.

BOTTOM LINE ADVICE:

Creative and practical: that combination is a requirement for success as a packaging consultant. You're producing a design that wraps up what "they" want, what will work, and what will sell. Intuition, skill, and artistic ability must mark your designs. As with many high-end consulting businesses, it will take time to become established, but eventually referrals will bring you a regular stream of work.

ADVICE FROM THE EXPERTS

What sets your business apart from others like it?

Andrea S. Mandel, President of Andrea S. Mandel Associates, Packaging Consulting Services in Robinsville, New Jersey, says her diverse experience is what counts. "I've worked for a number of different major companies in health care, personal care, foods, medical devices, and household products. This broad product experience facilitates technology transfer between areas. This is not commonly available inside a particular company."

Things you couldn't do without:

"A good computer and printer, modem, software, and extras as needed. You need at least one extra phone line, answering device, fax machine, and copier. Also, small measuring devices (calipers), and resource materials."

Marketing tips/advice:

Get on the Internet, says Mandel. "I have a good knowledge of computers and have been utilizing on-line services for a long time. Many independent consultants do not have this capability yet."

If you had to do it all over again . . .

"I would have come up with a different name for my company. I had felt my name in the title would have some equity, as I am somewhat well-known in the industry. However, the current name makes it too obvious that this is a one-person or very small company. This can be a disadvantage."

PAGING SERVICES

Start-up cost:	$10,000-$15,000
Potential earnings:	$30,000-$50,000
Typical fees:	Monthly fees range from $10-$30
Advertising:	Newspapers, radio, TV, direct mail, flyers
Qualifications:	Technical skill, organizational and sales skills
Equipment needed:	Computer paging system, office furniture, business card, letterhead, envelopes
Home business potential:	Yes
Staff required:	No
Handicapped opportunity:	Yes
Hidden costs:	Phone bills, insurance

LOWDOWN:

No longer limited to a few types of professionals, paging services now appeal to many businesses and individuals. Parents use them to keep track of children; sales people maintain a close link to their offices. In fact, almost everyone who works away from a home office can use a pager to increase productivity and maintain the highest possible level of responsiveness to customers. Creative marketing will connect your new paging services business to these emerging markets; excellent service will keep your clients linked to you for their mobile communications needs.

START-UP:

The required communications and phone equipment is quite expensive ($10,000 and up), and you may need an inventory of pagers as well. Set your monthly rates competitively to ensure maximum return.

BOTTOM LINE ADVICE:

Paging is trendy, and for good reason. You can ride the crest of this trend toward a successful business. It will take determination and responsiveness to your market to make your enterprise stand out from the competition.

PATIENT GIFT PACKAGER

Start-up cost:	$5,000-$10,000
Potential earnings:	$25,000-$40,000
Typical fees:	Gift baskets generally start at $15 each but can run as high as $35
Advertising:	Direct mail to hospital administrators; flyers to health care facilities
Qualifications:	Some creative flair, ability to market yourself
Equipment needed:	Decorative baskets, boxes, glue gun, shrink-wrap machine, filling, ribbons; products such as toothpaste, soap, and lotion; delivery vehicle
Home business potential:	Yes
Staff required:	No
Handicapped opportunity:	Yes
Hidden costs:	Insurance, vendor's license

LOWDOWN:

Creativity, organization, and the ability to visualize are all you need to have to make a go of this business. Build your market carefully—pinpoint hospitals, extended care facilities and even church groups (they often have members who regularly visit hospitalized parishioners). Who doesn't like to give a friend or relative a gift in the hospital, even if the basket just contains a get-well card and a few well-packaged toiletries? It makes both the gift-giver and the patient feel good. Gift baskets have caught on in the last five years, and this business is just a more specialized version. Most of your competition will be small shops, but even some of the larger retailers are doing it. Market yourself by getting in good with your local hospitals and nonprofit organizations. Donate a basket or two to a local charity event to get your name out there.

START-UP:

The initial start-up cost is in the relatively low range (around $5,000 for supplies), and you may already have some of your decorative items lying around the house if you're crafty. What will constantly keep you going after more clients is the need to maintain a high profit level—this business will not be substantial enough to support you if you aren't constantly on the lookout for new business. Find the private craft retailer who only sells to vendors. Their prices could be as much as 40 percent lower than public retail crafters. Even though this business is still relatively new, it's hot. You could wrap up an annual salary between $25,000-$50,000.

BOTTOM LINE ADVICE:

What a wonderful business to be in! Wouldn't it be a great feeling to know that what you are doing is making someone's day a little brighter, and getting paid to do it? However, this can be a very time-consuming occupation. If you decide to customize, be prepared to go on the hunt for specific requests. If you offer an assortment from which your clients can pick, make sure you provide enough variety. Don't forget—somebody has to deliver the baskets, too. If you can do it all, the better off you'll be.

PERSONALIZED CHILDREN'S BOOKS

Start-up cost:	$5,000-$15,000
Potential earnings:	$20,000-$40,000
Typical fees:	$15-$30 per book
Advertising:	Business card, bookstores, preschools, direct mail, flea markets
Qualifications:	Writing capability
Equipment needed:	Computer, laser printer, binder
Home business potential:	Yes
Staff required:	No
Handicapped opportunity:	Yes
Hidden costs:	Mistakes can add up quickly; proof your work carefully

LOWDOWN:

Customized picture books can brighten any kid's day—after all, what could be better for a kid than reading a story with his own name throughout? With these picture books, kids can actually be a character in the book they are reading—and many parents are more than willing to pay money for such a personalized item. You'll produce books using one of a few templates, and then simply drop in the child's name via computer. Then, you'll print the books out on the laser printer, bind them, and package them up for your customers. You can get the word out by advertising in community newspapers, or rent a mall kiosk during weekends or holidays to sell your services directly and in a place where you can produce products on the spot.

START-UP:

Your prices will range from $15-$25, depending on the length of the book. There will be an initial investment to get the book made (around $10,000 for your basic equipment setup and paper stock). If you're not great at creating your own stories, you'll likely be buying into a franchise. Expect to shell out a franchising fee of $30,000-$50,000, but if you do, you may be thankful for the support and the ease of production that results from such an affiliation. You'll have to use mock-ups or prototypes to sell your services, so don't forget to include a few sample books in your start-up plan.

BOTTOM LINE ADVICE:

This is a fun and entertaining venture—who doesn't love to make a child smile and get paid for doing it? The flip side of that is the frustration of working with difficult customers. It goes with the territory, since you'll likely be in a retail setting. Be prepared for little tantrums every once in a while.

PET BREEDER

Start-up cost:	$5,000-$10,000
Potential earnings:	$15,000-$20,000
Typical fees:	Purebred kittens and puppies cost about $300, more for very exotic breeds and show or breeding quality animals
Advertising:	Classified ads, specialty periodicals for your breed
Qualifications:	Love of animals, experience with care, breeding, and medical needs
Equipment needed:	Kennels, feeders, space, etc.
Home business potential:	Yes
Staff required:	No
Handicapped opportunity:	Not typically
Hidden costs:	Loss of young animals due to birth defects or disease, high vet bills, insurance, breeding fees

LOWDOWN:

Most people breed animals because they love them, and only secondarily to make money. If you really add up the cost in terms of your time and effort, you wouldn't find breeding your beloved shelties or Persians to be a good business deal. Yet many people fit breeding into the daily flow of their lives. If you have adequate space (you live on a farm, for example) and healthy purebred males and females, you can produce the adorable purebred puppies or kittens that find their way into more homes in America than children. Some kennels grow into large, full-time businesses providing working dogs, guide dogs, or animals for pet stores. You'll need adequate kennel space for these animals to live in while they are being weaned; some states require mandatory (and unscheduled) inspections of such facilities to avoid animal rights violations. Make sure you distinguish your service as a caring one.

START-UP:

The start-up cost will depend on where you live and what breed of pet you specialize in. Great Danes are a different proposition from toy poodles, and you'll sometimes need to present a "family tree" of the animals you're offering for sale. These costs, however, will be minimal compared to what you'll spend on a good dog pen or kennel ($5,000-$10,000, depending on how large you want your operation to be). Purebred dogs sell for $300 and up, with many in the $500-$700 range, so you can make some money if all goes well.

BOTTOM LINE ADVICE:

If you are still in awe of the miracle of birth, if you find a deep satisfaction in watching tiny creatures open their eyes and take their first wobbly steps into the world, if you love to put a warm puppy into the arms of a delighted child—consider making pet breeding your business. You'll be able to tolerate the mess, the dominance of the pets' life cycles over your human timetable, and the inevitable losses that come with the birth process. You may not grow rich, but you'll get by.

PET GROOMING/CARE

Start-up cost:	$5,000-$10,000
Potential earnings:	$25,000-$40,000
Typical fees:	$30-$60 per pet-primping session
Advertising:	Yellow Pages, direct mail, community bulletin boards, referrals from vets
Qualifications:	Experience, patience, knowledge of animal behavior patterns, familiarity with the grooming standards of different breeds
Equipment needed:	Grooming table, clippers, brushes, combs, bathing tub/shower accessories, shampoos, dryer, detangler, hair bows, business card
Home business potential:	Yes
Staff required:	No
Handicapped opportunity:	No
Hidden costs:	Supplies could get out of hand

LOWDOWN:

You have to really love animals to consider this business. But if you enjoy working with pets—many of whom may not enjoy taking a bath—you can build a decent business providing these services. Pet ownership increases each year in this country, but people have less free time than ever. What Afghan owners can really manage to comb out their pet's entire coat every day, as the books recommend? The popular white poodles need considerable grooming to present themselves in a clean, fluffy, well-trimmed coat. Aside from the pet's appearance, good health practices dictate cleaning and brushing the coat regularly. Once you establish rapport with Rover, you are likely to have regular repeat business from his owner. Giving cats their flea baths is another popular service (to the owner, definitely not to the feline). As an add-on, consider selling pet supplies and/or specialty products for the pampered pet.

START-UP:

Trying to do all this in your family bathtub is a poor idea. To make a go of the business, you'll need the setting and equipment to do a professional job without breaking your back. This may set you back around $10,000, but you stand a good chance of earning it all back in a year or so if there aren't many competitors in your area. Charge between $30-$60, depending on whether you're in the country or in a large city.

BOTTOM LINE ADVICE:

You may not be the only pet grooming service in your community, but you can be the best. You can offer pickup and delivery services, you can specialize in terrier coat stripping or caring for poodles, you can leave each "patient" happy and sweet-smelling. You'll need to make your customers feel that your service is the one that they can't live without. This is hard, physical work, but each grooming session leaves a beloved pet looking better—until he can get outside again.

Understanding Your Cash Budget

For those business owners who are "mathematically challenged," here is a quick breakdown of the items that should appear on your cash flow projection statements. Basically, you need to look at what's coming in and what's going out on a regular basis.

"In" column:

- Cash sales
- Accounts Receivables
- Funds from sales of assets or equipment
- Refunds (such as tax refunds)
- Collections (outstanding accounts)

"Out" column:

- Inventory/stock purchases
- Operating expenses
- Fixed expense payments
- Credit payments on long-term debt
- Tax payments (most often quarterly)
- Shareholder/stock payments

Taking a look at these items and how they change over a period of a year can provide you with a Profit and Loss statement that clearly shows you what your business is earning and spending.

You can use this information to build your following year's budget, by making educated assumptions based on what happened the previous year. For instance, if you had a bad winter quarter because your business is somewhat dependent on good weather, you'll know to build sales up in the fall to cover your winter operating budget and make sure the bills get paid.

PHOTOCOPYING SERVICE

Start-up cost:	$5,000-$15,000
Potential earnings:	$40,000-$60,000
Typical fees:	Prices vary; some copy centers charge as little as 4 cents per copy
Advertising:	Newspapers, Yellow Pages, flyers, direct mail, location
Qualifications:	Some graphics experience
Equipment needed:	High-quality photocopying machines, preferably with large-format capabilities; paper and toner stock
Home business potential:	No
Staff required:	Not initially
Handicapped opportunity:	Yes
Hidden costs:	Repairs, paper inventories

LOWDOWN:

This is a service needed by every business and almost every individual. You will need at least one machine capable of producing excellent copies, and a customer-focused attitude. Franchises (i.e., Kinko's, Sir Speedy, etc.) for copying services are available, or you can set up a small independent operation. Unless you plan to do all pickup and delivery work, you will also need an accessible location. And you must be creative about distinguishing yourself from the competition. Many successful copying businesses offer design and pasteup services in addition to the basic copying function. Having a range of papers available will add to the professionalism of your products. Personalized service may be enough to establish the value of your offerings over the national chain outlets.

START-UP:

This depends on the route you choose. With a franchise comes advice, assistance, and higher costs ($10,000-$50,000 or more for initial investment). If you're on your own, you will need to select the photocopying equipment needed, arrange for maintenance and repair contracts, and develop a marketing plan. Equipment costs alone will run you between $5,000-$10,000, but your per-copy rate will hopefully recoup your initial cash layout. Most copy centers charge at least 4 cents per copy (although some frequently run 2 1/2-cent specials); your income will be directly contingent upon how many clients you serve per month.

BOTTOM LINE ADVICE:

The market is huge. The background you need relates more to your desire to serve your customers than any technical training or work experience. People who enjoy a stream of customers, each with a different project to be completed, will find a that copying business can be rewarding. The downside is the competition. Just copying will not be enough when supermarkets and libraries have machines available for public use. It will take serious effort to develop services that seem valuable enough to draw customers in to your business.

ADVICE FROM THE EXPERTS

What sets your business apart from others like it?

Connie Delehanty, owner of a Sir Speedy Printing Center franchise in Fairlawn, Ohio, says: "A knowledgeable staff that asks the right questions and is able to get the job done right as a result. We have a commitment to customer service and quality."

Things you couldn't do without:

"We couldn't do without our staff and up-to-date technology such as interfaced computers with digital color output devices and laser printers."

Marketing tips/advice:

"Location, location . . . you need to be in a highly traveled path." Delehanty's print shop is located in a small shopping plaza near a major thoroughfare.

If you had to do it all over again . . .

"I'd start with more capital," says Delehanty. "Equipment costs can skyrocket in this technology-driven business."

POLITICAL MARKETING CONSULTANT

Start-up cost:	$5,000-$10,000
Potential earnings:	$50,000-$150,000
Typical fees:	Average fees are anywhere from $75-$150 per hour.
Advertising:	Referrals (it's who you know)
Qualifications:	Wide and deep experience with politics, demographics, marketing, statistics, and polling techniques
Equipment needed:	PC with modem and printer, software, fax, office furniture, cellular phone, business card, letterhead, envelopes
Home business potential:	Yes
Staff required:	Eventually you'll need a network of subcontractors, associates, etc.
Handicapped opportunity:	Yes
Hidden costs:	Telephone bills, on-line time, travel costs

LOWDOWN:

After the last presidential campaign, political consultants have achieved an almost mythological status in the U.S. We somehow respect them, even as we resent them for manipulating us. That's a tough public image, but the few political consultants who operate at the national level are not representative of the variety of skilled, knowledgeable people who offer this service on the local or regional level. Helping candidates present their messages clearly and effectively to the public can develop into a good business for you if you are savvy about language, political issues, government, and current affairs. It's a business of high highs and very low lows. Our democratic form of government requires reaching out to the people, and political marketing consultants provide a vital service in helping candidates do that.

START-UP:

Communication systems are central, as you will have to be reachable 24 hours a day. You will probably incur huge cellular phone bills. Your start-up costs, therefore, will be in the $5,000-$10,000 range, and will cover your computer and cellular phone (expect *high* phone bills).

BOTTOM LINE ADVICE:

Being involved with the political process is dynamic, interesting, and very hard work. You will need to know everything about your district, the issues likely to come up, and the views of the voters. You will be part of a tightly focused team during elections, and you can keep politicians and parties informed of public attitudes between campaigns. You'll need excellent connections and impressive experience to make a go of this kind of business.

PORTRAIT PHOTOGRAPHER/ARTIST

Start-up cost:	$5,000-$15,000
Potential earnings:	$20,000-$50,000
Typical fees:	$600-$800 for photos; $1,500-$3,000 for oil portraits
Advertising:	Brochures mailed to executives, networking, Yellow Pages
Qualifications:	Talent and the ability to capture a person's "essence"
Equipment needed:	Photographic equipment (essentially, a portable studio) can run as high as $10,000; oil paints can be as high as $500 or more
Home business potential:	Yes (but you'll be working on-site much of the time)
Staff required:	No
Handicapped opportunity:	Not typically
Hidden costs:	Be sure to have a refund policy in place, just in case customers are not happy with the work

LOWDOWN:

Ever walk into a large corporate office and see walls adorned with fancy portraits of everyone who's ever been anyone at the company? Yes, these folks did pay someone to preserve their mugs for posterity—but often, these portraits are gifts from those close to them, such as coworkers or family members. Market your services with each of these options in mind. Remember that you'll need to educate your clients to help them realize that, although this business requires artistic talent, it is highly specialized and not something any artist could necessarily do. Set yourself apart as an artist who is skilled at conveying a person's "essence" or spirit in each portrait, not just drawing a caricature or sketch (like those at county fairs). One last tip: since you'll be most often working with a wealthy clientele, set your fees at least 20 percent higher than you were thinking, and you'll be right about where you should be to compete with others in the corporate world.

START-UP:

Equipment and materials such as cameras, backdrops, film, paints, and canvas constitute much of your start-up costs ($5,000-$15,000). You'll need to spend at least $2,000 on printing up brochures with samples of your work, as part of your advertising campaign. Still, with your fees averaging between $600-$3,000, you could be sitting pretty in this profession.

BOTTOM LINE ADVICE:

Those who aren't skilled teach, it is often said, but you could boost your earning power even more if you teach the art of portraiture at a local university. It's not selling out, it's reaching out that in the end counts on your balance sheet.

PRIVATE DETECTIVE/
INTELLIGENCE SPECIALIST

Start-up cost:	$5,000-$9,000
Potential Earnings:	$50,000-$75,000
Advertising:	Direct solicitation, Yellow Pages, direct mail, speaking at meetings and seminars
Qualifications:	Experience in investigative work, people skills, writing ability, creativity and persistence
Equipment needed:	Computer with modem, printer, and software, fax; small tape recorder, pocket organizer, business card, video camcorder
Home business potential:	Yes
Staff required:	Not initially
Handicapped opportunity:	No
Hidden costs:	Some states require a license

LOWDOWN:

Private investigators dig up information that others want to keep hidden. There is a good market for solo practitioners who support lawyers working for both criminal and civil cases. Specialization is dividing this field, as with so many other businesses. Computer crime is rising, and those who can track it down are extremely valuable to a range of organizations, especially banks and businesses that are worried about employee theft or false workers' compensation claims. Background checks form another non-glamorous but profitable specialty.

Licensing is required in many parts of the U.S., and you will need experience with related types of work. Creativity is involved in finding the answers to puzzles that have troubled your clients, and well-developed listening skills are essential.

START-UP:

Outfitting your office will be your main outlay, along with a video camera or tape recorder for surveillance or interviews. Expect to spend at least $4,000 on equipment alone in the beginning; however, you will see a return fairly soon, because more clients than ever are flocking to private detectives to provide them with information that can be used against others (wrongful claims and philandering spouses).

BOTTOM LINE ADVICE:

This is your chance to play high-stakes *Unsolved Mysteries*. The real world of private detection does not mirror late-night movies, though. You may be on a crusade for truth, justice, and the American way, but you will find that many human beings out there don't see things your way. Your clients will value your services, of course, and you can build repeat business if you are an honest and effective investigator. Much investigative work genuinely helps people, by finding a lost family member, or preventing a crime. There may be a thrill of sorts to the chase, but resentment or even direct opposition will come your way in good measure. The hours are awful, and time management is almost impossible. Sometimes you will have trouble deciding whether the pressure or the tedium is worse.

PUBLIC PAY PHONE SERVICES

Start-up cost:	$5,000-$10,000
Potential earnings:	$20,000-30,000
Typical fees:	Income dependent on usage (high-traffic areas generate as much as $50 a day for each telephone installed)
Advertising:	Flyers, bulletin boards, location
Qualifications:	Communications technical skills, marketing ability
Equipment needed:	Pay phones, installation equipment
Home business potential:	Yes
Staff required:	No
Handicapped opportunity:	No
Hidden costs:	Insurance, repairs

LOWDOWN:

In many locations across the U.S. it is extremely difficult to find a pay phone. Small businesses are finding this niche in the huge telecommunications market. If you have telephone-industry experience, you may be able to ride this trend and create a viable business enterprise that fills in the gaps. An extremely refined marketing sense and skill at linking your callers to the network of major phone company services will define your ability to make a go of this. Some franchises are available.

To set up a public pay phone service, you need to first contact manufacturers of the phones to secure inventory. Equally important is your contact with the public utilities commission in your state. There may be regulations for you to comply with, so do your homework ahead of time.

A growing related service is prepaid phone cards, which can be imprinted with an advertiser's information. For instance, many drugstores now offer prepaid calling cards with their logo printed on the card; it's a good way for many companies to keep their name in front of their customers. You can market the same capability to as many companies as you can think of, then contract with a specialized card production house to finish the work.

START-UP:

Costs may be relatively high for a small business, depending on the type and configuration of services you plan to offer. Plan to invest at least $5,000 in this startup; and, if you decide to buy into a franchise, expect to pay an up-front fee of $10,000 or more. Earnings are dependent upon phone location and usage; prepaid phone cards generally retail for $5 and up.

BOTTOM LINE ADVICE:

This business will allow you to express your marketing agility to the utmost extent. It can be a real high to play the game that most people think is available only to telecommunications giants. The risks are significant, though, and there are a large group of businesses out there offering alternative types of communication services, from pager services to computer bulletin boards.

PUBLIC RELATIONS

Start-up cost:	$5,000-$10,000
Potential earnings:	$35,000-$75,000
Typical fees:	$50-$75 per hour, a bid-per-job basis, or monthly retainer
Advertising:	Networking and personal contacts, speeches before business or community groups, volunteer work for nonprofit organizations, telemarketing
Qualifications:	Strong communication and telephone skills, assertiveness and persuasiveness, ability to deal effectively with abstract concepts, high energy level
Equipment needed:	Computer with modem, printer, and fax, desktop publishing software, telephone headset, multiple phone lines with call-forwarding and conferencing features, office furniture, business card, letterhead, envelopes
Home business potential:	Yes
Staff required:	No
Handicapped opportunity:	Yes
Hidden costs:	Slow starting time; expect two years before profit

LOWDOWN:

As with so many other fields, the demand for PR is growing. At the same time, corporations are cutting their public relations staffs (usually the first to go in the age of downsizing). The work is definitely being farmed out, so public relations is ideal for a home-based business. Relationships with clients take time to develop, though, and depend in part on your network of contacts in the media. When a small company has a breakthrough new product, when advertising is too expensive, when an organization needs to get its message across to the public, or when a negative situation occurs that needs a positive spin, your PR services can be invaluable. To attract media attention and interest, you will need outstanding writing and speaking skills, a healthy dose of creativity, awareness of what the different types of media (trade journals, the nightly news shows) are hungry for, and an ability to put all the pieces together. It's fun, yet tough to do well unless you're an animal at networking with influential media types.

START-UP:

A very well-equipped office is a must, and you will need to present yourself and your business at the level of polish and professionalism you are selling for your clients. Expect to spend at least $4,000 on your office and equipment; bill at least $50-$75 per hour for your expertise.

BOTTOM LINE ADVICE:

For creative, dynamic, and above all energetic people, public relations is a wonderful field. If you thrive on relationships with many different individuals and organizations and love the stimulation of constant change, you should consider making PR your business. As a solo practitioner, you'll start with small projects and gradually expand your network and contacts to take on more complex projects. Not everyone has the skills and attributes to make a success of PR, although many people are out there trying. You will need to produce results; recognize that your business will take tremendous time and effort to grow. Marketing your own services must be a priority even as you complete one project after another for your clients. Media representatives can be fickle; getting publicity for your clients will require new angles and ideas each time to catch the media's attention.

ADVICE FROM THE EXPERTS

What sets your business apart from others like it?

Eric Yaverbaum, President of the New York City-based Jericho Promotions, says his soaring public relations business is unique because of how often the company itself is in the press. "We're on national TV regularly, and we've been written about in the *Wall Street Journal*. Our customers know we're in a league of our own in terms of creativity."

Things you couldn't do without:

Yaverbaum says he couldn't do without a fax machine, mailing list database, multiple phone lines, and E-mail.

Marketing tips/advice:

"Hire the right people to establish credibility . . . you're buying their experience and capitalizing on it. Doing that has saved me at least ten years of pounding the pavement. Also, when you lose someone, you can turn it into an opportunity to bring in new business. One of my people moved to a company that later became a client as a result of my professionalism in the matter."

If you had to do it all over again . . .

"I probably wouldn't do it . . . starting a business is a tough road for anyone. I guess I liked it best when the company was small enough to have a lot of fun."

PUBLIC SPEAKING CONSULTANT

Start-up cost:	$5,000-$10,000
Potential earnings:	$30,000-$45,000
Typical fees:	$75 per hour or a flat rate ($500-$1,500, depending on type of service provided)
Advertising:	Yellow Pages, business directories, association mailings, and direct mail
Qualifications:	Degree in speech communication
Equipment needed:	Resource/educational materials, TV/VCR unit, video camera (to tape your client and review afterward), basic office setup (computer, printer, fax, phone)
Home business potential:	Possibly (but unlikely)
Staff required:	No
Handicapped opportunity:	Possibly
Hidden costs:	Insurance, equipment maintenance

LOWDOWN:

Executives and other professionals are often called on to deliver speeches—only to fall flat on their faces due to inexperience or lack of preparation. That's where you come in. With your background in speech communication, you can help these floundering folks put together a presentation that is not only effective in its content, but also in its delivery. You can assist them in everything from written speech development and outlining to punchy delivery that gets repeated long after it's heard. The best part is, it's fairly easy work once you've established yourself. You can develop your own standard educational materials to coach professionals with, and you'll want to tape their "performance" to be able to critique. You will work with a wide array of professionals; from CEOs to physicians to engineers: the list of potentials goes on as far as your imagination permits. It's a straightforward kind of business, with many fixed rules and strategies for success. You'll really enjoy it best when you can deliver your own speeches—which you'll need to do sometimes to boost your business. Offer your services to associations and professional development directors.

START-UP:

You'll need some resource materials (books, tapes, etc.); purchase or lease a TV/VCR unit to allow playbacks of performances for review. Finally, you'll need to have some basic office equipment to run a smooth operation (include a computer, printer, fax, and phone system). With some hard work in the area of promotion, you can expect to earn $30,000-$45,000 per year.

BOTTOM LINE ADVICE:

Diversify yourself as much as possible—include small business owners who need to make presentations (contact your local Chamber of Commerce) and university officials who would like an outside opinion. If you have a degree in speech therapy, you could add on a multitude of services. The point is, you have a huge market—just be smart enough to fully develop it, and you'll do well.

RARE BOOK DEALER/SEARCH SERVICE

Start-up cost:	$5,000-$10,000
Potential earnings:	$20,000-$40,000
Typical fees:	$10-$15 plus a percentage of sale on book (based on your markup)
Advertising:	Yellow Pages, book industry publications, referrals from bookstores
Qualifications:	Good organizational skills and excellent follow-up ability
Equipment needed:	Computer, printer, fax/modem, phone with 800 number, on-line services
Home business potential:	Yes
Staff required:	No
Handicapped opportunity:	Yes
Hidden costs:	On-line services and phone bills

LOWDOWN:

Some avid readers will go to extraordinary lengths to find a used or rare book that they'd relish having in their private collection. Whether you're providing this service in addition to running a bookstore (as many searchers do) or running it as a separate business, you'll need to be highly detail-oriented and well-organized to make this business profitable. The good news is, there are plenty of publications that you can subscribe to, and these provide monthly listings of what books are currently available through other dealers. Sometimes, you'll be lucky enough to work out an even trade (and maximize your own profit on the book you're selling to the customer). Most often, however, you'll derive your income from a search fee ($10-$15 in some areas) and a sales commission on the book itself (which you will have priced accordingly to suit your bank account's needs). The older and more rare the book, the harder it is to locate—but if you can manage to drum up one yellow-paged copy, your earnings could be quite high on just one book.

START-UP:

It will take between $5,000-$10,000 to get you started with your computer and on-line searches; expect to spend $1,000 or so on advertising in your first year. If you are good at what you do, you can see income potentials of $20,000-$40,000 per year.

BOTTOM LINE ADVICE:

The stress level is actually quite low in this field, and you can pretty much search for a book at your own pace. However, you don't get paid as much for looking as you do for finding—so use computer on-line services to expedite your searches.

REAL ESTATE APPRAISER

Start-up cost:	$7,000-$15,000
Potential earnings:	$75,000-$100,000
Typical fees:	$300 per house, more for commercial property
Advertising:	Referrals from banks and mortgage companies, networking
Qualifications:	License or certification based on your state's requirements
Equipment needed:	Computer, fax, modem, printer, suite software, appraisal software, on-line accounts, office furniture, 35mm camera, pager or mobile phone, car, business card, letterhead, envelopes
Home business potential:	Yes
Staff required:	No
Handicapped opportunity:	Possibly
Hidden costs:	Tuition for required courses, insurance, license and renewal fees, organizational dues, mileage

LOWDOWN:

Real estate investment has made fortunes for people in the recent past—and it has brought down large institutions as well. Appraising the value of land and buildings is becoming even more important (particularly with the glut of refinances happening during lower-interest rate periods), and the licensing processes are producing more skilled appraisers. Once you pass through the certification process by your state, you will have the opportunity to provide a service needed by home owners, home buyers, investors, commercial property developers, and the institutions that lend money. You will conduct research on the trends likely to affect real estate values, and much of this can now be done on-line. Demographic statistics, finance issues, and changes in building construction methods can all be relevant. Of course you will also physically inspect the location and structures that you are valuing. You will need a working knowledge of architecture and building materials to help make good judgments, and your grasp of the big picture will help you compare the property you are appraising to the rest of the local real estate.

START-UP:

As with other professions requiring certification, start-up costs are as high as $15,000. The office equipped to develop and produce appraisal reports is also expensive to set up, although you could possibly get away with purchasing used appraisal equipment. Considering that you'll be billing customers $300 per house (and more for commercial properties), you'll be able to invest in nicer equipment in a relatively short period of time.

BOTTOM LINE ADVICE:

Sellers want the value to be high, buyers want it to be low. You will need errors and omissions insurance with broad coverage as you are in some danger of being sued if your assessment results in negative consequences for an investor.

RECREATIONAL COUPON DISTRIBUTOR

Start-up cost:	$5,000-$10,000
Potential earnings:	$15,000-$35,000
Typical fees:	Advertising rates vary from $150-$3,000 per client
Advertising:	Yellow Pages, direct mail to recreational facilities, health clubs
Qualifications:	Good organizational skills
Equipment needed:	Computer with desktop publishing software, laser printer, stationery and rate cards/contracts, perhaps a delivery vehicle
Home business potential:	Yes
Staff required:	No (but you may want to get some commission-only salespeople and hire someone to distribute for you)
Handicapped opportunity:	Possibly
Hidden costs:	Printing and paper costs are skyrocketing; keep a watchful eye to make sure your rates cover costs

LOWDOWN:

Everyone likes to have a good time—and everyone likes a good deal, too. That's why coupon books for recreational activities are such sure bets; they'll be read, kept, and used better than any other kind of coupon (except food coupons, of course). Your mission is to sell those in the recreation industry on giving some of their advertising dollars to you—then to make sure that your package is enticing enough to gain the interest of potential customers. If you produce the coupon books too cheaply, they'll get tossed like any other piece of junk mail; spend some money on a decent desktop publishing system that allows you to create your own innovative ads, then work with printers to get the best deals on paper and printing costs. Ask your printer early in the process how to best save money; familiarize yourself with the printing process so that you have a clear understanding of how and where you can save. Plan your distribution system well, and count on hiring at least one person to distribute. You won't have the time to do it all yourself.

START-UP:

You should be able to stay in the $5,000-$10,000 range to get this business off the ground; primarily, you'll be spending it on your computer system and travel/mileage or phone expenses you'll incur in trying to build sales. However, if you work hard and don't mind putting in lots of long hours, you could make $15,000-$35,000 or more at this one.

BOTTOM LINE ADVICE:

Your business will hinge on your reputation; you might want to join your local Chamber of Commerce for networking and credibility purposes, or become active in other community organizations.

REMANUFACTURING: LASER PRINTER CARTRIDGES

Start-up cost:	$5,000-$15,000
Potential earnings:	$30,000-$40,000
Typical fees:	$75 gross, per cartridge, is typical
Advertising:	Newspapers, trade journals, referrals, networking, direct mail
Qualifications:	Sales, marketing, and organizational skills
Equipment needed:	Delivery van, computer, printer, copier, fax, office furniture, storage area with shelving
Home business potential:	Yes
Staff required:	No
Handicapped opportunity:	No
Hidden costs:	Insurance, delivery costs, vehicle maintenance, inventory

LOWDOWN:

Laser printers are everywhere. The cartridges are extremely expensive, and a lively industry has grown to remanufacture used cartridges and replace them for businesses at a lower cost than purchasing a new one. Everyone from graphic designers to accountants are in need of your services, so you should have little trouble developing a client base if you can provide rapid response to orders and a range of related materials. This is definitely a niche market, but if you can find and service it, you can build your business into a profitable enterprise.

START-UP:

You will need to equip your own office, and you will need some way of delivering your products to the customer. Inventory is required but should be kept to the minimum needed for rapid response to customer calls. Since you'll charge an average of $75 per replacement cartridge, be sure to cover your own costs (such as mileage and materials) in your fee structure.

BOTTOM LINE ADVICE:

The market for your materials is there; your job is to find and serve it. Educating your customers about the ecological and financial rewards of recycling laser cartridges will be a challenge. It will take a determined marketing effort to develop this business—watch costs carefully.

RENTAL BUSINESS

Start-up cost:	$5,000-$15,000+
Potential earnings:	$30,000-$100,000+
Typical fees:	Depends on what you are renting and for how long (could be $15-$125 per rental)
Advertising:	Trade magazines, Yellow Pages, specialty magazines
Qualifications:	Good organizational and bookkeeping skills
Equipment needed:	Dolly, moving pads, truck/trailer (depends; the size of your rental equipment may range from chairs and tables to home hospital care equipment to Rototillers)
Home business potential:	Yes
Staff required:	No
Handicapped opportunity:	Yes
Hidden costs:	Repairs, insurance

LOWDOWN:

The rental business is a solid, recession-proof one because people always seem to need tools, equipment, or appliances on a short-term basis. If they don't happen to have a few hundred bucks lying around or a well-stocked neighbor to mooch off of, they'll need to come to you for that deep-cleaning vacuum or Rototiller. Salesmanship and advertising are going to be your best friends. Nail down the parameters of what it is you are interested in renting, and develop strong product knowledge. Be professional and capable about setting up any furniture or equipment once you've delivered it. You should be organized and efficient so you can turn around and make another delivery. The ability to keep books and track merchandise as it comes and goes will keep the money rolling in.

START-UP:

There could be a little or a lot in the start-up ($5,000-$15,000), depending on what you've decided to rent and whether you have a truck or not (you could even get by with a trailer at first). If you are doing home health care rentals, be prepared for the insurance companies to get their cut. Charge for use of the equipment by the hour plus mileage. You could earn in the range of $30,000-$100,000.

BOTTOM LINE ADVICE:

Let your people skills shine through and service your customers. You may need to give up your weekends and holidays and hire a second person to help with loading, but if you take care of your customers, word will get around and before you know it, you will have more business than you know what to do with.

RESIDENCE FOR THE ELDERLY

Start-up cost:	$10,000 (plus property cost or rental)
Potential earnings:	$15,000-$40,000
Typical fees:	$600-$1,000 per month per client
Advertising:	Referrals from community groups, church bulletin boards, word of mouth
Qualifications:	Excellent organizing ability, hospitable personality, genuine concern for the welfare of older persons, good reputation in the community
Equipment needed:	One or more easily accessible bedrooms, suitable furniture, bathroom with special handrails, dining space, efficient kitchen
Home business potential:	Yes
Staff required:	You will not be able to carry out 100 percent of the tasks required, 100 percent of the time but will need reliable backup workers occasionally
Handicapped opportunity:	No
Hidden costs:	Insurance, food (may have residents with special dietary requirements), possible home alterations

LOWDOWN:

In most regions of the U.S., there is an enormous need for housing for older people who do not wish to live alone but do not require nursing-home care. Many of the elderly cannot find affordable apartments or do not have family nearby and prefer to live with others. Making your own home or a second rental property into a residence for the elderly can be a rewarding business. You will rarely have a vacancy if you can "knit" your residents into a cheerful family unit and meet their day-to-day needs for food, shelter, companionship, and amusement. Many families who are caring for one or more of their own parents find that adding another elderly resident provides many benefits, including compatible company and increased family income.

START-UP:

Equipping your home for older residents may require few changes, or you may need to do extensive work. Be sure to check on state and local requirements when you are in the planning stage for your new venture. You may already own the furniture needed, or the residents may bring personal possessions, so the costs here will vary also (from $10,000-$100,000). Providing meals will challenge your budgeting and organizational skills, as well as your enthusiasm for cooking. At $600-$1,000 per month, you can expect to reap an income of $15,000-$40,000 or more.

BOTTOM LINE ADVICE:

Not everyone is aware of the possibilities that providing a residence for the "well" elderly can bring to an energetic, compassionate entrepreneur. Your challenges will come in planning the physical changes needed in your home, and in running the business so that it doesn't overwhelm your own life.

RESTORATION SERVICES

Start-up costs:	$5,000-$15,000
Potential earnings:	$30,000-$45,000
Typical fees:	Varied and dependent upon scope of project
Advertising:	Yellow Pages, local newspapers, business cards and flyers in antique shops and interior decorators
Equipment needed:	Sanders, strippers, steel wool, rags to start
Qualifications:	Thorough knowledge and skill in restoring a variety of surfaces
Home business potential:	Yes
Staff required:	No
Handicapped opportunity:	No
Hidden costs:	Insurance, chemical supply and disposal costs

LOWDOWN:

Many people value hardwood floors, old or antique furniture, antique ceramic fixtures, and old carpet—and would rather restore them than buy something new. These services are especially needed after a natural disaster—floods, earthquakes, and fires. For large clients such as offices, apartments, or hotels, repairing carpet and restoring tile and floors are preferable to replacing them. Refinishing floors, especially, can be time-consuming and labor-intensive, and people are often too busy or lack the know-how to bother with it. That's why there's a market for these services. You can start simply refinishing furniture with strippers, steel wool, rags, and stain, and later move into more complicated projects. You could opt for a franchise, some of which run close to $20,000. These often offer training, tools, and materials to start you off and are worth investigating.

START-UP:

Your start-up costs will largely be determined by your decision to go it alone or invest in a franchise operation. If you decide to wing it, be prepared to spend $15,000 or more in addition to the $5,000 initial investment you make to cover necessities such as EPA training for disposal of hazardous waste. Your fees will be varied according to the scope of each project, but could be as low as $100 or as high as several thousand.

BOTTOM LINE ADVICE:

Cultivate a variety of contacts—antique dealers, interior designers, building and operations managers of companies and hotels. Have a ready supply of business cards and a simple brochure or flyer outlining your services. If you have a knack for writing, submit articles to regional antique publications or send news releases to the antiques or home improvement editor of your local paper. When dealing with customers, get a deposit to cover cost of materials. Submit a proposal detailing the work you plan to do. After coming to an agreement with the customer, draw up a contract signed by the consumer before proceeding with the work.

10 Tips on Attracting Investors

1. Know what type of capital you can raise: equity capital (from wealthy individuals or venture capital companies), or debt capital (borrowing against cash flow or your business assets).

2. Know your investors' needs. Remember that investors have needs, too, and be sure you approach those whose needs you can fulfill.

3. Start with your own money, from savings, a second mortgage, etc. This demonstrates your commitment to the business. Spend it on preparing a business plan, building a prototype, executing a market study. Then show these to potential investors.

4. Know what you need. Plan to grow your business in stages, know what you need for each stage, and seek only that.

5. Minimize the risk to your investors, by minimizing your irreversible capital expenditures. For instance, buy off-the-shelf equipment that could, if necessary, be put to alternate uses.

6. Find a big name investor, someone with name recognition in your field, who will indicate to other prospects that you are promising. If Bill Gates were to invest in your computer business, other investors would follow.

7. Sell yourself as well as your business. Show that you are reliable, have honored former commitments, and have not abandoned ventures in midstream.

8. Anticipate objections. Real or imagined, objections to your proposals must be acknowledged, and you must explain your contingency plans.

9. Manage the process. Set a schedule; coordinate finding customers with finding investors; form a team with your lawyers, accountants, etc.; follow up on every approach and every agreement.

10. Follow through. Once you have the money, don't wait to get the business off the ground. This is no longer a hobby, and investors are looking for results, now.

RUBBER STAMP BUSINESS

Start-up cost:	$5,000-$10,000
Potential earnings:	$40,000-$60,000
Typical fees:	Anywhere from $5-$15 per stamp
Advertising:	Mail order, direct mail, newspapers
Qualifications:	None (you can be trained by a printing professional)
Equipment needed:	Computer with laser printer, photopolymer system (you can subcontract the larger orders that need to be made of rubber)
Home business potential:	Yes
Staff required:	No
Handicapped opportunity:	Yes
Hidden costs:	Materials can run high (as much as $1,000 per year)

LOWDOWN:

The rubber stamp business gets the stamp of approval from many entrepreneurial resources. Why? Because it's a relatively easy way to make steady money from a simple product. The variety of stamps you can produce is mind-boggling; think of the last time you went into a retail store and saw literally hundreds of choices (from frogs to stars to computers). Now think of the possibilities in the business world: small businesses need to have return address stamps; they're cheaper in the long haul than labels and more readily available as well. You can sell wholesale, retail, or mail order with this business, and expect to generate immediate interest if you introduce your company with introductory specials and discounts for new customers. You'll work with printers and graphics people who can provide you with all the background and technical information you need . . . so what's to lose from a product line so easy to produce?

START-UP:

You'll need to invest in some equipment ($3,000-$5,000) at the outset. If you're buying a franchise version of this business (which could provide you with all the training you'll need), expect to spend another $10,000 minimum on licensing fees. But, since you'll be marketing your inexpensive ($3-$15 each) product to the masses, you stand a good chance of making a go of this one.

BOTTOM LINE ADVICE:

The investment's not too high, the income potential is high . . . what more could you ask?

SALES TRAINER

Start-up cost:	$5,000-$8,000
Potential earnings:	$40,000-$60,000
Typical fees:	$2,000-$3,000 per engagement
Advertising:	Networking, referrals, trade journals, memberships in business and community groups
Qualifications:	Extensive record of success in sales, demonstrated effectiveness as a trainer, good ability to sell your own services
Equipment needed:	Office furniture, computer, suite software, presentation software, laser printer and/or color printer, cellular phone, fax, modem, business card, letterhead, envelopes, marketing materials, training materials
Home business potential:	Yes
Staff required:	No
Handicapped opportunity:	No
Hidden costs:	Preparation of training manuals and handouts, overheads

LOWDOWN:

Sales is a skilled profession, and as the hierarchy at most companies gets flatter, the managers have less and less time to train their vital salespeople in the techniques and approaches that really work. Your ability to transfer your wide experience and your repertoire of proven techniques for getting in the door, making a case clearly, and closing the sale will be your stock-in-trade as you respond to this growing corporate need. You may find it effective to focus on companies making the types of products you have sold (pharmaceuticals, toys, etc.), or you may target a certain size of company or region of the country. It can be very difficult to become established as a sales trainer. Among the most profitable are trainers who have continuing projects from one or two large organizations whose confidence they have gained. Be sure to plan for the cost and time you must spend on marketing as you develop your own business.

START-UP:

Equipping your office to function for your business and produce whatever training materials you plan to supply will be your main expenses (at least $3,000). Travel can also be costly, depending on your range of operations and ability to bill expenses to your clients. You can make $40,000 or more a year with this venture.

BOTTOM LINE ADVICE:

A effective sales trainer can make a significant difference in a company's sales figures. Salespeople, though, are a tough audience. They don't usually want to sit and listen; they want to get up and take over, or take off. You'll need excellent presentation techniques to keep you audience's attention and convince them of the value of your ideas. As you become successful, make sure that you track your results and use them in your marketing efforts. This will help set you apart from the many, many competitors in this field. Referrals and repeat business are the real key to a healthy bottom line for your enterprise.

ADVICE FROM THE EXPERTS

What sets your business apart from others like it?

Joan Thomas, a training consultant based in Akron, Ohio, says her ability to work with several different industries is paramount to her success. "I can work with anyone from banking to medical to manufacturing—and really listen to their needs before putting together a program for them."

Things you couldn't do without:

A computer with laser printer, fax machine, and index cards for brainstorming sessions are all Thomas says she needs to keep her business in business.

Marketing tips/advice:

"Network, network, network! Ask for referrals, and help others who can help you."

If you had to do it all over again . . .

"I would have more audiovisual products . . . in this business, you need stuff that's current, easy to transport, and yet economical."

SECURITY SYSTEMS CONSULTANT

Start-up cost:	$5,000-$15,000
Potential Earnings:	$65,000-$75,000
Typical fees:	$75/hour for established consultants
Advertising:	Networking, Yellow Pages, direct mail, writing articles
Qualifications:	Security or crime prevention experience, academic degree or experience with a police department, writing ability, ability to draft and read blueprints, knowledge of architectural software, knowledge of electronic equipment
Equipment needed:	PC with modem, printer, and software, fax; camera and tools, office furniture, business card, letterhead
Home business potential:	Yes
Staff required:	No
Handicapped opportunity:	No
Hidden costs:	Errors and omissions insurance, keeping up with trends in security technology through publication subscriptions and conferences

LOWDOWN:

Consulting about security systems is a subset of the security field (and of the consulting field too, for that matter). If you have the extensive background required, you can develop an extremely successful business in the design phase of security consulting. You will visit the location needing a security system—a museum, a store, an expensive home—and assess the security issues that must the addressed. Good drafting and writing skills are important, because your next step is to draw up architectural plans as they affect the security system you are recommending. A well-written report presents the results of your investigation to your clients. The need for this service is growing faster than the pool of individuals with the skills and experience to meet it.

START-UP:

Setting up your office with the computer equipment powerful enough to do architectural drawings and produce professional-looking reports is the principal cost. You'll typically spend between $5,000-$15,000 to get started, and bill out at $75 per hour after you're established.

BOTTOM LINE ADVICE:

Challenges and innovation make security systems consulting an exciting field. You will know that you are providing a much-needed service to your client organizations and individuals. You will need to plan for several years of development before your business becomes accepted and profitable. On top of all the qualifications listed above is the necessity to be very good. What you recommend has to work, in the real world. Many times you will be working under difficult circumstances or in crisis mode.

SEMINAR (SPEAKERS) SERVICE

Start-up cost:	$5,000-$10,000
Potential earnings:	$30,000-$50,000
Typical fees:	$125-$500 per speaking engagement; service earns 25-40 percent of this
Advertising:	Press releases to newspapers, radio, business/civic organizations
Qualifications:	Managerial and marketing skills, expertise in planning and promotion
Equipment needed:	Computer and printer, tape recorder and transcription equipment, business card, letterhead, envelopes
Home business potential:	Yes
Staff required:	No
Handicapped opportunity:	Yes
Hidden costs:	Transcriptions and tape reproduction costs

LOWDOWN:

If you have a sense of what trends are catching the attention of the public, you may be able to create a business by arranging for speakers on these topics. If you can organize appealing seminars and publicize them effectively, you can make a good living in this area. You can make some of the presentations yourself, but in order to be very successful you will need to have a list of speakers available who can make amusing or captivating presentations that stay with the audience long after they leave the meeting. Enjoyable seminars have a sense of give and take, with a lively speaker and active participation from the audience. These satisfied customers will be your best advertising; they will return with their friends for future sessions. An add-on business is sales of presentation tapes or transcripts. If you are a bit of a showman yourself, combine those skills with a good event planning skills and this business may be expressly for you.

START-UP:

Each seminar requires extensive planning and advertising. You will need a computer ($1,500-$2,500) to prepare materials and flyers, and to keep track of your database of effective speakers and satisfied customers. Mailings will cost you $500 and up for each event. Your speakers can earn $125-$500 or more for each speech they deliver, and your percentage of that could be as low as 25 percent and as high as 40 percent.

BOTTOM LINE ADVICE:

Bringing together a group of people for an enjoyable seminar is almost like putting on a play. There is a sense of excitement when a presentation goes well. You can get satisfaction from enabling people to learn something they need or want to know. You are also providing a service to your speakers, who rely on you to organize and support their work. Not all seminars are well-attended, though. You may have chosen the wrong topic, or bad weather may interfere with the success of the meeting. It takes a very detail-oriented person to make all the pieces come together in an event-promotional business like this one.

SHIPPING/CUSTOMS CONSULTANT

Start-up cost:	$10,000-$20,000
Potential earnings:	$50,000-$75,000
Typical fees:	$75-$150 per hour or a per-job rate
Advertising:	Yellow Pages, business publications, referrals
Qualifications:	Extensive background in foreign shipping regulations and international law
Equipment needed:	Computer with fax/modem and printer, phone and additional phone line to leave on for 24-hour business/information
Home business potential:	Yes
Staff required:	No
Handicapped opportunity:	Yes
Hidden costs:	Insurance, on-line services, other business resources

LOWDOWN:

Product manufacturers know a lot about making a good product—but often, they need help in getting it to their potential markets, particularly with the overseas opportunities that exist now more than ever before. As a shipping/customs consultant, you can help them learn the ins and outs of dealing with foreign distribution channels. Your expertise will be offered in everything from letters of credit to currency conversion and customs regulations (which do have a tendency to change according to the political climate in many countries). You're likely spend only a few hours with each customer. Your business will be heavily dependent upon word of mouth; referrals are your path to greater income potential.

START-UP:

You'll need about $10,000-$20,000 to get started in this business, mainly to cover your computer equipment and fax/modem line in addition to advertising. You will need to keep on top of changes in shipping regulations and international law, so a modem and on-line service would do you a world of good (even though it could become a little costly). Your income potential is $50,000-$75,000, based on a consulting fee of $75-$150 per hour; often, you'll opt for a flat per-job rate.

BOTTOM LINE ADVICE:

It is difficult, with all of the changes occurring daily in the world economy, to stay on top of every detail affecting international shipping and customs law. You'll really need to be on the ball, because one mistake could cost your reputation—especially on the Internet, where notes about good and bad services are often posted. Stay in control of your information.

SHORT-TERM AUTO RENTAL SERVICE

Start-up cost:	$5,000-$15,000
Potential earnings:	$25,000+
Typical fees:	$30-$40 per day
Advertising:	Radio, newspaper, direct mail, flyers, referrals from auto repair services and dealers
Qualifications:	Excellent organizational skills
Equipment needed:	Rental vehicles, office furniture, computer, printer, marketing materials, cellular phone
Home business potential:	Yes
Staff required:	Yes
Handicapped opportunity:	Yes
Hidden costs:	Insurance, vehicle maintenance and replacement

LOWDOWN:

In most communities, rental cars are available only at the busy, congested airport sites that serve long-distance travelers. But many people need to rent a vehicle for a short period and do not wish to struggle with the national chain car rental system. They would be glad to obtain a vehicle from your convenient, cost-effective service while their cars are in the shop. You could also be a subcontractor for dealerships and auto body repair services to provide the "loaner" cars for their customers. Other market niches would be vans, which are almost impossible to rent in many areas, and luxury cars, which many people would like to rent for a short period.

START-UP:

The type of vehicles you offer will define your costs (you could get by on about $5,000). Will it be rent-a-heap, luxury-for-less, or convenient compacts? Will you buy four-year-old cream puffs or lease several vans? Depending on your choice, you could earn $25,000 in the beginning (at a daily rental rate of $30-$40).

BOTTOM LINE ADVICE:

The challenge here is to distinguish yourself from the national chains. The excellence of your service will set you apart, and the convenience you bring to your customers' lives. You'll need to be creative in getting your message to your potential market. Finally, excellent management skills are required to keep track of services, drivers, billing, and costs.

SIGHTSEEING EXCURSIONS

Start-up cost:	$5,000-$10,000
Potential earnings:	$20,000-$45,000
Typical fees:	$5-$20 per person per trip
Advertising:	Local interest magazines, community bulletin boards, neighborhood flyers, newspaper entertainment sections
Qualifications:	Driver's license, enthusiasm, love of people
Equipment needed:	Van or bus
Home business potential:	Yes
Staff required:	No
Handicapped opportunity:	No
Hidden costs:	Insurance, vehicle maintenance

LOWDOWN:

Conducting a successful sightseeing excursion is more than getting a bunch of people into a bus and driving them around. Instead, you need a theme or idea, and you need to do a spoken presentation as you travel with your customers. Some excursion services tour Hollywood homes of the stars, while others take groups to places of historic interest such as Civil War battlefields. A sightseeing excursion can be a safe and fun way to explore a new city or to venture into the countryside. Depending on your area, you could offer fall foliage tours, visits to an Amish farm, or a tour of ethnic neighborhoods and bakeries. The way you frame your business will define advertising necessary to bring in customers.

START-UP:

The vehicle you rent, lease, or buy will be the main expense; with your advertising costs figured in, you may spend between $5,000-$10,000 getting this business off the ground. However, you could stand to make between $20,000-$45,000 annually, so your return on investment should have a quick turnaround.

BOTTOM LINE ADVICE:

You are going to have the most success at presenting the type of tour that you yourself would like to take. What are your own special interests? Can you spot a herd of grazing deer at dusk? Have you visited every antique shop within 50 miles? Do you know the twisted streets of the old part of your city like the back of your hand? You are the leader, the planner, the host of this experience. Making the excursion your own will make it wonderful for your riders.

SMALL BUSINESS CONSULTANT

Start-up cost:	$5,000-$15,000
Potential earnings:	$50,000-$150,000
Typical fees:	$900-$2,000/day
Advertising:	Word of mouth, referrals, presentations made to business groups, audiovisual materials, professional organizations
Qualifications:	Experience and expertise in all forms of marketing, management sense, communication skills, research, and planning ability
Equipment needed:	Office furniture, computer, suite software, printer, fax, business card, letterhead, envelopes
Home business potential:	Yes
Staff required:	No
Handicapped opportunity:	Yes
Hidden costs:	Make sure you get paid ASAP, as many of your clients who launch small businesses have little money to begin with

LOWDOWN:

As a small business consultant, you are the one with the knowledge and expertise to assess and solve many of the difficulties facing today's small businesses. Between complying with growing government regulations, integrating new technologies, and competing in a tightening economy, most small businesses are looking for consultants who have proved their ability to solve problems. This position offers variety, challenge, and respect—you are the bottom line.

START-UP:

A sizable time investment (and at least $5,000) is necessary to identify and approach your clients. Do research, send letters, do lunch. You should make at least $50,000 your first year.

BOTTOM LINE ADVICE:

You must know what you are talking about at all times. While you are selling your experience, companies are buying concrete solutions to their problems, even though the benefits from your work will not always be immediately apparent. Be able to apply your skills to your own business as well as to your clients'.

SNOW PLOW SERVICE

Start-up cost:	$5,000-$15,000
Potential earnings:	$25,000-$35,000
Typical fees:	$25-$40 per job
Advertising:	Yellow Pages, seasonally in newspapers
Qualifications:	Must have a driver's license
Equipment needed:	4-wheel-drive truck, snow blower, shovel, snow plow for truck; pager or cellular phone may be helpful
Home business potential:	Yes
Staff required:	No
Handicapped opportunity:	Not typically
Hidden costs:	Liability insurance

LOWDOWN:

There's nothing like the convenience of having a snow plow service remove the mountain of snow on your driveway—or your roof—in blizzard conditions—and convenience is the main reason you'd decide to be in this business in the first place. After all, if you've already got a heavy-duty vehicle that needs only a plow attachment, your start-up would be relatively small and the potential for earning quite high. You would be on-call for homes and businesses the majority of your winter time, and if you advertise in the right places, you could be in the enviable position of having to farm out some of your work to another service like yours. Obviously, you should only consider this business opportunity if you live in a climate with cold, snowy winters—since this business is dependent upon the white stuff. Still, you could intentionally make it a seasonal business, and paint houses in the summer. Many folks do exactly that.

START-UP:

You can start your operation small by investing only in a shovel and snow blower at a cost of approximately $500. However, you won't be able to clear anything larger than an average driveway or sidewalk with this equipment. To clear larger parking lots, you'll need a truck and a snow plow. Don't forget to set aside money for vehicle upkeep and repairs. Bill your services by the size of the job.

BOTTOM LINE ADVICE:

It's a great and necessary service you provide . . . and it can be profitable if you don't mind being out in Ice Station Zebra. However, this is a seasonal business, so be sure to make enough to stretch you through the warmth of summer!

SOFTWARE DEVELOPMENT/ CD-ROM PACKAGING

Start-up cost:	$5,000-$10,000
Potential earnings:	$25,000-$50,000
Typical fees:	$100 per hour, $1,000 average per-job fee, or percentage of profits
Advertising:	Shareware distribution, computer bulletin board systems, magazines and user groups, reselling by consultants
Qualifications:	Ideas for software that will work and appeal to a market; programming skills or ability to work with programmers
Equipment needed:	Computer, modem, fax, office furniture
Home business potential:	Yes
Staff required:	No
Handicapped opportunity:	Yes
Hidden costs:	Attendance at trade shows

LOWDOWN:

This is how many world-renowned software companies got their start. And some very well-known programs are based on a home-developed product. Another approach to this field is to develop an add-on utility for a popular program. You are most likely to have success in creating a software package for a field you already specialize in, such as accounting or database-building, or you could produce and publish a computer game. Your creativity and ability to make the most of new technologies such as CD-ROM will define your chances in this demanding field. The conventional business activities of networking, marketing, and selling are just as important here as in any other type of enterprise. The Internet may be all the avenue you need, though, to reach your market.

START-UP:

You'll need a high-end computer ($2,000-$5,000), of course, but you probably wouldn't even think of launching a business like this unless you already spend hours experimenting with programs and programming. Try to charge at least part of your fee up front; the computer software market is extremely volatile, and today's great idea could become tomorrow's canned project. If you could manage to get a $500 deposit per job, you'll cover at least some of your time.

BOTTOM LINE ADVICE:

If you've always wondered why no one has developed a program to make life easier in your industry, use CD-ROM technology in a dynamic way to illustrate home repair techniques, or blow up the galaxy in 3-D color, now is your chance to try it yourself. You can express your creative, practical, or imaginative side as you develop your program. Selling your program via the shareware route can be slow. This business is not a route to instant wealth. You will probably need to advertise, market, and network at trade shows to achieve success. Not everyone who is good at writing code enjoys these more social activities.

SOFTWARE ENGINEER/PROGRAMMER

Start-up cost:	$5,000-$15,000
Potential earnings:	$50,000-$100,000
Typical fees:	$50-$75 per hour or a 15 to 20 percent commission on end product
Advertising:	Personal contacts in trade and business associations, referrals from computer stores, opportunities to teach classes on programming to business people
Qualifications:	Two to five years of programming background in several languages and platforms, ability to understand and speak knowledgeably with clients about business needs, ability to learn quickly and keep up with new technologies
Equipment needed:	High-end computer with modem, printer, and network system file server, communications, compiler, and miscellaneous software, on-line services, office furniture, business card, letterhead, envelopes
Home business potential:	Yes
Staff required:	No
Handicapped opportunity:	Yes
Hidden costs:	Errors and omissions insurance

LOWDOWN:

Since so many companies are downsizing, programming is increasingly being done by freelancers rather than in-house. Your reputation for effective and efficient programming will make your business as a software engineer a success. You may specialize in adapting a commercially available package to meet the specific needs of your client organization. Other software engineers develop programs customized specifically for one business. Analysis of business issues is essential. What does your client really need, and what will be the best way of meeting those needs? Excellent business knowledge and the people skills required to learn enough about your client's operations will be necessary. Writing the program, loading it into the client's computer system, implementing it, and debugging it are the major elements of this field. You must be very familiar with the ever-changing world of hardware and software in order to develop a product that your client can take to market.

START-UP:

You'll need to set up an office for yourself, but if you have the expertise for this business, you probably have much of the hardware and software required already. Subscribe to as many computer publications as you can to stay on top of developments. Charge between $50-$75 per hour or negotiate a fair commission for your work on each project.

BOTTOM LINE ADVICE:

It is satisfying to produce a program that makes a client's business work. Knowing what information is needed and writing code or adapting a commercial package are high-level activities that can produce a real sense of achievement. As long as you understand the business language of the field in which you are working, you will be able to build on your successes and keep new projects rolling in. Your expertise will be highly valued and you can choose your hours. Marketing yourself can be difficult for the introverted people who excel at writing code. Projects can be long, so you need to develop a charging policy that keeps funds coming in. Judging what to charge for a complex project is not easy either. Most of all, this is often work done under pressure. Clients may be both demanding and unappreciative.

Dynamic Goal-Setting

If you want to succeed in business, you need to start with a good goal-setting program. Seek out professional help in this area if you are not sure how to identify and set your own goals.

Here are just a few tips to get you started:

1. **Remember to make your goals specific.** The only goals that stand a chance of being achieved are the ones that are clear enough to become part of a mind-set and visualization process. The clearer the goal, the easier to accomplish.

2. **Have a deadline for achievement.** You can have a terrific goal, but wander around aimlessly without a drop-dead date for its achievement. Someone once said that a goal is a dream with a deadline.

3. **Consider and anticipate your obstacles.** Know where the pitfalls might occur, and devise a plan to work around such impediments.

Above all else, make sure there is a personal benefit to achieving the goal, or it will not serve to motivate you. You need to reward yourself with a vacation if you sell one million dollars' worth of product, or you might not be able to see the benefit of working so hard to achieve that goal.

SURVEYOR

Start-up cost:	$5,000-$10,000
Potential earnings:	$35,000-$65,000
Typical fees:	Varies; can be as low as $125 or as high as several thousand per project
Advertising:	Business periodicals, referrals, relationship with architectural firms, civil engineering companies
Qualifications:	Degree/license in surveying
Equipment needed:	Surveying equipment, such as tripods and measuring devices
Home business potential:	Yes
Staff required:	No
Handicapped opportunity:	No
Hidden costs:	Travel, vehicle maintenance

LOWDOWN:

Surveyors are skilled in measuring land and buildings. They help landowners, mortgagors, municipalities, and real estate agents by determining the boundaries of parcels of land. Surveyors also assess the elevations of land for planning, construction, road projects, and so on. As a skilled surveyor you use your mathematical skills and detail orientation on a contract basis to supplement the work of organizations and governments. Land must be surveyed whenever it is sold, and inaccurate surveying has led to many lawsuits through the years. A mislocated fence or boundary wall can be a major problem to correct. Your surveying services will be called on by people and organizations anxious to avoid such disputes.

START-UP:

Your initial cash investment ($5,000-$10,000) will consist of surveying equipment and a vehicle. You'll also need to advertise your services, most likely through networking with city or township zoning officials. Have a decent set of business cards and present yourself well, and you could figure on an income between $35,000-$60,000 or more.

BOTTOM LINE ADVICE:

You will maximize your chance for developing a successful enterprise if you can make connections with active architectural firms, real estate agencies, and other organizations that often require surveying services. Accurate, on-time work will cement these good relationships.

TALENT AGENCY

Start-up cost:	$10,000-$15,000
Potential earnings:	$30,000-$50,000+
Typical fees:	10 percent flat fee of what your client makes
Advertising:	Industry trade publications, word of mouth
Qualifications:	You must be licensed by the state in which you operate. Some agencies must also be franchised by the labor union to which their talent belongs (such as Actors' Equity Association or Screen Actors Guild). In addition, some background in business, law, and/or entertainment would be useful
Equipment needed:	Computer, printer, fax, camera/video equipment, business card
Home business potential:	Yes
Staff required:	No
Handicapped opportunity:	Yes
Hidden costs:	Insurance, phone/travel expenses

LOWDOWN:

Talent comes in all shapes and sizes; your job is to figure out who's got it and who doesn't. Your representation may consist of actors, singers, writers, comedy acts, etc., or you can specialize in one area (such as modeling or animal performers). Some people will approach you, but in the beginning, you'll probably need to conduct some open casting calls. Advertise in local newspapers and through networking relationships with community theater directors and advertising agencies (both are likely candidates for providing talent for you to work with). It may also be helpful to align yourself with acting and vocal coaches, dance instructors, and other teaching professionals—they can provide you with a steady stream of talent, but can also help improve the talents of those you're already representing. The more added services you can provide, the better your chances of developing fine (and marketable) talent. In addition to a keen sense of talent, you'll need the ability to negotiate contracts, so some business and/or law background would be helpful.

START-UP:

If you own a talent agency, your fee has been predetermined by labor unions. This is to protect actors and others from getting ripped off by unscrupulous agents. You will receive a 10 percent (nonnegotiable) fee of whatever your talent makes, even if you did not book him. The only way you will be able to collect royalties and residuals is if you actually booked the talent yourself.

BOTTOM LINE ADVICE:

You get to meet people from all walks of life. Hopefully, you'll represent at least one future star who will take you along for a profitable ride. To really make it big, you'll have to go where the talent goes and that's to bigger cities. Be ready to handle unusual (and egomaniacal) personalities.

TAX PREPARATION SERVICE

Start-up cost:	$5,500-$15,000
Potential earnings:	$40,000-$100,000
Typical fees:	From $25-$50 per hour; more if complex
Advertising:	Referrals, networking, ads in local publications and Yellow Pages, direct mail
Qualifications:	An interest in people and their situations, patience, excellent math skills, thorough understanding of tax laws and calculations
Equipment needed:	Computer, phone, fax, office equipment (including copier), specialized tax software, reference manuals, insurance, business card, paper
Home business potential:	Yes
Staff required:	None
Handicapped opportunity:	Yes
Hidden costs:	Time and money for continuing education, if needed

LOWDOWN:

Income tax regulations and their associated forms are often too complicated for the average person to comprehend. Making heads and tails of tax forms, then, is a much-needed service and one that people often don't mind paying for (remind them that income tax preparation fees are tax-deductible, and you'll sell them even more on your service). You obviously need to have a thorough knowledge of tax law, tax preparation, and forms to succeed, but you don't need to study for a license unless you want certification as a CPA or other designation. This is complicated, detailed work; our tax laws are cumbersome and confusing. It would be quite beneficial to take a training course before you begin. This would not only ensure that your skills are adequate, but would give you a feel for whether this work is for you. Tax preparation can earn a talented, detail-oriented business owner a very nice income.

START-UP:

In addition to the usual computer and office equipment, detailed tax guides, special software, errors and omissions insurance, and a good quality printer and copier will be required. Depending on what you need, your office can be set up for as little as $3,500. Charge at least $25-$50 an hour for your services; more if the job looks complex.

BOTTOM LINE ADVICE:

Since people will always have to pay taxes, you will never run out of potential clients. IRS guidelines are complex and confusing to most citizens, so knowledgeable tax preparers are in great demand. To be a good preparer, though, requires constant upgrading of skills to meet the changes in forms and regulations. Tax preparation is seasonal, which means cash flow can be uneven; you might add other services to fill in the slower months.

TECHNICAL WRITER
(DOCUMENTATION AND ON-SCREEN TEXT)

Start-up cost:	$4,000-$8,000
Potential Earnings:	$30,000-$75,000
Typical fees:	$75+ per hour
Advertising:	Networking, trade publications, direct solicitation
Qualifications:	Writing and organizational skills, knowledge in specific technical areas
Equipment needed:	PC with modem and ink-jet or laser printer, word-processing and miscellaneous software, office furniture, business card
Home business potential:	Yes
Staff required:	No
Handicapped opportunity:	Yes
Hidden costs:	Time and expense in researching new technologies

LOWDOWN:

Technical writers usually take highly complex information and translate it into step-by-step instructions for the less skilled. Often, their work takes the form of manuals, proposals, software documentation, or even slide presentations for executives needing to explain or teach information to others.

This field covers two broad areas, print publications and on-line documentation. Both areas are growing explosively, and the supply of skilled writers, though high, does not meet the demand. While there are many kinds of freelance writers, there are relatively few who can produce technical materials. A technical writer needs technical knowledge (medical, engineering, etc.) in addition to verbal communications skills. The ability to explain technical products clearly, directly and effectively will set you apart. Marketing this skill must be an ongoing part of your business life.

On-line documentation is even more specialized. As anyone who has tried to use a computer "help" program knows, it's difficult to create one that can respond adequately to user questions. Many technical people cannot translate their vast knowledge into the simplest of terms, which is exactly what's needed in order for the new user to become expert enough in the program to write documentation. You will need to know everything about the technical topic or program and also have an acute awareness of how other people learn, read, and need to receive information.

START-UP:

Computer equipment will allow you to produce writing at your own office, but much of your work may be completed on your clients' premises. You should invest in a computer that is equivalent to or compatible with those of your clients ($1,500-$3,000). But, since you're billing out at $75 per hour and up, you'll be able to handle such overhead once you've got the clients rolling in.

BOTTOM LINE ADVICE:

This is the ideal field for people with excellent communications skills and a love of learning. Each new project takes you into a new area, connects you with new people in your client business, and asks the most of your ability to create and synthesize. Marketing your service is hard—and pricing projects can be even harder. It will take time to establish yourself; you must be able to produce good results under demanding, uncertain conditions.

Customer Service Tips

Getting and keeping customers is the challenge for any new business. Are your customers being serviced as well as they should be?

Here is a checklist of questions you can ask yourself from time to time:

❏ Are customers being helped in a timely manner? Are phones being answered promptly and cordially?

❏ Are your customer service representatives knowledgeable enough about your product or service?

❏ Do problems get resolved quickly and productively?

❏ Are your reps following up on a regular basis—especially to thank customers for their business?

❏ Are your customers receiving regular information, discounts, and other special offers from your company?

❏ Is your customer database being updated and added to constantly?

❏ Are your delivery services top-notch?

❏ Are all requests for materials (brochures, catalogs, etc.) being handled quickly and as professionally as possible?

❏ Is it easy for customers to order your product or service, or do they have to punch a million numbers into a phone to do so?

❏ Have you noticed a significant increase in referral business (a primary indication of excellent customer service)?

Customer service is not a one-shot deal; your business can only grow if you constantly maintain relationships and treat every customer as if he or she is a customer for life.

TELECOMMUNICATIONS CONSULTANT

Start-up cost:	$10,000-$15,000
Potential earnings:	$40,000-$75,000
Typical fees:	$50-$100 per hour
Advertising:	Referrals are the main source of jobs
Qualifications:	High-level telecommunications experience, business awareness, and interpersonal skills
Equipment needed:	Computer, software, printer, fax, modem, office furniture, business card, letterhead, envelopes
Home business potential:	Yes
Staff required:	No
Handicapped opportunity:	No
Hidden costs:	Business insurance, equipment maintenance, software upgrades

LOWDOWN:

You can offer what growing companies need but don't have in-house: superior electronic communications. As management flattens out and workers are spread across the country to be close to their customers, companies need more and more services to connect them. You will assess each client's needs, and advise them on which of the many services available are appropriate. Voice mail, video teleconferencing, and other telecommunications services are more and more in demand, and you will be able to build up a customer base of organizations needing the sophisticated services you can provide.

START-UP:

Telecommunications equipment is expensive, and you may need to acquire training in some of the growing areas for which you do not already have expertise. Initial investments of $10,000-$15,000 are not unheard of in this field. Being a valued technician, however, can earn you as much as $100 per hour (although, if you're just starting, you'll want to start at a more easily justifiable rate of $50 per hour).

BOTTOM LINE ADVICE:

People who have skills in the growing telecommunications field can build dynamic businesses offering the connections that their client organizations depend on. You will become a vital part of the businesses you serve; you will be operating on the leading edge of technology as you do so. Becoming established will be a challenge as the very organizations that need you the most will be the hardest to reach. Competition exists from a number of different types of services.

TELEMARKETING SERVICE

Start-up cost:	$6,000-$10,000
Potential earnings:	$40,000 or more
Typical fees:	$30 an hour
Advertising:	Yellow Pages, direct mail, business publications, membership in local business and civic groups
Qualifications:	Experience, persistence, ability to market your own service, writing skills for preparing script and reports
Equipment needed:	Telephone with headset, ergonomic office furniture, computer, suite software, printer, fax, modem, business card, letterhead, envelopes
Home business potential:	Yes
Staff required:	No
Handicapped opportunity:	Yes
Hidden costs:	Utility bills, marketing time and materials

LOWDOWN:

Telemarketing is a specialized and very focused form of marketing. No business can survive without effective marketing, and your challenge will be to reach the organizations that need to develop their customer base and show them how your service can help them grow. Telemarketing can be informational—a way of doing market research—but the major proportion will be focused on sales. As a small business, you may choose to offer a specific type of telemarketing: pharmaceuticals, commercial photography, wedding services, etc. This specialization will help you focus on your own marketing.

START-UP:

You'll need excellent telephone equipment and reasonably sophisticated computer equipment to track results and produce reports (about $6,000 to start). Once you get the hang of it, you can make $40,000 annually.

BOTTOM LINE ADVICE:

People skills are even more important to success as a telemarketer than they are in other types of small businesses. Listening well, speaking convincingly, and tuning the message to the receiver are all essential. You'll need experience writing effective scripts, and you'll need patience and persistence. It will probably take some time to develop the client base for your business. You can distinguish yourself from the run-of-the-mill telemarketers because you're not someone just hired off the street. You have experience, you're creating a proven track record, and you have an unquenchable enthusiasm for your clients' projects.

ADVICE FROM THE EXPERTS

What sets your business apart from others like it?

"While there are many marketing and advertising agencies, public relations firms, and telemarketing organizations, my company is a one-stop agency that has the capability of coordinating any and all aspects of a marketing plan," says Cheryl D. Cira, owner of Columbus, Ohio-based Marketing Dimensions. "I cannot stress how important it is to be honest and up front with your customers. Marketing Dimensions looks at each project and account as a long-term relationship."

Things you couldn't do without:

"Essentials include telephone equipment and office furniture. It also helps to have computers in order to enter large lists, track calls, pull up records, and run reports. Computers are also used for simple design work, database management, and mail merges," says Cira.

Staffing tips/advice:

"Telemarketing projects depend on the work and devotion of employees. And, because people are people, there are some aspects that cannot be controlled, such as employees quitting without notice, coming in late, and calling in sick time after time. My office manager is very good at juggling schedules and maintaining a strong pool of telemarketers, but it can get crazy at times."

If you had to do it all over again . . .

"I don't think there is any one thing of great importance that I would change or do differently. In general, however, I wish that I had had more hands-on experience in managing a large staff and more working knowledge related to personnel issues."

TELEVISION PROGRAM DISTRIBUTOR

Start-up cost:	$10,000-$15,000
Potential earnings:	$45,000-$75,000
Typical fees:	About 15 percent of the selling price per show
Advertising:	Business card, industry trade publications, word of mouth
Qualifications:	Knowledge of the television industry
Equipment needed:	Computer, printer, fax, cellular phone, letterhead, business card
Home business potential:	Yes
Staff required:	No
Handicapped opportunity:	Yes
Hidden costs:	Insurance, travel/entertainment expenses

LOWDOWN:

TV Program Distributor in layman's terms is a Program Sales Rep, hired by program producers to find the right matches in the television industry. Good selling skills and knowledge of how programs are bought and sold will help get your foot in the door. You also need to possess industry contacts including local, national, and cable. If you find that a group of programs are not selling, you can always launch your own network (provided you have the resources). Keep your business cards handy; you never know who you'll bump into at the drugstore.

START-UP:

Unless you have been with a reputable distributor already, your main expense will be to set up shop and market yourself ($10,000-$15,000). Keep a portfolio on the shows you've sold and how they fared in the ratings game; this will provide proof to the new client that you know what you are doing. If you are good at what you do, you could earn upward of $50,000.

BOTTOM LINE ADVICE:

This is probably the hardest job of the entire industry. Pounding the pavement to sell a TV program isn't for everyone. There will be long hours and lots of negotiating with some very high-powered clients. If you can stand the heat, you can work in this kitchen. If not, you'd better seek another profession.

TEXTILE BROKER

Start-up cost:	$10,000-$20,000
Potential earnings:	$40,000-$80,000+
Typical fees:	Usually a percentage of the sale (15 to 25 percent)
Advertising:	Trade/industry publications, direct mail, word-of-mouth, Internet
Qualifications:	Background in textile merchandising or wholesaling
Equipment needed:	Computer with fax/modem and separate line for international business (which tends to be a 24-hour prospect); phone system with additional cellular phone
Home business potential:	Yes (since you'll be on the road constantly)
Staff required:	No
Handicapped opportunity:	Possibly
Hidden costs:	Insurance, travel costs; also, fluctuating materials costs could make it hard to calculate a predictable income

LOWDOWN:

If the lure of traditional and exotic fabric has you wrapped in its infinite merchandising possibilities, a business as a textile broker could well be the "material" world for you. You will be the liaison between the textile mills and the clothing industry, selling materials to designers as well as manufacturers. Sometimes, it will be a specific type of cloth a manufacturer is looking for the best price on; other times, you will have established regular amounts of material to be sold to mass production houses. You will be competing daily on price and quality, and must establish key relationships early on to be sure you have an inside track. If you want to maximize your earning potential, you'll consider working in the global marketplace or on the Internet to strike some deals. At any rate, you will be doing a lot of traveling (to suppliers, to mills, and to trade shows to see what is new and hot).

START-UP:

You'll need to spend a lot of money traveling to supply houses first, and that may run you somewhere between $5,000-$7,000 alone. Don't forget to add in your computer equipment and international phone line costs (another $2,000 or so). Spend the rest on advertising and building relationships. If all goes well, expect to earn between $45,000-$80,000 or more (depending on whether you're selling domestically or internationally).

BOTTOM LINE ADVICE:

Traveling may get to you after a while, and so might the discriminating (and often changeable) tastes of the clothing designer/manufacturer. You might get tired of all the attitude you'll be expected to put up with, but (on the positive side) your income may greatly benefit from it. This is not a field for the weak.

THEATRICAL LIGHTING SERVICE

Start-up cost:	$10,000-$20,000
Potential earnings:	$30,000-$50,000
Typical fees:	$150-$1,000 per show
Advertising:	Industry trade publications, word of mouth
Qualifications:	Electrician, possible union contract required, handyman
Equipment needed:	Light board, lamps, gels, pipes, booms, business card
Home business potential:	Yes
Staff required:	Assistant required to keep track of the lighting changes in the scripts
Handicapped opportunity:	No
Hidden costs:	None

LOWDOWN:

The show has to go on, and the only way it can really go on is with great lighting. While it is often overlooked by audiences, lighting determines many things: how an actor looks on stage, the mood and time of day, the weather, and much more. You'll need to have experience scanning a script for your lighting opportunities, and carefully choose the right gels or special effects to create an atmosphere that works for the actors, the director, and the audience. You can get your start as a lighting technician for community theater or work with a lighting company before embarking on your own. You should have a well-developed eye for design. Knowledge of lighting gels and how they interact with fabrics and scenery is important, too. In the stage lighting business, equipment can be either sold or rented; once you start your own lighting business, you can save in the early stages if you work out short-term leases with other lighting companies. Networking will always be important to your profession; you'll never know whom you'll need later on, and you may need to farm out additional work as you become more and more in demand.

START-UP:

If you're planning on running your own company and buying all of your own equipment outright, you'll need large amounts of capital ($10,000-$20,000 or more). Unfortunately, this isn't a "I can get by on what I've got" business. Lighting can make or break a show, so you've got to have all the right stuff. Decide early whether you want to rent or buy your equipment. If you want to be in the lighting rental business, you can charge by the show. If you work hard and have a fine reputation, you could make at least $30,000-$50,000 per year; your fees will vary greatly depending on where you're working and the size or complexity of each project.

BOTTOM LINE ADVICE:

Lighting can involve long setup times. Broadway takes about two weeks to set up and smaller community shows take roughly five days. You work each and every show for the entire run of the production. Plan your time wisely.

TRAFFIC CONTROL CONSULTANT

Start-up cost:	$5,000-$10,000
Potential earnings:	$45,000-$100,000+
Typical fees:	According to size and duration of project, can range from $1,000-$150,000
Advertising:	Business publications, membership in civic and charitable organization, referrals
Qualifications:	Degree in field, experience and expertise, ability to market yourself, facility with design issues
Equipment needed:	High-end computer with large monitor, suite software, design and presentation software, laser printer, cellular phone, fax, modem, business card, letterhead, envelopes
Home business potential:	Yes
Staff required:	No
Handicapped opportunity:	Yes
Hidden costs:	Errors and omissions insurance, software upgrades, ongoing education, membership dues

LOWDOWN:

Many municipalities across the U.S. have poor traffic design. Towns often appear to have "just grown," with no overall planning. As the population expands, poor traffic control goes from being annoying to being extremely dangerous. Your skills in traffic control can be the foundation of a successful small business if you can find effective ways of linking what you know to the governments that need it. There should be a market among cities and towns that cannot afford a full-time traffic control staff but would benefit from better traffic patterns, cycled lights, clearer lanes, and better signs. The challenge will be to get your foot in the door and begin showing how your planning skills can get the rest of us where we're trying to go.

START-UP:

Your office must support the design side of traffic control consulting, and it must keep you in touch with your clients. You'll therefore spend between about $5,000-$10,000 getting started. However, since cities are growing at an unbelievable rate, you should be able to command a decent dollar for your expertise; charge at least $1,000 for each minor project and several thousand for the major traffic snafus.

BOTTOM LINE ADVICE:

As a traffic control consultant you will be in the same situation as other high-end consultants: it is very hard to get those first clients. You need a track record to attract business, which you can't get unless you have a track record. Becoming established will take time and effort, but eventually referrals will be an important proportion of your total client base. Projects may take you away from home frequently, as well. On the other hand, there isn't one traffic control consultant on each street corner, as there seems to be with accountants and management consultants.

USED BOAT SALES

Start-up cost:	$5,000-$10,000
Potential earnings:	$25,000 and up
Typical fees:	Percentage of sale price
Advertising:	Billboard, road signs, Yellow Pages, classifieds in local newspapers, possibly radio spots, referrals from boatyards and marinas
Qualifications:	Excellent consumer sales skills, wide knowledge of boats, engines, and marine equipment, ability to appraise motor and/or sailboats accurately
Equipment needed:	A lot for displaying the boats on sale; you may need cradles, trailers, and tarpaulins. Office space and equipment can be minimal but must allow you to keep the business records accurately
Home business potential:	Yes
Staff required:	Possibly
Handicapped opportunity:	No
Hidden costs:	Security, lot maintenance, boat clean-up in the spring

LOWDOWN:

Selling used boats comes almost naturally to some individuals who have a suitable property. This business may be an add-on to a yacht yard or marina, or even to a new car or boat dealership. To make a financial success in the used boat business, you will need to know everything there is to know about boats and about boat buyers. Purchasing a boat for recreation tends to be an emotion-driven action, and you need to understand how to help your customers choose what they want. You may also need to be something of an educator and teach your new buyer how to get his runabout back into the slip and how to maintain the engine.

START-UP:

Most used boat businesses are shoestring operations (around $5,000), and that is part of their charm. You'll need to figure out what works for you: a shoe box on the kitchen table, an office in an upscale yacht yard, or a trailer in a field. Annual income should be at least $25,000, depending on the amount of time put into your business.

BOTTOM LINE ADVICE:

This is not the route to great riches, even if you sell 60-foot Cigarette boats in Biscayne Bay. For the top of the market, new yachts are tough competition, and for the rest, the ups and downs of the economy will affect you so much that you really cannot count on a steady income. It's boom or bust. But it's outdoor work with the boats you love, plenty of opportunity to make friends with potential customers, and possibly a chance to rescue a wonderful piece of marine design and see it afloat once again.

USED COMPUTER SALES

Start-up cost:	$5,000-$15,000
Potential earnings:	$5,000-$100,000
Typical fees:	Used computers sell anywhere from $250-$3,000; your percentage could be a 50/50 split with the previous owner
Advertising:	Telephone marketing, word of mouth, networking
Qualifications:	Sales ability; energetic pursuit of buyers, sellers, and equipment
Equipment needed:	Computer, fax, modem, printer, office furniture, business card, letterhead, envelopes
Home business potential:	Yes
Staff required:	No
Handicapped opportunity:	Possibly
Hidden costs:	Building up inventory can be costly; be sure to figure in reconditioning costs if necessary

LOWDOWN:

There's definitely a market for used computers, but it's not an obvious one. To succeed in this business you will need to be the connection. You will be advertising in both directions, as a buyer of used equipment, and as a seller. Rapid changes in technology mean frequent upgrading of hardware by large organizations and even by many individuals. The "old" equipment may still function as well as it did when new, but need for a larger hard drive or more memory has made these machines seem obsolete. The previous generations of computers are very desirable to organizations that operate on a shoestring, to third-world companies, and to individuals who don't want to pay a lot to jump on the latest technology bandwagon. Your business opportunity arises from your ability to bring the used equipment together with its hidden market.

START-UP:

A great deal of advertising is required, and can cost you anywhere from $1,500-$5,000 per year. Inventory will be a variable but can lead to a considerable additional cost: where are you planning to store all of these units? Add rent if you build up too much inventory for your basement. In this field, you could make a nice percentage of each sale—your negotiation skills, however, will determine whether you can make a living doing this.

BOTTOM LINE ADVICE:

If you love a bargain and can attract the attention of others who share that view, you can take advantage of the technology whirlwind that is costing the rest of us so much money. As businesses upgrade, they will appreciate the opportunity you present to sell their previous hardware rather than just junking it. And you will enable canny buyers to obtain the computers they need at a fraction of the price for the glitzy models hot off the retailers' shelves. Time and effort is needed to educate both sellers and buyers. Finding exactly the equipment a customer wants can be very time-consuming and require you to have a network of sources. You will need to manage inventory costs carefully.

USED INDUSTRIAL EQUIPMENT SALES

Start-up cost:	$5,000-$11,000
Potential earnings:	$45,000-$100,000+
Typical fees:	20 to 40 percent commission on each sale
Advertising:	Classified ads in trade journals, Yellow Pages, newspapers, Internet (could have your own Web site)
Qualifications:	Sales background in a manufacturing environment would be especially helpful
Equipment needed:	Computer, printer, fax/modem, cellular phone
Home business potential:	Yes
Staff required:	No
Handicapped opportunity:	Yes
Hidden costs:	Insurance, occasional storage costs for machinery

LOWDOWN:

Many large manufacturers buy more equipment than they actually need. That's why the big guys unload equipment that may be obsolete according to their needs, but is affordable and usable for the fledgling manufacturer. Your job is to first locate those selling equipment such as lathes, deburring machines, or even robotics, then placing ads to sell the equipment from Manufacturer A to Manufacturer B. You should be a dynamic, yet extremely knowledgeable sales professional, because manufacturing types just aren't taken in by sales people who sound like they don't know how to actually use the equipment they're selling. You must create the impression that there is indeed dirt under your fingernails. Sometimes, you may have to pay to store individual pieces of equipment, but try not to do that unless it's an extreme emergency on the seller's part (and, even then, you should have a clause in your contract that states that the seller agrees to pay storage fees). One final tip: Be sure you have an "as-is/without warranty" clause in your buyer's contract—the last thing you need is a lawsuit against you when a piece of used equipment fails.

START-UP:

The first $3,000 of your start-up costs are all wrapped up in advertising the equipment you've got for sale. Of course, when you're starting out, you'll also be advertising that you're on the lookout for good, used equipment, so be sure to set aside an extra $3,000 or so to cover those costs. You'll need a basic office setup ($5,000), and your computer may become a valuable asset if you use it to sell on the Internet (tip: foreign countries are excellent outlets for used industrial equipment). You'll typically earn 20 to 40 percent of the asking price of each piece of equipment, and that could add up to $45,000-$100,000 or more per year.

BOTTOM LINE ADVICE:

Your background should be enough to sell your service, as long as it includes anything in the manufacturing realm. On the positive side, you could earn a great deal of money just placing ads and answering questions knowledgeably and professionally. However, if you're doing business with foreign countries, you'll need to spend time and money learning how to make a decent profit on international sales.

VACUUM CLEANER REPAIR

Start-up cost:	$5,000-$15,000
Potential earnings:	$25,000-$40,000
Typical fees:	$45 per hour is the usual rate; often, it's a set fee for the estimate and a negotiated fee for repair
Advertising:	Yellow Pages, local newspapers, supermarket and community bulletin boards, direct mail
Qualifications:	Strong technical knowledge and hands-on ability
Equipment needed:	Parts from a variety of manufacturers, including central vacuum systems (look for places that sell old vacuum cleaners for parts)
Home business potential:	Yes
Staff required:	No
Handicapped opportunity:	Not typically
Hidden costs:	Shipping costs for overseas parts

LOWDOWN:

How many times has your beater bar been completely filled with animal hair—to the point where it won't move anymore? The fact is, we've all experienced difficulty with our trusty vacuums from time to time. You'll have no shortage of customers, because every home has a vacuum cleaner and they all need service and parts from time to time. The problem is, your customers won't be thinking about your services until they definitely need them—so be aware of that in your advertising or marketing plan. Be where most customers will look for you, such as the Yellow Pages or in coupon books. You could, in fact, offer a free six-month checkup for early problem diagnosis and bring in instant business. Diversify as much as you can, too; by stocking replacement bags and commonly used parts you can make a tidy side profit.

START-UP:

From the start, you'll need to set up shop in a comfortable place with adequate lighting and a sturdy workbench. You can do this in your home, or spend $300 or more per month renting shop space. Whichever you choose, you'll need to advertise ($1,500-$3,000) and keep a fairly complete parts inventory. Charge at least $45 per hour for your time to be sure you're covering overhead and expenses.

BOTTOM LINE ADVICE:

Supplement that business by installing and servicing central vacuum systems, a feature in many new homes. Cultivate contacts among local developers and builders.

VIDEO TRANSFER SERVICE

Start-up cost:	$5,000-$10,000
Potential earnings:	$25,000-$35,000
Typical fees:	$250 for a 12-minute transfer (including music and character generation)
Advertising:	Industry trade publications, bulletin boards, direct mail, video retailers
Qualifications:	Background in video; experience in working with all types of film, including 8mm, 3/4", Super VHS, and VHS
Equipment:	Old projector, Super VHS camera, editing deck, audio equipment, character generator
Home business potential:	Yes
Staff required:	No
Handicapped opportunity:	Yes
Hidden costs:	You may eventually need a studio; start setting aside cash as early as possible

LOWDOWN:

People have a strong desire to preserve their memories, and video memory books have become a great way to keep those memories intact and in an easy-to-view medium. In most cases, you are hired to transfer old film onto the latest VHS tapes, but you might also have to shoot video of old photographs and put them more or less into documentary format. Work with writers to sell your clients on narration of their cherished memories or family histories; you can charge extra and split the profits with the writer. For the actual voice-overs, you could use the talents of college theater or communications students who will work merely for the experience (or for a nominal fee). You must have a strong background in video and know how to run audio equipment. If the client wants music behind the video, you must pick the appropriate track(s) and secure the right to use each song. You could also network with local musicians to provide suitable soundtracks that you can offer on a much less costly basis.

START-UP:

Start-up is high ($10,000 or more), but you could cut cost by buying used equipment. Just make sure it's not more than five years old or it will be obsolete. Starting out, your earnings could be in the range of $5,000-$20,000 per year, with a potential of $25,000-$35,000. Most video transfer services also offer other services such as video production and audio reproduction.

BOTTOM LINE ADVICE:

This can be a really fun business, but it can also be tedious. You have to be able to sit through lots of footage and try to pick out the most interesting parts. You're in the sentiment business here, preserving precious memories . . . tread carefully, because you're treading on people's lives. In other words, save every frame for your client.

WATER QUALITY SERVICES

Start-up cost:	$5,000-$15,000
Potential earnings:	$25,000-$40,000
Typical fees:	$60-$150 per job; more for commercial clients ($350+)
Advertising:	Referrals from related businesses, including well drillers, environmentalists, government departments
Qualifications:	Degree in biology, chemistry, or a related science, extensive lab and field experience
Equipment needed:	Well-equipped lab, computer, software, printer, office furniture, business card, letterhead, envelopes
Home business potential:	No
Staff required:	No
Handicapped opportunity:	No
Hidden costs:	Lab supplies, travel costs, mobile phone bills

LOWDOWN:

Your customers may deliver water samples to you for analysis, or you may provide the service of gathering them yourself. Highly developed lab skills are essential here as the most refined testing will be required to make an accurate report, which needs to include documentation regarding contamination, its properties, and how to get rid of them. Traces measured in parts per billion are being considered in the most up-to-date environmental plans. You will also need marketing skills to form business relationships, and these must be combined with the lab scientist's focus on detail and precision. Writing a clear, effective report will help set you aside from your competitors, as will the ability to perform your services quickly and efficiently.

START-UP:

Equipping a lab is a major outlay and must be completed before you can begin work. Depending on how extensive you want your services to be, you'll spend between $5,000-$15,000 on your lab and office. Once you get established, though, you should be able to find a steady stream of both individual and commercial clients. Charge them at least $60 per job (for individuals) and a larger flat rate for commercial clients.

BOTTOM LINE ADVICE:

Accuracy, on-time reports, and an attitude of strong customer service will help you build your water quality business. You will need a dedication to the process so that your lab work is precise, which can be challenging if you are not detail-oriented. You'll also need to be good at forming client relationships to keep business flowing in. Establishing your credentials and earning trust will take a lot of your energy in the early years.

Wilderness-Based
Therapeutic Programs

Start-up cost:	$6,000-$10,000
Potential earnings:	$15,000-$25,000
Typical fees:	A flat rate of $1,500-$3,000 per client/group
Advertising:	Referrals from therapists, seminars, and speeches for community groups, networking, direct mail, advertising in national and area-wide publications, radio spots
Qualifications:	Degree in related field, extensive outdoor experience, participation in group dynamics and leadership, excellent marketing and management skills
Equipment needed:	Camping equipment for self and group, office space with furniture, preferably a computer and printer, business card, letterhead, envelopes, high-quality brochures
Home business potential:	Yes
Staff required:	Possibly
Handicapped opportunity:	No
Hidden costs:	Insurance, equipment repair and replacement, transportation

Lowdown:

Setting up a successful small business that offers wilderness-based therapeutic programs will require a number of special talents and enthusiasms. To be more than just an Outward Bound wannabe, you will need to have, and to market, a special conviction in the efficacy of the therapy you provide, and in its relationship to the wilderness. If, for example, you specialize in treating depression in adolescents, you will be creating a wilderness experience that responds to the complex needs of this patient population. Your location will, to some extent, define the type of experience you provide—kayaking a seashore or mountain lake, hiking and camping in a hidden valley, or arranging a wilderness experience suitable for young people who have never been outside a suburb. You will probably need a support system, at least part-time, of helpers who can deal with transportation, food supplies, and challenging therapy situations that may arise. Once the structure of the business is developed, you should be able to draw many clients who can see the power of getting away, of changing to a new perspective, of getting back to the simple and beautiful things of life that can't be seen and felt from the parking lot of a mall.

Start-up:

The major expenses will be in equipment and marketing (at least $6,000). Until you become known for your work and for your effectiveness, you will be spending heavily on advertising and other types of marketing to build your client base. A profit of $15,000 can be expected at the end of the first year.

BOTTOM LINE ADVICE:

Creating the focus for your business will probably be the biggest challenge. Secondly, how specifically will you deliver your services? What age and other limits will you need to place on participants? What form of evaluation will establish the effectiveness of your efforts and support further marketing? How can you carry out the process without taking all the burdens on your own shoulders? Finding the right answers to these questions will define your success in combining your concern for the welfare of your clients with your love of the wilderness and your belief in its infinite power for healing.

Creative Idea-Generating

You have a business problem (or opportunity) staring you in the face; now, how do you come up with a suitable solution or answer in a short period of time?

Try one or more of these tactics:

- **Mind-mapping.** You draw a circle with the ultimate goal in the center, and lines extending outward like a sunburst. On each line, you write down one possible way to achieve your goal. Often, you map out all the smaller details of each method—leading to clearer goal-setting.

- **Brainstorming.** Invite a few business friends (or, better yet, fellow business owners) over for an evening of pizza and brainstorming. Listen to what others have to say, even if you like your own initial ideas more. Their feedback might influence you later.

- **Learn from others' mistakes.** Read trade journals and business publications—or e-mail other business owners in entrepreneurial or specialty business forums on on-line services.

- **Go where your customers are (if they're not with you).** If you have a resume service, you might hang out in the resume book section of your local bookstore to listen in to what your potential customers are needing and wanting.

The important thing to remember is that there isn't just one possible solution; the value of thinking creatively is that you can explore many different possibilities—and if one doesn't work, you still have others left to choose from.

WORD-PROCESSING SERVICE

Start-up cost:	$5,000-$15,000
Potential earnings:	$30,000-$45,000
Typical fees:	Many in this field charge $5-$10 per page
Advertising:	Yellow Pages, focus advertising in a 5-10-mile radius of your business location, direct mail, university bulletin boards, networking with business and professional organizations
Qualifications:	Fast and accurate typing skills (at least 65 words per minute), customer-oriented attitude
Equipment needed:	Computer hardware and software, laser printer, modem, copy machine, fax; optional: transcribing machine and scanner.
Home business potential:	Yes
Staff required:	None initially
Handicapped opportunity:	Yes
Hidden costs:	Equipment and software upgrades

LOWDOWN:

Despite the abundance of personal computers, demand for off-site word-processing services has steadily increased. Essentially, word-processing is a fancier (and more technically correct) phrase for typing service. You'll be doing all the same kinds of work, only you'll be using a computer instead of the great typewriter dinosaur. Customers will come to you with everything from reports and term papers to resumes and technical documentation. The ability to produce an attractive product with quick turnaround will ensure your success in this fairly competitive field. Remember that just about any Joe with a basic computer system and printer thinks of getting into this type of business; you'll have to be able to set yourself apart from these folks as well as the hundreds of secretarial services out there (who perform services that go beyond your own). Position yourself close to a university or in a downtown area, and you'll increase your chances of success by at least 50 percent.

START-UP:

Your start-up costs are going to be quite reasonable if you already own a computer and laser printer. Most of your initial expense will result from advertising and appropriate software purchases (set aside at least $3,000 for these). Charge a per-page rate of $5-$10 or an hourly fee for the larger jobs; it'll take you a while to get a feel for which projects are more labor-intensive.

BOTTOM LINE ADVICE:

Beware of underpricing your service. Consider adding a surcharge for handwritten or hard-to-read documents and materials that include charts or tables. If you can stand the repetitive motion of using a keyboard, and of typing other people's work, your income is limited only by your speed and the number of hours you want to work.

WORKERS' COMPENSATION CONSULTANT

Start-up cost:	$5,000-$7,000
Potential earnings:	$45,000-$60,000
Typical fees:	Monthly retainer fee of $1,500-$3,000 (depending on the size of the company)
Advertising:	Business periodicals, networking, referrals
Qualifications:	Ability to locate best rates for companies and ways to keep costs down
Equipment needed:	Computer, printer, office furniture, business card, letterhead, envelopes
Home business potential:	Yes
Staff required:	No
Handicapped opportunity:	Yes
Hidden costs:	Insurance, membership dues

LOWDOWN:

A workers' compensation consultant is an outside contractor who works with companies to reduce the incidence of workers' compensation claims, find better rates, and innovative ways to save money. You will investigate the circumstances of the manner in which the employer deals with these problems. You might even administer the claims process for a period of time, instead of having a company employee do it. Typical strategies to reduce claims include: 1) more thoroughly investigating the claim to determine whether it is indeed valid; 2) conducting regular reviews of workers' compensation benefits packages; and 3) recommending changes in the workplace to reduce injuries. The bottom line is, your nose for trouble can prevent a company from being taken advantage of—either by invalid claims or high rates.

START-UP:

Investigative tools and the equipment to write reports are what you will need; spend at least $4,000 equipping your office with computer and printing equipment. Your reports will need to be clear and easy to understand (after all, they hired you to clear up the red tape, right?), so buy a decent software package for all of your major communications. Most disability consultants work on a retainer (typically $1,500-$3,000 per month).

BOTTOM LINE ADVICE:

This is quite a lively field. To establish yourself you will probably need the experience gained from having been a workers' compensation specialist for an employer, or at least another consulting firm. If you show that you can conduct excellent investigations, write effective reports, and make productive recommendations for improvements in processes, you can build a very successful enterprise. You will not be everyone's favorite person as you uncover cheaters, but you will be improving your clients' bottom line.

START-UP BETWEEN $15,000 AND $40,000

AERIAL APPLICATOR

Start-up cost:	$25,000-$40,000
Potential earnings:	$30,000-$45,000
Typical fees:	$150 and up per spray job (depends on dimensions of area)
Advertising:	Direct mail, advertising in local farm journals and newspapers, Yellow Pages, membership in farmers' organizations
Qualifications:	Outstanding piloting skills, knowledge of agricultural chemicals, experience in aerial application
Equipment needed:	Crop duster, application equipment
Home business potential:	Yes
Staff required:	No
Handicapped opportunity:	No
Hidden costs:	Insurance, plane maintenance, airfield costs, fuel

LOWDOWN:

Crop dusters provide a service needed by almost every farmer in the country. Agribusiness executives and family farmers alike will need crop dusting with chemicals that keep their fields bug-free. If you live in a region with large acreage devoted to a certain crop, you will have your best chance of breaking into this market. Your task will be to develop relationships with farmers of enough acreage to support your very high overhead and still leave you with a profit. Two large uncontrollable factors will have effects on your business from year to year: the weather, and the world economy. But sure as death and taxes, the boll weevils are zeroing in on your customers' cotton, and disease-carrying spores are floating through the air toward their amber waves of grain.

START-UP:

Developing the skills necessary to fly a crop duster is expensive ($1,500 or more is not unheard of for flying lessons and certification). Of course the other large expense is the plane itself ($20,000-$45,000). But, you can charge your clients $150 and up per run—and they will most definitely bring you repeat business.

BOTTOM LINE ADVICE:

As you develop your business plan, you will need to factor into your projections the likely ups and downs of agriculture in your area. If the worst-case scenario leaves you with a reasonable expectation of profitable operation, you can launch into business and start marketing yourself. Careful attention to customer service may be enough to set you off from the competition. Aside from the vagaries of agricultural profitability, the biggest negative about this business is its danger. Crop dusting is not for the careless or the faint of heart. The chemicals that kill insects and mold can have bad effects on humans, too.

ANTIQUES DEALER

Start-up cost:	$20,000-$40,000 (depending on how large your inventory is)
Potential earnings:	$35,000-$65,000
Typical fees:	Varied; your pieces will sell anywhere from $10-$10,000
Advertising:	Yellow Pages, community newspapers, direct mail, show participation, location
Qualifications:	Should be knowledgeable about antiques and pricing
Equipment needed:	Storefront with cash register, computer for accounting/inventory purposes, printer, fax, retail display equipment
Home business potential:	No
Staff required:	Not initially
Handicapped opportunity:	Yes
Hidden costs:	Insurance, warehousing

LOWDOWN:

The lure of the old and priceless draws many a sentimental customer into an antique store, and you could start such a business with a dozen or so nice pieces of furniture, some antique china, and lots of old books and toys. All of these items tend to sell well, as they are collectible and worth increasingly more with each passing year. You'll need to develop a sizable stock or inventory of pieces to sell, and that can best be accomplished by combing thrift shops, flea markets, and estate auctions for the best and most interesting old items you can find. Watch the newspaper for garage sales, too—sometimes people will unknowingly unload a fabulous antique dresser at a steal of a price.

Basically, you should keep in mind that your business will need to be run just like any other retail establishment—and that means you'll need to price yourself well enough to cover your operating expenses in addition to building a profit. Tricky work, because folks will want to barter with you on price.

START-UP:

You'll need at least $20,000 and probably closer to $50,000 to get this business started properly, mainly because you need to have a significant inventory and a storefront to display and sell your products. Look to earn $35,000-$65,000, depending on three things: location, quality of product line, and price. Obviously, if you're in a quaint New England town, you might fare better than an antique shop in the middle of Kentucky.

BOTTOM LINE ADVICE:

It's a competitive market, and too many well-intended entrepreneurs make the mistake of thinking this will be an easy ride. If you've got sufficient working capital to buy the kinds of pieces that will build your reputation for the finer things, then you'll have little problem making a living. If you're undercapitalized, you'll be out of business before you know it, because you'll probably have bought way more than your operations can support.

ARCHITECT

Start-up cost:	$20,000-$40,000
Potential earnings:	$45,000-$65,000+
Typical fees:	Extremely varied; could be $5,000 to $30,000 for your designs
Advertising:	Referrals, Yellow Pages, newspaper advertising
Qualifications:	License after schooling and apprenticeship
Equipment needed:	Drafting table, high-end computer with computer-aided design (CAD) software, printer, blueprint-size copier, cellular phone
Home business potential:	Yes
Staff required:	No
Handicapped opportunity:	Not typically
Hidden costs:	Insurance, high number of requested changes from uncertain customers (charge for excessive requests)

LOWDOWN:

You have a knack for designing interesting buildings with plenty of airy, open spaces and aesthetically pleasing features. You know what people want from a building, and how to design one that encompasses many tastes and purposes. That's probably why you went to architectural college, right? Once you've gotten your license, you can put out your shingle and announce your availability, primarily to builders and contractors, but also to Realtors (who get asked nearly as often who the best architect in town is). You'll be competing against a dozen or more others in your area, so be sure to set yourself apart as a specialist in a particular area: for instance, you might enjoy designing ultracontemporary homes in affluent parts of town. (If that's the case, imagine the endless income potential.) More often than not, you'll be dreaming up more practical designs for doctors' offices, corporate headquarters, and possibly even manufacturing facilities. The commercial sector will provide you with larger, more steady income than residential might; it really depends on where you are located and how well your designs go over with the powers that be.

START-UP:

Start-up costs will be in the $20,000-$40,000 range (after your education and licensing). You'll need to purchase drafting and design equipment (including a computer with CAD capabilities), but your income ($45,000-$65,000 or more) should cover that fairly soon after you open your door to business; it shouldn't take more than two to five years to be in serious profit-making mode.

BOTTOM LINE ADVICE:

While the work is detail-oriented and technically precise, there is plenty of room for glamour. If you develop a reputation for terrific, inspiring work, you could find yourself in the spotlight (and, consequently, in the money) more often than you'd ever thought. Look at I.M. Pei and the Rock and Roll Hall of Fame . . . .

ART GALLERY

Start-up cost:	$15,000-$30,000
Potential earnings:	$40,000-$70,000
Typical fees:	20 to 40 percent commission on each piece sold
Advertising:	Newspapers, city magazines, art guides, universities
Qualifications:	Should be knowledgeable about art
Equipment needed:	Cash register, credit card processing systems, ample wall space (plus hanging materials/tools)
Home business potential:	No
Staff required:	None initially
Handicapped opportunity:	Possibly
Hidden costs:	Promoting of shows

LOWDOWN:

An art gallery is a place where folks come to see (and hopefully purchase) the new, the exciting, and even the surreal. To run a successful gallery, you can't just love art . . . you must also be able to promote it well; otherwise, you'll be running a museum instead of a retail establishment. Using whatever contacts you may have, you'll need to build a solid stable of artists to represent. National art publications feature the work of the more prominent modern artists, and you may want to invite some of them to submit slides and resumes. Of course, if you're a new gallery, the best way to offer a wide assortment of work is to invite art students to show in your gallery on a consignment basis. You'll keep anywhere from 20 to 40 percent of the selling price of each item for yourself, and many times the artists will let you know what they expect to receive for each piece and how much markup they'll allow for your profit. Your negotiation skills will determine what type of business arrangements you make with each artist. In the competitive '90s, you may want to pick a theme for your gallery instead of trying to offer everything (for instance, you might decide to be a nature gallery or one that features only local work).

START-UP:

Start-up costs can be considerably high in this high-profile "image" business. Since you're asking people to spend a pretty penny on original works of art, you'd better have your gallery in a classy place. Many artists are banding together and renting space in warehouses where they can offer their own wares in what amounts to an artsy shopping mall atmosphere. If you can place your gallery in a spot like that, you'll benefit from the traffic and save on rent, too.

BOTTOM LINE ADVICE:

True, art gallery openings are fancy gatherings for the "hipper-than-thou," but do these people sipping wine and nibbling on cheese really have the money to buy art? Yes, if you make sure you qualify those who have the cash to invest in art. If you don't take the time to build a hot prospect list, you'll lose money quicker than you make it—and that's not a happy situation.

AUTOMOTIVE PARTS REBUILDER

Start-up cost:	$20,000-$40,000
Potential earnings:	$20,000-$40,000
Typical fees:	$40-$50 per job
Advertising:	Enthusiast publications and membership in enthusiast organizations, Yellow Pages, auto show participation, referrals from reconditioners, restorers
Qualifications:	Excellent mechanical aptitude, experience with rebuilding, ability to manage sales and invoicing
Equipment needed:	Tools, parts, specialized diagnostic equipment
Home business potential:	Yes
Staff required:	No
Handicapped opportunity:	No
Hidden costs:	Materials, replacements for equipment

LOWDOWN:

Motorheads are everywhere across the U.S. Some of these car lovers are rebuilding an antique auto, or one with high sentimental value. For this group, total authenticity is highly valued, so the exact air filter that would have come new on a '79 Monza is important. You can meet and greet these enthusiasts at car shows, developing business for your rebuilding/reconditioning skills. The secondary market is less refined: simple replacement parts. Gas pumps, alternators, and other expensive parts can be reconditioned for resale to people getting a few more years out of their expensive vehicles. You may find that the best auto repair garage in town offers a market for your reconditioned parts.

START-UP:

The tools necessary to perform this work are relatively expensive, but you possibly have many of them already if you have developed the skills required to even consider starting an auto parts rebuilding business. You'll charge $40-$50 per job, and more for special parts needed to complete the job properly. Figure on an income potential of $20,000-$40,000.

BOTTOM LINE ADVICE:

A love of autos is usually behind a successful business like this. The pleasure that you take in mechanical devices will translate itself into a successful business if you also keep a good manager's head on your shoulders. Marketing, pricing, selling, and billing are also vital to the growth of your enterprise.

BANQUET FACILITY

Start-up cost:	$15,000-$25,000
Potential earnings:	$40,000 and up
Typical fees:	$350 and up per client
Advertising:	Newspapers, wedding planners/publications, direct mail, location
Qualifications:	Cooking experience, people skills, management and marketing experience
Equipment needed:	A building for banquets, kitchen equipment and utensils, dinnerware, cutlery, table linens
Home business potential:	No
Staff required:	Cook(s), dishwasher(s), servers, and cleanup help
Handicapped opportunity:	Yes
Hidden costs:	Meeting legal, zoning, and sanitation/hygiene requirements

LOWDOWN:

Running a banquet facility can be a satisfying career for the right person. It is a business that will be a good fit for someone who enjoys food and people, who can manage small but important details, and who is willing to work hard to get established. Be ready to do a lot of menu planning and cooking. Networking to obtain bookings for wedding, class reunions, and club parties is essential to getting started; you can send brochures or business cards to churches, the chamber of commerce, bridal shops, florists, and others who could make referrals. You might volunteer your catering services (working from your home at first) for a couple of parties to gain exposure and find out if this business is for you.

START-UP:

Start-up costs for a banquet business are not small: in addition to needing the kitchen equipment and facilities, you must buy or rent a hall in which to conduct the festivities (research the possibility of sharing a building with someone else at first). Also, you will need to get expert legal advice before starting your business; there are legal, zoning, liquor and food handling requirements to meet. You will also have labor costs and ongoing marketing expenses.

BOTTOM LINE ADVICE:

As long as there are people and occasions to be celebrated, there will always be a need for your banquet business. It can be very satisfying to provide people with good food and a good time. You will, though, work long hours, especially while getting established. You will be required to work evenings and weekends, since that's when most parties take place. Good management skills and an ability to market your business successfully will be essential. Although you will have bookings year-round, the business may be "feast or famine" because of the seasonal nature of many events, such as holiday office parties.

BIOFEEDBACK THERAPIST

Start-up cost:	$20,000-$50,000
Potential earnings:	$30,000-$45,000
Typical fees:	$150 per hour-long session
Advertising:	Yellow Pages, referrals from physicians and psychologists, advertising in community newspapers
Qualifications:	License or certification in your field
Equipment needed:	Biofeedback equipment (equipment for heart rate, pulse, breathing, and muscle movement)
Home business potential:	Not typically
Staff required:	No
Handicapped opportunity:	Not typically
Hidden costs:	Insurance (sometimes malpractice or liability insurance is suggested), equipment upgrades and maintenance

LOWDOWN:

Folks who suffer from chronic pain or complaints are often referred to biofeedback therapists who can connect sensitive pieces of equipment to various parts of the body to determine where pain is coming from and how to interpret stress. For instance, a heart rate monitor might tell what types of activities or conditions make a patient's heart rate rise, and what types lessen or eliminate body stress. The idea is to locate key centers in the body that are more sensitive than others to stress and high levels of activity. The results of each test are recorded and then interpreted by you or the referring physician or psychologist. Many times, you'll see that a patient is experiencing psychosomatic illness, and your test results will provide the proof of such imaginary illness. However, your services should not be used as a tool for committing the mentally unhealthy; rather, you provide a proactive service that helps people redirect their energies after being made aware of what stresses them out. They then have the opportunity to "teach" their bodies new ways of responding to stress; that is what the majority of your clients have been experiencing anyway (especially those with heart conditions).

START-UP:

You will need $20,000-$50,000 for your highly sensitive equipment, which will also need regular maintenance due to the risk of inaccuracy. Speaking of risk, you'll need to make sure that you have adequate liability insurance, too. If you are well-connected with other health care professionals who can provide regular referrals, you could make $30,000-$45,000 per year in this specialized profession.

BOTTOM LINE ADVICE:

If you enjoy working closely with people and in working with them to create more positive responses to stress, this business will give you everything you need (including a reasonable amount of financial security). On the other hand, getting insurance companies to cover your services might be trickier than you'd ever imagined; hire an administrator who knows the ins and outs of insurance claims.

BOAT OPERATION INSTRUCTOR

Start-up cost:	$25,000+ (depending on whether you own or lease a boat)
Potential earnings:	$23,000-$45,000
Typical fees:	$75 per person for a one-time class of four hours
Advertising:	Marinas, flyers, Yellow Pages, boating publications
Qualifications:	Captain's license, CPR certification
Equipment needed:	Computer, boat, safety equipment
Home business potential:	Yes (but you'll likely be out on the water all the time)
Staff required:	No
Handicapped opportunity:	Not typically
Hidden costs:	Insurance

LOWDOWN:

The water can be a very unsafe place these days. Most people who get behind the wheel of a boat are inexperienced and accidents are on the rise because of negligence. People are starting to hire boating operation instructors for their own personal safety. As an instructor, you need to know what the Coast Guard requires (life preservers, flares, fire extinguishers, etc.), boat safety regulations, chart-reading and meteorology. In addition, you'll need to have general seamanship knowledge and a good dose of common sense. Market yourself to local boat retailers with brochures and flyers—and get to know your water neighbors, so they can help spread your word with waves of referrals.

START-UP:

It is possible to be a boat operations instructor without a boat, since you could use your client's boat, but it would probably be a good idea to have one of your own. You will need to carry some type of insurance and probably legal counsel to draw up necessary papers for the client to sign absolving you from any type of negligence. Depending on where you live, you could teach for a possible 13 to 26 weeks and make a minimum of $23,000-$45,000.

BOTTOM LINE ADVICE:

Spring and summer will be your busiest seasons. If you love to teach without the confines of a classroom, then this water job is for you! Be prepared for some clients to not take you seriously, since people tend to be a little more relaxed with their leisure vehicles. Encourage them to stay with the program.

Franchising

A franchise is a mutually beneficial agreement between a franchiser (parent company) and franchisee (operator), which allows the franchisee to sell the franchiser's well-established product or service, while the franchiser collects agreed fees from the franchisee. The rules of operation vary from business to business, but generally the franchiser retains close control of the product in order to ensure uniformity.

A franchise can be an attractive way of becoming your own boss. Remember, however, that you will need a good deal of start-up capital. You may, for instance, have to own your own premises, and in running a franchise business, location is everything. Be aware, also, that you are not finally the only boss of your business: the parent company has its stake, too.

BENEFITS TO THE FRANCHISER

The parent company sees the franchise agreement as a cost-effective method of expanding the business. The explosion of franchise industries in recent years is attributable to the need for companies to expand while remaining lean. The franchiser can expand his business without the need for excessive capital and without adding extra layers of management that could compromise efficiency. The franchiser collects an agreed-upon revenue from each franchisee. This revenue varies, but can be as high as 20 percent.

BENEFITS TO THE FRANCHISEE

The franchisee can tap into economies of scale (in purchasing, for instance) that would normally be available only to a large corporation. The franchisee also gains from the parent company's advertising and promotional support, and from the franchiser's know-how.

PITFALLS

Most problems in franchising arise from the differing objectives of the franchisee and the franchiser. You, as franchisee, will be watching your bottom line, in order to maximize your profit. The franchiser, however, calculates his fees on your sales and will want you to maximize your sales even when (through discounting, remodeling, etc.) this cuts into your profits. Be aware that you are not the only person trying to make money from this enterprise, and that, while you may make a good living out of it, you won't take all of the profits.

BUILDING MAINTENANCE SERVICE

Start-up cost:	$20,000-$40,000
Potential earnings:	$45,000-$75,000
Typical fees:	Monthly contract of $150-$350 per client/building per month
Advertising:	Yellow Pages, direct mail to building owners and rental property managers, networking, cold calls
Qualifications:	Handyman experience (preferably with some background in electrical work)
Equipment needed:	Van equipped with tools, chemicals/solvents, ladders and small power equipment
Home business potential:	Yes (but you'll be working on-site)
Staff required:	No (but you will need additional staff if your business gets too large for you to handle your workload alone)
Handicapped opportunity:	No
Hidden costs:	Insurance

LOWDOWN:

Nearly all of the apartment complexes, office buildings, and universities in your community need to be maintained by someone—and, if you have a technical, hands-on background in building maintenance (or even more generally, as a "Mr. Fix-It") you can parlay that talent into a building maintenance service quite nicely and logically. After all, whom would you trust with your fix-up needs: a small service with an expert at the top or a large company of transient employees? That's exactly how you'll need to position yourself in this competitive business: as a small-but-mighty industry leader with stability and a commitment to keeping everything running smoothly. Of course, you can't promise that every single light switch will always work perfectly, but you can offer a pager accessibility and 24-hour service so that your clients can rest comfortably knowing that you're in charge of those three-o'clock-in-the-morning emergencies (and isn't that the time most things go wrong?).

START-UP:

Your costs to launch this business will be moderate ($20,000-$40,000) due to the fact that you'll need a good van filled with everything from wrenches and sockets to small pneumatic drills and large ladders. If you're a hard worker, as most maintenance folk are, you could make $45,000-$75,000 (depending on how many clients you serve). Of course, the more you make, the more likely you'll need additional staff, since one person can't simultaneously fix all the light switches and circuits in a dozen buildings.

BOTTOM LINE ADVICE:

Be prepared to spend long hours doing the kind of work that tinkerers like to do most of all: figuring out what went wrong with that blower or electrical system, and being the hero when the problem is solved. It's not a bad way to end each day, even if it is long.

ADVICE FROM THE EXPERTS

What sets your business apart from others like it?

Lillian Lincoln, President of Centennial One, Inc., in Landover, Maryland, says her company distinguishes itself from others by emphasis on quality. "We place a great deal of emphasis on giving our clients a comfort level that assures them that their building maintenance requirements will be adequately addressed."

Things you couldn't do without:

Vacuums, buffers, scrubbing and shampooing machines. "No equipment is needed until some work has been secured. No lead time is needed unless the job requires specialized equipment, so purchase only the equipment needed for each job as they roll in."

Marketing tips/advice:

"Industry knowledge as well as business acumen is a great asset. Too many people have the mistaken impression that this industry is a 'mop and bucket' business. Far from true! It requires knowledge of chemical and equipment usage, time management, human relations, and a number of other skills. For anyone going into this business, I advise them to work in the industry (preferably in the field) for a minimum of six months."

If you had to do it all over again . . .

"I would spend more time working in the field to learn more about on-site operations. I made some mistakes early on because I was not as knowledgeable as I should have been about the basics of the business."

BUNGEE JUMPING INSTRUCTOR

Start-up cost:	$25,000+
Potential earnings:	$35,000-$55,000
Typical fees:	$50-$100 for the first jump and $10 less for each additional jump
Advertising:	Yellow Pages, entertainment sections of local papers, brochures, visitor convention bureaus
Qualifications:	If you use a hot-air balloon, a pilot's license will be required
Equipment needed:	Platform of some type, harness, bungees, and insurance
Home business potential:	Yes
Staff required:	Yes
Handicapped opportunity:	No
Hidden costs:	Weather may cause some downtime

LOWDOWN:

The bungee jumping craze has got hundreds of people literally jumping off bridges—and most live to tell about it. If you are into the craze, and have teaching ability and a safety sensibility, you could probably take the plunge and launch your own specialized business. While it may seem like fun at first, you should remember that liability insurance for this type of business can be very high due to the high risk involved. One lawsuit could put you out of business in a nanosecond. Still, your customers are going to be the real thrill-seekers: people who simply aren't afraid to take the risk in the first place. Your marketing will be minimal because these thrill-seekers will usually come looking for you. Being registered in first aid and knowing CPR is essential and you should take every precaution you can to prevent injuries. Also, if you use a balloon as a platform, you will need a pilot's license to operate it.

START-UP:

Your start-up cost will directly relate to the type of platform you will use. A hot-air balloon or crane starts at $25,000. Some people get fancy and build their own, while others use isolated bridges (in some states this is illegal and isn't recommended). Your fee will be based on the number of jumps a person wants to take. Most are one-time shots of $50. For each additional jump the price is reduced by $10. Your typical earnings could range from $35,000-$55,000.

BOTTOM LINE ADVICE:

You do this entirely for the sport of it. There is no physical benefit except the "rush" you receive from jumping, but the adrenaline rush alone could cause your business to jump with steady repeat business. This would be a good sideline job especially in climates where it could be seasonal. Keep in mind that although bungee jumping has gained popularity, it has also caused some life-threatening accidents, as well as death.

BUSINESS FORM SALES AND SERVICE

Start-up cost:	$20,000-$40,000
Potential earnings:	$35,000-$60,000
Typical fees:	$25-$30 per form; more it's a complex custom design
Advertising:	Yellow Pages, classified ads, direct mail
Qualifications:	None
Equipment needed:	Printing equipment (or sub-contractor lined up), extensive color catalog of your goods, inventory
Home business potential:	Yes
Staff required:	No
Handicapped opportunity:	Yes
Hidden costs:	Cold-calling can get expensive

LOWDOWN:

This type of business is so standardized and easy for others to learn that it is among the top franchise businesses on the market today. All you need to do is find out what potential customers are using for business forms (such as inventory records, receipts, invoices, and other important documents). Then, you sell them on your customized service, quick turnaround, and easy terms. Remember, though, that you will be competing heavily against some fairly large organizations (Office Depot and Office Max plus other independents like yourself); you will need super sales skills to stay on top of it all and make your regular goals. Cold-calling is your primary way of finding new business, and it is extremely uncertain in the beginning (not to mention costly). Still, the income potential is great for those who can stomach the competition—and if you capitalize on your strong points, you should be able to come up with forms that make every customer happy (and, ultimately, result in your own profitability).

START-UP:

You'll need between $20,000-$40,000, particularly if you buy into a franchise operation. This investment will cover your catalogs, inventory, and training materials, and may also cover printing equipment (typically including specialized software). You'll charge $25-$30 per type of form; more if it's a complex custom design. In the end, you'll wind up making between $35,000-$65,000 per year—but that's only if you're working at this full-time and full-throttle.

BOTTOM LINE ADVICE:

There is probably no more straightforward, easy business to learn than this—but do recognize that you're going to need to be well-connected to get regular, dependable business. Network with anyone who's anyone, and make the daily fifty of so phone calls it may take to get one fresh lead. After all, you're competing against major office store chains, and you need to tell people just what's different about your business (in this case, it's the customized service).

CATALOG RETAILER

Start-up cost:	$15,000-$60,000 (depends on whether you're marketing your own or someone else's products)
Potential earnings:	$25,000-$50,000+
Typical fees:	Products can sell from $5-$500 or more; you'll charge a third more than list
Advertising:	Direct mail; advertising co-ops with other catalog retailers in national publications
Qualifications:	Sales/marketing background
Equipment needed:	Postage meter, computer, printer, fax/modem, phone with 800 number for ease of ordering, credit card processing equipment
Home business potential:	Yes
Staff required:	Not initially
Handicapped opportunity:	Yes
Hidden costs:	Insurance, purchase/lease of specialized mailing lists

LOWDOWN:

Catalogs have been around as long as there have been products to sell. But what seems to work best in the catalog/mail order business is to use niche marketing; that is, pick an area of specialization and only offer products related to that area. For instance, you might sell only products for golf lovers, or only baby items. Choose an area that is specific enough to catch instant attention, yet broad enough to include a wide variety of products. You'll build your customer base from lists you either rent or purchase; if you specialize, this will be an easy process for you (and cost less in the long run). Your days will be spent taking and filling orders in the most efficient way possible; you'll also be handling customer service and possibly returns. That's why, in addition to a terrific marketing background, you'll also need some accounting skills; it all gets to be quite complicated when you're dealing with hundreds of orders (which you'll need to break even). Make sure you have adequate storage space for at least some of the goods—your basement will run out of space quickly.

START-UP:

Your earnings potential is unpredictable because you're dealing with various products at different prices and hoping they will all sell within a short period of time. Because you'll need to send out a thousand or so catalogs to make your sales efforts pay off, and because you'll need everything from a postage meter to credit card processing equipment and a computer system to maintain and run your business, expect to spend $15,000-$60,000. It'll be closer to the high end if you're actually selling your own product line; obviously, it's a little cheaper to work out agreements with other manufacturers and get a percentage of their take (usually 15 to 20 percent). Don't forget printing costs, either (these could run as high as $10,000-$15,000 per issue). You could potentially earn $25,000-

$50,000 or more, depending on how interesting or different your product line is and how much of a price variance you offer.

BOTTOM LINE ADVICE:

On the positive side, you'll be able to work in your pajamas if you want to, since you'll be in your office most of the day. The downside is, you are your work—and if you're having a bad day, orders won't get filled and you'll wind up losing money. Also, be sure that you're selling quality products—ask for samples; it's good customer service.

Keys to Building a Profitable Consulting Business

Experts agree that there are a few major steps to building a successful consulting business. Of course, you must first decide what field you're an expert in yourself before embarking on your roadmap to success.

Once you've identified your niche market, you can focus your energy on the following areas:

- **Relationship-building.** It's the mantra of the '90s business professional: build relationships that last beyond the initial sale. Don't expend a lot of energy if it looks like you'll make only one sale; spending too much time with this kind of one-shot deal can blow a whole year of sales with another potential client.

- **Clearly stating your objective and strategies.** As a consultant, you'll be expected to solve some problems of a fairly large nature. You need to be as clear as possible in your proposal as to what you'll be providing for the price you're asking. How else can a company determine whether you're worth it? (P.S. Always remind the client in your proposal of why they're needing you in the first place.)

- **Present a polished, professional image.** You are in the image business, and your clients' perceptions of you are what ultimately bring in the sale. They need to see you as successful, in demand, and of the highest quality there is—so make sure all of your materials, from business cards to sample videos, convey the real you.

- **Don't be afraid to offer free, introductory sessions when you need to.** So often, consultants get caught up in thinking that every hour should be a billable one. Keep in mind that you need to build awareness of your services before you can sell folks on them (particularly if you are just starting out); the best way to get them interested is to hold a free information seminar once every quarter or so.

- **Charge by the hour, not by the job.** Too many consultants make the mistake of underestimating the number of hours a job will take. Make sure that although you have an hourly rate of $100 per hour, your estimate reflects additional hours that you project might occur. You can offer a 10 percent discount for timely payment—but never discount the value of your own time.

- **Update your client list regularly.** At least once per year, weed out those folks who only generate a tiny portion of your annual income. To be profitable, you need to focus on the bigger accounts—and constantly fill your time with more of them.

- **Remember to follow up with every client.** As a consultant, your job is never ending; once you sign on as an expert, you remain one for life (or until you make a mistake).

CATERER

Start-up cost:	$15,000-$23,000
Potential earnings:	$30,000-$80,000
Typical fees:	$800-$15,000 per event
Advertising:	Brochures, press kits, direct mail, networking
Qualifications:	Cooking and menu planning experience, knowledge about sanitation and safe food handling, good people skills
Equipment needed:	Cooking equipment and supplies
Home business potential:	Possibly
Staff required:	Not initially; may be needed to grow
Handicapped opportunity:	No
Hidden costs:	In many states it is illegal to sell food prepared in a home kitchen; a commercial kitchen (which can be rented and/or shared) may be required

LOWDOWN:

If you have the right mixture of cooking know-how, business and good communication skills, catering can be a profitable and enjoyable enterprise. Though a commercial kitchen may be required, most catering services begin at home because start-up does not require years of training, expensive equipment, or capital investment. One fast-growing segment of this business is food delivery—especially lunches—to offices and corporations. Catering opportunities also abound in preparing private banquets at hotels, furnishing meals to airlines, cooking for parties, fund-raisers, and other events, or serving as an executive chef in a company dining room. Specializing in a particular item, such as gourmet wedding cakes or chocolate chip cookies, is another option. Caterers must observe health, safety, zoning, product liability, and other laws and regulations. Detailed record-keeping is also needed.

START-UP:

Access to a commercial kitchen can range from about $8,000-$12,000; appropriate equipment (pots, pans, etc.) will be $500-$1,000. In addition, allow $3,000-$10,000 for insurance, legal and insurance fees, license, and advertising. You will also need a delivery vehicle. You will have to lay out the costs of your "raw materials," but you can charge them back to the customer.

BOTTOM LINE ADVICE:

Successful catering requires a lot of hard work and careful planning. You have to devote time to meeting with—and cooking for—potential clients even though you may not be chosen to cater their event. Social catering involves weekend and evening work, and is also often seasonal in nature. Keep in mind you also will be responsible for serving and cleanup, as well as menu planning and cooking, unless you hire others to do these tasks. On the other hand, cooking is fun! It's a creative process, one that nourishes the cook as well as those who eat the food. You can control how much or how little you work. And you'll always be welcome in everyone's kitchen!

CHILD ID PRODUCTS

Start-up cost:	$20,000-$40,000
Potential earnings:	$35,000-$50,000
Typical fees:	Varied according to type of equipment sold; can range anywhere from $350-$1,000 per sale
Advertising:	Direct mail to organizations sponsoring child ID programs
Qualifications:	None
Equipment needed:	Video cameras, fingerprinting equipment, background information forms to sell as a distributor
Home business potential:	Yes
Staff required:	No
Handicapped opportunity:	Yes
Hidden costs:	Insurance, equipment storage and shipping costs

LOWDOWN:

Sadly, too many children are disappearing . . . and many times, it's due to a bitter divorce and custody battle that went sour. That's why so many parents are making sure that their children can be easily identified by facial features, voice, and fingerprints—and you can supply the equipment to produce such critical information by rounding up the necessary video cameras, 35mm cameras, and fingerprinting equipment that can be used by police departments and other organizations sponsoring child ID programs through schools, malls, or churches. You'll especially want to include an extensive profile sheet on each child, with information chronicling birthmarks and/or special medical conditions. You'll market to organizations across the country that produce regular programs to help give parents peace of mind—it's a noble profession, and it can be quite profitable if you can work out exceptional deals with your own product suppliers.

START-UP:

Your start-up costs will be moderate ($20,000-$40,000) due to the fact that you will need to have some product inventory on hand; keeping well-meaning organizations waiting for their child ID products could have a negative effect on business. Your equipment inventory will include video cameras and 35mm cameras, fingerprinting equipment, and detailed information sheets that can be produced via desktop publishing. If you market aggressively, you could make between $35,000-$50,000 per year.

BOTTOM LINE ADVICE:

Marketing your services will be kind of tricky at first, since you're basically selling a service that is based on a negative need. The best thing you can do is tell as many success stories as you can—and recognize that parents everywhere will want to take preventive measures necessary to protect their children against crime.

COMPUTER-AIDED DESIGN (CAD) SERVICE

Start-up cost:	$15,000-$25,000
Potential earnings:	$30,000-$75,000
Typical fees:	$125+ per hour; some projects bill on a per-job basis
Advertising:	Yellow Pages, trade journals, referrals, networking
Qualifications:	Expertise in a specific field, knowledge of hardware and software
Equipment needed:	High-end PC with 200 meg hard drive, light pen or graphics tablet with a puck, high-resolution graphics video card, laser printer
Home business potential:	Yes
Staff required:	No
Handicapped opportunity:	Yes
Hidden costs:	Time and expense of keeping up with fast-changing field

LOWDOWN:

If you have an engineering or design background, you will have many opportunities to create a successful business. Many fields, from architecture to fashion to civil engineering, use computer-aided design (CAD) extensively to develop prototypes or detailed plans. CAD enables a designer to see a design from a more functional standpoint, creating an instant prototype on screen. You will be integrating the hardware and software of CAD with the needs of a field with which you should also be familiar. It's the dual nature of this expertise that separates the successful freelancers from the rest of the competition. Design skills, up-to-date computer hardware and software expertise, and the ability to work with your clients will establish you as the person to call for the next CAD project—and the one after that.

START-UP:

Costs are high because you will need the tools of the trade: high-end computer hardware including the CAD equipment itself, the latest software, a laser printer with 11" x 17" capability, and possibly a blueprint photocopier. Expect to spend anywhere from $10,000 on up for your computer equipment; expect to bill at $125 per hour and up for your services.

BOTTOM LINE ADVICE:

Creativity meets technology here. You can earn a high hourly rate once you develop your client base. This is a growth field, and the number of skilled people has not nearly met the demand. It will be a challenge to keep your skills current; you will be required to stay abreast with the trends in the profession or design field in which you specialize.

COMPUTER COMPOSER

Start-up cost:	$15,000-$30,000
Potential earnings:	$20,000-$40,000
Typical fees:	Bids can range from $500 for a small project to $10,000 or more
Advertising:	Bulletin board services, trade journals, referrals
Qualifications:	Composition plus technological awareness
Equipment needed:	Computer, peripherals such as CD-ROM player and speakers, tape deck, printer, modem, fax, office furniture
Home business potential:	Yes
Staff required:	No
Handicapped opportunity:	Yes
Hidden costs:	On-line time, software/hardware updates

LOWDOWN:

People with musical skill and a love of the leading edge in computer creations can produce the music that accompanies most CDs and many regular programs, principally games. You'll need experience in musical composition and with MIDI programs, especially at the popular level, and you'll need connections in cyberspace. It would be most beneficial to produce your own sample or demo that others could download and listen to before engaging your services. If you're one of the few who can connect with this developing market, you can become very successful. It's definitely on the cutting edge of creativity—and it could be quite an inroad to the future of the music world.

START-UP:

Costs relate to the computer equipment required; many composers have extensive MIDI equipment and composition software that is connected to actual instruments. Consequently, your costs could run as high as $30,000. Can you earn much of that back? It's a field that's too new to tell—and it really depends on the size of the project (in addition to who your client is).

BOTTOM LINE ADVICE:

Few people will ever enter this field, so it's wide open for you. Creating the sounds that are heard in millions of homes and businesses each day can be a rewarding experience, especially if you enjoy the team aspect of multimedia production. Only a few people and businesses make the market for this service, so you'll need to be creative in finding them. Try to work with the larger companies that have been around for a while, and you'll receive better pay for the same kind of work.

ADVICE FROM THE EXPERTS

What sets your business apart from others like it?

Michael Bross, Audio Producer/Music Composer for SoundPlanet in Latrobe, Pennsylvania, says his company provides very high quality audio and music for multimedia. "We work fast. I also believe that we understand the needs of multimedia developers better than other companies of this type."

Things you couldn't do without:

Broos couldn't do without the following: both a PC and a Macintosh computer, appropriate software for music composition and audio production, professional mixing console, multitrack recording system, effects processors, storage and backup memory storage for computers, sound modules and at least one sampler, MIDI keyboard, pro-level DAT machine, cassette deck, amplifier and audio monitors, soundcards, headphones, microphones, modem and printer, and a sound source library.

Marketing tips/advice:

"The work seems to pile up between July and December. Most developers are attempting to get their product on retail shelves for the Christmas buying season. The demands are very high during this time because many clients want to have work finished immediately."

If you had to do it all over again . . .

"I would learn computer programming. Also, I would have taken the time to develop a better marketing plan in the beginning."

COMPUTERIZED SPECIAL EFFECTS DESIGNER

Start-up cost:	$20,000-$40,000
Potential earnings:	$65,000-$150,000+
Typical fees:	$75-$150 per hour or a flat, per-project rate ($2,500-$30,000)
Advertising:	Yellow Pages, referral, direct mail, industry/trade publications, World Wide Web
Qualifications:	Extensive computer programming experience (in every programming language known to man) and ability to conceptualize, artistic background
Equipment needed:	High-speed, top-of-the-line computer system with multimedia production studio and exceptional monitors, backup tapes, and simulation software
Home business potential:	Yes
Staff required:	No
Handicapped opportunity:	Yes
Hidden costs:	Equipment maintenance and upgrades, resource materials and research time

LOWDOWN:

When a computer program needs to have special effects, such as a city-crushing giant spider or a flight simulator, software producers often turn to computerized special effects designers for expertise. But your client base isn't limited to just CD-ROMs or floppy disks—the market for computerized special effects in the film industry has been growing at a phenomenal rate. Movies like *Toy Story*, which was produced by computer animation, prove that computers have a bright cinematic future ahead—and, if you can get your name out there, you can jump on the bandwagon now. If you're working with a film producer, your turnaround time may be a little longer (six months to two years) than it would be with software producers (sometimes as quick as two months). Either way, expect there to be changes upon changes—and build them into the contract (to cover your time for the extra work). No matter who your clients are, you'll be spending huge amounts of your time researching (i.e., how exactly does a fighter jet operate?), developing visuals that look realistic and programming them into a particular project. The best way to get your company's services out there is to produce a dynamic simulation or special effects package on your own Web Site. Invite potential clients to visit your site via direct mail (post cards usually work best).

START-UP:

Your start-up is relatively high ($20,000-$40,000), but that's because you'll need to spend so much on a state-of-the-art computer/multimedia station with high-end graphics packages that allow you to program your intricate designs and bring them to life. Expect to update your equipment every year or so, as new developments occur frequently in the computer designer's world. If you're working mostly for small software companies and corporate productions, you could earn at least $65,000—but, if you're lucky enough to get film studio work, your earnings could be $150,000 or significantly more.

BOTTOM LINE ADVICE:

You're good at what you do—but, more often than not, computer geniuses are not too wonderful at promoting themselves. Hire a public relations professional if you can't sell yourself well, because in your field, image is everything. Take your first few jobs and turn them into sample presentations and get a Web Site going as soon as possible. Work is lonely, intense, and complex—yet it can be truly rewarding.

Knowing When to Move

Your files are constantly ending up on the kitchen table . . . and the work seems to follow you into your bedroom. It is time to move to an office space outside of your home?

If you're carrying your work all over the house with you, it probably wouldn't hurt to make a clean break. A new office, outside of your home, could do wonders in helping you to make the separation between work and home life (which we're sure your family will greatly appreciate). Too many entrepreneurs get caught up in their businesses to the extent that the work piles up and grows in the living room and other places in the home—even though there is a designated office space in the basement or studio.

Are you one of these types who can't stop working, even past 10 o'clock at night? Are you often at the center of family arguments about when to work and when not to? Or, is it just that you are overwhelmed by customers constantly invading your living space with their demands and needs?

If you answered yes to any of these questions, it would probably be a good idea to start looking for an office space, preferably close to your house but definitely outside of it.

If your business thrives on a homey atmosphere, there are

plenty of homelike spaces available; many older homes are being converted to office campuses, and you can rent space cheaply in these kinds of offices as opposed to the larger, more corporate spaces that rent out at $3-$5 per square foot.

It really depends on what your business's identity requires that you have; for many, there is nothing like the sound of a professional, high-profile business address (like 1 Corporate Center, or Prospect Place). You would do well to look into the possibility of renting space from a business incubator-type office complex, where you pay a flat monthly rent and share secretarial, copy center, and other services with fellow budding entrepreneurs.

Ultimately, the need to move is determined by two major factors: first, have you outgrown your current space, and second, can this growth support a regular rent payment. If you can substantiate the reason for moving, and can find a suitable space that allows for even more growth at an affordable price, you can build your empire in a classy space that could make you more productive—and consequently more profitable—than your cushy little space at home.

Sure, it's convenient to have a home office, but the price you pay in productivity is sometimes not worth it in the long haul.

CONCERT PROMOTER

Start-up cost:	$15,000-$25,000
Potential earnings:	$50,000-$100,000+
Typical fees:	25 to 30 percent of the concert gross
Advertising:	Promoters' magazine, industry trades, newspapers
Qualifications:	Should be well-connected in the music industry
Equipment needed:	Basic office setup, cellular phone
Home business potential:	Yes
Staff required:	Yes
Handicapped opportunity:	Yes
Hidden costs:	Insurance, travel/entertainment costs

LOWDOWN:

Rock, opera, classical, folk . . . there are as many different acts to promote as there are types of music. If you are a real go-getter and have had an extensive background in the music industry, you stand a chance of making it as a concert promoter. You'll need to be supremely well-organized and detail-oriented, since your business hinges on every little detail. You will solicit the agent by telling him or her that, if a particular group or star is brought to your town, you will promote them aggressively every place there is a space. Network with local media to ensure good public relations, but don't promise agents the moon if you can't deliver. This business is full of hyped-up promoters who are really rip-off artists. You can't afford to be greedy until after you've established yourself; once you have a solid track record of successful promotions, you can go for the big bucks.

START-UP:

Your start-up fee ($15,000-$25,000) will be wrapped up in getting your name out there and presenting a professional image. You have to be fairly well-known before someone will let you promote their act. Your fee will be 25 to 30 percent of the concert gross; if it's a big name, you could earn as much as $150,000 per show.

BOTTOM LINE ADVICE:

There are long hours involved this occupation—and a lot of socializing, too. Not necessarily a good deal for a person with a family, but it's workable if you have a strong support staff. Expect a lot of trial and error in the beginning; learn from each experience and improve yourself with time.

CONSULTING ENGINEER

Start-up cost:	$20,000-$50,000
Potential earnings:	$40,000-$85,000+
Typical fees:	Depends on length and extent of project; can be as little as $175 for a minor project and as high as several thousand for the larger ones
Advertising:	Trade journals, classified ads, federal publications, networking
Qualifications:	Degree and certification necessary (sometimes in each state you do business in)
Equipment needed:	Drafting equipment and reference materials, computer-aided design (CAD) software, perhaps surveying equipment
Home business potential:	Yes (but you'll be mostly working on-site)
Staff required:	Not initially, although you may want to hire an administrative type early on
Handicapped opportunity:	Possibly
Hidden costs:	Liability insurance, mileage

LOWDOWN:

When a big project is launched at a corporation or even in a municipal environment, the expertise needed to actually create the "great idea" isn't exactly in-house. That's where you can really carve a nice niche for yourself—as a "hired gun" to pull together all the necessary finishing touches for construction, manufacturing, or technical situations. Consulting engineers offer their opinions or "hands-on" abilities to bring special projects to fruition. This could involve anything from CAD designs to developing a better means of production for wiring harnesses. If you don't mind the pressure of coming into a potentially volatile (and political) situation, and particularly if you are amenable to long hours for a short-term project, this could be a perfectly workable business for you. You would likely be called in as an expert; perhaps you'll be solving a snafu between the manufacturing and design departments of a major manufacturer.

START-UP:

Your start-up costs (after, of course, your degrees and certifications are taken care of) will consist mainly of basic equipment. Expect to spend at least $20,000 (more if you're planning to have others working along with you). But if you're good at what you do, you'll be able to earn a considerable amount of money within the first year or two—perhaps as much as $100,000 or more.

BOTTOM LINE ADVICE:

The key to success as a consulting engineer depends heavily on your ability to establish yourself as an industry expert of some kind. The more well-known you are for solving manufacturability problems, for instance, the more calls you're going to get—and the richer you'll become.

DAMAGE RESTORATION SERVICE

Start-up cost:	$15,000-$20,000
Potential earnings:	$40,000-$65,000
Typical fees:	Varied according to damage; can be as little as $500 and as much as several thousand
Advertising:	Yellow Pages, coupon books, networking with Realtors and contractors
Qualifications:	Should have extensive knowledge about building structure and repair, codes and regulations regarding hazardous chemicals
Equipment needed:	A complete set of tools, painting/wallpapering equipment, varnishes and woodworking equipment, special solvents for cleaning up waste byproducts
Home business potential:	Yes (but, of course, you'll be working on-site)
Staff required:	Not initially
Handicapped opportunity:	Not typically
Hidden costs:	Insurance

LOWDOWN:

When a hurricane or other natural disaster strikes, any kind of professional who can fix homes or offices is called in to assess the damage, create an estimate, and work with insurance companies to get the job done. A damage restoration service is just one of the many services that can help fix the havoc that nature wreaked on a property. But it doesn't need to be a major natural disaster for your services to be called upon; more often than not, it is a fire or severe storm that warranted repair work to be done. Both fire and flood can cause structural damage to a building, but they can also ruin floors and walls. As a damage repair service professional, you'll spend the majority of your time fixing walls, ceilings, and floors, so you'll need to be familiar with every kind of chemical that cleans, repairs, or restores such surfaces. If peeling paint and waterlogged walls are up your alley, you'll enjoy each of the projects that comes your way. One thing is certain: this kind of work is never without its challenges.

START-UP:

The smartest thing you can do is lease your equipment (and possibly even your tools) until you're sure of enough business to cover expenses. Leasing can cost you between $150-$300 per month, as opposed to a large initial outlay of cash ($10,000 or more) for repair equipment. Your charges will depend on the extent of damage done to the building; some repair jobs bill at a mere $500, while others are costlier ($1,500-$80,000).

BOTTOM LINE ADVICE:

This business can be quite lucrative if you're in a hurricane-prone area, but sporadic if in other areas of the country. You might consider adding on related services, such as wallpaper installation or faux finishes, to keep the money rolling in.

Desktop Publisher

Start-up cost:	$15,000-$25,000
Potential earnings:	$20,00-$100,000
Typical fees:	$500 (newsletter) to $20,000 (for a large-run book or magazine)
Advertising:	Direct solicitation, Yellow Pages, local publications, word of mouth, networking, advertising in writers' magazines
Qualifications:	Computer skills, knowledge of typefaces, design, and layout, writing and editing skills, communication skills
Equipment needed:	Computer with scanner, laser printer, and CD-ROM, publishing, word-processing, and drawing software, fax, office furniture, business card, letterhead, envelopes
Home business potential:	Yes
Staff required:	No
Handicapped opportunity:	Yes
Hidden costs:	Marketing; keeping up with changes in software

LOWDOWN:

Desktop publishing (DTP) enables people who understand graphic design and typography to offer a range of services to clients. Skills with computer software will allow you to produce books, flyers, and almost every kind of printed material in between. Many small DTP businesses succeed by specializing; for example, they might create newsletters for a specific type of business. Others produce entire books or focus on annual reports. Most will provide only the camera-ready master and subcontract the larger printing jobs to a commercial printer. The DTP field includes many small and large businesses, but there is room for people who do excellent work, produce it on time, and focus on their clients' needs and expectations.

START-UP:

The computer equipment required can be very expensive, depending largely on the graphics capability you need. And you must have a work space that supports the complex nature of some DTP tasks. Figure marketing costs, too, of $1,000-$2,000 in the financial section of your business plan. Your income will be dependent upon how many clients you can win in a short period of time, so you'll need to advertise your services (unless your former employer has become a major client). Billing can be done hourly ($50-$75 per) or, more typically, on a per-job basis. Smaller jobs can net $50-$300; larger ones can bring in $5,000 or more.

BOTTOM LINE ADVICE:

Although working on several different creative projects at one time can be interesting and challenging, the pressure can be unbelievable. In the days of instant information and 24-hour turnaround, everybody expects their work done today. That can be a problem when you have 10 or more clients you're juggling—try to express realistic deadlines with your clients to avoid all-nighters and stress-filled days, and be sure to schedule time for yourself to complete the work.

ADVICE FROM THE EXPERTS

What sets your business apart from others like it?

"We produce healthy recipes and a common-sense approach to healthy living," says JoAnna M. Lund, President and CEO of Healthy Exchange, Inc., in DeWitt, Louisiana. "We appeal to the average person and offer quick, healthy recipes that taste good using easy-to-find ingredients."

Things you couldn't do without:

A computer and laser printer, plus a fax machine.

Marketing tips/advice:

It's challenging to stay on top of changes in your field, but it can pay you well to do so, says Lund. Make sure you're an expert on that which you're reporting about.

If you had to do it all over again . . .

"Nothing. I'm quite happy where I am."

DIGITAL IMAGING SERVICE

Start-up cost:	$20,000-$40,000
Potential earnings:	$25,000-$45,000
Typical fees:	$15-$45 per scanned-image product
Advertising:	Yellow Pages, mall kiosks and other high people-volume locations
Qualifications:	Training in equipment
Equipment needed:	Computer with scanner and video imaging capability
Home business potential:	No
Staff required:	No
Handicapped opportunity:	Possibly
Hidden costs:	Insurance, equipment maintenance and upgrades

LOWDOWN:

The digital craze is on—and it's not limited to musical instruments or compact disks. You can cash in on the trend by starting your own digital imaging service. You've probably seen such businesses in your local shopping mall or at a community flea market: the proprietor simply takes a video image of a person and places it onto a computer screen for printing on a color printer; the image is then transferred to a product (such as a felt banner, T-shirt, or coffee mug) and a personalized gift has been created. It's that simple, and the product generally sells itself if positioned in a high-traveled area. You can buy a franchise or start your own version if you are familiar enough with the equipment and can work with product vendors. Expect to market your service aggressively; you'll need to talk to people and have excellent sales ability to make enough money to cover your expenses (particularly mall rent). Still, it's a fun method of gift-giving for many consumers—and they will buy if you are visible enough.

START-UP:

You'll need $20,000-$40,000 for your equipment and space rental, slightly more if you buy a franchise. Your equipment will include a computer with color printer, video camera, and software that permits image transfer from video to computer screen to printer. Thermal transfer equipment will also be necessary to produce those personalized coffee mugs and T-shirts. On the plus side, you might see as much as $45,000 for little effort on your part.

BOTTOM LINE ADVICE:

Your business will fluctuate according to season; expect low times in the fall and spring, and a Christmas high (complete with long hours and heavy volume).

EDUCATIONAL PRODUCT DEVELOPMENT

Start-up cost:	$20,000-$30,000
Potential earnings:	$45,000-$65,000
Typical fees:	$25-$1,000
Advertising:	Yellow Pages, direct mail and cold calls to educational product distributors, teachers' stores, and school systems
Qualifications:	Degree in education would be helpful
Equipment needed:	Complete computer setup with laser printer, fax/modem, copier, phone system
Home business potential:	Yes
Staff required:	No
Handicapped opportunity:	Yes
Hidden costs:	Insurance

LOWDOWN:

For every workbook, handout, or overhead a teacher uses in the classroom on a daily basis, there is an educational publisher who developed and marketed it. If you have a background in education and/or publishing, then developing and producing a multitude of creative learning materials may be right up your alley. You could produce everything from bulletin board decorations to mathematics workbooks to individualized reading program material and textbooks, and all of it could be marketed through a catalog detailing your complete product line. You might be doing contract work for an educational distributor or publisher who needs you to develop a specific product for them, such as a series of overhead projection maps. Find a creative way to set yourself apart from your competitors. For instance, you might have unusual credentials yourself, or a nontraditional way of teaching children to solve problems via storytelling. Whatever your niche, you'll need to make sure that your materials are of the highest educational quality, and having a few teachers use and endorse your products will certainly help get you started.

START-UP:

It could easily cost between $20,000-$30,000 to establish yourself in the educational product development business, mainly because you'll need a complete computer system with desktop publishing capability and an excellent printer. Also, you'll need to produce your catalog, and that isn't going to be cheap (budget at least $10,000 for that alone). Still, if you have a solid client base or sell regularly enough from your own catalogs, you could pocket between $45,000-$65,000.

BOTTOM LINE ADVICE:

Your clients need innovation and excitement in their educational materials in order to compete with television and computer programs—if you can develop truly unusual materials that actually succeed in educating children, your only problem will be to tell enough clients about your products to make a sizable profit. Buy lists when you can. One last tip: since educational materials need to be precise and accurate themselves, be careful to ensure that there are no mistakes in your projects.

EMPLOYEE LEASING

Start-up cost:	$15,000-$35,000
Potential earnings:	$60,000-$80,000
Typical fees:	Mark up the going rates by 40 to 50 percent
Advertising:	Direct mail, networking in business and trade associations, publishing a newsletter
Qualifications:	Knowledge of and contacts in a specific field, excellent organizational skills
Equipment needed:	Office furniture, computer, printer, fax, telephone headset, business card, letterhead, envelopes, brochure
Home business potential:	Yes
Staff required:	No
Handicapped opportunity:	Yes
Hidden costs:	Liability insurance against employee misconduct

LOWDOWN:

While you may not be able to compete with the big general help agencies, a small employee leasing agency can provide workers with specialized skills who cannot be reached through the traditional temp services. This business produces good earnings relative to time and materials: you're not doing the actual work— just the organization. Build your database of specialists in a field you have experience with, then begin direct mail to your prospective clients.

START-UP:

Although the cost of building your initial database and center of operations is not high, you will need a sizable initial investment ($20,000) to cover the delays in cash flow between your clients and your employees. You could see at least $60,000 at the end of your first year.

BOTTOM LINE ADVICE:

You may need to consult an attorney to stay abreast of the laws regarding taxes, workers' compensation, and employment. Some types of temps will need to be bonded, and you will need to measure the advantages of incorporation over the extra costs and red tape involved.

ENTERTAINMENT DIRECTORY PUBLISHER

Start-up cost:	$15,000-$30,000
Potential earnings:	$35,000-$65,000
Typical fees:	Advertising income (rates from $125-$3,000 per issue)
Advertising:	High-profile shelf space (and plenty of drop-off sites), advertisement on buses and billboards, distribution at hotels and restaurants
Qualifications:	Previous publishing experience would be extremely helpful
Equipment needed:	Computer, laser printer, fax/modem, phone
Home business potential:	Yes
Staff required:	1-2 editorial or production types
Handicapped opportunity:	Possibly
Hidden costs:	Printing and rising paper costs

LOWDOWN:

Where do all the happening folk turn to for entertainment ideas in their community? They pick up a free entertainment directory from restaurants, hotels, and other hot spots around town. Despite the myriad of choices they'll have due to an influx of free newspapers and other publications, these fickle consumers will choose to read your publication as the source for what's truly hot and happening. You will solicit advertisements from every entertainment-related business you can think of in your community, from video stores to restaurants and concert halls—and, more than likely, you'll be able to sell them on the virtues of advertising regularly in your well-read pages. You will design a publication that looks inviting and entertaining itself—and you will set up a vast enough distribution channel to make advertising with you worth it. Words like "over 500,000 distribution points in the tristate area" will strike the right chords with potential advertisers. Create the product, get it printed as economically as possible, then wait to build consumer recognition. It could take more than two years, but if you work hard and stick with it, you could see a huge profit later.

START-UP:

It will cost you between $15,000-$30,000 to successfully launch an entertainment directory publishing business, mainly to cover printing and paper costs. It really depends, though, on how large your print run is; decide early what your demographics are telling you about your potential market for these directories, and budget accordingly for each issue you produce. If you can generate enough ad sales to cover printing costs, your income could reach anywhere from $35,000-$65,000.

BOTTOM LINE ADVICE:

You're competing against many other media in this field, including other entertainment directories. Set yourself apart by offering regular contests or an add-on service for your advertisers, such as a coupon-packaging service.

10 Steps to Managing and Motivating Your Employees Without Extra Cash

1. Be approachable: use employees' names; say "Hi! How are you?"; shake hands and smile.

2. Know your employees: ask someone to join you for coffee; inquire about workers' families; recognize important events in your employees' lives.

3. Be an active listener: make a note of others' ideas, and take those ideas seriously; accept differences of opinion, and say when you agree; express your feelings and recognize others'.

4. Ask for help: seek out problem-solving ideas.

5. Create an affirming environment: workers who feel competent are more likely to act competently.

6. Set helpful goals: see that your goals are quantifiable, realistic, and easily understood; have the worker help set them.

7. Give goals meaning: show employees where they fit into the broader company objectives.

8. Evaluate: measure employee productivity constantly.

9. Reinforce productive behaviors: even expected performance must be positively reinforced.

10. Inform: let your employees know how your company is doing.

FISH RESTOCKING

Start-up cost:	$15,000-$25,000
Potential earnings:	$30,000-$50,000
Typical fees:	$30-$50 per job
Advertising:	Sport magazines, direct mail, referrals
Qualifications:	Knowledge of fish breeding and nurturing, restocking practices
Equipment needed:	Land for a hatchery, tank vehicles for restocking, computer, office furniture, business card
Home business potential:	No
Staff required:	Yes
Handicapped opportunity:	No
Hidden costs:	Staff to feed the fish, conduct the restocking procedures, and maintain the property, insurance

LOWDOWN:

You will have two possible types of clients if you enter this field, governments and private fishing resorts. Governments at different levels have many rigid requirements and can be challenging to deal with. However, many government entities conduct fish restocking on a large scale, and this could be a good opportunity for the right business. Private fishing resorts also often need major restocking efforts, and it is possible that one of these might fund your operation's start-up costs. Detailed knowledge of fish is essential for success in this business.

START-UP:

Start-up costs are relatively high in this business as you must have not only the land and improvements needed, but also the vehicles for delivering fish stock across a fairly wide geographic area. Many fish restockers charge between $500-$1,000 for their services; it really depends on your area and the customer's needs. It might be a good idea to specialize in one kind of fish: this will keep your start-up costs down, especially for the first hatchings.

BOTTOM LINE ADVICE:

If you love the outdoors and the world of fishing, this business could be very appropriate for you. You will be establishing relationships with your clients, whether government or private, that may last for many years. You will also have a close involvement with the natural world. However, it can be difficult to find workers who share your enthusiasm for hard outdoor labor, especially in bad weather. And your business will be at the mercy of budget cutters in either the public or the private arenas.

FLORAL SHOP

Start-up cost:	$15,000-$40,000
Potential earnings:	$1,000-$5,000 per month
Typical fees:	Depends on what you sell (live fresh-cut, arrangement, wreaths, swags, etc.)
Advertising:	Yellow Pages, specialty magazines, business cards at bridal salons, funeral homes, and other places where people buy and use flowers regularly
Qualifications:	Some states require licensing
Equipment needed:	Building, floral tools, refrigerator, fresh, silk, and dried flowers, baskets, balloons, gift cards
Home business potential:	No
Staff required:	Yes
Handicapped opportunity:	Yes
Hidden costs:	Insurance, taxes, spoilage

LOWDOWN:

Nothing compares to the beauty of a single rose—or, better yet, an artfully designed floral bouquet. If you know your daisies from your day lilies, you can start a floral shop and work with your customers on nearly any project they present you with. This is truly creative work, and you'll enjoy the challenge of putting together an interesting array of the most gorgeous posies on the planet. You'll use three basic types of flowers: fresh cut, silk, and dried. A keen visual sense of what is pleasing to the eye and appropriate for the event is required. You must have the ability to preserve and sell flowers, take customer orders, and be as knowledgeable as any of your competitors. In this business, you will probably require a staff, especially to help you through the busy seasons.

START-UP:

Your start-up costs will be high (at least $15,000), because you will need a storefront that allows you to sell by window display. You'll have to price your merchandise according to type. Your peak period in the floral industry is November through May. After you've recovered your initial investment, the earning potential will still be slow until you've gained your niche. Expect $12,000-$24,000 the first year.

BOTTOM LINE ADVICE:

This job requires standing for long periods of time—sometimes 10-12 hours per day. The hours are even longer for weddings and holidays such as Christmas, Mother's Day, and Valentine's Day. The floral industry in general is usually closed on Sunday and sometimes Monday, but expect to work holidays and weekends. The faster you are in creating beauty, the more money you can make.

ADVICE FROM THE EXPERTS

What sets your business apart from others like it?

Personalized service, high quality, and reasonable prices are what set apart Pam Williams's florist shop, Pam's Posies, in Akron, Ohio. "We also have a pleasant atmosphere that's homey and inviting. We go one step further than any of our competitors by producing the most creative arrangements we can muster." Williams's business is located in a converted home in the middle of a busy commercial real estate parcel.

Things you couldn't do without:

"Employees, of course. But we also couldn't do without our coolers, decorative materials, fresh and silk inventory, knives, and cutters."

Marketing tips/advice:

"Be in an area where you already know a lot of people, first of all. Then, realize that whatever you send out is ultimately going to be your best advertising—so send out your best work!" Williams also participates in Welcome Wagon-type giveaways to bring people into the store for free flowers. "Once they've been inside, they almost always come back, so the free flowers are worth it."

If you had to do it all over again . . .

"I might have gotten more schooling before launching my own business. As it was, I had to learn everything on the job. Still, I think I handled my company's growth in the right way, growing in five- to seven-year increments rather than all at once."

HEALTH CENTERS FOR CORPORATIONS

Start-up cost:	$15,000-$35,000
Potential earnings:	$40,000-$65,000
Typical fees:	Monthly retainers of $3,000-$5,000 per project
Advertising:	Business publications, newspapers, direct mail
Qualifications:	Business background and extensive knowledge of the health and fitness field. Excellent managerial and selling skills
Equipment needed:	Well-equipped office, business card, letterhead, stationery, envelopes, high-quality marketing materials, demonstration video
Home business potential:	Yes
Staff required:	Yes
Handicapped opportunity:	No
Hidden costs:	Insurance, equipment repair

LOWDOWN:

For many employees, an on-site health center (or mini-clinic) convenient to work is the ultimate benefit. You can use your excellent managerial skills to develop and manage such centers for corporations that wish to increase the loyalty of their employees, and improve their health as well by making medical services more readily available to them. Balancing the costs against the fees will require an excellent business sense, and you will need outstanding employees of your own to run each center. Centralizing purchasing, marketing, and other services will enable you to offer these services to corporations at a competitive cost. With the current state of health care in America, how could you go wrong with a proposition such as this?

START-UP:

Start-up costs will be high ($15,000-$35,000 or more) for training/resource materials and your own office setup (with computer, printer, and fax/modem, and there will be a rise in expenses as each new corporate client is obtained and serviced. You'll earn every cent of the $40,000-$65,000 you get each year.

BOTTOM LINE ADVICE:

Once your business is established, you will have an innovative and highly profitable enterprise. Building the health center concept into an established business, though, will be enormously demanding. Your marketing and selling skills will be thoroughly tested. Keeping the centers operating well, safely, and profitably, will also be challenging. It's not a crowded field, and with these demands you can see why.

HOME INSPECTOR

Start-up costs:	$30,000-$40,000
Potential earnings:	$50,000-$75,000
Typical fees:	$200-$400, depending on size of home
Advertising:	Yellow Pages, real estate publications, local newspapers, networking with real estate agents
Qualifications:	Thorough knowledge of home construction and building codes or experience in contracting and building; depending on the area of the country, license or permits might be required
Equipment needed:	Electrical tracer, circuit tester, gas detector, basic tools like screwdrivers, flashlights, and ladders, computer, fax, printer
Home business potential:	Yes
Staff required:	No
Handicapped opportunity:	Not typically
Hidden costs:	Insurance, telephone bills, association dues

LOWDOWN:

In this litigious society, home buyers, sellers, and realtors are all looking for the best protection they can get. Learning the condition of a home up front from a third party ensures that buyers will know just what kind of home they are purchasing before the sale is complete. Unfortunately, home inspectors are often targets for litigation, too, so look into certification and licensing requirements in your area and protect yourself by either incorporating or affiliating yourself with a franchise organization. Whichever you choose, your work will change on a daily basis, as you'll be moving from one home to another to inspect everything from the condition of the wiring to shingles on the roof. You'll be checking off items in a large binder as you proceed, and this is what you will leave as a permanent record for the potential home owner. It's a necessary service in this buyer beware kind of market.

START-UP:

Mostly, you'll need the funds to either develop or secure rights to the information contained in each binder you provide your customers. This business will be much easier to get up and running effectively (and in a shorter period of time) if you pay a franchise fee (anywhere from $30,000-$50,000) to an already established company in this field. That way, you're also protected legally.

BOTTOM LINE ADVICE:

Don't underestimate the value of contact with real estate agents. Many of your best referrals will come from them. Likewise, thorough and honest inspections will result in satisfied home buyers, a valuable source of word-of-mouth advertising. You'll have lots of face-to-face contact with them, so excellent communication and people skills are a must.

HORSE/CARGO TRAILER SERVICE

Start-up cost:	$15,000-$30,000
Potential earnings:	$20,000-$30,000
Typical fees:	$40-$50 per trailer ride, plus mileage
Advertising:	Yellow Pages, word of mouth, business/farming publications
Qualifications:	Experience in animal transportation, clean driving record
Equipment needed:	Trailer with room to accommodate two to four horses
Home business potential:	Yes
Staff required:	No
Handicapped opportunity:	No
Hidden costs:	Insurance, equipment maintenance

LOWDOWN:

Horse owners often need to have their animals transported to shows, county fairs, and even to new owners, and they will pay you $40-$50 plus mileage to transport these animals for them—especially if they've got ten horses and only one two-horse trailer of their own. That's why it's so important for you to network well with local equestrians—often, there are equestrian associations where you can circulate your business card and meet with horse owners and trainers. These are the folks who will continually provide you with business.

START-UP:

You may need to shell out between $15,000-$30,000 to get your trailer (slightly less if you lease), but you can expect to earn a fairly decent living ($20,000-$30,000) if you promote heavily and subcontract to others like you during the heavy seasons (specifically, summertime—when most county fairs occur).

BOTTOM LINE ADVICE:

If you don't mind the hosing down you'll need to do after each equestrian delivery (horses tend to be quite messy when confined), this could be a relatively easy way to earn a living. However, until you get well-known, you won't be able to make enough to support yourself. Plan on the process taking two to five years to bring in any real money.

HOT AIR BALLOON RIDES

Start-up cost:	$15,000-$21,000
Potential earnings:	$45,000+
Typical fees:	$50-$75 per person (minimums of 4-6 are common)
Advertising:	Yellow Pages, word of mouth/referrals
Qualifications:	Pilot's license, good navigational skills
Equipment needed:	Complete balloon rig, insurance
Home business potential:	Possible, field/open space needed
Staff required:	Yes, for liftoff and return
Handicapped opportunity:	No
Hidden costs:	Liability insurance

LOWDOWN:

Up, up, and away in a beautiful (and profitable) balloon! Hot air balloon rides are fast becoming a popular entertainment form, especially for those thrill-seekers who aren't into bungee jumping or other potentially life-threatening adventures. From tethered rides to free-flying across the countryside at varying altitudes, the range of flight packages you can offer is wide. Many balloon ride businesses provide extras such as a picnic lunch or rides to special places of interest. You'll need to carry some costly insurance and regularly maintain your pilot's license, but think of all the interesting people you'll meet while cruising the friendly skies. Fees for a two- or three-hour tethered ride can be $800 or more, while a short champagne tour generally starts at $100. You'll need to come up with incentives to get groups of four to six people together at a time (to make your own time worth it).

START-UP:

The biggest expense in the "launch" of this business is initially in the purchase of a balloon rig (balloon and basket), which begins at $12,000. More luxurious models increase rapidly in price, but the average four-seater runs about $18,000. Obtaining a pilot's license can cost you anywhere from $2,500-$3,000; insurance premiums will vary according to where you live.

BOTTOM LINE ADVICE:

This business could be seasonal, depending on where you live. A love for flying is a must, as well as the ability to enjoy being around people all day long. Skill at helping others calm their fears could be an added benefit in situations when clients experience slight vertigo. There's no telling what can happen when you're flying along at 2,000 feet, so keep a cool head.

IMPORTING/EXPORTING

Start-up cost:	$15,000-$25,000
Potential earnings:	$100,000-$200,000+
Typical fees:	Percentage of each transaction
Advertising:	International business publications, on-line services, direct mail, referrals
Qualifications:	Extensive knowledge of everything from foreign business operation to letters of credit and legalities
Equipment needed:	Computer with high-speed modem and dedicated fax/modem line; foreign currency exchange resources (could be on-line), cellular phone
Home business potential:	Yes
Staff required:	No
Handicapped opportunity:	Yes
Hidden costs:	Insurance, on-line charges

LOWDOWN:

Import/export businesses have been on the rise since the late 1980s, when U.S. companies began to benefit from the dollar dropping against foreign currencies and foreign countries being more receptive to the idea of doing business with Americans. Now, with the global marketplace open for business on the Internet, there have never been greater opportunities for folks who have quality or high-demand products to sell to other countries; the moneymaking opportunities seem limitless. You can import or export everything from ball bearings to furniture—and even such large items as farm equipment. At first, it might seem like an easy proposition to call on foreigners for business exchanges, but you may find it challenging (not to mention exceedingly competitive) because virtually anyone with a modem can get on the 'Net and announce that they are open for business. However, if you can manage to learn about and stay on top of economic developments in other countries, and have a knack for getting along with people of different cultural backgrounds than yours, this could be an exciting and high-energy business for you to launch—and it could become easier and more profitable at the same time.

START-UP:

Your start-up ($15,000-$25,000) will include a computer with a high-speed modem, printer, and fax; you'll also need to have a dedicated line for the fax/modem, because you'll be doing business across many time zones. Phone bills will be somewhat expensive, but with the Internet you can communicate inexpensively with some of your overseas contacts. If you are well-connected and sell quality or high-demand products, you could earn $100,000-$200,000 in a relatively short period of time.

BOTTOM LINE ADVICE:

On the surface, this type of business seems like an easy way to become wealthy; in reality, it takes a great deal of time and effort to build the kinds of profitable contacts you'll need to build your empire. You'll need to stick with it while you build your Rolodex.

INTERNATIONAL BUSINESS CONSULTANT

Start-up cost:	$15,000-$40,000
Potential earnings:	$45,000-$150,000+
Typical fees:	$100-$500 per hour; sometimes a percentage of the deal (15 to 25 percent)
Advertising:	Industry and business publications
Qualifications:	Extensive travel experience, foreign language skills, and the ability to understand and work within other cultures
Equipment needed:	Basic office setup with cellular phone, laptop computer, strong, durable suitcases
Home business potential:	Yes, but you'll be doing lots of traveling
Staff required:	No
Handicapped opportunity:	Possibly
Hidden costs:	Insurance, travel, and cellular phone expenses

LOWDOWN:

The global marketplace is becoming increasingly important to large corporations looking to expand their operations, but small- to medium-size companies are also entering the global picture. That's where you come in, because your expertise will be in matching the needs and goals of one corporate culture to the world culture in general. In other words, you play matchmaker between one company and several possible expansion sites in other countries. You'll need to have a good handle on the economic, political, and especially cultural climate in each country, as well as the ability to communicate well to foreign officials as you try to negotiate intricate contracts. There's a famous story about Chevrolet's Nova and why it didn't sell well in Mexico: "no va" in Spanish means "doesn't go," and who wants a car that doesn't go? Remember that story as you approach different countries with products and concepts from the U.S. and beyond. Work within cultural boundaries and remember, too, to do in Rome as the Romans would do. On the plus side, imagine the Frequent Flyer bonus miles you'll rack up!

START-UP:

You'll need sufficient capital to advertise and travel in the right circles, so that you can meet with high-powered corporate officials who need your services. You might well spend $30,000-$40,000 getting this business off the ground, unless you already have 10-12 good client possibilities. Still, at $100-$500 per hour (depending on your level of expertise and track record), you'll be able to earn a highly respectable income for yourself—and you'd be wise to pencil in a percentage of the deal as well.

BOTTOM LINE ADVICE:

Traveling all over the world helping companies expand in the global marketplace can be glorious work when it goes well—and downright dismal when it doesn't.

LANDSCAPE DESIGNER

Start-up cost:	$15,000-$35,000
Potential earnings:	$30,000-$50,000
Typical fees:	Varied; anywhere from $40-$1,000 or more
Advertising:	Personal contact with landscaping companies and nurseries, ads in business and Yellow Pages, ads in local newspapers
Qualifications:	Thorough knowledge of different varieties of shrubs, trees, flowers and grass and soil that works best for each; a sense of aesthetics and ability to design plans that please the customer are essential
Equipment needed:	Basic office equipment
Home business potential:	Yes
Staff required:	No
Handicapped opportunity:	No
Hidden costs:	Phone and traveling expenses

LOWDOWN:

Do you have a love for the beauty of nature—and the skill to organize such beauty into a gorgeous landscape? If so, this could be the business for you. You'll be selling your services to landscape companies that will implement your plans—perhaps business owners and developers with grounds to beautify, or consumers who want to be surrounded by flora but don't know how to accomplish it. It will take excellent listening and communication skills to find out what your clients want. Drawing up plans that fit their budget and tastes and working with landscape companies that will implement your ideas can be challenging yet rewarding for those with the ability to create Monet's garden out of an otherwise grassy knoll.

START-UP:

Equipment will cost you in the neighborhood of $15,000-$20,000, especially if you don't already own a van or small truck. However, your business should be able to cover that in a relatively short period of time if you're charging $75-$100 per hour. (Note: most landscape designers charge by the project and not by the hour; however, you'll need to figure roughly what you'd like to earn per hour to correctly cover your expenses.)

BOTTOM LINE ADVICE:

Don't rely on business from home owners alone—they're likely to think of landscaping only during warm weather months. Big contracts will come from developers and landscape companies. Be prepared to offer your services to a broad geographic region; this might require some traveling.

LAWYER

Start-up cost:	$15,000-$30,000 (less if sharing space and resources)
Potential earnings:	$50,000-$80,000
Typical fees:	$125/hour outside the major cities
Advertising:	Yellow Pages, networking, referrals (many legal restrictions on lawyer advertising apply), organization memberships
Qualifications:	Law degree, persistence, people skills
Equipment needed:	Office space decorated in a professional (not necessarily ostentatious) manner, access to law library, computer, modem, fax, software, laser printer, business card, letterhead, envelopes
Home business potential:	Yes
Staff required:	Not initially (if you can type)
Handicapped opportunity:	Yes
Hidden costs:	Drain on your billable time from people wanting free advice, insurance, on-line time

LOWDOWN:

Abraham Lincoln did it, so why can't you? It has been fashionable to mock the "single shingle" lawyer, but opportunities to join huge firms right out of law school—and make huge bucks—have just about vanished today. One way to use the degree you have just suffered through is to start your own business. You create the clientele, you develop the specialty, you do the billing, you reap the rewards. Can you find a way to show total commitment to the success of small businesses in your area? Are you able to disentangle the affairs of wealthy individuals and keep them in control of their lives? Can you deal with the anguish of divorcing people and help them manage the separation process through mediation and negotiation? If you answered yes to any of these questions, you can make a go of your single-shingle operation and give up the frustrating struggle to be hired by someone else.

START-UP:

Many solo practitioners share office space, support staff, and other necessary costs of setting up in business. You'll need an appropriate and professional-looking space in which to meet your clients, and you must produce and store the paperwork. Spend at least $5,000 on your office and its contents (include an extra $3,000 for a high-power computer to make on-line searches less time-consuming and, hence, less costly). Bill out at around $125 to start; after your reputation is as good as old Abe's, you can start charging like the big boys ($200-$300 per hour).

BOTTOM LINE ADVICE:

Probably the most important factor in your success will be your connections to the community you hope to serve. The average Joe tends to have a negative view of all lawyers, and you're going to need to keep struggling against this stereotype.

Building trust is so challenging that you will have little chance for success unless you start with a network of people who know and like you. Eventually you will become known as the helpful, skilled lawyer to go to when a need for work in your specialty arises. Another difficulty is that you will be constantly asked to work for free. Everyone needs a lawyer from time to time, but many people are reluctant to pay for a lawyer's experience, expertise, and legal skills. It will be your job to track hours, send bills, and make sure the funds are collected. This is a tedious, time-consuming process. One tip: Consider offering prepaid legal services, which works much like insurance.

ADVICE FROM THE EXPERTS

What sets your business apart from others like it?

Stanford M. Altschul, sole practitioner based in Long Island, New York, says he picked a niche and set about servicing it with free information (in the form of marketing materials such as brochures and newsletters). "I market myself regularly to my clients, keeping my name in front of them via newsletters, brochures, and other direct mail pieces I produce myself."

Things you couldn't do without:

Altschul could not do without a computer and laser printer, telephone, copier, and fax machine.

Marketing tips/advice:

"You should definitely be networking with certain industries that will bring you referral business, such as accounting, real estate, and banking. All of these professionals are in regular contact with those who need your services."

If you had to do it all over again . . .

"I made a mistake in being in a partnership that wasn't a good partnership . . . It took me over twenty years to figure out that I prefer working alone."

MAIL-ORDER COMPUTER AND COMPONENT SALES

Start-up cost:	$15,000-$25,000
Potential earnings:	$40,000-$80,000
Typical fees:	Commission of 10 to 20 percent or higher
Advertising:	Computer magazines, newspapers
Qualifications:	Familiarity with consumer computing trends and product availability, marketing and distribution skills, access to inventory through a network of suppliers
Equipment needed:	High-end computer and software for entering orders, tracking inventory, and invoicing, telephone equipment adequate for taking orders, 800 number
Home business potential:	Yes
Staff required:	Possible need to add staff as business grows
Handicapped opportunity:	Yes
Hidden costs:	High phone bills can result if a few long-winded callers tie up your 800 number

LOWDOWN:

You will need to create ads that pull in orders. You also need to have direct access to inventory of the items you have chosen to sell. Set prices competitively so that people will choose to order from you instead of buying at their local computer retailer. You, or the person you hire to take phone orders, will need good telephone communication skills to answer customers' questions, recommend the best products for their needs, and record orders accurately.

START-UP:

Start-up costs are high in this field, but so are the prospects for earnings. The major expenses are advertising to bring in orders and equipment to respond to and fulfill those orders. The 800 number is your link to your market and can cost $8-$20 per month (plus the per-incoming-call rate). All of this could easily be offset by your income, since your commission can be as high as 20 percent.

BOTTOM LINE ADVICE:

Mail order is a special world. It enables you to create a business without all the challenges of developing a retail location, hiring salespeople, and so on. Computers and components are perfect mail-order products because customers do not need to see or touch them to understand what they want. The information you give over the phone is just as valuable as what a buyer could learn talking directly to a salesperson in the aisle of a store. In fact, your expertise is probably much higher than that available in most superstores, so you can educate your customers about what computer would best fill their requirements. The challenge here is to find the narrow price positioning that will keep your company competitive and still allow profitability.

MESSAGE RETRIEVAL SERVICE (ANSWERING SERVICE)

Start-up cost:	$15,000-$25,000
Potential earnings:	$20,000-$35,000
Typical fees:	$50-$75 and up per month
Advertising:	Networking and referrals, Yellow Pages, business publications
Qualifications:	A pleasant, helpful phone voice
Equipment needed:	Computer with internal fax/modem board, word-processing and contact management software, phone headsets
Home business potential:	Yes
Staff required:	Yes (usually 1-5 employees)
Handicapped opportunity:	Yes
Hidden costs:	Additional phone lines to handle more clients, personnel costs

LOWDOWN:

Answering services have been around for a long time, but the explosive growth in small service businesses has made them even more important than ever. You can take your pleasant phone manner and your good listening skills and create an excellent business opportunity. The latest software allows keyboard entry of caller information; pagers can connect you to the plumber or consultant who has hired you to be his "home office." A higher-tech approach is a voice mail system, with an options menu and the capability of recording and sharing long messages. This is increasingly a communications culture, and you can succeed by joining forces instead of competing.

START-UP:

Equipment required depends to some extent on the level of service you plan to offer. If you're using a phone system including a switchboard with headsets, you'll spend at least $2,000 on equipment in the beginning. If you opt for the high-tech voice mail system, you'll shell out $5,000 or more. At any rate, you will be billing a healthy monthly fee of $50 or higher, so the equipment, and cost of paying your staff, could pay for itself in a relatively short period of time.

BOTTOM LINE ADVICE:

You have a pleasant voice and care about people. You know how to filter out what is important from the background chatter. No one is better at keeping track of things than you. What can we say? You're a natural for this business. On the downside, this business does tie you down to your desk and phones. You will also have to work hard at marketing to develop enough customers.

MOBILE CAR INSPECTION/REPAIR

Start-up costs:	$15,000-$25,000
Potential earnings:	$30,000-$45,000
Typical fees:	$25-$30 per hour or a per-inspection rate of $125
Advertising:	Yellow Pages, local newspapers, news release announcing your service in automotive sections or special publications delivered free to residences, coupon books
Qualifications:	Must be a skilled auto mechanic (better to be certified)
Equipment needed:	Basic mechanic's tools, dependable transportation of your own
Home business potential:	Yes
Staff required:	No
Handicapped opportunity:	No
Hidden costs:	Insurance, mileage

LOWDOWN:

Convenience sells. Consumers today are often too busy to take their car to the shop so if you can come to them, you'd be saving them time—and for many busy professionals, time is money. Not only can you repair minor car troubles (such as windshield or minor electrical problems) on the spot, you can offer to help people inspect new or used vehicles before purchase. Assisting potential car owners with a good once-over can be a valuable service, especially if the car is used and being sold by an individual owner whom the buyer does not know. Women especially will appreciate the expertise of a mechanic who can inspect a vehicle and help them arrive at a good offer.

START-UP:

You'll need a good set of mechanic's tools and dependable transportation of your own (preferably something with your logo on it to get even more for your advertising dollar); expect to spend at least $15,000-$25,000 on launching this innovative yet necessary business. As a mobile car care or inspecting professional, you can charge an hourly fee ($25-$30) or a flat rate ($125) for each vehicle.

BOTTOM LINE ADVICE:

Your honesty and integrity are on the line. Backing those traits with a written, personal guarantee will help sell your service.

MOBILE PAPER-SHREDDING SERVICE

Start-up cost:	$15,000-$18,000
Potential earnings:	$20,000-$40,000
Typical fees:	$30-$50 per office visit
Advertising:	Local business periodicals, direct mail
Qualifications:	Marketing skills, excellent time management and scheduling ability
Equipment needed:	Van, paper shredder, computer, printer, and fax, cellular phone
Home business potential:	Yes
Staff required:	No
Handicapped opportunity:	No
Hidden costs:	Vehicle maintenance and repair

LOWDOWN:

Mobile paper-shredding services are just now beginning to grow in major U.S. cities. As information becomes more valuable, it becomes more important to certain types of businesses to maintain security. Banks, for example, have suffered great losses when criminals obtained and analyzed their discarded paper trash. Computer codes, product information, even customer records are essential to keep confidential. The value of your service is that it guarantees security; shredding is completed on the client's premises so that no possibility exists for loss of data and information. Shredding can be done within an office, but it is time-consuming and messy. You are saving time and trouble by bringing your shredding machine to your client's site on a regular schedule to perform this necessary but tedious task.

START-UP:

The van or truck is the major expense, at $15,000 or more. You, of course, will need a heavy-duty shredder as well (about $300). Charge $30-$50 per office visit; offer a monthly rate to more regular clients (attorneys and government officials, perhaps).

BOTTOM LINE ADVICE:

Try to get into this business fast if you intend to do so at all, before the crush of competitors limits your opportunity to make a fair profit by your labors. Marketing will need to include considerable education so that your potential clients become aware of the advantages to their organization of the mobile shredding services that you offer. Excellent customer service will maintain and increase your hard-won client base.

MOTOR VEHICLE LICENSE BUREAU

Start-up cost:	$15,000-$25,000
Potential earnings:	$25,000-$40,000
Typical fees:	Commission on each transaction (usually 5 to 20 percent)
Advertising:	Newspapers, Yellow Pages, good-size outdoor or window sign, location
Qualifications:	Good office management skills
Equipment needed:	Equipment for producing licenses, furniture, computers linked to the state registry of motor vehicles
Home business potential:	No
Staff required:	Yes
Handicapped opportunity:	No
Hidden costs:	Insurance, training for employees

LOWDOWN:

If you own a license bureau, you will take in a commission on each transaction your organization performs. You will be representing the state and offering the driver's licenses that almost everyone in the U.S. relies on to conduct our national love affair with the automobile. Specialized licenses for drivers of motorcycles, truck, and other types of vehicles will also bring in customers for your service. Some license bureaus offer the opportunity to take the driver's road test, while others do not. In our highly mobile society, people frequently need new licenses, replacements for lost licenses, or renewals on outdated ones. This means that your prospective market is a large one. To maximize your earnings potential, you may later decide to add on additional services, such as driver training and/or testing facilities.

START-UP:

Rent an office space accessible to the public, preferably with foot traffic and parking nearby. You'll need enough for appropriate fixtures/furniture, employee salaries, equipment to produce the photo licenses themselves, and materials. These will require a major outlay ($10,000-$20,000) at the onset of operations. With an average commission of 5 to 20 percent, it'll take a while to earn back your start-up money; however, you are in a recession-proof business, and should have a steady stream of clients if you locate wisely.

BOTTOM LINE ADVICE:

In a sense, a license bureau has a monopoly on the provision of its product within its service area. In some states you may even need political pull to get the opportunity to operate one. Your business will serve an incredibly high percentage of the total population of your area. Developing a workable process for providing the required services will be a challenge. You'll be working within a set fee structure; you will need to plan carefully to ensure that cash flow is adequate to meet immediate needs and that long-term profitability is reasonably assured. Make sure that you are not competing with a government office that offers the same services, and that your company is a legal entity for the private sector.

MULTIMEDIA SERVICE

Start-up cost:	$15,000-$30,000
Potential earnings:	$35,000-$80,000
Typical fees:	$500+ per project
Advertising:	Networking, Yellow Pages, direct mail, portfolio
Qualifications:	Good understanding of the technology, creativity, ability to stay abreast of rapidly changing market
Equipment needed:	High-end computer with MIDI, video, and CD-ROM hardware and software, printer, scanner, microphone, speakers, office furniture, business card
Home business potential:	Yes
Staff required:	No
Handicapped opportunity:	Yes
Hidden costs:	Purchasing and upgrading equipment to avoid obsolescence

LOWDOWN:

CD-ROMs have revolutionized the computer game industry. Now the market is turning to more practical uses: education, marketing, training, and communications. Business presentations are being enlivened by animation, 3-D effects and sound; some CD-ROM services specialize in free-standing products such as the kiosks found in malls. As a multimedia specialist you will draw first on your project planning skills. What does the client want, and what is the best means of achieving that goal? Writing a multimedia presentation is much more challenging than producing simple, linear text. Making full use of the capabilities of this medium will require you to have a lively imagination, graphics skills, and familiarity with multimedia authoring software. If you can do all of this, you have almost unlimited opportunities open to you.

START-UP:

The computer is the tool of your trade, with all the peripherals and software that express the "multi" in multimedia. Some specialists will work with their clients' equipment, but most will need a full range of the most up-to-date components available. Spend at least $10,000 on a powerful system that is upgradable; bill out your services at $500 and up per job (depending on size and complexity).

BOTTOM LINE ADVICE:

You're creative on many levels, a "techie" of major proportions. If you can communicate with business people to learn what they need and what they expect, even when they don't fully grasp the capabilities of multimedia, you've got an amazing opportunity here. Marketing and pricing will be your major challenges.

NANNY SERVICE

Start-up cost:	$10,000-$40,000
Potential earnings:	$40,000-$70,000
Typical fees:	$20-$35 per hour
Advertising:	Yellow Pages, newspapers, parents' groups, business associations
Qualifications:	None
Equipment needed:	Office equipment (phone, fax, etc.)
Home business potential:	Yes
Staff required:	Yes (about 20-30 nannies, ready and able to work)
Handicapped opportunity:	Yes
Hidden costs:	Liability insurance, personnel costs such as health benefits

LOWDOWN:

Not just your average baby-sitter, a nanny provides daily care for children in addition to helping with household chores. Obviously, then, nannies should enjoy being essentially another mom in a busy household. You need to carefully screen your nanny candidates (including running a background check with the police to make sure they have a clean record) and match them carefully to prospective households. Make sure that your client homes fill out a questionnaire detailing their preferences and exactly what kinds of work they expect to have done by the nanny. Also, since many nannies drive kids to soccer practice or other recreation activities, be sure that each nanny has a valid driver's license.

START-UP:

Your costs to start a nanny service are generally quite high for a number of reasons, including liability insurance, office overhead, and benefits. Once you factor in your advertising costs (a good-size ad in the Yellow Pages and flyers or brochures for parents' and professional groups), you've spent anywhere from $10,000-$40,000. It helps if you are in a large metropolitan area, because that's where most of your clients will come from.

BOTTOM LINE ADVICE:

It is a challenge to match the right nannies to each of your clients' households, but if you ask all the right questions up front, your chances of success will be high. Nannies are filling an important void in the lives of working families—and if the two-income family trend continues to rise, your service will be among the most profitable businesses to start.

OCCUPATIONAL HEALTH CARE SERVICES

Start-up cost:	$25,000+
Potential earnings:	$40,000 and up
Typical fees:	$35-$50 per hour
Advertising:	Newspapers and periodicals read by business people, networking, referrals, direct mail
Qualifications:	Health care degree and administrative experience, good connections in market area, well-developed knowledge of industrial hygiene issues
Equipment needed:	Office furniture, computer, suite software, printer, marketing materials, possible van and medical office equipment if mobile services are provided.
Home business potential:	No
Staff required:	Yes
Handicapped opportunity:	No
Hidden costs:	Recruiting costs, ongoing training for staff and management

LOWDOWN:

Occupational health care is a service that is needed by almost all companies, but especially by manufacturers and organizations with physically active employees—storage companies, delivery services. Another fact to the benefit of a small business providing this type of service is that only the very largest employers find it cost-effective to maintain in-house clinics to provide occupational health care. Businesses that offer this service can keep costs down by effective management and economies of scale. In today's changing health care climate, creating a profitable business that provides care to employees can be a real challenge. But if you're an innovate thinker and a dedicated marketer, the inevitable cutbacks in more conventional types of service may leave an opening for your enterprise.

START-UP:

Start-up costs will be high, (at least $ 25,000), which will include a clean, professional-looking office environment with a solid computer network system. You will need excellent visibility and credibility from the very outset. Plan carefully to contract for possible needed services—nursing, physician specialties, employee trainers—before you launch your marketing campaign. For mobile services, well-equipped vans are essential, and very costly. Establishing on-site clinics will entail related expenses, but you should be able to make $30,000 in your first year.

BOTTOM LINE ADVICE:

You may find it effective to target your market with a specific type of service: preventive training to strengthen back muscles and avoid injury, work processes designed to minimize carpal tunnel syndrome, or a quick-response service for on-the-job injuries. Outstanding customer service, high-quality medical care, and excellent business management will be necessary to distinguish you from the other types of providers competing in this market: hospitals, orthopedic physician groups, clinics.

OUTPLACEMENT SERVICES

Start-up cost:	$15,000-$30,000
Potential earnings:	$75,000-$150,000
Typical fees:	Retainer fees of $1,000-$3,000 per month
Advertising:	Yellow Pages, direct mail to human resource managers, trade shows, promotional items, networking
Qualifications:	A background in human resources
Equipment needed:	Computer, fax/modem, phone, letterhead, business card, corporate directories, career counseling/skills assessment materials
Home business potential:	Not typically
Staff required:	Not initially (but you may need extra help, depending on demand)
Handicapped opportunity:	Possibly
Hidden costs:	Insurance, phone bills, and time spent with each client (they'll want more of your time than is profitable for you)

LOWDOWN:

Needless to say, the late '80s and '90s haven't been exactly kind to the traditional workforce. Layoffs are coming faster, and with less warning than ever. That's why you need to promote your services, which help displaced individuals find new work elsewhere. Read the business pages daily to keep tabs on local companies. Generally, wherever there's a bad quarter, there's a layoff in the air. Your goal is to be the first (or the best) to approach these companies—at a time just before they actually need you. That way, your services can be in place before the downsizing is even announced to the employees; generally, that's the way companies prefer to do it, so that it looks like they've already got a plan for those employees caught completely off guard.

START-UP:

Your start-up costs are likely to be quite high, especially because you need to have a computer system with a high-speed modem for doing on-line job searches and similar research. Expect to spend between $15,000-$30,000 getting started (detailed corporate directories alone could run as high as $6,000 per set); expect to pull in between $75,000-$150,000 per year once you've established a name for yourself. It's a business that can be lucrative for those who have a good reputation—word of mouth travels fast in industry these days (especially via E-mail).

BOTTOM LINE ADVICE:

The best thing you can do in this business is stay on top of things—keep an ear to the ground (perhaps by networking closely with members of the Society for Human Resource Managers) and always get your materials in front of the vice president of operations or other key decision-makers before your competitors do.

OVERNIGHT DELIVERY SERVICE

Start-up cost:	$15,000-$40,000+
Potential earnings:	$40,000-$100,000+ (depending on size of fleet)
Typical fees:	98 cents is the going rate for mileage, plus what you will charge ($10 per pound is common)
Advertising:	Networking with office managers/secretaries, brochures, Yellow Pages, business publications
Qualifications:	Clean driving record, ability to read maps
Equipment needed:	One truck to start, PUCO license, loading dock
Home business potential:	Yes
Staff required:	Yes
Handicapped opportunity:	No
Hidden costs:	Maintenance, insurance

LOWDOWN:

Our business environment (and society in general) has become more and more dependent upon "instant" services: fast food, microwaves, and faxes. The overnight delivery service business is directly dependent upon the needs of people to have important items or documents delivered in a quick manner. The fact is, many of the major overnight delivery services are beginning to do something they never dreamed possible: downsize. Is that a bad sign for you if you want to launch this type of business? Not really, because it essentially ends the near-monopoly of the "big three" (Federal Express, UPS, and Roberts Express) and opens the door for smaller companies like yours to compete. Be prepared to give up sizable amounts of your free time; the delivery business is demanding and long hours come with the territory. The need to be accurate, punctual, and professional is critical. More likely than not, you will need a staff to run the truck(s) in shifts and someone to do the paperwork back at the office.

START-UP:

There will be a substantial start-up fee involved (at least $15,000 to cover your truck and license), even if you try to do it all yourself. So, it would be to your benefit to know what the competition is doing and price yourself accordingly. If you try to go it solo, expect to earn $20,000 or so the first year. If you invest in a fleet, you could earn upward of $100,000.

BOTTOM LINE ADVICE:

This is a highly competitive business. If you are late one time, it's one time too many. Hire a staff and avoid any early pitfalls. It's hard enough to start a business, let alone get off on the wrong foot by being late. Screen your applicants carefully to make sure they have a good driving record, can follow instructions, and are punctual. If you can hang tough and run a tight ship in this high-pressure profession, you can make a substantial amount of money.

PARAMEDICAL SERVICES

Start-up cost:	$20,000-$30,000
Potential earnings:	$50,000-$80,000
Typical fees:	$200 per run
Advertising:	Community bulletin boards, radio spots, penny savers, flyers, direct mail
Qualifications:	EMT training, business skills
Equipment needed:	Fully equipped response vehicle
Home business potential:	No
Staff required:	Yes
Handicapped opportunity:	No
Hidden costs:	Insurance, retraining, supplies

LOWDOWN:

Starting your own paramedical service will be possible in areas where gaps occur in coverage provided by fire departments or volunteer organizations. If you can spot the need, and if you have the medical training and the business skills, you can create an enterprise that provides this vitally necessary service. Consider affiliation with a local hospital network. This is a dynamic, demanding business, and making it a success will require quick response, excellent quality, and service precisely tuned to the needs of your client base.

START-UP:

Start-up costs are very high (at least $20,000 for the fully equipped ambulance), so excellent management will be required to achieve and maintain profitability. Possibility of $50,000 the first year.

BOTTOM LINE ADVICE:

You are a highly skilled, energetic individual, or you wouldn't even consider creating a paramedical services company on your own. With these personal characteristics, you can build a successful business, but you will need to focus on your links to the other health care providers in your service area. Serving them well, and receiving referrals from them, will be your keys to success. Or, market directly to a specific clientele of consumers by providing better service than the community hospital supplies.

PEST CONTROL SERVICE

Start-up cost:	$15,000-$25,000
Potential earnings:	$25,000-$45,000
Typical fees:	$150-$300 per treatment for a medium-size house
Advertising:	Newspapers, classified ads, Yellow Pages, direct mail, flyers
Qualifications:	Knowledge of pesticides, insects, and rodents
Equipment needed:	Sprayer, chemicals, pager or mobile phone, vehicle
Home business potential:	Yes
Staff required:	Not initially
Handicapped opportunity:	No
Hidden costs:	Materials, insurance, phone bills

LOWDOWN:

Almost every structure needs your pest control services, whether the owner wants to admit it or not. Needs vary in different regions, but the termites that gnaw on Louisiana plantations are happy to chew on Idaho log cabins as well. Pest control has an old-fashioned, grungy image, but you can make the buildings you treat into safer, cleaner environments. Environmental awareness has changed the world of pest control, and your selling point could be your controlled use of the least harmful agents to provide this very necessary service. Whatever you do, you'll need to have fairly extensive knowledge of chemical treatments.

START-UP:

The tools of the trade can become somewhat expensive, with equipment and chemicals starting at about $15,000. Some pest control specialists manage their businesses in person, receive immediate payment of $150-$300 per job, and do not have to set up a computerized office. A pager or cellular phone will help your customers reach you.

BOTTOM LINE ADVICE:

You love this work or you hate it. The advantages are that you are on the move, not tied to a desk. You are providing a service that everyone understands, and every property owner needs. It can be awkward and sometimes dirty, but it isn't really difficult once you have the knowledge. Exposure to your own chemicals may have negative health consequences. Clambering around in one dark, dirty basement after another can get you down. And there is a lot of competition, so you'll need to be creative in finding (or creating) a market niche.

ADVICE FROM THE EXPERTS

What sets your business apart from others like it?

"We have a real concern for the environment," says Leslie Wyman, Vice President of Marketing for EPCON, The Environmental Pest Company, in Akron, Ohio. "We rely less on pesticides and more on structural and behavioral modification."

Things you couldn't do without:

Chemicals, flashlight, stethoscope, BNG spray can, computer, and phone are all Wyman needs to keep her business running.

Marketing tips/advice:

"Get good training and state licensing first. Then, use cold call surveys to ask people what kinds of trouble they're having with pests. After that, it's pretty much: mail-call-mail-call-mail-call." You would do well, says Wyman, to pick a specialty area (such as mice) or an industry niche (such as health care).

If you had to do it all over again . . .

"I would have gotten started in this business much sooner. Also, if you've got a family-run business, you should always give your family a chance—but don't be afraid to go outside of your family network to hire additional staff if you need to."

PET TAXI SERVICE

Start-up cost:	$15,000-$25,000
Potential earnings:	$15,000-$30,000+ (with just one vehicle)
Typical fees:	Based on local rates and distance traveled
Advertising:	Local/community newspapers, Yellow Pages, veterinarians, dog groomers, Humane Society
Qualifications:	Commercial driver's license, travel cages, vehicle large enough to accommodate several animals at once
Equipment needed:	Van, two-way radio
Home business potential:	Yes
Staff required:	Yes
Handicapped opportunity:	Yes
Hidden costs:	Repairs, insurance, maintenance/cleaning

LOWDOWN:

We humans know when to call a cab, but what does Fido do when he needs a ride to the vet's office and his master can't take time away from work? Obviously, this is a highly specialized service that caters to the rich pet lover more than anyone else. Market yourself in upscale areas and target folks who work or go on extended vacations. Your vehicle will probably need to be a van or bigger. Know about pet care as well as some basics about farm animals (just in case you're servicing a rural area). Make sure you bring along clean-up materials in case of minor accidents; janitorial cleaning supplies work best to combat pet messes, and generally they run about $30-$40 for a three-month supply. To have a 40-hour work week, you'll initially need to knock on a lot of doors, but once you become established, your phone will start to ring—most of the wealthy share information about the cushier services they use.

START-UP:

The pay varies by hours and miles driven. In most cases, and just like taxi drivers, you will keep a percent of customer fares plus tips. One full-time taxi could earn $1,000-$2,000 per month.

BOTTOM LINE ADVICE:

Your service to some pet owners will seem like a frivolous luxury, but it's no easy task. You may be asked to let yourself in and feed the animal before you go or give Barney a quick walk around the block. You'll have to schedule carefully so you don't leave animals in the van, or decline work and risk losing potential clients. Of course, you've really got to be gentle and love being around animals—their owners will want you to be as crazy about their pets as they are.

POOL MAINTENANCE

Start-up costs:	$15,000-$30,000
Potential earnings:	$30,000-$50,000
Typical fees:	$75-$150 per total cleaning/shocking treatment
Advertising:	Flyers at pool sales and service centers, direct mail coupons, Yellow Pages, local newspapers
Qualifications:	Knowledge of maintaining and repairing inground and aboveground pools
Equipment needed:	Pool cleaning equipment (water vacuum, hose, etc.) and chemicals
Home business potential:	Yes
Staff required:	No
Handicapped opportunity:	Not typically
Hidden costs:	Insurance, phone, transportation

LOWDOWN:

Many people like the convenience of owning and using a pool, but who really likes the maintenance that pools require? You do—and you can earn a living providing this necessary service for busy pool owners who simply don't have the time (or energy) to clean or repair pools. You'll clean, repair, chemically shock and maintain each client's pool, either on a preseason/postseason basis or perhaps at regular intervals. Simply stated, you're selling convenience and peace of mind to the luxury-minded; they'll tell you how often they need you to come out. Of course, you'll do better if you're located in a part of the country, particularly the Sun Belt, where pools are common (and almost a prerequisite). In cooler climes you may have to offer your services in a wider geographic area to support your business, and that would mean increased travel expenses to and from customers.

START-UP:

You'll need the right cleaning equipment and chemical supplies to stock your van with; expect to spend at least $15,000 on all of these items from the outset. However, at $75-$150 per cleaning job, you could stand to make some decent money cleaning and maintaining pools. Spend a few hundred dollars on business cards to leave behind for repeat business and referrals.

BOTTOM LINE ADVICE:

By offering excellent service, you can build a customer base. Remember to call these people back periodically for repeat business—that follow-up could reap you thousands more dollars in the long run.

POWER WASH SERVICE

Start-up cost:	$15,000-$25,000
Potential Earnings:	$35,000-$65,000
Typical fee:	$300-$500 per medium-size house or office building
Advertising:	Business directories, personal contacts with fleet managers, building superintendents, painting contractors
Qualifications:	Willingness to work outdoors and clean the outside of buildings, large vehicles, and even airplanes
Equipment needed:	Pressure-wash system, van
Home business potential:	Yes
Staff required:	Possibly 3-4
Handicapped opportunity:	No
Hidden costs:	Insurance, transportation, workers' compensation

LOWDOWN:

Who cleans the graffiti from buildings or the exteriors of airplanes or large trucks? It can be you with some ingenuity and energy and desire to work outdoors. You can start little or buy into a franchise that could supply you with the equipment and van. You'll offer a service that literally washes off old peeling paint through high-pressure water systems, and the best part is, you don't necessarily have to paint the item or building (unless you want to add that on as an additional service). If you offer a superior service, you'll get repeat business—especially if you call those clients back. Just think how often we wash our cars. Trucks and airplanes must get dirty as often.

START-UP:

Your start-up costs could be small if you lease your equipment rather than purchasing it in the first year of business. If you lease, you could get away with $10,000 or slightly more; otherwise, expect to spend up to $25,000 making this one a go (add even more if you decide to employ a team). Charge between $300-$500 for medium-size buildings; more or less depending on the square footage of each additional project.

BOTTOM LINE ADVICE:

Getting a large contract could keep you in business for a long time. Check into building contractors, trucking companies, or businesses with fleets.

RECORDING STUDIO RENTAL

Start-up cost:	$15,000-$25,000
Potential earnings:	$35,000-$50,000
Typical fees:	$10-$75 per hour
Advertising:	Music stores, industry trades, local paper, flyers, direct mail, musicians' associations
Qualifications:	Knowledge of audio equipment and mixing processes
Equipment needed:	Microphones, amps, distribution amps, mixing boards, digital audiotape machine, multichannel capabilities
Home business potential:	No
Staff required:	Not initially
Handicapped opportunity:	Yes
Hidden costs:	Replacing obsolete /damaged equipment

LOWDOWN:

Local musicians and advertising agencies need to record their music and commercials somewhere, and why not at your studio? Running your own recording studio is pretty straightforward stuff, with sound mixing and engineering being your most critical functions; it can, however, become highly complex once you start adding state-of-the-art equipment such as MIDI systems and computerized music composition equipment. You can produce some great-sounding tracks if you have the absolute best in equipment; if you have a reputation for having the best, you'll likely get more business quickly (since the music industry is largely built on word of mouth). If you have all of the basic equipment needed to record and you're not using it all the time, rent your studio out to other sound technicians to bring in additional income. Market yourself in music stores and see if they will let you have their customer list.

START-UP:

Equipment will be your biggest expense and you'll have to build a soundproof room if your space doesn't have one. Your fee will depend on where you live, what type of equipment you own, and how long the studio space is needed for each project. It takes a long time to record (usually weeks or even months), so you could make $50,000 or more annually.

BOTTOM LINE ADVICE:

If you don't care who uses your studio as long as it's rented, make sure your insurance policy is up to date. Some of your equipment may become obsolete before you have a chance to pay it off. Computers have moved into the music industry, so an extensive MIDI system may be your next big purchase.

TELEVISION REPAIR

Start-up cost:	$15,000-$25,000
Potential earnings:	$20,000-$40,000
Typical fees:	$40-$50 per hour labor (plus parts costs)
Advertising:	Yellow Pages, local newspapers, direct mail coupons
Qualifications:	Thorough knowledge and skill in TV repair
Equipment:	Full array of testing equipment: oscilloscope, meters, soldering equipment, special devices for removing microchips
Home business potential:	Yes
Staff required:	No
Handicapped opportunity:	Not typically
Hidden costs:	Insurance, phone, transportation

LOWDOWN:

Your TV's on the blink again . . . and you don't want to miss your favorite soap opera. Or, the best play in the game is rudely interrupted by an annoying horizontal line stretched across the TV set. It's happened to nearly all of us, and what do we do? We call a TV repair service to take a look at it. There aren't many TV repair technicians around these days, so these services are valuable. If you're interested in starting this business, look into becoming officially qualified or certified to repair sets. This might involve a written test and a hands-on exam. Stock a variety of parts; most consumers don't want to wait to have a part ordered.

START-UP:

You'll need to spend at least $10,000 or more on parts, benches, tools, and diagnostic equipment to get a good start in this business. Also, your certification could cost anywhere from $100-$500. Charges for your services will vary according to what needs to be done, but as a rule, TV repair services bill $45 or more for each hour they spend.

BOTTOM LINE ADVICE:

In addition to servicing the general public, contact service centers and retailers who often farm out repairs rather than maintain an in-house repair operation. If you offer a free pickup and delivery service, you'll get even more business from sources like these.

TICKET BROKER

Start-up cost:	$15,000-$35,000
Potential earnings:	$25,000-$35,000+
Typical fees:	5 to 40 percent of each sale; it varies depending on whether you're selling nationally
Advertising:	Industry trade publications, newspapers
Qualifications:	Knowledge of state licensing requirements
Equipment:	Computer with specialized software program/hookup, 800 number phone line
Home business potential:	Yes
Staff required:	No
Handicapped opportunity:	Yes
Hidden costs:	Make sure you have in the contract that you're not liable for any unsold tickets

LOWDOWN:

How many times have you wanted to buy tickets for an event or a show, to find that it has been sold out? For those who simply can't get to the big tickets, ticket brokers provide a welcome relief by offering tickets, often at a discounted rate, and the convenience of purchasing by phone. Organization and responsibility are key to this business. Your job includes assigning seat locations, providing ticket sales information, making recommendations about ticket pricing according to the area or event, soliciting group sales, and keeping a customer ticket list. You'll need to purchase specialized software that allows you to search on-line for ticket availability and accept credit card orders over the phone. An accounting or book-keeping background would prove especially helpful, as there are a million little details that need to be managed on a daily basis to keep this one up and running.

START-UP:

Computers are a way of life for this occupation. You have to be able to hook up to the ticket distribution center. Your fee will depend on the event and place. Typically you get a 5 to 40 percent cut of each sale.

BOTTOM LINE ADVICE:

You may need to hire a staff to run this from your home; it all depends on how big you want to get. There may be some travel involved and you'll want to attend all of the trade shows so the industry knows you are out there. Most of the big tick-et brokers have been in business a long time and have a good reputation. Get to know them; you may need to network with them sometime.

TRANSPORTATION PROVIDER
(LIMOUSINE/VAN)

Start-up cost:	$15,000+ for van, $30,000-$90,000 for limo
Potential earnings:	$40,000-$65,000
Typical fees:	$50 per hour
Advertising:	Yellow Pages, local newspapers, brochures at bridal salons/tuxedo shops/hotels
Qualifications:	Proper licensing and insurance
Equipment needed:	A dependable fleet, short-wave radio for regular contact with dispatcher
Home business potential:	Yes
Staff required:	Not at first; you'll probably add a dispatcher early on, however
Handicapped opportunity:	Not typically
Hidden costs:	Liability insurance

LOWDOWN:

Business travelers and party-goers alike need dependable transportation services wherever they go. That's why the limousine and van service business has enjoyed a steady increase over the last decade. Also, because more and more people are investing in small indulgences, your investment in a decent fleet could net you giant profits. The mainstay for these types of transportation providers is airport service, but flexibility is key as rentals become more popular and affordable. The average fee is $50 per hour plus tips, and the customers range from wedding and prom parties to sporting events and wealthy tourists. A good way to establish yourself is by contracting overflow from larger limo companies.

START-UP:

Typically, newcomers to this business don't have enough money to outright buy several shiny new vehicles, especially when they run anywhere from $32,000-$90,000. This is why deciding upon one option to fit many needs is important in the beginning; you can always buy more vehicles as capital grows. Buying a new machine is important for reliability, because buying used often results in breakdowns and losing customers. The only exception, really, is when you have the mechanical ability and can handle any crises personally. Licensing and insurance regulations will vary from state to state. Be creative in your advertising; try to offer "extras" (such as a bottle of champagne) as incentives for people to use your service over others.

BOTTOM LINE ADVICE:

Good driving skills and a comfortable place for passengers are vitally important if you want to stay on top of the competition. A congenial disposition will increase the chances of your customers returning to you for service. As limo rentals increase, clientele will come from more varied backgrounds; be prepared to deal with a variety of personalities.

VIDEOTEXT SERVICE

Start-up cost:	$30,000-$50,000
Potential earnings:	$45,000-$75,000
Typical fees:	Can be as low as $500 for a low-budget feature and as high as $5,000 for a commercial motion picture
Advertising:	Trade publications, direct mail, Yellow Pages, word of mouth
Qualifications:	Technical training in videotext equipment; often, professional certification
Equipment needed:	Videotext equipment and film-editing/dubbing equipment, control panels, TelePrompTer™
Home business potential:	No (unless you've got a studio to work in)
Staff required:	Possibly
Handicapped opportunity:	Possibly
Hidden costs:	Insurance, equipment maintenance and upgrades

LOWDOWN:

Although we take it for granted as a viewing audience, those words you see printed across the screen for everything from commercials to major motion picture credits have to be input by someone; if you're in the videotext business, that's essentially the service you'll be providing. You'll enter whatever information, narration, or credits the producer requests, making sure that everything is spelled correctly and put into a readable format and order. You may even go so far as to suggest or write narrative, particularly if you're working with corporate clients who are producing their own in-house videos for training purposes. Essentially, you're a highly specialized, highly technical typing service for TV, film, and video producers. For this reason, you will have certification or training in your own field of interest, which is only a small piece of what the producers must study for their profession.

START-UP:

Your equipment costs will likely be in the $30,000-$50,000 range, because you'll need the basics of any small studio (minus the recording equipment). You could sensibly expect to earn between $40,000-$75,000 per year, depending on where you are located. For instance, videotext businesses in California and New York fare much better than, say, those in the middle of Iowa. You must be where the work is.

BOTTOM LINE ADVICE:

You will have ebbs and flows in your workload; try to compensate for the down-time by accepting subcontracting work from fellow videotext services. Network when you can so that, when the time comes, you'll have regular contacts to call when you need extra work.

VOICE MESSAGES SERVICE CENTER

Start-up cost:	$15,000-$20,000
Potential earnings:	$35,000-$75,000
Typical fees:	Monthly rate of $30-$75 per customer
Advertising:	Business publications, Yellow Pages, direct mail
Qualifications:	Organizational skills; knowledge of equipment and software
Equipment needed:	Computer with large hard drive, voice mailboard, software, business card, letterhead, envelopes
Home business potential:	Yes
Staff required:	No
Handicapped opportunity:	Yes
Hidden costs:	Reconfiguration and addition of phones lines to handle expanding client base

LOWDOWN:

Voice mail, like answering machines, started out with a negative image. Now the ability to leave a detailed message is valued by business callers. Many services offer the ability to send one message simultaneously to a group (i.e., a dispersed sales force). Responses can be made within the system, without the need for a separate phone call. This service follows trends affecting businesses across the U.S.—less administrative support, flatter organizations, and high expectations regarding communications links between customers and organizations, as well as within the organization. You can offer your customers the option of creating a menu system so that a caller can press a phone button to hear various kinds of recorded information or leave a message for a specific individual. To compete you'll need technical know-how and marketing skills.

START-UP:

Setting up this business requires high-end electronic equipment that runs in the neighborhood of $10,000-$20,000. Your income is decided by the rates you set—and, since this is an increasingly competitive market, you'll need to be sure you don't undercut yourself. Charge your customers a flat monthly rate for a pre-determined number of messages, or simply charge a flat monthly rate and unlimited messages. The market in your area will greatly affect your pricing.

BOTTOM LINE ADVICE:

You will be supplying a service that almost every business needs. The great increase in new small businesses should allow you to develop an adequate client base in almost all areas of the country. Keeping the system operating correctly takes technical skills, and it may be a challenge competing with answering services on the one hand and very large organizations (even the local phone company) on the other.

VOICE-ACTIVATED HOME AUTOMATION

Start-up cost:	$15,000-$25,000
Potential earnings:	$50,000-$80,000
Typical fees:	$75-$150 per client per month, depending on extent of system
Advertising:	Yellow Pages, community and metropolitan newspapers, direct mail (especially to builders and contractors)
Qualifications:	Training in installation/use of equipment
Equipment needed:	Home automation system units, van, complete set of tools
Home business potential:	Yes
Staff required:	No
Handicapped opportunity:	Not typically
Hidden costs:	Insurance, equipment maintenance/upgrades

LOWDOWN:

Microsoft Corporation's Bill Gates has one; so do many celebrities. Voice-activated home automation systems are the wave of the technological future, especially in the home market. However, even though this is a potentially hot market, it is not for everyone; at $75-$150 or more per month to keep the system running, it's easy to see why only the rich and powerful have systems they can literally "tell" what to turn off and turn on. Still, one franchise's 1994 sales figures indicated a $3 billion market for home automation systems, so there are probably more wealthy folks out there than you'd realize—your job is to locate them, send them a dynamite direct mail piece, and follow up to sell them on an installation. Each system can include the following components: security system, appliance and electrical system control, and even systems that "feel" people entering and leaving the room (and open and close lights accordingly). You'll sell, install, and maintain each system, suggesting upgrades when they seem appropriate and making sure each client is getting the maximum use out of each installed unit (recognizing, of course, that your business will largely grow out of a strong and happy referral base).

START-UP:

Your start-up fees will likely reflect a franchise or distributor fee of about $15,000 in addition to advertising monies; it wouldn't be unusual to spend as much as $25,000 getting this unique business going. In the plus column are the $50,000-$80,000 per year earnings you could achieve, if you market this service wisely.

BOTTOM LINE ADVICE:

While this seems to be a growing industry, it isn't exactly affordable and does come off as a luxury item. Your own sales figures may reflect a reluctance on the public's part to buy into what at first seems to be a fad. Concentrate on the security aspect heavily, because that's what will ultimately turn into dollars.

WINERY

Start-up cost:	$20,000-$50,000
Potential earnings:	Unlimited
Typical fees:	2-5 percent of gross from distribution channels
Advertising:	Newspapers, upscale magazines, restaurants, groceries, gourmet shops
Qualifications:	A very good knowledge of growing grapes, wine manufacturing, bottling, and marketing of the finished product
Equipment needed:	Depends on the size and scope of your business, but you will need plants, pruning and watering equipment, production, bottling and labeling equipment, and production/storage facilities
Home business potential:	Yes
Staff required:	None at first, except for help at harvest time
Handicapped opportunity:	Yes
Hidden costs:	Legal, food handling, and marketing costs

LOWDOWN:

The healthful atmosphere, the beauty of the grapevines, the perfume of the finished product, the joy of producing something that brings pleasure to many people—running a winery certainly has its romantic side. It also can be extremely lucrative, over time. The process of creating the wine from the grapes is technical but can be learned readily. Proper care of the vines is essential; so is a good working knowledge of wine growing, production, and marketing. If your business is small at first, you will have a better opportunity to gauge if it's the right business for you. It can be started at home if you have considerable acreage but may need more room to expand later on.

START-UP:

Start-up costs vary dramatically according to how ambitious you are. If you start small, experimenting with a few vines and a few dozen bottles of wine, you will incur minimal expense (and realize only minimal profits). A larger business will be expensive to start and will take awhile to become profitable. In addition, if you choose to offer more than one type of wine (as most vintners do), you will need more knowledge, more vines, and more processing and labeling equipment. Legal and zoning regulations can be costly, too.

BOTTOM LINE ADVICE:

For every moment of satisfaction with the beauty of the vines and the success of the finished product, you will have many moments of frustration and hard work. This is a demanding business, and a time-consuming one. It takes years for the vines to grow enough to produce fruit; you will need extensive knowledge to prune and care for them. In addition, the plants are very vulnerable to weather. Your wines must also age for months (or years) before they are ready to market. Wine making can be very rewarding, though, because it is truly a labor of love.

START-UP OVER $40,000

AIR CHARTER SERVICE

Start-up cost:	$1-$5 million+
Potential earnings:	$500,000-$1.5 million
Typical fees:	$150-$1,000 or more per flight
Advertising:	Yellow Pages, newspapers, billboards, word of mouth
Qualifications:	Pilot's license (twin-engine and instrumental license)
Equipment needed:	Fleet of turbo-prop, twin-engine airplanes or a Lear jet
Home business potential:	No
Staff required:	Yes
Handicapped opportunity:	No
Hidden costs:	Insurance, workers' compensation, training/testing fees, equipment maintenance

LOWDOWN:

From turbo-prop to Lear jet, you could be soaring with an air charter service if you're in a desirable enough location (New England, as on TV's *Wings*, perhaps)—or if you have the ability to fly special products to the rich and impatient. An air charter service out of Cincinnati, for example, regularly flies delectable ribs from the Montgomery Inn on the Ohio River to Palm Springs, where a well-known celebrity awaits with salivating anticipation. You could offer the same services, catering to the finer tastes of the upper echelon; or you could limit your charter service to the passenger-variety only. Either way, you'll be booking and flying regularly if you get the word out well enough from the start. Maybe you could promote your new business with ads in your local newspapers, or by doing a copromotion with a local bar or restaurant (perhaps a drawing for a free trip). When the customers start lining up, you can offer mini-travel packages, such as trips to gambling boats or to history-rich areas. Pick themes, as these are easiest to sell. Then, sit back, relax and enjoy the flight to success. One tip before you embark on this opportunity: keep your safety record as clean as possible; regularly test your equipment and run random drug screenings often. You can't afford a mishap in this business.

START-UP:

Your start-up costs will be incredibly high ($1-$5 million), because you'll need to secure a reliable fleet of airplanes or jets in addition to unleashing some heavy-duty advertising. Your income potential is high, though—at $150-$1,000 or more per flight, you could soar to the $500,000-$1.5 million range in no time.

BOTTOM LINE ADVICE:

While the start-up is extremely high and the insurance unbelievable, the income potential here is quite compelling. Once you pay off your investors, you could make a killing. What's not to like about that?

Taking Your Company Public

When your small business becomes successful and is experiencing rapid growth, you might want to look into offering the public shares of your business in exchange for more working capital.

Going public means finding new owners who will participate with you in the ups and downs of your business's future. They will add their dollars to yours to permit the new, larger enterprise to expand.

You can make money yourself by selling some of your shares to the public, but you should find a business-oriented lawyer to work with you since this is the most legal-intensive thing a business owner typically does.

You will need to be open with your financial statements, but in exchange you get the opportunity to become wealthier—particularly if your stock prices rise.

SHOULD I GO PUBLIC?

This is going to be a tough decision, and you should have the advice of lawyers, accountants, and other professionals. Some factors you'll need to consider are:

Advantages
- Access to a large amount of capital for the future. But remember that you may still be able to raise capital through private debt or equity.

- Greatly increased liquidity for your firm's securities.

- Wealth creation: taking your company public will establish its value, and (through a secondary offering of stocks), allow your founders and backers to sell some of their interest.

- Prestige: enhanced image with your customers, suppliers, and employees, as well as a sense of achievement for you.

Disadvantages
- Cost: going public is expensive both at the outset and in ongoing costs. But be aware of cost-saving SEC procedures such as Form SB-2.

- Public scrutiny: a public company must make financial and other information public, even when it would prefer not to.

- Change of focus: top management has to concern itself with pleasing Wall Street, while a private firm does not.

- Loss of autonomy: in a public company, the owners and managers are not the same people and may have differing priorities. There is also the possibility of a hostile takeover.

CHOOSING AN UNDERWRITER

Underwriters (investment bankers) are required to guide you through the process of making a public offering, and to sell your securities, in exchange for some portion of the proceeds. Talk to several underwriters, and take these factors into account in your final selection:

- Reputation: the underwriter's reputation will affect its ability to sell your stock.

- Distribution: be sure that your underwriter can get you the right spread of institutional and individual investors.

- Ongoing support: look for an underwriter who can give you continuing support and advice after the initial public offering.

DECIDING YOUR STOCK PRICE

Negotiation on stock price will run from your first discussions with your underwriter to, perhaps, the night before the offering. **Be aware of how your underwriter's interests differ from yours.** You want the best price you can get: the underwriter needs to be able to sell those shares, and offer its customers a good price. You will incur expenses during the course of registration: your underwriter may try to bring down your stock price by threatening to back out of the deal, leaving you with those expenses. Try to have the underwriter bear some of its own expenses (such as legal fees), so that it has something to lose, too.

OTHER DECISIONS

- Where to list: before choosing an exchange, see what its requirements are.

- Amount of primary offering: know how much your firm wants to raise.

- Amount of secondary offering: decide how much of their stake, if anything, your founders and backers are to sell. This will be their money, not your company's.

ARCADE/PARTY RENTALS

Start-up cost:	$75,000-$200,000
Potential earnings:	$50,000-$80,000
Typical fees:	Rentals vary according to product and duration, but generally start at $25-$30 per day
Advertising:	Billboards, radio spots, direct mail, Yellow Pages
Qualifications:	Ability to repair and maintain equipment
Equipment needed:	Computer, suite software, printer, marketing materials, party supplies and video games to rent, van
Home business potential:	No
Staff required:	Yes
Handicapped opportunity:	No
Hidden costs:	Replacement, storage, vehicle maintenance

LOWDOWN:

You have a stock of video games to rent to arcades, and you supplement this with rentals of party equipment such as tables, chairs, and punch bowls. You make a success of your enterprise by marketing vigorously, providing excellent customer service, and managing costs with an eagle eye. Timing is always a challenge: you'll need to have what your customers want, in the quantity they need, and at the time they expect to have it delivered. It will be important to keep aware of the shifting popularity of different video games, and the fashion for one type of party over another. Managing your delivery and repair people is also important, to minimize wasted time and maximize the service you can provide.

START-UP:

This is a capital-intensive business, relatively speaking. Expect to spend at least $75,000 to build a sufficient product base from which your customers may make selections. You will be charging at least $25-$30 (and maybe as much as $100) per day, depending on what kind of product you're leasing out. The key is to purchase only the kinds of equipment that are sure bets.

BOTTOM LINE ADVICE:

Once you become established, your business will be a part of the fabric of your community, supplying the equipment for wedding receptions, Christmas parties, and local arcades. Getting to this position will depend on the nature of the competition in your area and your ability to offer the products and services wanted by your specific market.

ASSEMBLY WORK

Start-up cost:	$40,000-$75,000
Potential earnings:	$60,000-$200,000
Typical fees:	$1,500-$5,000+ per job
Advertising:	Trade/industry publications, direct mail to manufacturers
Qualifications:	Hands-on assembly experience
Equipment needed:	Extensive tool collection and small assembly benches with equipment
Home business potential:	No
Staff required:	Yes (1-3 assemblers; more for large jobs)
Handicapped opportunity:	Not typically
Hidden costs:	Insurance, workers' compensation

LOWDOWN:

Many small- to medium-size manufacturers farm out their smaller assembly work to subcontractors; you can be on their list of possibles if you can demonstrate a thorough understanding of product manufacturing and a hands-on background in assembly. You'll need to circulate in the manufacturing world by attending as many trade shows, technical conferences, and association events as you can to make sure that you get your name out there as someone to contact when in need of subassembly work. Once you get established, you'll be taking calls from many different types of manufacturers (from small appliance makers to medical product manufacturers), each one asking you to perform a different, yet specific function. You'll need to be well-versed in manufacturability terms, as well as adept at turning around product in a short period of time; half the reason they're calling you is because they're behind schedule.

START-UP:

You'll need sufficient capital ($40,000-$75,000) to create a working environment, complete with assembly benches, tools, and assembly equipment. However, once you get established, you could earn as much as $200,000 per year.

BOTTOM LINE ADVICE:

Your turnaround times will often be quite tight, and the money could sometimes take longer than 45 or even 90 days to reach you for compensation. That's why it's entirely logical to work up a contract that demands at least a percentage of your fee up front. It's just smart business.

AUDIOBOOK PRODUCER/DISTRIBUTOR

Start-up cost:	$40,000-$100,000+
Potential earnings:	$50,000-$75,000+
Typical fees:	40 percent commission on selling price
Advertising:	Direct mail to publisher's representatives and retail outlets, cold calls, ads in magazines and travel publications
Qualifications:	Previous recording/engineering experience helpful
Equipment needed:	Extensive recording, dubbing and editing equipment, duplication equipment, tapes and tape boxes
Home business potential:	Not likely
Staff required:	Yes (1-2 to start with)
Handicapped opportunity:	Yes
Hidden costs:	Insurance, equipment maintenance and upgrades, excessive promotional costs

LOWDOWN:

Audiobooks are selling like hotcakes in the fast-moving society of the '90s. It seems we're all locked up in our cars, driving for hours and listening to our favorite books on the cassette deck. You can produce audiobooks based on actual books (by securing audio rights) or you can produce your own innovative series of tapes. For instance, one entrepreneur sells tapes that tell the local lore of a particular highway on the West Coast—guaranteed to appeal to those traveling down that road. Producing the tapes will require technical and sound engineering expertise, which you might have to subcontract if you don't have the talent yourself. Secure narration talent by hiring well-known celebrities (if you can afford them) or by screening local talent by holding regular casting calls.

START-UP:

You'll need between $40,000-$100,000 or more to launch this business, but it is a remarkably growing field and could bring you a sizable return on investment if you create unique or quality products. If your tapes are steady sellers, you could see earnings as high as $75,000 or more.

BOTTOM LINE ADVICE:

You can cash in on this vast consumer market if you can manage to produce tapes that will entertain, teach, or delight. What's not to like about that? Securing rights to existing material can be expensive, so price your tapes accordingly.

AUTOMOTIVE TESTING EQUIPMENT

Start-up cost:	$40,000-$100,000
Potential earnings:	$45,000-$60,000
Typical fees:	Equipment sells for $500-$10,000 or more, depending on how precise and advanced it is. Your cut is usually 30 to 40 percent
Advertising:	Automotive, dealer, and repair periodicals, newspapers, Yellow Pages, business publications, direct mail or sales representation to automotive manufacturers
Qualifications:	Familiarity with automotive testing regulations in your state, knowledge of testing equipment operations, marketing skills
Equipment needed:	An inventory of automotive testing equipment for sale or lease, office furniture, computer, suite software, printer, business card, letterhead, envelopes
Home business potential:	No
Staff required:	Probably
Handicapped opportunity:	No
Hidden costs:	Equipment repair and updating, transportation costs

LOWDOWN:

You are focusing here on a very narrow market niche. Your customer base will be drawn from garages in a state that has emission testing requirements. You will sell or lease the specialized equipment that assesses the quality and quantity of tailpipe emissions. Your ability to keep the equipment working, and working accurately, will make your service a very valuable one to many testing sites in your area.

START-UP:

Costs are relatively high ($40,000-$100,000) as you must obtain a reasonable inventory of this expensive equipment in a suitable warehouse, as well as the tools you need for maintenance, and have a means of delivering the equipment to your customers.

BOTTOM LINE ADVICE:

On the plus side, you're providing a critical service needed by many customers in a healthy, recession-proof field. But the downside is that you'll be upgrading your equipment constantly to keep up with industry changes and oft-evolving government regulations (such as freon level-testing, etc.).

BED & BREAKFAST

Start-up cost:	$60,000 (assuming you already own building)
Potential earnings:	$35,000-$175,000
Typical fees:	$125+ per room, per night (depending on season)
Advertising:	Yellow Pages, B&B directories, direct mail to travel agencies
Qualifications:	None
Equipment needed:	Beds, towels, dining tables/chairs, stationery/brochures
Home business potential:	Yes
Staff required:	Yes (but it could be comprised of family members)
Handicapped opportunity:	Unlikely (but not impossible)
Hidden costs:	Be sure your prices cover everything from electricity to food

LOWDOWN:

Large verandas for after-dinner strolls . . . billowy white curtains blowing in the wind . . . quiet meals by firelight. The sheer romance of owning and operating a Victorian-style B & B inn can be intoxicating enough to entice you into starting one of your own. If marketing trends are on target, more and more folks are looking for unusual escapes from city turmoil—and what better place to recuperate than a quiet little inn in the middle of nowhere (but within close driving distance to somewhere). You'll need anywhere from two to 12 extra rooms for guest accommodations, in addition to adequate kitchen and dining space. You will need to be meticulous in your cleaning and make sure that all prepared foods follow strict regulations. Also, be sure to educate yourself on all of the tourist attractions in your immediate area—you'll be surprised how often customers will count on your local expertise in devising their travel plans.

START-UP:

You'll need at least $100,000-$400,000 if you purchase a building; you may also look into buying an existing B&B and simply taking over the business (turnover is relatively high, as many owners burn out after a period of ten years or so). If you already have a building, put aside extra cash ($5,000-$10,000) for repairs and updates, in addition to another $10,000 to cover your initial operating costs. You'll spend between $1,500-$5,000 on your first six months of advertising as well. But, considering that you'll charge clients $125 and up per night, you should be able to develop a steady cash flow within the first five years of your business plan's projections.

BOTTOM LINE ADVICE:

You could easily be drawn in to the seemingly idyllic country inn lifestyle. But before you launder the sheets and open your doors to guests, give a lot of thought to the hard work ahead; most B&B owners will tell you that there are long hours of intense work (cooking, cleaning, and assisting guests in all of their needs). If you don't mind putting in a 60+ hour work week without the promise of grand riches, a bed & breakfast inn can be a great match.

BEER BREWERY

Start-up cost:	$100,000-$1.5 million
Potential earnings:	$300,000-$2 million
Typical fees:	Varied according to distributor agreements
Advertising:	Direct mail to distributors, ads in newspapers and magazines, articles in beer brewing magazines, participation in beer clubs, event sponsorship
Qualifications:	An avid interest in beer
Equipment needed:	Brewing equipment, brewer's yeast, other key ingredients
Home business potential:	Possibly (but only temporarily)
Staff required:	Yes
Handicapped opportunity:	Possibly
Hidden costs:	Insurance, licensing from state liquor boards in every state in which you plan to distribute

LOWDOWN:

Beer brewing is one of the hottest trends of the entrepreneurial future; virtually all beer aficionados believe that they can make the best brew on the planet. There are actually beer clubs where members taste-test beers from all over the country (and sometimes the world), then rate them according to their flavor. Yours could be one of the top-rated if you know how to brew beer properly (and tastefully). Beer conventions are a great place for you to check out all the competition before sinking your investment capital into a brewery of your own; you can see what's out there, then set about figuring out how to make your product truly stand out. Perhaps you could open a restaurant next to your brewery to give yourself an immediate outlet and niche for your product; several breweries have done this successfully. However you choose to produce and market your beer, you will need to make sure you set up strong distribution channels from the get-go; in the beverage business, it's where you are (including shelf placement) that truly determines how successful you'll be.

START-UP:

Your start-up is high ($100,000-$1.5 million), because you'll need lots of specialty beer brewing equipment and plenty of space to produce your product. You'll also need licensing from each state you plan to sell in, and you'll need certification from the health and food safety arenas as well. However, you should be able to make a good living brewing beer (perhaps as much as $2 million per year)—to beer lovers, there can never be enough of the good stuff.

BOTTOM LINE ADVICE:

This is a fiercely competitive business to be in right now, mainly because it looks so easy. Recognize that a huge amount of work goes into successful beer brewing—that it is an art that took several centuries to truly perfect.

Boosting Sales

One thing you can never have enough of is sales. But how do you drive sales up in the fastest way possible? What methods tend to bring results for small business owners?

Here are just a few things you might try, especially if you've never really considered yourself a salesperson:

1. **Listen before you talk.** Ask what your potential customer's needs are, and listen. As many sales pros will tell you, there's a reason you have two ears and only one mouth.

2. **Find out what the client's problems are.** Too many novices don't listen well enough to their customers' problems, which are the real keys to selling. If you know what's going wrong at a client's place of business or in their home, you stand a much better chance of coming up with a quick solution. You are in the business of making your customers' businesses or lives run better, with whatever products or services you can offer.

3. **Match your best solutions to each problem.** After you've identified your client's problems, dive into your list of solutions. But don't offer all of them as potentials; spend time highlighting the ones that seem the most viable and compatible with your customers' needs.

4. **Offer your services as a continual process.** Your services are not over when you finish the job; you must also convey the idea that you are an expert whose services and advice can be depended on for a time that lasts much longer than the initial sale. If you want repeat business, you have to build a long-lasting relationship with your client—one that is based not only on the problem-solution orientation, but also on the human level. Get to know your customer on a personal level; find out the things he or she enjoys in life and remember to talk about them every time you meet.

5. **Remember to always say "thank you."** No sale is ever complete until it is fully acknowledged by some show of appreciation. Two simple words can bring in a lot of residual and repeat business.

Getting and keeping customers is not easy work, and even the pros need to have regular workshops on increasing sales effectiveness. So, if your first few attempts at sales don't go as smoothly as you'd like, don't give up. It takes a while to perfect the "art of the deal!"

BOAT TOURS

Start-up cost:	$50,000-$80,000+
Potential earnings:	$45,000-$75,000 (depending on whether your business is seasonal)
Typical fees:	$4-$20/trip
Advertising:	Yellow Pages, radio spots, billboard, newspapers, magazines
Qualifications:	Possibly a pilot's or mariner's license, good people skills
Equipment needed:	Boat with seating, rest rooms, snack bar, dock, parking area, ramp
Home business potential:	No
Staff required:	Yes
Handicapped opportunity:	No
Hidden costs:	Maintenance and fuel, marine insurance, dry dock/storage fees for winter

LOWDOWN:

Boat tours are a family favorite for vacation activities. Almost everyone who can walk can take a boat tour, even if they aren't fit enough for more vigorous water sports. You'll need a dock, or docking rights, in a central location that has available parking. Obviously, the type of tour you offer will depend on your area: city tours on rivers can offer a fascinating glimpse of familiar territory from a different perspective. Harbor tours take people around the giant container ships, yachts, and even naval vessels like aircraft carriers. Some tours focus on the magnificent estates lining the shore, as in Newport, Rhode Island. Others focus on whale watching, seal spotting, or environmental education. The nature of your tour will dictate the appropriate advertising. You'll need helpers on shore to sell tickets and interact with potential passengers. And you'll need at least one deckhand to help with docking. Sales of snacks can be a big contribution to your bottom line.

START-UP:

Start-up costs are high, and so is ongoing maintenance. You'll shell out $50,000-$80,000 or more for a decent rig, and you'll probably need to add even more for liability insurance. The biggest determinant of your success in this field is whether you live in a place where your business would be seasonal. Obviously, the folks who build their business near Lake Erie won't make as much of a killing as those in Miami.

BOTTOM LINE ADVICE:

Showmanship has to be mixed with seamanship in the boat tour business. Many people just enjoy the opportunity to get out on the water, but your line of patter about the sights around your vessel will add a lot to the experience. Your business plan must allow for the effect of the weather. No one wants to go out on the ocean in a gale, and extremely hot or unseasonably cold weather can cut down on expected ticket sales.

CANOE LIVERY

Start-up cost:	$65,000-$150,000
Potential earnings:	$45,000-$60,000
Typical fees:	$5-$10 per rental, depending on length (usually rented by the hour)
Advertising:	Entertainment and outdoors magazines, recreation guides, sporting goods shops, referrals
Qualifications:	Experience with all aspects of managing a water-oriented business, canoeing skills
Equipment needed:	Staging area, canoes, paddles, life preservers, van for return of canoes
Home business potential:	No
Staff required:	Yes
Handicapped opportunity:	No
Hidden costs:	Insurance, maintenance, replacement of canoes and paddles

LOWDOWN:

If you have land access to a suitable river, you can make your love of canoeing and the outdoors into a steady, although fairly seasonal, business. You will need quite a few experienced, reliable helpers, and it may be difficult to find such people if you must hire them only part-time. Everyone involved in the business must focus on safety. You will be teaching safe canoeing practices and gently enforcing these behaviors with your customers. But the most important factor in your success will have been provided by Mother Nature—the beautiful, soothing river with its interesting eddies and graceful tree branches leaning down over the banks.

START-UP:

Equipping your enterprise will be more capital-intensive than for many types of small businesses, but continuing costs will not be too great. You should be able to rock steady around the second or third year of business—and could earn up to $60,000 if you're a savvy marketer.

BOTTOM LINE ADVICE:

Many successful canoe liveries are family enterprises. There are times when many willing hands will be needed to do maintenance, deal with several busloads of teenagers arriving at once, and drive the canoes and paddlers back to the staging area after their trips. The attractiveness of your piece of the river will draw groups of people to your business, and marketing to schools and church youth groups may also be a successful tactic.

ADVICE FROM THE EXPERTS

What sets your business apart from others like it?

Mel Reinthal, owner of Pleasant Hill Canoe Livery in Perrysville, Ohio, says coming up with a gimmick that works is what ultimately brings in business. "I made up a story about Perrysville being named after Commodore Perry, and made up a whole humorous tale about the good commodore. You'd be surprised how many people ask about that—we even had a Japanese tourist once!"

Things you couldn't do without:

"I couldn't do without eighteen-year-olds with strong backs to carry the canoes, a telephone and, most important, good weather!"

Marketing tips/advice:

"Nothing beats good word of mouth, but we also do direct mail pieces and advertising co-ops through tourist associations. It helps to have access to low-cost advertising through group deals."

If you had to do it all over again . . .

"I would issue a warning about relatives and partners . . . and would encourage others to really do their research first."

CAR WASH

Start-up cost:	$50,000-$250,000
Potential earnings:	$75,000-$250,000
Typical fees:	$3-$5 per car
Advertising:	Print media, radio, flyers, discount coupon distribution, location
Qualifications:	Business and financial management knowledge; a technical background might be helpful
Equipment needed:	Washing and drying equipment for full-service, self-service hoses and brushes, water reclamation system, vacuum system
Home business potential:	No
Staff required:	Yes
Handicapped opportunity:	Yes
Hidden costs:	Security for self-service stalls, change machines for self-serve, insurance coverage for workers and customers, maintenance cost for machinery; water usage will increase as equipment wears

LOWDOWN:

Since southern California receives fewer than 20 days of rain each year, it is an ideal place for starting your car wash business! However, operating a successful car wash does not mandate moving to the West Coast. There are over 20,000 automatic washes in operation today. It is preferable to consider a geographic location with approximately 250 rain-free days a year. Nationwide, there is less business during the months of June, July, and August with more people washing their own cars in the warmer weather. Northern climates do more business in the winter months as car owners strive to keep their cars free from corrosive road salts. Remember, morning or night rain usually does not hurt business. In fact, the day after a heavy rain is usually better than normal because cars are quickly dirtied by sloppy roadways.

START-UP:

Land costs can hike your initial cost significantly. Excluding land costs, you can start a four-bay self-service car wash for approximately $140,000. A full-service car wash requires an investment ranging from $100,000-$300,000 down, with loans from $400,000 to $1 million.

BOTTOM LINE ADVICE:

With the increase in double-income families and the constant struggle to find more time in one day, who wants to wash their car? Busy professionals would rather spend a Saturday afternoon relaxing than soaping up the family vehicle. Car washes are more popular than ever. Your hardest decision will be to build or to buy. In either case, be aware of possible shifts in demographics and large expenditures for replacing major components.

CHILD DEVELOPMENT CENTER

Start-up cost:	$40,000-$80,000
Potential earnings:	$35,000-$50,000
Typical fees:	$150-$300 per month per child
Advertising:	Community newspapers; church and school bulletin boards, referrals from pediatricians, teachers, and counselors, direct mail, seminars to community groups, brochures
Qualifications:	Advanced degree in a related field, several years of experience counseling or teaching the type of child targeted
Equipment needed:	Facility that meets the codes and requirements for your state, child-size furniture, appropriate play materials, teaching tools, office equipped with computer and printer for producing sheets, forms, business card, letterhead, envelopes
Home business potential:	Yes
Staff required:	Possibly
Handicapped opportunity:	No
Hidden costs:	Insurance, redecorating frequently to maintain good appearance of space

LOWDOWN:

Knowledge about the developmental needs of children is growing rapidly. There is an intense focus on the problems that prevent many children, especially boys, from doing well in school. Increasingly, parents find that the overcrowded public schools cannot meet the needs of their children, and they are turning to child development centers for the services that will enable their kids to make better progress. Individuals with the background and ability to assist young people in learning and feeling better about themselves can make a child development center into a very successful business.

START-UP:

Start-up costs will be substantial ($40,000-$80,000) because you must have a fully equipped center before the first fees ever arrive. Just the process of getting the necessary permits and insurance can be quite expensive. Marketing to get the new enterprise launched can cost a considerable amount. Still, at $150-$300 per month per child, you could earn $35,000-$50,000 and make a decent living expanding the minds of children.

BOTTOM LINE ADVICE:

If you are skilled at helping children with developmental needs, your services will be in demand in most areas of the U.S. As parents and schools become more overburdened, the demand for assistance with children's problems is rising. As the first year or so of your business goes by, you will discover where to focus your services: children with reading difficulties, attention-deficit disorder, special gifts and talents that make traditional school inappropriate, etc. Managing your organization, managing your own time and energy, and keeping up with new developments in the field will all be challenges. Pricing your services to make an adequate profit will also be difficult. This business could be the way for a gifted teacher or counselor to make a real difference in the lives of children who desperately need the assistance.

10 Ways to Expand Your Business for Little Cash

1. Get on the Internet. For just a few dollars per month, you can market your services worldwide. Who can beat that?

2. Trade services with a franchisee prospect. You could work a deal where a potential franchisee's buy-in fee would be cut if they helped produce the operations manual; this way, you use one franchisee to get more franchisees. The payoff comes later.

3. Hire commission-only sales reps. You only need to pay them what they earn.

4. Hire interns from colleges and universities. They often work for free or next-to-nothing, and get college credit in return.

5. Participate in business organizations where you can network for free.

6. Find inexpensive ways to advertise your company on a regular basis (such as asking all family members with a car to sport your company logo).

7. Join forces with a compatible business. For instance, you could merge with a secretarial service if you are a resume service.

8. Put on seminars, charging a fee for teaching others your own skills.

9. Sponsor trade shows or other events.

10. Develop a program or system for your business that can be marketed and sold to others. You could write a book or develop a software program for mass production.

COIN-OPERATED LAUNDRY

Start-up cost:	$50,000-$100,000
Potential earnings:	$30,000-$60,000
Typical fees:	25-50 cents per load; additional services such as folding can be charged by the pound (usually $1-$3 per)
Advertising:	Yellow Pages, coupon books, location
Qualifications:	None
Equipment needed:	Heavy-duty washers and dryers, laundry detergent dispensing machines
Home business potential:	No
Staff required:	Yes (2-4 people)
Handicapped opportunity:	Possibly
Hidden costs:	Insurance and equipment maintenance

LOWDOWN:

Wherever there are apartments, there are Laundromats. It's a recession-proof business, and one that may never be affected by technological advancements. Oh, the equipment may get better, and there may be electronic key cards used instead of coins in the laundries of the future, but until dirt-free clothes are invented, there will continue to be a need for this kind of business. Many innovative entrepreneurs are expanding their coin-operated laundries to include other services that help customers escape the monotony of washing, drying, and folding clothes—they're including bars with big-screen TVs, or tanning booths or video game arcades. Of course, you could also offer additional services, such as folding or even washing the clothes for your customers (usually these services are priced per pound). But the basics of running a Laundromat are very cut and dried, so to speak: you rent or buy space, install 25-50 washer/dryer units, and hang up your sign (which, by the way, will be your primary means of advertising).

START-UP:

Your start-up costs will be high to accommodate the large amounts of space and equipment you'll need; expect to spend at least $50,000 during your first year of business. Spend another $1,000 or so on advertising for your first six months, and tack on $1,000 extra if you have any add-on services which might appear in different sections of the newspaper or Yellow Pages. The markup is typically 25-50 cents per load; $1-$3 per pound for special services such as folding. Of course, the more services you have, the more money you'll make.

BOTTOM LINE ADVICE:

You'll be dealing with different types of people each day, and to some that's a plus, to others it's a negative. Make sure to assert some sort of policy against loiterers, or your Laundromat will look like a flophouse.

COLOR SEPARATION AND FILM ASSEMBLY SERVICES

Start-up cost:	$100,000-$200,000
Potential earnings:	$75,000-$250,000 per year
Typical fees:	Varies; could range from $150-$3,500 per project (depending on size and complexity)
Advertising:	Trade journals, business card, word of mouth
Qualifications:	Graphic design, photography background
Equipment needed:	Highly specialized camera, darkroom, photo enlarger, processing chemicals
Home business potential:	Yes
Staff required:	No
Handicapped opportunity:	Yes
Hidden costs:	EPA guidelines for disposal of chemicals

LOWDOWN:

The film production business is a very technically precise one, so be sure you have had thorough training before embarking on a full-time career. Considering that, if you have an interest in this type of business, you likely have some equipment to begin with, it should be relatively easy to set up your production studio. What will you do all day? You'll be handling a wide variety of projects for an array of clients, ranging from magazine photos to motion picture film. Basically, you'll shoot a picture of a picture being laid out for a publication (or even shoot an entire page so that it can be taken to the printer in sheets ready for reproduction), then prepare photos using the standard four-color process. In terms of your personal expertise, you should have knowledge of two processes for this job: color separation and the development of film.

START-UP:

To be successful, you need to have all of the equipment and space to maintain it, including chemicals (around $100,000). The EPA requirements that go along with the disposal of these chemicals can also be costly, yet a necessary evil. The good news is, your potential income after your initial investment will also be high—in the ballpark of $75,000-$250,000.

BOTTOM LINE ADVICE:

The one bad thing about this business is that your expensive equipment may become obsolete before you have paid it off, so it might take you a while before you see any sizable profit. Also, people who go into this business tend to become full-service, so add a printing press to your list of equipment.

COMMODITIES BROKER

Start-up cost:	$100,000+
Potential earnings:	$1,000,000+
Typical fees:	The difference between what you pay when you buy and what you get when you sell
Advertising:	None
Qualifications:	Awareness of everything that affects commodities prices, from famine to genetic engineering of new grain types, knowledge of human psychology
Equipment needed:	Communications equipment (pager/beeper/phone), access to stock market via computer, seat on commodities exchange in either New York City or Chicago
Home business potential:	Yes
Staff required:	No
Handicapped opportunity:	Yes
Hidden costs:	Insurance

LOWDOWN:

Being a commodities broker is the ultimate entrepreneurial activity: it's you against the market. Commodity investments are notorious for their danger. You can lose everything, or more than everything, that you have, or you can become enormously wealthy. By their nature, commodities (agricultural and mining products) are much more volatile than stocks and bonds, even junk bonds and over-the-counter offerings. Commodity prices vary with popular attitudes (otherwise known as "the market"), the weather, the effectiveness of farming techniques in a certain season, and government (actions such as President Carter's grain embargo), just to name a few factors. Successful commodities brokers gather enormous amounts of such information, assess its influence on the market for a specific commodity, and buy or sell shares of stock (not the actual product) accordingly. This is a very high-stakes way to make a living.

START-UP:

The cost of your seat on the exchange and your need for working capital make entering this business a very expensive proposition, perhaps to the tune of $100,000 or more. However, if you're good at it, you could become a millionaire.

BOTTOM LINE ADVICE:

Many people thrive on risk. If you are guiding their commodity trades, you need to have the people skills to work with them as well as all the financial skills to operate in this dynamic world. Everything is heightened here: the possibilities, the danger, and the opportunity to balloon your bank account.

CREATIVE ARTS DAY CAMP

Start-up cost:	$50,000
Potential earnings:	$20,000-$35,000
Typical fees:	$50-$100 per child for two weeks
Advertising:	Local newspaper, bulletin boards, flyers at schools, organized groups (i.e., Girl Scouts)
Qualifications:	License to run a camp, background in arts and crafts (degree or teaching certificate would be helpful)
Equipment needed:	Building or place to hold camp, art/craft supplies
Home business potential:	No
Staff required:	Yes
Handicapped opportunity:	Yes
Hidden costs:	Insurance, transportation, first aid, miscellaneous fees

LOWDOWN:

Day camps are extremely popular these days, primarily because most families are two-income and don't have the time to keep kids occupied in interesting, healthy hobbies during the summer. This is a great way to get kids involved in an activity during the summer that's worthwhile, and you can make a nice second income if you promote your day camp in a creative way—aim for the community publications and align yourself with school officials early on so that you can tap into your ready-made market in the easiest, most direct way. Your curriculum could consist of as many as 16-20 different activities throughout the week, from basket weaving to ballet. Imagine the fun you'll have teaching the children how to paint landscapes (or even portraits of one another)! You probably will need a staff of at least two more people, and you may need to provide lunches (if so, don't forget to build that into your cost).

START-UP:

Start-up cost will be relatively high, especially if you do not own a lot of land (maybe as high as $50,000). You'll need a shelter (which you can rent from local parks if you reserve early enough) and it should have adequate bathroom facilities and a kitchen. Since you will likely need a staff, you might consider rounding up people interested in educating children too, such as stay-at-home moms or student teachers looking for practical experience. It might be a good idea to have a nurse on staff or on call during camp hours. Where you live will determine the fee per week. Once you get established in a good area, you could make upward of $35,000.

BOTTOM LINE ADVICE:

This is a great job to consider if your own kids are sitting around saying, "What's there to do?" The best part is, it doesn't have to get stale after the first couple of sessions. Each day can be a different, unique, creative experience. Plan to explore different cultures or time periods by making art or crafts the way natives did. On the downside, even though this business can be fun, it is also a commitment. Even if you're under the weather, the kids will still get dropped off and the show must go on. That's why it's such a good idea to have a backup staff.

CUSTOM EMBROIDERY

Start-up cost:	$50,000-$150,000
Potential earnings:	$30,000-$250,000
Typical fees:	$5-$150 per item
Advertising:	Local newspaper, bulletin boards, direct mail, parks and recreation, YMCA, schools
Qualifications:	Skills needed to run embroidery equipment
Equipment needed:	Embroidery machine, ironing press, threads
Home business potential:	No
Staff required:	Yes
Handicapped opportunity:	Yes
Hidden costs:	Workers' compensation, fluctuating materials costs

LOWDOWN:

Companies everywhere have been using custom embroidery services for as long as they've been available—for T-shirts, hats, and jackets with their corporate logos or slogans proudly displayed on them. As a custom embroiderer, you would take specific orders from your customers, help them choose the article of clothing that would be most appropriate for their purposes, and then reproduce their logo on as many of the items as the customer has ordered. You'll likely run specials for large orders. If you are extremely knowledgeable about the process of custom embroidery and know how this type of business should be run, you can start it up yourself. If you don't, but think it would be something you would like to try, you might look into buying a franchise.

START-UP:

Investing in a franchise would call for a high start-up investment ($50,000 or more), but it may well be worth it in the end. Your earnings could range anywhere from $30,000-$250,000; however, this will depend on the quantities you sell and whether you're able to secure lots of repeat business. It would be wise to get involved with school systems, YMCAs, and parks and recreation bureaus in addition to local businesses. Put your bid in early for big-ticket items like letterman jackets and jerseys, etc. Your prices will vary extremely; you can charge as little as $35 and as much as $300, depending on how extensive the work is.

BOTTOM LINE ADVICE:

Your community involvement will spread your good name and get you more business; work hard at building a strong network of people who can help you bring in the customers. With this business, you have a little flexibility to be creative; however, be prepared to work long hours and weekends to fill all of your orders.

DAY SPA

Start-up cost:	$50,000-$100,000
Potential earnings:	$65,000-$100,000
Typical fees:	$75-$150 per day, plus or including lunch (you decide)
Advertising:	Newspapers, women's magazines, Yellow Pages, coupon books
Qualifications:	A cosmetology license may be required
Equipment needed:	Massage tables, sauna/tanning equipment, standard hair salon equipment
Home business potential:	No
Staff required:	Yes
Handicapped opportunity:	Possibly
Hidden costs:	Insurance

LOWDOWN:

It's the ultimate working person's fantasy—a whole day of relaxation and escape at a place where nothing gets in the way of pure pampering. Customers at a day spa can expect to spend their time in a soothing sauna, followed by a relaxing massage, and perhaps a facial and makeover session. Light lunches can also be offered as part of the package, as can hotel suites laden with goodies for an overnight stay (presumably for the extremely stressed-out). To get business to come to you, you may want to offer coupons or special packages (i.e., a romantic couples' getaway with free champagne or a working woman's package with a motivational speaker as a highlight). You'll need to take every step necessary to provide the ultimate in service for your clients to make sure their fantasies become reality—and that will require you to think creatively: what would you want if you had $150 a day or more to burn?

START-UP:

If you're going to offer a slice of the finer things in life, expect to have a large initial investment in your business long before you see a profit. Any kind of luxury service is going to require a huge amount of capital—and since your equipment and space rental costs will run anywhere from $50,000-$100,000, you should make sure you have an airtight business plan to sell bankers or investors on. Fees generally start at $75 per day for this service; you may decide to set a half-day fee of $40-$50 to offer clients more options.

BOTTOM LINE ADVICE:

You'll be spending money hand over fist in the beginning stages of your business . . . but if you can wait for the return, you could make a fortune for your patience. Luxurious escape-type businesses are on the rise in the harried '90s.

DEMOLITION/WRECKING CONTRACTOR

Start-up cost:	$65,000-$100,000
Potential earnings:	$50,000-$70,000
Typical fees:	Depends on job (but can be as high as $10,000)
Advertising:	Yellow Pages, classified ads, trade associations, networking, referrals
Qualifications:	Extensive experience, knowledge of construction methods, ability to operate and maintain the required heavy machinery, project planning skills, knowledge of explosives
Equipment needed:	Wrecking ball, radio equipment, bulldozers, and Dumpsters
Home business potential:	No
Staff required:	Yes
Handicapped opportunity:	No
Hidden costs:	Licensing, insurance, maintenance, overtime pay for crew, workers' compensation

LOWDOWN:

Demolition is a highly skilled occupation. If you live in a densely populated area of the country (which you probably do if you have developed the experience necessary to consider this business), there will be many opportunities for sub-contracting demolition work. Getting the old out of the way so the new can take its place is a profitable business for many small operators. Awareness of up-to-date approaches to environmental issues may give you an edge in the field. You will also need an ability to organize the wrecking process so that it occurs on time, in coordination with the other activities related to the project. A simple crash-and-smash approach is no longer acceptable in most municipalities. Recycling as much as possible and disposing of the rest have become an integral part of each operation.

START-UP:

The equipment you will need demands a heavy capital outlay before any revenue can flow back in to the business (sometimes as high as $100,000). If you can raise the capital, charge your clients on a per-job basis; perhaps an hourly rate of $75-$100 would be applicable.

BOTTOM LINE ADVICE:

There is a man-in-the-street fascination to the process of destroying something as big as a building. Behind all the rumbling and dust, though, is a careful plan and a lot of tedious preparation. Once you show you can do demolition with precision, you will draw referrals to new projects. Keeping a capable crew can be difficult. There is undoubtedly some danger in even the most well-planned wrecking project as well. In many areas the business may be seasonal.

DIAPER SERVICE

Start-up cost:	$45,000-$60,000
Potential earnings:	$40,000-$55,000
Typical fees:	$30-$50 per client per month
Advertising:	Yellow Pages, parent's publications, local newspapers, flyers, direct mail
Qualifications:	Some states require licensing or adherence to sanitation regulations
Equipment needed:	Heavy-duty washing, drying, and ironing equipment, delivery vans, plastic diaper pails, and inventory
Home business potential:	No
Staff required:	Yes (4-25 people, depending on the size of your market)
Handicapped opportunity:	Possibly
Hidden costs:	Insurance, workers compensation, cost of lost diapers, high utility bills

LOWDOWN:

New parents love everything about their little bundles of joy—until they have to contend with dirty diapers. That's where you come in. Your diaper service will provide these harried parents with a service they will love, not to mention respect (if they are the least bit environmentally conscious). Although the cloth diapers you rent will use more fuel to keep clean and sanitized, they do cut down on the number of diapers filling up landfills. That's your first selling point. The second is convenience, since you will send a delivery person out to each customer's home on a weekly basis to pick up the dirty diapers and drop off clean ones. Your delivery team will drop off pails, liners, and a specific number of clean diapers (based on the average number dirtied per week), then bring back the dirty ones to be washed, dried, and ironed by your cleaning team. Buy your initial mailing and phone lists from hospitals (who often let companies like yours know of new births each week or month); then, sell your services by making cold calls or sending direct mailings to each new parent's home. It's really a recession-proof business.

START-UP:

You'll need some heavy-duty washers and dryers to begin with, along with a large ironing press and a small fleet of delivery vehicles. Add to that your basic office set-up (computer, fax, phone, copier) and you're looking at a start-up of $40,000-$55,000. You will have lots of staff overhead costs, too. But if you're looking for a dependable means of making a living, you could do a lot worse that $35,000-$55,000 per year.

BOTTOM LINE ADVICE:

It's a dirty job, but somebody's got to do it. Just make sure that you use strong air-freshening chemicals in your plant, and provide your employees with the proper masks, gloves, and gels to keep the smell away from the more sensitive noses!

DISTRIBUTOR

Start-up cost:	$40,000-$60,000+
Potential earnings:	$50,000-$150,000+
Typical fees:	Varied, depending on what type of product you're distributing
Advertising:	Yellow Pages, business-to-business
Qualifications:	Knowledge of retail/wholesale practices; some training will likely be provided for you if you purchase a distributorship from a licensing agent or corporation
Equipment needed:	Computer, printer, fax/modem, possibly delivery vehicle
Home business potential:	Not likely
Staff required:	No
Handicapped opportunity:	Possibly
Hidden costs:	Insurance, price wars, mileage

LOWDOWN:

Distributors are the lifeline of any manufacturing business; they provide the vital link between manufacturer and consumer, selling products to the right channels to ensure that the consumer has the best chance to purchase the item. If you decide to purchase or become a distributorship, try to choose a product with which you have at least some experience. For instance, if you have a background in electronics, selling satellite dishes as a distributor would not be a huge leap in your credibility. However, keep in mind that many companies offering distributorships will train you as thoroughly as they have been trained so that you can maximize your sales potential for them. They, after all, have a vested interest in your success. You can look for a distributorship to purchase in an entrepreneurial publication or via on-line services; be sure to check out the company you'll be doing business with, as the magazines themselves often print disclaimers relinquishing responsibility for claims made in advertisements.

Once you find a solid company to represent (and preferably a product you really believe in), you'll set weekly contact goals and monthly sales goals. All the rest of your work is selling product (whether it be satellite dishes, prerecorded videotapes or even specialty petroleum products) and making sure it gets to the right selling points.

START-UP:

You'll need between $40,000-$60,000 to purchase a distributorship with a company that has a great reputation; less if it's a start-up or unknown business or product. Somewhere in that figure should be your advertising costs ($3,000 or so) and the office setup you'll need to succeed (computer, printer, fax/modem, copier, and phone—all under $5,000). If you're good at making the right contacts, you could earn $50,000-$150,000 or more.

BOTTOM LINE ADVICE:

It seems easy enough to pitch a product to selling outlets and individuals, but the work is hard and the hours tend to be much longer than one would think. If you're a hard-working professional, you should have no trouble. It's the novices who tend to have the biggest struggle.

Two Sides to Successful Leadership

COMMUNICATE:

- **your company's vision.** Create a mission statement. Show how your employees are contributing to the vision, and how it influences your decisions.

- **by example.** Remember, you set the standard in integrity, dependability, and commitment.

- **your expectation of success,** at every level of your business. Be ready to redefine success as the goals change.

- **where the company is.** Be prepared to share with your employees information about what goals have been met, what problems have arisen, what opportunities exist.

LISTEN:

- **in a way that establishes trust.** Let your employees speak to you openly, without fear of retribution. Encourage informal conversations and casual e-mail messages.

- **before you make any decision.** The decision will remain yours, but you will make it more constructively by listening to employees, customers, vendors, etc.

- **to diverse ideas.** Acknowledge when you use an employee's idea, even if not in the form it was given to you.

- **as you prepare for the future.** All the information you can gather from your market, your vendors, your employees, and your business network will help you to be ready for tomorrow's challenges.

DRUG TESTING SERVICE

Start-up cost:	$50,000+
Potential earnings:	$45,000-$75,000
Typical fees:	$125-$300 per test
Advertising:	Yellow Pages, direct mail, ads in specialized trade journals or newsletters
Qualifications:	Laboratory technician background
Equipment needed:	Highly sensitive testing equipment to run blood and urine specimens through
Home business potential:	Not likely
Staff required:	Two or three lab technicians and one administrator
Handicapped opportunity:	Yes
Hidden costs:	If test results aren't conclusive, you may have to retest at no additional charge: invest in state-of-the-art equipment the first time

LOWDOWN

Accidents and costly mistakes happen all too frequently in the workplace due to employees involved in drugs or alcohol. As a preventive measure, then, it makes incredibly good sense for companies to ask potential and current employees to participate in random drug testing. As a drug testing service, you would provide such corporations with the information necessary to prevent disasters from occurring. You would possibly travel to the client company's own site to collect and label blood and urine specimens, then run them through your own equipment to determine whether drugs or alcohol are present in the employee's system.

START-UP

Equipment and office space, in addition to personnel overhead, set your start-up costs at a minimum of $50,000. You'll also need to advertise your service in industry newsletters and business newspapers—so add another $1,000 or so to cover six months of those costs.

BOTTOM LINE ADVICE

The value of working independently can be immeasurable to those who enjoy it, so that's where your major reward is (aside from terrific earning power). If you like precise, technical work, this is the perfect opportunity to work at something you enjoy. On the downside, precise results will always be expected of you—and your reputation will be challenged with every mistake.

DRY CLEANING SERVICE

Start-up cost:	$75,000-$125,000
Potential earnings:	$45,000-$60,000
Typical fees:	Many charge on a per-pound basis ($5 per pound in some areas); otherwise, fees are extremely varied depending on item needing to be cleaned
Advertising:	Yellow Pages, location, coupon books, community newspapers, billboards
Qualifications:	Training in use and care of dry cleaning equipment
Equipment needed:	Dry cleaning equipment
Home business potential:	No
Staff required:	Yes (to cover many shifts)
Handicapped opportunity:	Possibly
Hidden costs:	Insurance, equipment maintenance, workers' compensation

LOWDOWN:

Dry cleaning businesses have been around for such a long time, mainly because of special fabrics always being in style. But the rise in women entering and climbing in the workplace has also meant an increase in business for dry cleaners, since these women don't have the time to wash finer fabrics at home. Also, there are certain items (such as draperies and comforters) that are too large to be washed in most home-size washers and dryers. Your service is a most practical one, servicing nearly anyone in your community. The challenge is to set yourself apart from other dry cleaners and laundry services in your area; run regular specials (since it's largely a price-driven business) and try running a creative promotion from time to time (trip giveaways are always nice). You'll spend your days in your hot location, windows steamed and brows furrowed; but, if you don't mind the labor, the profit is surely worth the strain.

START-UP:

Start-up will be high because you need so much capital equipment to begin with; expect to spend $75,000-$125,000 or more on equipment ranging from your cash register to ironing presses and steamers. Of course, your advertising budget should be set around $10,000 for your first year (and that's modest). Expect to earn $45,000-$60,000 per year.

BOTTOM LINE ADVICE:

The work is hard, the hours long (especially in the beginning, when you have a limited staff). If you don't mind any of that, this could be a perfect match; but, do keep in mind that you'll need to hold your costs down and promote heavily at all times to be able to make a regular, decent-size profit.

EARTHQUAKE PRODUCTS/SERVICES

Start-up cost:	$75,000-$150,000
Potential earnings:	$45,000-$85,000
Typical fees:	Varied according to product or service; could be as low as $500 for a consultation or as high as several thousand for earthquake-sensitive equipment
Advertising:	Yellow Pages, ads in business publications, referrals, offering your expert opinions in the media as often as you can
Qualifications:	A degree in seismology or environmental geography
Equipment needed:	Inventory of earthquake sensors and related seismographic products; delivery van equipped with tools/maintenance equipment; basic office setup (computer, printer, fax/modem and phone system); you may also need a cellular phone (for field work)
Home business potential:	Possibly (although not typically)
Staff required:	No
Handicapped opportunity:	Possibly
Hidden costs:	Equipment upgrade/maintenance, travel expenses for continuing study in seismology (often, you'll want to travel to earthquake sites, and your clients probably won't cover those expenses)

LOWDOWN:

The West Coast is always experiencing some kind of geologic activity, whether it be flooding or earthquakes. Earthquakes, of course, are more common in California than anywhere else, so a sizable portion of your market will likely be based there. Keep in mind, however, that the Midwest and East Coast both experience small tremors from time to time, and meteorological services in those areas need your products and services, although not nearly as much. As an earthquake product distributor and service business, you'll be selling extremely sensitive earthquake-detecting products and seismographs—but you'll also be offering your expertise in earthquake safety and protection. You can evaluate buildings for their ability to withstand major earthquakes, and assign them a rating for insurance or related purposes. Or, you can teach seminars on how to prepare for earthquakes and protect oneself. The best thing you can do to get your name out there is to position yourself as an earthquake expert—offer your name to the media on a regular basis so that they call on you when the "big one" happens.

START-UP:

Since so much of your equipment is highly specialized and of a delicate nature, you'll need to build up a sensible inventory and store it in a secure environment; expect to spend at least $75,000-$150,000 on stock and storage space, along with a delivery/maintenance vehicle and your marketing materials. The good news is, you can look forward to an income potential of $45,000-$85,000 or more per year.

BOTTOM LINE ADVICE:

You're selling folks on peace of mind, and trying to turn a violent natural event into something somewhat less threatening. Remember, you're providing products that help people to prepare for the worst, and that's not always a very happy business to be in. Your challenge is to admirably walk the fine line between fear and disaster.

Keeping the Records You Need

Probably the most important device for managing the paperwork of your business is the circular file. Do not keep any piece of paper unless you are sure that you want it, or need it. Hanging a "Bless This Mess" sign over your desk is no solution. Instead, plan how you will manage your paper and just do it. You want to spend your time on profit-making tasks, not on searching through mountains of unorganized material for that one vital receipt or order slip.

What records are you required to keep? The IRS has issued certain guidelines: "Your permanent books (including inventory records) must show not only your gross income, but also your deductions and credits. In addition, you must keep any other records and data necessary to support the entries in your books and on your tax and information returns." This information includes paid bills and canceled checks. The IRS lets you decide how to store this material, as long as you choose an "orderly" approach.

For very small businesses, the checkbook register can be enough of a financial record, with one shoe box for receipts and another for invoices. Most organizations move rapidly past this stage, though. Spend a small amount of time planning for storage, and prevent yourself from wasting hours and hours at year-end as you prepare your figures for your accountant. Set up a filing system you feel comfortable with, and stick to it during the year. Color-coded file folders in hanging files are appropriate for almost all types of organizations.

There's nothing glamorous about file folders in a box, but this kind of system can expand as you grow. It lets you put your hand quickly on the paper you need and efficiently store the records you must keep. It gets stuff off your desk when you're not working on it, and it lets you have it back when you need it.

A popular approach is to devote one color to each major business topic. Marketing, for example, could be blue. You'd set up a tabbed hanging folder, in blue, for whatever marketing papers you have now. Later, you will probably need to subdivide the hanging folder with different tabbed blue file folders for your plan, your market research, new ideas, special promotion plans, sales forecasts, and so on. And remember that labeling the file folders is just as important as labeling those computer disks you probably have sliding around on your desk.

Further refinements to the filing system depend on the nature of your business. For salespeople, a tickler file system arranged by date may be essential: two weeks from now, which accounts should be called on? What should be done six months from now? For services, you may need files of information and concept-oriented material arranged by topic area: employee motivation, training systems, new approaches, etc.

Most businesses keep client files alphabetically. Your clients or customers are the lifeblood of your business, and you need a quick, efficient way of storing and retrieving their information: desires, wants, needs, buying history, future possibilities. The IRS may not care about this aspect of your business, but it's the basis of the ongoing marketing relationship that supports everything you do.

So choose a system, put it together, and put away every piece of paper you have kicking around your company. Keep using the files all year. Then you can stop thinking about this boring topic and get busy with the action steps that lead you toward your business goals.

Fiber Optic Transmission Systems

Start-up cost:	$800,000-$1.5 million
Potential earnings:	$100,000-$1 million+
Typical fees:	$1,500-$5,000 per fiber optic network, per month
Advertising:	Direct mail to potential clients (such as long distance telephone carriers)
Qualifications:	Fiber optics experience and access to cable burial sites
Equipment needed:	Heavy-duty cable, tools, fiber optic technology, computer, printer, fax/modem, copier, cellular phone
Home business potential:	No
Staff required:	Yes
Handicapped opportunity:	Not typically
Hidden costs:	Insurance, workers' compensation, subcontracting fees, related maintenance

Lowdown:

Some of the nation's largest long distance services depend on fiber optics to carry their customers' voices clearly over the entire world—so why shouldn't this be an area ripe for business opportunity? Of course, you should keep in mind that this area is so highly specialized only those with experience should really attempt a go at it. That being said, your fiber optics transmission service will provide a near-perfect means for transmittal and receipt of electronic and voice messages for telephone carriers and related communications businesses—primarily by transmitting impulses through extremely sensitive fiber optic cable. Your own background should include telecommunications experience and sales ability (to help you promote your company's services to large players in the communications field). Be prepared to spend a lot of long hours supervising the initial installation of the fiber optics network; you may opt to subcontract much of this work to other specialists in the field.

Start-up:

Start-up in this industry is quite high (in the $800,000-$1.5 million range), mainly because the equipment and related accouterments are of an intricate, complex nature and they need to be placed in the most conducive environments possible (usually under water). You'll probably pay a pretty penny for your burial site, in addition to regular maintenance that will be required. Keep in mind, too, that you'll have plenty of staff overhead, particularly if you do not choose to subcontract installation work. Still, this business should be able to take you into the millionaire realm, if you know the ropes of promoting your services over a competitor's.

Bottom Line Advice:

Remember that fiber optic cables are buried under the sea—and that sharks and other sea creatures sometimes can cut through the cables with their teeth. Of course, there are newer materials that prevent such mishaps, but be sure to investigate all of your options thoroughly. In order to stay profitable, you need to stay durable.

FITNESS RENTAL EQUIPMENT

Start-up cost:	$50,000-$150,000
Potential earnings:	$20,000-$60,000
Typical fees:	Monthly rentals of $15-$25 per piece of equipment, plus service charges
Advertising:	Direct mail, Yellow Pages, newspaper ads in the sports section
Qualifications:	Ability to market your services
Equipment needed:	Various exercise equipment (stair stepper, weight machine, stationary bike)
Home business potential:	Yes
Staff required:	No
Handicapped opportunity:	Not typically
Hidden costs:	Insurance protection against theft or damaged equipment

LOWDOWN:

The fitness craze is on—and you can capitalize on it if you are knowledgeable about the types of equipment that are popular, safe, and produce results. If you know the difference between a StairMaster and a Nordic Track, and can teach others how to use this equipment, you can not only market your rental business but also tack on lessons for a small additional fee. Depending on what you buy and how much of it you do, it will take at least one year to break even on investment. You need to sell your customers on the service issue and the convenience of using the equipment in the privacy of their own home—a big selling point for those "cocooners" identified by Faith Popcorn in her marketing bible for the future, *The Popcorn Report*.

START-UP:

Initial investment ($50,000-$150,000) might seem high compared to first-year earnings. However, keep in mind you should start your business with at least four to five different varieties of equipment and have two of each type. You will want to purchase well-built equipment so that it lasts longer. Research different options to find the equipment at wholesale cost. You will want to rent the equipment out on a monthly, possibly a weekly, basis—charging at least $15 a month. You probably cannot charge more than that because joining a health club is another option for these clients, for just a few dollars a month more.

BOTTOM LINE ADVICE:

This business might be slow getting off the ground—be persistent. Emphasize the fact that delivery is included in the rental contract and that customers can exercise in private without having to leave their homes. However, these are probably one-time only customers, so get the word out.

FRAMING SERVICE

Start-up costs:	$40,000-$60,000
Potential earnings:	$40,000-$50,000
Typical fees:	$15 per hour for custom work plus materials; materials only for frame-it-yourself
Advertising:	Yellow Pages, local newspapers
Qualifications:	Understanding of operating a retail business plus skill in framing and training a staff, ability to teach customers to frame
Equipment needed:	Framing supplies, special cutters for glass, wood, mats, cash register, retail space
Home business potential:	No
Staff required:	Yes
Handicapped opportunity:	No
Hidden costs:	Insurance and materials costs

LOWDOWN:

This business is lucrative because many people buy prints and other artwork or want to frame their own pieces. Some people don't have the time or patience to frame, so the custom aspect should not be ignored. Take into consideration, however, that about 60 percent frame their own, while 40 percent request custom framing. Material costs fall somewhere around 26 to 32 percent, and gross profits about 68 to 74 percent.

START-UP:

You'll spend at least $30,000 launching a frame shop, primarily because you'll need lots of storage space and work area with sufficient lighting. More than likely, you'll rent space somewhere close to an art gallery. Charges will vary according to size and make of frame.

BOTTOM LINE ADVICE:

Be mindful that this is a retail establishment, so take into consideration the size of the shop, location, rent. You might want to sell some ready-made frames and prints to supplement the framing business.

FRANCHISEE

Start-up cost:	$40,000-$100,000 or more (depends on the type of business)
Potential earnings:	$10,000-$50,000 (or more)
Typical fees:	Depends on size and type of business
Advertising:	Newspapers, brochures, direct mail, location
Qualifications:	Ability to produce and/or sell the service or product; marketing skills
Equipment needed:	Depends on the product or service
Home business potential:	Many franchises can be started from home
Staff required:	Usually none at first
Handicapped opportunity:	Yes
Hidden costs:	Depends on the franchise. All franchisees, though, will incur some legal costs for contracts. It is important to explore the specific opportunity you're considering to be sure of your expenses and liabilities in starting up

LOWDOWN:

Food franchise businesses are very popular in the U.S. One need only look around any shopping area to see all the "brand name" businesses out there. That name recognition gives you a powerful boost. Everyone knows your product, so marketing is off to a good start. You also have a wide variety of businesses to choose from: anything from cookie shops to ice cream parlors to restaurants. Franchisees can learn how to avoid many first-time-business-owners' mistakes because a large part of what they purchase is the franchiser's experience. It is very important to research the company thoroughly, before signing on the dotted line. Make sure you understand what (if any) marketing, purchasing, and other assistance you are entitled to. Demographics are very important, too: make sure the geographic area you want for your business is one that can support it.

START-UP:

As mentioned above, the costs vary considerably depending on the type of business you choose. Some enterprises have modest start-up requirements; others are quite expensive. Marketing and legal fees can run as much as $10,000 or more, depending, again, on the product and the structure of the franchise offer.

BOTTOM LINE ADVICE:

One concern about franchises: the legal ramifications. It can be very tedious plowing through all the legal issues surrounding your franchise, but you must do your homework: read all documents concerning the business thoroughly—and seek legal counsel before signing anything. Also, health regulations must be considered in any franchise involving food. Having a franchise business can be wonderful—the support of the franchise company is invaluable in getting started. But the long hours and hard work common to all start-ups will still be yours—and you may at times feel restricted by some of the guidelines of your franchise.

FREELANCE TV PRODUCER

Start-up cost:	$40,000+
Potential earnings:	$50,000-$150,000+
Typical fees:	$10,000-$50,000 per project (more if you have the reputation to command big bucks)
Advertising:	Industry trade publications, word of mouth; the best advertising is to produce one great TV show
Qualifications:	Degree in telecommunications would be helpful; ability to write grants, along with excellent marketing and selling skills
Equipment needed:	Computer, printer, fax, phone, letterhead, business card
Home business potential:	Yes
Staff required:	No
Handicapped opportunity:	Yes
Hidden costs:	Insurance, union fees, travel and entertainment expenses

LOWDOWN:

As a freelance TV producer, you are responsible for every phase of production—including raising the capital to produce in the first place. Affiliate yourself early on with casting directors, talent agencies, and writers (you can find them through writers' unions such as the Screenwriters Guild). Pass your card along to anyone you meet in the industry, and work hard to build a solid stable of projects instead of focusing on only one. There's a good reason to spread your interests across a few projects at a time: namely, your chances of actually selling a studio or network on one project greatly increase by number. You'll need to find good scripts, hire everyone from actors to pages, and know what goes on in the actual pre- and postproduction stages. Experience in the television industry in all phases is essential; hopefully, you've worked your way up to this position of power and tremendous responsibility. In addition, you'll need good marketing and sales skills.

START-UP:

If you are lucky, a studio will back you in your endeavor. If not, brush up on your grant-writing skills, lean on your rich friends, and plan to empty your savings account. It's going to take every penny you can muster to get enough capital to get the show off the ground, since most productions cost between $75,000-$300,000 to produce (and that's a modest budget). After you've raised your capital, you have to wisely decide how to spend it; of course, you won't forget to factor your own salary in your budget plan, right? Your fee to produce a television show will range from $45,000-$150,000+.

BOTTOM LINE ADVICE:

This profession requires a great amount of responsibility. If the show flops, you flop. If it's a hit, you're the next up-and-coming producer. It's a hard way to live, from one project to the next . . . but, if you're up to the challenge and don't mind a few disappointments, you can manage to make a decent enough living.

FUNERAL HOME

Start-up cost:	$50,000 and up
Potential earnings:	$100,000 or more
Typical fees:	Usually a flat fee: $3,000-$10,000
Advertising:	Billboards, advertisements in program books for fund-raising events, newspapers, local magazines
Qualifications:	License, training, experience
Equipment needed:	Mortuary equipment, fleet of vehicles including a hearse and a limousine, suitably furnished rooms for services, an office for counseling, an equipped business office, letterhead, envelopes, marketing materials
Home business potential:	No
Staff required:	Yes
Handicapped opportunity:	No
Hidden costs:	Utility costs, donations to community charities

LOWDOWN:

Establishing a funeral home is a considerable project. You will need to plan carefully for the market you hope to serve. The contemporary focus on respect, care, and counseling may allow you to create an enterprise that stands above other old-fashioned funeral homes, which may have a dubious reputation or which have not kept up their premises. In today's fragmented culture, many people live far from family and friends. When a death occurs, they need far more support and guidance than the usual funeral home provides. You can offer planning, grief counseling, and a range of support services that may extend over a period of time to ease the inevitable feelings of loss. Finding a way to achieve clarity about costs and payment will also help set your business apart as different from, and better than, the competition.

START-UP:

Start-up costs are clearly very high (you will need at least $50,000 to get you started), relative to the expense of beginning a "typical" small business. But you are establishing an enterprise that will be woven into the fabric of the community you serve, for the long term. You should be able to make close to $100,000 once your business gets off the ground.

BOTTOM LINE ADVICE:

The need for funeral home services is great, in any community, but you must overcome many negative assumptions, fears, and prejudices before you can develop your clientele. Community standards will define, to some extent, the way you can express your message about the positive differences you offer. Most of all, your claims must be supported by reality. If you say, "We care," you must show it to the community by your involvement in charitable activities, service to the elderly, or similar philanthropic actions.

GEOLOGIC DRILLING SERVICE

Start-up cost:	$45,000 or more
Potential earnings:	$35,000-$60,000
Typical fees:	Varied according to length of job (average daily rate of $600-$1,000)
Advertising:	Referrals, partnerships with related businesses, advertising in trade periodicals
Qualifications:	Extensive experience, knowledge of drilling equipment operation, ability to read geological survey maps, interpret field reports
Equipment needed:	Specialized drilling equipment, heavy truck(s)
Home business potential:	No
Staff required:	Yes
Handicapped opportunity:	No
Hidden costs:	Insurance, equipment maintenance and replacement, travel costs to distant locations, workers compensation

LOWDOWN:

Oil and gas companies are constantly on the lookout for dependable drilling services to help them locate energy sources. They need extensive wells in order to have strong, regular supplies of oil and gas. Once a potential site is located, you will be called in to drill and set up the well. Your experience and skills will enable you to carry out the complex drilling process in a cost-effective, productive manner. Each well is different, and you will need a sophisticated understanding of geologic formations and the environment to make a success of this heavy-equipment enterprise. You will usually be a subcontractor on a larger project that includes site identification and the management of the well's production. Other types of drilling could provide an add-on or a subspecialty.

START-UP:

Drilling is very capital-intensive to get started, and the payoff may be slow in coming, requiring considerable operating funds at the beginning of the enterprise. Even when billing $1,000 per day, it will take a while to earn a sizable return on investment.

BOTTOM LINE ADVICE:

Forming relationships with businesses that use your drilling services will be vital. This is your main marketing avenue. Once you have an established customer base, you will likely receive ongoing business. Clearly travel is necessary to the different well sites, and paying your crew will be expensive as they need to be quite skilled. Drilling can be hard, dirty work, but it has its satisfactions, too. You will be in close contact with beautiful places around your region, and outdoors for the better half of each business day.

GROUND WATER ASSESSING

Start-up cost:	$40,000-$65,000
Potential earnings:	$40,000-$60,000
Typical fees:	$350+ per job
Advertising:	Referrals, trade association memberships, networking, business relationships with related services
Qualifications:	Extensive experience, scientific background in water quality testing, knowledge of heavy equipment operation, report-writing skills
Equipment needed:	Trenching or drilling equipment, truck, computer, printer, office furniture, business card, letterhead, envelopes
Home business potential:	Yes
Staff required:	Possibly
Handicapped opportunity:	No
Hidden costs:	Maintenance, lab fees, insurance

LOWDOWN:

Water constantly flows through the "solid" ground under our feet. It's one of our most valuable natural resources. With more than 260 million people using water daily in the U.S., providing an acceptable water quality is no longer simple. Pollution is a growing problem, and your ground water assessment service can highlight the location of water in addition to the nature of any contamination. Even if most of the houses in an area use a municipal water supply, tracing the purity of the ground water is essential—especially in areas where new building is a critical part of the local economy.

START-UP:

The level of the water table will define the type of equipment you'll need to reach and sample it. Minnesota is entirely different from New Mexico. In either place you will need a lab or the ability to subcontract lab services, and you must be able to write and print out a professional-looking report. Expect to spend anywhere from $30,000 on equipment; expect to bill your services at a minimum of $350 per job.

BOTTOM LINE ADVICE:

You don't want to vegetate behind a desk for the rest of your life. You love the outdoors and have a lively interest in what lies under the surface of the earth. If you have a relevant scientific background, you can take these attitudes and use them as the basis for this business. Quite a lot of capital should be available. You will have a high initial outlay and may need several years before you can establish your name and reputation for accurate, on-time work. Building a customer base will be challenging. In northern states this may be somewhat of a seasonal business.

HEALTH CLUB

Start-up cost:	$40,000 and up
Potential earnings:	$40,000-$70,000
Typical fees:	$300-$1,000 per membership
Advertising:	Word of mouth, bulletin boards, coupon books and mailings that offer corporate discounts, location
Qualifications:	Some background in management and recreation
Equipment needed:	State-of-the-art exercise equipment, location
Home business potential:	No
Staff required:	Yes
Handicapped opportunity:	No—there is lots of demanding physical work
Hidden costs:	The markup on equipment can be quite high; be sure you're getting the most for your investment

LOWDOWN

The rise in health clubs during the 1980s as a meeting place for singles has given way to health-conscious clubs with services beyond mere workout equipment. For instance, some clubs offer free on-site day care for members, while others have combined physical fitness with mini-wellness centers to offer a more complete, holistic approach to staying fit for life. Whatever you decide, you'll face some interesting challenges and plenty of competition, so you'll need management experience in order to best direct the growth of your club and its staff (which can range from 10-50 people, depending on the size of your club). The nice thing is, you can hire your staff as you grow—and there are always plenty of college students who can get certified to teach aerobics. Make sure you have met all municipal and state requirements, and secure any certificates you'll need to operate.

START-UP:

Start-up for a health club is expensive, mostly because of the need for a large enough space to accommodate bulky exercise equipment and areas for aerobics instruction. You can count on spending at least $15,000 on equipment alone (and that's with just a few starting pieces—imagine a complete room full of equipment at about $1,000 each). Look to lease a space with sturdy floors and add another $2,000 and up per month in rent. By the time you add in salaries, advertising/promotional costs, and liability insurance, you've spent a great deal of money—but all of this could take care of itself if you price your rates competitively.

BOTTOM LINE ADVICE

While the fast pace and new faces will "pump you up," stiff competition from larger chains could leave you feeling deflated. You need to come up with innovative ways to set your club apart from the big guys—and offer people a real incentive for coming to your facility (discounts, or special services such as on-site day care, etc.). In this competitive field, you'll be spending long hours doing flips and twists to stay ahead.

Home Health Care Service

Start-up cost:	$40,000-$150,000 (depending on size and location)
Potential earnings:	$50,000-$100,000
Typical fees:	$40-$50 per hour
Advertising:	Newspapers (especially those geared toward seniors), hospitals, direct mail
Qualifications:	Should be a licensed or registered nurse or other medical professional
Equipment needed:	Standard office equipment, plus pagers or cellular phones
Home business potential:	Yes (but most have outside offices)
Staff required:	Yes (usually 30 or so RNs or LPNs and 2-3 administrative types to handle insurance claims and billing)
Handicapped opportunity:	Yes (for supervisory position)
Hidden costs:	Liability insurance

Lowdown:

When it boils down to it, who really wants to be in the hospital—even when you are sick? That's why visiting nurse services are rapidly becoming available in many areas across the country. By caring for patients who can be treated at home with medications and follow-up, you could offer a personal touch to an otherwise sterile health care industry. Also, with the high cost of hospital care, more and more people will be turning to your type of service. There are a lot of incentives for people to use this service aside from mere financial benefit; for instance, many working couples need a nurse to care for an elderly parent.

Start-up:

You'll need to secure an office and maintain a staff of anywhere from 20-30 nursing professionals; these costs alone could run you $20,000. You'll also need to advertise in high-profile places (such as large metropolitan newspapers), so add in another $15,000 for an advertising budget. One tip to help curb advertising costs is to place ads in the less-pricey newspapers aimed specifically at senior citizens. Most important of all, however, is the liability insurance you must carry—and there are different minimum amounts of coverage required by each state.

Bottom Line Advice:

Visiting nurse services are the medical wave of the future, particularly because more and more insurance companies are requiring shorter stays at hospitals. Make sure, in addition to your own medical background, that you also have a clear business sense and the ability to manage several people simultaneously—or you'll wind up pulling your hair out over issues such as personnel management and cost control.

INDOOR PLAYSPACE

Start-up cost:	$50,000-$150,000
Potential earnings:	$50,000-$75,000
Typical fees:	Admission is usually $8-$10; you can make more money by adding concessions
Advertising:	Newspapers, magazines, Yellow Pages, parents' groups
Qualifications:	None
Equipment:	Indoor playground equipment (i.e., Junglegym™, sliding boards, and places to swing and jump)
Home business potential:	No
Staff required:	Yes
Handicapped opportunity:	Possibly
Hidden costs:	Liability insurance, employee overhead, and equipment costs could be considerably high

LOWDOWN:

Starting a place for children to come for a great time can be extremely rewarding, both personally and financially. First, there is the joy of seeing laughing kids chasing one another around; second, their parents will be paying you for the experience. With such high-profile success stories as The Discovery Zone™ cropping up across the country, it's no wonder that indoor play centers are no longer considered child's play. You should have a background in recreation or management if you really want to push for success, but basically all you need is the start-up funds to launch this fun—and profitable—business.

START-UP:

Since your initial investment is considerably high, and because you'll have a staff of 10-20 employees, it will take a while to roll in the profits. However, there is such a critical need for children's recreation facilities that are clean (and offer extras such as birthday party services), your chances of success are probably higher than you can imagine. At $8-$10 a head, your earnings could become quite considerable after your company's first few years.

BOTTOM LINE ADVICE:

There's nothing cuter than a group of kids having a ball—and several Kodak™ moments are likely to occur at your facility. However, this is a competitive business—and your competitors are not just other indoor playgrounds, but just about anything that draws the attentions of young ones (from television to computer games). Your challenge is to come up with innovative ways to turn their heads to you.

INSTANT SIGNS

Start-up cost:	$65,000-$100,000 (depends on whether you're buying into a franchise)
Potential earnings:	$20,000-$45,000
Typical fees:	$15-$150 per sign (depending on size and complexity)
Advertising:	Yellow Pages, coupon books, and signs of your own (including a storefront)
Qualifications:	None, except short-term training on equipment
Equipment needed:	Computer, printer, color foils, specialty paper/sign materials
Home business potential:	Not typically
Staff required:	Not initially
Handicapped opportunity:	Yes
Hidden costs:	Insurance, workers' compensation; watch your advertising dollars, as they could melt quickly

LOWDOWN:

From garage sales to small businesses, lots of folks need good (and inexpensively produced) signs that meet their particular needs. Whether it be a mom-and-pop flea market or an incorporated car repair service, it won't matter—your customers will come from all walks of life and each, in the end, will pay decently for your services. They may need a magnetized sign for their company vehicle, or simply a banner that announces a special sale or promotion. Whatever their need, you'll have an easier time producing the goods if you have either previous expertise in this field or a backing franchise operation with training and 24-hour support. If you can get financing (either through a bank or through the franchise itself), do it. You can then rest your advertising on the company's corporate history—and that buys you the kind of credibility you'll need to compete. However, if you don't have enough funding necessary to franchise, consider joining the Better Business Bureau or similar organization to get the credibility boost you'll need in the beginning.

START-UP:

You'll need to purchase a computer system with specialized software that allows you to produce nice-looking signs, so expect to spend at least $50,000 on those items in addition to your retail space and advertising budget. Your charges will vary greatly ($15-$150) according to what needs to be done, but you can expect an annual income of $20,000-$45,000.

BOTTOM LINE ADVICE:

Signs all point to profit—if you're reputable and produce high-quality signs for your customers. Consider offering packages of signs for various needs (such as garage sales or a special promotion value pack) to price yourself more attractively.

KEY CONTROL SYSTEMS
MANUFACTURER/DISTRIBUTOR

Start-up cost:	$50,000-$100,000
Potential earnings:	$40,000-$120,000
Typical fees:	Varied according to product; can be as low as $125 and as high as $1,000 for a key control station at a large manufacturing facility
Advertising:	Business/trade publications, Yellow Pages, direct mail
Qualifications:	Manufacturing and sales background
Equipment needed:	Sheet metal, key tags, and small hardware; possibly a production area; computer, printer, phone, fax, copier
Home business potential:	Not typically
Staff required:	Yes (for assembly, unless you subcontract)
Handicapped opportunity:	Possibly
Hidden costs:	Insurance, workers' compensation, fluctuating metals costs

LOWDOWN:

How many times have you been locked out of your home or office—and you can't remember where the additional keys are? That happens every day in the work world; from hotels/motels to large manufacturing facilities, people simply misplace keys. One of the best ways for your customers to stay organized in such matters is to have a centralized location for keys. As a key control system manufacturer/distributor, you can provide items to accomplish just that—from small key hooks that clip onto a door to large key cabinets with several compartments. You develop a professional-looking catalog of your products and then advertise in industry publications to assess your market size and sales potentials in each territory. Then you follow up with direct mail or independent sales representatives who stay in tune with your customers' needs. Like many manufacturing businesses, yours is fairly straightforward; you can quickly teach your production staff how to assemble product, or you can save some time by subcontracting the work to a job shop.

START-UP:

You'll need at least $50,000 to secure a suitable inventory of sheet metal and other raw materials, but expect to spend closer to $100,000 when all is said and done. That's because you'll still need an office setup (with computer, printer; customer tracking, accounting and/or inventory control software). At $125-$1,000 or more for a key control system, you can expect to earn anywhere from $40,000-$120,000 per year. Expect at some point to employ or retain outside sales help, as your market is nationwide.

BOTTOM LINE ADVICE:

You are providing a much-needed service, and yet it is growing increasingly obsolete with the emergence of electronic key card systems. Sell your customers on the benefits of using products that will never fail in an electrical storm—or add electronic key cards to your product line.

LEAK DETECTION SERVICE

Start-up cost:	$40,000-$60,000
Potential earnings:	$50,000-$100,000
Typical fees:	$50-$75 per appointment
Advertising:	Business-to-business advertising, networking, referrals
Qualifications:	Ability to work with and maintain the leak detection equipment, self-marketing skills
Equipment needed:	A wide range of equipment, depending on the specialization of the business
Home business potential:	Yes
Staff required:	No
Handicapped opportunity:	No
Hidden costs:	Insurance, equipment repair and updating

LOWDOWN:

This is a growing business across the country. Building codes require inspections before a roof is repaired, and the need to keep costs down makes detection of problems more and more important. Hurricanes and earthquakes have produced a great deal of business for leak detectors, and in many areas the importance of conserving fresh water gives another boost. Gas leaks must be contained before they damage the environment or endanger people; even swimming pool leaks can cause serious trouble unless they are detected early. Leak detectors work closely with plumbers, maintenance supervisors, and others. Some have an add-on business of carrying out the needed repairs when a leak occurs. Some leak detection practices require strength and skill with various pieces of machinery, including carbon dioxide detection equipment, while others result in a computer printout of the problem area in a roof.

START-UP:

Training and equipment can be quite expensive, but once you become proficient you can expect a good return on these investments. You'll need to advertise in the Yellow Pages, so expect to spend at least $1,000 annually on that alone. However, you'll be billing several clients per month at the rate of $50-$75 per consultation.

BOTTOM LINE ADVICE:

This is a big, exciting business that will involve you with major projects. You will be providing a much-needed service and can expect to see it grow as you become established and develop working relationships. The downside can be having to work under constant pressure. Regular maintenance is less significant in leak detection than responding to a problem, so you may find yourself too busy at times, and not busy enough at others. The work can be physically demanding and you could end up in some hazardous environments.

LONG-DISTANCE PHONE SERVICES

Start-up cost:	$100,000-$500,000+ (depends on how extensive your market is)
Potential earnings:	$50,000-$150,000+
Typical fees:	Percentage of each phone call made, plus a monthly service fee (always changing, to be competitive with going rates)
Advertising:	Direct mail, radio/TV ads, or simply free trial phone cards (usually with five free minutes to try your services)
Qualifications:	A background in management and/or finance would be especially helpful
Equipment needed:	Extensive telephone system with an 800-number for customer service, fax/modem, computers and printers on a network system
Home business potential:	Not typically
Staff required:	Yes (you'll need 24-hour customer service to compete)
Handicapped opportunity:	Yes
Hidden costs:	Workers' compensation, payroll administration, and technical service

LOWDOWN:

Deregulation in the long-distance telephone services sector has opened the door for many new companies offering huge discounts on airtime; never before have consumers been able to shop around for the best rates (and change services so often to get them). You'll need to have a certain brilliance with the financial aspect of this business, since it is so price-driven; if you aren't on top of fluctuations in your market, you'll lose out immediately. Your biggest challenge is to get this one off and running with a solid, trustworthy image, since people are reluctant to change over from the larger long distance services to a virtually unknown one like yours. Many new services market to a specific population, and this might be your ticket to separate yourself from the bigger companies. That's why you'll have to spend so much on advertising and promotion in the beginning—you need it to build credibility and a name for yourself. Once you get started, you'll offer your services via direct mail, phone solicitation, or free promotions (such as a five-minutes-free phone calling card). Then, you'll develop your customer service staff as you go, so that they are ready to handle any question or complaint that might come through. Essentially, your staff is what's going to make this a high-investment proposition, since you'll be carrying all the resulting overhead. Once you've got good people working with you, however, you stand more than a chance of making it all work.

START-UP:

At $100,000-$500,000+, this is an expensive business to start, to say the least. You'll need to first secure your equipment (an extensive phone system with monitoring and billing capability) and then you'll have to spend a small fortune on advertising to get your name out there in this competitive field. After you've done those things, however, you could pull in between $50,000-$150,000 annually for your efforts. (Of course, that figure reflects your own personal income—your employees will have fair salaries, too.)

BOTTOM LINE ADVICE:
This is an increasingly competitive business, and only the tough (and well-financed) survive. Get proper backing to begin with, and don't skimp on anything where your customer will notice it (for instance, a phone service too cheap for an 800-number for customer service will send up a major red flag to any would-be consumer). On the plus side, this can be a very lucrative field for the aggressive.

More Networking Tips

■ **The best time to make new contacts is when you don't need them.** It's best to call on others in happy times so that your business image is positive, and new contacts will respect you before you need help.

■ **Don't forget to follow up.** Most of all, never forget to say "thank you."

■ **Set up a good filing or business card management system.** Choose one that will actually work for you, not one that merely sounds good.

■ **Weed out nonproductive relationships every six months.** But don't throw away a card if you can help it. You never know when you'll need that person in the future.

■ **MOST IMPORTANT, ALWAYS BE YOURSELF.** We all have different styles of networking, and there are no real hard-and-fast rules when it comes to the joy of meeting new people—and making new friends.

MACHINERY REBUILDING/REPAIR

Start-up cost:	$50,000-$150,000+
Potential earnings:	$100,000-$500,000
Typical fees:	Varied according to project; ranging from $500 to several thousand
Advertising:	Business directories, direct mail, Yellow Pages, word of mouth
Qualifications:	Mechanical aptitude and an understanding of manufacturing equipment
Equipment needed:	Repair equipment pertaining to your area of specialty; often, welding equipment is needed
Home business potential:	No
Staff required:	Yes
Handicapped opportunity:	No
Hidden costs:	Insurance (accidental damage), long payback periods

LOWDOWN:

Serious downtime can result when a piece of machinery breaks down in a manufacturing plant. That's why it's so critical for a manufacturer to be tied into a service such as yours; you can work on-site or have the equipment moved to your own facility for repair when something goes wrong. Keep in mind that you'll need to choose an area of expertise; for instance, if it's robotics you know the most about, that's the area you should concentrate in. It's all too often a mistake to try and repair everything for everybody (and it could wind up costing your reputation). You should have a mechanical ability, technical mind, and manufacturing experience to be able to talk the same language as your clients and convince them that you're the right one to help. It is not a fiercely competitive field, so you should have little trouble finding work if you're connected and produce quick results for your clients. The hard part might be growing too quickly to meet the needs of your clients, who experience machinery downtime much more frequently than they'd like to admit.

START-UP:

You'll need sufficient capital to buy your own repair equipment (what you'll buy will depend largely upon your area of specialty, but expect to spend $50,000-$150,000 or more). Although each individual job will bring a different fee, you could easily make $100,000-$500,000 per year (think about all of the additional fees you'll tack on for quick turnaround and emergency calls).

BOTTOM LINE ADVICE:

You're going to be on call basically 24 hours a day, and you may need to work on equipment at times when others are not. That means you should expect to spend a lot of wee hours of the morning getting equipment back on track; if that doesn't bother you, this will be a happy and profitable experience for you.

MAILBOX RENTAL SERVICE

Start-up cost:	$50,000-$80,000
Potential earnings:	$35,000-$65,000
Typical fees:	$15 per month
Advertising:	Yellow Pages, direct mail to home-based entrepreneurs, newspaper ads, radio spots
Qualifications:	None
Equipment needed:	Post office boxes, scales, parcel packaging equipment, cash register, security system for after-hours
Home business potential:	No
Staff required:	Yes (could be part-time, to cover shifts)
Handicapped opportunity:	Possibly
Hidden costs:	Insurance, security (vandalism could be costly)

LOWDOWN:

Mailboxes are a booming business in the age of entrepreneurism; home-based businesses benefit from having your service more than anyone else around, largely because they rely on establishing a professional-sounding address. Using your services, they can get a suite number (actually their P.O. Box number) for a low monthly rental of $15 or so (depending on metropolitan area). It's a straightforward, easy-to-manage business for those who have even a limited retail background; with training in postal regulations, you can become quite knowledgeable in a short enough period of time to be up and competing in four months or less. Your largest competitor, of course, is the United States Postal Service—but they don't offer as many add-ons as you could and as high a level of customer service, do they?

START-UP:

Your start-up investment ($50,000-$80,000) will likely involve buying into an existing franchise, although you can go it alone if you are familiar with shipping and receiving procedures and have the ability to procure your own equipment. If you buy into a franchise, you'll get technical and managerial support as well as a procedures/operations manual that could solve most of your early start-up problems. It's worth it to at least investigate a few franchises. If you choose an area close to students and home-based entrepreneurs, you'll earn somewhere between $35,000-$65,000 per year.

BOTTOM LINE ADVICE:

You would be especially wise to locate your service in a busy shopping complex; even though the rent is higher than most other spots, your location itself can be a profitable method of advertising—and you need visibility more than anything else with this business.

MANUFACTURER OF LICENSED PRODUCTS

Start-up cost:	$50,000-$150,000 (more if you have extensive manufacturing facilities of your own)
Potential earnings:	$200,000-$500,000+
Typical fees:	25 to 30 percent of gross profit
Advertising:	Direct mail, referrals, Yellow Pages
Qualifications:	Manufacturing and/or sales background
Equipment needed:	Depends on product you're producing; computer, printer, fax/modem, phone, business card
Home business potential:	Not likely
Staff required:	Yes (primarily production workers)
Handicapped opportunity:	Possibly
Hidden costs:	Workers' compensation, legal fees

LOWDOWN:

An extremely lucrative field—after all, what kid doesn't want a Mickey Mouse sweatshirt or a Big Bird dinner plate? These products are all manufactured by someone, and it might as well be you if you've got the manufacturing and market- ing ability to attract the attention of licensing agents. Any character can be incor- porated into virtually any type of product, from dinnerware to clothing or even food products. Your expertise will be to help the customer decide which type of product(s) might sell best, then to go about producing such a product line in the least expensive way possible (which could entail overseas production). You need to recognize, however, that the license to produce products bearing the name or likeness of any character rests solely with the licensing corporation—you can't go on producing and selling items beyond the number stated in the contract. Legal fees will result from your production contracts if you exceed the limit.

START-UP:

You'll need $50,000-$150,000 for some no-frills manufacturing equipment (lease, buy it used or, better yet, subcontract production) and basic office setup (computer, printer, fax/modem, and phone). Obviously, you'll need to have a warehouse for receiving and shipping product, so part of your start-up fee reflects that overhead. If producing in-house, you'll need a production staff (and with it comes additional overhead). Still, since the demand for licensed products (which often become highly collectible and hence, worth something later on) is high, you can expect an income potential of $100,000-$500,000.

BOTTOM LINE ADVICE:

This can be an exceptionally competitive field. Be sure your quality is top-notch. Otherwise, the Disney Corporation may turn to a competitor for their next project and your name could turn to mud in the industry. With such high overhead, you can't afford the luxury of a cheaply produced product—you'll wind up paying for it later.

MANUFACTURER OF SELF-ADHESIVE PRINTED LABELS

Start-up cost:	$40,000-$50,000
Potential earnings:	$25,000-$40,000
Typical fees:	$5-$10 per roll of 1,000 labels
Advertising:	Newspapers, Yellow Pages, direct mail
Qualifications:	Knowledge of printing, marketing skills
Equipment needed:	High-speed, low-heat printer; adhesives applicator, computer, printer, fax, phone
Home business potential:	No
Staff required:	Possibly
Handicapped opportunity:	Yes
Hidden costs:	Pickup and delivery time

LOWDOWN:

You're focusing on a very narrow niche here. Your marketing will be direct and uncomplicated, though demanding in terms of time and effort. Self-adhesive labels are used very widely, and your ability to print them on time for a competitive price will be your major selling point. You will need to enjoy selling to keep up your enthusiasm for the marketing process. Eventually you will probably receive much repeat business, but the initial effort to compete with other types of printing companies will require dedication to marketing and sales.

START-UP:

This business is not a shoestring start-up. Equipment and supplies are an investment you must make, although you can seek out used equipment in professional publications special to your industry. Be prepared to spend at least $30,000—expect to earn at least $25,000 your first year, and more each successive year.

BOTTOM LINE ADVICE:

The best advice to hold costs down, at least initially, is to either lease your equipment or subcontract the actual printing. This way, if your business doesn't take off in this rather competitive field, you'll be liquid enough to get out of it soon—without losing your shirt on the equipment costs.

MANUFACTURER/RETAIL ITEM

Start-up cost:	$1 million-$3 million
Potential earnings:	$2-$15 million+
Typical fees:	Varied according to product
Advertising:	Business/trade publications
Qualifications:	Manufacturing, design, purchasing experience
Equipment needed:	Various types of machinery pertaining to mass production (depends on what type of product you're manufacturing)
Home business potential:	No
Staff required:	Yes (possibly 2-3 shifts)
Handicapped opportunity:	Not typically
Hidden costs:	Insurance, workers' compensation, warehousing and costs relating to inventory, production and product design

LOWDOWN:

Whether you're a manufacturer of clothing, shoes, kitchen products, or tools, you'll need to have a solid product design and plenty of space for manufacturing facilities and warehousing. That's why your start-up is so high—you'll need to produce a high enough volume of product to be able to see the kinds of profit margins you'd like, and all that product has to be made and stored somewhere. Often, you can have manufacturing and warehousing at the same facility; it is more common, however, to subcontract your manufacturing to an overseas facility and store product in a warehouse here in the U.S. Right or wrong, it is cheaper to have product made in countries such as Korea and China, and that's why so many manufacturers do so. Still, if your product line is small enough, and your volume limited at first, you could produce your own products offered at retail shops within a limited geographic area. Your market is as vast as you'd like it to be, provided you have proper distribution channels and the opportunity for high visibility.

START-UP:

You're going to need quite a bit of capital to get started in retail product manufacturing; at least $1 million but more likely $5 million for your capital equipment expenses, employee-related costs, and manufacturing/warehousing facilities. If all goes well, you could make $15 million or more; if your product dries up before it saturates the market, your profits will be closer to $2 million (or even less).

BOTTOM LINE ADVICE:

It's a volatile market—you never know what will sell well and what won't. It's not uncommon for a manufacturer to spend millions on a product line that winds up on the 75 percent off rack somewhere. On the positive side, when things go well, they really go well (financially speaking, of course). You could become a multimillionaire if you produce a good product.

MAP PUBLISHER/DISTRIBUTOR

Start-up cost:	$40,000-$65,000
Potential earnings:	$40,000-$80,000+
Typical fees:	30 to 40 percent of list price
Advertising:	Direct mail/catalogs, sales calls
Qualifications:	Surveying and/or publishing experience
Equipment needed:	Computer with map-making software program (often custom-designed), printer, fax/modem and (sometimes) surveying equipment
Home business potential:	Yes
Staff required:	No (but you'll likely contract with sales representatives)
Handicapped opportunity:	Possibly
Hidden costs:	Insurance, costly mistakes

LOWDOWN:

We all use maps on a regular basis, but rarely do we think of the work that went into producing them. True, a map maker of the '90s is basically updating the work of previous map makers, but in today's volatile world where countries redefine their boundaries on what seems like an annual basis, it is important to be able to respond to those who need to travel. You'll likely use older maps to generate the new ones, but you'll need to use some design software (possibly custom-produced to suit your needs) to change boundaries and town names where appropriate. It's very detail-oriented work. Your income potential will be even greater if you can manage to get your maps on a piece of computer software; such programs are beginning to sell quite well for the travel-minded.

START-UP:

You'll need at least $40,000 to get started in this business, mainly because you're going to need some high-end computer equipment to produce the kinds of maps that can be reproduced clearly and easily. Not only that, if you're producing smaller maps for private clients, you may need surveying equipment (unless you subcontract with a surveyor). If you set up solid distribution channels, you could earn $40,000-$80,000 or more per year.

BOTTOM LINE ADVICE:

The only problem with this type of business is that it is a fairly narrow niche; when there's work to be done, you'll be quite busy—but expect there to be some downtimes. Use the quieter moments to plan ahead or produce computer versions of your product (that seems to be the wave of the future for map makers).

MESSENGER SERVICE

Start-up cost:	$40,000-$65,000
Potential earnings:	$45,000-$60,000
Typical fees:	$35-$50 per delivery run
Advertising:	Yellow Pages, business publications, promotional items (such as pens, magnets, or notepads)
Qualifications:	Driver's license
Equipment needed:	Fleet of delivery vehicles, bicycles or (yes) Rollerblades
Home business potential:	Yes
Staff required:	Yes
Handicapped opportunity:	No
Hidden costs:	Insurance, workers' compensation (this is a high-risk profession, particularly for bicyclists and Rollerblade delivery people in large metropolitan areas)

LOWDOWN:

What happens when you have an important message or document that absolutely, positively has to be there . . . well, sooner than overnight? You call a messenger service to run it over to the appropriate local business. Maybe the messenger service is made up of a small fleet of vehicles, or maybe it's comprised of a bunch of college students on Rollerblades, skateboards, or bicycles. However you determine to power your own fleet, you'll be wise to invest in safety gear and perhaps even first-aid training for each of your employees. It's a dangerous world out there, particularly in the big city, and even though it is definitely faster to deliver an envelope via bicycle as opposed to vehicle in a large, congested city, the high cost of personal injury may make this business a little more costly than you'd anticipated.

START-UP:

You'll need a good fleet and lots of delivery people to make this one work profitably. Ideally, you'll have a small staff that works quickly enough to tackle several runs per hour—making your profit margin higher than most of the larger, better-known delivery services. You'll charge $35-$50 per delivery (and may have a surcharge for speedier runs), so you can expect an income potential of $45,000-$60,000 per year.

BOTTOM LINE ADVICE:

Make sure your staff is physically fit, able to handle multiple tasks, and just plain quick about it. You'll make lots more money if your staff can manage to get through the streets safely.

MINIATURE GOLF COURSE

Start-up cost:	$75,000-$150,000
Potential earnings:	$50,000-$75,000
Typical fees:	Admission fees of $5-$10 per person; percentage on concessions
Advertising:	Billboards, local magazines, coupon books, flyers
Qualifications:	Design and building skills, creativity
Equipment needed:	Clubs, balls, maintenance equipment
Home business potential:	Yes
Staff required:	Yes
Handicapped opportunity:	No
Hidden costs:	Maintenance, insurance

LOWDOWN:

If you have a piece of land with a reasonable amount of drive-by traffic, you can probably draw customers for a miniature golf course without too much advertising. Creativity in the course layout will mean that your customers will return. Some miniature golf courses have a theme, while others focus on the complicated holes featuring loop-the-loop shots and the standard windmill. Miniature golf is appealing to almost everyone, from young kids to their grandparents. By entering this business you are keeping up a wonderful tradition of fun for the whole family.

START-UP:

How much of the construction can you and your family do? Minimizing expenses for labor and materials will make a big difference in the start-up cost. If you need to have most of the work done by contractors, expect to spend between $75,000-$150,000 from the get-go. At a few bucks per admission, it may take you five years or so to earn back your return on investment, but amusement-type businesses do seem to have a recession-proof nature if they're not too trendy. Here, you have a timeless pastime.

BOTTOM LINE ADVICE:

You'll be working when everyone else is recreating: evenings, weekends, and most other days when the weather allows. It can be hard to get away unless you have reliable assistants to cover for you. The other principal disadvantage is that this type of enterprise is not the road to untold riches. It's a good, seasonal business, but it won't fill your garage with BMWs.

MUSICAL INSTRUMENT LEASING

Start-up cost:	$50,000-$100,000
Potential earnings:	$50,000-$65,000
Typical fees:	Lease payment per month, depending on instrument type (can range from $40-$100 per month)
Advertising:	Yellow Pages, referrals from band leaders and music teachers
Qualifications:	Familiarity with all types of instruments, ability to perform basic repairs, good managerial skills
Equipment needed:	Instruments to lease, display area, basic office setup
Home business potential:	Yes
Staff required:	No
Handicapped opportunity:	No
Hidden costs:	Replacement and repair of instruments and cases

LOWDOWN:

Areas with active high school music programs, especially marching bands, will support a musical instrument leasing business. Leasing makes sense because children grow, change interests, and become able to play more sophisticated instruments. Some companies make an excellent profit on leasing quarter- and half-size violins as children progress through Suzuki programs in the elementary grades. Other enterprises focus on band instruments, some of which are much too big and expensive for purchase by individual students (bass drum, tuba). Your connections with band directors and other music teachers will be essential to your marketing. The other source of customers is parents who are reluctant to purchase an instrument until they are sure their child has a genuine interest in playing it; they can lease an instrument with option to purchase.

START-UP:

Costs for your inventory of instruments will be high, perhaps even in the $50,000-$100,000 range. It really depends on how many types of instruments you plan to lease, and how high a quality you want to shoot for in terms of product line. Your rental fees will range from $40-$100 per month or more (again, depending on whether you're leasing a Strad or just a plain old fiddle).

BOTTOM LINE ADVICE:

A love of music is a wonderful thing. Your business allows children, young adults, and parents to work with instruments they cannot purchase outright. As the lessons continue, a proportion of the leasers will probably become committed instrumentalists interested in a purchase. Keeping track of all this will be challenging. Be sure your bookkeeping and other records are always up to date and that you can get the information you need easily. Otherwise, profits may dribble away without your being aware of the problem.

900-NUMBER SERVICE

Start-up cost:	$50,000-$100,000
Potential earnings:	$60,000-$150,000
Typical fees:	$3 to $5 per minute, per customer
Advertising:	Newspapers, magazines
Qualifications:	None
Equipment needed:	Telephone centers or special phone codes or hookups to allow your staff to work from their homes
Home business potential:	Yes
Staff required:	Yes (at least 5-10 to manage incoming calls)
Handicapped opportunity:	Yes
Hidden costs:	Insurance, workers' compensation

LOWDOWN:

Believe it or not, there are some 900-number services that don't cater to the sexually depraved—although, admittedly, that's where the biggest money can be made. Singles classifieds and sex-talk lines get the biggest bang for the buck, so to speak, so if you're in it for straight cash, that's the kind of 900-number service to offer. Once clients get on the line, they have to be encouraged to stay on, and that may require a script of sorts to keep hangers-on from hanging up. Time is definitely money, and the longer folks stay on, the greater your own reward. If the "talk-dirty-to-me" set doesn't appeal to you, or if you have highly specialized information you'd like to sell over a 900 number, you can exercise that option instead—although it may hamper your earnings potential considerably.

START-UP:

You'll need lots of capital to get your phone system up and running, plus sufficient funds to cover initial salaries (before the bucks start rolling in); expect to spend at least $50,000 and possibly as much as $100,000. But, your income potential can be as high as $150,000 or more, so it shouldn't be long before you earn back your investment. Just make sure you spend a fair amount on print or television advertising ($10,000-$25,000 per year).

BOTTOM LINE ADVICE:

While it's not the kind of business you'll want to tell your parents about at Thanksgiving, you can make a small fortune with a well-visited 900-number service. Just tell the folks you're into telemarketing, and you'll be playing it safe.

PILOT/FLYING LESSONS

Start-up cost:	$45,000-$125,000+
Potential earnings:	$3,000-$5,000 per month
Typical fees:	$75 per hour
Advertising:	Yellow Pages, entertainment sections of local papers, brochures, visitor convention bureaus
Qualifications:	Federal Aviation Administration (FAA) license, 20/20 vision, 1,500-3,000+ hours flying time
Equipment needed:	Plane and appropriate safety equipment
Home business potential:	No
Staff required:	No
Handicapped opportunity:	No
Hidden costs:	Fuel, maintenance

LOWDOWN:

Believe it or not, there is more to being a pilot than just climbing into the cockpit. You need to have the ability to work with words and numbers; follow procedures and read the instrument panel; be alert and ready to make decisions; and communicate accurately. If you decide that you'd like to teach others to fly the friendly skies, you must be incredibly thorough and have a great many hours in the air yourself. The more 'fly time' or experience you have the better teacher you will be. Skipping over any details could cost your students their lives, and that's a heavy amount of responsibility for anyone to take on. Still, if you have a high degree of knowledge and know how to convey that information in an accurate, concise way, you could make this business soar—particularly if you live in an area where the weather cooperates regularly.

START-UP:

The plane itself is the major cause of your start-up being so high (at least $35,000). Chances are good, though, that if you are looking into this field, you already own or have access to a plane. The rest of your overhead will be wrapped up in insurance and advertising. Your typical annual earnings will be in the neighborhood of $36,000-$60,000.

BOTTOM LINE ADVICE:

The good part is you're up in the sky enjoying the tranquility and breathtaking views. The bad part is you are working in a confined space and your instructions must be very accurate. A mistake in teaching could be life-threatening, and turnover could be low because of the extensive training involved.

PINBALL/ELECTRONIC GAME ARCADE

Start-up cost:	$50,000-$75,000
Potential earnings:	$45,000-$60,000
Typical fees:	25 cents to $1 per play
Advertising:	Location
Qualifications:	None
Equipment needed:	Pinball/electronic games, token or change machine
Home business potential:	No
Staff required:	Yes (1-2 to cover shifts)
Handicapped opportunity:	Yes
Hidden costs:	Insurance, maintenance

LOWDOWN:

You don't have to be a "pinball wizard" to make a go of a pinball/electronic game arcade—all you need are the most popular games out there and a good token or change machine. You don't even necessarily need a storefront of your own, because many shopping malls rent out floor space in their corridors precisely for games like yours. If you're in an accessible, highly trafficked area, you can probably earn a pretty penny while doing minimal work to maintain your machines. If you start out small enough (with one to four games in a mall corridor setting), you can earn a great deal in a short period of time. Obviously, your hours will be the same as the mall's—and when they're busy (weekends and holidays in particular), you'll be busy. Just make sure to drop by every few hours to collect your money or make sure the machines are running properly.

START-UP:

Your start-up costs will mostly be in the equipment purchases themselves—and pinball/game equipment isn't cheap. If you buy some used equipment, you could save money, but then you run the risk of shelling out money on potentially obsolete or less-popular games. Invest wisely and sensibly ($50,000-$75,000 for eight to ten units) and count on a payback period of four to five years. That's not too bad, really, because you don't have to work too hard to maintain this business and your overhead will be low as a result.

BOTTOM LINE ADVICE:

With this business, you have the freedom and flexibility that many others are after—but your income depends on how many games you have running simultaneously in different places. In this case, the more machines you have, the merrier (and wealthier) you'll be.

PREFAB HOME SALES/CONSTRUCTION

Start-up cost:	$75,000-$150,000+
Potential earnings:	$40,000-$80,000+
Typical fee:	$10,000 more than the cost of materials and labor
Advertising:	Yellow Pages, local newspapers
Qualifications:	Thorough skills and knowledge of construction and building codes, management ability
Equipment needed:	Construction equipment, materials, plans
Home business potential:	No
Staff required:	Yes
Handicapped opportunity:	No
Hidden costs:	Insurance, equipment maintenance, workers' compensation

LOWDOWN:

Prefab homes are considered by many to be the housing wave of the future, largely because they are far less expensive than custom-built homes and provide homeowners with the ability to live in their own house at a cost similar to apartment rent. You may be required to purchase the components (many are manufactured in Elkhart, Indiana, a good place to check out before plunging into this business), and assemble them at the customer's lot. You might have to purchase a large lot yourself to display some of the homes you are selling and to store the components prior to installing them on a lot. You could use one of them as a model home and as your office.

START-UP:

Your initial investment will be quite high ($75,000-$150,000), as you'll need to cover items such as materials, supplies, insurance, workers' compensation, and transportation or shipping of the prefab home itself (or rights to the plans if you're doing the construction yourself).

BOTTOM LINE ADVICE:

These homes have to be transported with tractor-trailer rigs. Be sure to hire truck drivers with excellent safety records. Also look into lease options for these vehicles—you might need a few of them yourself, and it could save you money in the long run.

PROFESSIONAL DIVER

Start-up cost:	$40,000-$50,000
Potential earnings:	$25,000-$45,000 (on the higher side of teaching)
Typical fees:	$25 per hour for diving services; classes usually run $35-$50 per unit of instruction
Advertising:	Yellow Pages, flyers, word of mouth
Qualifications:	Certification and CPR training
Equipment needed:	SCUBA diving gear/tanks, wet suit, and possibly a boat
Home business potential:	Not typically (although you can set up a one or answering service there)
Staff required:	No (unless you need a boat operator)
Handicapped opportunity:	No
Hidden costs:	Insurance, cost of renting additional equipment for classes

LOWDOWN:

Divers are not just surfers looking for additional recreation; they provide a critical service to police and rescue personnel when emergency situations arise. As a professional diver, you can have the best of both worlds: on the one hand, you can help save lives or solve mysteries by locating important items (or better yet, people); on the other hand, you can have the low-stress job of teaching others how to diver properly and safely. If you want this kind of high- and low-stress mix, diving could provide you with the perfect balance. Most of your business will come from police departments looking for help that only your expertise can provide; you will receive sales from referrals more often than from advertising when folks are seeking your services as a diver. However, to find students, you will have to post flyers in appropriate places (such as surf shops and related businesses near water) in order to gain the kinds of clients you're after. Once you are certified as a professional diver, you can start your business on your credentials and the investment needed to purchase your equipment.

START-UP:

You'll need to invest in SCUBA gear and equipment, so plan on at least $30,000 to cover equipment costs and insurance. You could make between $25,000-$45,000 per year, and you'll be charging $25 per hour for diving services or $35-$50 per class for teaching.

BOTTOM LINE ADVICE:

Imagine getting paid to do something you enjoy! Diving can be fun, relaxing, and even inspiring—but it can also be physically demanding, strenuous, and incredibly stressful (especially if you're looking for a dead body). Are you up to the task—no matter what you're diving after? You should be able to answer than question well before embarking on this profession.

REAL ESTATE INVESTOR

Start-up cost:	$40,000
Potential earnings:	$50,000 and up
Typical fees:	There's no "typical"; each deal is different; however, your percentage could be as high as 40 percent
Advertising:	Real estate publications and networking through investing clubs, banks and the Board of Realtors
Qualifications:	None required unless you need to borrow money to get started, in which case credit-worthiness is mandatory.
Equipment needed:	None
Home business potential:	Yes
Staff required:	No
Handicapped opportunity:	Yes
Hidden costs:	Appraisals, interest, finance fees, eviction costs

LOWDOWN:

Real estate (both commercial and residential) is a good, solid investment to make in the first place, since value only tends to increase with time. Imagine your potential to earn two or three times the value of your property by becoming an investor! Your research, knowledge, business sense, and awareness of real estate market trends are the basis for your income. You will focus on land suitable for a strip mall, apartment buildings that can be upgraded and made more profitable, or recycled factory buildings. What real estate investors do may look easy from the outside, but serious work and considerable risk-taking are involved. Success requires a dedication to learning, patience, and constant research. There are no "easy pickings" out there; instead, opportunities exist for those investors who can recognize and exploit them.

START-UP:

You'll need sufficient investment capital and excellent credit—not to mention the capability (with money or "sweat equity") to fix and maintain your properties. You could earn as much as 40 percent off your investments—or, if primarily renting spaces, your income could easily be between $30,000-$50,000 annually (depending on what you own and—particularly—where it is).

BOTTOM LINE ADVICE:

If you know your community like the back of your hand and have a sense of the value that the people put on their places and spaces, give this type of business serious consideration. If you're good, there are no limits on what you can financially achieve for yourself. The flip side of the coin is that maintenance can be very costly if you don't keep up; also, some tenants force you to evict them (and that can get costly, too).

REPAIR SERVICE

Start-up cost:	$40,000-$65,000
Potential earnings:	$35,000-$50,000+
Typical fees:	Varied according to service provided; can be as little as $3-$5 and as much as $150 or more
Advertising:	Yellow Pages, newspaper ads, referrals, coupon books
Qualifications:	Skills training in specialty area
Equipment needed:	Sewing/mending equipment, leather repair kits, repair equipment specific to industry being served
Home business potential:	No
Staff required:	No
Handicapped opportunity:	Not typically
Hidden costs:	Insurance, fluctuating materials costs

LOWDOWN:

Even the best products need to be repaired at some point, and that's why repair businesses continue to be such an economic mainstay. After all, in our busy, two-income society, who has the time to repair anything? You'll be filling a niche, such as golf equipment repair, vacuum repair, or even the timeless shoe/purse repair; picking a specialty area is the only way to set yourself apart and not spread yourself too thin (although the idea of an all-in-one repair shop would be a happy thought for many a consumer). You'll need to have a small shop or storefront so that your customers can easily reach you as they circulate in their area; you would do well to invest in a spot near a shopping mall or some other heavily traveled area so that your sign becomes your main form of advertising. People are looking for convenience in finding you as well as in your service itself.

START-UP:

You'll need to start with about $40,000-$65,000, which will cover your equipment, rent, and advertising costs. What you'll earn in this business depends largely on what area you choose to specialize in; obviously, repairing golf clubs is going to be more lucrative than repairing shoes and purses. Expect to earn somewhere between $35,000-$50,000.

BOTTOM LINE ADVICE:

The hours can get long very quickly, and you'll find that you're competing in a fast-food society where everyone wants their product fixed on the spot. Calm their nerves (and yours) by adding a surcharge for speedier service; it works as a deterrent, and your customers should be willing to wait for your good service and attention to detail, right?

RESALE SHOP

Start-up cost:	$40,000-$100,000
Potential earnings:	$35,000-$80,000+
Typical fees:	Varied according to products you're reselling; you could sell items from $5-$5,000, but often you split the profit with a consignor
Advertising:	Yellow Pages, community newspapers, coupon books, location
Qualifications:	Previous retail experience is helpful
Equipment needed:	Cash register, retail display cases, computer, printer, fax, phone
Home business potential:	No
Staff required:	Possibly
Handicapped opportunity:	Possibly
Hidden costs:	Insurance, cost of sales

LOWDOWN:

Resale shops of all kinds abound in the shopper's market; Goodwill Industries and Salvation Army paved the way for resale shops because they did so well in sales that others decided to move resale into the for-profit zone. You'll need to advertise somewhat heavily at first, so that you can encourage enough folks to bring their stuff in to your shop; with each customer, you'll negotiate a contract to sell said items at an agreeable percentage split (usually 60/40 or 50/50). Remember, too, that you should only accept things that you feel will sell well—there's nothing worse than a resale shop filled with useless items that take up valuable floor space. You'll have lots of repeat business, especially from collectors; they regularly comb the aisles of every thrift and resale shop they can find to locate items that they, too, can resell at a profit. Your products might include everything from clothing and jewelry to office furniture or even record albums.

START-UP:

There are franchises available in the resale shop business; if you decide to purchase one, you'll spend at least $50,000 for the buy-in alone (not including your advertising, office equipment, and store location). If you decide to go it alone, you'll spend at least $40,000, but probably closer to $100,000, to get your location stocked with quality products to sell.

BOTTOM LINE ADVICE:

The lure of selling used items has drawn many into the resale business; how many stay in business is quite another story. Actually, you may survive the cut if you are adept at buying low and selling high, which is what you always must do in this business.

RESTAURANT

Start-up cost:	$50,000-$1.5 million
Potential earnings:	$50,000-$75,000
Typical fees:	3-5% of gross
Advertising:	Word of mouth, newspaper ads, phone directories, Location
Qualifications:	Good business management and marketing skills; knowledge of cooking
Equipment needed:	A location for the business, cooking and serving equipment, cash management system
Home business potential:	Not in most cases
Staff required:	Yes
Handicapped opportunity:	Yes
Hidden costs:	Liability insurance fees, legal advice, decorating costs, possible remodeling of facility to meet your needs

LOWDOWN:

With the continuous increase of two-income households, people have no time to cook and more money to spend at restaurants. Providing people with good food and a nice atmosphere can be satisfying to the business owner. Your restaurant can be anything you like, from a cafeteria-style establishment (which won't require serving personnel) to an elegant, haute cuisine bistro. Depending on whether your restaurant is in the city or the suburbs, and what kind of cuisine you offer, your costs will vary accordingly.

START-UP:

Start-up costs vary greatly. Consider your own geographic area, where the restaurant will be located (suburb? upscale neighborhood? downtown?), the cost of labor (how many employees will be required?), the type of menu you wish to offer (sandwiches and soup? French cuisine? burgers?), marketing requirements, legal and health requirements, etc. Obviously, you will need cooking equipment, seating for your patrons, signage and lighting, in addition to foodstuffs and beverages. If you plan to serve liquor, you will also have to obtain a liquor license.

BOTTOM LINE ADVICE:

The restaurant business is a volatile one. Restaurant owners face a myriad of challenges on an everyday basis. Finding and keeping good employees can be difficult; getting people to try your restaurant may take time (word-of-mouth is your greatest marketing tool); zoning and health regulations must be met; working hours are usually long. If you relish a busy, high-stress working environment and can handle multiple tasks at once, a restaurant business may suit you.

Types of Business Insurance

- **Property Damage:** Covers fire, storm damage, vandalism, etc., for the replacement costs of the contents of your business.

- **General Liability:** Provides protection from personal injury and property damage.

- **Product Liability:** Protects from claims for damages or injuries related to defects in the products you make or sell. Regardless of outcome, litigation in these cases is time-consuming and expensive. Judgments often run to multimillion-dollar sums.

- **Disability:** Provides income replacement should you miss work through injury or illness. This is important if you are the major income source for your family.

- **Workers' Compensation:** Covers employees for loss of income and for medical costs arising from a job-related injury or illness. This coverage is required by law in all fifty states. You are legally required to: 1. provide a safe workplace, 2. hire competent employees, 3. provide safe tools, and 4. warn employees of existing dangers. Check the coverage of any contractor you hire.

- **Business Interruption:** Covers extra expenses and loss of income caused by an interruption of normal business due to an unforeseen event, such as fire. Lost income is defined as the difference between normal income and the income earned during the interruption of normal business.

- **Key Person:** Protects your business in case of the death or disability of an owner, partner, or key employee.

- **Health or Medical:** Protects against the costs of major medical expenses.

- **Special Insurances:** Many special types of insurance are available, such as automobile, crime, computer, life, malpractice, and glass insurance. Take a close look at your business to see what may be advisable.

- **Financial Insurances:** Depending on the structure of your business, you may need Sole Proprietor Insurance, Partnership Insurance, or Shareholder Insurance. Fidelity Bonds protect against loss from embezzlement.

RESTAURANT EQUIPMENT AND SUPPLIES

Start-up cost:	$40,000-$70,000
Potential earnings:	$40,000-$60,000
Typical fees:	$5-$5,000 per item
Advertising:	Trade publications, newspapers, direct mail, Yellow Pages
Qualifications:	None
Equipment needed:	Display models of the items you plan to sell
Home business potential:	No (yes if you're selling catalog or direct-mail only)
Staff required:	One to five employees
Handicapped opportunity:	Yes
Hidden costs:	Investments in the equipment you sell can be costly; always check to make sure you're getting the best deal and terms

LOWDOWN:

There are literally hundreds of restaurants in each metropolitan area (not to mention a constant surge in new ones), so the opportunity to sell these establishments new or improved equipment can be lucrative and seemingly endless. You'll need to be constantly on the lookout for opportunities, and may have to hire a sales representative to call on restaurant owners. If you have a background in the restaurant field, use it as a marketing point; if not, stress the benefits of using your product line and perhaps include information regarding the manufacturer's reputation for quality. There are thousands of products you can stock and/or sell to your customers, from bulk napkins to industrial-size ovens. Be aware, however, that there are as many of your own competitors as there are restaurants.

START-UP:

Your display equipment alone can run as high as $10,000-$20,000, while advertising costs could add another $10,000 or more per year (especially if you choose to display your wares at industry trade shows). Still, with the markup on equipment generally quite high, you could stand to be profitable—especially if you price your products competitively or add incentives for restaurants to do business with you (perhaps 10 free consultation hours per year, for example).

BOTTOM LINE ADVICE:

While it can be stressful to manage and sell a huge product line in an extremely competitive market, you can generate business if you provide potential customers with satisfactory products. Use incentives, develop marketing programs that create interest in your company and, most of all, hang in there. It takes a year or two to start making money in this field.

RETAILER

Start-up cost:	$500,000-$10 million
Potential earnings:	$150,000-$20 million
Typical fees:	40 to 100 percent markup on list price
Advertising:	Print, TV/radio ads, newspaper ads, billboards, World Wide Web site, location
Qualifications:	Previous retailing experience would be helpful; degree in merchandising
Equipment needed:	Cash registers, scanning equipment (for bar codes), retail equipment/fixtures, credit card processing equipment
Home business potential:	No
Staff required:	Possibly
Handicapped opportunity:	Possibly
Hidden costs:	Insurance, medical benefits, workers' compensation, high turnover costs

LOWDOWN:

In retailing, two things count: timing and pricing. You will live on the competitive edge, constantly dreaming up schemes to keep the dollars flowing in. It could be that you're in the clothing retail business, where you'll need to slash prices regularly in order to compete with fellow retailers in your geographic area. Or, you could be in the bookselling business, where added services (such as espresso bars and music-listening areas) are hot. Whatever you choose to sell, you'll need to do it at a fair enough price to bring in a sizable profit and not lose your shirt on a regular basis. There will be times when you'll need to sell at cost just to clear inventory for newer, more popular products. Your biggest challenge is not pricing, however; it is getting your name on the tops of every consumer's mind. For that, you'll need to advertise quite heavily in just about every medium there is; expect to shell out a few million dollars on advertising alone.

START-UP:

You'll need a huge amount of capital ($5-$10 million or significantly more) to launch a retail business; most likely, you'll have venture capitalists or bank investors involved in your operation (perhaps more so than you would like, since they could have a controlling or large interest). If your store fares well in the stormy retail market, you could pocket $150,000-$20 million per year (depending on your size and whether you're selling franchises of your own business).

BOTTOM LINE ADVICE:

Retailing is a rough way to make a living, but it can be very profitable for those who do it well. Choose a well-established retailing name if you're going to buy into a franchise; if you're building your own retail empire, prepare for an uphill battle for at least five to seven years.

ADVICE FROM THE EXPERTS

What sets your business apart from others like it?

Ingredients standards and an emphasis on organics are what set apart the Mustard Seed Market in Akron, Ohio. Chairman and CEO Margaret Nabors, who co-owns the health food grocery store with her husband, Phil, says: "We don't allow any harmful chemicals to come in contact with our foods, and we sell only cruelty-free products (such as cosmetics)." The Nabors's grocery store is unique in that it also houses a health food restaurant.

Things you couldn't do without:

"Our management staff . . . they're the essence of our business. Also, we need tremendous amounts of refrigeration and restaurant equipment, fixtures."

Marketing tips/advice:

"You should definitely work for someone else for a while, and build a high level of commitment to your beliefs. Owning a health food store is a belief system, not just a business. Phil and I are lucky to be paid for doing something we believe in so deeply."

If you had to do it all over again . . .

"I would have hired my management staff much earlier. Our business manager transformed us from an idea to a viable business—we were just not as focused on that kind of growth as she was."

SATELLITE EQUIPMENT/SYSTEMS (WHOLESALE)

Start-up cost:	$150,000-$500,000
Potential earnings:	$75,000-$100,000
Typical fees:	$3,000-$5,000 per installed system
Advertising:	Yellow Pages, trade publications, direct mail, referrals
Qualifications:	Electrical contracting experience would be helpful, specialized training in installation and repair of satellite equipment is essential
Equipment needed:	Parts and product stock, van
Home business potential:	No
Staff required:	Yes
Handicapped opportunity:	No
Hidden costs:	Insurance, workers' compensation, mileage, equipment maintenance

LOWDOWN:

With literally hundreds of channels available today, and only one way to truly get all of them, your satellite equipment business should have no problem making money. Actually, it's staying on top of the competition and keeping ahead of demand that will be your biggest challenges. As a systems wholesaler, you'll be selling to distributors and installations professionals who in turn install the systems in hotels/motels, office complexes, and private homes. Therefore, you'll need to provide excellent training and technical support to those who resell your product.

START-UP:

Your start-up costs will be high ($150,000-$500,000), mainly because your product is expensive to produce. Once you're established, however, you can cut costs by working out special deals with your parts suppliers. Look for an annual income between $75,000-$100,000—but remember, too, that you'll need at least one additional staffer (so figure that into your budget accordingly).

BOTTOM LINE ADVICE:

The hours are long, and your work isn't exactly easy—after all, you need to sell your distributors on your product's quality and your ability to outservice the competition, and those items are simply not a given in the satellite jungle. Set yourself apart by offering incentives for people to do business with you.

SHIPPING/FREIGHT FORWARDING SERVICE

Start-up cost:	$80,000-$150,000
Potential earnings:	$800,000-$2 million
Typical fees:	Commission percentages from shipper, carrier, insurance company
Advertising:	Yellow Pages, direct mail, referrals
Qualifications:	Previous background in shipping industry would be helpful; excellent organizational and communication skills
Equipment needed:	Computer, printer, tracking software, fax/modem, copier, phone system
Home business potential:	Yes
Staff required:	No
Handicapped opportunity:	Yes
Hidden costs:	You may have to carry transit or cargo insurance on commodities

LOWDOWN:

What do you do when you are a manufacturer who needs a shipment sent out to the back roads of West Virginia with a load too small for a large trucking business to care about? You call a shipping/freight forwarding service, which then finds a suitable carrier with an already partial load to carry your product safely and economically to its final destination. If you decide that this is the kind of business you'd like to be in, be prepared for logistical challenges on a daily basis; none of your loads is going to be easy to place with a carrier, and it may take several phone calls to find any trucker (independent or affiliated) who's going your way. You'll need to have expert time management, organizational, and communications skills, as you'll be dealing with three different "clients": first, the company needing your services to ship their product; next, the carrier you link up with to transport the load; and, finally, the insurance company earning money from your referrals.

START-UP:

You'll need a sizable start-up investment ($80,000-$150,000) to cover your own liability insurance, office equipment (computer system with tracking software), and advertising. The best part is, you'll make your money three different ways, earning a commission from the shipper of products, a finder's fee from the carrier, and as bonus cash from insurance companies who benefit from your client's need for their services. That's a win-win-win.

BOTTOM LINE ADVICE:

The greatest difficulty will be securing the proper times and carriers to transport when the delivery is scheduled; often, you'll need to work extra hours trying to find the perfect match. Still, the rewards when you do find a good transporter are worth the extra effort you put in, and you could make a sizable fortune in a short period of time.

SPECIALTY PAPER
PRODUCER/DISTRIBUTOR

Start-up cost:	$600,000-$1.5 million+
Potential earnings:	$80,000-$2 million
Typical fees:	Varied according to product; usually $16-$20 per 100 sheets
Advertising:	Direct mail (catalogs) to hundreds of businesses
Qualifications:	Previous experience in printing
Equipment needed:	Four-color process printing equipment, desktop publishing design equipment
Home business potential:	No (you'll need a warehouse)
Staff required:	Yes (20-50 people to run presses, design papers, handle customer service)
Handicapped opportunity:	Not typically
Hidden costs:	Maintaining inventory

LOWDOWN:

Nearly every office manager or design professional gets barraged daily with catalogs containing hundreds of styles of preprinted stationery, all of which could be used with existing computers and printers to create truly professional-looking letterhead, business cards, and brochures. Prior to the days of the laser printer, these self-promotion items would have cost a small fortune to produce. Now using papers such as yours, with individualized designs and colorful presentation, a business owner or professional can develop his or her own materials—beautifully, and in a short period of time. You'll develop an extensive product catalog, complete with photos of each type of paper you offer; you'll also need to develop a sample kit for those who would like to see paper samples up close. It's an increasingly competitive business—one that even photocopying businesses are getting into, so make sure that your designs are unique and attractive to many different types of professionals.

START-UP:

Start-up for a preprinted specialty paper business will be incredibly high—possibly higher than $1.5 million—mainly because the cost of the paper itself. You'll need to contract with a paper mill for the best prices and paper availability. If you market aggressively and competitively, you could see earnings as high as $2 million.

BOTTOM LINE ADVICE:

Rising paper costs have made this a tricky industry to excel in; also, you'll really need to keep a handle on your customer service professionals. If you hire only the least expensive employees to greet and serve customers, you'll wind up losing in the long run because there are plenty of competitors who treat their customers with greater respect. Your business is about getting and keeping customers—if you do a good job with their first order, they'll be back for repeat orders.

SPORTS EQUIPMENT SALES/SERVICE

Start-up cost:	$40,000-$100,000
Potential earnings:	$80,000-$150,000+
Typical fees:	5 to 15 percent commission
Advertising:	Print advertising, direct mail/catalogs, cold calls, sports equipment fairs
Qualifications:	Sales experience
Equipment needed:	Computer, printer, fax/modem, phone system, cellular phone
Home business potential:	Yes
Staff required:	No
Handicapped opportunity:	Not typically
Hidden costs:	Insurance, mileage

LOWDOWN:

Any parent knows how large and profitable the junior and senior high school market is for sports equipment; all they have to do is look at their checkbooks. But parents aren't the only market for sports equipment sales and service businesses: you'll also be selling to the school systems themselves. They'll depend on you to sell them quality equipment at a competitive price, and their sports departments will probably seek special deals for purchasing in large quantity. You will likely have worked out a distributorship or sales representative contract with one or many sports equipment manufacturers, and your income will be directly tied into how well you are able to sell each product line. Set yourself realistic goals, research your market, and then get out onto the playing field—literally.

START-UP:

You may need a large amount of capital to get into this business, especially if you purchase a franchise; expect to spend $40,000-$100,000. Included in these figures are the office equipment you'll need (basically, a computer, printer, fax/modem, copier, and cellular phone). If you are able to establish regular customers and constantly increase volume by doing sports equipment fairs, you stand a good chance of making anywhere from $40,000-$100,000 or more (depending on your geographic location).

BOTTOM LINE ADVICE:

Sports equipment fairs are becoming increasingly popular; these are excellent venues for you to sell your wares at high-volume, competitive prices—and you don't have too much overhead because the companies you're representing will likely provide samples of each product (or even a certain number of products on a consignment basis).

STOCK PHOTO SERVICE

Start-up cost:	$50,000-$75,000
Potential earnings:	$45,000-$65,000
Typical fees:	$30-$500 per photo, per use
Advertising:	Direct mail to businesses, publishers and ad agencies, ads in related trade publications
Qualifications:	Photography/marketing background
Equipment needed:	Computer with desktop publishing software, printer, fax/modem, and phone with 800 number for customer service/ordering; storage for photographs/slides
Home business potential:	Yes
Staff required:	No
Handicapped opportunity:	Yes
Hidden costs:	Percentages/royalties

LOWDOWN:

As a stock photo service, you'll be serving individuals who need your photos for a specific purpose (such as a presentation or a class) as well as business professionals. Advertising agencies (especially the smaller, home-based ones) need your services in place of an expensive in-house art studio. You'll have a stable of photographers steadily providing you with black-and-white or color photos generic enough to be used by virtually anyone in any industry. Or, you can specialize in different subject matters, like movie stars or travel-themed photographs. All you have to do is rent enough photographs to make it worthwhile—and the best way to do that is to offer discounted prices if customers sign on for a monthly rate. To interest photographers in your service, you'll need to advertise in *Photographer's Market* (published by Writer's Digest Books) or in professional photographers' publications; you'll also need to pay them a percentage or royalty for each photo used (usually, this is 5 to 10 percent).

START-UP:

You're going to spend a lot of money promoting this business; ads for initial solicitation of photographers, followed by catalog production, will drive costs up to $30,000 or so. Add to that your own advertising, direct mail (and resulting postage costs) and follow-up calls, and you'll wind up with a start-up cost closer to $75,000. But, if you market well to the right people, you can make $45,000-$65,000 your first year alone.

BOTTOM LINE ADVICE:

Production costs are your biggest overhead—so be cautious and conservative when producing your first catalog. Test the market first with a smaller version of what you eventually hope to send out. The only downside to embarking on a stock photo service is that you'll need to constantly come up with new images while making sure you've got enough inventory of the old stuff—someone will inevitably want that one picture you've just run out of.

Advice from the Experts

What sets your business apart from others like it?

Howard Mandelbaum, President of the New York City-based Photofest, says his business is unique because it specializes in the performing arts. "Our customers get better research here because we're all experts in the entertainment industry."

Things you couldn't do without:

"Believe it or not, we don't have a computer yet. Our most important pieces of equipment are the telephone, fax, and a light box."

Marketing tips/advice:

"Don't look down on what might be considered trashy . . . the fact is, trashy often sells best. Also, try to get as much as you can and worry about aesthetics later."

If you had to do it all over again . . .

"I would've bought more at thrift shops and flea markets, where a lot of celebrity photos are sold for next to nothing. False thrift kept me from doing that, but now I realize that even the smallest things can be surprisingly useful."

STORAGE SERVICE

Start-up cost:	$50,000-$150,000 (depending on whether you buy a franchise)
Potential earnings:	$40,000-$60,000
Typical fees:	Varied (rental space starts at $25 per month and runs as high as $150 per month)
Advertising:	Yellow Pages, community newspapers, bulletin boards
Qualifications:	None
Equipment needed:	The storage building and property itself; computer, fax, phone, master key box, credit card processing equipment
Home business potential:	No
Staff required:	Yes (at least 1-2 to cover shifts)
Handicapped opportunity:	Possibly
Hidden costs:	Insurance and security systems

LOWDOWN:

Comedian George Carlin once did a routine called "A Place for My Stuff"; in it, he talked about how we as Americans spend a lot of our time making money so that we can buy stuff . . . and we buy so much stuff that we need to buy larger houses so we can buy more stuff, and so on. Funny as it may seem, it definitely rings true. We just don't have enough room for everything we own these days. That's why storage services provide the answer. For a relatively small monthly fee, customers can rent a small garage to store anything from an antique car to barrels of junk. You're providing a service that is primarily one of convenience, and the only inconvenience to you is that you must have a large enough space to accommodate everyone else's stuff. Storage centers are often offered as franchises, and this may be a better way for you to get started, since the franchiser provides everything you need to get this business up and running efficiently. Often, they'll provide at least some of the financial assistance to launch the business. At any rate, your building should typically accommodate 50-100 or more customers, each paying $25-$150 per month for rental space. They will have 24-hour access to their space, so you'll need to make sure you install a security system to keep out others.

START-UP:

As stated, start-up is quite high for this business due to the need for a large enough building and property. You'll spend at least $50,000 on a building alone, then fork over another $25,000 or more for employee overhead. Add your advertising costs ($1,500-$3,000) and you've got a sizable investment. However, this is a fairly stable business—it's a necessary convenience that never really goes out of style.

BOTTOM LINE ADVICE:

If you're able to get financing to pull this off successfully, go for it! You'll enjoy the ability to make money without doing much legwork. The people may be difficult—and sometimes criminals use storage spaces to conceal loot. Be prepared to work with the police at times.

TANNING BOOTH OPERATION

Start-up cost:	$50,000-$75,000
Potential earnings:	$45,000-$65,000
Typical fees:	Varied ($25 per half hour is common)
Advertising:	Yellow Pages, newspapers, bulletin boards, coupon books
Qualifications:	Familiarity with health codes/regulations
Equipment needed:	Tanning beds, heat lamps, sanitizing equipment
Home business potential:	No
Staff required:	Possibly
Handicapped opportunity:	Possibly
Hidden costs:	Insurance and equipment maintenance

LOWDOWN:

The sun's direct rays are becoming more dangerous than ever due to a reduction in ozone protection, and that's why more people in search of the perennial tan flock to tanning beds. Of course, it's also pretty convenient to slip into a tanning bed at a time that's comfortable. You'll need to advertise heavily due to competition, and you'll have to lay out large amounts of cash for equipment. However, since this field is a constantly growing one, and since it has the potential for add-on services such as a hair salon, massage therapy service, or even a Laundromat, you can convince a banker of your financial worthiness if you've got a solid business plan that allows for such expansion. Once you've got the word out about your tanning booth, all you need to do is schedule appointments, accept payment, and turn the machines on for those who wish to sun their buns.

START-UP:

Tanning booth equipment can start at $50,000 or more; investigate the used equipment market first (and take a mechanical expert with you to be sure the equipment is functional). Advertising will run $3,000-$5,000, and a staff could cost you thousands more. Set your fees in the $25 per half hour or $40 per hour range; more, if that's what you're competitors are charging. Price-shop well for this business before setting your own fees; it's competitive and changeable.

BOTTOM LINE ADVICE:

While some folks see this business as a real opportunity for success, others frown upon it for health reasons. It hasn't been proven that tanning booths cause skin cancer, but it is questionable nonetheless. P.S. You will be inspected regularly by the Board of Health, so be prepared.

Taxi Service

Start-up cost:	$50,000-$75,000
Potential earnings:	$35,000-$50,000
Typical fees:	Based on local rates and distance traveled
Advertising:	Local paper, Yellow Pages, magnetic signs for your cars, business cards
Qualifications:	Commercial driver's license
Equipment needed:	Car, two-way radio
Home business potential:	Yes
Staff required:	Yes
Handicapped opportunity:	Yes
Hidden costs:	Repairs, insurance, workers' compensation (if you have employees)

Lowdown:

To make any money in this business, you need to be on call 24 hours a day, seven days a week (including and especially on holidays, since some folks just can't help but overindulge). You will probably need to hire a dependable staff to make this business work long-term; most taxi services run in three shifts so that each person has a 40-hour work week. Good vision is as important as knowing the area you are going to service; also, make sure your staff has a clean driving record. You'll need someone at home to radio back to you where your next pick-up will be, so be sure to set aside some bucks for that employee.

Start-up:

Prepare to spend about $50,000 to get started with a small fleet and some radio equipment. The pay will vary by hours and miles driven. In most cases, taxi drivers keep a percent of customer fares plus tips. One full-time taxi could bring in $1,500-$3,000 per month. If you can get clients to share a taxi, you can carry up to four people and offer special fares.

Bottom Line Advice:

You will have to constantly deal with all types of people, and heavy traffic can be exhausting. You'll need to have an extremely flexible schedule (including early mornings, evenings, weekends, and holidays). The good news is that this is a growing industry, and with just one additional car you can double your earned income.

TEMPORARY EMPLOYMENT AGENCY

Start-up cost:	$60,000-$150,000+
Potential earnings:	$200,000-$450,000
Typical fees:	$1,000-$1,500 per employee per project
Advertising:	Yellow Pages, direct mail, newspaper ads, billboards, referral
Qualifications:	Previous employment agency experience would be helpful; business background and ability to match candidates successfully is paramount
Equipment needed:	Computers (four to six) with printers and fax/modems, phone system, scheduling/billing software
Home business potential:	No (image is everything, and your office shows your success)
Staff required:	Yes
Handicapped opportunity:	Yes
Hidden costs:	Workers' compensation

LOWDOWN:

It used to be that temporary agencies specialized only in clerical types—but the age of corporate downsizing has led to an increase in professionals entering the "temp" field, from marketing communications professionals to product designers and even attorneys. It's a $33-billion-dollar industry, mainly because the large companies that employed thousands a few years ago are now using help only as they need it. After all, from their point of view, why pay the huge benefits packages and salaries for work that can be done on a project-by-project basis? From your standpoint, this philosophy makes perfect sense; you're making your money on the fact that both workers and corporations are seeking less permanent commitment; workers are beginning to see the positive side of nonpermanent employment (they can freelance, launch businesses of their own, etc.) and the companies see the obvious benefit of saving money where possible. It's a win-win . . . all you have to do is match the right temp to the right assignment, and make sure that all of your employees are trained and able to work on short notice. You'll do an extensive background check and intake (including typing tests, computer aptitude assessments, etc.) and ensure that each temporary employee has sufficient credentials and/or experience to do a fine job. Then you'll sit back and reel in the money—particularly if you choose to specialize in a specific, in-demand area (such as nursing or engineering).

START-UP:

You'll need $60,000-$150,000 to buy into a franchise; possibly more if you decide to go it alone (because you'll need a comprehensive benefits plan, several computers, and the placement staff or account executives to manage each account thoroughly and professionally). This is an extremely lucrative field, and you can make anywhere from $200,000-$450,000 if you develop enough contacts and build a fine reputation.

BOTTOM LINE ADVICE:

You can dig yourself an early grave if you don't spend enough time preparing; know that your competitors are out there, that they have just as many good candidates as you, and that all you have to do is set yourself apart by advertising the uniqueness of your service. That's why a niche would work wonders for you financially—it gives potential clients a way to pigeonhole you in a positive way, so that they associate your company name with whatever specific need they have (i.e., Acme Personnel = engineering specialists).

ADVICE FROM THE EXPERTS

What sets your business apart from others like it?

"We have a personal approach and a high level of applicants to choose from; in that sense, we're a cut above the rest," says Fran Doll, President of Superior Staffing, Inc., in Akron, Ohio, and recognized Ohio Entrepreneur of the Year.

Things you couldn't do without:

Doll says her business thrives on a telephone system, a computer, and fax machine. "If our phones go down, we're dead," she says.

Marketing tips/advice:

"You need to have worked in this industry for a while before embarking on your own. It's not as easy as it looks. Also, be sure you have enough capital or you'll have cash flow problems because you're underfinanced."

If you had to do it all over again . . .

"I would be more careful about the accountants I chose to work with. I had two accountants who really messed me up."

TOW BOAT OPERATOR

Start-up cost:	$35,000-$70,000
Potential earnings:	$45,000-$75,000
Typical fees:	$50 to tow one boat with a membership, $300 for nonmembers
Advertising:	Marinas, flyers, Yellow Pages
Qualifications:	Captain's license
Equipment needed:	Tow boat with radio, insurance
Home business potential:	Yes (but you'll obviously be out at sea)
Staff required:	Depending on the body of water you plan to service, you may need a crew
Handicapped opportunity:	No
Hidden costs:	Maintenance of boat, insurance

LOWDOWN:

Your love of the water will draw you to this specialized (yet seasonal) business, where you'll simply tow boats to higher ground or out of precarious situations. Besides loving the high sea, you have to be on call 24 hours a day, seven days per week. You must be extremely familiar with the body of water you plan to service and if it's large, you may need to hire an experienced crew and have adequate equipment. Be prepared to handle any type of water situation, such as a boat capsizing, a fire on the boat, or even a 'man overboard' situation. Keep in the good graces of the competition, as you may need to call on each other for help in the busy season. Getting to know the boating retailers and businesses along the shore will help spread your reputation. Try to work with the boat licensing bureau or other retailers to see if they would be willing to pass out your flyer or brochure.

START-UP:

First and foremost, you need a tow boat, so your start-up cost will run on the high side of $35,000. Most of your income will come from up-front prepaid memberships, usually $50 per year. Otherwise, an average tow runs around $300. It's helpful to know that most insurance companies will cover only the first $50 of the tow, so you'll have to bill out the rest. If you need a crew, plan on shelling out more for a payroll, insurance, and benefits.

BOTTOM LINE ADVICE:

If you're in this business by yourself and your own boat breaks down, you're out of operation until the boat is repaired. In some cases, this could paralyze your business. You'll probably want to live near a body of water that needs this type of service year-round, since it's a big investment to do only part-time. Be prepared to deal with insurance companies. On the upside, if you hate being on land and have a yen for adventure, this could definitely be the job for you.

TROPHY/ENGRAVING SERVICE

Start-up cost:	$40,000-$75,000
Potential earnings:	$40,000-$65,000
Typical fees:	Can be as low as 40 cents and as high as $100 or more per piece
Advertising:	Direct mail, Yellow Pages, networking with business and civic organizations as well as schools
Qualifications:	None (but you will need initial training on the engraving equipment)
Equipment needed:	Engraver, molds, and stencils
Home business potential:	Yes
Staff required:	No
Handicapped opportunity:	Yes
Hidden costs:	Insurance, workers' compensation

LOWDOWN:

For nearly every school, association, or organization, there is a trophy or an award to be given to its members. For every business, there are name badges to be made for the employees. Think of the potential, then, for your engraving business—it's a bottomless cup, isn't it? You'll need to be a strong networker, as much of this business has already been soaked up by those established much earlier than you. But, to compete, you can set yourself apart by offering unique products to engrave—or even by reselling recognition products from other sources, such as the retail shop and catalog outfit, Successories. Sell people on your exceptional eye for detail and customer service abilities—and, if you can, throw in quick turnaround. Often, your clients will need an award or trophy to be made on a tight deadline—so you can reap an additional fee for 48-hour service, if you think you can handle it.

START-UP:

You could spend anywhere from $40,000-$70,000 or more on your engraving equipment, depending on how high-tech you get and how large a company you'd like to be. Your best bet is to seek out good used equipment first. In terms of earning power, you could make between $40,000-$65,000 if you work hard and build the right contacts.

BOTTOM LINE ADVICE:

You'll be singled out as a winner yourself if you can keep up with your orders in an accurate, timely manner. The best thing you can do is to send samples to folks with their names or company logos already printed on it—nothing appeals more to a person than a little ego boost (wasn't it Dale Carnegie who said that there is no sweeter sound than the sound of one's own name?).

TRUCKING BROKER

Start-up cost:	$50,000-$75,000
Potential earnings:	$70,000-$100,000+
Typical fees:	Commissions of 5 to 10 percent per load
Advertising:	Yellow Pages, referrals, print advertising in business/manufacturing publications
Qualifications:	A background in trucking or shipping would be useful
Equipment needed:	Computer, printer, fax/modem, tracking software, phone
Home business potential:	Yes
Staff required:	No
Handicapped opportunity:	Yes
Hidden costs:	Insurance, phone expenses

LOWDOWN:

A trucking broker is actually a smaller piece of the shipping/freight forwarding business; here, you're providing only a linkup service between manufacturers needing product shipped and those freight lines able to transport. You will not handle the insurance aspect of shipping at all. Logistics of matching a shipper to a carrier are your primary day-to-day concerns, and it isn't always easy to find a suitable carrier for each load. Still, if you can manage to keep up with the fast pace of being basically on-call for shippers in need, you can make a profitable living in this liaison-type service.

START-UP:

You'll need between $50,000-$70,000 to get started, mainly because your business will require high insurance premiums and some computer equipment (i.e., printer and fax/modem) with tracking software to help maintain information pertaining to carrier whereabouts. Expect to earn $70,000-$100,000 for your efforts.

BOTTOM LINE ADVICE:

Your days will be spent searching for rigs en route to the same destination that your shipping client has targeted, and your nights will likely be spent handling your accounting and other daily chores (unless you manage your time exceptionally well or hire someone to take care of the details).

UNIFORM SERVICE

Start-up cost:	$150,000-$300,000
Potential earnings:	$50,000-$150,000+
Typical fees:	$500-$1,500 per client per month
Advertising:	Yellow Pages, direct mail, cold calls, coupon books, newspaper ads
Qualifications:	Previous dry cleaning/delivery service experience
Equipment needed:	Heavy-duty, industrial-size appliances (washer, dryer, dry cleaning equipment, and sterilization chemicals), pickup and delivery vans, inventory of uniforms
Home business potential:	No
Staff required:	Yes (a staff of 10-12 initially, from drivers to dry cleaners)
Handicapped opportunity:	Not typically
Hidden costs:	Insurance, workers' compensation, excessive mileage, equipment maintenance

LOWDOWN:

Businesses as diverse as restaurants, institutions, hospitals, and mechanic's shops all use uniforms for their employees, mainly to protect the employee's regular clothing from anything from wine stains to patient blood or automobile grease. Your service provides crisp, clean uniforms for groups of employees as small as 10 and as large as 1,000—and you will regularly pick up and deliver clean ones. This service usually costs the average medium-size client in the vicinity of $500-$1,500 per month, and your own costs will cover a multitude of equipment in addition to the cost of the uniforms themselves. Work out terrific terms from your own suppliers, then pass along the savings to your clients. Because this is a price-driven field, you'll need to try every trick in the book to keep your costs down while providing quality uniforms and personalized service. It's not an easy balancing act, but one you'll need to perfect in this competitive business.

START-UP:

You'll need to spend a significant amount of money ($150,000-$300,000) up front to cover your delivery vehicle and cleaning equipment costs. You can expect to spend $10,000 or more of that money on advertising your services, since yours is a competitive business that sells on price as well as great service. If you can manage to keep many clients in close proximity, you can cut your travel expenses and see a higher-than-average profit. Expect to earn anywhere from $50,000-$150,000 or more, depending on the size of your metropolitan area (and how much of that market you control).

BOTTOM LINE ADVICE:

Finding good help may be your biggest obstacle; your need to contain costs may hold you back from getting the kind of dependability your business needs to rely on from its employees. You might consider hiring retirees as delivery personnel for that reason.

USED CAR LEASING

Start-up cost:	$40,000-$80,000
Potential earnings:	$40,000-$65,000+
Typical fees:	Varied; lease payments are often $100-$300 per month, depending on the size and condition of the vehicle
Advertising:	Yellow Pages, auto clubs, community newspapers, small business publications
Qualifications:	Organization/management skills; it may be helpful to have mechanical ability to do your own repair work
Equipment needed:	Fleet of decent used cars, minivans, and vans
Home business potential:	No
Staff required:	Not initially, but you may want to add 1-2 staffers once the phone starts ringing
Handicapped opportunity:	Possibly
Hidden costs:	Insurance, advertising, and maintenance can all add up more quickly than you expect; plan ahead

LOWDOWN:

With the price of new cars rising steadily, it is easy to see why leasing is becoming a more popular option. It's affordable, and it allows the customer to grow into a better car in a shorter period of time. But what if you can't afford a brand-new car to lease? You turn to a company specializing in leasing used vehicles. In this business, you would assist financially impaired individuals in securing dependable transportation—and you can also offer a lease-to-own program for those interested in keeping the vehicles once they've passed their mileage limit or their term. The biggest problem is developing a big enough fleet to service your customers; you'll have to make a sizable investment before you see any significant return. However, if you plan well and are able to secure financing, you should have no problem finding suitable vehicles at auctions and even through other car rental agencies—once their cars reach a certain mileage limit, they are sold and replaced with new vehicles. You could work out quite a deal with these companies.

START-UP:

The large equipment investment notwithstanding, you'll also need to consider how to spend your advertising dollars. A sensible amount would be $3,000-$5,000 per year, to cover Yellow Pages ads and regular advertising in newspapers. You could network with auto clubs to bring in more business. Your leases will bring in anywhere from $100-$300 per month, depending on the size of the vehicle and whether it's a one- or two-year lease.

BOTTOM LINE ADVICE:

Position yourself as an economical alternative to traditional leasing programs and you'll get a regular stream of responses from your advertising. If you can't tell a peach from a lemon, take along an expert when making purchasing decisions . . . a bad car could cause you more trouble than it's worth.

VIDEO PRODUCTION COMPANY

Start-up cost:	$40,000-$100,000
Potential earnings:	$45,000-$100,000+
Typical fees:	A simple duplication of videotape can run $150-$300 and production of a video (from script to finished copies) could run several thousand dollars
Advertising:	Yellow Pages, business publications, direct mail
Qualifications:	Degree or experience in TV/radio production
Equipment needed:	Complete video production studio (with cameras, mixing/dubbing/editing equipment)
Home business potential:	Not typically (can be done if you build a studio in your home)
Staff required:	No (use freelancers for the extra work)
Handicapped opportunity:	Not typically
Hidden costs:	Studio construction costs (rent if you can), insurance

LOWDOWN:

Businesses and organizations in and around your community frequently need the services of a small production house, and your video production service can assist them. You may offer everything from scriptwriting to rounding up local talent to assisting with purchase of airtime. You need to decide up front how extensive you'd like to have your services become, and then make sure you have the pool of talent to help you achieve it all. The best thing you can do is build a strong stable of freelancers (from writers to actors and production people) who can pick up the slack for you and allow you to be out selling. Corporate clients will likely be your best bet, because they tend to produce many in-house training videos and sales/promotional tapes per year. Don't discount the smaller folks, though, because they are the ones who will constantly return with more projects if you treat them well the first time. A final tip: You'll be able to locate inexpensive talent at universities and community theaters; audition folks even when you don't need them in order to build a talent file, so that you can save precious time when ready to film.

START-UP:

If you decide to make a total investment in this business, you'll need $100,000 or more to build a fine studio with all of your taping/editing/dubbing equipment. You can make $45,000-$100,000 or more, depending on how many corporate clients you manage to snag.

BOTTOM LINE ADVICE:

You'll be able to make a sizable profit if you can manage to keep your overhead low; so often in this field, entrepreneurs go crazy over "image," spending more money than they make in order to impress clients. Know that to really make the big bucks, keep quality high and pomp low.

VIDEO-ON-DEMAND

Start-up cost:	$80,000-$100,000+
Potential earnings:	$75,000-$150,000
Typical fees:	$300-$500 for installation and a percentage each time the video is watched
Advertising:	Hotel trades, service conventions
Qualifications:	Some states may require an electrical contract permit
Equipment needed:	Electrical tools, cables, jacks, satellite dishes, van(s) for transport
Home business potential:	Yes
Staff required:	Yes
Handicapped opportunity:	Yes
Hidden costs:	Workers' compensation

LOWDOWN:

Hotels and motels by the thousands are installing video-on-demand services for their guests. These systems operate through regular TV sets, but offer the viewer the chance to pick and choose which movies to watch and when to watch them. Unlike channels like Home Box Office or The Movie Channel, video-on-demand lets the viewer decide when it's convenient to watch a particular movie. You'll work long, hard hours at the initial system installation, but the good news is, most jobs will be a one-time shot with minimal follow-up service. You're basically installing a cable system and a satellite dish, although sometimes you'll be asked to come up with a more elaborate system (so that Rooms 315 and 325 can play Nintendo against each other). Be prepared for such requests by constantly reading up on your industry and keeping in step with what's new and hot. You'll need good marketing skills for this, but your service skills must be outstanding, since it is a competitive field.

START-UP:

Your start-up fee will be expensive ($80,000-$100,000 or more) because you need to lease the movies. After that, you can pass the leasing on to the hotel, who may pay you a fee for installation plus a percentage on the movie each time it is watched. Look for your earnings to be between $75,000-$150,000 (depending on the size of your market).

BOTTOM LINE ADVICE:

There is a high turnover rate in this field, so screen your people well. In order to keep your business thriving, you'll need to travel extensively (and so will your staff, so your payroll may need to be automated). You'll also have to price your service competitively or offer an extra bonus or service.

WEIGHT LOSS CENTER

Start-up cost:	$75,000-$150,000
Potential earnings:	$45,000-$80,000
Typical fees:	$65-$150 per client per program; more if additional services are provided (such as an exercise program)
Advertising:	Yellow Pages, print advertising, radio/TV ads, location
Qualifications:	A degree in nutrition would be helpful; you may need to be state-certified
Equipment needed:	Complete diet and exercise regimen (workbooks, videos, exercise equipment, display equipment for related sales items)
Home business potential:	No
Staff required:	Yes
Handicapped opportunity:	Yes
Hidden costs:	Insurance, legal fees

LOWDOWN:

Considering that most Americans are at least 10 percent over their ideal body weight, the market for businesses aimed at helping "trim the fat," so to speak, is considerably warm. Think about all the exercise equipment, health clubs, and over-the-counter stimulants that the weight-obsessed buy each year—then think about how your weight loss center can benefit from the trend. Perhaps the best (and most credible) way to get into this business is to purchase a franchise operation; here, you'll get all of the operations and management training you'll need, along with expert assistance in learning weight loss methodology. You'll likely have a retail-like storefront, complete with a reception area and offices plus a classroom or exercise facility; expect to spend some big bucks ($60,000 or more) on your location and furnishings alone. Still, since your image is just as important as the one your clients are hoping to achieve with a new body, you'll need to shell out more than most small businesses for your business location. The payoff could be worth it, however, since this is (and traditionally has been, in spite of some bad publicity) a profitable industry.

START-UP:

You'll likely spend $75,000-$150,000 or more on your location, since your credibility and professional appearance are of utmost importance in bringing in the dollars. If you affiliate with a well-known and respected franchise, you could earn anywhere from $45,000-$80,000 per year helping others lose weight.

BOTTOM LINE ADVICE:

Since this is a high-risk liability business, the downside is that you'll spend more on insurance premiums (and possibly legal fees). On the plus side, there will never be a shortage of potential customers; as long as there are fast-food restaurants, folks will need to burn off what they put on.

WHOLESALER

Start-up cost:	$50,000-$80,000+
Potential earnings:	$100,000-$150,000+
Typical fees:	Varies according to list price; based on percentage of markup
Advertising:	Yellow Pages, direct mail, cold calls, word of mouth, ads in trade publications
Qualifications:	Background in merchandising
Equipment needed:	Computer, printer, fax/modem, copier, phone, delivery vehicle (optional)
Home business potential:	Yes
Staff required:	No
Handicapped opportunity:	Yes
Hidden costs:	Insurance

LOWDOWN:

Wholesalers deliver goods to retail outlets so that they can be sold to the consumer; these are the sales professionals who strike the deals between manufacturers and retail outlets. For instance, a wholesaler would be the key negotiator in a retail clothing business, selling the maximum amount of clothing to a store at a competitive bulk rate. Therefore, the wholesaler's income is actually a percentage based on markup on list price. As a wholesaler, you'll be working in the trenches of the retail market; you'll spend long hours meeting with retailers trying to strike the best and most profitable deals for both of you on items ranging from office equipment to clothing. Expect there to be lots of give and take; there is a lot of bartering in this field.

START-UP:

You'll need some seed money to secure deals with product manufacturers as well as furnish your office with some basic equipment; expect to spend anywhere from $50,000-$80,000 getting this business started. You'll also need some money for advertising, so set aside an additional $5,000 or so for your first year. You could earn $100,000-$150,000 or more if you are shrewd and sales-oriented.

BOTTOM LINE ADVICE:

Wholesalers are starting to open their own shops—offering goods at near-cost prices and raking in even bigger bucks. You'll do well to consider your market for its maximum potential—then pick the option that suits your financial needs best. For many, running a wholesale shop is a profitable way to go—and it does run inventory through quite rapidly.

X-RAY INSPECTION SERVICE

Start-up cost:	$40,000 or more
Potential earnings:	$50,000-$75,000
Typical fees:	$50-$80 per X-ray
Advertising:	Trade journals, direct mail, business association meetings, referrals
Qualifications:	Appropriate degree in radiological technology, knowledge of business issues
Equipment needed:	Mobile X-ray equipment, van, office, furniture, business card, letterhead, envelopes, marketing materials
Home business potential:	Yes
Staff required:	No
Handicapped opportunity:	No
Hidden costs:	Equipment maintenance, repair, and replacement

LOWDOWN:

For shippers, storage firms and other businesses that must handle packages of unknown content, an X-ray service provides a "look unto the unseen." Increasingly in this day of terrorism and confusion, analysis of packages is required. If you are located in a large urban area or near any major shipping facility, you can develop an X-ray service that meets the highly specialized needs of this market. Many of your potential clients are old-fashioned in their modes of operation, and you will show them how your services can improve the safety and efficiency of their operations, at less cost than they had experienced previously.

START-UP:

The costs of the equipment and of the start-up marketing to develop a loyal client base will be the largest drains on your new-business budget (about $30,000 to get you started). With perseverance you could make $50,000 the first year.

BOTTOM LINE ADVICE:

Getting your foot in the door will be the challenge. Your potential clients are likely to have done things the same way for a generation or two, and learning something new (like why they should call in your company) will be slow for them. Once you show that your service meets a real need, one that can be met no other way, or not at such a good price, you will build up referrals and repeat business. Marketing must focus on the practical advantages of your service.

PART III

APPENDICES

LISTING OF BUSINESSES
BY CATEGORY

ARTS & CRAFTS

Airbrush Artist, 17
Candle Maker, 35
Caning Specialist, 36
Cartoonist, 37
Collectibles/Memorabilia, 304
Creative Arts Day Camp, 550
Custom Embroidery, 551
Doll Repair Service, 46

Floral Shop, 494
Ice Sculpting, 59
Jewelry Designer, 62
Jewelry/Clock/Watch Repair, 196
Patient Gift Packager, 399
Personalized Children's Books, 400
Silk Flower Arranger, 98
Stenciling Service, 250

AUTOMOTIVE

Auto Maintenance, 118
Auto Paint Touch-Up Professional, 23
Auto Swap Meet Promotion, 288
Automobile Window Stickers, 289
Automotive Detailing, 290
Automotive Marketing and Training, 291

Automotive Parts Rebuilder, 463
Automotive Testing Equipment, 537
Car Wash, 544
Mobile Car Inspection/Repair, 507
Short Term Auto Rental Service, 427
Used Car Leasing, 615

BUSINESS

Abstracting Service, 107
Art Broker/Corporate
    Art Consultant, 113
Barter Systems, 28
Business Broker, 130
Business Forms, 471
Business Plan Writer/Packager, 298
Buyers Information Service, 131
Consumer Researcher, 148
Coupon Distributor, 45
Direct Marketing/Sales, 158
Efficiency Expert, 326
Factory Locating Consultant, 166
Franchise Idea Center, 338
Franchisee, 565
Home Office Consultant, 351
Incentive Programs/Promotional
    Material, 353
Incorporation Service, 61

Information Consultant, 354
International Business Consultant, 501
Inventory Control, 359
Lead Exchange/
    Business Networking, 363
Liquidator, 199
Management Consultant, 371
Manufacturer of Self Adhesive
    Printed Labels, 581
Market Mapping Service, 374
Marketing Consultant, 375
Meeting Planner, 204
Middleman, 381
Mobile Paper-Shredding Service, 508
Multilevel Marketing, 80
Office Equipment Leasing, 392
Packaging Consultant, 396
Payroll Administration Service, 220
Personnel Safety Consultant, 223

COMPUTERS

COMMUNICATION

Printing Broker, 227
Public Relations, 410
Public Speaking Consultant, 412
Satellite Equipment/Systems, 600
Seminar Service, 425

Specialty Paper Producer/Distributor, 602
Stock Photo Service, 604
Telecommunications Consultant, 439
Translation Services, 257
Voice Messages Service Center, 526

EDUCATION/CHILDREN

Child Care Referral Service, 38
Child Development Center, 545
Child ID Products, 476
College Application Consultant, 40
College Internship Placement, 141
Day Care Service, 156

Educational Product Development, 489
Home Schooling Consultant, 56
Nanny Service, 511
Parenting Specialist, 219
Private Tutor, 92
Standard Test Preparatory Services, 249

EMPLOYMENT SERVICES

Assembly Work, 535
Association Management Services, 114
Athletic Recruiter/Scout, 21
Career Counselor, 298
Corporate Trainer, 316
Economic Development
    Consultant, 161
Employee Benefits Consultant, 328
Employee Harmony Consultant, 163
Employee Leasing, 490
Executive Search Firm, 329
Human Resources Services, 352

Interviewer, 192
Job Hotline, 362
Labor Relations Consultant, 197
Motivational Speaker, 210
Networking Services, 388
On-Line Job Search, 216
Outplacement Service, 513
Relocation Consultant, 234
Resume Service, 236
Sales Trainer, 422
Secretarial Service, 245
Temporary Employment Agency, 609

ENTERTAINMENT/ARTS

Acoustical Services, 276
Art Broker, 113
Art Gallery, 462
Art Restoration Services, 284
Art/Photo Services, 285
Background Music Leasing, 120
Band Manager, 25
Casting Director, 300
Color Consultant, 142

Comedy Writer, 43
Commercial Actor, 143
Concert Promoter, 483
Fan Club Management, 167
Freelance TV Producer, 566
Literary Agent, 70
Mobile Disc Jockey, 383
Motion Picture Research
    Consultant, 387

ENVIRONMENT

FINANCIAL SERVICES

FOOD/BEVERAGE

Food Manufacturing Consultant, 176
Herb Farming/Flowers, 185
Herbal Products Distributor, 349
Nutrition Consultant, 83
Personal Menu Service, 89
Restaurant, 595

Restaurant Equipment and
  Supplies, 597
Retail Bakery/Specialty Food
  Store, 238
Taste Tester, 101
Winery, 528

HEALTH CARE

Ambulatory Service, 280
Biofeedback Therapist, 465
Childbirth Instructor, 39
Counselor/Psychologist, 150
Doula/Midwife, 323
Drug Testing Service, 557
Emergency Response Service, 162
First Aid/CPR Instructor, 48
Forensic Consultant, 177
Gerontology Consultant, 51
Health Centers for Corporations, 496
Health Club, 570
Home Health Care Service, 571
Lactation Consultant, 64
Medical Claims Processing, 378

Medical Management Consultant, 203
Medical Products Manufacturer, 379
Medical Transcriptionist, 380
Occupational Health Care
  Services, 512
Paramedical Services, 515
Pharmaceutical Returns
  Consulting, 224
Residence for the Elderly, 418
Respiratory Equipment Repair, 235
Stress Management Counselor, 100
Weight Loss Center, 618
Wilderness Based Therapeutic
  Programs, 452
X-ray Inspection Service, 620

HOME IMPROVEMENT

Architect, 461
Carpet Installation, 299
Carpet/Upholstery Cleaning, 133
Chimney Sweep, 135
Construction Services, 314
Damage Restoration Service, 485
Decks/Outdoor Furniture, 321
Electrical Contractor/Electrician, 327
Fabric Coverings, 331
Framing Service, 564
Furniture Refinisher, 339
Gardening Consultant, 340
Handyman Network, 55
Home Inspector, 497
Home Office Consultant, 351

Interior Designer, 188
Landscape Designer, 502
Lawn Care Service, 68
Locksmith, 368
Maid Service, 369
Mini-Blind Cleaning Service, 382
Pool Maintenance, 519
Power Wash Service, 520
Prefab Home Sales/Construction, 590
Restoration Services, 419
Television Repair, 522
Upholsterer, 262
Vacuum Cleaner Repair, 449
Window Treatment Specialist, 266
Window Washing Service, 267

MISCELLANEOUS

PERSONAL SERVICES

PETS & ANIMALS

Animal Broker/Dealer, 281
Animal Registration/ID Services, 18
Dog Trainer, 160
Feed Consultant/Broker, 171
Fisherman, 337
Horse Trainer, 57
Horse/Cargo Trailer Service, 498

Invisible Fencing Sales/Installation, 360
Pet Breeder, 401
Pet Grooming/Care, 402
Pet Psychologist, 91
Pet Taxi Service, 518
Taxidermist, 253
Tropical Fish Service, 261

PUBLIC SERVICE/LEGAL

Accident Reconstruction Service, 275
Adoption Search Service, 110
Arbitration Service, 112
Disability Consultant, 159
Expert Witness, 330
Fund-Raising Firm, 182
Government Contract Consulting, 183
Grants/Proposal Writer, 184
Law Library Management, 67
Lawyer, 503
Legal Cost Control/Litigation
    Management Service, 364
Licensing Agent, 198
Lie Detection Service, 366

Lobbyist, 200
Mediator, 376
Motor Vehicle License Bureau, 509
Notary Public, 82
Paralegal, 218
Political Campaign Management, 225
Political Marketing Consultant, 406
Pollster, 226
Private Detective/Intelligence
    Specialist, 408
Security Systems Consultant, 424
Speech Writer, 248
Trademark Agent, 256
Workers Compensation Consultant, 455

REAL ESTATE

Apartment Preparation Service, 19
Architect, 461
Boardinghouse Operator, 30
Building Maintenance Service, 468
City Planner, 136
Construction Management Service, 147
Demolition/Wrecking Contractor, 553
Draftsman/Blueprinting Services, 324

Property Management Service, 230
Real Estate Agent/Home
    Researcher, 94
Real Estate Appraiser, 414
Real Estate Investor, 592
Residence for the Elderly, 418
Surveyor, 434
Traffic Control Consultant, 445

RECREATION

TRANSPORTATION

WHOLESALE/RETAIL

Alphabetical Index

for growing your business

Adams Streetwise® Customer-Focused Selling
by Nancy J. Stephens
8" x 9 1/4", 388 pages, two-color, illustrated, $16.95
ISBN: 1-55850-725-6

Adams Streetwise® Business Tips
by Bob Adams
5 3/8" x 6", 256 pages, $8.95
ISBN: 1-55850-778-7

Adams Streetwise® Independent Consulting
by David Kintler
8" x 9 1/4", 388 pages, two-color, illustrated, $16.95
ISBN: 1-55850-728-0

Adams Streetwise® Do-It-Yourself Advertising
by Sarah White & John Woods
8" x 9 1/4", 408 pages, two-color, illustrated, $16.95
ISBN: 1-55850-727-2

Adams Streetwise® Managing People
by Bob Adams et al.
8" x 9 1/4", 388 pages, two-color, illustrated, $16.95
ISBN: 1-55850-726-4

Adams Streetwise® Hiring Top Performers
by Bob Adams & Peter Veruki
8" x 9 1/4", 452 pages, two-color, illustrated, $16.95
ISBN: 1-55850-684-5

Available wherever books are sold.

How to order: If you cannot find this book at your favorite retail outlet, you may order it directly from the publisher. BY PHONE: Call 1-800-872-5627 (in Massachusetts 781-767-8100). We accept Visa, Mastercard, and American Express. $4.50 will be added to your total order for shipping and handling. BY MAIL: Write out the full title of the book you'd like to order and send payment, including $4.50 for shipping and handling to: Adams Media Corporation, 260 Center Street, Holbrook, MA 02343. 30-day money-back guarantee.

Visit our exciting job and career site at http://www.careercity.com

for growing your business